ROADFOOD

Also by Jane & Michael Stern

Trucker: A Portrait of the Last American Cowboy

Roadfood

Amazing America

Auto Ads

Douglas Sirk

Friendly Relations

Horror Holiday

Goodfood

Square Meals

Roadfood and Goodfood

Real American Food

Elvis World

A Taste of America

Sixties People

The Encyclopedia of Bad Taste

American Gourmet

ROADFOOD

The All-New, Updated, and Expanded Edition

Jane & Michael Stern

HarperPerennial

A Division of HarperCollins*Publishers*

HarperCollins books may be purchased for educational, business, or sales promotional use. For information, please call or write: Special Markets Department, HarperCollins Publishers, Inc., 10 East 53rd Street, New York, NY 10022. Telephone: (212) 207-7528; Fax: (212) 207-7222.

FIRST EDITION

Designed by Cassandra J. Pappas

Library of Congress Cataloging-in-Publication Data

Stern, Jane.
    Roadfood: the all-new, updated, and expanded edition of the classic guide to America's best diners, small-town cafes, BBQ joints, and other very special eateries serving great, inexpensive regional food / Jane and Michael Stern.—1st HarperPerennial ed.
        p.   cm.
    Includes index.
    ISBN 0-06-096599-1 (pbk.)
        1. Restaurants, lunchrooms, etc.—United States—Guide-books.
    2. United States—Description and travel—1981– —Guide-books.
    I. Stern, Michael, 1946–. II. Title.
    TX907.2.S84 1992   91-50519
    647.9573—dc20

92 93 94 95 96 MAC/RRD 10 9 8 7 6 5 4 3 2 1

CONTENTS

ACKNOWLEDGMENTS

Sometimes we accidentally find a good restaurant. More often, we come to it because someone gave us a tip. There is no way we can enumerate the hundreds of *Roadfooders* who have sent us their suggestions over the years; but you know who you are, and we do thank you for sharing your advice and experiences.

There is more to writing *Roadfood* than navigating from breakfast to lunch to supper. We are indebted to Nach Waxman, who would not let us rest until we revised this book, to our friend and editor, Rick Kot, for his belief that the world would be a better place if it had an all-new *Roadfood,* and to our publisher, Bill Shinker, for the last word in country pie shops. And thanks to Binky Urban, a wonderful agent even if her idea of Roadfood is a lobster sandwich at The Quilted Giraffe.

We also want to salute two special friends and *Roadfood* connoisseurs, Bob Gottlieb and Martha Kaplan, with whom we have shared a happy decade's worth of meat loaf and marshmallow salads in cafes all across America.

INTRODUCTION

We want this book to take you to places all over the country that we believe serve really good, cheap food. Even if you are not planning to eat your way from coast to coast, we hope our descriptions convey the flavor of the American road that has fascinated us for the last fifteen years. *Roadfood* is a guidebook, but it is also a kind of journal that we have been keeping as we roam: a catalogue of the pleasures that has made exploring this land our passion as well as our job.

Back in 1976 we wrote the first edition of *Roadfood* out of desperation. We had spent two years on highways and back roads researching a book about truck drivers, and had eaten enough ghastly hash house meals to realize that our truck-driving pals definitely did not know all the good places to eat, as they were supposed to do. We were convinced that there were plenty of regional specialties worth seeking out, but there was simply no handy way for travelers like us to find them. Where were the roadhouse taverns with their skillet-cooked fried chicken and where were the backwoods barbecues with succulent pork ribs and smoky brisket? Where were the mile-high meringue pies, the four-alarm Texas chili, the colorful cafes called Mom's, and the sleek diners that still made blue-plate specials? Because we couldn't find a book with the answers, we resolved to research and write one ourselves. We have been writing and re-writing *Roadfood* ever since.

The more good things we have found to eat, the more we know that this is a project that will never end. The diversity and range of local specialties—from Frito pie and Hopi blue corn piki bread in the Southwest to steamed cheeseburgers and Grape-Nuts pudding in New England—is flabbergasting; and the style of restaurants—including pancake parlors, crab shacks, boardinghouses, tea rooms, and taverns—makes finding and eating this food a continuing adventure. What's best about America's popular cuisine is how easily accessible it all is, and how cheap. If you know where to go, you can savor the soul of this country—usually for five dollars or less, no reservations required.

For us, the *Roadfood* trail is the only way to travel, because it leads to so much more than food. You will not feel like a stranger for long when you sit with the overall-clad townsfolk at the Anchor Inn in Farragut, Iowa, and watch as owner Emily Bengtsen pulls her fabulous cinnamon rolls out of the oven to a chorus of oohs and aahs. Likewise, it is a revelation to sit shoulder to shoulder with locals and travelers at a big round table in a Mississippi boardinghouse where the motto, stitched in a needlepoint sampler on the wall, is *Eat 'Til It Ouches:* By the time you leave, you will have made twelve new friends and had the best chicken and dumplings of your life.

Roadfood is a very personal book. Our goal has always been to celebrate a part of American culture that we like very much, not to judge restaurants the way a critic does. Of course, delicious food is our Holy Grail, especially when it is accompanied by generous helpings of local color; but the last thing in the world we would ever want to be about this subject is objective. We are frankly partial to certain kinds of meals and eateries—big breakfasts, plate lunch in the South, cafeterias, old-fashioned soda fountains, delis with crabby waiters and good rye bread, any place with the regulars' coffee cups hung up on the back wall. We are suckers for a cafe patronized by small town sheriffs or farmers in overalls; and you can be sure we'll pull into any diner if its parking lot is filled with local pickup trucks (or, as on one memorable occasion during the wheat harvest in Nebraska, with tractors).

As complete as we try to make *Roadfood*, and as much as we endeavor to find great things to eat wherever we go, sometimes we simply strike out. America is a big hunk of land to cover, and there is no way we can even pretend to be fair and sample food in every region with impartial detachment. So if we slight the great restaurants of the Badlands and write excessively about the good things to eat in the Ozarks, it is only because—at least this time around—we spent so much time enjoying Arkansas baked beans and catfish suppers that we didn't have time to re-evaluate the sour cream raisin pie at Ed's cafe in Douglas, Wyoming.

As much as we depend on tips, suggestions, and advice of friends, we don't rely on anybody else to actually eat in restaurants for us. We do it all ourselves: all the eating, all the traveling, even all the indigestion are ours; and for better and worse, so are all the opinions about what's good to eat and where's good to eat it. So, to paraphrase a sign that we have seen in many cafes along the way, If you are satisfied, please tell others. If not, tell us. And tell us, too, if you have a favorite restaurant you think we ought to sample. We are always looking for a good place to eat.

HOW TO GET THE MOST FROM ROADFOOD

This book is different from other guidebooks, and to get the most out of it, please remember:

Roadfood restaurants are not the dining room at the Ritz.

For one thing, they are cheaper. Because you can eat at nearly any place in this book for under ten dollars (in some cases, *way* under), we do not list prices for dishes or meals. However, there are a few restaurants here—steak houses, mostly—that are more expensive. In every case, we have tried to make note of this fact in the text.

Similarly, we trust it is obvious that you won't need reservations to dine at Putz's Creamy Whip or Pink's Chili Dogs. Still, there are a few *Roadfood* eateries that do require reservations in advance: a summertime fish boil in Door County, Wisconsin, for example; or Friday night supper at Rancho de Chimayo outside of Santa Fe. This, too, is a policy we note where it seems necessary to do so; but if you are in doubt, please call ahead.

Like reservations, the dress code in *Roadfood* restaurants tends to be casual; but again, we ask that you use your good judgment. It would be embarrassing, if not technically illegal, to eat Sunday fried chicken dinner in Indianapolis dressed in shorts and a Teenage Mutant Ninja Turtle T-shirt among crowds of people in their after-church pastels. Likewise, you might feel a little silly if you wore a pin-striped banker's suit to chow down on hot guts and brisket in a backroom barbecue in Elgin, Texas.

Hours of operation are not included in these listings. Because so many of the places we favor are personal, if not downright idiosyncratic, the times they are open can be impossible to know precisely. At Totonno's in Coney Island, the kitchen stops serving food every evening when they run out of that day's pizza dough. Mama Lo's in Gainesville, Florida, is usually open through the supper hour, but regular customers all know that the best vegetables are gone before five in the afternoon. Such tips are included with each restaurant's write-up, wherever appropriate.

It is our belief that listing exact hours in earlier *Roadfoods* gave travelers a false sense of security: we know some disappointed people who, for example, arrived at Mosca's in New Orleans at a time we said the place was open, only to find that the management had decided to go on vacation that week. Therefore, we are batting this ball into your court. We have indicated, wherever it makes sense, which restaurants maintain consistently unusual hours of operation (barbecues only open on weekends, strictly breakfast cafes); but it is up to you to make certain a place you aim to eat at is open when you aim to eat there. When you call to check (we always include a phone number), use the opportunity to get directions and to reserve a slice of your favorite kind of pie.

Happy *Roadfood*ing!

ROADFOOD

ALABAMA

ARCHIBALD'S
2602 FOSTERS FERRY RD., NORTHPORT, AL (205) 758-9219

A back-roads adventurer named Betty Eilson first suggested we try Archibald's, although she warned it was likely we would get lost trying to find it. "It's the best, and the best-kept secret barbecue anyone I know has ever had," Betty wrote. "There are no side dishes other than white bread and potato chips, but the thin sauce on this meat is 'spicy enough to make you slap yo' mammy.'"

We sure did get lost looking for the run-down, whitewashed concrete building in a backyard behind a shopping center across the river from Tuscaloosa; but when we spotted it, we reckoned *Roadfood* greatness was at hand.

There was a stack of hickory logs in the driveway/parking lot, and a blackened chimney sent perfumed, pork-scented haze into the air. Inside, facing a tin-covered pit, where shoulders and ribs slow-cook for hours over charcoal, we found a counter with five stools, which is Archibald's entire dining room. Meat is served from a cutting board attached to the pit: racks of ribs or sandwiches of sliced pork along with sauce, Sunbeam bread straight from the plastic bag, potato chips, and soda pop.

These humble ingredients are the makings of a sublime meal, because

1

the ribs are ambrosial. Their meat, which is lean but audibly succulent when bitten, fairly slides away from the bone with the gentlest tug of your teeth. The red sauce applied to them before they are served does not seem quite as nasty as tipster Betty had suggested, but it does add a tangy, tomato-flavored twist to the exquisite flavor of Archibald's smoke-laced pork.

AUNT EUNICE'S COUNTRY KITCHEN
1004 ANDREW JACKSON HIGHWAY NORTHEAST, HUNTSVILLE, AL (205) 534-9550

There really is an Aunt Eunice. Eunice Merrell is her name, and breakfast is her fame. Her low-slung brick cafe out Andrew Jackson Highway has been a favorite morning haunt among Huntsville chowhounds for the last forty years. We called her one day about 4 A.M. to find out if she was open yet and she said, "Come on! The biscuits will be ready when you get here." We were on our way to Auntie's place.

Breakfast is the only meal she serves, starting before dawn and continuing until noon, every day but Tuesday. There are eggs, of course, and they are perfectly well made, whatever way you like them; but it's the ham and gravy, grits and biscuits that put this country kitchen on America's good-eats map. There are two kinds of ham (sausage and bacon, too); country ham is the good stuff—cured until it is chewy and packed with flavor. Aunt Eunice fries it, so the halo of fat that encircles the dignified pink meat turns translucent and verges on brittle crispness; the lean parts develop a mottled skin and begin to bead with moisture. You need a good knife to slice it; and will want to slice it small—it is powerful. But once you have savored ham such as this, no blubbery city ham can ever satisfy.

Ham in these parts is seldom served plain. On the well-worn oilcloth that covers Aunt Eunice's tables are set bowls of red-eye gravy, made from ham drippings and black coffee, and cream gravy (known as sawmill gravy), which is thick, rich, and peppered. Spoon a little on the ham; or better yet, use one or both of the gravies as a dunk for the tender-textured, hot-from-the-oven biscuits (or cheese biscuits) that are served with every meal.

To wash it all down there is strong coffee, to which customers are invited to help themselves if they want seconds. Fair warning, though: it is customary when the tables in this cozy eatery are crowded, as they become around the time the sun rises, for anyone who pours himself a refill to help Aunt Eunice out and offer seconds to everyone else in the restaurant.

DREAMLAND DRIVE-INN
JUG FACTORY RD., TUSCALOOSA, AL (205)·758-8135

The Dreamland is good eating pared down to basics: a cinderblock and tar-paper hutch in the middle of nowhere on a country lane south of town, with six tables, a pot-bellied stove, a few booths, and a bar on one side. We found it thanks to traveling gastronome Joe Heflin, who was inspired to write us with an unmitigated rave. "The best BBQ'd ribs in America! Truly without equal," Joe adulated, adding that the restaurant itself is "simply the funkiest, nastiest, raunchiest looking dive around. Inside the light is so dim you can barely see the twenty or so seats, yet the line stretches out the door for yards into the parking lot."

Accommodations are limited to a short counter, a few booths, and unclothed tables; ribs are all there is to eat. They are available by the whole slab, or on a disposable plate with white bread, pickle slices, and potato chips. "You ain't seen anything like 'em anywhere else," the menu insists; and they are indeed beautiful. Succulent and moist, crusted with sauce, they are the kind of satisfying chew that will engage your tastebuds and send you into a barbecue reverie for the entire meal, then set an afterglow on your tongue that lasts for hours.

The Dreamland beverage list is nearly as short as the menu: beer or soda pop. That's the way it's been at this happy hole in the wall since 1958 when John Bishop and his wife Lillie opened for business; and thousands of satisfied customers wouldn't want it any other way.

FULLER'S CHAR HOUSE
92 KNOLLWOOD BLVD., WAUGH, AL (205) 272-3995

When Terry and Char Jeggie of Cincinnati wrote us a note extolling Fuller's Char House (after scolding us for praising what they considered to be inferior five-way chili parlors in their home city), their tip included mention of the fact that some Alabamians liked Fuller's so much they had gotten married there.

No brides and grooms were evident when we stopped in, but their absence in no way spoiled the pleasure of this lunchroom that is clearly the local people's choice. The Jeggies marveled at the length of Fuller's foot-long hot dog ("at least eighteen inches," they speculated), but it was pork they recommended, pork with a zest so delightful that it wants hardly any of the mild sauce provided. The ribs are especially tender and easy to eat;

the extraordinarily lean chopped meat is the familiar medley of crust and succulence from the outside and inside of the roasted butt.

Side dishes are southern paragons. You get a choice of two with any dinner: fried okra, pole beans, black-eyed peas, potato salad, turnip greens, cole slaw, baked beans, or French fries. For a little extra, you can replace one of your vegetable selections with a portion of the hearty slumgullion known as camp stew, a traditional companion to barbecue at pig pickin's throughout the South. As for dessert, that, too, is proverbial: lemon ice box pie, pecan pie, meringue pies (chocolate, coconut, or lemon), and a balmy banana pudding.

The Jeggies, who regularly eat their way around the country, worried that places like Fuller's are getting rarer all the time. "It has survived by the locals," they wrote. "And it remains, thankfully, for us travelers, too." Our thanks to you, Jeggies: this place is a real find.

HOTEL TALISI
SISTRUNK ST., TALLASSEE, AL (205) 283-2769

H ere is a page from our little black book of way-out-of-the-way Americana. There is nothing else quite like the Hotel Talisi. Northeast of Montgomery, a good drive off the interstate, a little bit below Thurlow Dam and this side of the Tallapoosa River, the town of Tallassee is a mere dot on the map. It has one main street (Sistrunk), and one good place to eat and stay.

The Hotel Talisi is a plain brick building with a simple sign hanging over the street corner, and a few nice pots of flowers near the entrance. It has no penthouse or elevators or health spa, no concierge or twenty-four-hour room service or mini-bars in the rooms. What it does have is a working baby grand player piano in the lobby, reeling out tunes by Irving Berlin and Tommy Dorsey. And there is a pump organ near the staircase, too. That's about it for amenities.

What has drawn customers to the Hotel Talisi for more than a quarter century is the dining room. Breakfast, lunch, and dinner are served Monday through Saturday; breakfast and dinner (until 3 P.M.) Sunday. Service is help-yourself from buffet tables replenished throughout the mealtime. Pay one price and eat all you want.

If you come on Sunday—the most cornucopic day—you may have to wait a spell for your turn to pile up a plate. The groaning boards at the Hotel Talisi are a gastronomic Circe for hungry students from nearby

Auburn University, families from Montgomery and Tuskegee and Phenix City, and a few savvy traveling chowhounds who know about the hotel by word of mouth.

The spread is a vista of Dixie cooking. Fried chicken is always the star attraction, supported by a second main course such as roast beef, sirloin tips, or pork loin. Side dishes are invariably luscious, from recklessly goopy macaroni and cheese to sweet potato soufflé streaked with marshmallows. There are supersweet squash soufflés, richly seasoned platters of rice and gravy, purple-hulled peas, peppery casseroles of chicken and dressing, innumerable salads, relishes and watermelon pickles, hot rolls, biscuits, and muffins. For dessert, there is pie: chocolate custard, apple, or lemon icebox.

JOHN'S
112 21 ST., BIRMINGHAM, AL (205) 322-6014

John's belongs to a relatively unexplored but praiseworthy class of restaurants found throughout Dixie: the deluxe cafe. Included in the top ranks of deluxe cafes are such venerable establishments as Weidmann's of Meridian, Mississippi; Pappy and Jimmie's of Memphis; and the Elite of Montgomery, Alabama. By deluxe, we do not refer to appointments, which in most of these places consist of ordinary booths and minimal, or at least unpretentious, decor; in fact, John's of Birmingham, with its blinking neon sign outside, is as plain as any town lunchroom. In deluxe cafes the dress code is casual (however: no shirt, no shoes = no service!); John's staff consists of friendly ladies in nylon uniforms, who tote meals without pomp or pretense through the big, rambling (and frequently crowded) eatery.

What *is* deluxe about John's and the handful of distinguished southern cafes in its league is the food they serve—always a few rungs up the culinary ladder from plate lunch. John's repute is for seafood, including great slabs of sweet-fleshed flounder, red snapper, and crisp-fried shrimp, as well as lobster, crab claws (fried) and zesty crab cakes, oysters, trout, and scallops. Okra gumbo, an intriguingly swampy stew sided by steamy corn sticks, and slews of fancy, well-cooked vegetables every day are sure proof of John's southern flair, as is a short but very sweet dessert roster that includes chocolate pie, lemon pie, and coconut pie. There is a fancier dessert, too, recommended to us by a waitress who described it as suited to "silk-stocking sweet-tooths": cheesecake, topped with strawberries. It was fine, but the coconut pie is better.

OLLIE'S BARBEQUE
515 UNIVERSITY BLVD., BIRMINGHAM, AL (205) 324-9485

Ollie McClung, Sr., started serving meat cooked over charcoal in 1926. Ollie Jr. followed; and although their original pork parlor on the south side of Birmingham is gone, the two Ollies' fine food is still one of the city's gastronomic treasures. The new Ollie's is a spanking clean, multi-room establishment built around a pit in the middle so that all the customers can see the meat being made while they eat.

Sliced pork, cut from a Boston butt, is the meal of choice: a great mottled heap of crunchy-edged, tender wedges piled up on a plate or in a sandwich, dressed with a bewitching vinegar-tomato sauce that is only faintly sweet, powerfully hot, and thin enough to seep into all the crevices and fissures in the smoky meat. There is beef, too—delicate-textured and especially delicious when dabbed with that powerhouse sauce. The sleeper on Ollie's menu is the half chicken, which is cooked over coals until it acquires a faintly chewy skin that encases stunningly succulent white and dark meat.

Alongside the pork, beef, or chicken take your choice of tossed salad, cole slaw, potato salad, beans, or French fries. For dessert there are pies—chocolate, coconut, lemon, and apple. They are good, homemade pies, but for a tongue that has been elated by Ollie's four-star meats and sauce, they are an anticlimax.

SYKES BAR-B-QUE
1724 9TH AVE., BESSEMER, AL (205) 426-1400

Many years ago there were fourteen Bob Sykes barbecues around Bessemer; now there is one. Ever since we hit the road in search of good things to eat, this Bob Sykes has been high on our list of prime pork parlors. When you enter, you can see the raison d'eat here: ribs, along with mahogany-red pork shoulders, on a hot grate to the right of the order counter. The xylophonic lengths of rib are cut into smaller slabs when ordered; the pork shoulder still sizzles as it is forked from the grate and carved, oozing little dribbles of porcine juice as its darkened crust is pierced by a knife.

The ribs are what made us fall in love with Bob Sykes. They have a chewy crust that pulls away from the more luscious meat closer to the bone; and this crust is imprinted with a mottled skin of heat-blistered red sauce. The shoulder meat is available one of two ways: inside or outside. The inside pieces are baby-food tender, pale and sweet. Outside pieces are firm, some nearly crunchy, and they radiate the taste of smoke and sauce. A combination of the two on a bun is just about ideal. You can also get them both, along with baked beans, cole slaw, and potato salad or biscuit rolls, as part of a barbecue dinner. In addition, Sykes prepares carry-out orders sized from "five people or two hawgs," to "twenty-four people or twelve hawgs." (The latter is one entire pork shoulder and a half-gallon each of slaw, beans, and potato salad.)

Barbecue this good is entirely satisfying all by itself; its lingering sweetness is practically dessert. But if you are very lucky, there will be some real dessert: Mrs. Sykes's lemon meringue pie on a crushed ginger-snap crust. The commanding presence in this pie is not sugar; it is lemons, abetted by zest from ginger in the crust. It is crisp and spicy and cool, an ideal way to put an exclamation point at the end of a thrilling meal.

UNCLE MORT'S
HIGHWAY 78, JASPER, AL (205) 483-7614

Uncle Mort's serves breakfast from before dawn until ten at night. It is a rustic barn-board building by the side of the highway that we first discovered about fifteen years ago when we read a review in a *Birmingham* [Al.] *News* food column (entitled "Cordon Bleu & Barbeque") that rated Uncle Mort's as a three-pig-snout restaurant. The trio of snouts was awarded out of a possible five, but a five-snout rating, the column's sidebar advised, was reserved for "classic restaurants in Europe, New York, etc."

To this day, we don't understand why Uncle Mort's didn't earn four or even five snouts. Honestly, we don't know of any restaurant in Europe or New York that serves biscuits this good; they are tall and pale with steamy insides that are pure fluff and with delectable crusty bottoms. (They are accompanied by margarine; maybe that's the explanation for the missing snouts.) With the biscuits, you want pig meat. Uncle Mort's serves all kinds, including smoked-here pork tenderloin, fairly dripping with juice ready to get mopped up by a torn-open biscuit. Sausage (made here, too, available smoked or not) is zesty; country ham is lightly cured; or choose bacon or smoked pork chops. Along with the ham and biscuits, an "Uncle Mort's Special" breakfast gets you grits or hash browns, red-eye gravy for dunking, and sorghum syrup, plus eggs.

There is a big menu of other things at Uncle Mort's—fried seafood, steaks, and sandwiches; but it is strictly short-order. "How's lunch? Is it good?" we asked our waitress as she poured our seventh cup of coffee and replenished our supply of biscuits and sorghum. She scrutinized the table where we had laid waste to breakfast and shook her head. "It's fine," she answered. "But there are no vegetables, and no all-you-can-eat biscuits. Y'all wouldn't get enough to eat."

WAYSIDER
1512 GREENSBORO AVE, TUSCALOOSA, AL (205)345-8239

A little old house with cafe curtains on the windows, pleasant waitresses in white uniforms, quiet radio music in the background, fans spinning slowly overhead, and good, hot biscuits throughout the meal: that's breakfast at the Waysider, one of Alabama's premier *Roadfood* restaurants.

For nearly thirty years now Archie Farr and his parents before him have served two meals a day (no supper). Lunches of fried chicken, smothered steak, and the like are accompanied by lots of southern-style vegetables such as buttered okra, field peas, squash soufflé, fried corn, and corn-on-the-cob, and followed by handsome pie or fruit cobbler; but it's the morning meal that puts the Waysider on our map. Those biscuits that keep coming to the table are tiny and featherweight, and their warm powdery aroma perfumes the dining room along with the more earthy smell of grits that come with nearly every meal, accompanied by a pitcher of honey.

The two great things to order for breakfast are both pig meat. Elegant country ham, brick red and with only a muffled salty punch, is served with red-eye gravy (just right for biscuit-dunking). There is less salty, sugar-cured ham available, too; but it doesn't have the breeding of its country cousin. Streak o' lean, served with brown gravy and biscuits, is a lot like bacon, only more so. You get four sections of it, about a quarter-inch thick, fried crisp. The word "luscious" does not do justice to the overwhelmingly rich quality of this pork, streaks of which are chewy but most of which just melts away on your tongue.

WINTZELL'S
605 DAUPHIN ST., MOBILE, AL (205) 433-1004

There are signs, slogans, announcements, and cartoons hung everywhere inside and outside Wintzell's. On the front wall above the sidewalk three anthropomorphic oysters are depicted in various stages of edibility. The fried one sits in a pan, fanning himself, sighing "Whooo-whee!" The stewed one appears drunk. The nude one looks embarrassed as he stands on his half shell and tries to hide his private parts. Inside the Formica eating hall approximately ten thousand of the late Mr. Wintzell's homilies, jokes, and *bons mots* are tacked, taped, and hung everywhere. To wit: "Eat, drink, and be merry, for tomorrow you may run out of credit." "If you want home cooking, stay home." Stools at the oyster bar are labeled: "Emily Post fainted here." "Edward Kennedy can sit on a tack."

Wintzell's is a goofy place, an unabashed shrine to bad taste. But that doesn't mean the oysters taste bad. Indeed, this is a princely place to eat oysters, especially if you like them on the half shell by the dozen.

Wintzell's nude Dauphin Islands are a silken mess, their big half shells strewn about a tray, ice sprinkled around and on top of them. Wintzell's also sells Mobile specialties like baked deviled crab, breaded crab claw tips, and a delightful invention called West Indies salad—nothing but a bowl of marinated lump crabmeat. There are also oyster loaves (that's a po' boy loaded with crisp fried oysters, mayonnaise, and relish) and gumbo, catfish with hushpuppies, and a roster of fried and broiled Gulf Coast seafood.

Unlike ordinary restaurants that provide privacy to customers, Wintzell's is a gregarious place where it seems only natural to socialize as you eat your dozens. If you can beat the current record of twenty dozen in twenty-five minutes, you win twenty-five dollars. However, the management advises that all challengers must warn shuckers in advance of their attempt to beat the record, and one of Wintzell's signs reads "Not responsible for bellyaches."

ARIZONA

EL CHARRO
311 N. COURT AVE., TUCSON, AZ (602) 622-5465

If it is true that you can judge a cafe by the number of calendars that hang on its walls, then El Charro must be the finest place to eat on earth. Each year since 1946, the Flinn family, which runs the place, has printed up a souvenir calendar emblazoned with a stunning artistic tableau: swarthy, muscle-bound deities wearing loincloths stand atop mountain peaks looking heavenward; handsome caballeros and their ladies fair gallop off into the sun. Years' worth of such mythical visions cover the walls at El Charro, and they create the right mood to indulge in magnificent Sonoran-style Mexican cooking.

Unlike Tex-Mex or New-Mex, this is a relatively mild cuisine. A lot of it comes wrapped in soft flour tortillas or oozing warm cheese with peppers providing provocative zest but no pyrotechnical concussions. For example: "Mexican pizza," which is a frequently served appetizer in this part of the world, is listed on the El Charro menu simply as a tostada. It is a wafer-thin tortilla topped with melted cheese and your choice of guacamole, shredded chicken, or carne seca (dried beef). A perfect and truly appetizing combination, especially if accompanied by a pitcher of El Charro's sangria.

A lot of Tucson-style Mexican food is rolled in tortillas, the most famous example of which is the deluxe fried burrito known as a chimichanga, which was (by some accounts) invented in Tucson in the 1950s. El Charro's "chimi" is a beaut—a hefty dude surrounded by beans, guacamole, and sour cream, venting wisps of palate-teasing steam. El Charro's nonfried burros are terrific, too, available with all the usual stuffings.

The one dish we like best from this kitchen, and it is something we haven't seen elsewhere, is known as a topopo salad. It is literally a monumental plate of food, arranged in a shape reminiscent of an ancient Mayan pyramid. Cool lettuce and shredded chicken adhere together with peas and cubed carrots atop a warm base of refried beans on a soft tortilla encircled by avocado slices. What a taste, texture, and temperature delight!

Handsome dessert: almendrado, a tricolored meringue effigy of the Mexican flag gilded with velvet-soft almond-vanilla sauce. Or you can get a deep-fried fruit twist topped with whipped cream.

Although the calendars go back to the forties, El Charro is much older than that. In fact, it is the oldest Mexican restaurant in the United States, open since 1922 when the current Flinns' grand-aunt, Carlotta Dunn Flores, opened for business just a decade after Arizona became a state. In those days, it is said, Mrs. Flores used to take customers' orders, run to a nearby grocery for ingredients, then run to the kitchen to cook the meal. Today, the restaurant has an uncommon vintage charm. It is a little whitewashed building in the old part of town with a small terrace for outdoor dining, lots of hanging plants, and Mexican pottery. There are some swell T-shirts for sale near the cash register, including one with an anatomically correct diagram of a chili pepper, inside and out.

HOPI CULTURAL CENTER RESTAURANT
RT. 264, SECOND MESA, AZ (602) 734-2401

There isn't another restaurant on earth that serves Nok Qui Vi and Ba Duf Su Ki, so if you are a seeker of arcane culinaria, you must come to this singular establishment in the Arizona desert, surrounded by Hopi mesas, near the ancient village of Shungopovi. Here is an opportunity to sample genuine Native American food, from rolls of parchment-thin ceremonial piki bread to blue-corn-meal griddle cakes for breakfast, served forth by a kitchen that also makes deluxe cheeseburgers and triple-decker club sandwiches.

Rare and curious as the Indian dishes are, it is likely they will shock you less by their weirdness than by their blandness. Nok Qui Vi is traditional lamb stew, made with puffy hominy corn and mild green chilis. It is earthy and laden with chunks of lamb, more satisfying to the stomach than the tastebuds. How strange it is to eat a restaurant meal that is truly as unseasoned as nursery food. The stew is served with triangular hunks of good fry bread, like sopaipillas, which are accompanied by plastic bubble packs of honey. Hopi tacos are like Navajo tacos but, in this case, meatless. Made atop fry bread rather than inside corn tortillas, these tacos are topped with gently seasoned beans and lots of lettuce, tomato, and grated cheese. Hopi chili, which goes by the name of Chil-Il Ou Gy Va, is a pleasant-tasting stew of ground beef, beans, and lovely earth-colored red chili sauce. A baby could eat it, and might just like it.

We have never been able to get anything uniquely Hopi for dessert; but we are content topping off our meal at this place, known to its natives as The Center of the Universe, with a piece of carrot cake à la mode or a nice bowl of red Jell-O.

JACK'S ORIGINAL BARBEQUE
5250 E. 22ND, TUCSON, AZ (602) 750-1280

The "Original" in the name of this restaurant is significant, according to the family of Jack L. Banks, who opened his pit in Tucson thirty-five years ago, because for a short while a few years ago the business was in the hands of lesser culinary lights, and the quality of the ribs, sauce, and sweet potato pie ebbed.

We loved Jack's place when we came through town in 1982; we were especially smitten by the ribs. Pork ribs they were, encased in a mahogany-colored crust, the lean meat inside almost shockingly tender, subtly imprinted by the flavor of a superior, rich, red sauce and by the even more elusive taste of pit smoke.

Last year when we ate at Jack's the ribs were every bit as good as we remembered them; and we once again believe that this modest drive-in restaurant with its handful of al fresco dining tables is a beacon of soul-food barbecue in the Southwest. In addition to ribs, Jack's makes delicious, plump, peppery hot links; with that sauce and some good cumin-spiked beans on the side, they are the fixings of a gloriously oozy meal. There is brisket, too, ridged with crunchy blackened crust around a center of mild, smoky meat. Sliced or chopped, it is served with some of Jack's sauce on top—a touch of tangy sweetness that adds just the right dose of luxury to the almost severe simplicity of the beef.

Peach cobbler and sweet potato pie are Jack's traditional desserts. We like the latter—a fine, buttery burnished gold pie in a flaky crust. It is velvety and comforting to a tongue that has just experienced the fire of a grand smoke pit meal.

TUBA CITY TRUCK STOP CAFE
JUNCTION OF ROUTES 160 & 264, TUBA CITY, AZ (602) 283-4975

We like to come to the Tuba City Truck Stop for Navajo tacos whenever we are wheeling our way through the sandy buttes of northern Arizona. They are sights to behold, these plate-size meals, the best in the West. A thick piece of puffy fry bread gets topped with meaty (and beany) chili, a deluge of runny yellow cheese, lettuce shreds, and tomato chunks. The amazing thing about it is that when you fork down below the greens and beans and meat and cheese, the bread below has stayed intact—chewy, rugged-textured, with crisp golden crust and a significant wheaty flavor. This is good eating! There are lesser versions of it available—fry bread topped with nothing but chili; or you can get a "Navajo ham sandwich" made on fry bread rather than ordinary baked white.

Last time we were in Tuba City, we decided to be more adventurous. Instead of our old favorite tacos we ate chicken-fried steak and pork chops and ordered a Hopiburger. The steak was fine, but nothing to remember; and we won't be eating pork chops here again. As for the Hopiburger, which we had expected to be served atop one of those great rounds of fry bread, it also disappointed us and arrived on a stupid, spongy bun.

Eating Navajo tacos at the Tuba City Truck Stop Cafe is an experience beyond simple culinary satisfaction. The old place has inimitable southwestern ambience, from its cinderblock walls and dusty front windows that look out toward the highway, to the regular clientele, who are mostly locals from the nearby Hopi village of Moenkopi. Outside, a sign exclaims "Let's Eat."

ARKANSAS

B & J FINE FOOD
HIGHWAY 67, ASH FLAT, AR (501) 994-2101

We learned about B & J Fine Food a couple of years ago thanks to an article that Celia Marks wrote for the *Senior Neighbor News*, in which she described it as "the Waldorf-Astoria of Ash Flat, Ark." At the time, it was called B.J.'s Drive-In (although it was not, in fact, a drive-in, having started life as a Laundromat), and Mrs. Marks was so enthusiastic about her find that she wrote, "If arbiters of taste still award stars or forks for excellence, this eatery deserves a whole handful."

Although "Fine Food" had been added to the name by the time we visited Ash Flat, the restaurant was still Formica-table and linoleum-floor plain with cattle-brand decor on the walls; and despite the fact that the menu did evince glimmers of upward mobility (orange roughy and sautéed mushrooms, anyone?), we were able to enjoy some skillfully prepared, meat-and-potatoes meals. There were big, juicy pork chops with the kind of sweet elegance that pork never has north of the Mason-Dixon Line. On the side came a vegetable combination dish of rice, peas, and okra in tomato sauce (here called hoppin' john, but not at all like the traditional version of the dish), cool cole slaw, a slew of hefty, golden-crusted deep-fried mushrooms, a block of cornbread, and a salad with chunky Roquefort cheese dressing. We have also eaten B & J's catfish with onion rings on the side and chicken-fried steak topped with peppery gravy; and we even tried—and relished—that orange roughy, a firm-fleshed, delicate-flavored fish that was baked in a pepper-needled lemon butter sauce.

Portions are big in this small town cafe, and there is no dessert other than ice cream. As we were leaving after an evening meal at B & J's, the waitress regaled us with stories about breakfast: biscuits and gravy, country ham and sausage. It sounded terrific; and we are eager to return for a taste, because, to tell the truth, the dinners at B & J's were a whole lot better than anything we have eaten at the Waldorf-Astoria. Thanks for the tip, Celia!

BUBBA'S
HIGHWAY 62W, EUREKA SPRINGS, AR (501) 253-7706

At the sign of the pig in Eureka Springs, Bubba's is a barbecue parlor with a whiff of sophistication. For one thing, it has a menu; for another, the menu lists foods other than barbecued meat: both amenities would disqualify this establishment from the exclusive A-lists kept by the purest-souled barbecue hounds. However, if you like succulent, sauce-crusted baby loin back ribs (those are the smaller, most tender ones) or shoulder meat sopped with the lush, natural juices pork maintains only when it is slow-roasted over hickory coals, put this restaurant on your Arkansas itinerary.

With ribs, you want barbecued beans—sweet and sloppy; and good French fries; and crisp cole slaw; and iced tea. There is no faulting this meal; it's a classic. The shoulder meat, sold as a dinner with beans, slaw, French bread, and butter, is also available on a sandwich, topped with cole slaw. A large sandwich is huge—nearly a full meal. One other pit-cooked item worth knowing about: a hot link. For true pork junkies, this tube of drippingly fatty, highly spiced, hickory-flavored ground meat is terminal pleasure. You can get it in a sandwich, or as a "Bubba link," smothered with meaty chili and gobs of melting cheddar cheese. If the ribs and pork shoulder weren't so good, we'd eat Bubba links every time.

CATFISH 'N'
DARDANELLE DAM RD., DARDANELLE, AR (501) 229-3321

C atfish 'N' is just a quick hop off I-40: a wood-shingle building with a spanking-clean interior where Formica-topped tables are lined up in rows for serious eating. Picture windows in the dining room overlook the Arkansas River. It's just the view to properly gear one's appetite for eating a feast of catfish.

This is superb catfish—grain-fed but not at all wimpy or devoid of flavor the way some farm-raised cat can be. Hefty oval steaks are enrobed in a well-seasoned, sand-colored crust that breaks with an emphatic crunch when you crack into it. The meat inside is juicy, delicate-textured, and strong-flavored the way catfish connoisseurs prefer, and there are a few bones to contend with. Catfish-eating wouldn't seem real without a bone or two.

With these sturdy steaks come terrific hushpuppies, laced with bits of onion, sweet and steamy. And French fries with real potato flavor. And cool cole slaw to refresh the palate. And pickles and onions and lemons and peppers. Help yourself. Catfish 'N' is an all-you-can-eat buffet, and on weekend nights, the line to get at it stretches out the door.

COY'S PLACE
2908 N. COLLEGE, FAYETTEVILLE, AR (501) 442-9664

C oy's ribs are beautiful. Get a slab and wrench one free. It is huge, but there is a daintiness about the meat, which pulls away from the bone in moist ribbons that are so intensely colored you want to call them infrared. The meat is opulent, dripping juice and flavor, some of the best deluxe barbecue in Arkansas.

There is barbecued *everything* on Coy's menu. Sliced pork, redolent of the green hickory logs over which it has been cooked, is pale and tender, much easier to eat than the ribs, but not as deeply satisfying. Sausage is a sensation. It is pepper-hot and loaded with spice, tightly packed and bursting with juices. (Mild sausage is available, too.) By comparison, barbecued beef is a letdown, with none of pork's succulence. However, it can be brought up to snuff easily—by a generous application of Coy's opaque, dark-red, grainy sauce.

These barbecued beans are the kind of beans you don't get anywhere but mountain country—sweet and smoky, loaded with chunks of meat (ham, sausage), brilliantly peppered. They could be a meal all by themselves; but they are just one of the side dishes that come with a platter of barbecue, along with garlic bread and cole slaw. Barbecue salad is also on the menu (at lunch only), and Coy's is one of the most impressive variations of this odd regional favorite. It is a huge chef's salad topped with beef or pork (your choice), then barbecue sauce or salad dressing (your choice again). If you are going to try it, we recommend pork topping with barbecue sauce.

In addition to barbecue, Coy's has a high-ticket dinner menu that includes such swank items as prime rib, Cornish game hen, and steaks with sauce béarnaise. Coy's is not a funky barbecue parlor. It is a nice restaurant with a full bar, a beer list from around the world, polite service by helpful waitresses, and comfortable seating in a tableclothed dining room. But don't let any of those amenities distract you from Coy's glory—hickory-cooked meats.

CRAIG'S BAR-B-Q
ROUTE 70, DE VALLS BLUFF, AR (501) 998-2616

"Mild, medium, or hot?" you will be asked when you place an order at this roadside smokehouse. Even the mild stuff packs a pleasant punch; medium is very spicy; hot is diabolical, enough to set your tongue aglow for hours. It was quite a sight to watch local boys in overalls come to Craig's for "extra hots" at lunchtime, and quickly ingest two or three big sandwiches nonstop before hopping in their trucks and driving back to work. Not a one of the big fellers combusted from the heat.

This is superior Q; mild or hot, the lean slices of pork are irresistibly tasty even before their red-orange, peppery sauce is applied. The way most people seem to like it served at Craig's is in a bun as a sandwich, wrapped in wax paper and stuck together with a toothpick. Stuffed into the bun atop the pork is cool cole slaw, providing a truly sensational balance. And on the side, there are some superior Ozark-style beans, silky and sweet, cosseted in a lovely amber emulsion.

Much of Craig's business is take-out, although a scattering of tables across the slick floor inside provides space for eating in. For dessert, drive to the other side of Route 70 and get a piece of Mary Thomas's pie at the Family Pie Shop. It is a sublime denouement to one of Craig's climactic meals.

FAMILY PIE SHOP
ROUTE 70, DE VALLS BLUFF, AR. (501) 998-2279

Across the highway from Craig's Bar-B-Q is the Family Pie Shop, one of three four-star restaurants in De Valls Bluff's constellation of superior dining establishments (see also Murry's, p. 21). It is known to Arkansans as Mary's Pie Shop after its owner, Mary Thomas. The Pie Shop is not really a restaurant. It is more an annex of Mrs. Thomas's home, built out of a former bicycle shed, now filled with tools of the baker's art. Mrs. Thomas starts baking every day at six and by late morning there are half a dozen varieties available, usually including pineapple, apple, lemon, cream, coconut, and sweet potato, all laid out in gorgeous golden brown crusts that rise up like fragile pastry halos around their fillings. Her Karo nut pie (southern cooks' name for what the rest of the world knows as pecan pie) is a tawny temptress packed with halves of nuts in a profoundly sweet suspension. The meringues on her cream pies are snow-white, decorated with tiny grid mark swirls at their cloudy peaks. Fried pies—individual-serving half-moon pockets filled with apples or peaches—shatter into ethereal fragments as soon as they are hit by fork or teeth.

Mrs. Thomas has been selling pies to the public for the last dozen years. Her customers include pie hounds from all the nearby towns as well as devotees who drive from as far away as Little Rock (or in some cases send their chauffeurs) for whole pies to take home. Others wander over from across the street in search of something sweet and soothing (such as the sublime sweet potato pie or chocolate pan pie) after a bout with fiery barbecue. She used to sell every kind of pie she made by the slice, but now she obliges those of us without a nearby dinner table by selling mini-pies, about two slices' worth, to passers-by. If you will be traveling through De Valls Bluff and crave a particular variety, call ahead to make sure Mrs. Thomas bakes it that day and saves it for you.

FRED'S FISH HOUSE
HIGHWAY 62E, MOUNTAIN HOME, AR (501) 492-5958

If you are under three years old or over ninety, you definitely want to know about Fred's, where toddlers eat free and nonagenarians eat "free on lifetime gift certificate." We're not sure what that gift certificate business is all about; but to tell the truth, we have no intention of waiting until we are ninety to return to Fred's. It's too good not to enjoy whenever we are in the vicinity of Mountain Home, even if we have to pay full price, which is less than ten dollars for a meal.

You can buy catfish fillets by size, from a little five-ouncer to a ten-ouncer; but for those intent on satiation, Fred's menu suggests a strategy entitled "The Ole Grandaddy." Grandaddy is an endless supply of fried catfish fillets—their heavy meat dripping with sweet savor, enveloped in a nice, gritty crust. With these excellent fillets there are plenty of accompaniments, and they are good, too: moist-centered hushpuppies; cole slaw; extra-large French fries; pickled tomatoes, onions, and pickles.

Catfish is definitely the thing to eat. Fred's menu boasts that only the finest Arkansas-grown fish are allowed in the kitchen, and that they are dressed daily and fried in the finest peanut oil available. (Also from that clean, clear oil come some very nice fried shrimp.) After catfish, there is only one dessert to know about, and we're not going to spoil the fun by telling you too much about it. Just the name: "Five Layer Delight Pie."

Fred's is a fitting place to munch catfish. It is casual, clean, and modern, with strange wood-weave-patterned wallpaper and an even stranger rug on the floor that looks like patio rocks. The dining room provides an unobstructed view of Lake Norfolk and the Arkansas countryside.

JIM LEWIS CAFETERIA
3400 ROGERS AVE., FORT SMITH, AR (501) 783-4569

If there were a Jim Lewis Cafeteria where we live, we would eat at it every day. There wouldn't be any need for other restaurants. If we go to heaven, we expect it to be a cafeteria a lot like this one, with chicken and dumplings puffing wisps of tantalizing steam into the air and buttermilk chess pie for dessert.

Some people raised in the South have taken our advice to eat at Jim Lewis and come back to tell us that we are exaggerating. They think it's fine, but they aren't as impressed as we are. Perhaps appreciation of the quality and scope of what is served here demands an outsider's eye. For example, okra. Arkansans or Texans may be blasé about fried okra this crisp-skinned, this fresh and zesty and joyful to chew, but to us it is a marvel. And chicken-fried steak. To those who grew up eating it, it's ordinary food; and a lot of chicken-fries you get in truck stops and second-rate cafes are worse than ordinary; but Jim Lewis' chicken-fried steak is a wonder of the *Roadfood* world, its wide, wavy golden crust enclosing a slab of meat that is tender but not too tenderized, its juice-heavy fibers a sublime companion for the crunch and chew of the crust that hugs it. On the side, there are Texas potatoes, a dish about which no spud lover could ever be nonchalant. These are cross-sections of potato, fried with onions until some of the onions blacken and many of the potato discs turn crisp while others stay floppy, soft as butter.

We won't rave on about all the good things there are to eat at Jim Lewis. As in the finest cafeterias of the South (and the Midwest), there is a vast selection every day: dozens of salads, pies (note in particular the German chocolate pie), vegetables, and meats. The bread selection is stunning: whole sweet pineapple-studded loaves, jalapeño cornbreads, corn sticks and corn muffins, cinnamon twirls, baking powder biscuits, white rolls, wheat rolls, dinner rolls, and Texas toast. We want to swoon just thinking about the choice from the handsome array; and if you are a traveler who loves to eat, you, too, will feel weak-kneed when you begin your journey through this awe-inspiring cafeteria line.

MC CLARD'S BAR-B-Q
505 ALBERT PIKE, HOT SPRINGS, AR (501) 623-9665 OR 624-9586

We raise our milk-shake glasses high to salute traveling chowhound Mitchel Zoler, who directed us to McClard's Bar-B-Q with a recommendation no false modesty can keep us from repeating: "Mr. and Mrs. Stern, thank you for the humanitarian work you have done writing *Roadfood*. Allow me to suggest McClard's. Their beans are beyond description."

Mr. Zoler was right. There is no way mere words can adequately convey the complex chili zest of McClard's beans, which are at once hot, sweet, tangy, and pillowy soft. So we won't try. Simply let us say that you have not tasted Ozark beans until you have tasted these. The really good news is that the superlative beans are merely a side dish for barbecue—beef *and* pork *and* pork ribs—that is stratospherically delicious . . . and even harder to describe.

But seeing as how it's our job, let us try to tell you what this Q is like. The beef is sirloin, slow-sizzled over smoldering hickory until it begins to disintegrate, crusty and rugged outside but soft and yielding within, heavy with natural juices, shot through with the kick of smoke and glazed with dizzying sauce that achieves balance among pepper's heat, sugar's sweetness, lemon's zest, the plushness of tomatoes, and the pungency of vinegar. It isn't quite as stunning to taste pork so succulent; but at the risk of running out of adjectives, we must tell you that McClard's pork is rich indeed—tender, steamy-sweet pieces brought to pig epiphany by that sauce; and ribs whose meat yanks off the bone in long, luscious strips.

With the meat and beans, McClard's dishes out lovely crisp French fries and cole slaw; and you can even eat excellent versions of that Mississippi Delta specialty, hot tamales, available on the side or as the centerpiece of a hot tamale spread with beans, meat, sauce, and chips. To wash down these spicy foods, choose beer or a thick milk shake.

There is a nice story behind McClard's beginnings. It seems that back in 1928, when the McClards ran a tourist court, they had a boarder who offered them a sauce recipe instead of his ten-dollar rent. They took the recipe, opened a barbecue pit adjacent to their motor court, and within a few years barbecue was their profession, built upon the secret recipe, which has been followed to the letter by their children and now their grandchildren. The McClards' business card boasts "Bar-B-Q: best in the state since '28." No one who eats their food could possibly dispute that claim.

MURRY'S CAFE
CYPRESS ST., DE VALLS BLUFF, AR (501) 998-2247

Senator Dale Bumpers once gave a picture of himself to Mr. Murry, autographed to "the best cook in Arkansas." For about half a century, Murry's Cafe in De Valls Bluff has been a beacon among serious eaters in the mid-South. Nearly everyone comes for catfish with all the fixin's.

The old Murry's was quite an amazing site: a helter-skelter collection of manufactured homes and makeshift dining rooms situated way back on a side street. There was no sign outside, but no one needed one. Any night of the week, starting after four in the afternoon, all you had to do was follow the legions of hungry customers and hope that you could find a place among the crowd. The new Murry's is tidier—a green-and-white house on Cypress Street—but it is still an unlikely setting in which to discover some of the finest shrimp, oysters, frog's legs, and catfish for miles around.

Mr. Murry's expertise is deep-frying. His catfish fillets are gorgeous lengths of fish, moist and profoundly luscious inside their shatteringly brittle crusts, accompanied by a hot corn cake, French fries, and good cole slaw. Shrimp and oysters are delicious, too, especially the latter, which are so fragile once you crunch through their crisp-fried breading. Fish frowners can order steak or quail at Murry's, and we hear they, too, are very good. But it seems to us that eating anything other than catfish at Murry's would be a little like going to a bakery in Paris and asking for Wonder Bread instead of a croissant.

ROCKHOUSE BAR-B-QUE
416 SOUTH PINE (HIGHWAY 7), HARRISON, AR (501) 741-1787

The Rockhouse is genteel. It looks like a picturesque rock-house cabin from the outside. Inside, the floors are gleaming polished wood, and the paneled walls are hung with impressive full-size quilts. Tables are covered with red-checked oilcloth. And there is actually a cute printed menu (decorated with cartoons of cavorting pigs), listing many items other than barbecue, including fish and steaks broiled over hickory and a variety of "gourmet burgers" topped with "natural cheeses."

It is barbecue that draws the customers, particularily on weekend evenings. Mike Warshauer, a spelunker who runs a bakery in Mountain View, Arkansas, and who tipped us off about the Rockhouse, explained that the food is actually more delicious on weekends. "Perhaps it's just a nuance of interpretation," he suggested, "but the fires are hotter then. The ribs are perhaps a notch better."

They are loin back pork ribs, sold by the rack or half rack, their crusty meat fairly glowing with baked-in spice. Only a gentle tug is required to pull succulent strips of pork clean off their bone. There are other kinds of barbecue, too—beef brisket, sliced pork loin, ham, chicken, and Polish sausage—but it is ribs you want to eat.

The other thing to order, a dish referred to by Mr. Warshauer as "a Platonic masterpiece," is onion rings. They are quite an amazing creation: individual giant-size O's with a fresh-fried crunch and a distinctive tang to their faintly sour, buttermilky batter. If onion rings are too tame or ordinary for your taste, the Rockhouse offers a whole roster of deep-fried things, including dill pickles and jalapeño peppers.

Other regional specialties to enjoy at the Rockhouse: barbecued salad, which is the Ozark version of a chef's salad, made here with three kinds of smoked meat; beverages served in one-pint Mason jars; pit-cooked beans laced with shreds of ham and onion; and stupendously delicious cornbread. This bread is moist and jalapeño-hottened, dished out in big squares on plates, so quiveringly tender that you are best off eating it with utensils, like spoonbread.

STUBBY'S HIK-RY PIT BAR-B-Q
310 PARK AVE., HOT SPRINGS, AR (501) 624-2484

Barbecue, cafeteria-style: the line forms at the door and proceeds past a hot oven pit and cutting boards where ribs are chopped, beef and pork are sliced, baked potatoes are dressed with gobs of butter, and crocks of beans are fetched from deep within the pit.

Stubby's barbecue is smoky and sweet, and nearly everything they make here is strongly flavored. The sauce is dark cinnabar red and as rich as molasses, hot and peppery. Poured onto a cardboard basket full of lean flaps of beef strewn with little shreds of blackened crust, it will set your tongue aglow. The sauce is baked into the ribs, which are lean and meaty and benefit from a quick dip in some of the extra sauce that comes with every tray of food.

The beans are real Ozark vittles, served in a small stone crock that is positively loaded with big, luscious shreds of ham. And the potato is a treat, too. Cooked in the pit until its skin is about as tough as leather but the insides are pure, spuddy fluff: a perfect, gentle white counterpoint for the delirium of sweetness and spice that is Stubby's barbecue.

WAR EAGLE MILL
HIGHWAY 98, 13 MILES EAST OF ROGERS, AR (501) 789-5343

The scenery around the War Eagle Mill is bucolic: pastures and grazing cows, and a steady-moving river dotted with canoeists and fishermen. On the top floor of the mill is a place to eat called "The Bean Palace." Here you can sit down to breakfast of whole-grain buckwheat cakes and sausage, cracked-wheat cereal, biscuits and sausage gravy with sorghum molasses on the side, and good old-fashioned grits.

Lunch at the Bean Palace is a small repertoire of Ozark cooking with an emphasis on healthy, whole-grain breads and rugged-textured, granola-style cookies and pies. What sweet memories we have of dipping our steamy hot wedges of cornbread into individual pots of pork and beans, then forking up the porky corn and bean mélange, punctuated by big gulps of sweet iced tea served in individual Mason jars. Even the ham sandwich at the War Eagle Mill is memorable: good, smoked Ozark ham, served on slabs of whole-grain bread in country high-style, on a blue-marbled granite-ware dish.

The War Eagle Mill really houses a working, eighteen-foot water wheel with a triple set of buhrs that grind wheat and corn slowly (unlike modern high-speed steel rollers, which heat it up during grinding), producing whole-grain flour and cornmeal that contain all the natural germ, oil, and bran: nothing added, nothing taken out. You can see the mill at work every Saturday and Sunday, when visitors with grain of their own are asked to phone ahead if they'd like to have the miller grind it for them.

(The Bean Palace is not open for dinner: breakfast and lunch only.)

CALIFORNIA

BEADLE'S CAFETERIA
825 E. GREEN ST., PASADENA, CA (818) 796-3618

If you appreciate cafeteria cuisine as much as we do, Beadle's is bliss. It has been about fifteen years since we first were smitten by its fine food, and although the place itself has been relocated (to make way for an office building) and remodeled, the food hasn't changed a bit. The entrée station of the line is still anchored by magnificent twin landmarks: a roast beef and a ham, ready to be carved to order.

As always, the line begins with a comprehensive selection of salads, including fruited Jell-O, slaws of every description, Waldorf salad, apple-date mélange, and bowls of stewed prunes. Breads, muffins, and rolls are hot and homemade. Vegetables are real (including excellent mashed potatoes to go with that roast beef). The dessert station features cake, fruit pies, and a choice of chocolate, vanilla, or rainbow ice cream.

A few urgent recommendations beyond roast beef and mashed potatoes: corned beef hash, a dark, serious mishmash with savory snap; macaroni and cheese, the comfort food *pièce de résistance;* apple fritters, big tender buns gilded with a microthin sugar glaze; and asparagus on double-thick toast with rarebit sauce.

If you are a fan of polite, old-fashioned kinds of cake (from an era before such vulgar concepts as chocolate decadence and flourless blackout cake), there is no way you will be able to resist Beadle's coconut cake—a triple-decked tower at least six inches high, spread thick with sweet white frosting.

Aside from the satisfying food, another reason we like Beadle's is its civility. Serve yourself, then a hostess comes around to refill your coffee cup, and busboys help remove your tray. Silverware, doled out at the beginning of the line, is bundled in thick white napkins. The clientele tend to be a polite segment of society, nice people.

Beadle's has long been a favorite among oldsters, who appreciate the low prices, mild seasonings, and prunes. But we recommend this grand dining room to anyone of any age who has a taste for honest American food.

CAFE BEAUJOLAIS
961 UKIAH ST., MENDOCINO, CA (707) 937-5614

Among those of us for whom breakfast is the most eagerly anticipated meal of the day, Margaret Fox's restaurant in a 1910-vintage Victorian house on a side street in Mendocino is a siren song. Breakfast this good is sure to put anyone in the right frame of mind to face the day; the fact that you walk out of the cafe into the ocean-scented air of the northern California coast makes it one of our favorite eating experiences anywhere. "When I die and go to heaven," one anonymous fan wrote to Ms. Fox several years ago, "there had better be a Cafe Beaujolais there, or I'm not going."

Waffles: crisp, slightly sour, steamy hot. They are served with maple syrup, but you only want a drizzle, just enough to add a pinch of sweetness to the tang of buttermilk and grainy bite of cornmeal and oatmeal from which these lovely golden pastries are laced together. Even the most ordinary items on Cafe Beaujolais's morning menu are extraordinary. Creamy omelettes are filled with fresh mushrooms and sour cream, or wondrous herbed cream cheese, or linguica sausage or—on one well-remembered occasion—ricotta and Gruyère cheeses and sautéed sweet peppers. Fried potatoes to go with eggs are served with sour cream, or with jack cheese melted into them.

Granola, presented with pieces of gorgeous fresh fruit fanned out across the top, is studded with sunflower seeds and loaded with chunky cashews, and has a snowy texture unlike any other granola we have tasted. Of course there is a full array of freshly made muffins, rolls, almond croissants, and coffee cakes, including a poppy seed apricot Danish to die for.

There are handsome-looking lunch and dinner menus at Cafe Beaujolais, including such totems of modern upscale dining as Chinese chicken salad, baked polenta, and all manner of grilled fish and local lamb. And Margaret Fox is famous for her nutty Italianate confection, panforte de Mendocino, as well as such killer desserts as chocolate sin and a buttercream caramel bar sundae. Sounds great, but we have yet to come to Cafe Beaujolais for dinner because we always route our travels to be here early in the morning, for the best breakfast in the West.

CARL'S BAR-B-QUE
5953 PICO BLVD., LOS ANGELES, CA (213) 934-0637

Sawdust is strewn across the floor. There is a disorderly pile of hickory logs against one wall. The air is so heavy with cooking smoke it makes your eyes water. What a welcome scene!

Several years ago when we heard that Carl's, a venerable Los Angeles soul-food eatery, had moved to a new shopping center location, we worried that it would sanitize itself and in doing so lose its soul. On the contrary. If anything, Carl's is better than ever. And while not exactly genteel, it's definitely friendly.

Even when the place seemed more daunting to timid souls like ourselves, we frequented Carl's, as did fans of smoke-cooked food from all over Los Angeles, who know that the kind of finger-licking meatstuffs dished out here could never be attained in a restaurant with a too-dainty temperament.

Ribs are the thing to get: half a small-end slab. Heft a bone. Rip into the pork. Tear it loose. It's tender, the lean parts heavy with juice that long hours in the pit have coaxed from its veins of fat.

As you savor this extraordinary succulence, another sensation begins to tickle your tongue, then gradually fill your mouth. It's the sauce, magnificent sauce, whether you get it regular or hot. Like all great sauces, this one builds. It sets your mouth aglow. By the time you have finished a half-slab of ribs, you feel its warmth from your lips to your stomach. This sauce and these ribs constitute one of the essential eating experiences Los Angeles has to offer.

There is more to eat at Carl's, all of it distinguished. Many customers know the restaurant as Carl's Dirty Rice for its version of the kaleidoscopic Cajun specialty that joins rice with chicken gizzards, spice, et cetera, to make a profound side dish or a meal. All of the barbecue companions are good: gloriously thick macaroni and cheese, fall-apart tender yams, baked beans or black beans, black-eyed peas, outstanding potato salad. Carl's also offers collard greens and cole slaw. Two vegetables, plus greens, dirty rice, and corn bread come on the side with any "soul dinner."

Those who don't spring for the whole soul dinner can satisfy major appetite with a sandwich. Carl's sandwiches are giants, big enough to nearly cover a plate, virtually impossible to eat without significant spillage, bun disintegration, and vast quantities of napkins.

The thing to get for dessert is one of the individual sweet potato pies, another classic of the soul-food kitchen. On one occasion we remember, the other after-dinner offering was sock-it-to-me cake, a classic of the modern convenience food kitchen. We didn't try it, but knowing the magic touch of Carl's, it wouldn't surprise us a bit to discover that even it had been exquisite.

CASSELL'S
3266 W. 6TH ST., LOS ANGELES, CA (213) 480-8668

Want to know how good Cassell's hamburgers are? Johnny Carson and Clint Eastwood have eaten here. Liza Minelli, too. Carl Reiner and Peter Boyle once ate here together. In Los Angeles, stars' endorsements can be a restaurant's greatest asset, and Cassell's has been blessed by many heavy hitters; but it isn't stardust alone that puts it on the map. It's the fact that the hamburgers actually are excellent—and that Cassell's dishes them out with that unique devil-may-care panache that makes the street food in this city so much fun.

You are not allowed to tell the servers you want a two-thirds-pound cheeseburger with the works or a one-third-pound hamburger, rare. A sign on the wall instructs customers to order strictly by the number that corresponds to what they want: a twenty-one, or a thirty-three, or a twenty-seven. Appetizing, isn't it?

Never mind the formalities. Cassell's burger is a beaut, best described by the artificial word first uttered by Jayne Mansfield in *The Girl Can't Help It: divoon.* Each patty is made from prime steak, double ground daily, broiled on a special slanted rack so excess grease drips away. It is charred nearly black, pocketing enough juice to make your chin glisten at the first jaw-stretching bite, and served on a large sesame-seed-spangled bun. We definitely recommend the two-third-pound patty over the one-third-pounder. The big one can be cooked all the way to medium and still keep plenty of juice in its rosy center; the smaller one can dry out fast.

This is a superior burger, but check out the buffet of extras, too: homemade mayonnaise and red relish, sliced tomatoes that actually taste like tomatoes (remember them?), the best potato salad in town, pineapple chunks and peach halves, cottage cheese, and Roquefort dressing. Cassell's aficionados pile on everything, making the Platonic patty the ground floor of a tremendous, only-in-California condiment salad.

CLIFTON'S BROOKDALE CAFETERIA
648 SOUTH BROADWAY (AT 7TH), LOS ANGELES, CA (213) 627-1673
(4 OTHER LOCATIONS IN LOS ANGELES AND VICINITY)

The original Clifton's Pacific Seas Cafeteria (since 1931) closed in 1960, but there are five other Clifton's still going strong in Los Angeles, including the Brookdale, which was built in 1935 and remains the largest open-to-the-public cafeteria in the world. Designed to remind visitors of California's redwood groves, the Brookdale is a multi-tiered stage set with granite cliffs, boulders, tree trunks, a babbling brook and waterfall, and transparent forest scene murals on the mezzanine walls. Three separate cafeteria lines disperse customers toward tables; and at mealtime, the place is a clamorous symphony of plates clanking and boisterous eaters from all walks of life plowing into trays full of good, old-fashioned, institutional food.

The cuisine of Clifton's is as satisfying in its own way as anything you will find anywhere in Los Angeles: fried chicken and buttermilk biscuits, turkey with all the trimmings, meat loaf and mashed potatoes, Jell-O molds galore, and wondrously corny desserts such as millionaire pie (whipped cream, pineapple chunks, sugar, and nuts), ice cream with jamocha sauce, and pumpkin-nut crumble cake. We especially appreciate the wide array of vegetables available in the cafeteria line. There are innumerable pans of roasted, whipped, and fried potatoes, as well as various cheese-enriched casseroles and one gelatinized wonder known as "spinach soufflé gelatin" whipped up from spinach, mayonnaise, lemon gelatin, and cottage cheese.

The price of a meal is ridiculously low (about three dollars), and Clifton's stated policy is "No check too small; no service too great. Pay what you wish, and dine free unless delighted." If you like square meals, and appreciate the flavors of American cookery at its most ingenuous, you *will* be delighted!

THE COTTAGE
7702 FAY, LA JOLLA, CA (619) 454-8409

$\mathcal{S}$ ome people like to stop and smell the roses. We prefer to stop and smell the coffee, especially if it is strong espresso and it is being brewed at The Cottage of La Jolla, and it is accompanied by an aromatic, hot-from-the-oven muffin and a farm-fresh fruit cup.

Early in the morning, you could walk in the door of The Cottage blind-folded and guess the entire muffin menu just by inhaling. You might smell baked apple and oatmeal, blueberries, carrots, cornmeal, or bran. The aromas might also include yeasty cinnamon rolls, coffee cake, and the hefty, gnarled "health muffins" which are surprisingly unsweet and genuinely healthy-tasting. The muffin we like best is a pale gold one made with peaches and poppy seeds. Behind the bakery case where the muffins are displayed are all the appurtenances for brewing espresso and steaming milk to make cappuccino and Cottage Cafe mocha—a blend of espresso, steamed milk, chocolate, and cinnamon.

Breakfast is the meal to eat at The Cottage. It is served until eleven in the morning Monday through Saturday, and Sunday from eight to two. In addition to the bakery goodies, there are omelettes of all kinds, from machaca (shredded beef) to one called "The Pope's Favorite" (kielbasa and cheddar cheese) and the luxurious California combo of avocado, bacon, Monterey jack cheese, and sour cream. There are Belgian waffles, served plain or with bananas and/or strawberries. You can get *huevos rancheros,* granola with steamed milk or yogurt, or eggs-and-cheese enchiladas.

The Cottage is open for lunch, too, when they serve sandwiches, quiche, soup, and an array of salads that includes Hawaiian chicken salad (with honey poppy seed dressing), a traditional Cobb salad, taco salad (with beef, beans, and corn tortilla, topped with sour cream), and a rainbow-hued fruit salad (its ingredients sliced to order) with yogurt or cottage cheese. They make a nice mild chili here, listed on the menu as "My Mother's Chili," served with cornbread. To accompany lunch (or breakfast), The Cottage makes its own version of that Southern California specialty, the smoothie—a kind of healthy milk shake blended from fresh orange juice and fresh fruits, with a raw egg added on request.

The dining room of The Cottage is cute and casual, with about eight small tables and four booths. Silverware comes wrapped in a paper napkin; coffee is served in tall, graceful mugs; specialty coffees come in glass cups. Overhead, ceiling fans help circulate the good aromas. Many customers never see the dining room. They come to sit on the broad front patio at an umbrellaed table, basking in La Jolla's perpetually glorious weather, reading the paper, sipping coffee, eating good food, and generally relishing the Good Life.

THE DINER
6476 WASHINGTON ST., YOUNTVILLE, CA (707) 944-2626

B egun in the 1970s by Cassandra Mitchell and her friends, the Diner is a converted bus depot conceived as an ode to real American food. It is a happy place by the side of the road, not as snazzy as an actual stainless steel diner, but comfortable and inviting, with a counter and stools and big booths, and air that smells like bread baking, bacon grilling, and hot fudge sauce brewing. The menu includes a notable repertoire of soda fountain delights, big hamburgers, breakfast (served all day), and a selection of expertly made and quietly seasoned California-style Mexican food (evening only).

The meal that first made us smitten with this Napa County treasure is breakfast, which features homemade sourdough rye, raisin wheat, wheatberry, or potato bread and a spectacular side dish modestly titled "seasoned potatoes," which is a heap of skin-on disks, some sizzled crisp and others butter-soft, woven with limp bits of sautéed onions and festooned with melted cheddar cheese. The potatoes create a problem: they are fine companions for eggs and omelettes, but they don't really go with pancakes, and The Diner's pancakes are swell. We especially like the banana-nut pancakes with maple syrup, or buttermilk corn cakes sided by sausage patties seasoned with herbs from The Diner's backyard garden. There are also potato pancakes made from finely shredded spuds and some of those homegrown herbs. Also on the breakfast menu is a colossal burrito stuffed with eggs and chorizo sausage. The coffee is good and strong; and if you've got time to linger, you might want to sip on a Mimosa, made with freshly squeezed orange juice and locally bottled champagne.

The midday menu is a roster of reassuring lunch-counter fare: grilled cheese sandwiches, "humdinger hamburgers" (on an English muffin), BLTs, avocado BLTs, daily blue-plate specials, and some good soups and salads. What we like about lunch is the soda fountain menu, which includes flavored Cokes (chocolate, cherry, lemon, vanilla, or a combination of all syrups known as "the suicide"), sundaes (deluxe and midget size), sodas and banana splits, and every kind of milk shake or genuine malt you could hope for (including even a buttermilk shake that does a good impersonation of liquid cheesecake). The fudge for the hot fudge sundaes, by the way, is homemade and sensational—dark, grainy, dizzyingly intense.

Now, dinner. At nightfall a whole other menu, titled "El Diner," makes its appearance, and the specialties of the house become such robust Mexican-style things as chicken and cream enchiladas, carne asada (grilled steak strips with salsa), chicken molé, and *tostadas grande.* The accompanying guacamole is especially memorable, at once thick and creamy, merely the essence of avocado heightened by a temperate infusion of mashed garlic. If you don't want a hot fudge sundae for dessert (you do, you do!), El Diner's menu also lists flan—smooth as silk, and just as sweet as it ought to be.

DOIDGE'S
2217 UNION ST., SAN FRANCISCO, CA (415) 921-2149

A cheerful, always-crowded storefront, Doidge's serves lunch every day and dinner a few nights a week, but breakfast is the meal we like best, when the able cafe kitchen sends forth some spectacular and delicious presentations. Baked eggs arrive in cups formed from Motherlode bacon. Eggs benedict are topped with ethereal hollandaise sauce. Corned beef hash is a dazzling mélange of coarsely cut, highly seasoned beef mixed with fresh mushrooms, flavored with onions and parsley and gobs of sour cream, sharpened with parmesan cheese, capped with a perfect poached egg. On the side come crusty fried potatoes and a sourdough roll.

You want French toast? Choose your bread: white, whole wheat, light rye, dark rye, honey wheat, or raisin nut. The toast is available topped with bananas, walnuts and cinnamon, fruit and sour cream, or fresh fruit alone. Doidge's omelette list is endless, including peach and walnut chutney, black olive and Monterey jack cheese, avocado and cream cheese, and all kinds of peppers. Orange and grapefruit juice are freshly squeezed; coffee is extraordinarily good.

There are many places to eat a magnificent breakfast in San Francisco. Doidge's is in the Pantheon.

DUARTE'S
202 STAGE ROAD, PESCADERO, CA. (415) 879-0464

Duarte's is a small-town tavern where locals come to eat at mismatched tables and chairs in a knotty-pine-paneled dining room. When it's crowded—as it usually is at mealtimes—strangers share tables. Geezers hold court; babies squall; townsfolk trade gossip; and travelers are made to feel right at home.

Down-home dinner, California-style, doesn't get much better than this. There are pork chops served with homemade applesauce and chunky mashed potatoes; pot roast; beef stew; roast turkey with sage dressing. Depending on the time of year and how the fish are running, you can dine on the finest-textured local seafood—sand dabs or rex sole. If you are an oyster lover, you haven't lived until you've tasted Duarte's Pigeon Point oysters, baked in puddles of garlic butter. Even the house salad—a perfunctory gesture in so many restaurants—is a bounty of beets, onions, carrots, beefsteak tomatoes, and lettuce that all taste like they were pulled, picked, or plucked from a nearby garden.

Artichokes are a specialty of the house because the farmland around Pescadero is thick with the thistle-topped stalks of artichoke plants. In fact, Pescadero isn't far from Castroville, which lays claim to the title "Artichoke Capital of the World" (and boasts a restaurant called The Giant Artichoke, with a menu that includes not only boiled and fried artichokes, but even artichoke cake!). The Duarte family has their own patch; at their cafe, they make maximum use of the garden's yield, serving them simply steamed or elaborately stuffed (with fennel sausage), in omelettes at breakfast, and as the foundation of artichoke soup that accompanies every full-scale dinner.

For serious feasting, we recommend a visit to Duarte's on Friday or Saturday night, when the kitchen prepares a grand version of San Francisco cioppino, a symphonic red-sauced fisherman's stew made with clams, prawns, mussels, cod, and Dungeness crab. Cioppino is served with hard-crusted sourdough bread, and second helpings are included in the price of dinner.

To conclude any meal at Duarte's, you want pie—blue-ribbon pie reminiscent more of some great mythical mom's home cooking than of restaurant fare. Olallie berries, rhubarb, apricots, and apples are sweetened and heaped into feather-light crusts that are all the more delicious for being so homely rather than symmetrical. Such homemade pies using local produce

have been a tradition in this extraordinary dining room ever since Frank
Duarte opened for business ninety-eight years ago.

DUKE'S
8909 SUNSET BLVD., WEST HOLLYWOOD, CA (213) 652-9411

Duke's is still a dump, thank goodness. Those who relish Hollywood's
haute hash houses got nervous back in 1987 when the Tropicana
Motel, a fleabag to which Duke's was connected, got demolished and
Duke's was forced to move out on its own. It is indeed scary when you first
see the new location on Sunset Boulevard. It looks clean and polite! And
there is a sign outside announcing ATTENDANT PARKING, in back, for a dollar. Has Duke's gone uptown?

No way. At heart it is the same democratic canteen it always was.
Rock-and-roll pix and posters are still taped helter-skelter on grubby white
walls. There is counter seating and there are tables. The tables are lined
up mess-hall style, so no matter where you sit you are uncomfortably close
to a motley crew of tinseltown characters you might not want to be so close
to. (But gosh, it's fun to eavesdrop!)

The management has added metal rails along the entry ramp to
restrain people waiting for a precious place in the dining room. Above this
holding pen, a Magic-Markered sign instructs, "Please Do Not Sit On
Rails." Duke's is crowded every morning, especially on weekends, because
it is a place to see and to be seen.

It remains the premier breakfast spot for celebrities and would-be
celebrities who feel the need to *get real*. Duke's is the Polo Lounge of the
blue-jeans set, where counterculture connoisseurs come to get away from
the supercilious gastronomy that pervades the upper echelons of the West
L.A. eating scene.

Although some customers come only to be part of the morning proces-
sion, there is another good reason to patronize Duke's: excellent food. That
hasn't changed either. Despite its impolite airs, Duke's dishes out some of
the prettiest good-tasting breakfasts you will ever eat. Glorious pancakes:
fluffy but substantial, the batter loaded with sliced bananas or apples or
strawberries; lovely omelettes, made with all the usual ingredients, or
sunny original combos such as peach chutney, walnuts, raisins, and sour
cream.

Duke's makes the best blintzes in town: tissue-thin crepes rolled
around pot cheese and fresh fruit, gobbed with mounds of sour cream.

Good French toast, good muffins, great high-calorie beverages such as fruit smoothies and pineapple-coconut shakes. And, of course, freshly squeezed orange juice.

The food is good. The scene is fun. The waitresses are sassy and sexy. If you live in L.A. or if, like us, you come only to sightsee, this is a restaurant to inscribe in your little black book. Duke's is a Hollywood original. Where else would you see a sign scrawled on the cash register, in these exact words: "Back by Popular Demand, Appearing Night and Day: Frozen Snickers."

EL INDIO
3695 INDIA ST., SAN DIEGO, CA (619) 299-0333

El Indio, a great place to feast on Mexican food, is just north of the airport alongside Interstate 5 in San Diego. It has a tortilla press turning out big, warm wheaty ones for burros and chimichangas; there are hot corn tortillas, freshly fried and super crunchy; there are chimichangas, quesadillas, tacos, and taquitos. There are lush pork carnitas, combo plates topped with gobs of sour cream, and crisply fried fruit burros dusted with cinnamon sugar. El Indio is the place to savor nearly all the good varieties of Tex-Mex food—or, more properly, Cal-Mex food.

The cuisine of this kitchen is based on the food of Sonora in western Mexico, which means that most of the cooking is not too spicy, and it includes copious amounts of drippy cheese and mild peppers, as well as fresh avocados, sliced as garnishes and mashed into exemplary guacamole. Cups of hot sauce come with nearly every meal, and although the fresh-tasting sauce is zesty, you don't have to worry about scorching your tongue. Food can be ordered by the piece—taco-by-taco, wheat tortillas by the dozen; or as lavish suppers that come garnished with rainbows of bright tomatoes, peppers, avocados, and always lots of sour cream.

Dining at El Indio is very informal. In fact, there is no indoor seating at all. It's just a bunch of take-out windows and a long (but fast-moving) line of customers waiting to place their order. Across the street, however, El Indio maintains a sunny, fenced-in patio to which many people carry their heaping take-out plates, along with cups of cold soda or Peñafiel to drink. Here you sit, serenaded by cars passing on the raised highway, as well as the festive sounds of customers at their Styrofoam plates, plowing plastic forks into utterly authentic western chow.

Above the windows where you order your food at El Indio are portraits of fierce Mayan gods, including the god of war, the gods of rain and wind, and the god of Mexican food, who according to this portrait goes by the name of El Indio. We aren't up to date on our Mayan theology; but there is no doubt in our minds that El Indio is indeed the god of Mexican food, at least in San Diego.

FOG CITY DINER
1300 BATTERY ST., SAN FRANCISCO, CA (415) 982-2000

The Fog City Diner *is* a diner, all shiny silver and neon with the classic configuration of a long counter as well as some tables and booths farther out by the windows. Like an old-style diner, service is fast and efficient; you can come for a big meal or a small snack; and prices are relatively low. However, this is a diner with an elevated consciousness. No ordinary roadside beanery will ever serve you gorgeous crabcakes like they make here, accompanied by sherry-cayenne mayonnaise; or baked buffalo mozzarella and peppers with pesto on toast; or cold rare sirloin salad with onions, asagio, anchovies, and zesty olive tapenade.

Don't worry, there are some fine blue-plate classics on the menu, too. You can get an excellent hamburger or a "cheese hamburger" (they come with *homemade* catsup); you can get French fries or onion rings (more elegant than you have ever seen or tasted in your life); and there are root beer floats, turtle sundaes made with homemade ice cream, and chocolate malted milk shakes (all superb). Pickles are actually pickled here; and if you want something different with your hamburger or chili dog or pork chop, ask for a mashed potato pancake—it is unpardonably delicious.

Some of the Fog City specialties are clever variations on familiar themes: a Cobb *sandwich* (rather than a salad) of smoked turkey, avocado, bacon, and sharp Gorgonzola cheese on a homemade poppy seed roll; grilled calf's liver, but with pancetta instead of bacon, and tomato pesto for a garnish; leek and basil bread (rather than garlic bread), toasted crisp and dripping butter, heaped with fresh herbs.

We love this modern food and place as much as any of San Francisco's more venerable eateries; and oh, what torture it is to live three thousand miles away. When you are in the Bay Area, do yourself a favor and give it a taste. Reservations are advised, especially if you want one of the plush booths. (We actually prefer the counter, where you can watch the activities of the open-kitchen staff, who are as agile as short-order chefs, but considerably more artistic.)

HOB NOB HILL
2271 FIRST AVE., SAN DIEGO, CA (619) 239-8176

In a world of mercurial food trends, Hob Nob Hill is a gastronomic Rock of Gibraltar. To eat here is to come home for dinner.

Actually, it's breakfast, every bit as much as dinner, that has won people's loyalty to this comfy coffee shop for the last half century. Hob Nob Hill opens at seven, and by nine there is almost always a line waiting to get in. The line leads inside past glass cases crowded with such fresh-baked wonders as cherry cashew bread, orange pecan and other varieties of bundt cake, and various fruit breads, loaves, and rolls.

When you get a seat, you are set upon by a team of waitresses who couldn't move any faster if they *flew* through the aisles. Now comes the hard part: choosing from a repertoire that includes truly excellent pecan waffles, pigs in blankets (buttermilk pancakes rolled with ham, sausage, and sour cream), blueberry hotcakes, grilled smoked pork chops—plus a bakery's worth of coffee cakes, wondrous muffins (try carrot), and a not-to-be-missed pecan roll. Even little amenities are special: syrup is served warm; jelly comes in hollowed-out orange halves; coffee is strong and rich—and hottened-up throughout the meal.

At dinner, it's meat-and-potatoes time: leg of lamb with sage dressing and mint jelly, chicken and dumplings, roast tom turkey with giblet gravy, corned beef and cabbage, pot roast and buttered noodles every Sunday. There are turkey croquettes with cranberry sauce, a nursery-nice breast-of-chicken curry, and baked ham with fruit sauce and yams on Thursday. It is all expertly prepared, accompanied by such homey and out-of-fashion side dishes as warm applesauce (homemade, of course), marinated bean salad, and puffy yeast rolls.

Every city ought to have a Hob Nob Hill. But this place is San Diego's alone, a one-of-a-kind journey back to gastronomic innocence.

JO-ANN'S CAFE
1131 EL CAMINO REAL, SOUTH SAN FRANCISCO, CA (415) 872-2810

Tucked into our file cabinet of tips, in the California section, is a napkin on which we long ago wrote these words: *Buttermilk shake at Jo-Ann's—Harvey Steiman says the best.* Nobody knows more about San Francisco restaurants than Harvey Steiman so this was a hint we took seriously. Not only did he extol the milk shakes; he sang praises about the home cooking; he rhapsodized about featherweight omelettes; he implored us to eat a plate of pancakes. "Jo-Ann's is your kind of place," he assured. After a few breakfasts there, we are happy to report that he was right.

The first few times at Jo-Ann's, we were so mesmerized by breakfast that we forgot all about the milk shakes. You will see what we mean if you arrive about seven or eight in the morning, when the muffins are out in their trays near the cash register. Who can resist these big-topped beauties? Blueberry, apple, banana: the options vary; our favorite is raisin-nut, a tawny hulk that looks just grand when you pull it apart and set some butter on it to melt.

Another fresh-baked breakfast attraction is orange bread, which is sliced thick and made into French toast. There are superior pancakes, too—the batter spiked with mashed bananas or pumpkin; or you can get a stack of buckwheat cakes. Jo-Ann's granola is a lavish harmony of nuts, raisins, honey-flavored grains, brown sugar, and fruit. And there is a pleasingly direct item on the menu known as "Jose Pappas." It is a mound of home-fried potatoes topped with cheddar cheese, hot salsa, and sour cream.

Then there are omelettes. Name your filling: Italian sausage, Cajun sausage, bacon, turkey, cheddar cheese, Monterey jack cheese, Swiss cheese, cream cheese, blue cheese, parmesan cheese, jalapeño peppers, chili peppers, bell peppers, mushrooms, green onions, caviar, sour cream, or black olives. A three-egg omelette comes with your choice of any two ingredients. If you want more than two, you pay ninety-five cents per addendum. The first time we visited Jo-Ann's, the blackboard above the counter listed a special omelette of the day: spinach, ground beef, cheddar cheese, tomatoes, and olives. It had no name, but anyone with an interest in arcane Bay Area cuisine could spot it as an omelettized version of the weird local dish known as a "New Joe Special," which San Francisco's Italian restaurants have been concocting since the 1930s. New Joes vary from place to place, but they are basically a jumble of ground beef, spinach, and eggs. Customarily, all the ingredients, including the eggs, are stirred together in a frying pan. Here at Jo-Ann's (no relation to any other Joe's), the eggs form a pocket for all the other ingredients.

Now, about that buttermilk shake: it is silky sheer heaven, a glass of liquid moo that reminded us of four-star cheesecake somehow reduced to its thick flavor essence. It wouldn't taste right at breakfast, and it is so luscious it hardly seems proper to drink it alongside any other food. But all alone, with only a glass of water to occasionally refresh the palate, it is a lesson in monotone greatness.

JOHN'S WAFFLE SHOP
7906 GIRARD AVE., LA JOLLA, CA (619) 454-7371

We kept a souvenir menu from the Waffle Shop. It is made of paper, folded in thirds to resemble a letter. On the outside, in flowery type, it says, "A Special Invitation to You. . ." It seems so very civilized.

That's the way the Waffle Shop is. The interior is shaped like a diner, and service is diner-fast, and prices are diner-low; this is, nonetheless, a mannerly place to eat a wholesome breakfast (or lunch). For singles, it's great because the counter stools are comfortable, and they afford a ring-side-seat view of the cook in his tall white toque as he flips flapjacks, fries eggs, and extracts steaming hot waffles from the iron. Shoppers and local business people crowd the dining room by nine in the morning, filling the row of small tables opposite the counter.

Waffles are, of course, the favorite breakfast stuff; and they are superb. Jumbo Belgian ones are available, topped with ice cream and/or strawberries or hot, cinnamon-flavored apple wedges. They're good, but not our idea of breakfast food.

We prefer the flatter, more familiar waffle, of which John's offers a couple of interesting variations: with nuts, or made from a batter enriched with honey and wheat germ. It's the latter that won our hearts, although to a first-time visitor we would probably recommend the plain everyday waffle. It is perfectly cooked: crisp but not brittle, thin enough to be called elegant, yet with enough tender inside heft to sponge up plenty of melting butter and syrup. It's available in all the good configurations: with bacon, ham, sausage, or eggs (or à la mode).

After a few waffle-centered visits to John's, the time comes to branch out to other agreeable parts of the menu. Pancakes, especially. There are all kinds, and they are *good:* banana nut, buttermilk, cinnamon-raisin, blueberry, and chocolate chip. Get them three at a time, a short stack of two, or by the dozen—silver-dollar size.

The syrup provided with pancakes and waffles is listed on the menu as "John's Homemade Maple Syrup." The waitress assured us, "They *do* make it here, but to tell the truth, I don't think it's authentic." We weren't sure what that meant, but we can tell you that it is an intriguing blend: not pure maple syrup, but a clever fusion of what seems like maple flavor and vanilla. Especially when combined with whipped butter (which the kitchen supplies in abundance on all waffle and pancake orders), it's swell.

Egg dishes include not only omelettes but breakfast burritos with refried beans and salsa, scrambled eggs with chorizo sausage, and poached eggs perched on a sizzling mound of corned beef hash.

Lunch would put John's into our little black book even without waffles. It's fine Southern California coffee shop fare: sandwiches, salads, a burrito, chili, even hot plates such as liver and onions and country-fried steak. What's extraordinary is the kitchen's generous hand. For instance, the BLT. You know how most lunch counter BLTs treat bacon like caviar, doling out only a few measly strips? Not John's. There's plenty on this BLT, maybe even too much (is that possible?).

A final regional recommendation: smoothies. They're California's version of a milk shake, made with orange juice or strawberries. Rich as sin, but virtuous-seeming.

MAX'S DINER
311 3RD ST., SAN FRANCISCO, CA (415) 546-6297; CALL 546-0168 FOR DINNER RESERVATIONS (ADVISED)

It used to be that a diner was a lowly place to eat. It was known as a greasy spoon, a hash house, or—in trucker lingo—a choke and puke. Diners were where the city's fallen angels went for a cup of mud (coffee) and a sinker (a doughnut) beneath fluorescent lights; where night hawks and wandering hoboes whiled away the wee hours. As for the food at diners, it was strictly for the crude of palate—heavy on the starch, grease, and gristle.

You still might find an occasional diner like that if you scour the fringes of cities in the Northeast; we even know of a few rare and treasured back-road diners where they actually serve good food. But mostly, the great authentic diner has vanished from the land.

If you are feeling a twinge of nostalgia for that naughty stainless-steel-and-neon ambience, if you crave to indulge yourself in an evening's entertainment in which the theme is grade-B movie gastronomy, we recommend a trip to Max's of San Francisco, a diner fantasy come to life: diner as dinner theater. Although it is not in any way like any real diner you have ever seen, everything about it is meant to evoke nostalgic thoughts of blue-plate specials.

The primary difference between Max's and real diners is the food. Max's is better. Indeed, Max's food, although not pretentious, is consistently first-class. Turkey (for hot turkey sandwiches with mashed potatoes and cranberry-applesauce, or for turkey dinners with dressing, spuds, and succotash) is cut fresh from an expertly roasted bird. The mashed potatoes are superb, served in a volcano shape, with "crater gravy" spilling down the side. There are two kinds of meat loaf, three kinds of hash (sausage, corned-beef, or pastrami-chicken), and you can choose between normal-size hamburgers and baskets of little White Castle–style "sliders." For dessert, there is a long list of pastries, cakes, pies, homemade ice creams, and sauces "made in New York," according to the menu, "by a certified chocoholic who refuses therapy."

Aside from the good food, Max's differs from real diners in its cleanliness and polite manners. It sparkles. It is big and streamlined, with comfortable booths (and of course a counter, too). Waitresses, in crisp black-and-white uniforms, do not sport tattoos (at least none are evident) or chew gum or sass the customers.

The dining areas are a veritable museum of pop cuisine, including heroic paintings and pictures of diners on the wall, thick white dinner plates plainly labeled Meat Loaf Plate, and stacks of Bazooka bubble gum boxes at the take-out counter (meals conclude with a complimentary block of Bazooka for each customer). The menu warns "We reserve the right to refuse service to anyone using the word *nouvelle.*" Checks promise "More Calories for Your Money." And the house motto is "Everything You Always Wanted to Eat."

MUSSO AND FRANK GRILL
6667 HOLLYWOOD BOULEVARD, HOLLYWOOD, CA (213) 467-7788

A few years ago we arrived at Musso's for the Wednesday special of sauerbraten and potato pancakes, and were regaled by the parking attendants in the lot out back who were offering a running commentary on which movie stars and celebrities were inside, and how long ago they had arrived. Sure enough, sitting in a booth not far from us were Bob Seger and several members of his band—eating meat and potatoes.

Now that meat and potatoes are back in fashion, Musso's almost seems trendy. Hollywood's first restaurant (since 1919) is a square-meals classic, where you can sit down at a linen placemat for a low-priced lunch of flannel cakes (flannel-thin pancakes) or outrageously priced abalone, sautéed *meunière.* The menu is printed every day, but Musso's is known for dowdy kinds of meals: those flannel cakes (for lunch), Welsh rarebit, chicken pot pie on Thursday, classic corned beef and cabbage every Tuesday, lamb shanks, baked ham, chiffonade salads.

There are so many things we love to eat from this kitchen's extensive repertoire; but pay special attention, please, to the potatoes. Eleven different kinds are listed, from mashed and boiled to lyonnaise and candied sweet. Steaks and chops, cooked on an open broiler for dinner, are grand. From the dessert list, note bread-and-butter pudding, and its deluxe variant, diplomat pudding—topped with strawberries.

Many gourmets of our acquaintance do not understand the appeal of Musso's. They compliment its antique Tudor decor and comfortable red leather booths but complain that the food is ordinary. Yes, indeed! It is some of the tastiest ordinary food anywhere.

THE ORIGINAL PANTRY
877 S. FIGUEROA ST., LOS ANGELES, CA (213) 972-9279

What aficionado of cafe cookery could resist one whose boast is "Since 1924, Never Closed, Never Without a Customer"? The Original Pantry is a straight-shooter just north of the Los Angeles Convention Center where the seating capacity is a mere eighty-four, but where they boast of feeding up to three thousand people every day. They feed 'em fast, cheap, and well—a process facilitated by the practice of taking waiting people's orders *before* they sit down, so that as soon as their rear hits the chair, the food is presented by the staff of white-shirted, bow-tied waiters, many of whom have been working here for decades.

Sourdough bread is a house specialty, and it, along with rye, white, or whole wheat, can be part of an especially noteworthy breakfast. (The bread is baked fresh daily; according to a brochure dispensed by the management, eggs are supplied by "two thousand energetic laying hens.") Along with the bread and eggs, there is homemade sausage or extra-thick bacon and heaps of fried potatoes.

Because it is always open, and the breakfast hour begins at two in the morning, many customers think of The Original Pantry only as a breakfast place; but dinner is swell. It begins with dowdy relishes: carrots, radishes, and celery. Then cole slaw and sourdough bread by the half loaf. Then square meals: liver and onions with pan-fried potatoes or lamb chops or beef stew or ham hocks or roast beef, followed by hot apple pie with rum sauce. Prices are low, service is fast, food is good: what more do you want?

PHILIPPE THE ORIGINAL
1001 N. ALAMEDA ST., LOS ANGELES, CA (213) 628-3781

The floors are strewn with sawdust, waitresses wear tiny, starched cup-cake hats atop sculpted hair-don'ts, and coffee is a dime a cup. Philippe's is a public mess hall straight out of a Raymond Chandler novel with clientele to match: perpetual coffee hounds, civil servants on a breather from the nearby post office, grizzled students of the day's racing forms, plus cheap-eats epicures and scholars of Southern California culinary history, of which Philippe's is a cornerstone. Philippe's invented the French dip sandwich in 1908.

The French dip is the western version of what is known in Kansas as "beef Manhattan," in Buffalo as "beef on weck," in Chicago as "Italian beef," and in Philadelphia as a "cheese steak" (but without the cheese). It is thin-sliced roast beef on a hard roll; in this case, the inside of the roll is dipped in natural gravy before it pockets the beef. One local historian told us that the sandwich was invented for a toothless patron who couldn't chew his bread unless it was softened by gravy.

A French dip sandwich as dished out at Philippe's, which calls itself "the Original," is tender and mild-tasting until you lay on a gob of Philippe's own mustard, a stinging lather that is also sold by the bottle (at a gorgeous glass and oak candy counter) to take home. With mustard, the French dip sandwich is a well-nigh perfect combination: the roll and beef are brought to perfect consonance by the bite of hot mustard. All you want to put a point on this blue-collar feast is a heap of Philippe's cole slaw and a dose of that ten-cent coffee.

In addition to French dip beef sandwiches, Philippe's will also French dip ham, pork, or lamb for you; and they will gild the sandwich with American, Swiss, or blue cheese. You can eat stew or chili, even pigs' knuckles. (Philippe's menu boasts that they sell more pigs' knuckles than any other restaurant in Los Angeles; do you doubt them?) For dessert, there are thick wedges of gooey-filled fruit pie or big, falling-apart baked apples that can be flooded with cream.

The pleasure of eating at Philippe's is relishing the atmosphere along with the food. It is a big restaurant with seating for a couple of hundred customers at a time, not bright enough to be cheerful, yet not depressing either. There is a beguiling nostalgic haze in the dining room that seems rich with Los Angeles history, culinary and otherwise. You eat in ancient high-backed wooden booths or at communal waist-high tables alongside the regulars, a collection of characters who seem to have materialized out of a Preston Sturges movie: dime-a-cup coffee hounds, geezers, letter carriers between rounds, neighborhood loafers. It is a cast as obsolete and fossilized as Philippe's pickled eggs.

PINK'S CHILI DOGS
711 N. LA BREA AVE., HOLLYWOOD, CA (213) 931-4223

Step right up and and meet a hot bow-wow every street food scholar ought to know: Pink's chili dog, an all-beef wiener topped with mustard and onions, then a load of chili sauce. This dog is a beaut, steamed until it seems ready to burst out of its crackling skin. It is normal-size, so you won't likely see it beneath all the topping. It tastes great, just garlicky enough to have some punch but not overwhelm the rest of the package. It is muscular, juicy, a rewarding chew.

The chili sauce that crowns it is all beef (no beans), hot but not incendiary, thick enough so it stays on top of the dog and inside the bun if you remember to hold the whole savory load in a reasonably horizontal position. The mustard, onions, and bun are all ordinary. Indeed, the bun is pretty awful if you come at the wrong time of day and get a stale one.

Los Angeles being the city of baroque customization of all things, Pink's sells wild varieties of chili dog, such as a Guadalajara dog topped with mustard, relish, onions, tomatoes, and sour cream. There are cheese dogs, burrito and bacon dogs (wrapped in a tortilla), double-size Polish sausages, and chopped dogs in baked beans. It's all prize stuff if you have a craving for raunchy wieners; but first-time visitors really ought to sample the usual configuration of hot dog, mustard, onions, and chili. It is a model, two-fisted feast.

What else is there to eat? Actually, a couple of pretty decent items. The baked beans are very good, even without the chopped hot dogs in them. And the potato salad is extraordinary. It's hot (thermally, not spicewise), with a vivid pickly snap to the slithery disks of sliced potato.

One of the endearing things about Pink's, other than its superlative wieners, is its insolent ambience. Eat your tube steak on the street standing up in front of the open-air stand, or at one of the few scattered tables under a flimsy roof along the side. Many customers park in the red zone along the curb and down dogs in their cars. Then there is the service, which is always fast, and can be disarmingly brusque. It is not unusual for the men behind the counter to turn hot dog preparation into a demonstration of lunch-counter dexterity. Watch them heft the wiener from its steam bath, whip it up toward the ceiling, then nab it midair with a bun. Then watch as the condiments get spread in perfect formation, and the chili is unloaded instantly, but without a drop spilled. (Would that we could say the same about our skills eating chili dogs! Extra napkins are *de rigueur*.)

It isn't always a razzle-dazzle show behind the counter; but even if the guys aren't tossing and catching wieners in the air, Pink's glows with sass and impudence that, in our book, represent the best of America's street-corner cuisine.

SAM'S GRILL
374 BUSH ST., SAN FRANCISCO, CA (415) 421-0594

Sam's Grill is a restaurant we dream about, hungrily, whenever we antici-pate a trip to San Francisco. Open since 1867, and a uniquely San Franciscan blend of elegance and informality, Sam's is a benchmark of the kind of splendid West Coast cuisine that never goes in or out of style: fresh Pacific seafood, grilled or pan-fried, accompanied by hearty salads, a loaf of brittle-crusted sourdough bread, and fresh vegetables. It looks the way you want a great old California restaurant to look: outfitted with yards of thick white linen and brass hooks for coats. Although this isn't Sam's origi-nal location (that was in the Old California Market), its bygone atmosphere is genuine; nothing affected about it.

For all the dining room's decorous trappings, Sam's menu is simplicity itself, printed every morning at ten, *after* they have been to the fish and produce markets to find what's fresh. The kitchen turns out a huge roster of straightforward American food, including two dozen specials and almost a hundred à la carte selections every day. It's possible to order charcoal-grilled steaks and chops, or short ribs of beef with horseradish sauce, or just bacon and eggs; but nearly everybody comes to Sam's for the seafood.

One whole portion of each day's menu is devoted to "Casseroles à la Sam," many made with Dungeness crab meat from the northern coast. There are crab creole and crab curry, crab au gratin and creamed crab with noodles. One longtime Sam's specialty we especially like is a sunny-hued casserole of cream and crab and sherry known as deviled crab à la Sam—not nearly as devilish as its name implies, but a truly tasty mustard-tweaked heap of old-fashioned comfort food.

As is characteristic of so much new California cuisine, most of Sam's seafood is plainly cooked. This is the place to sample Pacific rarities that seldom make it east, like genuine Hangtown fry (an omelette made with Northwest oysters); rex and petrale sole grilled over charcoal; and the delicate, white-fleshed local fish called sand dabs—about a half dozen sweet little fillets sauteed in lemon butter.

Sam's is a quirky establishment, the way venerable oldsters are entitled to be. Open only on weekdays, only until 8:30 P.M., it caters to a clientele of people who work downtown and come every day for lunch, or for an early dinner before heading home. At noon, it is mobbed with successful-looking types jockeying for a table, or crowding three deep against the bar. Reservations are not accepted, nor are credit cards. Once you get a table, it is an immensely comfortable place to eat. The staff of formally dressed waiters are consummate professionals, not even blinking when they bring a second loaf of bread to a certain greedy twosome who pocketed their loaf to take with them on the trip north up the coast.

SAN DIEGO CHICKEN PIE SHOP
2633 EL CAJON BLVD., SAN DIEGO, CA (619) 295-0156

Jell-O is always on the menu at the San Diego Chicken Pie Shop. It comes in a square block, red, yellow, or green, filled with little chunks of no-color fruit. Cottage cheese and canned fruit is another item you can count on from this menu. To get a fix on the kitchen, consider also the vegetable that frequently comes with dinner: a spill of the medley known as "mixed vegetables." You know mixed vegetables, don't you? They're like fruit cocktail, only smaller: miniature cubes and spheres and rectangles that have the appearance of carrot bits, peas, and corn kernels.

Are we doing a good job explaining why we are enamored of the San Diego Chicken Pie Shop? Perhaps if we tell you about the chicken pie, you will understand. What you appreciate, as you fork up this pie, which is nothing but meat and gravy and crust, and tear into the big soft dinner rolls that come with it, is that this meal doesn't want to be home cooking; and it certainly isn't trying to convince anyone it's swanky. But gosh, it's nice to eat. We also like the hot turkey sandwich with whipped potatoes and gravy. And the hot roast beef. And the dinner of chicken giblets in gravy inside a patty shell. It's all coffee shop food, nothing more; but it tastes fine, and it exudes the same warm, democratic aroma of mealtime at a dime-store lunch counter. In a land of restaurant overachievers, there is much to be said for such probity.

We also like the waitresses in their maroon tunics. They "Hi, hon" you and bring the grub at hypersonic speed. Ours volunteered the information that she was having a calendar of boudoir photos made for her boyfriend, but had to stop after the "April" photography session when she came down with shingles.

SEAFOOD GROTTO
605 BROADWAY, EUREKA, CA (707) 443-2075

"We ketch 'em, cook 'em, serve 'em" brags the sign outside The Seafood Grotto. This restaurant on the coast of northern California is owned by Eureka Fisheries. Behind the dining room they also operate one heck of a retail fish market, which sells a harvest of Northwest seafood that includes ready-to-eat hunks of smoked salmon and albacore tuna, as well as whole and picked crab, cod, and cod cheeks. Up front, near the cash register, exotic fish (strictly decoration) swim in a large aquarium.

If you suspect that the Seafood Grotto is a good place to eat seafood, you are right. However, what we like even more than its cuisine is its informality. Tables are set with disposable placemats and paper napkins. The menu is plastic-laminated. The china is heavy-duty, and your thick coffee cup will be filled as soon as you hit your seat. Waitresses, clad in black nylon uniforms and orthopedic-soled shoes, are fast and ingratiatingly fresh. Get a window seat, and the view outside is of trucks rumbling past on Broadway.

There is nothing romantic about a meal here. It makes us think of dining in a company cafeteria. Prices are low; and although the variety of seafood available is vast, the kitchen has no epicurean aspirations. At noon, most people come for a cup of chowder or bowl of cole slaw and a quick plate of clams or oysters or fillet of rockfish or grilled rex sole; then it's back to work. Customers who are under twelve or over sixty-five years old have a special section of the menu all to themselves, listing shrimp and crab Louis, hamburger steak, and fish sticks.

The chowder is Northwest style—thick, creamy, and abundantly clammy. It is sold by the cup, bowl, large bowl (a satisfying meal), and by the pint or quart (to go). On the Formica table you will find a bowl full of garlic croutons which are nice to sprinkle on top.

Heading the long roster of local seafood is Dungeness crab, served in big creamy-white chunks on a bed of ice or mixed with dressing into a giant-size crab Louis (or combination shrimp and crab Louis). You can get hefty Pacific oysters, too—chilled, grilled, or deep-fried.

Flatfish are the real treasures on this menu: the Grotto lists the delicate little sweeties known as sand dabs, as well as rex sole and broiled salmon steaks or fillets. Most are available with wine sauce or egg sauce, but what we look back upon most fondly is a simple and unadorned slab of petrale sole, filleted and grilled to moist perfection.

For dessert, there is mousse cake, cream pie, ice cream, or good, heavyweight cheesecake.

SEARS FINE FOODS
439 POWELL ST., SAN FRANCISCO, CA (415) 986-1160

California bon vivant and radio personality Paul Wallach once called Sears "the breakfast capital of the Western Hemisphere." There are more inventive and more dazzling restaurants in the Bay Area, but you cannot really say you have eaten San Francisco's best until you have forked your way through a plate of Sears's Swedish pancakes—eighteen limp, ethereal, golden disks served with plenty of whipped butter and a choice of syrups that includes blackberry, loganberry, boysenberry, and maple. While you are here, you must also eat Sears's French toast. It is made of sourdough bread, soaked in eggs and cream until the texture verges on that of junket, but retains a vague bready chew and the tang of ancient yeast, delectably complemented by Sears's strawberry preserves.

And there is more: excellent smoked ham or sausage for side dishes and truly fresh fruit cup for an hors d'oeuvre. There are pecan waffles, banana nut bread, big baked apples, Swedish coffee cake, and omelettes with crisp hash-brown potatoes. In addition, there are lunch and dinner and some famously good pies. But it's breakfast that has been Sears's glory for nearly ninety years now, and the reason people line up on Powell Street every morning well before the place opens at seven.

SUNSET EAST CAR WASH
2040 W. SUNSET BLVD. (AT ALVARADO), LOS ANGELES, CA
(213) 484-0821

Los Angeles's most significant contribution to American gastronomy is its street-corner dives. No city has a more colorful and eccentric population of holes-in-the-wall dishing out grubby eats—from chili dogs (Pink's, p. 44) to Bucket Burgers to the soft steamed tacos of Cocina Corina. For a couple of bucks, this taco stand in front of a thriving car wash will sell you some remarkably tasty Cal-Mex food: steamy soft burritos stuffed with pork, beans, hot sauce, and cilantro; or tacos loaded with oozy, sweet-pork carnitas and four-alarm chili verde. Of course, there is no place to sit down, and you have to compete with cars exiting from the adjacent car wash for a place to park, and the employees barely speak English ("pig stomak tacos" were the advertised daily special one day last summer). But to the connoisseur of counterculture, such crudeness only amplifies the pleasure.

SWAN OYSTER DEPOT
1517 POLK ST., SAN FRANCISCO, CA (415) 673-1101

Fairly expensive, and worth every dollar you fork out, Swan Oyster Depot is a marble-topped oyster bar with a rickety row of stools and a menu honed to little more than shellfish. Oysters from the East and West coasts are served on the half shell. There are cold prawns, too, and some delicious smoked salmon, available on rye or French bread. Also, chowder.

Dungeness crab is served in season (generally, mid-November through May), available "cracked," meaning that you get sections of cooked, cooled claw, leg, and body ready to be unloaded of their sweet meat. This most famous Pacific crustacean is also available as crab Louis, a regal dish (invented in San Francisco, it is believed) in which large chunks of pearlescent meat are cosseted in a condiment compounded from lemony mayonnaise spiked with relish and olive bits, enriched by hard-cooked egg. Crab Louis, a length of French bread, and a cold beer: what else is there to want from life?

TILLIE'S
1500 WEBSTER ST., ALAMEDA, CA (510) 523-1737

Tillie's is a big, happy coffee shop in Alameda that serves three meals a day but specializes in jumbo breakfasts. "NOTICE!" warns the menu. "Our three egg whopper breakfasts have been known to have brought husky Canadian lumberjacks to their knees!!! Maybe you're next."

The breakfast specials are titanic indeed, each triple-egger hoisted from the kitchen to the counter or booth in a capacious copper skillet with room not only for the eggs, but also spiced stewed apples, hash-brown potatoes, toasted French bread, plus your choice of corned-beef hash, sausage, ham, sirloin steak, or pork chops. If that doesn't sound like enough food for you, there is the officially designated "Whopper Breakfast" of juice, four eggs, five slices of bacon, potatoes, apples, and three slabs of bread. Traditional omelettes can be had, too, each made with three eggs that the giddy, laminated menu describes as "happily mixed-up, laid by stunted, frustrated ostriches."

Among Tillie's delirious morning specialties, the one we like best is a three-egg concoction called "Steak Bitts N' Eggs" (*sic*), featuring small pieces of sirloin sautéed with pepper and onions, accompanied by hash browns with melted cheese and sawmill gravy, plus three pieces of Tillie's sweet French bread. We also have fond memories of a heap of "Bloody Mary Eggs," which are scrambled and laced with sharp yellow cheese and pieces of chopped tomato.

Breakfast is the only time we have eaten at Tillie's but we like the looks of the dinner menu, too, especially on Monday (corned-beef-and-cabbage day), Wednesday (meat loaf), and Sunday (prime rib or chicken fricassee). There are long lists of sandwiches, salads, diet plates, and hot meals each described with a panache that makes just reading the menu fun. Jell-O is "shimmering"; the chili is so hot that "even the crackers hurt"; and a grilled ham-and-cheese is listed, oddly, as "unclaimed happiness." The egg salad sandwich is "for beginners," and a cheeseburger gets the lout's treatment: "Da same old garbage, but with TWO slices of delicious cheese." For burger fanciers with ambition, Tillie's offers a bacon-Swiss cheeseburger: "That beautiful flavor for the high and mighty!"

COLORADO

BUCKHORN EXCHANGE
1000 OSAGE, DENVER, CO (303) 534-9505

Start with Rocky Mountain oysters (bull's balls) sliced thin and deep fried, then move on to steak: a T-bone, pan-fried, or a big, not-so-juicy slab of buffalo. Pardner, you are now in the American West, a fact you'd have to be blind not to notice in this rather horrific environment filled to the rafters with five hundred heads of dead animals, all shot by former owner Shorty Zietz.

You don't have to begin your meal with a plate of testicles. There are good buffalo sausages and cheddar cheese. And there is a thick, satisfying ham-and-bean soup—chuckwagon grub *par excellence.* All sorts of normal sandwiches are available at lunch, including patty-melt burgers and a good hot pot roast as well as a nontraditional Reuben on pumpernickel bread, made with shaved, smoked buffalo instead of corned beef. The lunch crowd at the Buckhorn includes a lot of local businessmen who don't think of the place as a woolly relic. (It opened for business in 1893, when the oak bar was installed and Colorado Liquor License #1, displayed above it, was issued.) They come to eat here because it is comfortable and the food is good and the bar serves normal drinks as well as sarsaparilla.

Dinner is mostly meat—T-bones, tenderloins, pork chops, or buffalo steak, as well as split and sautéed quail and Rocky Mountain trout. On the side you get your choice of a baked potato or Saratoga chips (a.k.a. potato chips). There is ice cream or cheesecake for dessert, but the best bet is apple pie, available à la mode, with cheddar cheese, or accompanied by cinnamon hard sauce. A dinner such as this can easily run fifty dollars for two; lunch will be half that.

CONWAY'S RED TOP
1520 S. NEVADA, COLORADO SPRINGS, CO (719) 633-2444
(ADDITIONAL LOCATIONS AT 3589 N. CAREFREE AND
390 N. CIRCLE DRIVE)

Conway's motto, referring to its hamburger, is "One's a Meal." The colossi they dish up in these restaurants are *real* whoppers—half a foot across, served on broad-domed buns, accompanied by shoestring French fries and titanic pitchers of soda. Panavision-wide but not gourmet-thick, they are happy lunch-counter patties with enough oily smack to imprint the bun with their savor. They are sold whole or half, topped with regular cheese (or, as the ingenuous menu advises, "a generous serving of Velveeta cheese") or zestier jalapeño cheese, or served as a "Hickory Dickery Top" infused with smoke flavor and smothered with chopped onions and barbecue sauce.

One definitely is a meal, especially if accompanied by good, shrivel-tipped French fries and a large soda. But it would be a shame to visit the Red Top without a taste of the soups and stews that are still made from the original recipes of Grandma Esther (Phyllis Conway's mom). The navy bean soup, for example, is a stout brew with a profound, long-simmered flavor redolent of hickory-smoked ham and spice. With its accompanying sourdough roll, it is hearty enough to be a filling lunch (with a minuscule price tag). Beef stew is another classic—hours in the making, so all the juices of the beef and vegetables have a chance to mellow and blend and soften. It is so thick you only need a fork to eat a bowlful. We concur with the menu's description of it, which promises a stew that is "delicious, nutritious, and healthy."

The Red Tops have been a family operation since 1962 when Norb Conway bought the hamburger shop he worked in and he and his wife and ten children went to work. The Conways instilled an unshakable pride in the business that is as much a part of this restaurant's charm as are the giant hamburgers. After all, the Red Tops aren't really much more than hamburger shops, with waitresses in red hats and blue uniforms who deliver the check with your meal and provide the kind of quick service one expects. The honest menu, homemade food, and genuine hospitality are delightfully old-fangled.

DADDY BRUCE'S BAR-B-Q
1629 E. 34TH AVE., DENVER, CO (303) 295-9115

D addy Bruce Randolph is Denver's godfather of barbecue, so esteemed that 34th Avenue outside his restaurant has been officially renamed Bruce Randolph Avenue. Mr. Randolph, whose car sports a sign saying "God Loves You and So Does Daddy Bruce," has built his reputation upon a majestic sauce that will set your lips on fire as soon as you begin to work your way into a row of ribs. You get the same sauce on hot sausage links, copiously dotted with hot pepper seeds, or on beef, or mixed into the starchy beans that perfectly complement everything on the menu. This is consummate southwestern-style barbecue, the fire of pepper and spice balanced by the sweet tenderness of beans.

For a denouement to the heat of the meat, soothe your palate with sweet 'tater pie—glowing orange, clove-scented, lush with sugary sweet potatoes.

Daddy Bruce's is in the wrong part of town, and the street can be scary, but we have always found perfect hospitality once we get inside the Day-Glo orange building. The staff is accustomed to helping pilgrims from barbecue-deprived regions of the country. Most of Daddy Bruce's business is take-out, but there are some tables and chairs for eating here.

THE FORT
19192 HIGHWAY 8 (AT JUNCTION WITH HIGHWAY 285), MORRISON, CO
(303) 697-4771

H ungry, but a little low on cash? No problem if you are in the vicinity of Morrison, Colorado (on the southwest side of Denver). Simply catch yourself a few beavers, skin them, and bring their pelts to The Fort. Beaver pelts are accepted in lieu of currency as payment for meals. Credit cards are okay, too.

Payment in pelt, however macabre, makes some sense at The Fort, as do the southern Cheyenne calico costumes on the waitresses, and the five-inch Green River knives you get to slice your steak (beef or buffalo). Built twenty-six years ago as a replica of a fur trader's fort, the red adobe restaurant attempts to create a romanticized taste of frontier history—and succeeds deliciously well.

The Fort is outfitted with working black powder cannons, a couple of capacious fireplaces and an open-air campfire, and rugged wooden tables and chairs set across a floor made of congealed dirt and beef blood. There is also a canvas tepee in the courtyard in which couples can dine seated on buffalo rugs, serenaded by owner Sam Arnold playing the saw. From outside, the view of Denver is dazzling. Inside, the vittles are unique.

The cuisine of The Fort is Wild Western, duded up for modern American palates. Frankly, we doubt if any cowpokes or even ranchers or land barons ever dined this well. Even the drink list adds fashionable coolers such as daiquiris and piña coladas to historical exotica that range from "the hailstorm" (mint julep in a pint Mason jar) to the "Santa Fe Original Gin Cock Tail," and Chimaja whiskey flavored with wild mountain parsley.

Hors d'oeuvres can be as familiar as guacamole and chips or as weird as buffalo tongue (a nineteenth-century delicacy featured in the finest restaurants in New York and Europe). The tongue is served along with "prairie butter" (buffalo marrow) and boudies (a lean buffalo sausage) on what the menu calls a "Historian's Platter" of gamey appetizers. One can also begin a meal with bite-size peanut-butter-stuffed jalapeño peppers, Rocky Mountain oysters (sliced, fried sheep's testicles), or a relatively tame shrimp-and-avocado cocktail.

Of course, there are all kinds of steaks to eat—sirloins, pepper-stuffed sirloins, strip steaks, prime rib, even a nearly fatless "Texas longhorn" cut. You can eat buffalo or elk or lamb chops, or a brace of quail or trout broiled Taos Indian style—topped with bacon and mint.

The best-known dish served at The Fort is Bowl of the Wife of Kit Carson. Technically, the true name for this lusty soup/stew (known to regulars at The Fort as the "K.C. Bowl") is "caldo tlalpeno"; but Sam Arnold says that Kit Carson's granddaughter, Miss Leona Wood, told him that she ate it as a youngster. Many years ago, when he first opened The Fort, he named it for her.

HOMESTEADERS
45 E. MAIN ST., CORTEZ, CO (303) 565-6253

Cortez bills itself as the place where the mountains meet the desert, but its arid climate and golden sun make it feel like a pure cowboy kind of place. For meals to match the wide-open western feel of the landscape around the town, the place to go is Homesteaders on Main Street, a western-decorated eatery frequented by ranchers, oilmen, and local buckaroos as well as hungry tourists looking for good, inexpensive, unfranchised food.

Come for breakfast and you can feast on such real western vittles as biscuits and gravy, stacks of buttermilk griddle cakes with bacon or sausage on the side, and omelettes loaded with cheese, ham, or sautéed vegetables. At lunch and dinner, the menu is about equally divided between Mexican and American fare. We have enjoyed strapping chimichangas, brilliantly seasoned tacos, and enchiladas nearly as well-made as the paradigms of New Mexico. But the truth is, our preference is for Homesteaders' mainstream American cookery: steak with French fries or slabs of liver smothered with onions and sided by mashed potatoes with gravy. Even the hamburger we ate was memorably good—the kind of juicy, flavorful patty of high-quality meat that bears no resemblance to the flattened ones portioned out by fast-food restaurants.

Now, dessert: that is special, too. Pies are served in titanic slices; and while we would never call them aristocratic, they are unmistakably homemade and indisputably tasty. We have enjoyed Dutch apple and cherry flavors, as well as a generous slice of plain but heartwarmingly classic chocolate cake.

JUNIPER VALLEY RANCH
ROUTE 115, SOUTH OF COLORADO SPRINGS, CO (719) 576-0741

A low-slung adobe house on the old road to Canyon City, open only in the summer, only for dinner, and only if you have a reservation (generally three to four days in advance), Juniper Valley Ranch serves some of the nicest food in the West. In a region where most culinary highlights are four-alarm hot or cowpoke-crude, here is a place to sit down with a serene, square meal and a glass of iced tea. It is a family-style retreat with antiques around the fireplace and a menu that lists the same two entrées every day.

Start with curried consommé or spiced apple cider. Then have skillet-fried chicken or baked ham in an oval casserole. These satisfying entrées are accompanied by hot biscuits and good apple butter, cole slaw, okra-and-tomato stew, and delightfully fluffy riced potatoes. Help yourself to seconds, thirds, as much as you like, then top things off with the home-made dessert of the day: bread pudding, fruit cobbler, or cake. It is a simple meal, the same year after year, served on faded calico tablecloths and seasoned with the rare and irresistible ingredient of tradition's charm.

CONNECTICUT

ABBOTT'S LOBSTER IN THE ROUGH
117 PEARL ST., NOANK, CT (203) 536-7719

A bbott's is such a nice place to eat lobsters and clams that sometimes the crowds make it nearly impossible to get in. On a warm summer's day, customers come to the village of Noank by boat and by car, pushing up to Abbott's order window in quest of the unimprovable pleasures of a shore dinner in the rough, served on plastic trays and eaten on picnic tables. The seating is al fresco, the atmosphere is salt air breezing in off the ocean, and background music is provided by gulls screeching in the sky.

Abbott's provides all this warm-weather ambience to go with plump-fleshed, sweet and faintly briny lobsters of nearly any size you want. The hot red beauties are served with cole slaw and drawn butter and a bag of potato chips. They are cooked when ordered—steamed in massive tanks for about twenty minutes, a delay that cannot be avoided: once again, be prepared to wait.

How about raw littlenecks (five at a time), mussels, steamers, or chowder in the meanwhile? The chowder is true southern New England style—an elementary clam-juice-based broth, made with a few finely chopped vegetables and a bracing panoply of clams. According to Abbott's owners, Ruth and Jerry Mears, its formula was devised over thirty years ago by their predecessors, Ernie and Doris Abbott, and it has legions of fans who return for it every summer. The Mearses told us, "Woe to those who even contemplate change in this mystical mixture!"

Another noteworthy Abbott's *pièce de résistance,* and one of the few regional specialties unique to Connecticut: the lobster roll. This is nothing more than *hot* buttered lobster meat (as opposed to lobster salad, made with mayonnaise, which is also available, as are shrimp and crab salad rolls) piled into a sesame-seed-spangled bun and usually so well buttered that the bun is nothing but glistening shreds of bread by the time you are two-thirds through. Sheer summer luxury.

BETHEL PIZZA HOUSE
206 GREENWOOD AVE., BETHEL, CT (203) 748-1427

The Bethel Pizza House menu, a single-page yellow flyer suitable for attaching to the refrigerator with a magnet (for take-out inspiration), is decorated with a picture of the Parthenon. Specialty of the house is Greek-style pizza, an unofficial and seldom-appreciated but thriving and delicious branch of pizza-ology in New England.

Greek pizza parlors don't advertise their pies as anything different from the usual Italian variety; and aside from the occasional feta cheese salad or stuffed-grape-leaf appetizer, their repertoire is as focused as that of any reliable town pizzeria: small, medium, and large pies, hot-oven grinders, and cold soda. However, there is a difference between Greek and Italian pizzas. A Greek pizza is made using dough that is flattened out to rest (and slowly rise) in a rimmed pan well before it is assembled and baked. You will see stacks of these pans, dough ready, martialed all around the counter where the *pizzaiolo* works.

Once ingredients are piled on and the pan goes in the oven, the baking pizza is worried constantly by a man with a long, double-tined fork. He pokes hard all around the crust as it bakes, at once deflating the dough's ascension and creating little holes that allow wisps of heat to escape and give the finished round of bread an unruly crunch. Because of its long set in the pan, it has a strong, yeasty flavor and more body than an elegant Italian-style pizza crust. We wouldn't say we like Greek pizza better than Italian; but there are times when its extra punch is a wonderful change of pace.

When we crave it, Bethel Pizza House is where we go. What a fine dive! There are exactly three booths, and the last one is usually occupied by ceiling-high stacks of empty pizza boxes, as most of the business is take-out. The front two booths are murderous in the winter because the wind whips inside whenever the door opens, as it does at least every five minutes during mealtime. Do not think, however, that no attention is paid to dining ambience at Bethel Pizza. There is plenty of decor, and not all of it is frightful. The two wagon-wheel chandeliers hanging above do a valiant job of balancing the ghastly greenish light from fluorescent tubes. And note, please, the leitmotif of woodgrains throughout the pint-size pizza parlor: white laminated woodgrain walls (sort of French provincial), brown knotty pine at the counter where you stand to place an order, paper plates with a red woodgrain design, and a free-form wooden plaque above the oven with "No Checks Please" burned into its varnished surface.

Pizzas arrive at the table on cardboard disks that do a good job of soaking up grease as you pull slices. They are huge pizzas and truly beautiful—modern-day Greek classics heaped with far more and better ingredients than the low-low prices would lead you to expect (a seventeen-inch, three-item pie costs under twelve dollars). All the usual toppings are available; we especially recommend the excellent sausage and fresh garlic, although not necessarily together. The pies all sport mighty mozzarella with a fine rich flavor and a unique mouth-watering chewiness that complements the crunchy dough tableau below.

CLAIRE'S CORNER COPIA
1000 CHAPEL ST., NEW HAVEN, CT (203) 562-3888

Claire's Corner Copia is an off-the-wall soup kitchen, a vegetarian-Mexican cafe, a stronghold of motherly Italian cooking, a hangout for street people and students, and maybe the best home-cooking restaurant in New Haven.

Where should we begin? How about soup? That's the thing; above all, that makes Claire's glow. Every day she offers two or three varieties. The split-pea soup is thicker, richer, more flavorful than you ever hoped split-pea soup could be (we guarantee it). Seafood bisque is as opulent as a twenty-dollar lobster casserole. French onion soup is a snarl of melted veins of cheese, clods of broth-sopped bread, and sweet onions. And the French peasant soup is a majestic banquet of spuds, beans, vegetables, and herbs.

Each soup is a meal, particularly because it is always accompanied by a mini-loaf of Claire's homemade bread. This is real bread, freshly baked, tender but with enough oomph so you can dip big shreds of it into your soup and it will come out intact, burdened with a massive infusion of the savory liquid. It is white, dark, rye, or wheat; occasionally it arrives as a braided combination of a couple of doughs.

Bread and soup are really all you need to know about, but not all you will want to eat. Try Mexican: burritos, tacos, tostadas, eggplant Vera Cruz. They are all made with sharp cheese, substantial salsa, top-quality tortillas, but always without meat.

Claire's serves some celebrated sandwiches, too, many of them stuffed cornucopia-like inside pita breads: melted cheese, tabbouleh, greens, and veggies of every description.

Any time anything Italian is on the menu, try it. Claire is Italian, and if there is one thing she knows how to do spectacularly well (other than soup), it is homespun but sumptuous dishes like cavatelli dumplings in marinara sauce, parmigianas, and manicotti. Many a morning, if you come in for a scone or muffin (hot out of the oven, natch!), you will see Claire and her helpmates stirring great pots of sauce for these Italian specialties.

Service is cafeteria-style, sort of. You go through the line, picking and choosing some of the things you want (we haven't even mentioned the intoxicating buttercream-frosted cakes that are her dessert trademark) and placing orders for others, which are subsequently carried to your table by a member of the kitchen staff who strolls the dining room calling out your name above the lunchtime din.

Claire's is a raucous place, sometimes brusque, even impolite. If quiet dignity and impeccable service are what you seek, avoid it. On the other hand, if you want gratifying food at low prices, served with enthusiasm in a street-corner cafe in the heart of a bustling city, Claire's has few equals anywhere.

COFFEE AN'
343 N. MAIN ST., WESTPORT, CT (203) 227-3808

If you crave good doughnuts—aristocratic doughnuts—some of the best doughnuts in a region where fried, sweet dough is serious business, we've got a hot tip for you: Coffee An' in Westport, Connecticut.

The time to eat at Coffee An' is between seven and nine in the morning. It will be crowded: that's part of the fun. Observe the regulars at the twin counters on either side of the store, and at the seats along the front window. They've got their dunking-sipping-reading-the-paper routine down pat. Few of them eat just one doughnut; personally, we find it hard to limit ourselves to two. It is hard not to pig out when each variety—chocolate, cinnamon, plain, and glazed—is a paragon.

The genius responsible for this sweet morning excellence is Derek Coutouras, whom you will see in the back room every day (starting at 4:00 A.M.) working at the fry kettles, hanging freshly cooked donuts on dowels to cool, drizzling on the glaze, and sprinkling sugar. Up front, the counters and cash register of the tiny cafe are staffed by Mrs. Coutouras and a team of lightning-fast waitresses.

The kind of doughnuts that made us fall in love with Coffee An' are the chocolate ones. Understand, please, that we are not chocoholics, so we don't automatically like them just because they're fudgy. Indeed, what's amazing about them is more texture than flavor. They are crusty with lush insides, with all the heft and chaw of cocoa pound cake encased in a sweet sugar shell.

The glazed, plain, jelly-filled, and powdered-sugar doughnuts are all quite wonderful, too; but the other thing you *must* sample at Coffee An' is a cinnamon bun. It is a billowing, yeasty spiral gilded with a faintly brittle glaze of sugar and veined with lodes of dark, sweetened cinnamon. Each bun is about six inches wide and three inches high: too big for dunking or even for picking up whole. Just tear at it for half an hour, and imbibe three or four cups of good coffee alongside.

DR. MIKE'S
158 GREENWOOD AVE., BETHEL, CT (203) 792-4388

We cannot tell a lie. Sometimes we hate Dr. Mike's ice cream. Sometimes it's just too rich, too butterfatty, too chock full of Chocolate Lace candy or malt powder or whole dark Bing cherries or whatever it is supposed to be full of, and there's too much whipped cream on top of the sundae, and the fudge sauce is so potent it makes us dizzy. Believe us when we tell you that this is some of the most opulent-tasting ice cream in creation, and there are occasions—rare occasions—when it simply is too, too much of a good thing.

Most of the time, the cones and cardboard cups dished out by the little shop in an alley way off the main street of Bethel are perfect. Several of the flavors set standards unequaled by any other brand. The longtime standard-bearer, "rich chocolate," for example, is stunningly flavored, cocoa-brown, and more deliriously chocolatey than a pure plain Hershey bar, but with the added luxury of all that high-butterfat cream. We must warn you, however, that sometimes it gets scooped from the tub cold and hard; and the flavor does not blossom until it is on the verge of melting. This makes for an unbelievably messy cone, and a good possibility of dark chocolate stains on your hands, face, and clothes (somehow, this chocolate ice cream leaves smears that are far more conspicuous than any other brand); but you *must* wait until the rich chocolate ice cream is soft. If you do, bliss is yours.

"Chocolate lace and cream" is another Dr. Mike's exclusive flavor, using a luxurious chocolate-covered hard candy that is made in big webbed sheets by a local confectionery. The candy is broken into bite-sized pieces and suspended in a pure white emulsion of sweetened cream: another dreamy experience, but in this case our warning is to get it in a cup. The crunch of the candy conflicts with the crunch of a cone.

We've named our two favorite flavors. Don't hesitate, though, if you find your personal favorite among the approximately six varieties available on any particular day. Each one is made the old-fashioned way, using cream from dairy buckets, in five-gallon batches; and we have fond, fond memories of Dr. Mike's coffee, coconut, cinnamon, Heath Bar crunch, even prune, dazzling vanilla, and some real tongue-stunners made with fresh fruits in the summer.

After you have tasted the ice cream in its unadulterated state, please return to Dr. Mike's for a milk shake (none thicker this side of St. Louis) or a hot fudge sundae. The fudge is dense, faintly granular, and a glorious complement to any of the light colors and fruit flavors. And the pure, sweet whipped cream is heaped on with a trowel.

GAIL'S STATION HOUSE
3 SIDE CUT ROAD, WEST REDDING, CT (203) 938-8933;
SECOND LOCATION: 378 MAIN ST., RIDGEFIELD, CT

Before we rave about Gail's cheddar-corn pancakes, freshly baked unsprouted wheat bread, homemade soups, and giant brownies, let us tell you about the parrot crisis. A couple of Octobers ago, an escaped scarlet-lore Amazon parrot found its way to a tall ash tree behind the Station House cafe, where it learned to scavenge for food with a gang of crows. Gail was distraught because the weather was getting cold, and there was no way the neotropical bird could survive winter. Miguel, who works in the kitchen and used to be a tree surgeon in Costa Rica, climbed the ash tree and set a cage fifty feet up in hopes of trapping the wayward parrot with a bowl full of Gail's homemade granola. Nearly every morning, customers from inside the Station House cafe would stand under the tree whenever the parrot was roosting and sing tunes at it, offer it apples and warm muffins and pieces of buttered buckwheat pancake, and otherwise try to tempt it down to warmth and safety. At one time, Gail spent a morning whistling the theme song to "The Andy Griffith Show" because someone had told her about a local pet parrot who was enthralled by that particular tune. Nothing worked. The bird was having too good a time flying free. By November, when the nights turned freezing cold, it was gone. Although some people wept when it became obvious the parrot was lost, it was not an altogether sad occasion. "He was a nice bird," Miguel pronounced at the end when he brought down the empty cage, and Gail's regulars (ourselves included) shared a lot of sweet memories of the bright green vagabond flapping merrily alongside its crow companions through the red and yellow leaves of the Connecticut autumn.

Even before the parrot crisis, we had a soft spot for the Station House cafe, and not only because of its good food. It's such a nice place, a real country kitchen in an old wooden building along the railroad tracks with a short counter, a handful of tables, an open porch in front for nice-weather dining, and a blackboard that lists specials every day with a fancifully scripted colored-chalk menu. The food is hearty and the waitresses are friendly; and because it is only miles from our house, Gail's is the place we go whenever we want to relax à *deux* or give visitors a scenic and cozy (as well as delectable) taste of New England.

Gail Gilbert, who runs the place along with Nancy Bariluk, is a vegetarian. Her menu is filled with such healthy things as carrot juice squeezed to order and vegetable-and-brown-rice casseroles. There are peanut-butter-and-banana sandwiches on thick slabs of toothsome-textured bread, fruit smoothies to drink, and even veggie burgers. But in addition to the virtuous foods (which actually taste great), there are plenty of naughty ones, such as beefy hamburgers (quarter-pounders or half-pounders) served with thick, fried wedges of potato and draped with oozing blankets of cheddar cheese and strips of bacon—all on homemade buns, of course.

Breakfast is the great meal of the day, including different kinds of muffins every morning, Gail's honey-sweet granola, double-thick French toast, all the usual omelettes, and a trio of gorgeous egg specialties served in small cast-iron skillets. "Texas Pink" is a combination of red-skinned hash browns, jalapeño peppers, scrambled eggs, salsa, sour cream, and a wedge of grapefruit; "Barney's Breakfast" is melted cheese and Canadian bacon with scrambled eggs and an English muffin; "Leo's Skillet" is eggs scrambled with nuggets of Nova Scotia lox and green onions, served with a bagel and cream cheese.

Best of all are pancakes: plain ones and buckwheat ones, pancakes with blueberries, bananas, or chocolate chips—all available, of course, with bacon or sausage. Our favorites are cheddar corn cakes, their tawny surface mottled with spots where cheddar cheese has turned crusty on the grill, the buttery batter inside studded with corn kernels. Drizzle on some syrup and you have a plate of four-star food, all the more enjoyable for the country comfort of the friendly cafe that serves it.

GOULASH PLACE
42 HIGHLAND, DANBURY, CT (203) 744-1971

You will thank us for recommending the Goulash Place when you find it. But first, you might decide you want to kill us when you go looking for it and get lost somewhere in Danbury. We have been there dozens of times (it's just miles from our house), yet we lose our way every time we go. The problem is that it is not in a business district. The Goulash Place is a home in a neighborhood on a street corner; and you can drive right past and miss it if you aren't looking carefully. Don't worry, though. You *will* find it. Just ask anyone in the general vicinity to point you to the Goulash Place (a.k.a. Goulash Diner).

It is a snug little inn fashioned out of an annex to the owners' home. Each place setting is marked with white Scotties napkins; and there are a few pieces of Hungarian folk culture placed around the dining room to help create a mood. You will have no trouble getting in the spirit of things when you meet Magda, who is not only the waitress but also (with her husband, John) the cook and owner. Magda has never lost her Transylvanian accent; and she approaches customers with all the panache of an experienced diner waitress. "Are the mashed potatoes real?" you naïvely ask. She scoffs and gives you a dirty look as though you just asked her to serve you a Quarter-Pounder. Not only are the mashed potatoes real, they are *real good*—somehow enriched and super-seasoned so they taste even better than ordinary spuds.

There are so many good things to eat—all at low, low prices (about five dollars for a hearty lunch), and all heartwarmingly homemade. Start with soup. Each broad bowlful is accompanied by a separate saucer holding three saltine crackers and a spoon. Chicken soup is pale gold, threaded with thin noodles; bean soup is staunch, enriched with chewy little dumplings; the best of the soups is mushroom, a powerful broth heavy with shreds of pork and tiny dumplings.

There are at least three kinds of goulash (a generic term for shepherd's stew), including Transylvanian (made with pork and sauerkraut), veal goulash, and the classic paprika-accented beef soup known as Hungarian goulash. Hungarian goulash is great either as an appetizer before a hearty dinner or as the main course at lunch—accompanied by the Goulash Place's pickled red cabbage or a marinated cucumber salad.

Main courses include such hearty fare as wiener schnitzel, chicken paprikash, stuffed cabbage, and (on weekends) roasted duck, most of them accompanied by heaping portions of buttery little nockerl dumplings and/or those swell mashed potatoes. For dessert, there are strudels, rum cake, and palascintas (also known as crepes) wrapped around apricot, cheese, chocolate, or nut fillings.

If you like home cooking, cozy cafes, and low prices, put this neighborhood restaurant of ours in your little black book. We'll see you there.

JERRY'S PIZZA
885 WASHINGTON ST., MIDDLETOWN, CT (203) 346-5335

In a small storefront in a common shopping center on the road into Middletown there is majestic pizza to be eaten. It is Jerry's "white Sicilian." Baked in a square pan, it has a crust that is medium-thick, rising up in glistening, oil-gilded golden puffs around the edge. It's got a bit of crunch before its chew, and at the outermost edges, it is brittle; but in the center of the pie, it is a lush pillow of taut, yeasty bread. If it seems as though we are paying inordinate attention to the crust of this pie, just wait until you see and taste it—a match for the most elegant focaccia you ever ate. Atop it, Jerry spreads a finely chopped mélange of garlic, anchovies, and fresh parsley, to which he adds a spritz of oil and a fine dust of parmesan. That's all there is on a white Sicilian, and it is pizza pie perfection.

One time we asked Jerry if he could make one with anchovies only on half to satisfy an anchovy-phobe among us; and he answered simply, no, he could not make a white Sicilian any way other than the right way. Then when the pie came to the table he pointed to one quarter and explained that he had indeed tried to make part of it as we wanted. Jerry is that kind of guy—a real sweetheart. However, we've got to warn you that the part without evidence of actual pulverized anchovies still had their distinctive salty smack. In fact, the whole restaurant smelled of anchovies and garlic once our pie emerged from the oven. This is one of the most powerfully odoriferous foods in creation. And after eating this pie, we, too, smelled like a pizzeria (a *great* pizzeria) the rest of the day.

Jerry's makes other things: fine thin-crust pizzas, whole or by the slice; foot-and-a-half hot oven grinders (eggplant parmigiana is especially lovely); and plates of unstylish red-sauced spaghetti. But the white Sicilian is Jerry's triumph. It takes a full hour from the time it's begun—the dough has to rise, a process that cannot be short-cut. We suggest you call ahead to place an order or plan some interesting activity while you wait, such as driving to O'Rourke's (p. 69) downtown and having a steamed cheeseburger hors d'oeuvre.

LENNY & JOE'S FISH TALE RESTAURANT
86 BOSTON POST RD., WESTBROOK, CT (203) 669-0767;
ALSO 1301 POST RD., MADISON, CT (203) 245-7289

There are two Lenny & Joe's; one is a restaurant with waiters, the other a wait-in-line, self-service affair. Both are feed-the-family eating barns with easy-wipe bare tables, paper placemats, and walls decorated with this year's model of Lenny & Joe's garishly colored T-shirts; both are crowded and noisy at suppertime during the summer (although both are open year-round); and, to the point, both are choice places to eat maximum amounts of top-quality shoreline food at minimum prices.

Start with chowder. It's New England style: white, abundantly clammy, with a strong ocean smack. There are lovely plates of raw clams and oysters on the half shell, and a quartet of giant, snapping-fresh boiled shrimp in the shrimp cocktail. The menu (which is printed each day) suggests starting dinner with fried seafood; but we recommend you save the fried stuff for your main course. There aren't many kitchens that know how to fry fish as well as Lenny & Joe's.

Clams: available whole or as "strips" (without the gooey part), they are sheathed in a fragile, tender crust that isn't particularly brittle, but tastes great. The whole-bellied ones (our favorite) are behemoths—big, weighty clods of luscious, nectareously tender clam encased in their breading, proffered in great piles by the clam roll (on a toasted bun), single order, double order, platter, and super platter. Whichever size you order, you inevitably get more than you expect. With platters (of shrimp, scallops, scrod, calamari, oysters, too), you also get good cole slaw, dinner rolls, and a choice of potato: French fries, which are fine, or an unexpected but welcome companion for fried food, boiled red potatoes, which are smooth, silky, mild, and a clean contrast to the raunchy main course. You must pay extra for onion rings, and they are well worth it—big crunchy hoops with a real onion sweetness that goes well with any fish.

Not all the food at Lenny & Joe's is fried. We have eaten superb hunks of char-broiled, smoky-flavored swordfish steak, clean and sweet fillet of sole, homely but satisfying casseroles of broiled shrimp with garlic, Connecticut River shad in the spring, and even a swell plate of shrimp baked and stuffed with crab and cheese. And then there is the lobster roll: it's rich. Presented in a long, butter-grilled split wiener roll (like HoJo's used to serve, but better), it is loaded with pieces of lobster meat that are bathed in so much butter that the bun is quickly reduced to a buttery wad of breadstuff. It comes in a cardboard boat, but even so, by the time you are halfway through this plush sandwich, it is likely you will be picking and poking at the mess on your plate with the relish of a hungry vulture.

LOUIS LUNCH
261 CROWN ST., NEW HAVEN, CT (203) 562-5507

There is a lot of discussion about who invented the hamburger, and where and when the great event occurred; but whether you believe it was the Tartars, the Earl of Salisbury, or sailors from Hamburg who first grilled a patty of beef and ate it between two pieces of breadstuff, you've got to tip your hat to Louis Lunch of New Haven. Even if the hamburger was not invented here in 1903 by Louis Lassen as a thrifty way of doing something with leftover trimmings from the steak sandwiches he sold at his lunch wagon, Louis Lunch today, operated by fourth-generation Louises, is a real taste of hamburger history.

A small brick building with school-desk seats and an ancient wooden counter with years' worth of initials carved into it, Louis Lunch cooks hamburgers an old-fashioned way. A gob of ground steak is flattened into a patty, then placed inside an armature inside a vertical broiler that holds it suspended between two heat sources and allows the grease to drip away as the meat sears. When it is done, the hamburger is put on a piece of toasted bread, not a bun (toast smeared with Cheez Whiz, if you wish), and another piece of toast is put on top. There it is: a primitive and truly delicious American classic.

MARBLE PILLAR
22 CENTRAL ROW, HARTFORD, CT (203) 247-4549

Does anyone but us realize that Hartford, Connecticut, has its own culinary specialty? It isn't unique to Hartford, but the few old-line restaurants that remain in the city still make a big deal of it; and somehow, there
is something so correct about it being the gastronomic symbol of America's
insurance capital. We are talking about chicken pie, as served at the Marble Pillar, Wednesdays only, at lunch.

It vents wisps of steam as the waitress hurries it to the table in its foil
tin. She flips the tin and dumps it out on a plate. A mess, but this is truly a
widow's-and-orphan's-friend kind of meal: big squares of tender white
chicken meat, peas, carrots, potato chunks, sunny yellow gravy, and strata
of crisp, tan crust. What could be more comforting?

The rest of the Marble Pillar menu pretty much follows suit. This
ancient kitchen is a treasury of bygone lunchroom cuisine, from chowders
and cream soups to beef liver and onions, meat loaf, and pot roast, as well
as an array of cold sandwiches for quick meals and delightfully dowdy rice
pudding or bread pudding for dessert. When they used to serve dinner
here, the kitchen specialized in German food, and there are still some
mighty good remnants of it at lunch: bratwurst, goulash, sauerbraten.

As for ambience, the dining room of this institution (now more than
125 years old) is arrayed with communal tables and utilitarian coat hooks
on the walls. The kitchen is near enough so that when the restaurant is
crowded waitresses don't have to go all the way back to communicate with
the food-prep people. They can stand in the midst of the lunchtime crowd
and bellow out their order above the customers' clamor.

NOAH'S
115 WATER ST., STONINGTON, CT (203) 535-3925

Hop off I-95 at the eastern border of Connecticut, follow the road south
as it twists and turns, and you will soon be meandering along the narrow one-way main street that is the picturesque village of Stonington.
Homes, shops, and artists' studios are close together, their clapboard sid-
ing weathered by age, their windows underhung with flower boxes. There is
a fancy restaurant in this town called the Harbor View; and there is
Noah's—the local lunchroom.

Noah's is two rooms. The one you enter serves as an art gallery, community bulletin board, and display case for pastries. It is casual, with lots of plants, haphazard but clean. The next room is where you eat, at one of several unclothed wooden tables spread in a random pattern across a creaky wooden floor. Windows provide a view of the street; old advertisements and travel posters decorate the walls.

Also on the wall is a blackboard listing Noah's daily specials. There is a regular menu, too; but look to the board first. Here are listed the various fish of the day, pasta, and quiche. One November when we stopped in during an Indian pudding–hunting expedition, the board listed, of all things, chicken croquettes. These dowdy old tea room favorites were delicious, accompanied by mashed potatoes and gravy. Most full meals come with bread, but if yours does not, order some. Noah's is known for brawny homemade loaves of white, wheat, or rye, served with a crock of spreadable-temperature butter, and for Portuguese sweet bread available by the loaf, to go.

Unless you are here for breakfast or allergic to mollusks, you really ought to start whatever meal you have with clam chowder, which Noah's sells in three sizes, from six-ounce cup to eighteen-ounce bowl. It is a milky brew, not too briny. Mild, chock full of tender cubed potatoes and little bits of clam, it is persuasive Yankee comfort food.

For dessert, look to the blackboard on the wall, where about a dozen different things are listed every day. From the simplest homemade lemon ice cream to a dazzling rum-soaked Jamaican banana cake, the repertoire is plain and fancy, although never too elaborate or sinfully rich. We especially appreciate the regional specialties on the dessert menu: there is always a pudding, almost always a good berry pie. If you are lucky, you will have a chance to sample Noah's exemplary apple brown Betty, the classic down-east dessert that is apple pan dowdy's cousin, but crumble-topped rather than biscuit-doughed.

O'ROURKE'S DINER
728 MAIN ST., MIDDLETOWN, CT (203) 346-6101

O'Rourke's is a 1946-vintage, neon-ribboned stainless steel diner on Main Street in Middletown. It is a fine place to eat blue-plate chow (meat loaf and mashed potatoes, chili dogs) in an atmosphere of neon lights, worn Formica tables and ancient marble counter, and a rocking jukebox (one at each booth); but that's not all. Brian O'Rourke, nephew of the original Mr. O'Rourke, also makes refined food to suit the tastes of the Wesleyan personnel who venture away from the campus for a taste of real life. Nothing on O'Rourke's menu costs much over five dollars, not even the smoked salmon croissant, the chicken breast sautéed on a toasted bagel with brie cheese and smoked bacon, or the Florentine supreme omelette filled with sun-dried tomato pesto.

Please, don't be scared by the aspiring sound of some of these fancy-pants dishes. Believe us when we say that O'Rourke's hasn't sold its soul to the trendies. It's just that Brian likes to have fun in the kitchen and try new things. In fact, we have had some of his roasted plum tomato soup (with pesto) and it was delicious, as was the wild duck and wild rice soup (which he made because a friend gave him some fresh-killed ducks). One day last spring, shad and shad roe were featured on the menu (for the top price of $5.45 for either), and Brian explained that the reason he could sell them so cheaply was that he had been down by the river that morning, bartering meal tickets with the fisherman who had just caught them. On weekends, O'Rourke's offers an array of stupendous breakfast items, the likes of which you would never find in a strictly classical diner: griddle bread pancakes (like scones) topped with honey, butter, jam, and heavy cream; French toast made from Irish soda bread; omelettes filled with the likes of fresh asparagus, Gorgonzola cheese, diced Italian sausage, or smoked salmon; and also four-star muffins (banana-chocolate chip, blueberry cream cheese, morning glory).

Honestly, though, as much as we appreciate the high quality and low prices of O'Rourke's upscale cooking, it's the funky stuff that always brings us back. As we said, the meat loaf is excellent and the mashed potatoes are real. French fries are thin, wispy ones, gloriously greasy and good to eat. And—here is the *pièce de résistance*—O'Rourke's makes the best steamed cheeseburger on earth.

Unless you've spent some time in Middletown or Meriden it is likely you've never heard of a steamed cheeseburger. Central Connecticut is where it was invented about half a century ago, and central Connecticut is where it has stayed—unknown in cities as close as Hartford or New Haven. The process is simple. A patty of ground beef is set on a metal tray and put in a steamer about the size of a microwave oven. After it steams for two minutes, the cook puts cheddar cheese on top, steams it a few seconds more, and it's done. It tastes different than a fried or grilled burger. The cloddish qualities of a hamburger are diminished by the steam bath: the patty that emerges is juicier and meatier. The steam-melted cheese works its way into all the crevices of the cooked meat. Combined with a crusty hard roll, a slice of sweet Bermuda onion, and plenty of bright yellow mustard, this is one scrumptious sandwich.

Exactly when and why the restaurants of central Connecticut invented this peculiar cheeseburger is a gastronomic mystery. In their investigation of the topic for *Connecticut* magazine a few years ago, Janelle Finch and John Columbus quoted Jack Duberek, son of Ted of Ted's Restaurant in Meriden, as believing it was invented at a now-defunct diner named Jack's in Middletown, where it began as a steamed cheese sandwich. When local factory workers wanted a more substantial meal, meat was added. To this account, we would add our own observation that there was great concern during the 1920s that fried food was unhealthy and blocked normal digestion. (In those days, Crisco began advertising itself as "the digestible shortening.") Steaming might have been an ingenious Yankee solution to the problem of greasy burgers.

In any case, O'Rourke's steamed cheeseburger is the *ne plus ultra* of the genre: a hefty patty of coarse-ground but tender-textured meat topped with an immense portion of high-quality cheddar cheese and served on a good, crusty roll. A unique treat for burger-lovers; and with a heap of the slippery French fries, it is a grand *Roadfood* meal.

For dessert, O'Rourke's will be happy to set you up with a piece of pie. It is homemade, and it is superb, especially the rhubarb-nut pie in the spring and apple pie any time of year. If you ask nicely, they will put your slice of pie in the steam box, lay a hunk of their good cheddar on it, and steam it until the cheese softens just enough to cling to the flaky top crust of the pie. It's an old custom at O'Rourke's, and the only logical conclusion to a steamed cheeseburger meal.

PAT'S KOUNTRY KITCHEN
JUNCTION OF ROUTE 154 & MILL ROCK RD., OLD SAYBROOK, CT
(203) 388-4784

L obster may be king of seafood on Yankee shores, but it is clams that are the people's choice. New Englanders adore clams, and have devised a thousand ways to eat them. Clam chowder, fried clams, clams casino, stuffed clams, deep fried clam fritters, baked clam casseroles: from raw on the half shell to the top of thin-crusted pizzas, the almighty bivalve is as common hereabouts as turnip greens in Dixie or Frito pies in Santa Fe.

One of the most delicious ways with clams happened as an accident about ten years ago. Pat Brink, who used to run a small coffee shop in Old Saybrook, had recruited her children to help her make the clam chowder. The young ones shucked a mountain of clams, but instead of carefully saving the briny broth inside the shells, they kept only the meat. Chowder cooks know that you cannot make clam chowder without clam liquor. "What to do with two bushels of clams and no broth?" Pat wondered.

The answer to her question was clam hash, a spur-of-the-moment invention which has since become the signature dish at Pat's Kountry Kitchen—a family-size restaurant that grew out of her popular town cafe. Like chowder, the hash is made from the big clams known as quahogs (say *co-hogs*), too chewy to eat whole. They are chopped up, mixed with potatoes and onions, then griddle-fried until crusty brown outside, with a moist, ocean-scented center.

Pat told us that many new customers, especially those from clam-deprived regions of the country, don't cotton to the idea of clam hash right away—especially for breakfast. That's why she always offers strangers a sample. "I bet I've given out 10,000 tastes of clam hash since we started making it," Pat grinned, telling us about hungry travelers from all over the country, as far as California, who come back for hash every summer.

The Kountry Kitchen is a genuine hash house—the only place we know that regularly makes not only clam, but corned-beef hash, too. And every weekend, the menu lists an old down-east favorite called red flannel hash—chopped-up corned beef, potatoes, onions, etc., turned vivid red by the addition of beets. Pat's version is further pepped up with pastrami.

At breakfast, Pat's is packed with hash hounds who accompany their crusty hot-off-the griddle slabs with eggs and home fries and crumbly blueberry muffins. Coffee comes from the school of the bottomless cup, replenished throughout the meal.

The first time we sat down, it was a hectic weekend morning, but Pat recognized us as newcomers and zeroed in as we read the menu, advising us to be sure to order our hash well-done. Then she table-hopped among her regulars (some of whom told us they come here for three meals every day), offering them tastes of her freshly baked Pilgrim pie (apples, raisins, cranberries) or vanilla chip pie or Grape-Nut tapioca pudding. The pies are exuberant, and there are many varieties; but in our experience they are prettier than they are good.

Pat's is a happy place, imprinted with the personality of its owner, who watches over the boisterous dining room with all the sass of a diner moll. The decor is a hodgepodge of Pat's favorite bric-a-brac, including a teddy bear collection, antique implements and china, and a sign in the lobby asking "Next to the flag, whom do you love?"

PEPE'S PIZZERIA NAPOLETANA
157 WOOSTER ST., NEW HAVEN, CT (203) 865-5762
(PEPE'S ALWAYS CLOSES FOR TWO WEEKS AFTER LABOR DAY.)

New Haven pizza—Wooster Street pizza in particular—is a matter of crust: brittle-skinned, but with a chaw so brawny that half a large pie can make your jaw ache the morning after. The circumference of the pizza, a circle of bread unladen with any of the stuff in the middle, rises in rugged puffs, occasionally charring to a crackable black blister at the outermost burst of stretched skin. Look underneath: the crust is speckled with grains of charred semolina flour. Semolina is used on the oven floor and baker's peel like tiny ball bearings, so the pizzas slide in and out easily. As they burn, the grains absorb the flavors of the smoke and sizzling pizzas, and many of them cling to the bottom, creating a friable web beneath the dough. It's an ugly, raunchy underside, sometimes greasy in spots where a previous pizza has oozed excess olive oil; but it is this lagniappe of oven grit that gives the Wooster Street pizzas their extra measure of soul.

At Pepe's, the greatest (and original) of Wooster Street's pizzerias, you walk into a room with an open kitchen in back where white-aproned pizzaioli reenact the ritual originated by Frank Pepe nearly seventy years ago: bombs of dough are flattened on a marble table, clouds of spice are strewn in an instant, and six-foot wooden baker's peels inject pizzas deep into the wood-fired oven. It is a hypnotic scene, untouched by time or fashion.

The most delicious irony of Pepe's is that Frank Pepe, New Haven pizza's Zeus, was allergic to mozzarella—and to tomatoes! His favorite pizza was olive oil and oregano on a bare crust, dotted with little bits of anchovy. To this day, Pepe's premier pizza is made without mozzarella or tomato sauce. It is called a white clam pie, and it is available only when the kitchen can get the good, little clams from Rhode Island. It is elementary food—nothing but crust, freshly shucked littleneck clams, olive oil, garlic, oregano, and a dash of grated parmesan. Without a mozzarella mantle, the dough develops wicked resilience, its mottled surface frosted gold with grated cheese.

If the warden gave us one last meal, anything on earth before he flipped the switch to fry us, we would ask to have it served in a booth at Pepe's. We would inhale the aroma of the coal fire, of garlic and clams sizzling in hot oil, and of yeast flexing up gluten in the puffy halo of crust. After a white clam pizza and a pitcher of beer on Wooster Street, we could die happy.

THE PLACE
891 BOSTON POST RD., GUILFORD, CT (203) 453-9276

The Place is as plain as its name: an open-air clambake by the side of Route 1 with tree stumps for chairs and massive wood cable spools for tables, all randomly arranged in a sunny clearing around a smoky wood fire where seafood is cooked by the shirtsleeved staff. Tents are erected when it rains, and music is provided by a portable radio that dangles from a low tree branch. If you want wine or beer, bring your own. (There are liquor stores nearby.)

The menu is fundamental shoreline fare, like a traditional clambake, but all à la carte. The best dish is littleneck clams roasted over wood, split open, daubed with hot sauce and heated just until the sauce and clam juice come together in perfect, picnic harmony. There are steamer clams, too; also lobsters, which taste just wonderful when cooked outdoors. And don't forget corn-on-the-cob. It is cooked in its husk and swabbed with melted butter.

The Place is open only in the summer, starting the last weekend in April; on a nice weekend day it can be maddeningly crowded. But come on an off-hour or a weekday, and it can be a happy retreat from the bustle of shoreline shops and traffic.

SEA SWIRL
ROUTE 1, EAST OF MYSTIC, CT (203) 536-3452

A former soft-serve ice cream stand on an unsightly strip of Route 1 as you exit Mystic, Sea Swirl at first might seem like an unlikely place to find four-star food. But on the *Roadfood* roster, the fried clams dished out across this stainless steel counter are tops. Sweet and faintly oily with a zesty marine snap to the meat inside their brittle crust, these are the best clams anywhere this side of the North Shore of Massachusetts. They are everything fancy-pants gourmets dislike, and everything fried seafood ought to be: greasy, raunchy, luscious, salty, powerfully oceanic, and a kick to eat by the plateful, with French fries and a sweet, ice-cold soda on the side.

As for atmosphere, it couldn't be better. Picnic tables provide a full view of muscle cars cruising Route 1. And gulls who can find nothing good to scavenge over at Mystic Seaport (where refuse is considered an eyesore) hover in the air above, hoping to dive-bomb a table and steal a French fry or neglected clam.

STICK TO YOUR RIBS
1785 STRATFORD AVE., STRATFORD, CT (203) 377-1752;
ALSO 1308 E. MAIN ST., STAMFORD, CT (203) 348-6700

Barbecue in the Northeast is usually as appetizing as fried clams in Amarillo; but here is one worthy exception. Since it opened about ten years ago, Stick to Your Ribs has earned a reputation among traveling eaters far and wide as a stronghold of Texas-style (and also North Carolina–style) meats, and fine fixin's to go with them.

Ribs resonate with the nutty sapidity of pork that has sucked in the perfume of hickory and oak wood and just enough sauce to give the meat a nip. Beef ribs are much bigger than pork, almost scary to look at—big rectangles of meat and bone. But the meat is surprisingly gentle, mellow-textured and fine-flavored, pulling easily into juicy, fibrous hunks as you lift it toward your mouth.

The "North Carolina–style" pork is the style of western North Carolina, which is to say chopped up, well-sauced, at once tangy and sweet. Regular pork shoulder (not North Carolina–style) is our choice for the best dish in the house—moist beyond belief, flavorful, and a great-looking mottled mess of inside and outside pieces from the roast. Like almost all the meats, it is served on plates or in sandwiches made from dusty-crusted, chewy Portuguese rolls that Stick to Your Ribs gets from a Bridgeport bakery. Another good breadstuff here is cornbread, which is rugged-textured, but with a winning mellow taste.

There are four levels of sauce from which to choose: mild, medium, madness, and mean. Even mean isn't horrendous, but unless you are a chilihead, you ought to start with madness or medium. The sauces don't have a lot of interesting flavor, but they come in handy to provide the degree of heat you want, and to moisturize the beef brisket which, although packed with good flavor and gorgeous to look at and unbelievably tender, tends to dry out as it sits on a plate.

The original Stick to Your Ribs location off Exit 31 from I-95 in Stratford helped give this place a cachet among skeptical barbecue purists. It was, and is, a supreme dump in a no-man's land surrounded by barbed-wire factory lots, and with nothing but a few picnic tables for accommodations. Most business is take-out, and it isn't at all unusual to see a dozen cars in the parking lot filled with people gnawing ribs and eating sandwiches off their dashboards. The new location on the Stamford-Darien town line, while in no ways uppity, is civilized. There is a sit-down dining room with interior decor (bleached bones on the wall; eight-by-ten photographs of the West) and actual table coverings (oilcloth). There is even a full bar, and credit cards are accepted. But please, don't let any of these refinements dissuade you from eating here. The beef and pork transcend them, as they transcend the Yankee location of this quality barbecue.

SWANKY FRANK'S
182 CONNECTICUT AVE., NORWALK, CT (203) 838-8969

S wanky Frank's is a roadside shanty with the lowest possible amount of class and high-concept weenies. It has been a dump for years; even as the personnel behind the worn-out counter have changed, the hot dogs and recreant roadside ambience have, like fine wine, aged and improved. Sit at a wobbly table in the annex to the left or at the counter to the right and call out your order. There are hamburgers and clams and tuna salad and such on the menu, but at Swanky Frank's, the hot dog is king. Here sit truckers, working people, and junk-food connoisseurs scarfing them down two at a time, their assemblage of paper plates also holding tawny-skinned, made-here French fries alongside soda pop or cartons of homo milk.

The dogs are nasty critters—hefty tubes of well-garlicked porcine pink meat fried in hot oil until they develop a crackly darkened skin. If you pay two bits extra you can get yourself a lite version—the frankfurter is bisected and cooked on a grill—but this has none of the wicked charm of the oily one. Relish, onions, mustard: pile 'em on. A Swanky Frank is strong; no amount of condiments can disguise its authoritative character.

THE SYCAMORE
282 GREENWOOD AVE., BETHEL, CT (203) 748-2716

A genuine drive-in restaurant. Pull into the parking lot facing the low white building with the neon sign on top, then flash your lights or beep your horn. In a jiffy a carhop will be at your window. Maybe there are written menus; we couldn't tell you because we always order the same thing, and anyway, the side of the building is garlanded with lists of all the different hamburgers the Sycamore makes. Our meal is always burgers, French fries, and root beer. Place the order, and in about five minutes out comes the carhop once again, this time toting a tray full of food to attach to the window. Tune to your favorite radio station and sink your teeth into a blast from the culinary past.

The burgers arrive wrapped in wax paper, which is a good thing if you order one of the sloppy ones and care about your car's upholstery. The Sycamore's tour de force, known as a Dagwood burger, is two patties of meat blanketed with cheese tucked inside a bun with catsup, mustard, mayonnaise, pickle slices, lettuce, and tomato: an unholy and irresistible mess.

The meat patties themselves are extraordinary. They are not gourmet burgers, nor are they elegant in any way. They are thin, greasy, and infused with the flavor of a grill that has been sizzling patties of ground steak for decades. If you ever go inside The Sycamore (there are booths and counter seats, too), you can watch the man at the grill make them. When an order comes in, he grabs a round gob of chopped meat a little bigger than a Ping-Pong ball and slams it down on the hot grill. He then immediately presses it down hard, flattening it into a vaguely round patty so thin at the outer edges that you can practically see through it. The center remains somewhat thicker, perhaps a quarter inch, but not much more than that. The first side of this flattened patty cooks until it is crusty brown, meaning that the other side barely needs any time on the grill at all because it has virtually cooked through. The result is a skinny hamburger with one soft, tender side and one righteously crisp one: a tantalizing configuration, especially if you get two such patties on one bun, the layers of meat festooned with melted American cheese. The doubling-up provides a memorable textural variety as you sink your teeth into the sandwich.

To go with your hamburger, you want French fries (better than the fairly ordinary onion rings) and a root beer. They actually make their own root beer at The Sycamore, and they serve it in big, chilled mugs that arrive at your car encased in a lovely sheen of frost. Depending on whether your serving comes from the top or bottom of the barrel, it can range from sugar sweet to urbanely dry. Whatever the vintage, it is good root beer, and a perfect companion for a hamburger.

There are other things you can eat at The Sycamore. A few years ago, they even expanded their repertoire from the basic roster of hamburgers, hot dogs (good ones), chili, and short-order breakfasts to include a variety of sandwiches and even salads. Honestly, we have never eaten a salad at The Sycamore, and have no intention of doing so. How could one possibly fork into a bowl of lettuce with a steering wheel in the way?

VONETE'S PALACE OF SWEETS
262 MAIN ST., DERBY, CT (203) 734-2061

When was the last time you plunged your spoon into a tutti-frutti sundae or a banana royale? Do you ever crave a well-made egg cream or an orange flip? They are all here in this truly fabulous antique candy store on Main Street in the Naugatuck Valley city that time forgot—Derby.

Vonete's (say "von-ET-ees") opened for business in 1905. Despite its name, it is hardly a palace. It is a small, time-worn storefront with a tin ceiling and walls painted in Easter-egg pastels, a floor of teeny-weeny tiles, a counter and a few tables in back. Candy is weighed out in an antique scale that is no affectation. In addition to candy, ice cream, and a vaulting repertoire of soda fountain specialties (the very names of which induce nostalgia), you can come here to eat lunch: skinny hamburgers cooked on a tiny grill.

It's the sundaes we like best, especially any one that is topped with chocolate sauce or hot fudge. Vonete's chocolate topping is thin and sweet; you almost want to call it aristocratic. The fudge is rich and thick and so intensely fudgy it will cause a powerful thirst. No problem: have them spritz you out a glass of seltzer to accompany any sundae made with fudge.

WHISTLE STOP MUFFINS
BRANCHVILLE STATION, GEORGETOWN, CT (203) 544-8139

Lovely muffins: a panful, hot out of the oven, sometimes looks like one unbroken cake until proprietor Lolly Turner cuts the sheet into separate squares, each knobby umbrella capping a small, moist loaf. Many's the morning we have sat at one of the three tables in the Whistle Stop dining area (the waiting room for a commuter train) and watched a customer remove the top from a muffin as gingerly as splitting an Oreo, then eat the two halves as if they were separate courses.

The daily repertoire of about a dozen different kinds includes a granular and not-too-sweet corn, cakelike blueberry, raisin-dotted bran, gingerbread, sour cream almond, and seriously black chocolate chip, which is especially delicious later in the day as an after-dinner sweet when they serve it warmed, cut open, and à la mode with a scoop of made-here ice cream.

Since she opened her muffin hut in the old wood-walled train station several years ago, Lolly's menu and her enterprise have expanded. There is a nearly identical branch of Whistle Stop at the next station down the line in Wilton (not quite as adorable); and in addition to muffins, the menu now includes scones, coffee cake, cinnamon rolls, and big, goop-topped sticky buns. Also, naturally, you can buy coffee to drink and a newspaper to read while you eat; and now you can leave your dry cleaning with the muffin ladies early in the morning for guaranteed one-day service.

YANKEE DOODLE SANDWICH SHOP
260 ELM ST., NEW HAVEN, CT (203) 865-1074

Fast food has a bad name because most places that serve it are insipid, and the food is all the same. The Yankee Doodle Sandwich Shop on Elm Street in New Haven is a good place to restore your faith in short-order cookery and cheap eats.

Open from six-thirty in the morning to two-thirty in the afternoon, the Yankee Doodle consists of a twelve-stool counter in a skinny cafe that is truly a hole in the wall. Its sign, hanging over the sidewalk, depicts a white-uniformed waiter rushing to deliver food, posed in the same big-foot-forward "Keep on Truckin'" stance popularized in R. Crumb's underground comics in the late 1960s. Yankee Doodle's logo was around long before that. The tiny front window has some nice neon signs advertising cheap breakfast and fast lunch; but the signs are often out of commission; and the window is frequently fogged up from the furious cooking activity that goes on just inside. If you can see through, you will see dozens of eggs martialed in big cartons, and a grill on which the eggs, burgers, pigs-in-blankets, and cheese sandwiches sizzle.

At mealtime, it is likely you will arrive and find all the stools occupied. Don't be discouraged. Service is practically instantaneous, and most people don't come here to linger. Above the work area, where signs for the various house specialties are posted, is a series of bulletins in the poetical Burma Shave genre, that address the problem of a full house:

> NO SEATS? IN A HURRY? THINKING OF GOING ELSEWHERE?...
> BY THE TIME YOU DECIDE...
> WHERE, GET THERE, GIVE YOUR ORDER, GET YOUR FOOD...
> YOU CAN WAIT ONE MINUTE AND HAVE...

BETTER FOOD, FASTER SERVICE, FOR LESS MONEY…
BY DINING AT THE DOODLE.

Prices are ridiculously low. A breakfast of eggs and toast is eighty-five cents; a hefty omelette is just over two dollars. The most deluxe sandwich in the house—a Dandy Doodle Double-Double Cheeseburger, on a hard roll with lettuce and tomato, onions, and bacon—is about $2.50. In addition to sandwiches, the Doodle offers a nice selection of lonely-guy cuisine, in the form of individual canned soup and stew for one, as well as individually wrapped sets of crackers-and-cheese and Oreo cookies.

Twenty years ago, when we first dined at the Doodle, we were seduced by the small enthusiastic sign behind the counter that advertises the Yankee Doodle pig-in-a-blanket. After describing the ingredients—a frankfurter, melted cheese, bacon, and barbecue sauce—the sign concludes with an exclamation: YOU WILL HAVE MORE! Sure enough, we did; and we still do, any time we hit a counter stool with a hankering for a good and greasy wiener. If you sit up front, you can watch the counter man make the Yankee Doodle pigs-in-blankets. A porcine frank is slit and stuffed with cheese, then wrapped with bacon and cooked on a hot grill until the dog blisters and the bacon is crisp. This luscious tube steak is slapped into a toasted and buttered bun, accompanied by a small paper cup of hot relish, and sold for a little under a dollar and a half. We have found that two or three make a satisfying meal.

Other than the cuisine, we like Yankee Doodle for its ambience, which is so deliciously déclassé. The smell of the grill perfumes the air, and diners are serenaded by a dishwasher that periodically belches forth a rude, rumbling clamor down at the far end of the counter. One griddle man does all the cooking, and one waitress handles the counter. Customers' bills are slapped down on the Formica right along with their meals.

ZIP'S
ROUTE 101 & 12, EXIT 93 OFF I-395, DAYVILLE, CT (203) 774-6335

Zip's bills itself as "New England's Finest Dining Car," and it is a real looker. From Route 52, especially at night when the neon "EAT" sign is burning, it is a vision of roadside allure, circa 1954; the inside is spanking clean, sunburst-pattern steel and pink-pastel Formica. At either end of the counter, black-and-white photo murals of Dayville's Lake Alexander provide a touch of art and nature to appreciate. Even the waitresses fit the picture: outfitted in neat white nylon uniforms and bright red aprons that match the menus.

What's to eat at Zip's? Diner food with a Yankee accent. Pot roast is *Yankee* pot roast, whatever that means; and whatever it means, it is fine in a dinery sort of way: gray, tender, juicy, with lots of beefy flavor in the gravy. We longed for better potatoes on the side. Most of the menu is basic diner eats: meat loaf, liver 'n' onions, triple-decker sandwiches and hamburgers (including a Zipburger on a hard roll with cheese, bacon, lettuce, and tomato and a Dayville Special with sautéed onions), as well as fine coconut cream pie for dessert. Some locals like to come here on Sunday for roast stuffed turkey with all the fixin's (available every day). Regional specialties on the menu include baked beans and franks, clam chowder, strawberry shortcake on a crisp biscuit, and a repertoire of dowdy baked puddings for dessert, including rice pudding, bread pudding, butterscotch pudding, and that Northeast favorite, pudding made with Grape-Nuts cereal.

DELAWARE

HADFIELD'S SEAFOOD
192 S. DUPONT HIGHWAY, NEW CASTLE, DE (302) 322-0900

For travelers hurrying up or down I-95, Hadfield's is a gift from the sea—an easy place to eat it and beat it. There is no charm here, none whatsoever. This overbright, oversize seafood market is strictly functional, and a vast majority of its sales are of raw fish (wholesale and retail). In fact, there is really no place to eat here, so bring your own picnic table or be prepared to eat in the car. That's what we and thousands of travelers like us do, because Hadfield's is equipped to fry or steam most of the fresh fish displayed in the glass counter. Or you can get local clams and oysters on the half shell and buy cocktail sauce by the cup to accompany them.

The soups are noteworthy. There is good snapper soup, but we especially like the hefty Manhattan-style clam chowder. It is spicy, sweet, loaded with chunks of clam, bits of carrot, onion, potato, and tomato. Steamed clams are good and briny. The fried fillets of fish are well-seasoned (maybe too much so), but there is no faulting their quality or freshness. There may be better versions of these foods elsewhere; but one of Hadfield's indisputable charms is how easily accessible it is for those times when going elsewhere is impossible. Many's the time, late at night as we were speeding north toward home, that a cup of Hadfield's chowder and a dozen freshly boiled shrimp have saved our lives.

MRS. ROBINO'S
520 N. UNION, WILMINGTON, DE (302) 652-9223

M rs. Robino's daughter is now in charge of the kitchen at this rare and charming eatery, but the cooking is utterly motherly—just as it has been since it opened in 1948 (since which its loyal fans have come to know it as "Mama Robino's). Mama's place is a truly quaint, venerable family restaurant with floors that list a bit with age, checked cloths on the tables, and placemats that appear to be decades old.

Service is friendly, ambience is casual, prices are low, and portions are enormous. You won't find anything unexpected on the menu (except perhaps separate listings for homemade and store-bought pasta), but let us tell you, everything this kitchen makes is exemplary: good, old-fashioned, red-sauced Italian-American cuisine, and plenty of it. Lovely ravioli are cooked al dente and blanketed with marinara sauce that our tipster, Diane C. Lanctot, correctly described as "addictive"—wonderful for mopping up with good Italian bread. There are spaghetti and meatballs, monumental platters of eggplant parmigiana, good plates of antipasto to begin, and strong coffee at the end of dinner. With that coffee, choose from a proverbial dessert list that includes spumoni, tortoni, cheesecake, and a moist, memorable cake roll. As we said, there are no surprises; but with food this consistently excellent, who wants to be surprised?

DISTRICT OF COLUMBIA

FLORIDA AVENUE GRILL
1100 FLORIDA AVE., NW, WASHINGTON, DC (202) 265-1586

We once made the mistake of meeting someone at the Florida Avenue Grill to talk. It was impossible on two counts. First, it was in the summer and the air-conditioning units that keep this little diner cool were running full blast, making quiet conversation impossible. Second, as soon as the food arrived no one wanted to talk about anything else. No one wanted to talk at all. There was serious eating to be done.

We asked the waitress what was good that day. "Pig feets," she answered. Yes, you can come for feets or chitterlings, but unless you are a feets aficionado already, we suggest you begin with more familiar things to eat. Spare ribs, for example, glazed with breathless hot sauce, rugged and satisfying: these are not yuppie baby back ribs; they are food that make you work, and when you do, they deliver tidal waves of flavor. Pork chops are like that, too: highly seasoned, meaty, and substantial. For a tender meal, how about meat loaf? The loaf, particularly with a side of real mashed potatoes and a heap of pungent collard greens, is one of this kitchen's unexpected triumphs, its coarse-textured meat shot through with brilliant spices. True to southern custom, there are lots of vegetables to accompany the entrees: candied sweet potatoes, rich macaroni and cheese, lavish potato salad, rice, beans, peas, and always sweet cornbread for mopping up a plate.

For many fans of the Florida Avenue Grill, the best meal of the day is breakfast. That's when you can eat stacks of pancakes, onion-laced corned-beef hash, cornmeal muffins, squares of scrapple, crusty fried potatoes, stewed spiced apples, buttermilk biscuits, grits, and gravy.

If you value soul food and soulful eateries, this humble restaurant with its sprung-spring booths, pink counter, and red plastic stools is choice. It is cheap, fast, and the motherly waitresses make even us pale-faced strangers feel right at home.

SHOLL'S CAFETERIA
1990 K STREET, NW, WASHINGTON, DC (202) 296-3065

When gourmets talk about eating in the nation's capital, they tend to rave about the many fabulous Third World (and Second World) restaurants. It all sounds very interesting, and in some other lifetime maybe we will explore the many wonders of Afghani and Far Eastern and even French cuisines to be found there. But during this lifetime, we are quite happy having discovered Sholl's Cafeteria.

Here is about as conventional a slice of edible Americana as you will find in D.C. or anywhere. The ambience is slightly faded tea room; and the clientele ranges from bargain-conscious singles and families (the prices here are rock-bottom), to loiterers for whom cafeteria dining is a form of entertainment, to Jane and Michael Stern, for whom a place like this is culinary nirvana.

Name a corny dish, and it is likely they serve it at Sholl's. There is simple, falling-apart-tender oven-baked chicken, so good with hot, high-top biscuits. There is beef stew: get some cornbread to crumble into it. We will have meat loaf please, with *real—real good—*mashed potatoes, and peas and buttered corn and cole slaw and warm dinner rolls and Jell-O and apple pie. It is honest food, and it is good food—made by expert cooks, well seasoned, and never, in our experience, the victim of prolonged exposure on the steam table. Even the fish is astonishingly good for something dished out of a cafeteria pan. Fillet of haddock and bluefish are about as tasty as any we have had in a regular restaurant in this town, and about one-third the price.

Whatever else you pile on your tray, leave plenty of room for dessert. Sholl's is famous for its pies. Last time through the line we inventoried cherry, blueberry, peach, apple, rhubarb, coconut cream, chocolate cream, banana cream, and Boston cream. Plus about a half-dozen kinds of cake, plus puddings: custard pudding, rice pudding, chocolate pudding, tapioca pudding. They never heard about mousse at Sholl's.

Finally, we pay our respects to the management's noble effort to make dining a civilized experience. Every table is provided with a little card to encourage customers to pause and reflect before they dig in. It is titled "Thanksgiving Before Meals" and provides a suitable prayer for Catholics, Jews, and Protestants.

FLORIDA

BRANCH RANCH
PLANT CITY, FL (BRANCH-FORBES EXIT OFF I-4, NORTH 3/4 MILE TO SIGN,
TURN RIGHT ON THONOTOSASSA RD.) (813) 752-1957

Mary Branch began serving meals to paying guests in the TV room of her family home thirty years ago. Her makeshift eatery became known to an ever-increasing circle of friends; and as new people crowded in for dinner, Mrs. Branch enlarged her dining room and kitchen. Today the Branch Ranch is a sprawling complex that can serve a thousand customers a day. In its reception room, where throngs wait for a precious weekend table, the walls are plastered with a million calling cards of customers who have come from around the world to partake of the legendary Florida feasts.

And yet, for all the noise and commotion, despite the silly "I.Q. Test" pegboard set on tables to amuse the kids, this place is *for real*. There are few restaurants in the South or anywhere in the United States that offer such an unadulterated taste of true country cooking.

The meal begins with a relish tray: pickly beets and tangy bread-and-butter pickles that would do any farm cook proud. Chewy buttermilk biscuits, warm from the oven, are accompanied by tart orange marmalade and jam made with whole, tender-textured strawberries. Everything is from scratch, the kind of blue-ribbon stuff you cannot buy in supermarkets or even in gourmet stores.

Main courses are country ham, fried chicken, or steak, and they're all just fine. But the best part of a meal is the arrival of the tower of side dishes. The stack of pans is a yard high: candied sweet potatoes, scalloped eggplant, pole beans and white potatoes, baked yellow squash, and dumpling-topped chicken pot pie. These, we repeat, are merely the *side dishes!* And of course there are more biscuits, too.

Serve yourself, family style; or designate one person at the table to dish out the food, just like Dad does at home for Sunday dinner. For dessert, tradition demands peach cobbler or white cake topped with grated coconut. And if you like those pickles or homemade jams, we suggest you buy some to take home with you. Believe us when we tell you that after eating relishes here in Plant City, no store-bought ones will ever taste the same again. (You can also buy them by mail.)

Surrounded by orange groves and farmland, the Branch Ranch remains one of America's great rural restaurants. Size and popularity have done nothing to diminish its glow.

THE CATFISH PLACE
2324 13TH ST., ST. CLOUD, FL (407) 892-5771

One of many inconspicuous shops along the main highway in St. Cloud east of Orlando, this wood-panel and Formica roadhouse features a menu with a long list of regional specialties including turtle, 'gator tail, frog's legs, snapper, shrimp, and catfish. One side of the restaurant is occupied by a horseshoe-shaped raw bar, where the prices are low enough to down 'em by the dozen. In the vestibule, dividing the oyster bar from the dining room, the management maintains a lively saltwater aquarium. Other than the tank of exotic fish, decor is minimal: a few Floridian murals on the walls.

It is food, not atmosphere, that makes The Catfish Place well-liked by locals as well as tourists. Portions are large, the fish is fresh, side dishes are praiseworthy, and the price is right.

Catfish is sold as an all-you-can-eat dinner, including hash browns or French fries, cole slaw, and hushpuppies. It is easy eating, without bones: the catfish are filleted in the kitchen, cut into thin strips, dipped in seasoned stone-ground cornmeal, and deep fried until golden brown. If you've never eaten catfish, or if you find whole, bone-in fish a bit scary, you can learn to love it here. These hassle-free crisp strips are mild, sweet, and moist. We especially like Catfish Place hushpuppies. They are a little sweet and oniony, small enough to pop in your mouth whole.

For more adventurous eaters, the menu also lists catfish fingerlings: whole small fish with (edible) bones. And for explorers who want to eat Florida foods they won't likely find back home, there is much, much more. The "house special" dinner, for example, is an immoderate feast featuring not only familiar fried foods such as oyster, catfish, scallops, and shrimp, but these decidedly local items: turtle chunks, 'gator tail, and frog's legs. Neither turtle nor 'gator tastes very good. They are chewy and without any distinctive flavor. And the frog's legs seemed rather repulsive: just too plump and fatty-tasting for us. Our waitress, who recommended them highly, explained that their bulk was due to the fact that "when it comes to frogs, Florida's legs are better than anybody else's."

Not all the food at the Catfish Place is fried. There is an ample list of boiled and broiled seafood, including shrimp, red snapper, rock shrimp, and frog's legs broiled in butter. But it is the fried food we recommend, especially those strips of fried-crisp catfish.

DIXIE CROSSROADS
1475 GARDEN ST., TITUSVILLE, FL (407) 268-5000

S hrimp in Florida are bigger, cheaper, tastier, and more interesting than anywhere else in America. At Dixie Crossroads in Titusville, which happens to be one of the state's premier shrimp-eating restaurants, they always serve at least three kinds.

Rock shrimp, caught just east in the waters of the Atlantic Ocean, are small and hard to break into, but yield a rich, lobstery meat. Royal red shrimp, also caught in the Gulf Stream off Cape Canaveral, are bigger, dark red, succulent, and sweet. Cape Canaveral golden brown shrimp are bigger still: huge, prawn-size beauties with more shrimp flavor per piece than you ever thought possible.

Each variety of shrimp is available however you like it: fried, broiled, or steamed. The fried ones are shatteringly crisp, with barely any batter but with a resounding crunch of a crusty halo. Steaming is a preparation best with rock shrimps, which have a powerful sweet marine flavor all by themselves. Broiled is the best way to enjoy the golden browns. You can get two dozen—that's right, two dozen—for $6.95; and if you think that means these are small shrimp, think again. They are huge. Two dozen, crowded close together on their jumbo plate, are about as much meat as you would get if you ordered a large prime rib. But the flavor is far more intriguing, especially if you dip them in the drawn butter that comes alongside.

The other great Floridian flavor on the Dixie Crossroads menu is mullet, skinned and filleted, then broiled or breaded and deep-fried. Mullet is a rich-flavored fish, a staple of the local everyday cuisine that is affectionately known hereabouts as "cracker cooking." It has never gotten popular outside of Florida, but it is a fish lover's delight, particuarly if you get it broiled and sizzling the way they make it here. If shrimp or mullet is not your dish, there are good crab cakes and fried scallops; but beyond such basic items, the menu is limited. This is a restaurant for seafood lovers only.

Along with the stellar seafood specialties, the kitchen provides each customer with a dish of fresh cole slaw and a plate of powdered-sugar-dusted corn fritters. The meal begins with soup—your choice of vegetable or a savory shrimp bisque that is a simple and well-nigh perfect combination of rock shrimp, potatoes, onions, celery, and chicken stock. For dessert, there are Key lime tarts.

Despite its proximity to I-95, Dixie Crossroads calls itself "the locals' seafood restaurant," and it does have a down-home feeling. It is a big, modern place, all varnished wood and nautical decor with generous waitresses who are happy to supply second baskets of corn fritters when you eat all of the first batch (as you likely will!).

FLORA AND ELLA'S
ROUTE 29, LA BELLE, FL (813) 675-2891

When we asked the waitress at Flora and Ella's if the ice tea came presweetened, she was practically insulted. "Honeys, don't you know where you are?" she asked. "This is the nation's sugar bowl." Of course, the tea is sweetened—extremely so. LaBelle must also be the nation's tomato bowl, judging by the beautiful, full-flavored sliced beefsteaks that came alongside our big, sunny bowl of chicken and dumplings.

There are lots of tasty reasons to visit this corner cafe in a sleepy town just off Highway 80. Do you like southern-style vegetables? How about a bowl of black-eyed peas with rice and onions, accompanied by a hunk of cornbread. That was a lunch special one day last spring. It was delish. The day's roster of vegetable side dishes included English pea salad (with relish and bits of hard-boiled egg), potato salad, mashed potatoes, green beans, buttered carrots, whipped sweet potatoes, pickled beets, sliced pineapples, and marinated vegetable salad. On the other side of the plate you could have fried grouper or flounder, crab cakes, or roasted turkey. All meals are accompanied by biscuits and cornbread; and there is a menu of handsome "mile-high" pies and soda fountain sundaes for dessert

Flora and Ella's has nice oldfangled atmosphere. Tables are spaced far apart for privacy and elbow room; and in the back of the dining room, an old cabinet holds a good stock of patent medicines. Three high fans circle slowly over the gray and pink tables, which are, no surprise, covered with boomerang-patterned Formica.

HALF SHELL RAW BAR
1 LANDS END VILLAGE, KEY WEST, FL (305) 294-7496

In a vintage building at the shrimp docks, the Half Shell Raw Bar is simple, cheap, tasty, and a nice place to sit and soak up atmosphere. The blackboard menu lists what's to eat, and although the hamburger here is really good, most people come for such briny delights as Key West shrimp, crabmeat-stuffed Florida lobsters, barbecued tuna, deep-fried squid rings, shark nuggets, or the well-seasoned, crusty conch fritters. There are always clams and oysters on the half shell, and if you want to linger over a few dozen of them and some slow, cool beers, the Half Shell has an outdoor screened porch for just such casual relaxing. The single best dish in the house, and a local specialty that ought not to be missed, is conch chowder, made with finely chopped pieces of the Keys' distinctive mollusk. It is a smooth-textured brew, but with a zest and marine savor that seems only distantly related to the more familiar chowders made from regular clams in the North.

HOPKINS BOARDING HOUSE
900 N. SPRING ST., PENSACOLA, FL (904) 438-3979

Arkie (Mrs. G. J.) Hopkins opened up her boardinghouse and dining room over forty years ago. She had nine people for lunch. The next day she had seventeen. Today, you might have to wait to get a place at one of the broad tables in her tall-ceilinged dining room. When we first stopped by for a meal, about fifteen years ago, there was a fellow on the front porch who boasted to us that he had been living at the boardinghouse for a quarter century, and hadn't once missed a meal—three squares a day!

Mrs. Hopkins's cooking, although emphatically regional, is not in any way bound by purist notions of tradition. Yes, of course there is classic fried chicken on the table at most meals, as well as barbecue and drippingly delicious turnip greens and oven-hot biscuits. But you will also find blissfully calorific convenience-food wonders such as heavenly hash salad (made from mini-marshmallows, canned fruit cocktail, canned coconut, pecans, pineapple tidbits, and canned Bing cherries).

As is true at so many southern cafes and cafeterias, vegetables are the most memorable dishes produced by the Hopkins kitchen. Sometimes they are fresh and simple: sweet corn, pole beans, or baby peas. There are always a few vegetable casseroles on the table: squash, rutabaga, and an oozingly luscious (and outrageously unfashionable) broccoli-rice combination stuck together with plenty of Cheese Whiz and canned cream of mushroom soup.

Hopkins Boarding House has been high on our list of favorite restaurants for years. Any time we know of someone traveling along Florida's Gulf Coast, we recommend it in the strongest terms possible. But a funny thing happens every time we steer people its way. The travelers return and accuse us of not telling them just how *really* wonderful Hopkins is. We have concluded that no mere superlatives can express the magic that happens when one eats in this special place, because there are so many intangibles, beyond the food, that make a meal here wonderful. Sit down among strangers who, as you eat, become friends. Help yourself, and when the serving bowls get low, more food is brought from the kitchen. And when you've had your fill, mosey out to the front porch and find yourself a rocking chair. Relax a spell, relishing the afterglow of a real downhome meal.

JOE'S STONE CRAB
227 BISCAYNE ST., MIAMI BEACH, FL (305) 673-0365
(NOTE: JOE'S IS OPEN ONLY DURING STONE CRAB SEASON, BETWEEN MID-OCTOBER AND MID-MAY)

When Joe Weiss moved to Florida in 1913, there was no place to eat in Miami Beach. Joe, a former waiter from New York City, opened a restaurant in a small wood-frame house, where he and his wife cooked shore dinners for the sprinkling of tourists who came to visit. They served oysters, pompano, shrimp, yellowtail, and every variety of south Florida seafood—with the exception of stone crabs.

Although plentiful in the waters of Biscayne Bay, stone crabs were not popular food seventy-five years ago. For one thing, they are difficult to catch. They hide themselves in sand and mud; their claws pinch *hard*. And once captured, their shells are tough to crack.

But ten years after opening his restaurant, Joe put stone crabs on the menu. Business boomed. He moved to a larger white stucco building, renamed Joe's Stone Crab. Since then, Joe's restaurant has come to symbolize everything delicious and unique about old-fashioned Florida seafood meals. And stone crabs have become one of the famous local delicacies.

"They now sell by the karat," Damon Runyon once wrote, referring to their high price tag. He lamented that they were all gobbled up by visitors, leaving none for Florida natives. "A certificate of at least four years' residence in Dade County should be required of every person desiring stone crabs," he suggested.

In fact, the population of stone crabs diminished not so much because of all the people eating them, but because the harbor where they lived was dredged as Miami boomed in the 1920s. The crabs moved south to the Keys. In order to insure their survival today, when a stone crab is caught, only one claw is broken off (claws are the only part worth eating). The crab is then thrown back in the water, where it will grow another claw large enough to be harvested in about two seasons' time.

As the fame of Joe's Stone Crab spread, Joe Weiss launched his own fleet of boats; the restaurant went through half a ton of crabs on a good day. Arthur Godfrey paid homage to the landmark restaurant innumerable times on his "Talent Scouts" television show. And Miami Beach grew up to the north of Joe's.

Joe's son Jesse took over the business; now Joe's granddaughter, Jo-Ann Sawitz, runs the place; and although the waiters all got new tuxedos a few years ago, not much else has changed. Despite the high cost of stone crabs, Joe's is not a ritzy dining establishment. They still take no reservations, so at any ordinary mealtime, everybody waits for a table. In rustic fish-house style, the white walls are decorated with photographs of Florida and Miami Beach that go back to the time when Joe's was young ... you had to take a boat to get here from Miami. High ceilings make for a booming, hustle-bustle noise level in the dining room.

Stone crabs arrive cool, five or six claws to an order. Their color scheme—coral pink, tipped with ebony—is distinctly Floridian. The hard shells, of course, have been precracked in the kitchen, allowing for easy extraction of plump, succulent segments of meat with the long fork provided. On the side, you have a choice of two dips: plain drawn butter or Joe's tangy mustard sauce, an inspired complement for the moist, sweet meat.

Beyond crabs, the menu is classic south Florida cooking, with a few special twists that Joe's fans have come to love over the years. Red snapper, mackerel, and pompano are as fresh and good and expertly prepared as you will find in any restaurant. Hash-brown potatoes are the usual accompanyment, but many regulars know to order Joe's special cottage-fried sweet potatoes, a delectable companion to a large fillet of yellowtail and a side of cool cole slaw. For dessert, choose Key lime pie or chunky apple pie with a wedge of cheddar cheese.

JULIA MAE'S TOWN INN
HIGHWAY 98, CARRABELLE, FL (904) 697-3791

Julia Mae's is a roadhouse nestled among a grove of tall evergreens along Route 98 southwest of Sopchoppy and Tallahassee. If you are looking for a taste of what locals refer to as "cracker cooking," this is the place. Most visitors to Florida, especially those who head directly to the cosmopolitan cities of the south or the west central coast, never know cracker cooking, a style of cookery that is Florida's alone. It is distinctly rural, deeply southern, and based on groceries that are uniquely Floridian.

Oysters by the dozen, local fish, turtles, alligator tail, plus Dixie favorites from grits and hushpuppies to banana pudding are all part of the repertoire of the cracker cook. Whatever the ingredients, true cracker cooking is never fancy or expensive. It is proud to be an of-the-people cuisine.

That is why Julia Mae's Town Inn is the perfect place to eat it. Rumble on in to the dusty gravel parking lot, saunter inside, and find yourself a booth. The seats are molded plastic; the walls—draped with a few seashells and fish nets—are made of woodlike panels reminiscent of a well-kept mobile home. If there was any music playing, we couldn't hear it: our visits to Julia Mae's have always been in the summer, when the multiple air conditioners groan full blast.

Along comes a waitress, who sets down a card announcing "Hello, my name is Toni." Every table in the house is set with tartar sauce: gentle, creamy white, with just a tad of pickle smack. Cole slaw is served in a Styrofoam cup. The menu lists local specialties such as scamp, Florida lobsters, grouper burgers, even fried grouper throat (which Toni explains is the meat from behind the gills).

We have feasted on shrimp "Franklin," in which each pink crescent comes wrapped in bacon with broiled tomato, also on spicy deviled crabs served in an aluminum shell, accompanied by a formidable Greek salad loaded down with a mountain of feta cheese. Portions are country style—enormous!

The most delicious local specialty we have sampled at Julia Mae's is fried mullet—rich and smoke-flavored, with a sharp crunch to its breading, accompanied by tubular hushpuppies, French fries, and cole slaw. All of Julia Mae's seafood is served with wedges of lime to bring out the fish's natural sweetness.

Julia Mae's pies are designed as a grand climax, piled high with toasty-topped meringues, cut into jumbo wedges guaranteed to satisfy. The lemon meringue is sharp, tart, and jiggly. Our favorite is chocolate—creamy smooth and dizzyingly chocoriffic, a fitting end to a lusty, sleeves-up meal. Words to the wise: the pies are made fresh every Friday, so they are terrific weekend treats; by midweek, you don't want to know about them.

LA TERESITA
3248 W. COLUMBUS DR. (AT LINCOLN), TAMPA, FL (813) 879-4909

"Strong enough to make the rooster crow" is how one nearby La Teresita regular narrated the arrival of small cups of inky espresso to our place at La Teresita's counter. It *is* powerful brew, with enough body to deliver a wallop even when you order it *con leche.* In the morning many customers sit at this counter with their newspaper (in Spanish or English) and drink cups of *con leche* with lengths of toasted and buttered Cuban bread. It is elegant bread—crisp with fluffy insides—and needs nothing more than butter to attain a certain simple perfection. With coffee, it is a great breakfast.

At lunch, the long tubes of bread become the foundation for Cuban sandwiches, and shorter lengths are served alongside such Latin specialties as *bistec palomilla* (sirloin steak, thinly sliced, pan-fried and served with yellow rice), black beans with white rice, and the lush pot roast known as *carne asada.*

There are no tables at La Teresita. All seats are arrayed around three horseshoe counters, where whole families line up on the rows of stools at dinnertime.

LATIN AMERICAN CAFETERIA
2740 SOUTHWEST 27TH AVE., MIAMI, FL (305) 445-6040
DAILY 7 A.M.–1 A.M. (FOUR OTHER LOCATIONS IN MIAMI)

The Latin America Cafeteria is one of five open-(nearly)-all-night eat-shops by the same name, each owned by a member of the Galindo family. These places can be an adventure if you speak only English, but don't worry; it isn't difficult to point and gesticulate and thereby make the point that you want deep-fried pork chunks, with white rice and black beans on the side, or a breaded steak, or best of all, what may be the finest Cuban sandwich in town.

Foodlore says that the Cuban sandwich was invented by José Sacre, a Cuban from Lebanon who ran a cafeteria west of Havana in the 1930s. It has since migrated to Florida, Miami and Tampa in particular, where it is as popular in the Cuban parts of the cities as burritos in Los Angeles or bagels in New York. It is a Caribbean version of a hero sandwich, and when you enter Renaldo Galindo's cafeteria on 27th Avenue, you can see the Cubans being assembled. For a basic Cuban, the sandwich-maker starts with a split and buttered length of fluffy-textured, hard-crusted Cuban bread. Into that he layers ham, roasted pork, Swiss cheese, and pickle disks. The sandwich is then warmed in a toaster just long enough to turn everything inside limp and barely crisp (but not brown) the bread. Deluxe versions of the sandwich can be ordered with other kinds of cheese, extra portions of pork, or fancy Virginia ham. One tipster at a nearby table in the Latin American Cafeteria watched us ingest a couple of these warm torpedoes, then informed us that such a Dagwood is known hereabouts as "the midnight special."

MALAGA
740 S.W. EIGHTH ST., MIAMI, FL (305) 858-4224 OR 854-9101

Named after the city in which Picasso was born, Malaga is a comfortable and gracious Iberian restaurant with a tree-shaded courtyard in back and private dining rooms for small parties. It is family-run and casual, and the Spanish-accented kitchen turns out memorable but relatively inexpensive feasts from squid in its own ink and a truly august paella Valenciana weighted with good shellfish all the way down to simple and savory roasted chicken with yellow rice, the Latin hash known as picadillo, and even a seemingly ordinary (but actually quite wonderful) omelette.

Most of the ethnic meals served at Malaga are brawny fare: black bean soup, *carne asada mechada* (pot roast) accompanied by fried bananas, and boiled smoked ham hocks with rice. It is also possible to eat lighter, regionally accented meals of Gulf Coast seafood such as red snapper, pompano, or shrimp with Creole sauce. To accompany dinner, have a pitcher of sangria or icy daiquiris. And don't miss the rice pudding for dessert.

MAMA LO'S
618 N.W. 6TH ST., GAINESVILLE, FL (904) 372-3034

A hunkering whitewashed building near the police station, with two wood-paneled dining rooms (one offering a pool table), Mama Lo's is a favorite haunt of students and townsfolk alike. It is a place to eat soul food cheap, known for its succulent, sizzling pork chops with peppery dressing, its fall-apart-tender baked chicken, garlicky smoked sausage, and chitlin's.

Every meal comes with a square of cornbread, and the real fun is choosing vegetables, each of which is dished out in its own little dish. Mama Lo offers at least a dozen selections daily, listed on the handwritten sheet of blue-lined notebook paper that serves as a communal menu. They are well-cooked, southern-style, not *al dente* vegetables, many of them embellished with buttered bread crumbs, cheese, pot likker, and other assorted sweeteners and enrichments. Our personal favorite is broccoli casserole, for which the florets are encased in a mighty baked mélange of cheese, eggs, sugar, and white bread. The yams (to accompany that pork chop or smoked sausage) are gloriously sweet. There are pungent collard greens, squash and cabbage casseroles, mashed potatoes, whole potatoes, macaroni and cheese, black-eyed peas, okra and tomatoes, fried corn or corn on the cob, even fruit cocktail (unadulterated).

After so spectacular a selection of meats and vegetables, dessert is simplicity itself: cake, available plain or gilded with a blob of whipped topping. There are soft slabs of golden-crumb pound cake, triple-layer coconut cake, and shortcake made with strawberries or peaches.

Warning: basically a lunch place, Mama Lo's frequently runs out of the day's vegetables by late afternoon.

MANNY & ISA'S
MILE MARKER 81.6 ON HIGHWAY 1, ISLAMORADA
(UPPER MATECUMBE KEY), FL (305) 664-5019

K ey lime pie is one of America's most famous regional dishes, offered by
dozens of restaurants in the Florida Keys and beyond; but the real
thing is hard to find because Key limes are rare. Tahiti limes—the familiar
bright green ones sold in every American supermarket—are far more common because they are easier to grow and harvest. Most people agree that
Key limes have a more satisfying, profoundly limey flavor; but nearly every
restaurant that sells "Key lime" pie is actually selling "Tahiti lime" pie.
The counterfeit pies can taste quite all right; but they don't have the poise
of the real thing, for which Key lime juice is combined with condensed
milk to produce a pale yellow chiffon that precariously teeters on the line
between sweet and tart.

If you want to taste real Key lime pie, head out Highway 1 a couple of
hours south of Miami to Matecumbe Key. Here is Manny & Isa's restaurant.
Manny Ortiz, the proprietor with his wife, Isa, grows all his own Key limes
in a small lot along with mangoes, avocados, and sour oranges. He squeezes
the limes himself—about thirty gallons' worth (at 250 limes per gallon)
each year, which is enough not only for his pies, but to provide some leftover juice for the Matecumbe sauce he uses to marinate red snapper.

Before you dig into authentic and original Key lime pie at Manny and
Isa's, you will definitely want to eat a whole meal. This comfortable roadside cafe specializes in Caribbean cooking from the Ortizs' home, Cuba,
and from the waters of the Florida Keys. Feast on conch chowder spiced
with herbs from a backyard garden, zesty Cuban picadillo, conch fritters,
and stone crab. And top it all off with a piece of the famous pie accompanied by a cup of strong Cuban coffee: few elementary combinations of flavors are as satisfying.

SHORTY'S BAR-B-Q RANCH
9200 SOUTH DIXIE HIGHWAY, MIAMI, FL (305) 665-5732

"A thirty-five-year-old artifact surrounded by the shopping plaza
sprawl of Dadeland," is how *Roadfood* reader Steven Zwerling
described Shorty's in his letter of recommendation, telling us to go there for
the ribs, chicken, and baked beans "almost as good as Ridgewood's [Ten-
nessee]—very high praise!"

A faux log cabin with half-round logs stuck on its outside walls and a neon sign perched on the roof, Shorty's is indeed a jewel of Georgia-style barbecue where you least expect it. Dine at long picnic tables in a screened room reminiscent of summer camp. It's an elbow-to-elbow feast, and on the weekend night we visited, the place was packed; spirits were high; and the smell of seared meat was in the air.

The menu lists pork and beef sandwiches, beef ribs, and chicken, accompanied by pit beans and cole slaw. The ribs are weighty fellas, packed with meat that yanks free easily. The meats are served with two different sauces, each of which has a unique character, and which taste great when applied equally together. There is smoky-flavored but fairly mild stuff presented in a shaker jar, and there is hot, tangy sauce in a squeeze bottle. It tastes like there is some of each in the truly excellent beans, which are also liberally laced with meat and smoke flavor, and are available for sale in bulk at the take-out counter, in sizes that range from a pint to a gallon.

SILVER RING CAFE
1831 EAST 7TH AVE., TAMPA (YBOR CITY), FL (813) 248-2549
(SEVERAL OTHER LOCATIONS IN AND AROUND TAMPA)

The Silver Ring Cafe has been in business for a little over half a century, having opened about the time the Cuban sandwich was invented outside Havana. In recent years it has earned a reputation as the best Cuban sandwich shop in Tampa, hence—because Tampa is Cuban sandwich central—the best on earth.

You can stand on the sidewalk outside the Silver Ring, surrounded by the bustle of Ybor City, and watch the sandwich makers construct these behemoth Dagwoods by stuffing meats and cheeses inside toasty lengths of fragile-crusted, fine-crumbed white bread. The standard "Cuban" configuration is boiled ham, roast pork, Swiss cheese, and pickle slices; but these expert countermen will customize a sandwich nearly any way you choose, always providing what seems to be a maximum amount of ingredients without going over the line into sloppiness. One thing about a Cuban, unlike many kinds of grinders and submarines: it always must be neat; ingredients have to stay within the bread; major spillage is not allowed.

As for atmosphere at the Silver Ring, there is none; at least there is nothing extraneous. It is a plain but not the least bit colorless little luncheonette, perpetually in need of a good paint job. Find a place, get your sandwich, and listen to orders called across the counter (mostly in Spanish) and the sounds of meats being sliced and sandwiches slapped together. It is an appetizing place to dine.

TED PETER'S FAMOUS SMOKED FISH
1350 PASADENA AVE. SOUTH, SOUTH PASADENA (ST. PETERSBURG), FL (813) 381-7931

R oll down the window when you drive along Pasadena Avenue, and you won't likely have any trouble finding Ted Peter's Famous Smoked Fish restaurant. Just sniff. When you catch the heady aroma of Gulf Coast seafood slow-cooking over burning wood, you will have found one of the Gulf Coast's exemplary places to have lunch or dinner.

Every year over a hundred thousand pounds of mackerel and mullet are smoked in the little shack adjacent to the dining area. Mullet is a Gulf of Mexico delicacy virtually unknown north of Florida. There are restaurants throughout the panhandle and along the Gulf Coast that specialize in it. Most of them, like Ted Peter's, are informal places that serve it on disposable plates with plastic forks, and bottled longneck beer on the side to wash it down.

One of the most delicious things Ted Peter's does with mullet is to mash it into smoked fish spread, which many customers buy in bulk to take home and serve as hors d'oeuvres. If we had a way of keeping it cool in the car for weeks on the road, we would have a pantryful every time we return from Florida. For those of us who can't take fish spread home, the best way to enjoy mullet is portioned out in big hunks on a plate. It is a lush fish, and during the hours it spends over smoldering red oak wood, its oily meat absorbs the sharp tang of fire, creating an unimprovable confluence of succulence and smoke.

Ted Peter's is not a fancy restaurant. Reservations are not accepted, nor are credit cards. The cozy little dining area (which does have a fireplace to provide warmth when the weather is cool) is the height of happy-go-lucky informality. Some folks like to eat at the shaded counter; some choose a picnic table outside, where seagulls loiter looking for scraps. Many customers come only to take food home. There is even a loyal contingent who patronize the place not for fish, but for hefty hamburgers, which, along with the mullet and a top-secret family-recipe German potato salad, have helped make Ted Peter's a local favorite since 1950.

TOM'S PLACE
7251 NORTH FEDERAL HIGHWAY, BOCA RATON, FL (407) 997-0920

Tom's new red-brick building seats nearly three hundred customers and has chandeliers hanging from the ceiling. It is so refined—a quality usually in inverse proportion to ribs' taste—that *People* magazine once declared it the "Most Unlikely Spot to Find Good Barbecue." It *is* good barbecue, though: butter-tender baby back ribs, glowing with the taste of hickory smoke and a fragile-flavored sweet tomato sauce. There are pit-cooked sliced beef and chicken pieces, too; and all the meats may be accompanied by choice from a side-dish selection that is truly deluxe by pit standards, usually including French fries, potato salad, porcine black-eyed peas, collard greens, corn-on-the-cob, cornmeal muffins, and hush-puppies. On weekend nights there are even some nonbarbecue items on the menu, including whole, deep-fried catfish from Lake Okeechobee and conch fritters.

Despite the extensive menu and an extraordinarily well-mannered air about the place, Tom's meals are served with a welcome, wipe-your-hands-on-your-jeans informality. Customers sit elbow-to-elbow at long wooden tables; and there is no disguising the impolite sound of happy people gnawing ribs.

WOLFIE COHEN'S RASCAL HOUSE
17190 COLLINS AVE., MIAMI BEACH, FL (305) 947-4581

Among the ethnic eatfests to be savored in Miami is a sandwich with a plate of pickles and a cup of borscht and a piece of cheesecake at Wolfie Cohen's Rascal House at the north end of Miami Beach. The Rascal House is a taste of Miami Beach that seems to have changed little in over three decades. This is the place to eat world-class delicatessen fare from a gigantic menu of sandwiches, hot plates, traditional soups, luncheonette salads, smoked fish appetizers, and a few dozen pies and cakes.

Begin with a schmeck from the bowl full of pickles and pickled green tomatoes—pungent, puckery food. There is slaw, too: strong and pickly. Then come onion rolls, dinner rolls, slices of sour-crusted salt-spangled rye bread, pumpernickel rolls—superb bread, aromatic and flavorful, that goes well with any dish on the menu.

Whatever else we order at the Rascal House, we like to start things off with a bowl of borscht, Borscht is cold beet soup; its color—flamingo pink—seems especially appropriate in this location. It is a grand hot-weather cooler to start any meal. For a dollar extra, you get it with a big, boiled potato which, with sour cream, makes for a sumptuous combination of tender flavors.

Pastrami is lean and garlicky, rimmed with spice—sensational when piled high and slathered with mustard between pieces of Wolfie Cohen's first-rate rye bread. Blintzes are made to order: big plump golden crepes rolled up around sweetened pot cheese and fried in clarified butter. (Get them with sour cream on the side.) Chopped liver, enriched with gobs of chicken fat and lots of hard-boiled egg, is Heartburn City—gloriously good if you've got a constitution that won't fight back.

Opened in 1954, the same year as the grandiose Fontainebleau Hotel at the other end of the beach, this oversized sandwich shop is done in shades of flesh pink tile and aqua upholstery with wood paneled walls. It is a huge couple of rooms with a big counter and big booths (as well as close-together tables-for-two that make eavesdropping on neighbors unavoidable). Service is provided by an appropriately brusque staff of white-uniformed waitresses, each of whom is outfitted with an effulgent personalized hankie pinned to her left shoulder.

Wolfie's is usually crowded, which means you wait in line for a seat; actually, you wait in one of five lines for a seat: one for couples who want a table; one for parties of three or four who want a table; one for parties of five or more who want a table; one for singles willing to sit at the counter; and another for couples who want counter seats. Although service is fast and people at the Rascal House tend to eat fast, it takes a while before you reach the chain barrier at the head of your line, opened each time an appropriate seating arrangement becomes available.

The time spent in line affords you an unparalleled opportunity to study variations in style among Sans-A-Belts, those shiny beltless slacks in pastel, wrinkle-free fabrics preferred by a majority of the elderly Jewish gents who eat here. It seemed to us that the older the man, the higher the pants: the oldest of the Sans-A-Belt set belt theirs just below the armpit, leaving barely room for two shirt buttons between waist and neck.

THE YEARLING
ROUTE 325, CROSS CREEK, FL (904) 466-3033

South of Gainesville in the hamlet of Cross Creek, tucked between Lochloosa and Orange Lakes, The Yearling is a vision from Florida's pre-condo days. Named after the novel by Marjorie Kinnan Rawlings, the town's most famous resident, it is an inn and restaurant adjacent to Miss Rawlings's restored home (where she wrote *Cross Creek Cookery*), and a good place to sample such Floridian fare as frog's legs, speckled perch and bass, pan-fried quail, catfish, alligator tail, and pan-fried cooter (soft-shell turtle). You can also get fresh ocean fish, shrimp, and oysters, or a plate of nearly everything, known as the Cross Creek special, including tender-center, brittle-crusted hushpuppies. For dessert, there is good Key lime pie.

The dining room of The Yearling is a civilized place, even if most of its cuisine is inherently rustic. There is a full bar with a wine list, even a gift shop with souvenirs (and Marjorie Kinnan Rawlings books). The management takes credit cards and reservations are advised, especially for weekends. The price of dinner can top twenty dollars. So it is hardly *Roadfood* in the raw. But if well-prepared native food in a bucolic setting reminiscent of Florida long ago will make you happy, no other eatery comes close.

GEORGIA

THE BREAKFAST CLUB
1500 BUTLER AVE., TYBEE ISLAND, GA (912) 786-5984

"Good morning, Americans," declares the menu of The Breakfast Club, which is practically as memorable for its exuberance as for its edibles. The food is fine; you won't see handsomer omelettes for miles; they are available with a choice of any or all of eighteen different ingredients, ranging from expectable peppers and tomatoes to Polish sausage and corned beef hash. Eggs are cooked all ways, accompanied by every breakfast meat known to humankind as well as regular grits, cheese grits, hash browns, home fries, toast (white, wheat, rye), or English muffins but no biscuits or bagels. There are waffles and pecan waffles, a Happy Face breakfast for kiddies (an omelette with a ketchup smile), and eggs Benedict on Sundays.

If you are in the market for a seriously big morning blowout, you might want the meal known as "The Grill Cleaners' Special," or alternately, "Helen's Solidarity" (because the Breakfast Club's original owner, Helen, used to feed it to the boys who cleaned her grill). It is a heap of diced spuds with peppers, onions, and Polish sausage scrambled with eggs and two kinds of cheese. The house special is one egg Florentine on a slab of whole-wheat toast, the egg poached in a bed of spinach and topped with Swiss cheese and mushrooms. According to the menu, this one was "discovered by accident by the current owner when he dropped an egg on top of some hot spinach. Instead of trashing the whole lot, he decided to doctor it up a little—WALA!"

So, if you are a purist in search of authentic American regional cuisine, we do not recommend The Breakfast Club. It is too cute and the cuisine is more all-American than coastal Georgian. On the other hand, if what you seek is satisfying breakfast accompanied by a sizable side order of shenanigans, this is a fine place to know about.

DILLARD HOUSE
HIGHWAY 441, DILLARD, GA (404) 746-5349

You need to bring two things when you come to dine at Dillard House: patience and appetite.

Patience because, at most mealtimes, the place is packed. Throngs of vacationers mill around in the vestibule waiting for their number to be called. As your stomach grumbles in anticipation, you can contemplate a blackboard on which the day's vegetables are written. It makes interesting, even exciting reading because the list is always changing. If fried okra is on the board when you arrive, there is a possibility it will be crossed off before you get your table. Creamed corn might get written, then vanish in only an hour or two. The Dillard House kitchen is always cooking different things; and when they run out of a particular dish, it is simply unavailable until they make more. When your time comes and you are seated at a table, you get some of everything that is available at that exact time. You don't order or select; it is all brought to the table on big, communal platters and in bowls designed to get passed around the table, family-style.

That brings us to the second requirement for eating at the Dillard House: appetite. It simply is no fun to come here if all you want is a light meal. The point is to stuff yourself, to plow through an extravagant feast of fried chicken, country ham, and pork along with about a half a dozen such lusciously cooked vegetables as rice and gravy, squash soufflé, black-eyed peas, and stupendously rich steamed cabbage. Also, there are dinner rolls, biscuits, peach cobbler for dessert, and iced tea in Mason jars. The meal is *prix fixe;* eat 'til you bust.

Tables may be shared by strangers during peak summer hours; but that doesn't inhibit anybody from having a wildly good time tucking into these groaning-board banquets. The dining room is loud, boisterous, and delicious-smelling: a real party if you love to eat.

Aside from the lavish food, Dillard House's claim to fame is the surrounding north Georgia landscape, which includes awe-inspiring waterfalls, enchanting backwoods cabins, hiking trails, and picturesque highways that served as scenery in numerous good-ol'-boy movies starring fast cars and Burt Reynolds, whose signed eight-by-ten, along with wife Lonnie Anderson's, hangs on the wall somewhere near the vegetable board.

FRESH AIR BAR-B-QUE
U.S. 23 SOUTH OF JACKSON, GA (404) 775-3182

Hams are cooked over smoking hickory logs for a full twenty-four hours, by which time the succulent, sauce-basted meat is ready to fall into shreds if you look at it hard. The meat is pulled and hacked with a cleaver, and the chopped-up mélange, a stupefying variety of tenderness and crunch, subtle pork flavor and bang from the sauce, is piled on buns and moistened with a tart-sweet tomato sauce. Get it with Brunswick stew on the side: a magnum opus of a meal.

Fresh Air is a shack that has been in business, in the same location, operated by G. W. Caston and his progeny, for sixty-three years now. It was remodeled once, back in the 1950s, when a concrete floor was put down and pine paneling was nailed on the walls; but other than that, it is the original establishment, still deep in the woods, where barbecue smoke smells especially good. *Roadfood* bloodhound Ort Carlton, who first clued us in to its charms, wrote, *"This* place found *me."*

THE GA PIG
EXIT 6 OFF I-95 IN BRUNSWICK, GA (912) 264-6664

The GA Pig is just about the most convenient good barbecue restaurant in America. You could almost stretch a pitchfork out the window of your car and impale a slab of ribs as you whiz past on the Interstate. EZ-on, EZ-off is not generally the mark of good eating, but this place, however odd, is the real thing. It is a genuine, and genuinely hokey, restaurant next to a gas station with souvenirs for sale and old-tyme atmosphere in the form of picnic-table seating, cypress bark shavings on the walkway, and the smell of pine trees from a grove outside. Its owner, Ed Powers, has long held a dream of franchising GA Pigs all over the country; but the last time we heard, he hadn't had much success. Good barbecue demands far too much work, not to mention skill.

The meat is what puts this place in the Pantheon. It is cooked slowly in a brick pit over a fire of oak and hickory logs and basted with a luxuriously sweet sauce that it imbibes along with the perfume of burning wood. Torn off the bone in chunky shreds, inside tender pieces mixed with crusty shreds from the outside, it is brushed once more with the tangy sauce. The result is divine barbecue, every bit as good as the best you will find in a scary, impossible-to-locate city barbecue parlor. According to a souvenir brochure we picked up last time we ate at the GA Pig, "Georgia barbecue connoisseurs still think the very best-tasting barbecue is that which is roasted in a pit over a hickory wood fire, and served fresh cut and hot from the pit." Amen. The brochure includes a review from *The Brunswick News* that notes, "People from as far away as Boston, Mass., have come to the GA Pig."

Wherever you come from, if you eat this connoisseur's Q along with a serving of the kitchen's molasses-sweet barbecue beans you will find yourself in pig heaven, even if the view from the front porch is of vacationing families filling up their cars with gas.

GREEN SHUTTERS TEA ROOM
OLD HIGHWAY 441 SOUTH OF CLAYTON, GA (404) 782-3342

The man tending the biscuits at the wood-burning cookstove told us that the Green Shutters Tea Room's season had been the same for the last four decades: open from the day school stops until the day school starts, or until it gets too cold. This is a paradisiacal place, especially in the autumn when the leaves turn color. Our first meal was breakfast; we arrived early one morning and sat at a table on the back porch overlooking a meadow with a split-rail fence and watched the rising sun cast a veil of brilliant light across dew on the grass where horses grazed and a rooster crowed.

We ate crisp-crusted biscuits with homemade jelly and honey just off the hive; pan-sizzled country ham; buttered grits; eggs and coffee. We walked out into the clean mountain air, took a deep breath that smelled of fallen leaves, morning air, baking biscuits, and frying ham, and set off on a gorgeous drive through the mountains. It was a breakfast to remember.

Next time through, we had lunch. We sat in the indoor dining room, at a table with a green-checked cloth, and ate crusty fried chicken, country ham, more biscuits, and slews of good, southern vegetables, including peas and beans and greens and yams. All the dishes were served country-style, in bowls for passing around the table. The Green Shutters also serves dinner, which we are eagerly looking forward to.

MARY MAC'S TEA ROOM
228 PONCE DE LEON AVE, NE, ATLANTA, GA (404) 875-4337

A feed-'em-fast plate lunchroom that first appears to have no more grace than a prison mess, Mary Mac's is one of the great city restaurants of the South. With little fanfare and at low prices, it provides an eating experience that anyone who cares about regional food will savor. How many other restaurants do you know that always feature pot likker and cracklin' cornbread on the daily menu? Where else can you go for soufflés of sweet potato and sweet corn like this? Or chicken pan pie jambalaya? Or a local conceit called Carter Custard, made with peanuts and named after the peanut farmer who is well remembered in his home state.

Much of the fun of Mary Mac's is the sleeves-up, but civilized, atmosphere. After waiting in line (there is *always* a line) and being led to a plain laminated table in one of the cacophonous dining areas, you peruse the day's menu, printed on pastel paper, then write your own order on a tiny pad. The waitress zooms to the table, says a quick howdy-do, snatches the order, and before you can read this warning on the menu—"Mary Mac's is the place for good food—for fast service. Mary Mac's is NOT the place for a leisurely luncheon"—she is on her way back to the table with your food.

The thing you want to eat is fried chicken. Giant pieces are sheathed in a most wonderful dark golden crust, their insides steamy moist and drippingly delicious. Some of the usual entrées listed on the menu include chicken and dumplings, baked chicken with dressing, chicken pan pie, country ham, rainbow trout, red snapper, shad roe, steaks, and stews; but other than the fried chicken what you are likely to remember best are Mary Mac's vegetables. There are well over a dozen different ones available every day, from the simplest macaroni and cheese or stewed corn to deluxe casseroles of squash or yams. The spruce-green pot likker, served in a cup with a cornbread muffin on the side, is a breathtaking experience, the essence of turnip greens with a nice, piggy flavor from the hambone with which they have been simmered. It is as invigorating as food can be.

Desserts at Mary Mac's are less distinctly southern than they are tea-room classics: puddings, cobblers, custards, pies, and pretty Jell-Os—all sweet and nice and easy to eat.

MELEAR'S
GA. 85 (NOT THE INTERSTATE), FAYETTEVILLE, GA (404) 461-7180

For the last thirty-five years Melear's has been the premier barbecue outpost on the road south out of Atlanta. Before that, Kenneth Melear's father and grandfather were barbecue men; and if you have any doubt that this family knows its P's 'n' Q's, just dip a bit of bread in the sauce—the hot version—and savor its character on your tongue. It is ferociously hot with the bite of peppers, but alluringly complex and shot through with a perfectly balanced harmony of sweetness and vinegar's pucker.

The barbecue on which you want to sprinkle this sauce is hickory-and-oak smoked, mild and gentle-textured. Pork is the meat of choice (there is beef, too). It is hacked up and served in sandwiches or as a dish with the lovely name "bowl of pork," or on trays in portioned plates along with potato chips, pickles, bread, and a rib-sticking Brunswick stew. To accompany these fine smokehouse meals, Melear's serves spectacular iced tea—extremely presweetened, as is the custom in this part of the country, presented in tumblers that are a full foot tall and about half as wide at the mouth. When you get to the bottom of this tub, it is refilled on the house; and it will continue to be refilled for as long as you are parked in a high-backed chair at one of Melear's aged wood tables eating barbecue.

MRS. BONNER'S CAFE
MONUMENT ST., CRAWFORDVILLE, GA (404) 456-2347

About a dozen years ago we breezed into Crawfordville at eight in the morning in search of Mrs. Bonner's Cafe. It had been described in a letter from Mrs. Harold Uttley of Charlotte, North Carolina, as "something from yesteryear." She had written that Mrs. Bonner's sweet potato pie was the best she had ever eaten, a declaration that called for some intensive reconnaissance work as we headed east out of Atlanta.

We found the right street, but where was Mrs. Bonner's? A passerby directed us to a plain storefront on the town square identified only by a small sign that read *Cafe*. Its windows were draped with heavy curtains. Overhead fans spun slowly above the booths in the high-ceilinged dining room. A wisp of a lady appeared from the back, carrying coffee in two weathered mugs that must have served thousands of cafe customers through the years. This was Mrs. Bonner, proprietor since 1926.

"I didn't make any biscuits this morning," she announced without a hint of apology in her voice. "I'm lazy today."

"Too lazy to make sweet potato pie?" we asked.

She fixed us with a hard gaze. "Are you sure you know what that is?"

"Yes, and we would like two pieces for breakfast."

"Well, fine," Mrs. Bonner smiled, toddling back to the kitchen and returning with two slim triangles of pumpkin-colored pie. She explained to us that many of her regular customers have a piece of pie after breakfast. "That's the way real country folks like it," she added cheerfully, including us in the elite club of morning pie eaters despite our out-of-state license plates.

We dug in. A meditative silence descended over the table as we savored Mrs. Bonner's country wonder in a crust. Its mellowness explained why almost every unaffected southerner says *tater* rather than *potato* pie. *Potato* is sophisticated-sounding, a three-syllable word. *Tater* is infantile, appropriate for pie that is as yummy as one's best remembered high-chair food. Mrs. Bonner's pie is the balmiest pie in the South.

Each time we pass through Georgia, we route ourselves into Crawfordville for a nice plate lunch—meat loaf, pork chops, baked chicken—or at least a couple pieces of pie and a morning visit. Last time we called ahead to make sure Mrs. Bonner was still in business and that she would have some of the noble pie the day we were planning to come. "You call the day before you visit," she told us. "I'll be sure to bake some warm for you that morning."

MRS. WILKES BOARDING HOUSE
107 W. JONES ST., SAVANNAH, GA (912) 236-9816

West Jones Street is a boulevard of antique brick houses with curving steps and graceful cast-iron banisters. At eleven o'clock each morning a line begins to form at No. 107. There is no sign on this house, nothing to indicate why people start to gather here just before lunchtime. (No supper is served.)

Any Savannahan who likes to eat can tell you what is going on. At eleven-thirty, Mrs. Wilkes will ring the dinner bell, and those who have waited in line will enter and find a seat at one of the large oval tables, shared by strangers. Mrs. Wilkes says grace, then all assembled will dig into one of the most abundant feasts in Georgia.

The tabletops are crowded with great platters of fried chicken and cornbread dressing, sweet potato soufflés, black-eyed peas, okra gumbo, corn muffins, and biscuits. And nobody is shy about helping themselves. This is one place where a boardinghouse reach is quite appropriate.

Passing the platters back and forth, chatting with friends and table-mates, heaping your plate with seconds and thirds of whatever you like best: what a party! This is a social event at which the cast of characters is always changing—townspeople, traveling families, and chowhounds of every description drawn together by the lure of fried chicken, red rice, bis-cuits, and fruit cobbler.

Because so many of Mrs. Wilkes's customers are regulars, the menu changes each day. There is *always* fried chicken, with alternate entrées like pork sausage and hot peppered rice, or country-style steaks, smoth-ered in onion gravy, or peppery crab stew, spiked with sherry.

As at any southern feast worth its cracklin' cornbread, there are con-stellations of vegetable casseroles: great, gooey, buttery bowlfuls of squash au gratin and scalloped eggplant, cheese grits, corn pudding, pineapple-flavored yams topped with melted marshmallows, creamed corn enriched with bacon drippings, green rice (mixed with broccoli and celery); brown rice (with mushrooms and soy sauce); and the low-country legend, Savan-nah red rice. Mrs. Wilkes intends to put some meat on your bones!

There aren't many boardinghouse meals like Mrs. Wilkes's left. Inter-state highways have passed boardinghouses by. For adventurous eaters, the few such kitchens that do survive are some of this land's finest culinary treasures. Dining at the oval tables in the brick house on West Jones Street is a taste of a bygone way of living—and eating—that Savannahans hold dear, and a few travelers through the South are lucky enough to know.

SCONYERS BAR-B-QUE
2511 WINDSOR SPRING RD., AUGUSTA, GA (404) 790-5411

L arry Sconyers's car has a license plate that reads "NO. 1 PIG." Barbe-cued pork is his business and his pleasure, and he claims to have invented a unique way of cooking the whole hams and ribs—standing upright rather than lying down over wood coals. This process makes the tenderest pork, Mr. Sconyers says; and legions of customers would likely agree. Since his father opened for business in 1956, Sconyers Bar-B-Que has grown from a help-yourself cinderblock shack to a sprawling six-room,

full-service restaurant brimful of pig memorabilia, including pictures, statuettes, and whole mounted heads, where up to three thousand people a day
come to gorge on Q.

Chopped pork is the best dish, an ambrosial mélange of tender hunks
and shreds cosseted in a zesty red sauce, available on a plate or in an ele-
phantine sandwich. Get the plate, which comes with some of Sconyers's
hash, a potent brew made from barbecued meats of all kinds—pork, chick-
en, and beef—shredded with tomatoes, potatoes, onions, and spice and
cooked until fall-apart tender. Dolloped on a mound of rice, hash is a traditional accompaniment at a Dixie pig pickin'. And although Sconyers's
ultramodern, ultrabig barbecue is anything but old-fashioned, its flavors
are impeccably true to the unchanging ritual of the smoke pit.

THE SMITH HOUSE
202 S. CHESTATEE, DAHLONEGA, GA (404) 864-3566

You cannot make a dinner reservation at the Smith House; service is
strictly first-come, first served. On weekends, the place is packed.
What an elbow-to-elbow eatfest! Tables are communal, shared by families,
local folks, and strangers, who all behave as though they were at a party
with best friends and relatives, passing platters back and forth, chattering
happily about the delicious food.

Pay one price and eat your fill. There is no menu to look at; there are
no choices to make. Everything the kitchen has prepared that day is
brought to the table in large serving dishes. Count on fried chicken, supplemented by Brunswick stew or catfish and hushpuppies; plenty of southern-style vegetables, including brandied chestnut soufflé, turnip greens,
and fried okra; and always warm breads: cracklin' cornbread, blueberry
lemon muffins, angel biscuits.

Smith House history starts before the Civil War, during Georgia's gold
rush, which attracted prospectors from all over America. One such adventurer was an already-wealthy Vermonter named Captain Frank Hall, who
staked a claim just east of the public square—and struck a fabulously rich
lode. Dahlonega authorities, so the legend goes, would not allow their
town's heart to be stripped open. The ornery Yankee declared that if he
couldn't have his paydirt, neither would anybody else. So he promptly built
an ostentatious mansion, complete with carriage house and servants' quarters, smack on top of the vein.

In 1922, long after Captain Hall's feud with Dahlonega ended, Henry and Bessie Smith bought the house to run it as an inn, where for $1.50 travelers got a room and three square meals a day. Mrs. Smith was a sensational cook, and word spread fast about her fried chicken, country ham, and platters of fresh vegetables. By 1946, when Fred and Thelma Welch took over the kitchen, the Smith House was known for its family-style feeds.

Forty years later, the rooms have been modernized, but the food on the tables in the dining room is old-fashioned north Georgia cooking, just like it has always been. To our knowledge, nobody has yet mined Captain Hall's gold.

SPRAYBERRY'S BARBECUE
U.S. HIGHWAY 29 NORTH, NEWNAN, GA (404) 253-4421

Thirty-five miles south of Atlanta, exit I-85 onto Highway 29 in Newnan. Roll down the windows and inhale deeply. When you begin to smell the aroma of pork sizzling on a pit over hickory and oak wood, hit the brakes. Pull into the parking lot at Sprayberry's, push up your sleeves, tuck a napkin in your collar, and prepare to feast on barbecue, Georgia-style.

Use a fork to heft a heap of smoke-laced pieces of pork shoulder so succulent that they hardly need the sauce Sprayberry's provides (and sells by the quart, to take home). Among the tender shreds and nuggets are crusty bits from the outside of the roast, glowing with the flavor of smoke and sauce. Get a barbecue platter, which supplements the motley heap of delectable pig meat with the starchy vegetable dish known as Brunswick stew (also available by the quart), as well as French fried potatoes, salad, bread, and pickles. And if you really want to go whole hog, get hot-from-the-fryer onion rings on the side, too. The traditional beverage to accompany this immensely satisfying meal will be a tall tumbler full of iced tea—presweetened, if you please.

Pork is not the only thing Sprayberry's sells. They also barbecue beef and mutton, and the menu lists an "aristocratic hamburger" as well as fried chicken, steaks, oysters, catfish, and shrimp, all the usual breakfasts, and even "hot weather specials" such as chicken salad. First-time visitors, however, are required to try the barbecued pork. That is what has put Sprayberry's on the map since it opened for business sixty-two years ago, and it is the dish most highly recommended by Jill Dabbs, the Alabama *Roadfooder* who first clued us in to this regional treasure a couple of years back.

Not many people can think of dessert after a plunge into pig heaven such as provided by this venerable barbecue parlor, but Sprayberry's provides a few sweet things worth saving room for. They have good ice cream, and there is a frosty lemon ice box pie to cool a palate overheated by too much barbecue sauce; and there are superb fried pies.

Many people who haven't eaten their way through the South do not know about fried pies. Served after barbecue and plate lunch meals throughout Arkansas and Tennessee, as well as in the barbecued mutton belt of Kentucky and parts of Georgia, fried pies—also known as half-moon pies—are a southern cook's way of maximizing the lusciousness of dessert. They are individual-serving half-circles (providing the greatest amount of good crust) that are baked, deep fried, or sizzled on a griddle until flaky and gold and crisp. Packed with sweetened peaches or apples or mashed sweet potatoes, served hot with maybe a scoop of ice cream melting fast on top, they are an authoritative conclusion to the kind of grand, informal smokehouse feast that Sprayberry's does so well.

SWEAT'S
I-16 AT GA 29, SOPERTON, GA (912) 529-3637

Each table at Sweat's has a well-stocked spice and condiment rack for doctoring the meat, but all you will likely want is a sprinkle of hot sauce. Sweat's barbecued pork is packed with flavor, not only of pit smoke and the sweet meat itself, but of the nippy sauce with which it was basted when it cooked. It is available sliced or chopped; we recommend the latter. Piled up in one sector of a partitioned plate, the meat is a mélange of soft, juicy pieces from the inside of the roast and fibrous, chewy, high-flavored shreds from its exterior.

The plate's other partitions hold a scoop of cole slaw or potato salad (neither memorable) and Brunswick stew, which is a hearty gallimaufry of peas, bits of carrot and potato, and shreds of meat in a well-peppered gravy. White bread comes on the side.

For dessert there are some dandy pies: coconut or lemon ice box. The pecan pie that used to be so good has been absent from the menu the last two times we visited, alas. Our waitress said she, too, missed it but couldn't promise it would ever return.

Once a funky smoke shack, Sweat's is now a nondescript rectangular roadside building made of cinderblocks; its interior is all wood paneling and easy-wipe tables, with a prosaic salad bar in the center of the room for customers who eat meals of steak, shrimp, or fish. Forget those things. For decades now, it has been the barbecue that has kept generations of hungry Georgians coming back to Sweat's.

THE VARSITY
I-75 AT NORTH AVE., ATLANTA, GA (404) 881-1706

The Varsity has no wine list, no maître d', no fine china, and no linen napery. It has, however, atmosphere galore. The Cokes are cold; the chili is hot; the onion rings are crisp; and the fried pies are sweet as sugar. And there is plenty of free parking. In fact, the Varsity restaurant of Atlanta is actually the Varsity Drive-In, which has been dishing out chili dogs and all the fixin's since 1928.

"Gimme a yellow steak, a sideways dog, a ring, and two strings," the counterman shouts back to the kitchen, using some of the most cultivated hashslinger slang you'll find anywhere in the U.S.A. Within seconds, out come a hamburger with mustard, a hot dog with onions, an order of onion rings, and two orders of French fries. To say service is fast at the Varsity is an understatement. It is *instantaneous*. Starting at seven in the morning (yes, chili dogs at 7:00 A.M.!), customers queue up in the hamburger lines, hot dog lines, sandwich lines, and family group lines. The lines move nearly as fast as you can walk, turning out forty-five customers per minute into vast dining rooms (each equipped with its own color TV, each tuned to a different channel).

Hot dogs, chili dogs, hamburgers, onion rings, French fries, and fried pies are the great things to eat at the Varsity. To drink with this grub, there's a full menu of reliable southern favorites: ice cold buttermilk, gigantic cups full of Coke, PCs, and frosted oranges. PC is Varsity lingo for chocolate milk ("plain chocolate") as opposed to a chocolate milk *shake* (with ice cream). Frosted orange is Atlanta's version of a California smoothie, reminiscent of a Creamsicle-in-a-cup. With or without chili dogs, frosted oranges are one heck of a way to keep cool.

You want facts? How about 16,000 customers per day, 30,000 when Georgia Tech plays football at home. How about a kitchen that goes through a ton of onions and a ton of potatoes every day. How about a two-acre, double-decker curb-service parking lot with room for 600 vehicles. The Varsity bills itself as the world's largest drive-in, and claims to sell more Coca-Cola than any other restaurant on earth.

There are two other branches of the Varsity, one in Atlanta on Lindbergh

Drive at Cheshire Bridge Rd., N.E., one in Athens, Georgia, on Milledge at Broad.

YE OLDE COLONIAL RESTAURANT
108 E. WASHINGTON ST., MADISON, GA (404) 342-2211

There is nothing obviously Colonial about this popular town cafe on the square in the small Georgia town of Madison. It is located in an old Victorian bank building with a beautiful interior of wood-paneled walls and flocked red wallpaper, with high arched windows that provide a view of the street and town square outside. Meals are casual and inexpensive, eaten in booths and at round tables in the center of the room, each of which is set with a large pitcher of presweetened iced tea so customers can help themselves.

There are no waitresses wearing colonial uniforms. In fact, there are no waitresses. Food service at Ye Olde Colonial is by means of a small cafeteria line at the back of the room. The choice of dishes, while by no means pre-Revolutionary, is certainly classic.

Every day at noon there is a choice of three meats available, including baked or fried chicken, fish fillets, and some kind of pork. Barbecue is our favorite—great, sodden shreds of smoky-flavored pig, infused with peppery red sauce, mustered into a mound on the plate by the serving person, who then passes the plate along for cornbread sticks (crisp and steamy), and selection from an array of vegetables and vegetable casseroles that would make any southern cook proud. Feast upon buttery mashed yams, crisp fried okra, collard greens drenched in pungent pot likker, black-eyed peas, or rutabagas. We found our Holy Grail as soon as we tucked into a great, quivering heap of custard-rich squash casserole. For dessert there is resoundingly sweet fruit cobbler.

Pay on your way out: at about five dollars per trayful, this place is a real bargain, and a mother lode of genuine Dixie cooking that seems not to have changed one bit since current owner Jimmy Cunningham's parents started Ye Olde Colonial restaurant thirty-eight years ago.

IDAHO

WOLF LODGE INN
FRONTAGE RD., 8 MI. EAST OF COEUR D'ALENE, ID (208) 664-1176665

We told Wally Wickel, proprietor of the Wolf Lodge Inn, that we were glad to see that nothing had changed since our last visit. The steaks were still juicy and flavor-packed—aged behemoths cooked on an open pit over cherry wood; and the krebel bread was every bit as good as we remembered. "This is the way it's been for twenty years," Wally said. "This is just the way we like it."

If you are traveling the wide-open spaces in search of real western meals, you will like it, too. The Wolf Lodge Inn, a capacious restaurant where broad tables are spread throughout a comfortable, carpeted dining room with two fireplaces and an impressive steak pit, has genuine sagebrush ambience but is reassuringly civilized.

Steaks are the star of the menu—ranging from a one-pounder (the smallest, named "Lil Dude") to two-pound T-bones and a majestic two-and-a-half-pound porterhouse. Cooked over the hardwood fire, the heavy-textured beef, aged eighteen days and never frozen, develops a sizzly, blackened crust to pocket its juices. The tang of aging and the flavor of the charcoal fire create a memorable piece of meat. There are other main courses on the Wolf Lodge menu, including lobster tails and tiger shrimp;

117

and we actually like the lobster. Of course it doesn't compare to a whole one like you'd eat in Maine; but tails have their own sumptuous charm—easy to eat, pearlescent luxury, bathed in butter.

There are good salads and an interesting breadstuff called krebel (German fried bread), a bun of sweetened dough twisted into a figure eight; but the side dish adventurous eaters want to know about is Rocky Mountain oysters—testicles of bulls sliced into half-inch disks, breaded and deep-fried. Pat Wickel, Wally's wife, told us that some customers come to the Wolf Lodge for nothing but testicles; but on her advice, we have always gotten one order to split between us. Nice as they may be, we need room for potatoes and beans, both of which are excellent. The spuds are called Belgium bakers—pressure-fried wedges with crusty skins and fluffy insides; and the beans, in a sweet tomato sauce, are a fine, sophisticated gloss on chuckwagon cookery.

ILLINOIS

AL'S BAR-B-Q
1079 W. TAYLOR, CHICAGO, IL (312) 226-4017

A l's is not a barbecue in the usual sense of the word. It is an Italian beef stand, where the specialty of the house is a great heap of shredded, gravy-sopped, garlic-scented roast beef piled into a long section of crusty Italian bread, topped with a pungent medley of chopped vegetables known as *giardiniera,* garnished with a choice of sweet or hot roasted peppers, and served with plenty of lunch-counter sass. This sandwich is one of Chicago's gastronomic splendors.

Like a lot of America's best neighborhood cookery, the fun of eating Italian beef at Al's has a lot to do with atmosphere. Neighborhood folks know the place as "Little Al's"; and it is a favored meeting and greeting spot among devotees of cheap eats. We have never come here when there weren't at least a couple of Chicago police cars in the lot and officers kibitzing inside and out as they ingest their mammoth sandwiches. Out back, flocks of plump pigeons expect to be thrown pieces of bread; and the counter inside is frequently mobbed with customers and noisy with back-and-forth patter as the beef men keep up a lightning pace.

Beef's the thing at Al's, but it's not the only sandwich that is worth

119

ordering. They make wonderful sausage—muscle-bound, crackle-skinned tubes of pork roasted over charcoal and served inside Italian bread either by themselves or as part of a half-and-half, with beef. And the French fries—greasy, hot, and delicious—are not to be missed.

There isn't really any place to sit and eat at Al's, but that bothers no one. You can stand at a counter inside or eat off the hood of your car.

THE BERGHOFF
17 WEST ADAMS ST., CHICAGO, IL (312) 427-3170

The Berghoff is a grand old relic of normal food with a German accent. This is the place to savor long-cooked pot roast with plump, buttered noodles; roast turkey with dressing and mashed potatoes; lamb stew; pork shank; sauerbraten and potato pancakes; corned-beef hash browned in a skillet with a poached egg on top; zesty creamed spinach; heaping, hot portions of profound bread pudding with a custard-rich vanilla sauce.

There are notable regional specialties on the menu, including broiled whitefish from Lake Superior and that odd, damp, vividly garlicked Chicago concoction, shrimp de Jonghe. You can eat such European delights as Alpen ragout or beef rouladen; or American classics from fried catfish to New York cheesecake. Fried chicken, crusted with beer batter, is an iconoclastic triumph. We especially like anything served with the Berghoff's excellent mashed potatoes (open-faced hot turkey sandwich for lunch; roast beef with sour cream sauce for dinner). There are few restaurant kitchens anywhere in this country as straightforward as this one, which has been dishing out square meals since 1898.

Nor are there many dining rooms that exude such old-fashioned savoir-faire: dark aged wood, portraits of Berghoff ancestors, stained glass, a maroon linoleum floor, and high chandeliers stocked with clear bulbs whose filaments infuse the restaurant with an antique glow. Everybody waits in line for a table; no credit cards are accepted; and prices are low. People-watching, especially at lunch, is great fun here, because so many people actually come to eat rather than to have meetings: hungry businessmen seem to have no interest in conversing when they tuck napkins into starched white collars, tear a piece of crusty fresh sour rye, heft a stein of Berghoff's own draught beer, then plow into meat-and-potatoes meals nonpareil.

BIG JOHN'S
MARTIN LUTHER KING DR. & KUMPF BLVD., PEORIA, IL (309) 674-4158

There are formal and informal photographs of Big John Robinson on the wood-paneled walls, with and without celebrities, as well as a nice hand-tinted picture of Pat O'Brien in priest's garb, and various plaques and commendations from local and state officials. There is easy-to-listen-to soul music piped into the dining room, and a credit card machine by the cash register. Such a nice, polite restaurant!

Then you taste the sauce and your head explodes. "Real hot" is what the waitress said when we asked if there was something a bit zestier than Big John's usual, red-orange, delightfully tart—but fairly mild—sauce that accompanies plates of ribs, beef, and pork. We ordered the "real hot," and after the first shock, relished it—in small doses—on handsome slabs of hickory-scented brisket and on lean, crusty ribs. With one dinner we got French fries, which were good, crunchy logs of speckled-skin brown potato; with the other came balmy potato salad. A plate of spongy white bread was set in the center of the table, and the ribs were accompanied by an extra plate to hold bones denuded of their meat.

Big John's is about the tidiest barbecue parlor we know. From the well-kept Formica dining room where people sit gnawing ribs and savoring brisket, you can look through a plate-glass window into the kitchen and see men hoisting hunks of cooked beef and sizzling ribs onto counters and hacking at them. Only outside the restaurant do you smell the telltale aroma of hickory logs smoldering in the pits.

BYRON'S DOG HAUS
1017 IRVING PARK RD., CHICAGO, IL (312) 281-7474

As plump Polish sausages sizzle on the grill, the Dog Haus counterman dips a ladle into the fryolator (whence commeth the French fried potatoes) to get some hot fat to pour over the grilling tube steaks. The grease helps give them a blackened, crisp skin; it also gives them a look of glistening, sinfully swollen avoirdupois. These are some of the most cumbrous Polish sausages in a city where Polish sausages, along with their beefy brothers, hot dogs, are matters of serious culinary consideration. If you are a Polish sausage fanatic, it isn't likely you will be blasé about the big, charred tubes they serve up at Byron's Dog Haus; you will love them or hate them.

The hot dogs are more civil; and we can recommend them to anyone who likes a substantial, all-beef frank. They are Vienna-brand beauties, perfectly steeped to plump succulence, with a faint crackle as you sink your teeth into them. Our only complaint is about the buns. These buns, alas, are a bore—small, plain (no poppy seeds), forked right out of their plastic-wrapped container (not well-warmed), and therefore redolent of cardboard and plastic wrap.

On the other hand, Dog Haus condiments are gorgeous: eleven different toppings are advertised on the outside wall of the tiny cubicle restaurant (the same sign that proclaims Byron's motto, "Thee Hot Dog"). The available toppings include strips of green pepper, cucumber discs, piccalilli, squeeze-on yellow mustard, onions, sport peppers (hot!), and virtually whole tomatoes that happen to have been cut into slices. Yes, there resting atop your hot dog and all its other condiments is one tomato, not quite still round, because it has been cut into slices; but because the slices don't go all the way through, it stays in one piece . . . until you try to eat the dog, at which time—unless you are one of Chicago's semi-professional hot dog eaters—everything falls into a splendid mess. The tomato is customarily gilded with a sprinkle of celery salt.

Alongside this outstanding specimen of frankfurter pulchritude, you want French fries. They are skinny and crisp—an ideal spuddy companion to the highly seasoned sausages that are this restaurant's specialty; and they are served forth in a big paper cup. One order is plenty for two.

There are other Byron's at 850 W. North Ave., 1701 W. Lawrence, and 6016 N. Clark St.

CONNIE'S ITALIAN BEEF
1732 N. HARLEM, ELMWOOD PARK, IL (708) 453-3994

Someone stole the portrait of Telly Savalas that used to hang on the wall of Connie's. When we pointed out to the management that we missed it, they accused us—jokingly, we think—of having stolen it. We didn't; but we cannot honestly say the thought hadn't crossed our mind. We miss the picture; and to be honest, we miss the old Connie's on North Avenue. The new, air-conditioned one, in a strip mall, has tables to sit at (the old one was strictly stand-up-and-scarf) and no more Telly, both of which take away from the original's sassy charm; but still, if you are looking for great Italian beef sandwiches, you must come here and feast.

Chicago has an abundance of restaurants that sell Italian beef sandwiches, which are second only to hot dogs as the city's favorite proletarian food. Many connoisseurs get it spiced with the traditional Italian beef condiment, pepper-hot *giardiniera,* a pickly vegetable relish for which Connie's uses an especially piquant recipe.

Serious Italian beef eaters demand a sandwich overloaded with beef—to the extent that they do not even bother to try to eat it like a sandwich. Veteran Connie's patrons have adapted their old, stand-up eating style to the new tables: you will see them with their sandwich set before them, unwrapped and splayed open as they pick and tear at it with their fingers, hefting shreds of beef, clumps of bread, and blobs and dribbles of *giardiniera.* The bread in these sandwiches is so fresh it smells like a bakery; and it has enough body to soak up and hold plenty of oozing gravy yet still stay intact. The beef is simply the best in town: so thin and tender it almost falls apart as it is lifted with tongs from the gravy trough, yet has a heady savor that is ready to yield even more beefy smack when you chew. It is super-lean, super-juicy, shaved as thin as possible, then sopped in a garlicky, pan-drippin' natural gravy that is so delicious itself that many customers come for nothing but a "gravy sandwich" (soaked bread).

FATHER AND SON PIZZA
2475 MILWAUKEE AVE., CHICAGO, IL (312) 252-2620

You likely already know about Chicago's famous deep-dish, thick-crusted pizza—invented at Uno's and served in all its high-rise splendor at several good pizzerias around town. Now we are going to tell you about the thinnest crust in Chicago, and a lesser-known pizza parlor that all pizzaphiles ought to inscribe in their little black book.

Cracker-crisp, surprising your teeth with a quick, subtle resilience before it shatters, Father and Son's tour de force crust is astoundingly sturdy considering its elegance. Top it with a heavy load—even oddities like pineapple or taco beef, or wet things like sliced fresh tomato—and it hangs tough to the last slice. Father and Son will also sell you Chicago-style pies with a breadier crust, "New York–style," which is medium-thick, and "gourmet pizzas" festooned with eggplant parmigiana, broccoli and almonds, sirloin steak, or omelettes. Anywhere else, such fanfaronade would seem like boutique-pizza pandering. At Father and Son, charter member of the Chicago deep-dish pantheon (since 1947), it seems only right and good that pizza creativity marches on.

HALE'S RESTAURANT
OFF ROUTE 3, GRAND TOWER, IL (618) 565-8384

It has been some fifty years since Ma Hale opened a restaurant in her wood-frame home on a side street in Grand Tower. Ma is long gone, but the Sunday dinners to which families came from miles around are still a big draw. Eat in the living room at long tables that may be shared by strangers on occasions when the lines outside are especially long. The decor is old-lady rustic, including many of Ma's vintage pictures on the wall.

The menu is proverbial: fried chicken or ham every day, supplemented on Sunday by turkey and dressing. The chicken is deep-fried and so not as aristocratic as that turned in a skillet, but we like its flavor; ham is cut into thick steaks with a strong (but not overwhelmingly so) flavor. With the main course you get plenty of family-style fixin's, including mashed potatoes and gravy, buttered hominy, green beans, cole slaw, and dinner rolls. There are gooey cream pies and sweet fruit pies for dessert. It is in no way an elegant meal; but it is a taste of family-style dining that is ever more rare, even here in the southernmost Midwest.

LEON'S
1640 E. 79TH ST., CHICAGO, IL (312) 731-1454
(3 OTHER LOCATIONS ON THE SOUTH SIDE OF CHICAGO)

Dinner is served from behind bulletproof glass. Hand your cash underneath the inch-thick pane, and barbecued ribs are delivered via a carousel that protects the server from bandits. Dine on the front seat of your car, or standing up in the parking lot, off your trunk; or find a friend in Chicago where you can take your meal and enjoy it sitting down at a table. In any case, you will not need utensils.

Amenities are scarce in the heart of barbecue country on Chicago's South Side, but that only encourages true devotées to make the pilgrimage to Leon's for what many consider to be the city's finest ribs.

They are spare ribs, large and brawny, dripping juice as soon as your teeth cut down below the crust. The pork is sweet and tender-of-spirit, infused but not overwhelmed with the taste of smoke. They are so nicely cooked that you can easily pull individual ribs off the rack, providing yourself a dozen good mouthfuls of porcine paradise per bone.

Some Leon's fans leave their ribs plain. Ourselves, we wouldn't want them without a generous application of the hot sauce. There is mild sauce, too, but it's a bore. The hot, in concert with the gentle pork ribs, creates a harmony that only South Side barbecue can sing. The tang of the sauce seems to wake your tastebuds to nuances of the pork you might not otherwise know. The pork is the cushion that gives the heat of the sauce a pleasurable sting instead of a painful one.

Slabs and half slabs are served in cardboard boats, ribs at the bottom. On top of the ribs come a mess of crinkle-cut French fries, which by the time you open up the package have virtually meshed with the sauce to become a kind of starchy greasy glaze. Atop the fries is a sheet of wax paper, and on top of that, two slices of clean, spongy white bread. You would not want this bread for any other meal (unless you, like us, demand blah bread for baloney and Miracle Whip sandwiches); but as a salve between bouts with barbecue, it's exactly what the pitmaster ordered.

There are other items on the menu, and they're good, although not in the stratosphere with the ribs. You can get hot links, hacked-up rib tips, and sliced barbecued beef. Chicken is sold whole or half, or by the wing. It is crusty gold and well-spiced. The beverage list is limited to "Jolly Good" brand sodas.

As we found our way to Leon's one afternoon, we noticed a billboard advertising a local ham. "So good it will haunt you until it's gone," the sign said. Leon's is different. Long after the ribs are gone, their flavor haunts you . . . and will continue to do so until you get back to the South Side of Chicago for a flavor sensation found nowhere else.

LOU MITCHELL'S
560 W. JACKSON BLVD., CHICAGO, IL (312) 939-3111

W e miss Lou Mitchell greeting customers at the door of his coffee shop and offering each lovely lady who enters a personal-size box of Milk Duds or a donut hole. Lou still occasionally mans the entryway; but now most of the time his nephew, Nick Noble, carries on the assignment—and a fine job Mr. Noble does of giving out the Duds. But we are sentimentalists, and Lou Mitchell's restaurant isn't quite the same when he himself, in suspenders and bow tie, isn't at the door.

Still, if you want breakfast in downtown Chicago, this glass-fronted, green-awning coffee shop at the northwest edge of the Loop is the hottest spot in town. It's got the same wacky charm it has had for years, as well as low prices and terrific food.

Let's start with the food. There are fourteen omelettes on the menu, including a splendid one made with feta cheese and spinach; eggs are served in their skillet, which is presented, still sizzling, on a wooden trivet. They are accompanied by thick-cut toast made from tender-crumb Greek bread. Ham is the pig meat we like best to accompany any meal. It is fried to crusty red lusciousness. Some other side dishes worth knowing about: clove-scented prunes, tart homemade marmalade for that toast, freshly squeezed orange juice, and coffee made from "triple filtered water," which apparently is the same mouthwash-colored stuff that froths vehemently in big tanks up by the front of the restaurant. Whatever it is, it makes a brawny, satisfying cup of java.

There is more: muffins, donuts, Danish pastries, and giant-size pecan rolls baked here every morning, and served still warm from the oven; waffles made from batter enriched by malt powder; truly elegant pancakes, dished out with stewed fruit and sour cream or honey-flavored yogurt.

As for ambience, Lou Mitchell's is just about the most sociable place in Chicago. The friendly folks who serve the food seem to share in the kitchen's spirit of generosity; and the chowhounds with whom you sit elbow-to-elbow at Lou's crowded, communal tables (there are booths, too) come not merely to feed, but to relish eating. If you enjoy hearty meals in the company of fellow lunch-counter connoisseurs, it is impossible not to delight in breakfast at Lou Mitchell's.

MANNY'S COFFEE SHOP
1141 S. JEFFERSON ST., CHICAGO, IL (312) 939-2855

The first signal of a four-star restaurant in our book is that it smells great. Walk into Manny's Coffee Shop at the southernmost edge of Chicago's Loop and the mingled aroma of hot beef stew and roasted chicken is an overwhelming invitation to eat hearty. These homey perfumes are accented with spice and zest, in the form of steaming corned beef, lusciously oily liver and onions, and a hint of sliced dill pickles.

We like the sound of Manny's, too. Men behind the counter call out above kitchen clatter to get customers' orders. At tables in the two big dining rooms, people chatter noisily the way happy eaters tend to do. There is a lot of table-hopping among them. Manny's clientele are old friends: police officers, cabbies, local business people for whom this place has been a home-away-from-home for years.

Manny's is a Jewish (but nonkosher) restaurant with all the good food of a traditional deli, dished out cafeteria-style every day starting at five in the morning. The variety of choices along the lunch line is tremendous, including such Old World favorites as knishes (potato dumplings), kasha (buckwheat groats) with bow-tie noodles, and prune tsimmes (a sweet vegetable stew). The chicken soup is gold in color, luxuriously thick with schmaltz (chicken fat), and holds a big fall-apart-tender matzoh ball. Blintzes (order by the piece) are tender crepes rolled around faintly sweetened pot cheese, sizzled in butter, then garnished with cool sour cream.

Manny's is famous for its behemoth corned-beef sandwich: three or four inches of hot, lean, glistening, rose-pink, thin-sliced corned beef stacked between slices of sour-crusted rye. These are so popular there are usually a half-dozen of them already assembled atop the counter at the sandwich station in the cafeteria line. Other sandwiches are acclaimed, too. One enthusiastic customer insisted to us that Manny's made the best egg salad in Chicago. We confess we were too busy eating hot meals and corned-beef sandwiches to try the egg salad, or the chopped liver, or the tuna; but next time, we will: deli greatness springs from these humble sandwich ingredients every bit as much as from the more profound comfort foods.

Along with sandwiches, instead of French fries or chips, Manny's serves magnificent potato pancakes: oval patties with gnarled skins encasing white pillows of shredded potato with a trace of onion flavor. Potato pancakes are terrific on the side not only of sandwiches, but of any stick-to-the-ribs main course, especially a pot roast. Or they are good all by themselves, accompanied by chunky apple sauce and/or sour cream.

There are all-American lunch-counter favorites, too: turkey drumsticks every Wednesday, franks and beans on Saturday, macaroni and cheese on Friday. Or how about chicken pot pie; or a slab of meat loaf with mashed potatoes; you can even order that dowdy hodgepodge known as American chop suey. Manny's is a temple of honest food that tastes great but is not the least bit fussy or prettied-up.

MARY LOU'S
114 S. ILLINOIS, CARBONDALE, IL (618) 457-5084

Mary Lou's is a beanery with an attitude. Who would want their beanery any other way?

The walls are lined with pictures of celebrities and unknown people, most of whom accompanied their autograph by a declaration of love for this chow dump next to a dime store in Carbondale.

It used to be a *real* dump—a tiny diner with a counter and stools, beloved by Southern Illinois students for its cheap eats and Mary Lou Trammel's willingness to let them put a piece of chocolate cream pie or a plate of biscuits on the cuff until their parents sent money. Now it is a dump *manqué:* too big and too clean to pass as an unrepentant hash house, but still with all the trappings of a blue-collar eatery where the food is cheap and the service is sassy.

The kitchen is now in back, but there is still a counter—thirty-two stools; and there are tables. The menu is pretty much the same: country cookin' (before expansion, we wouldn't have dropped the *g*). Meat loaf. Pork chops. Turkey and dressing. Chicken and dumplings. Cream pies and cobblers for dessert; occasionally, a Mary Lou invention called poor-boy pudding, made with devil's food cake mix. This part of Illinois is pork country, so we generally go for pig meat at Mary Lou's. She makes a fine, crisp tenderloin sandwich. There are sausage patties cooked and served like hamburgers (with or without melted cheese on top). And you cannot get more authentically regional than this kitchen's ham and bean lunch, accompanied by cornbread suitable for crumbling on top.

Mary Lou's closes by midafternoon; and there are many of her fans who even turn up their noses at lunch. They come only for breakfast, when the kitchen clatters out such hearty fare as griddle cakes and ham, eggs and omelettes of every kind, and a traditional rib-sticker that is probably the truest expression of Mary Lou's culinary soul: a plate of biscuits smothered with cream gravy, accompanied by strong coffee.

MR. BEEF
666 N. ORLEANS, CHICAGO, IL (312) 337-8500

Italian beef is such a common feature in Chicago's gastronomic landscape that most Chicagoans (M. Stern included) never know it is anything special until they move away, then realize with horror that you cannot get it anywhere else, certainly not in Italy. It is roast beef, slow cooked and vigorously seasoned, sliced thin and sopped in natural gravy, loaded into sturdy crumbed bread torpedoes, garnished with either roasted peppers or hot pepper *giardiniera.*

Of all the Italian beef sandwiches in town, we put Mr. Beef right up there at the pinnacle of excellence. Its meat is lean, rare, maniacally garlicked, and oozes vast quantities of natural gravy into the greedy jaws of bread that surround it. For a special treat, we suggest a Mr. Beef "combo sandwich"—that's beef plus a length of tough-skinned, juicy, sweet sausage.

As for atmosphere, Mr. Beef's is superb: picnic tables provide a view of the parking lot and the Scala Packing Company across the street, where much of Chicago's finest beef originates.

OBERWEIS DAIRY
945 N. LAKE ST., AURORA, IL (708) 897-0512

Oberweis Dairy sells no cooked food at all; just sundaes, shakes, sodas, malts, and ice cream cones. There isn't even a counter to sit at, merely a handful of tables with a view through a glass wall to a room in back where milk is bottled (in the morning) and ice cream packaged (in the afternoon). Find a seat, look over the menu, then tell the waitress what you want.

The selection is canonical: single-, double-, or triple-dip ice cream sundaes, topped with chocolate, pineapple, marshmallow, caramel sauce, or strawberries. You can get an orange float or a black cow, a "cheery cherry" milk shake, a banana malt, or a "lusty lemon" super soda. Then there is a list of "special sundaes," for serious pigging out. Rocky road: chocolate marshmallow ice cream topped with marshmallow topping and spanish peanuts. Banana royal: vanilla, chocolate, and strawberry ice cream heaped with fudge and bananas, plus strawberries and pineapple.

All the sundaes come crowned with a billowy cloud of Oberweis's glossy smooth whipped cream, and a single maraschino cherry. Ah, what bliss!

One of the greatest things to eat at Oberweis Dairy is plain vanilla ice cream. It is silky white, elegant, and refined—nothing like the grossly overrich designer ice creams that sell for twice the price.

"Only for the big spender!" warns the menu about the turtle candy sundae (although at under three dollars for the triple-dip version, we gladly splurge every time). "Turtle," of course, refers to Turtle candies, in which caramel and pecans are bound in chocolate. As children, we always craved Turtles because they seemed like rich man's food, costing two or three times as much as ordinary candy bars. There is still something fine and fancy about the triple-whammy ingredients on a turtle candy sundae, even though they are as gloppy as all-get-out.

PIZZERIA UNO
29 E. OHIO, CHICAGO, IL (312) 321-1000

W e're schizo on the subject of pizza. Is it any wonder? We met and fell in love over pizza in New Haven, and to this day contend that it's the world's best. However, to be frank, each of us is troubled by gnawing doubt. Jane, after all, is from New York, where America was introduced to pizza in the 1890s, and where the broad, flat pies and pizza-by-the-slice are terrific. Michael is from Chicago, where deep-dish pizza was invented about fifty years ago, and where pizza's evolution and development is taken more seriously, by more restaurants, than any other place on earth.

The place where Chicago-style pizza was born is Pizzeria Uno. Although there are now many excellent pizza parlors around the city, many of them creating more spectacular, overburdened, deeper-dish, and even healthier pizzas, there is something about the original deep-dish pizza, as dished out by Uno's, that is incomparable and unsurpassed. And we don't just say that out of respect for history or hometown pride.

Look at the crust on this pizza—faintly granular with cornmeal, thick and substantial with a profound crunch, at once lusciously oily but clean-flavored, spread out in the pan like a brawny pastry composed of reefs and shoals of delicious breadstuff. Atop this magnificent platform there are clots of sweet tomato (not red sauce), dripping gobs of cheese, and—if you order it—some of the most distinctive sausage to be found on any pizza. It is sweet, coarse-ground, and really tastes like pork with a fennel kick. Eating an Uno's pizza is the kind of culinary experience that inspires reverie and transcendence. It is simple, inelegant, and perfect.

Due's Pizzeria, down the street at 619 North Wabash, is a branch of the original operation that serves identical pizzas. However, Pizzeria Unos in other cities are of varying quality; none, in our experience, even vaguely replicates the greatness of the original.

SOLLY'S DRIVE IN
1982 N. CLYBOURN, CHICAGO, IL (312) 248-7233

I f you live and regularly eat in Chicago, you can skip this entry. You probably already have your favorite place to chomp into gyros, Italian beef, sausage, red hots, and Polishes. Indeed, there are places in town that we believe serve better beef and red hots than Solly's; but there is something about this joint at the three-way intersection of Clybourn, Cortland,

and Racine, with its scattering of al fresco picnic tables and short stand-up counter and basic eat-with-your-hands menu, that is the essence of Chicago's best vulgar cuisine.

In particular, we like the gyro: that weird, pulverized and reconstituted, highly seasoned lamb, sliced and heaped on a broad pita loaf and served with shockingly garlicked sauce.

The Italian beef is satisfying, although not aristocratic. Shaved thin and wallowing in a gravy trough until served, it is mighty juicy; you would almost call it fatty it is so succulent; and its gravy is nicely flecked with little bits of red pepper. It soaks its roll very quickly and makes a grand, uncouth feast.

There is fine Italian sausage—plump and peppery with a taut, charred skin and juicy insides, needing only roasted peppers inside the bun to attain completion.

That's practically the extent of the menu (plus hot tamales, hamburgers, and chili by the pint); except we ought to note that nearly everything Solly's serves is available as a double: double hot dogs, double burgers, double sausage sandwiches, and, most delectable of all, the beef *and* sausage combo sandwich—a wanton union that elevates colloquial food toward baroque delirium.

SUPERDAWG
MILWAUKEE AVENUE AT DEVON, CHICAGO, IL (312) 763-0660

More than any other city in America, Chicago is crazy for hot dogs, or as they are known hereabouts, "red hots." The dogs are all-beef, firm, and brightly spiced—superlative tubes of firmly packed meat; but what makes them soar into the culinary stratosphere are Chicago's buns and condiments. An exemplary case in point is Superdawg, where you want to order your red hot "dragged through the garden." That means it will be served to you buried under a lush landslide of mustard, picallili, onions, peppers, pickle spears, sliced tomatoes and/or pickled green tomatoes, and a sprinkle of celery salt. The bun is poppy-seeded, soft, and fresh—a big mitt in which you try to hold the dog and its toppings.

Superdawg's logo is a lounging wiener clad in leopardskin who offers "thanks from the bottom of my pure beef heart for stopping." Order yours with fries (homemade crinkle cuts) and the take-out box advises, "Your Superdawg lounges inside contentedly cushioned . . . in Superfries." Good burgers and ultrathick (impossible to suck up a straw) milk shakes, too: all served in a genuine drive-in with "Order Matic" carhop service. Hot dog, indeed!

WALKER BROTHERS ORIGINAL PANCAKE HOUSE
153 GREEN BAY, WILMETTE, IL (708) 251-6000

There are many good kinds of pancakes at Walker Brothers, but the top of the line is the apple pancake. It is a baked pancake, bigger than a large plate, a satisfying meal for at least two hungry people. Think of it as a cake rather than a flapjack. It truly is gorgeous—a great puffed promontory of caramelized apples and sugar and butter and cinnamon and cake that arrives at the table still sizzling and gusting clouds of sweet steam into the air. Slice into the stupendous mountain and you discover strata of cooked, eggy dough, soft pillows of apple, and untold amounts of sweet, mahogany-colored goo. This is breakfast for the gods.

Years ago, when we were more experimental types, we used to order other things at Walker Brothers, too, and they were great. On occasion, we still do get bacon; and like the famous pancake, it is a superior version of a common dish: thick-cut, sweet, and smoky-flavored. Ham, too, is hickory-smoked and truly delicious. Among the other breakfasts we recall with fondness are the German pancake (also oven-cooked, but without the apples), silver-dollar sourdough 'cakes, elegant Swedish pancakes, and pecan waffles; also omelettes with onion-scented hash-brown potatoes. But honestly, you are nuts to come to this restaurant and eat anything other than the apple pancake.

Big problem: Walker Brothers is nearly always hideously crowded. If you can't stand to wait in line, come just before it opens at seven in the morning or at an off-hour.

WITZ RESTAURANT
RT. 146, E. CAPE GIRARDEAU, IL (618) 661-1644

Sunday at noon is the time we recommend you pull off Route 146 just east of the Mississippi River bridge that connects Missouri and Illinois. Here on the south side of the road is the Witz Restaurant—a sprawling multi-dining room establishment surrounded by a parking lot. Inside, customers sit at tables covered with woven-look oilcloth, at places set with paper mats and napkins. Although the atmosphere is utilitarian, Witz is a folksy place, with a menu that makes you feel at home.

Arrive with a big appetite if you come on Sunday, because that is when Witz Restaurant serves Sunday dinner: baked ham or fried chicken, chicken and dumplings or chicken and dressing. We especially enjoyed Witz's smoked pork barbecue, served without any sauce: just a heap of motley minced pieces of lean meat that goes so well with Witz's crusty, tender-center corn sticks. We also had some brittle-skinned fried chicken, accompanied by whipped potatoes, turnip greens dotted with little diced chunks of turnip, and a bowl of blackeyed peas.

Dinners come with slews of spuds and vegetables, corn sticks, and Homeric slaws and salads the likes of which one finds only in the heartland—including German potato salad, served hot, and layered lettuce, which is a multi-tiered mélange of greens, cabbage, and a few other assorted ingredients that some farm cooks know as "24-hour salad" because that is how much time it spends in the refrigerator before it is ready.

To top off a big meal like this, you need major-league dessert, and Witz delivers. Each pie, cake, cobbler, and pudding available on a particular day is listed on an eight-by-ten-inch placard posted on a huge board at the front of each dining room, suggesting the stage set of some television gastronomic game show. During one visit, the board held cards for chocolate, banana, and coconut cream pies, rhubarb pie, apple pie, lemon pie, egg custard pie, raisin pie, peach or blackberry cobbler, and bread pudding with vanilla sauce.

WOLFY'S
2734 W. PETERSON AVE., CHICAGO, IL (312) 743-0207

Wolfy's is a plasticine hot dog stand reminiscent of a McDonald's franchise, but with a giant, skewered wiener for a sign instead of golden arches. Despite the sanitary appearance, the hot dogs and Polish sausages, as well as the munificent and all-important (in Chicago) condiments, are superb.

When you walk in the door you can see the sausages stacked like logs near the grill, where they sizzle and develop a scrumptious blackened skin. These meaty links, made of pork and beef, are fully three times the size of an ordinary hot dog and they extend far beyond both ends of their buns. They audibly crackle when you bite into them, and juice spurts. The red hot is all beef and smaller than the Polish, but emphatically tasty, with a lean, concentrated flavor.

Wolfy's buns are some of the best—Rosen's poppy-seeded jumbos, invariably so fresh that they have a doughy deliciousness all their own. Inside these buns, along with your red hot or Polish, "the works" includes slimy fried onions (not everybody's taste, but good for oil junkies), jade-green picallili, mustard, tomato slices, a couple of pickle spears, and tiny super-hot sport peppers. It is this presentation that puts Wolfy's among the greats. Once smothered with all these things, each tube steak becomes a Fauvist masterpiece—bright, clean, colorful, and appetizing. It is nearly impossible to raft to your mouth without major spillage; but that's the way of the wiener in Chicago.

Wolfy's also serves nachos, cheese dogs, and chili dogs. You can eat in a plastic chair or in your car.

INDIANA

COURTESY COFFEE SHOP
202 S. MERIDIAN, WINCHESTER, IN (317) 584-1851

A tip of the hat to Jean Jacobs of Peru, Indiana, who directed us to the Courtesy Coffee Shop, just off the town square in Winchester. Our first visit was early one summer morning and most of the town was still waking up; by ones and twos they arrived in cars and pickup trucks and walked in under an appealing old neon sign hanging outside the Beachler Apartment Building announcing "Courtesy Coffee Shop." The entrance to the restaurant is through the lobby of the apartments.

When we entered, we sighed with joy at what we saw and the food we sniffed. Customers were arrayed on pink stools at a short counter, and on pale green kitchenette chairs at tables covered with boomerang-pattern Formica. In a big open kitchen at the back, ladies were hard at work mixing salads, popping breads in the oven, squeezing glasses of orange juice one by one. A rack held pie crusts so hot from the oven they were still steamy in the cool morning air, wafting the perfume of cooked, sugared berries into the air.

For us, the scene was love at first sight, and we inscribed this place in our register of culinary treasures as much for the country feeling of the place as for the great buckwheat cakes we ate. Sorry to say, the Courtesy

Coffee Shop no longer serves buckwheat cakes or any breakfast at all—just lunch and supper, six days a week; but those meals are every bit as endearing. Service is cafeteria-style, help-yourself from a buffet line that features such country vittles as pan-fried steaks, meat loaf, and our favorite—chicken and dumplings, which go great with the kitchen's jiggly raspberry Jell-O salad and a slab of blueberry pie. It occurred to us as we plowed into exactly this square meal in the heart of Indiana that its color scheme was red, white, and blue.

DODD'S TOWN HOUSE
5694 N. MERIDIAN ST., INDIANAPOLIS, IN (317) 257-1872

Jim and Betty Dodd started serving good food to the public at the Flag Pole Restaurant back in the 1940s. Twenty years after that they moved to the Town House, a former tavern in a residential neighborhood on the north side of Indianapolis. Since then, the Dodds' place has developed a sterling reputation near and far for pan-fried chicken, thick steaks, and farm-fresh pies. Jim and Betty retired a few years back, and their son David took over. The last we tasted, the twenty-ounce T-bone was delicious and the pie crusts as flaky as ever.

The Town House skillet-fries steaks so the meat develops a wickedly savory crust to pocket its juices. Slice into that T-bone or pound-and-a-half porterhouse, or even a smaller one-pound strip or "ladies' ribeye," and the natural juices spurt, then ooze onto the plate. That's just fine, because it is a delight to push big hunks of chewy-skin baked potato, or even one of Dodd's toasty French fries, along the plate to mop up all the juices. On the side of these all-American vittles comes a suitably all-American salad—a mound of iceberg lettuce with sweet and sour garlic dressing, or creamy cole slaw.

Nobody dresses fancy to dine at Dodd's; but somehow everyone who comes looks nice and acts polite. Service is fast but never brusque; and there is a feeling of well-worn familiarity about the whole experience. Most customers are regulars who have been dining with the Dodds for years, as well as a loyal clientele of out-of-towners (ourselves included) who wouldn't think of coming to the heart of Indiana without a visit to this wonderful old eatery.

No matter how much steak and potatoes or fried chicken you eat at Dodd's (and you will eat plenty), it is required that you have dessert. Pies like these you don't find too many places any more: real blue-ribbon beau-

ties, with feathery-light crusts and fillings rich with cream or with locally
grown berries in the summer. You never know which pies will be available
any particular day, but among the well-known specialties are chocolate
cream, blueberry, and buttermilk, the latter a lesson in how to make something spectacular out of basic ingredients. Sugar, eggs, butter, buttermilk,
and a sprinkling of lemon zest and vanilla flavor are combined in a crust
and the result, so utterly simple, is sheer felicity—a fitting conclusion to a
meal in a restaurant where dinner always tastes like coming home.

DOGTOWN TAVERN
OLD HENDERSON ROAD, CYPRESS (SOUTH OF EVANSVILLE), IN
(812) 423-0808

A t the southern tip of Indiana along the Ohio River, in the southern end
of the city of Evansville, there is an area locals know as Cypress,
named for the trees that grow along the riverbank. There is one part of
Cypress some folks still call Dogtown, named for reasons no one we asked
could remember. Dogtown is not a place most sightseers accidentally find
themselves; but if you are moseying through the southern Midwest (indeed,
a lovely place to mosey) and have a hankering for real American food, we
suggest you seek it out. In particular, look for the Dogtown Tavern. And be
prepared to eat hearty.

"Over 100 years of home-style cookin'" boasted the small advertisement for the tavern we spotted in the Evansville newspaper the Sunday
afternoon we were passing through. The ad also promised "You won't leave
hungry." When we found our way to Dogtown, we had no problems locating
it. The Dogtown Tavern looks a hundred years old. It lists with age, and it
has been appended with extra rooms and enclosed porches over the years.
Inside, belt-driven ceiling fans spin slowly above gray Formica tables and
vinyl-covered chairs. Next to the bar, on a refrigerator, the chef had taped a
list of the day's pies. In one big dining area, large groups of people surrounded tables and ate their meals family-style, passing food and gabbing
like it was Thanksgiving.

The menu is one-hundred-percent blue-ribbon Americana: plenty of
meat and potatoes, as well as catfish and fried chicken, as well as the
unusual (but locally beloved) specialty, a brain sandwich. Brains are big in
these parts—deep-fried in a golden-batter crust and served on a bun with
pickles and mustard—but we went brainless and focused on the more common menu items. A prime rib dinner was hanging-off-the-plate huge,

juice-dripping luscious, and butter-knife tender . . . albeit a bit bland the way prime rib can often be. A brace of catfish were snappingly seasoned in a fine brittle crust.

Our most vivid taste memories of the Dogtown Tavern are of its side dishes and potatoes. There is terrific cole slaw—tart and vinegar-spiked; sweet cinnamony applesauce; delectable American fried potatoes with onions or, best of all, Kate's potato (Kate is owner Rosie's mother): an enormous spud-in-a-bowl that is chopped up with butter and bits of pickle.

When we polished off a couple of big meals, the waitress advised us that Monday through Thursday were family-style dinner nights, meaning once you sit down, you don't get up until you've eaten your fill of just about everything you want, except the catfish, which is too precious to serve so freely.

FRANK AND MARY'S
21-25 EAST MAIN ST. (STATE ROAD 136), PITTSBORO, IN (317) 892-3485

Since Frank and Mary's Tavern opened for business back in 1945, the specialty of the house has been fried fish. Originally it was codfish, cooked in an iron skillet and served as a sandwich; but in the early 1950s, about the time they moved to the present location, they started serving fresh, natural (not farm-raised) catfish from Florida; and since then catfish, a.k.a. fiddlers, have been Frank and Mary's claim to fame.

You can get whole fish or filleted tenderloins. Either one comes encased in a crackling-crisp crust, nearly a pound's worth per order. Catfish epicures generally consider the whole fish better and more succulent; but for novices, it can be some work to retrieve the meat from the bones. Fillets are easy to eat; and although Frank and Mary's does not offer an all-you-can-eat supply like many Deep South catfish parlors, a dinner's worth won't leave you hungry. According to the extremely informative menu (where we learned the history of the business as well as of Frank and Mary Herring's family), excellent catfish is the kitchen's holy grail. Whenever possible, they continue to serve the natural kind, which are considered tastier, rather than farm-raised fiddlers, although there are occasions when they simply cannot get enough natural ones to meet customers' demands.

Frank and Mary's is one of the nicest places we know to eat catfish, fried chicken, and ribeye steaks with peppermint ice cream for dessert. Service is fast and sociable; accommodations (in a building that used to be an Overland auto dealership) are at long, modest tables in a big old dining room populated mostly by Hendricks County regulars and pilgrims from Indianapolis to the east, who come to Pittsboro because it has become a custom among families who relish down-home cuisine. A word of warning is in order, however: on Friday and Saturday evenings, it can get mighty crowded. Actually, that's the way we like it. There is a special flavor to a big, sweet catfish meal when you sit down to share it with a throng of happy Hoosiers.

GRAY BROTHERS CAFETERIA
555 SOUTH INDIANA ST., MOORESVILLE, IN (317) 831-3345

Gray's Restaurant serves a million customers every year and bakes two thousand pies the day before Thanksgiving. But it is not for magnitude that we recommend this popular restaurant; it is for Hoosier food.

Fried chicken is what nearly everybody comes to eat. It is crisp, nearly greaseless, and expertly seasoned, accompanied, naturally, by mashed potatoes as well as delicious buttered corn kernels and hot blueberry or apple-walnut muffins. If you don't like your chicken fried, plow your fork into a dish of heartwarming chicken and noodles. There is a selection of other entrées including roast beef, meat loaf, etc.; but we have no idea what they taste like because we have never come to Gray's for anything other than the chicken.

After chicken dinner in central Indiana, everybody eats pie. Raspberry, coconut, buttermilk, chocolate, apple, blueberry, and strawberry are almost always available at Gray's.

Despite its size, Gray's is a comfortable kind of place with carpeted dining rooms, displays of antique china and brass, and a big fireplace. On Sunday prepare to wait in line: families from all over the state have made dinner here an afternoon tradition.

HOLLYHOCK HILL
8110 N. COLLEGE AVE., INDIANAPOLIS, IN (317) 251-2294

In 1928, on a quiet street at the northernmost outskirts of Indianapolis, a restaurant named The Country Cottage opened for business, featuring family-style chicken dinners. The city has grown around it and the name was changed to honor the hollyhock bushes on the lawn, but the specialty of the house is still fried chicken dinners.

The great time to experience the character of this place is Sunday, after church. The pastels on the ladies and gentlemen echo the flowery murals in the fairy-tale dining room, which is partitioned with trellises and wrought iron the color of Easter eggs. Tables are draped with linen, and some of the really big ones have lazy Susans in the center so members of big families can spin the wheel and grab what they want.

The meal people come to eat is a ritualized banquet that begins with pleasant enough but unmemorable pickled beets and cottage cheese and iceberg lettuce salad with sweet and sour vinaigrette, then upshifts to unforgettably good chicken. It is pan-fried and mighty-crusted, served with pan gravy. To go with it there are bowls of mashed potatoes, green beans, and kernel corn, as well as hot breads with apple butter. All these trustworthy selections are replenished for as long as anyone at the table wants to keep eating them, but it's only the chicken that makes you want to eat 'til you bust.

Dessert is ingenuous and fun: Make your own sundae. Sauces of butterscotch, crème de menthe, and chocolate are provided, as is Indiana's favorite ice cream—pretty pink peppermint.

LAUGHNER'S

WASHINGTON ST. E. AT I-465, INDIANAPOLIS, IN (317) 356-3388 (THERE ARE SIX OTHER LOCATIONS: CALL 783-2907)

We are smitten. Laughner's makes us swoon. If you like good square meals and civilized cafeteria-style dining, you will love it, too. Here is a restaurant (actually seven restaurants) that after more than a century in business knows exactly how to make customers happy.

First, let's look at the food. It's gorgeous. Overhead lamps shine down on gleaming muffin tins overflowing with swirly buns and rolls; focused lights for close-up carving make the great round of beef glisten, and expose the juice-heavy texture of each pink flap as it is severed from the roast; Jell-O salads seem to glow like oversized gelatinous gems—emeralds, rubies, and sapphires that have magically ingested nuts, carrot or cabbage shreds, raisins, sliced olives, or sweetened coconut.

Part of what makes dining at Laughner's so appetizing is the wait. Every Sunday and many weekday meals, too, chances are you will spend some time slowly inching forward in line before you get to the food. But the proprietors of this place are clever folks. Instead of leading you along some boring corridor, their line doubles back along itself, snaking you right past the food waiting to be chosen. That, friends, is a killer: watching people way ahead of you in line, yet close enough so you could snatch a buttered new potato off their tray, receive plates heaped with turkey and dressing or baked ham and sweet potatoes. The menu is an awesome roster of culinary Americana from Hoosier fried chicken and warm cinnamon buns to a blue-ribbon repertoire of fruit pies, cream pies, custard pies, nutmeat pies, cakes and shortcakes, puddings, and pastry confections.

The Laughner family has gotten cafeteria service to a science since J.W. Laughner started in the restaurant business in 1888. In the early 1900s, J.W. decided to open an efficient kind of eatery at which customers would select their own food from a steam table, carry their trays, and find their own place—either at a marble-topped table or in individual school chairs with side-arm tables. His place was called Laughner's Dairy Lunch, and was one of the first cafeteria-style restaurants in America.

Business has been good these last hundred-odd years. The Laughner family now reigns over seven cafeterias in central Indiana. As cafeterias go, they are the height of elegance: fireplaces, fine draperies, thick carpets, stained-glass windows, Colonial wallpaper and oil paintings, comfortable upholstered chairs. Although it isn't really necessary, many customers dress for dinner at Laughner's: it's that swell.

NOBBY GRILL
213 E. 4TH ST., MARION, IN (317) 662-6029

"They are so giant that they look like a spaceship has just landed on your plate." So began a breathless ode to tenderloin sandwiches we received a few years ago from *Roadfood*er Jill Maidenberg of Madison, Wisconsin. Jill's tribute included not only an elaborate account of the perfect 'loin ("ordered with everything, including pickles"), but detailed illustrations of how to eat one. (They are so large you cannot pick them up in two hands like an ordinary sandwich, so she suggested cutting the breaded pork cutlet in half or folding it over itself inside the bun, then eating the sandwich as a double-decker.)

Her letter concluded with a recommendation—the Nobby Grill in Marion, Indiana, home of "undoubtedly the best tenderloin in Indiana." We allowed her some poetic license, considering she once waited tables at The Nobby; but her enthusiasm was infectious. She wrote, "Being a former Hoosier, I ought to know. They also serve a mean slab of homemade cream pie. Try the butterscotch or banana cream!"

We were on our way. The Nobby was listed in the local phone book on

4th Street, just east of the town square. When we found it, however, the sign outside read "Pyramid Pizza." Oh-oh. Was the Nobby Grill out of business? The mimeographed sheet of paper that served as a menu seemed to list nothing but pizza, submarine sandwiches, and stromboli (the local name for a lovely concoction of sausage meat topped with pizza sauce, onions, peppers, cheese, etc.).

Then we flipped the menu over. And there it was, listed as a House Specialty: "Our Giant Tenderloin—the all-time favorite of the Nobby crowd." We ordered one, and sure enough, a spaceship was soon launched our way from the back of the little luncheonette. The breaded and deep-fried pork cutlet was so large it covered both halves of an opened burger bun. It was a real, hand-breaded cutlet, slim but moist and succulent inside its crusty golden skin. We ate it like a couple of rubes—with knife and fork, then set our sites on those pies that Jill had recommended.

The day's selection included coconut cream, banana cream, butterscotch, strawberry, and a chocolate–peanut butter wonder listed by its brand-name inspiration, Reese's Pieces pie. Each type we sampled was a beaut, but it was the chocolate–peanut butter combo that made us weak-kneed—its velvety chocolate filling swirled with veins of peanut butter, heaped with whipped cream, and dotted with chocolate chips.

We never did get to try the pizza; and we were too distracted by pie to remember to investigate why the Nobby Grill now seems to have an alias, and recently we heard from Jill that the name had reverted to its original, the Nobby Grill. Whatever it is called, we definitely recommend the Nobby, a.k.a. Pyramid Pizza, to all adventurous eaters passing through north central Indiana.

SHAPIRO'S
808 S. MERIDIAN ST., INDIANAPOLIS, IN (317) 631-4041

Funny, Shapiro's doesn't *look* Jewish—at least not like the familiar Jewish delicatessens in New York or Miami or Los Angeles. It looks like a modern midwestern cafeteria-style restaurant, with ample parking outside and a spacious interior dining room with plastic chairs and Formica tables. Instead of the platoon of crabby old Jewish men who traditionally staff deli counters in the East, the servers here are a heterogeneous group of men and women—some young, some black, some rather pleasant.

If we hadn't been tipped off by passionate Shapiro's fans from around the country, we might have driven right past. They told us that despite

Shapiro's modernization into a somewhat anonymous-looking eatery, it is still the finest delicatessen in town, and one of the best in the Midwest. Perhaps even those superlatives are understatements. We would stack Shapiro's corned-beef sandwich against any corned-beef sandwich from anywhere. The meat itself is lean but not too lean—succulent enough so each rosy slice, rimmed with a thin halo of smudgy spice, glistens underneath the fluorescent lights of the dining room. The butter-tender slices are piled high and heavy inside extra-thick slabs of rye bread with a shiny, hard, sour crust that encases a tan interior redolent of yeast and rye flour pungency. Slather on the mustard, crunch into a dill pickle to set your tastebuds tingling, and this sandwich will take you straight to deli heaven.

Get some latkes (potato pancakes), too. They are double-thick, moist, and starchy: great companions to a hot lunch of short ribs or stuffed peppers; Shapiro's supplements ordinary latkes with cinnamon-scented ones—wonderful when heaped with sour cream. And soup: bean, lentil, split pea, and chowder are daily specials; you can always order chicken soup with rice or with matzoh balls.

Shapiro's serves breakfast every morning, including classic platters of bagels and lox with cream cheese, onions, tomatoes, and olives; also salami omelettes, fried matzoh, cold corn flakes, and hot oatmeal. Even after breakfast, desserts here are mighty fine. We like a gigantic slice of cheesecake with a cup of coffee; but if you want an end for your meal that is more midwestern than Jewish, Shapiro's peanut butter pie is grand.

PHIL SMIDT & SON
1205 CALUMET AVE., HAMMOND, IN (219) 659-0025; IN CHICAGO: (312) 768-6686

Enter the Rose Room at Phil Smidt's and you have left normal proportion behind. It is a cloister with sensuously curved seats of wood and red leather. Light filters in through glass bricks, surrealizing movement in the hallway on the other side. Smoked mirrors don't reflect so much as they refract the room. The walls are rose-colored, except for the luminous black one, an eight-foot Phil Smidt version of an Ad Reinhardt painting, overlaid with a towering image of a pink rose in full flower. Napkins are pink, white tablecloths are edged in pink. Water glasses are etched with pink and black letters and a rose. Waitresses in black nylon uniforms (an exact match for the glossy background of the rose mural) all wear stickpin name tags, festooned with rhinestones that glitter back the staggering pink and black decor. Smidt's high style is reflected by the clientele—an interesting mixture of foodies, hairy-chested honchos with Guccione-style jewelry, and suburban ladies with the latest fashions in fingernail art.

Aside from the majesty of the place and its opportunity to people-watch, the reason you want to come to Smidt's is perch, pan-fried, the formal name for which is "a mess of perch" (usagistically similar to a "bucket of chicken" or a "brick of Velveeta"). They sell it whole, boned, buttered, or boned and buttered. Old-timers do their own boning and make it look easy. The rest of us get fillets, swimming in butter. They are small sides of fish, pan-crisped, firm, freshwater luscious. Plates of perch are preceded by five relish trays, lined up in formation on the table: potato salad, kidney bean marinade, pickled beets, slaw, and cottage cheese. Custom demands unlimited supplies of everything: more relish when a bowl is empty; more perch until you've had your fill.

This is the definitive meal of the Calumet region southeast of Chicago. It goes back three-quarters of a century, when Hammond was a vacation spot for waterfowlers and fishermen, and Phil Smidt's was a tavern where customers brought their own local catch: perch, pike, and frog's legs. A lot has changed since then: as Hammond pumped iron, Smidt's glamorized.

So if we tell you that this restaurant is "on the lake," understand that Hammond, Indiana, home of American Steel Foundries and Federated Metals, is not exactly a beach resort any more. From the bar at Phil Smidt's, the view is not of water, but of an even more midwestern tableau, stunning at nightfall: the railroad right-of-way, and rolling stock heading west.

VILLAGE INN
104 S. MAIN ST., MIDDLEBURY, IN (219) 825-2043

You may have some trouble finding a place to park in the lot next to the Village Inn. At mealtime, many of the spaces will be taken up by somber black buggies and the horses that pull them. The town of Middlebury is where local Amish farmers come to shop for dry goods and hardware. When it is time to eat, they crowd into a town lunchroom called the Village Inn for plowman's meals served mostly by Mennonite girls in organdy caps.

How about a huge plate of cornmeal mush, accompanied by head cheese, for breakfast? There are ordinary egg breakfasts, too, but even they seem twice as hearty as anything you would get in an ordinary diner. Lunches are even bigger: chicken and noodles or meat loaf or beef stew and mashed potatoes, smothered steaks and stuffed peppers, all served with plenty of richly dressed slaws and salads and well-cooked vegetables enriched with bread crumbs, butter, and cheese.

You cannot say you have truly partaken of this monumental heartland cuisine unless you follow breakfast, lunch, or dinner by a piece or two of pie. Pies are the decisive Amish food—rich, sweet, calorific, and always available in abundance. They offer at least a dozen different kinds every day at The Village Inn, including blueberry (from locally picked berries), lattice-topped raisin, and the pie known among Indiana farm folks as O.F., meaning "old fashioned": little more than sugar, eggs, and cream, whipped into a jiggly custard perched atop a flaky pastry crust. Whole pies can be ordered in advance, to go.

VOGEL'S
1250 INDIANAPOLIS BLVD., WHITING, IN (219) 659-1250

Vogel's dwarfs all other restaurants. Compared to it, the Pool Room at the Four Seasons is a mere puddle. When you enter the lobby, you want binoculars to see the dual bouffanted hostesses, waiting at the other side. To their right, you spot a stuffed grizzly bear, then among Polynesian jutting rocks, a menagerie of exotic animal heads and heavily impastoed paintings of reclining nudes. Once you journey to a proprietress's pulpit, she may try to seat you in the lounge, a relatively ordinary room for newcomers and blasé Hammondites. Wrong! You want The Crown Room.

The Crown Room is an indoor stadium with a domed ceiling. From heaven above hang octopus-armed chandeliers that occasionally flicker and dim—a reminder of the heavy power conductors that buzz outside serving the factories and mills that surround Vogel's. Windows, swathed in scarlet drapes, allow no light in. The eating hall is scattered with what the hostess calls booths, but which are, in fact, free-standing banquettes, each large enough for two giants, aligned at a table opposite two broad chairs. Upholstery is monstrous orange Naugahyde, even more jarring against the green vinyl brocade wallpaper and green brindle rug.

Start your meal with a cocktail; that's what most of Vogel's regulars seem to do, and there is a lovely rendering of a martini on the sign outside. In this dizzyingly outré establishment, though, we prefer something more drastically out of fashion: a Manhattan, extra-sweet with four maraschino cherries. Now, here comes the food, which is the ritualized perch dinner that has put northern Indiana on the *Roadfood* map. It begins with five trays of relish—pickled beets, cole slaw, potato salad, cottage cheese, and bean salad. Then you are brought a pan of boned and buttered perch, nine dainty fillets to an order, their skin crisp from the frying pan, their flesh firm and sweet. If you eat all of them, more will be brought to you.

There are other things to eat at Vogel's, and we are sometimes tempted by the monumentality of the steaks, chops, and surf 'n' turf platters we watch carried past our table to other diners. But to be honest, the perch is so good that we have never ordered anything else.

WOLF'S BAR-B-Q
6600 FIRST AVE., EVANSVILLE, IN (812) 424-8891

Nowhere in America is barbecue terminology more esoteric and precise than around Evansville, Indiana, which is one of about half a dozen cities that claim to be the barbecue capital of the country. When you come to Wolf's or its former rival, Mac's (now a branch of Wolf's), you'd better know if you want beef pit or beef and sauce, pork pit or pork and sauce. At least you don't have to know about soaks, because they don't sell soaks at Wolf's (but they do at Porky's at 6224 Booneville Highway).

Now, pay attention: Soaks are similar to what Kansas Citians know as brownies. They are shreds, scraps, ends, chunks, and odd-lot pieces of meat that are heaped together and simmered in sauce. Similar to soaks, but less sloppy, are the items Wolf's calls beef sauce and pork sauce. For these, the meat of choice is precut and long-simmered in sauce until the meat and sauce are nearly indistinguishable. It's like barbecue bouillon, meat and sauce reduced to a saturated essence. Beef pit or pork pit refers to meat that is sliced when you order it, and only then brushed with sauce. Whereas the already-sauced stuff verges on flavor overdose, beef pit and pork pit are by comparison almost elegant, and have a certain discreet poise that allows you to actually savor the taste of the fire that has seared the meat.

Wolf's serves barbecue according to exacting procedures shared by many pits of the southern Midwest and adjacent parts of Kentucky. When you order a "plate," beef or pork, sauce or pit, you get your meat of choice along with the most peculiar slices of bread, which are vaguely tan and precisely square, known as rye but actually every bit as bland—and suitable for barbecue-mopping—as Wonder. You also get pickle, onion, and a bag of chips.

YODER POPCORN SHOP
COUNTY ROAD 200S, TOPEKA, IN (219) 768-4051

If you are a serious popcorn aficionado, we recommend a visit to Elkhart and LaGrange counties in northern Indiana, an area known as "Heritage Country," where they grow some of America's best popping corn. It is great country to travel through, past Amish farms, herds of dairy cows, work horses pulling plows, on roads you share with people steering horses-and-buggies. There is good eating (pies especially) to be done in many of the local cafes; but for popcorn in all its glory you've got to head south out of Middlebury toward Honeyville. Just off County Road 200S, you will see a sign for the Yoder Popcorn Shop.

It is hardly a store, at least not like a store one would find in a town. It is a small room in the back of a popcorn farm—down the gravel driveway, past black Amish garments flapping on a clothesline, toward the corn cribs and barn.

A hot corny aroma perfumes the room. Before you have a chance to look around the pint-size office, the girl behind the counter looks up from her ledger book (her records are kept in longhand) and offers a small bag of freshly popped corn. Now, browse among the inventory of popcorn-related items: poppers, oils, and special salts, plus peanut brittle and locally put-up pumpkin butter.

For the connoisseur, Yoder's sells several varieties of popping corn. Of course there are white or yellow kernels, but have you ever seen *black* popcorn? Here it is, called "black jewel," a strange genetic mutation that doesn't really taste different, but sure looks odd. The cream of the popcorn crop is what Yoder labels "T.T." corn, meaning "tiny tender" kernels from the tip of the ear. These little pearls pop into an elegant, featherweight snack almost (but not quite) too fragile for gobs of butter.

ZAHARAKO'S
329 WASHINGTON ST., COLUMBUS, IN (812) 379-9329

Zaharako's is a gastronomic treasure: a working soda fountain where they still know how to concoct a Green River, a black cow, and a double chocolate malt.

It opened as a confectionery in 1900. Five years later, the Zaharako brothers brought back a couple of soda fountains from the St. Louis Exposition. The fountains were ornate fixtures, set into a backbar of solid mahogany, Italian marble, and onyx pillars. The Zaharakos installed a counter of Mexican and Italian marble, and a Tiffany lamp on an onyx stand. Today, everything looks as it did back then, but haloed with a fine patina of age. It is a dazzling experience to walk into Zaharako's for the first time and confront the gleaming silver and polished wood in the front room, or to continue beyond the fountain, through the trellised wood divider, toward the tables in the back room, surrounded by walls covered entirely with mirrors.

At the back of the back room is the most spectacular of Zaharako's antiques: a full concert German pipe organ, purchased in 1905. It features 185 pipes and complete orchestration: trumpets, bass drum, snare drum, cymbals, flutes, and a triangle. The organ is played like a player piano, with punched paper rolls, each five to ten minutes long. It still works perfectly, providing Gay-Nineties background music for sipping sodas and eating sandwiches.

The menu at Zaharako's is limited to soda fountain specialties and sandwiches. The only cooking utensil in evidence, other than the mixological instruments, is a small grill. It is used for making grilled cheese sandwiches and a unique item listed on the board above the serving area as a cheese-br-ger. If you guess a cheese-br-ger is like a cheeseburger, you'd be almost correct. But there is a difference. A cheese-br-ger is made with meat sauce instead of a meat patty; the sauce, along with a nice slab of Velveeta cheese, gets grilled inside two slices of white bread instead of a bun. The secret of its goodness is the spice in the sauce—a Greek-accented combination of sweet and hot reminiscent of Cincinnati five-way chili.

A cheese-br-gr and a black cow in an ancient wooden booth, serenaded by John Philip Sousa: what could be more deliciously, midwesternly American?

IOWA

ANCHOR INN
610 HARTFORD ST., FARRAGUT, IA (712) 385-8333
(OPEN ONLY FOR NOONTIME MEALS MOST DAYS.)

When we tell you the cinnamon buns Emily Bengtsen bakes are big—
hot, yeasty swirls veined with cinnamon sugar and dripping white
sugar glaze—please try to imagine them, then quadruple the size you have
imagined. These buns are giants approximately six inches square and four
inches high, and they are delectable. Ms. Bengtsen, whom most of the customers of her Anchor Inn know as Emmy, explained their secret as we sat
at a table and tore into a couple of hot ones: "Potato water with all those
nice potato goodies from the bottom of the pot." Potato water—water in
which potatoes have been boiled—rather than plain warm water gives
Emmy's buns a softness and flavor that make them, in our cinnamon-bun-
eating experience, the best in Iowa—a state where cinnamon buns reign as
the supreme bakery treat.

Emmy has plenty of potato water available because she and her small
kitchen staff peel, boil, and mash lots of potatoes. Most of the plate lunches
Emmy serves come sided with potatoes—honest mashed ones, usually
smothered with good brown gravy. Spud-lovers like ourselves could make a
meal of them. And, oh boy, what a fine chicken-fried steak Emmy makes:

crisp-crusted, tender enough inside to be a pleasant chew, but with real beef flavor that overly tenderized meat never has. Emmy is proud of her steaks' girth; and during dinner she called across the big, open dining room to a man who had ordered—and eaten—two of them. He was an Iowan who had spent some time in Texas, which is famous for chicken-fried steaks. "Ever have one this big down there in Texas?" Emmy asked. With a mouth too full of pie to speak, the man gleefully shook his head to indicate no, then later stopped by our table to offer witness to the excellence of Emmy's food.

Also on the daily menu—which is a blackboard posted on the wall for all to see—were Polish sausage and sauerkraut and roast beef dinners. There aren't a lot of entrées from which to choose, but what is there is real farm cooking: fried chicken, meat loaf, ham loaf, chicken 'n' biscuits. Alongside come vegetables—vegetables from a vegetable garden, cooked and bathed in butter. We had carrots, and darned if they weren't some of the tastiest we ever ate.

Cinnamon rolls cost a dollar apiece; we saw people coming in to Emmy's (which is generally open only for the midday meal, known hereabouts as dinner) for cinnamon buns to take home or to their place of business. With dinner you get a different kind of superb bread: yeast rolls. These are golden-topped beauties baked in a pan, soft enough to serve as a mop for gravy.

Emmy apologized for her pies. Because she knew we were easterners, she assumed we were sissy nutrition fanatics and therefore figured we liked modern-style pie crusts made with vegetable shortening. "These are made with pure, old-fashioned lard," she admitted. Praise be, they were; and they were as elegantly flaky and fine as only a true, old-fashioned, farmhouse pie crust can be. Some were double-crusters, some were piled high with cream or custard. They were inelegant pies, and blueberries or apples cascaded from within the crusts, and even the custard wanted to ooze out onto its plate as soon as it was touched by a gentle fork. Our favorites were the custards, especially those topped with sugar-crusted meringues. Sheer blue-ribbon heaven!

Put the Anchor Inn on your Iowa itinerary. It's a small-town cafe beloved by folks from miles around, and a treasure for any traveler in search of heartland square meals.

THE CANDY KITCHEN
CEDAR ST., WILTON, IA (319) 732-2278

F *iz Biz,* the quarterly journal of the National Association of Soda Jerks, recently noted that although Gus Napolous opened the Candy Kitchen in Wilton in 1910, town records indicated that there has been a soda fountain on the spot since the mid-1880s, which makes this place "a strong contender for one of the nation's oldest existing soda fountains."

They don't hand-make candy as they once did, and the egg malted milk is no longer on the menu as a morning special for those who didn't have time for breakfast, but the Napolous family continues to serve ice cream treats as it has for over eighty years. Their customers include not only people from Wilton and surrounding towns and serious devotées of sugar-sweet mixology, but widening numbers of regular highway travelers and vacationers who have staked out The Candy Kitchen as one of I-80's handy treasures.

There are a few modern boinging games to play inside, and an unaffected menu of cold cut and tuna salad sandwiches ("no greasy stuff," a waitress assured us), but it's the old-fashioned things that make a visit worthwhile. The soda jerks here can make a green river (lemon and lime syrup, sugar, and soda water over ice), a brown Jersey (ice cream and syrup sprinkled with malt powder), and a black cow (vanilla ice cream floated in root beer), as well as all the traditional sundaes, sodas, splits, fizzes, malts, shakes, and dipsy doodles. No backwards-streaking time machine could be more effective.

COFFEE CUP CAFE
SULLY, IA (515) 594-3765

T he clock and the coat hooks are shaped like coffee cups, and it seems to be a popular morning ritual in the town of Sully to linger over a few morning cups in this small cafe on the square. For travelers, it is a comfy place to sit, eat, listen, and observe as village life passes by.

Breakfast on banana bread or warm pecan rolls or featherweight pancakes with peppery homemade sausage. Have lunch of meat loaf and potatoes along with the house special "Dutch lettuce" (iceberg lettuce salad topped with a hot mustard and celery seed dressing, then sprinkled with bits of hard-boiled egg and bacon). Or come Friday night for pizza made from scratch. Pie is the thing to eat for dessert, preferably rhubarb: made on the premises and loaded into a flaky crust, heaped with whipped cream.

What we like best about the Coffee Cup is the way customers at different tables talk to each other, and easily bring strangers into conversations. The first time we visited, we had a discussion with owner Linda Zylstra, the town postman, and a few other assorted locals about the correct address of the Coffee Cup. None of them knew if it had a street address, not even the postman. In a town like Sully, they explained, numbered addresses weren't needed. "Just say 'on the square,'" Linda advised.

DERBY RESTAURANT
MAIN ST., DERBY, IOWA (NO PHONE; SMORGASBORD MEALS ARE THURSDAY AT NOON AND 6:00 P.M., AND SATURDAY AT NOON. MON., TUES., AND WEDS. THE RESTAURANT IS OPEN 6:00 A.M.–2:30 P.M., FRI. AND SAT., 11:00 A.M.–2:30 P.M.)

There is no sign outside, but it is easy to find the Derby Restaurant once you find Derby, Iowa. Of the three buildings in town, it is the one that is not the Derby Opera House and not the Derby Post Office. When we first opened the door of the Derby Restaurant, we were rendered speechless. Before us stretched a scene that we can only describe as the *Roadfood*er's gastronomic holy grail.

In contrast to the street outside, the restaurant was noisy, even boisterous. There were big tables up front, shared by six or eight or ten—mothers, children, grannies, spinsters, farmers in overalls. Toward the back, there was more seating at long counters that faced each other across the wide, wood-floored room. And there was the food, all laid out in Tupperware bowls, electric skillets, pie plates, Pyrex casseroles, and crock pots. The way it works is this: you pay five dollars, grab a plate, then help yourself.

The food is farm-wife cooking: a happy hodgepodge of freshly baked breads, sweet rolls, and coffee cakes alongside pastel Jell-O molds and homey casseroles, vegetables galore, *real* mashed potatoes, four kinds of pie and a couple of cobblers, all anchored by serious main courses of baked chicken, ham, and roast beef.

It is hard to describe the ambience of the Derby Restaurant, because it is like no place else. The best thing about it is its mess hall high spirits. Most conversations stretch from table to table, and across the counters. It's like a town meeting, at which everybody knows everybody. And if you are a stranger, as we were, they'll be curious.

"Where're you from?" one farmer asked across two counters.

"Connecticut," we answered.

"It's a long way to come for a meal," the man's wife commented, with a large forkful of peanut butter pie on the way from her plate to her mouth.

"Yup," a nearby man said, laughing as he watched the farmer's wife eat the pie with gusto. "But it sure is worth it!"

As for local color, there is plenty: pictures of the Derby High School graduating class of 1937; jars and jugs, baskets and knickknacks that are old, but not quite antique; calendars of yesteryear; slow-spinning fans overhead. No inventory of decor or list of menu items, however, could possibly convey the sense of community and goodwill imparted by a meal in this singular restaurant.

GREEN GABLES
1800 PIERCE ST., SIOUX CITY, IA (712) 258-4246

Green Gables is a genial place; most of the customers at dinner are family groups, and nearly everyone seems to know everyone else. For strangers and travelers heading west, it provides a friendly dining experience that will last a thousand miles.

On Saturday night you might have to wait for a table. This place is that popular among the locals; it has been a Sioux City favorite since it opened a little over sixty years ago. The dining room is casual but polite, brightly lit, and decorated with an illuminated mural of Sioux City on one wall. Study the menu, which is mimeographed daily on green paper, then write your own order on the small pad provided. Food arrives at tables on rolling carts pushed from the kitchen by the staff of uniformed waitresses.

Steaks or chops seem to be the people's choice: ribeyes, T-bones, sirloins, pork chops, or lamb chops. There are good slabs of ham; and barbecued ribs, infused with the taste of hickory wood, are delicious. So is Chicken in the Gables, which is half a crusty-fried bird served surrounded by French fries, rolls, and slaw. They also serve nice fillet of walleyed pike, simply broiled with tartar sauce on the side.

Our favorite meal was "Oriental chicken chow mein," which was a mountainous serving of stir-fried and cornstarch-thickened vegetables atop a bed of crisp noodles, topped with shreds of well-salted chicken and strips of egg. It was not like any chow mein we have eaten in a Chinese restaurant, but we liked it: it was real Chinese-American food, with an emphasis on the American flavors and presentation. On the side, we drank lemonade—made with the juice of real lemons and sugar, decorated with half a maraschino cherry, and served with a flexible straw. Meals were preceded by a basket of dark and white rolls that arrived under a layer of plastic wrap. The price of dinner also included a demure square of marble cake; or you can buy a wedge from one of the day's pies, or a piece of cheesecake or bowl of Jell-O with whipped cream; but we had better things on our minds for dessert.

By the time our plates were cleared, we were ogling the back of the Green Gables menu, where we had found an irresistible roster of soda fountain specialties: sundaes, sodas, and malts of every variety, including peppermint ice cream hot fudge sundaes served with their fudge sauce on the side, in a small, serve-yourself pitcher. The top-of-the-line treats get deluxe names, like "The H-Bomb" (an extra-plush soda), the Harem Share'm (a flaming extravaganza made with three kinds of ice cream and chocolate syrup), and the Goshawful Gooey (vanilla ice cream, orange sherbet, and marshmallow sauce). Give us a restaurant where they serve lemonade with a flexible straw and Goshawful Gooeys for dessert, and we are devotées for life.

GROVE CAFE
124 MAIN ST., AMES, IA (515) 232-9784

John Stanford, an Iowan who clued us in to the Grove Cafe back in the mid-eighties, noted a sign on the wall announcing, "The Grove Cafe. Just Like Home—You Don't Always Get What You Want." That may be true, but this place comes pretty darn close to exactly what a lot of travelers seek in the way of heartland eating places.

When we walked in the first time, it was noon on a weekday and nearly every booth and table were occupied by a diverse clientele of gents in overalls, white-collar businessmen with ties, ladies in white pumps and pantyhose, and even a few double-dome types from the university. Ames isn't exactly a small town (at least not compared to the *really* small towns of the Corn Belt), but this place near the train tracks had the unmistakable feel of a village cafe, mostly because it seemed as though everybody felt free to share in the same communal conversation, in this case about the lousy officiating at a recent Cyclones basketball game.

We ate meat loaf: hunky slabs, coarse-ground and well-seasoned, accompanied by heaps of mashed potatoes and gravy. Then we had chocolate cream pie for dessert. Other than ice cream with chocolate or strawberry sauce, it was the only dessert available (Jim, the chef, hadn't made a fruit pie today, his wife, the waitress, apologized); but it was just about perfect.

Next time through Ames, we came to the Grove for breakfast; and we discovered pancakes that were beyond mere perfection. It was Saturday, mid-morning, and we had to wait for a table. It was a long wait because once someone secures a place here on Saturday, they might hold forth for hours, guzzling coffee and visiting with friends who come and go at their own or adjacent tables. Nearly everyone in the cafe was eating pancakes. Gorgeous pancakes: tawny, pumpkin-colored ones as big as a plate, available singly, as a short stack (two) or a full stack (three). They were delicious; and they are Jim's specialty, made not only as big circles for adults, but in a festive shape *du jour* (it changes each Saturday) for children.

Our tipster Mr. Stanford described the Grove Cafe as "a taste of Americana I wouldn't trade for the fanciest restaurant anywhere." Nor would we.

HAMBURG INN NO. 2
214 LINN ST., IOWA CITY, IA (319) 337-5512

The sign outside Hamburg Inn No. 2 (No. 1 is defunct) says "Hamburgers—Chicken." The hamburgers are served every day, and they are made at least a dozen ways, on buns and off. Last time through Iowa City, we enjoyed a bunless mushroomburger accompanied by mashed potatoes and a hearty bowl of vegetable beef barley soup. Usually, we like our burgers here on buns, with a pile of grilled onions. As for the chicken part of the repertoire, the prime day for that is Sunday, when it seems like half of Iowa wants to crowd into this little snack shack for chicken dinners with all the fixin's. ("Please share booths during rush hour," a sign advises.)

Most of what is served at the counter and the booths is satisfying plate-lunch food: broad grilled cheese and bacon sandwiches, catfish dinners, ham steak with scalloped potatoes. But the really great meal to know about isn't plate lunch or chicken or hamburgers. It is breakfast, served all day: pancakes, omelettes galore, and splendid "American fried" potatoes to accompany eggs. It's the spuds that we like best about Hamburg Inn No. 2—a chunky pile of them fried with enough grease so they darken and turn brittle on their edges as they suck in character and flavor from a grill that has been aging deliciously for some forty years now.

LOVING SPOONFUL CAFE
502 W. BURLINGTON, FAIRFIELD, IA (515)472-4613

The name has changed, but the tenderloin is still a giant one. Years back, we had been sent to the K.C. Cafe of Fairfield with a recommendation by former midwesterner Sylvia Carter, who said the tenderloins in this roadside diner were among the pick of the field in a state that thinks about tenderloins as lovingly as northern Michiganders think about their pasties. We came, we ate, and we were conquered by a breaded and fried, pounded-thin slab of pig meat that was indeed giant (although not grotesquely so), crusty gold, sweet and moist, served on a bun with lettuce, tomato, and Russian dressing, sided by a cup of bright yellow mustard. It was a beaut, and delicious.

When we came back for seconds, we were nervous to see that the K.C. had become the Loving Spoonful, but relieved when we sank our teeth into a nearly identical giant loin on a bun. It's still among the best of the Midwest. If the idea of a giant one is daunting, you may want to consider the Loving Spoonful's pork fritters, which are essentially a downsized version of the big boy. Not much else about this old-fashioned roadside hash house has been changed. They still make a swell colossal cinnamon bun for breakfast in the morning; and although they had sold out of our favorite pickle-pea-cheese salad the afternoon we stopped by, they did have some other fine ultra-luxurious salads on the menu, including an especially good ham salad, as well as cauliflower salad and a creamy five-cup ambrosia.

In addition to blue-ribbon pies that were always part of the dessert repertoire (cherry, rhubarb, pecan, etc.), the waitress offered us a special that she called by its brand name, "Jell-O cake," but which we recognized by its moistness and sweetness as none other than the Jell-O chef's delight, poke cake, for which just-mixed gelatin is infused into a cooked cake and set, creating a colorful appearance and squishy texture that few Cordon Bleu pastry chefs could ever hope to match.

PANTRY CAFE
CENTRAL AVE. & 1ST ST., NE, LEMARS, IA (712) 546-6800

Of all the good ways to start the day around the country, none are quite as awesome as Iowa's. Even before dawn in cafes all across the state, bakers start pulling freshly baked cinnamon buns from the oven. Sweet, sticky morning rolls are popular coast to coast, but nowhere else do customers expect them to be as shockingly huge as they are at places like the Anchor Inn in Farragut, Mary's Cafe in Casey, and the Pantry of LeMars. Pantry "sticky rolls," hot from the oven every morning, are a full four inches across and two inches tall—puffy clouds of sweet, yeast-risen dough infused with a buttery syrup of cinnamon and sugar. They are a meal unto themselves (unless you cannot resist the Pantry's excellent, downy-textured pancakes with sausage links), and a genuine taste of true Iowa cookery.

Lunch is the real thing, too: pork chops and potatoes (baked, broasted, hash browns, or French fries), grilled pork chops on toast, brittle but juicy fried pork tenderloins on plate or sandwich. Pork is number one, but it isn't the only thing on the menu. We have eaten swoonfully tender baked chicken with dressing as well as a tasty and delightfully outré deviled egg sandwich. One curious item on the menu one day that we didn't sample: "prime rim dinner." For dessert, of course, there is pie and plenty of it—about half a dozen kinds every day, each cut into jumbo slabs as is the Iowa custom.

The Pantry's booths are ancient wood, each provided with a diamond-shaped mirror on the wall; the woodgrain tables are edged with silver bands; the floor is a lovely retro-chic pattern of tiny six-sided black-and-white tiles. It is a nostalgic eatery, like a set from a movie about a midwestern childhood long ago.

PENN PHARMACY
SIDNEY, IA (712) 374-2513

The last report we got from Evelyn Birkby, our midlands cinnamon roll and pork chop tipster, about the Penn Pharmacy on the main street of Sidney was that a team of inspectors from the National Association of Soda Jerks had been through town and proclaimed it to be Iowa's oldest. Small towns throughout the Midwest used to have neighborhood shops like this one, which was founded in 1863 by John Newton Penn of Pennsylvania—places where you could come not only to fill prescriptions, but also to buy school supplies, stationery, and other sundries, and to sit at the counter or at a table and sip a soda or eat a sandwich in the company of other townsfolk.

Many of these friendly places have closed in recent years, but Penn's is thriving. A while ago we were there on a Tuesday morning, just about dinner time (as the midday meal is known). There wasn't a free seat at the twelve-stool counter, and all three tables in back were occupied. The men and women of Sidney and environs were here for such familiar lunch-counter fare as peanut butter sandwiches (ninety cents), ham on whole wheat, liverwurst, and the top-of-the-line meal, a chicken salad sandwich, which sells for all of $1.80. One thing we especially liked about our meal here was that nearly everyone in the place participated in the same, communal conversation—on this occasion about the recent heavy rains. It wasn't required to join, and there were a few folks eating silently; but it seemed natural to chat from table to table; and even strangers like ourselves were soon drawn into the neighborly discussion.

Most regular customers sipped coffee at the end of their meal; but for *Roadfood* fanciers, the true pleasure of a visit to Penn's—in addition to its friendliness and historical importance—is ice cream: a simple dishful with chocolate syrup, a giant-size sundae topped with whipped cream and chopped nuts, a banana boat, or best of all, an ice cream soda, which the mixologists in this place can make in nearly as many colors as there are in a good-size pack of Crayola crayons. The soda is served in a tall, broad-mouthed, fluted glass, crowned with a scoop of ice cream and a billow of whipped cream and a bright red cherry. It comes with a straw and a spoon. It is *good*—all the better for the casual charms of the pharmacy dining area. One more thing: if you come to Penn's on your birthday, and you can prove it is your birthday, you will receive an ice cream soda on the house.

STONE'S
507 S. THIRD AVE., MARSHALLTOWN, IA (515) 753-3626

Stone's has been a way station for hungry travelers since 1887, when it first became known among crews on passing steam trains for its roast beef sandwiches and double-size wedges of pie. According to *Midwest Living* magazine, which recently honored Stone's for its lemon chiffon pie (which is now *more* than double-size), the canteen had a slight change of character back in the 1930s when it went from a lunchroom known for jiffy meals to a polite restaurant that served family-style food. That is what it has been ever since.

Sunday is the great day to dine here, either at an oilcloth-covered table in one of the carpeted dining rooms (we especially like the one with the floral display in the wall niche) or at the U-shaped counter in the smaller front room, under a tin ceiling and slowly spinning fans. Sunday is buffet day in this vintage eatery, when your roast beef and baked ham are cut on a board while you watch; then you pile on plenty of all-you-can-eat accompaniments including breads and potatoes and a selection from a truly resplendent salad bar (marinated vegetables, pasta salads, bean salads, relishes, slaws, pickles, ambrosias, etc.); then after that, you choose your pie. There are lots of different cream pies available, also grasshopper pie and an admirable ice cream-caramel-fudge turtle pie, but the house specialty is the illustrious mile-high, fluff-topped (genuine!) lemon chiffon.

Don't worry if you cannot come to eat on Sunday. They always have their pies; and every day there are homespun and tasty specials, ranging from truly recherché ("tender young beef heart" is a regular menu item) to merely eccentric (the Robert E. Lee sandwich of chicken, bacon, and olives on homemade rye, with white sauce on the side—named because the bacon and olives are arranged to look like the Confederate Stars and Bars). Meals come with terrific fresh cole slaw and warm, aromatic cornbread and dinner rolls.

Monday is our favorite weekday at Stone's; that is when they make chicken and noodles and meat loaf and rivel soup (broth with tiny dumplings known as rivels). We've never eaten Tuesday's ham and scalloped potatoes or Wednesday's chicken casserole, but we have feasted royally on Friday's beef and homemade noodles, as well as on Thursday's roast loin of pork with dressing. While any day is a fine time to eat at Stone's, we do recommend an evening meal rather than lunch. Here in Marshalltown, the salad bar comes out only at night.

WHITE WAY
8TH AVENUE (ROUTE 6), DURANT, IA (319) 785-6202

H ere are three good reasons to eat at the White Way: pork, salad, and pie.

First, pork: there are grilled chops, smoked chops, and "Iowa" chops. Iowans give their state name to pork chops that are cut double-thick. At the White Way these meat mounds are baked and smothered in mushroom gravy that is nothing but canned mushroom soup. But please, don't be a food snob. The soup is a great complement for the pillows of pork, which are more tender than pot roast, sweet, juicy, and unpardonably luxurious. Other good kinds of pork: country sausage, grilled ham, sauce-crusted barbecued ribs, braised ribs. The one sorrowful caveat we must add is that the mashed potatoes, made from powder, are second-rate.

Salad: Here is a memorable lesson in true Midwestern cuisine, not the dolled-up facsimile thereof sometimes sold in expensive city restaurants. White Way proprietor Carroll Marshall gets his salad recipes from his mother and from locally printed, spiral-bound cookbooks published by PTAs and church groups. (He told Susan Puckett, author of *A Cook's Tour of Iowa,* that he likes Catholic church cookbooks best because their recipes, designed for larger families, are easiest to adapt to restaurant sizes.) All the salads are prepared in the kitchen and marshaled at a salad bar in the White Way dining room—about a dozen different bowls buried up to their rims in shaved ice. Among the splendors we have eaten from this bar are pickly pea, egg, and cheese salad (an Iowa favorite), cauliflower pea salad, beef-and-bean taco salad, sweet and sour cucumbers, clove-tinged pickled beets, carrot-raisin slaw, three-bean salad, sweet-dressed spinach, dizzying pineapple-marshmallow-Cool Whip ambrosia (known as White Fluff), pink and sweet rice salad, and ordinary iceberg lettuce topped with extraordinary celery seed dressing. Among the salads you will also find bowls of chocolate pudding, cheddar cheese spread, and pork spread. And to the side is a soup bar which, we must confess, we have never had the inclination to sample.

Now, pie. It was pie that first led us here—a tip from a cross-country trucker who said he never went through Iowa without fortifying himself with a piece of sour cream raisin pie at the White Way. Back then, Carroll Marshall's mother was the pie chef. Since her death, Mr. Marshall has continued the tradition, mastering her recipes and maintaining his cafe as a pie-lover's mecca of the Midwest. Made with fruit or custard, double-crusted, lattice-topped, or crowned with meringue, his are mammoth beauties, baked in deep crusts and served in half-pound pieces. The sour cream raisin is a thick, ultrasweet mound of pabulum for mainline pie junkies only; there are somewhat more demure meringue-topped wonders—coconut, banana, etc.; and even the pecan pie we sampled last time through was mighty good. A word to the wise: order your pie at the beginning of the meal; the kitchen frequently runs out of its most popular varieties.

The White Way opened in 1967 before Interstate 80 was complete. It was named after Route 6, which used to be known as the Great White Way through the heartland.

KANSAS

BROOKVILLE HOTEL
BROOKVILLE, KS (913) 225-6666

People drive for hours, from as far away as Wichita and Kansas City, to eat supper or their midday Sunday meal at the Brookville Hotel, which has been serving celebration-size banquets in the Kansas prairie since 1897, when Brookville was the roundhouse town for the Central Pacific Rail Line. The town is now pretty quiet except for the hotel and a few general stores with antiques for tourists and provisions for locals; but on weekends the sidewalks are crowded with people: hungry ones about to eat and sated ones walking off their feast.

The meal everyone comes for is fried chicken—*skillet-fried* chicken, which is the only right way to do it here in the middle of America, where connoisseurs of this all-important subject look upon buckets of franchised, pressure-fried chicken with about as much appetite as they would muster for a bucket of live bait. Frying chicken in hot oil (preferably at least half lard) in a heavy skillet gives it a brittle, golden skin and allows the meat inside to stay drippingly luscious and radiant with natural chicken flavor. At the Brookville Hotel, they serve this country classic by the platter; and guests eat it at tables set with Blue Willow china.

The fancy old Victorian dining room is crowded every Sunday with happy eaters passing and grabbing serving platters piled high with mashed potatoes (sadly, not made from scratch), creamed corn, baking powder biscuits with whipped butter and strawberry preserves, sweet-and-sour cole slaw, and cottage cheese, plus plenty of gravy to ladle on the chicken and potatoes. It's an eat-'til-you-drop affair: Whenever serving platters start looking empty, they are filled again.

CHICKEN MARY'S
RR 1, PITTSBURG, KS (316) 231-9510
(SUPPER ONLY; SUNDAY FROM 11:00 A.M.)

"It's crazy, isn't it," Chicken Mary's son mused to us one hot summer day. "What's all this fried chicken doing out here anyway?"

It was a rhetorical question. The man knew perfectly well why the narrow lane off Highway 69 between Frontenac and Pittsburg, Kansas, is known as the Chicken Dinner Road; but he also knew that a couple of strangers highballing up toward Kansas City had to wonder: why, in the middle of nowhere, are there two flourishing restaurants—Chicken Mary's and Chicken Annie's (not to mention Chicken Annie's Annex)—that specialize in identical dinners of deep-fried chicken?

Mary and Annie have long ago gone to their reward, so Mary's son—no spring chicken himself—explained how it happened.

It was the hard times of the 1930s. His father and Annie's husband both worked in a nearby mine. In 1934, Annie's husband lost a leg in a mine accident. To make ends meet, Annie opened a little restaurant and served her specialty, fried chicken.

Only a few years after that, Mary's husband had to quit work, too, because of a bad heart. "There were three of us kids to feed," the old man recalled. "And my mother could see how well Annie was doing selling chicken dinners out here. She took a hint and opened her own place, Chicken Mary's, just down the road."

A tradition was begun. The rivalry has made this unlikely farm road a chicken-lover's paradise for the last half century. The meals are ritualized family-style feasts: plenty of deep-fried chicken and mashed potatoes or German potato salad, with slaws, beans, etc. on the side and ice cream for dessert. (Poultry-frowners can order chicken-fried steak.) It is very tasty chicken, although to our tongues not as delectable as the skillet-fried variety they serve up north in Kansas City.

Honestly, it isn't the food that we relish about a visit to the Chicken

Dinner Road. It is experiencing this strange little pocket of tradition. Some of the signs for the restaurants, painted long ago on the sides of aged barns and teetering billboards, are peeling with age. The dining rooms are well-worn and congenial. There is something so comfortably dilapidated about it all.

In particular, we enjoyed meeting Chicken Mary's son's dog, Buddy, who was then a happy pup who scampered around as we chatted in the parking lot. Buddy, we learned, eats nothing but chicken bones. We worried: "Aren't chicken bones supposed to be bad for dogs? Our veterinarian tells us we should never let a dog crack into a chicken bone."

"What do veterinarians know?" Chicken Mary's son asked. "Chicken Annie had a dog that lived sixteen years and never ate anything but bones his whole life!"

Despite the testimonial, we wouldn't give our tender-throated pooches a chicken bone, and we don't recommend such a diet for anybody else's dog. For humans, on the other hand, we do recommend a taste of real midwestern fried chicken—on location on the Chicken Dinner Road of southeast Kansas.

COZY INN
108 N. 7TH, SALINA, KS (913) 825-9407

Thick, juicy hamburgers are very good. But the hamburgers we like best are so thin you can practically see through them. We don't mean White Castles, which are perfectly fine in their skinny way; we are talking about the original, exquisite thin-as-a-nickel, eat-'em-by-the-dozen hamburgers, as made and served at the Cozy Inn of Salina, Kansas, for the last seventy years.

Cozy burgers are dangerous. After you have eaten one, you become aware that you have tasted something that no other food can match—not a ten-dollar Salisbury steak, nor a twenty-dollar T-bone. When you get the craving for a Cozy burger, you simply must have one; nothing else will satisfy. Cozy burgers are to hamburgers what caviar is to eggs: the smallest and the best (however *not* the most expensive).

The first great thing about Cozy burgers is their aroma. When you walk into the Cozy Inn, which is the one and only place where the supreme slider can be tasted in all its glory, breathe deep the smell of grilling onions and beef with a hint of dill pickle. Sit at the Cozy counter on one of the six stools for a twenty-minute lunch of maybe a half dozen burgers, a bag of potato chips, and a bottle of Coke, and that smell will saturate your hair and clothes and stay with you the rest of the day. Freeze a bag of Cozies, then heat them in the microwave oven six months later, and their perfume will billow out when you open the oven door.

The other exceptional thing about them is their taste. It is, to be frank, just right. Meat, bun, pickle, mustard, catsup; here is a consecrated combination—so sacred, in fact, that, according to Cozy Inn folklore, some years ago when a Cozy cook tried to put a piece of cheese on his own, personal burger, he was fired on the spot.

The best way to eat a Cozy burger is straight from the grill (which holds fifty-five at one time), at the counter in Salina, anytime between nine-thirty in the morning and eleven at night, Monday through Saturday, and eleven to eleven on Sundays. (It has been reported that the management will ship Cozy burgers packed in dry ice to desperate people elsewhere in the country; but it is not a house policy.) As always, the price is right: Cozy burgers, which started selling for a nickel apiece when the Inn opened in 1922, now go for forty-three cents, or six (a nice-size meal for one) for $2.43.

DOC'S
1515 N. BROADWAY, WICHITA, KS (316) 264-4735

Doc's steaks and garlic salad have been the toast of Wichita since the 1950s when Dwight L. "Doc" Husted (brother of Ted Husted, the brains behind Wall Drug of South Dakota) opened a steak house in a few rooms of a private home on Broadway. Doc's eatery prospered and expanded, and even after he sold it in 1963, the strict menu he created lived on. Today Doc's is a fine place to eat—a peculiar one, let us tell you, but appetizing.

About that garlic salad: it is cole slaw. Cool, creamy, finely chopped, served in a mound on a bed of shredded iceberg lettuce, and exceptionally redolent of garlic. It is at once killer-strong and refreshing—a unique, inspired idea. We have actually tried "double garlic salad" at Doc's, but twice the punch does not equal twice the pleasure. Garlic salad comes with all of Doc's "complete meals" (unless you opt for bland cottage cheese). You also get a choice of French fries or (foil wrapped) baked potato.

The entrées of choice are steak: small T-bone, large T-bone, sirloin, filet mignon wrapped in bacon, or chicken-fried. Doc's is so proud of its steaks that there is a sign posted in the lobby listing the kitchen's current

meat suppliers and promising that none of the beef served in these premises has been frozen, tenderized, marinated, or otherwise adulterated in
any manner. We enjoyed our big T-bone and filet mignon. The former was a
wide, thin slab of meat with good flavor; the filet was thick and tender, with
a balmier beef taste. These are not luxurious cuts such as those served in
high-priced city steak houses; they require some chewing, and yield the
satisfying flavor that is so often lacking in the ultra-tender, higher-priced
cuts. We can also recommend Doc's fried chicken, which is nicely crusty,
but don't much like the chicken-fried steak, which is served plain without
gravy or mashed potatoes.

As we said, Doc's is a strange place: comfortable with well-upholstered
high-backed booths and swift, nylon-uniformed waitresses, but a bit dis-
concerting. The lighting inside is indirect, some of it is eerie blue, and at
least one wall seems to be tilting outward at a strange angle. There is an
unearthly quality about the ambience: cool and untroubled, but very weird.
Then there is the menu, which is rigid to the point of being harsh, warning
against substitutions, checks, and credit cards, and heaping contempt
upon split orders ("defined as more than one person, adults or children,
sharing the same meal"), then promising retribution, in the form of a sur-
charge, if customers disobey and proceed to share. The explanation for the
strict rules is that Doc's aims to fight inflation, which is an admirable goal;
but couldn't they be a little nicer about it? We're not complaining. We really
like Doc's. Its cranky personality is very much part of its charm.

HAYS HOUSE
112 WEST MAIN ST., COUNCIL GROVE, KS (316) 767-5911

D r. Malcom Muir, Jr., of Tennessee wrote us to recommend the Hays
House, lamenting that he had arrived in Council Bluffs too late for
dinner, but did manage to have a superior breakfast, including "the only
white flour gravy I have ever enjoyed."

We have never eaten the morning meal that inspired Dr. Muir, but we
will gladly vouch for this kitchen. We came on a Sunday, which is feast day
in Council Grove; and the Hays House dining room brimmed with bunches
of eaters from Salina, Topeka, and beyond. Beautiful beefsteaks, slabs of
ham, and pork chops were being carried to tables all around us, but we had
a hankering for pan-fried chicken, which was good and crusty, served with
potatoes, gravy, vegetables, and oven-hot bread. We also ate Hays House
beef brisket, cut into soft, heavy slices that dripped gravy when lifted from

the plate. The menu is a big one, and lists various seafood meals as well—none of which we have tried, or would want to. There is also a salad bar, featuring not only do-it-yourself components, but composed salads of only-in-the-heartland complexity and creativity.

Of course there is pie for dessert; and the house pie list reflects the complex taste of modern Plains cooks. In addition to old-fashioned fruit pies, there were grasshopper pie and Kahlua pie, both of which are pretty, unsophisticated, and recklessly sweet. To top the pies, Hays House ice cream *du jour* when we stopped by was chocolate-marshmallow-pecan.

The atmosphere of the Hays House is old western, and it can seem a little corny until you realize that it is genuine. A century and a half ago, the town of Council Grove was the final outpost before utter wilderness for pioneers heading west on the Santa Fe Trail. The Hays House was built in 1857, and is now the oldest restaurant west of the Mississippi River. We suspect the frontier people who came through town back then would have been perfectly familiar with a lot of the good vittles on the Hays House menu, in particular the fried chicken and beef brisket. Grasshopper pie might have surprised them, but we bet they would have enjoyed it, too.

KEARBY'S
STATE ROAD 24E, MANHATTAN, KS (913) 539-1332

C hicken, fried, with potatoes, mashed: they are what has made Kearby's not only a favorite cafe for Manhattanites but also a treasured way station for travelers along I-70 who don't mind a detour north for a classic, and unbelievably cheap, chicken dinner. Mr. Kearby, the proprietor and chef, is a chicken fanatic, a point that is obvious as soon as you see the sign outside, across from the sale barn, where a top-hatted hen beckons customers to stop and eat. Inside Kearby's informal lunchroom, the motif is inescapable: chicken pictures and stitched samplers hang on the walls, figurines and statuettes roost on nearly every available display surface.

If brittle-crusted hunks of white and dark meat, accompanied by mashed potatoes (or baked), brown and white gravy, and such vegetables as broccoli-cauliflower-carrot-cheese casserole or black-eyed peas are not your dish, Kearby's far-flung buffet table always includes about half a dozen other main courses, ranging from Italian casserole and fish cakes to meat loaf and chicken-fried steak. We like the chicken best, but it was not within our powers to resist a plateful of this devil-may-care kitchen's delightfully démodé stuffed frankfurters (loaded with cheese and wrapped with bacon). There are soups each day (minestrone and ham and bean are typical) and there is a surprising selection of desserts. Surprising because, in addition to the very nice white-frosted chocolate cake, butterscotch pudding, and cream pies, you can choose fresh fruits and melons: strawberries, honeydew, and cantaloupe one fine day last summer.

All this is available on an all-you-can eat basis, for the grand total of $4.75, plus tax, as of late 1991. If even that sounds too expensive, you can skip the buffet and get a table-service mini-meal, which consists of one meat from the buffet, one serving of potatoes, and one vegetable for $3.10. At the other end of things, if you want to splurge, we will pass along the suggestion of our enthusiastic waitress Gay (she's the one with red hair): come to Kearby's on Friday night, when the weekday buffet is supplemented by ham and roast beef, carved to order. Grand total cost for the big feed: $6.15.

LEONA YARBROUGH
2800 W. 53RD ST., FAIRWAY, KS (913) 722-4800

L eona Yarbrough's restaurant is a sanctuary of gracious food. Kansas Citians come to these comfortable tables, banquettes, and booths to eat egg salad sandwiches on whole-wheat toast, turkey divan on English muffins, and apple pie with a lattice crust made the old-fashioned way, with lard. Culinary trend-seekers won't likely discover tomorrow's fad by eating Leona's seafood tetrazzini or dowdy old prune whip, but such vintage normalcy is our most compelling culinary temptation. This honorable food, which is all made from scratch and as homey as any granny's, is portioned out modestly, on pretty floral-patterned plates.

Leona has always been a great cook, but she learned the food service business from her predecessor, Ann Peterson, who sold Leona the restaurant about a quarter century ago. "Ann didn't cook," Leona told us. "And my nine-year-old son thought the desserts could be better. So I asked to do the baking. I came in every morning at three." Now Leona, a stately blonde in a clean white apron, is on hand every day to make sure the kitchen does everything right, and that the dining room runs smoothly.

The restaurant functions like a tea room, meaning that a small order pad and pencil are provided for customers to write their own ticket. Service is swift; and of course no liquor is served. Iced tea is the beverage of choice.

The lunch menu has a lot of sandwiches, all on homemade bread, whole wheat or rye. Spinach salad, topped with warm sweet-and-sour dressing, is sided by a block of luxuriously moist, high-flavored cornbread. Dinner is bigger, but every bit as conservative. Leona's is famous for skillet-fried chicken, each piece enveloped in a seasoned breading as fine as gilt. Aromatic braised lamb shanks are served with mint jelly and parsleyed new potatoes. Baked tenderloin is a tender piece of sweet pork topped with cream gravy and accompanied by whipped potatoes and buttered corn kernels.

In such a bastion of tradition, desserts are especially pleasant: blue-ribbon pies and gooseberry cobblers, fresh apple cake, rice custard pudding, devil's food cake, that veritable antique, prune whip (a froth of shredded prunes suspended in a cushion of whipped egg whites), and dainty little chocolate sundaes. When you walk out into the street after a Leona's meal, you cannot help but feel like a card-carrying nice person.

LONE STAR CAFE
606 N. 12TH, MANHATTAN, KS (913) 537-9077

In earlier editions of *Roadfood*, when we arranged the states by region, Kansas always troubled us. Gastronomically speaking, only Kansas City really has the flavor of the heartland. When we ate at the cafes and lunch counters farther west—in Wichita, Coffeyville, and Dodge City—the Sunflower State tasted much more like the great Southwest. Manhattan, Kansas, which bills itself, alas, as the Little Apple, has a very good example of what we mean: the Lone Star Cafe.

Ever since Tex-Mex food got popular a while back, Lone Star Cafes have probably opened up in every medium to large city in America, including New York. Here in Kansas's Manhattan, in this restaurant in the area called Aggieville, the name does not seem like an affectation. Although the restaurant and its clientele have a raised consciousness about the Texas shtick (imported beer is popular with nachos; instead of lardy refried beans you get wine-laced *frijoles borrachos*), most of what is served is true to Texas ideals; more important, it tastes good.

There are several kinds of chili. We'll ignore the "Gringo Chili," which is made with beans, and tell you about the fine Texas-style chili made from chunks of lean sirloin without any beans. It is hot, but it has much more than heat: real flavor, the smack of spice and chili peppers. Fans of highly spiced food will also want to know about Lone Star's enchiladas: shredded beef, chicken and tomatillos, chili and cheese. They are freshly made and dazzlingly seasoned, served with Spanish rice and beans.

Something for everyone on this menu: fajitas (beef or chicken), chicken molé, red snapper Vera Cruz (broiled over mesquite, topped with tomato-herb sauce), good guacamole for an hors d'oeuvre and an eye-opening margarita pie for dessert. There is barbecue, too; and although the brisket does not measure up to Texas standards, the pork ribs are succulent and infused with what the management immodestly calls "killer sauce." It did not slay us, but it sure made our tongues happy. Our vote for the best dish on the menu is Lone Star's chicken-fried steak—a hand-breaded giant fried until crusty brown and served with a mantle of peppery cream gravy, with curlicue French fries on the side. That's good eating, Texas style!

MRS. PETERS' CHICKEN DINNERS
4960 STATE AVE., KANSAS CITY, KS (913) 287-7711

Of the many four-star chicken dinner houses in Kansas City, Mrs. Peters' just might be the homiest. Not architecturally—the place itself is a nondescript food service building on a business strip; but decoratively. It is loaded with knick-knacks, most of them chicken-themed, like the work of an impassioned collector for whom chicken abundance equals happiness. The chickens are set among gingham and antique tools that give the dining rooms a feeling of a happy farmhouse on a Sunday, its tables set with the good linen napkins and old family silver. Decor at Mrs. Peters' is changed to fit any proximate holiday—pastels for Easter, orange and black and pumpkins for Halloween, etc.

People come to Mrs. Peters' to celebrate occasions; they come by fours, eights, tens, and dozens to eat—what else?—chicken. Fried. Four crusty pieces to an order, served with country cole slaw, a gone-bonkers variegated eight-bean salad, mashed potatoes and cream gravy, biscuits with honey butter and rhubarb-strawberry preserves, plus a trio of hot vegetables (corn, beans, carrots), iced tea or lemonade to drink, and pie, cobbler, or ice cream sundaes for dessert. Once we ate pork chops, and they were good; and country-fried steak is also available, as is catfish on Thursday nights; but if it's your first time, it's chicken you want. KC is a fried-chicken town, and Mrs. Peters' place is a pillar of its dinner culture.

NORTH STAR INN
1100 NW 25TH ST., TOPEKA, KS (913) 296-9470

Don't worry. It's okay. This really is the place. It does not look like a great restaurant; from the outside, it is about as plug-ugly as a food service establishment can be. It is a weather-beaten clapboard bunker with a single sign hanging outside, which shows a neon five-pointed star (like a sheriff's badge) encircling the word "North." There are no windows. This roadhouse, which looks more like a saloon than an eatery, happens to serve the best steaks in Topeka.

Once you are inside, and once your eyes adjust, it turns out to be a comfortable supper club with a hostess who is perfectly polite and waiters in black bow ties and clean white jackets who are consummate professionals. You *can* drink liquor here, which means, according to local law, that the North Star must operate as a private club; but most of the time, that is not a problem for travelers: membership fees are waived when you show them your out-of-state driver's license. (Warning: for a spell last year, because of problems with the liquor control commission, the North Star Inn was not able to allow nonmembers in. Call first, and ask for Donna, to make sure the coast is clear.)

It is not drinks that have lured customers to the North Star Inn for some fifty years now. It is steaks so tender that they are served with butter knives. Porterhouses and boneless clubs are veined with juice that is redolent of a distinguished, emphatic beef flavor that steaks somehow never have when you eat them on either of this country's coasts, away from the heartland. With the blue-ribbon steaks there are two kinds of potato offered, and they are each stupendously good. The French fries are equal to any in Kansas City: crusty honey-colored logs of spud are served in baskets, fresh out of the hot oil, and they are just exactly salty enough to bring out the luxurious flavor of the potato inside their fragile crust. Or you can choose hash browns, cooked with onions until the onions get all frizzled and lend their sweetness to the potatoes. Both kinds are accompanied by bowls of peppery gravy for dipping.

That's all there is to know about the North Star Inn, except that they do serve shrimp and, occasionally, fried chicken, for beef-frowners; and there is no dessert.

PORUBSKY GROCERY

508 N.E. SARDOU, TOPEKA, KS (913) 234-5788

"A lunch hideaway that locals frequent and out-of-towners track down" is how Jan Witkoski of the Topeka *Capital-Journal* described Porubsky's Grocery, a thirty-six seat, wood-paneled, Formica-tabled tap-room that's been serving sandwiches since 1947. Charlie and Lydia Porub-sky serve pastrami, ham, turkey, or cheese sandwiches, plates of cold cuts, and chili (the latter during chili season only—October to March), along with beer and RC Cola, to a clientele that includes a number of Kansas politicians and other public types whose autographed pictures, inscribed with praises of the place and its proprietor, line the walls.

The sandwiches are generously apportioned and low-priced, and the pastrami and Swiss on rye is a real beauty; but it's the extras that make lunch at this inconspicuous storefront worth a detour off Highway 70. The most famous of the extras are Charlie Porubsky's pickles, which are guaranteed to snap your taste buds to attention. They are "known far and wide for their industrial-strength fire," according to Ms. Witkoski, who managed to pry their secrets from Charlie: horseradish, mustard, and hot peppers. But even extraordinary pickles aren't what pack the little eatery six days a week from eleven-thirty in the morning until early afternoon (then again at night, when people come for beers and snacks). People love it because of its atmosphere: it is a real neighborhood tavern where customers come to chat 'n' chew and enjoy Charlie and Lydia's hospitality.

ROY'S

STATE ROAD 96, HUTCHINSON, KS (316) 663-7421

Roy's cooks about a quarter ton of meat every day (except Sunday and Monday), starts selling it at eleven-thirty in the morning, and locks the door when everything's been eaten, which is generally about six in the evening. If you come to eat Roy's meat, you will be seated at Roy's table. There is only one in the restaurant, but it is a capacious one, holding what an employee told us was "about a dozen, or less if they're real big." The table is round, so the view as you dine is of your tablemates gnawing ribs.

The ribs are chewy, beaming with the taste of hickory smoke, and are a lot of work to eat, but yield dazzling flavor and set taste buds tingling for hours. Their intensity is complemented by a dark, sweet-hot sauce. Pork and turkey are creamier meat than that you will tear from the ribs, and they seem to taste less like hickory and more like their gentle selves. There is some truly ambrosial beef brisket, cut into heavy, moist chunks, and there are two kinds of sausage links—mild and (very) hot. Most of this meat is available piled up by itself or in a sandwich, on big slabs of griddle-cooked toast.

To go with the four-star meat there are baked beans and a little salad bar with such palate-balms as macaroni salad, potato salad, slaws, and relishes.

KENTUCKY

BOONE TAVERN
ROUTE 25, BEREA, KY (606) 986-9358

The Boone Tavern Hotel, which began as a guest house for visitors to Berea college, is a place to see—and savor—the unique nature of a Berea education. Its rooms and lobby are furnished with walnut and cherry wood reproduction antique furniture made by students in the Woodcraft program. Decorative touches are supplied by student weavers. The registration desk and the dining room, as well as the kitchen, are staffed almost entirely by students in the hotel management program.

In the beginning, most Berea students were Appalachian. Now they come from around the world, so if you dine at the Boone Tavern, you might just as easily be served by a boy or girl from Zimbabwe as from Zebulon (Kentucky). The dining experience, however, remains distinctively southern—graciously paced and rather formal (men wear jackets at dinner), and expensive. The staff is mostly kids; and their good cheer gives the high-tone airs a reassuring cheerfulness—like Sunday dinner at the home of a rich grandparent who is a stickler for good manners.

There is *lots* of service at a Boone Tavern meal. Student waiters swarm through the dining room, offering dinner rolls, clearing plates, bringing new courses, checking to make sure customers are happy. While not all the food they serve is totally delicious (there are students in the kitchen, after all!), it is impossible not to enjoy their earnest efforts at making dinner into a grand event.

The feast always begins with a relish tray, presented by a waiter who doles out whichever ones you choose: watermelon pickles, marinated carrots, etc. He (or she) is followed by another member of the staff carrying a hot bowl full of spoonbread. Quickly, clean your plate of relishes, because you want to spend some quality time with this spoonbread. It is the dish that most Boone Tavern dinner guests remember best: a moist cornmeal soufflé, hot and fluffy, faintly granular, just a wee bit buttery, delicious with nearly any meaty main course.

What follows the spoonbread is a menu of classic Kentucky cookery. One of the aims of the college is to sustain and celebrate mountain culture, but in the case of the dining room, that does not imply a menu of such Ma and Pa Kettle vittles as hog jowls, baked beans, or scalded mush balls. The bluegrass cuisine of the Boone Tavern is more refined than that. In fact, some of it is downright baroque—such as chicken flakes "Elsinore," a creamy Dixie belle of a meal served in a nest of potatoes. There is wonderful honey-cured ham gilded with sweet lemon clove sauce. ("Is it country ham?" we asked our waitress before ordering. "I don't know," she answered. "I'm from Africa.") There is native turkey served with dressing, giblet gravy, and fresh cranberry relish. And to end the meal, the kitchen offers such impressive sweet-tooth fancies as homemade ice cream, French vanilla custard, rhubarb pie, and red velvet cake the color of a 1969 pop art shag rug, topped with ultra-rich hard sauce and a cascade of nutmeats.

DEL'S
HIGHWAY 60, STANLEY, KY (502) 764-1152

The sign says "Truckers Welcome," and although it is possible that regular customers of Del's might give you a steely once-over when you walk into the big plain room, it's worth a bit of discomfort to get plates full of mutton and the meaty stew called burgoo, those two regional specialties unique to this part of Kentucky. If you don't feel comfortable dining under fluorescent tubes on Formica among a room full of gearjammers, Del's can make your meals to go.

About this mutton: it is get-down good, rich and oily, sweet and smoky, edged with a savory burned crust and with a maximum amount of flavor packed into every fall-apart tender bite. It is available chopped or sliced.

For us, the "chopped" is too disintegrated; "sliced" is actually what we would call "chunked," reminiscent of a deliriously flavored pot roast. Strangely—considering the extravagant zest of the mutton—Del's burgoo is fairly mild. You do taste the strong lamb out of which it is built, as well as perhaps three other kinds of smoked meats—all of which are pulverized nearly beyond recognition—but their punch is tempered by plenty of vegetables and a temperate orange stock. Del's sells burgoo by the bowl, quart, and gallon.

DIXIE CHILI
733 MONMOUTH ST., NEWPORT, KY (606) 291-5337; FOUR OTHER LOCATIONS

Dixie is a small chain of inconspicuous serve-yourself restaurants in the vicinity of Cincinnati that make some of the finest five-way chili anywhere. The strata of noodles, beans, onions, and cheese of which it is composed are all standard-issue ingredients; but the meat sauce is remarkable. Faintly flavored with cinnamon, richly meaty (rather than soupy), it has a resonance that makes all the other flavors and textures in this complex dish come together in a great, symphonic chord of cheap eats grandeur. By comparison, lesser chilis seem confused and random.

Forget the meatless vegetable soup on the menu; and the chili salad, similar to a taco salad, is an idea whose time is never; and the sandwiches are uninteresting. There is only one reason to come to Dixie Chili, but it is a compelling one.

GEORGE'S BAR-B-Q
E. 4TH & MONTGOMERY, OWENSBORO, KY (502) 926-9276

George's serves first-class mutton. It is dished out in juicy, fibrous shreds that are saturated with fiery red sauce, accompanied by a useless heap of the wiggle-edged French fried potatoes that look like miniature concertinas. In addition to mutton, which is the western Kentucky pit meat of choice, George's also serves fine platters of barbecued pork shoulder, beef, ham, chicken, and pork ribs.

Good as they are, none of these meats on plate or sandwich is what draws us back to George's whenever we are eating our way around Owensboro. The choice item on the menu is burgoo, and it contains nearly all the pit-cooked meats, and then some. Burgoo has been a favorite Kentucky meal since it was invented by a Confederate chef during the Civil War; and although its origins as a wild game stew (with squirrel, opossum, and whatever birds could be killed) are history, the folks in these parts still love to make huge caldrons of it for public events that range from beer party picnics to Derby Day luncheons.

Not too many restaurants make burgoo because it requires so much effort and is, no matter how delicious, incurably rustic in nature. That is why we appreciate George's, which has it on the menu all the time—at low prices and without ado. Workmen and businessmen alike crowd into this small, wood-paneled eatery for burgoo by the bowlful, accompanied by a Coke or a draught of beer. It is a kaleidoscopically spiced, tomato-red slumgullion loaded with vegetables and shreds of meat, including enough pit-cooked mutton to give it smoky gusto. A lively country-western jukebox provides just the right background music.

MOONLITE BAR-B-Q INN
2840 W. PARRISH AVE., OWENSBORO, KY (502) 684-8143

The flavor of mature lamb blossoms when it slow-cooks for hours in a pit, imbibing smoke and sauce but never losing its own characteristic tang; and there is something especially delectable about the texture of this meat when the cooking process has turned it from tough to luscious. After mutton, beef and pork can seem wan.

The premier mutton restaurant of western Kentucky's mutton belt is the Moonlite Bar-B-Q Inn, a veritable mutton mansion featuring a staggering help-yourself buffet at which the choices also include barbecued chicken, beef, and pork; a slew of assorted vegetables; cornbreads and yeast rolls; potatoes; beans; salads; even burgoo; as well as pies, cakes, puddings, and ice cream (from a soft-serve machine). It's the mutton that everybody comes for—a jumble of variegated chopped meat, ranging from butter-tender hunks to succulent, leathery shreds, cosseted in a fairly mild tomato sauce. To adjust its flavor and heat, the Moonlite offers three sauces that range from a basic steak condiment to a fiery one labeled "very hot." Pay one price and eat your fill of everything.

The Moonlite is a cavernous eatery; its multiple wood-paneled dining rooms can hold more than three hundred customers at a time, and its kitchen can turn out four thousand pounds of mutton on a good day. Owner Ken Bosley, whose father started the business in 1963, advised us in no uncertain terms that thanks to its insatiable appetite for mutton, Owensboro, Kentucky, has become the barbecue capital of America, if not the world.

OLD HICKORY PIT

338 WASHINGTON AVE., OWENSBORO, KY (502) 926-9000

Old Hickory is deceptive. It looks about as soulful as a muffler shop. Order a mutton plate, however, and you will savor the kind of soul that only the most distinguished barbecue delivers. This new, nondescript edifice off 25th was planned by the Old Hickory pitmaster, a Mr. Foreman, to make great smoked meats and serve them efficiently. Mr. Foreman knows a thing or two about barbecue, having learned from his father, who learned from his father, who learned from his father, who began cooking mutton for a living in 1918.

Mutton is really the only thing you need to know about on the Old Hickory Pit menu, although there are other meats for sale. In fact the pork and pork ribs are really very good; we would recommend them anywhere else. And the side dishes, especially the beans and onion rings, are tasty indeed. And the peach and blackberry cobbler are exemplary desserts. But it is the mutton that you will remember long after a meal at Old Hickory. It is served sauceless—"off the pit," in mutton-lover's lingo. The thick, chunky slices are lean, whisperingly smoky from their spell over the burning logs, and each bite packs a juicy vigor that beef and pork simply do not have. There is sauce if you need it, but you don't. This meat is so moist and its flavors are so complex and satisfying that all it needs for completion is an eager tongue to taste it.

OLD STONE INN

U.S. 60, SIMPSONVILLE, KY (502) 722-8882

A living antique. Built in 1791 as a stage stop, opened as a restaurant in 1924, the Old Stone Inn is a taste of a vanished way of serving meals along the American road. White tablecloths and thick napkins, wood floors that creak when you walk across them, grand old antique furniture spread out through fourteen eccentric (and romantic) rooms, and genuine old Kentucky meals served by old Kentucky waiters: if you like tradition, you will love this place.

The menu, posted on a board in the great vestibule, has stayed pretty much the same for decades. The thing to eat is ham—aged, country ham with a salty smack and real character; or chicken—fried, of course, but unlike Colonel Sanders' version (which was invented just a few miles away), this chicken is fried in a skillet, and is very good. If you cannot decide between ham and chicken, the management offers a half-and-half plate. Or there is an occasional super-genteel version of chicken, called chicken Jerusalem, made with cream gravy and artichoke hearts.

Many travelers remember their meal at the Old Stone Inn by the side dishes, which are brought to the table throughout the meal by the venerable waiters. The best of them are luxuries such as eggplant casserole and corn pudding—both cream-rich, mild, and aristocratic. For dessert, there is always a crusty-sweet mélange of fruit cobbler.

SHADY REST
HIGHWAY 60 EAST, OWENSBORO, KY (502) 926-8234

"If it fits the pit we will barbecue it," a sign at Shady Rest announces, and the menu includes barbecued pork shoulder, pork ribs, ham, beef, and chicken; but the barbecue of choice in this part of Kentucky is mutton. That's what we recommend you eat at Shady Rest: the Old Kentucky Hickory Smoked Barbecue Mutton Plate, which includes, in addition to the meat, a hearty heap of barbecued beans, potato salad, slices of onion, pickles, and beige bread suitable for pushing food around the plate.

Unless you tell the waitress differently, the mutton comes already bathed in good barbecue sauce, the thick slices as tender as prime rib, but with the vivid flavor wallop that only old ewes pack. For a slight extra charge meat can be ordered "off the pit," which means sliced but unsauced, allowing customers to customize their own from the three different strengths of sauce that are brought to every table.

Shady Rest sells burgoo, another tasty western Kentucky inclination, made with some of all the barbecued meats (except pork), including enough mutton to give it the unique zest, as well as corn kernels, lima beans, potato chunks, tomatoes, and spice. Sold by the bowl, quart, or gallon, burgoo is a party meal unto itself, or a nice way to round out a mutton meal.

To complete the Ohio River Valley taste sampler, Shady Rest makes fried pies for dessert: thin envelopes of crust folded around tender stewed and spiced apples, then sizzled in butter on a griddle. A scoop of vanilla ice cream melts fast on top of this warm, sweet pillow; and the combination is ambrosial.

SKIN HEAD'S
1021 S. 21ST ST., PADUCAH, KY (502) 442-6471

L ong ago when we first hit the road, it was at Skin Head's that we had our first real taste of southern style breakfast: biscuits, gravy, country ham, hash browns, and eggs. We are happy to report that nearly a quarter century later, Skin Head's serves the same good food, and is every bit the déclassé cafe it has always been. A squat cinderblock building with a metal awning that looks like it was used for car-hop service years ago, a sign outside proclaims it to be "The Breakfast House of the South." The inside is still a spill of rattle-legged booths and tables, wood-paneled walls, overhead fluorescents. "Remember now," the menu says, "short, fat, thin, or tall, 'Ole Skin Head' will try to feed y'all."

The roster of morning meals is immemorial, each made to perfection. There are eggs and potatoes, of course. Slabs of griddle-fried country ham, their scarlet centers edged with halos of translucent amber fat, are accompanied by viscous red-eye gravy. Buttermilk biscuits, the menu brags, "are made from Sunflower Self Rising Flour, not that stuff they are calling scratch." However they are made, they are hot and good, made for dunking—either in the red-eye, made from ham drippings, or into bowls of thick, rib-sticking, pepper-tweaked sawmill gravy. "At Skin Head's," the menu boasts, "breakfast is a full-time job—not a sideline . . . seldom equaled, never excelled, imitated but never duplicated."

Great as breakfast is, this is a noteworthy lunch stop, too. Every sort of Paducahan from truck driver to prom queen to local businessman comes for down-home blue-plate specials of skillet-fried catfish, crisp tenderloin sandwiches, or Skin Head's cheap and wonderful mid-American ploughman's lunch of white beans, corn sticks, hot sauce, and a slab of onion.

STARNES BAR-B-Q
JOE CLIFTON DR., PADUCAH, KY (502) 444-9555

U ntil we ate at Starnes, we always pretty much assumed that blah white bread was a vital part of all good barbecue. Its spongy texture makes it right for dunking into sauce and slurping up maximum amounts of flavor; it is pliable and therefore well-suited to mopping a plate; its blandness provides an innocuous, cushiony presence that is a nice foil for pyrotechnical spices and the subtle taste of smoke; and most important of all, it's traditional. Barbecue greatness is almost always inversely proportional to the character of the bread served with the meat.

When you peek at Starnes' food-prep area, this venerable establishment (since the fifties) appears to be no exception to the rule. There are long loaves of cotton-soft white bread for sandwiches. But get this: warm meat from the pit is piled between two pieces of this bread, the meat is sprinkled with a bit of peppery red sauce, then the sandwich is toasted on a grill. What a clever innovation! It takes some getting used to—lifting a sandwich wrapped with hard tiles of toasted bread rather than the usual mitt-like slices; but you discover when you bite down into it that because the bread was grilled on one side only, rather than toasted, its interior portions are still soft and spongy enough to sop up juice and sauce.

About the meat in this sandwich: it's swell. Pork, beef, or ham, chopped fine, with a nice hickory sizzle, is generally served unsauced (unless you tell the waitress otherwise). Applied in small amounts, however, the sauce is an essential part of the formula and brings the meat—the beef in particular—to a perfect consonance of protein's heft and spices' jingle, so don't neglect it.

Starnes is diminutive: two booths and a horseshoe counter, with the pit out back. The menu is nothing more than barbecued meat, accompanied by potato salad and cole slaw, and you can see the beverage list by looking in the drink case. Dessert is displayed next to the drinks: a small selection of packaged cupcakes, Twinkies, and candy bars.

THOMAS' F & N STEAK HOUSE
ROUTE 8, DAYTON, KY (606) 261-6766

If you happen to be anywhere near Cincinnati when a serious beef craving strikes, here is the place you want to know about: Thomas' F & N Steak House, just over the Ohio river in Dayton, Kentucky.

Established in 1929, Thomas' is a higgledy-piggledy roadhouse that looks like it has expanded in random fits and starts for the last sixty-odd years. Its multiple dining rooms are loaded with memorabilia, souvenirs, antiques, and just plain junk. Photos from the 1950s share wall space with Victorian prints; there is a wooden cookstove in one room, a million statuettes in another; six fireplaces altogether. Booths are as large as a roomette, their leatherette cushions nearly soft as down, with the kind of spreading-out space demanded by a mighty meat meal.

Thomas' steaks are aged and cut on the premises. You have no doubt, at first bite, that they really are *aged,* with the heightened flavor smack that a couple weeks on the hook gives to beef. (It is possible to order nonaged beef if you prefer a callow cut of cow.) They are served with an iceberg lettuce salad, baked potato, long-cooked string beans, and a warm loaf of bread that arrives impaled by its cutting knife. The most memorable dish in the house, other than the meat itself, is an extra-cost appetizer of French-fried eggplant. Cut in thin strips, served with fiery horseradish-spiked cocktail sauce, the eggplant is especially savory, and a good munchie to accompany pre-dinner drinks.

The F & N menu also lists fish and lobster, baby back ribs, and barbe-cued chicken, but it is steak that has established this place as a landmark for carnivores: delmonicos (ribeyes), chopped steaks, chunked and skew-ered tenderloins, T-bones, two-pound porterhouses, filets mignon, and our personal favorite, the New York strip—described on the menu as "man-size."

LOUISIANA

BLACK'S OYSTER BAR
311 PERE MEGRET ST., ABBEVILLE, LA (318) 893-4266
(CLOSED IN THE SUMMER THROUGH JULY)

A happy little cypress wood-paneled cafe with ceiling fans overhead and stuffed game fish on the wall, Black's is oyster-eater's heaven. Freshly shucked, raw on the half shell, by the dozen, is the preferred way to eat them—"Live Longer! Love Longer!" the menu promises to those who eat enough. The table has a little lazy Susan crowded with a panoply of local hot sauces to sprinkle on the oysters. This is real hot sauce country, just miles from Avery Island where the McIlhenny family grows many of the peppers that go into Tabasco sauce; and the combination of fresh, salty-flavored oysters and throat-clenching heat from "Cajun Power Garlic" or "Aunt Hallie's" or "Frank's" or classic Tabasco is addictive. All you need is a few bottles of beer on the side and an occasional fistful of crackers to give your taste buds a breather.

Beautifully breaded shrimp, encased in a faintly spiced envelope of crunch, are another specialty of the house at Black's; and the fried oysters, too, are wonderful. Cooks in this part of the world have made an art of fried seafood. The way most locals eat it at Black's is as a combination sand-wich: shrimp and oysters, both fried to a golden crisp, stuffed into a long, soft hamburger roll along with mayonnaise and mustard. Abbeville's version of a po' boy, which is actually an oyster loaf, was declared by Amy Wilentz, writing in *Traveler* magazine, to be "perfect."

BOUDIN KING
906 W. DIVISION ST., JENNINGS, LA (318) 824-6593

Boudin King is no idle title in this part of Louisiana. Each year the town of Broussard chooses an accomplished hot link maker to wear the crown. Ellis Cormier, founder of the Boudin King restaurant in 1975, has been a sausage suzerain many times over, not only in swamp country, but at fairs and food festivals throughout Louisiana and the south; and in 1979 the Louisiana House of Representatives officially declared Jennings to be the "Boudin Capital of the Universe," specifically lauding the "quality and excellence" of Mr. Cormier's boudin. There is no better place to eat this singular sausage, a southern Louisiana bomb made of pork and pork parts, onions, parsley, and a fierce hail of pepper and spice.

Buy it by the pound, mild or hot, to eat here or to go. One pound equals approximately one link, and it is a frightening sight, even more daunting when you first taste how hot it is. This is uncompromising food, vigorously seasoned and unabashedly unctuous—and a genuine, rare treat to eat. Monsieur Cormier says he sells two tons of it every week.

It is all the more surprising to enjoy such an authentic piece of regional Americana when you consider the surroundings. Boudin King is not some funky butcher shack attached to a small-town grocery store. It is a modern, drive-in restaurant with a full menu of fried chicken family packs (about a hundred times better tasting than Kentucky Fried franchise stuff) and fried catfish by the bucket, throwaway flatware, and easy-wipe Formica surfaces throughout.

You will not give a hoot about the overly efficient ambience, however, when your tongue is catching fire from the boudin, or if you spoon deep into a murky bowl of Monsieur Cormier's four-star chicken and sausage gumbo, or crunch down on fried crawfish tails (in the spring). This food is real Acadian; and if you doubt its authenticity, buy a pound of Boudin King's freshly made hog's head cheese on your way out. We dare you.

THE CABIN
JUNCTION OF HIGHWAYS 44 & 22, BURNSIDE, LA (504) 473-3007

An all-in-one taste of old Louisiana: you can admire genuine antiques on display, buy souvenirs at the adjacent general store, listen to Cajun music in the background, and eat red beans, sausage, and rice. A few centuries ago The Cabin was one of ten slave quarters on the Monroe Plantation; today it is a restaurant catering to tourists in search of local color as well as to locals in search of a good hot lunch.

The house specialty is a magnum opus known as the pirogue, named for its resemblance to the cypress canoes used to navigate through the bayous. A long loaf of bread is hollowed out and stuffed with a heap of oysters, shrimp, and nuggets of fish (all fried), and dressed to your liking. It is served with a choice of French fries and cole slaw or red beans and rice. There are all kinds of po' boys on the menu, which are like a pirogue but not as spectacular: roast beef and ham, sausage (mild or hot), barbecued beef, even hamburger. Other Cajun specialties of the house include gumbo, jambalaya with white beans, shrimp creole, and bread pudding with rum sauce. For locals who eat here all the time and therefore aren't so interested in local food, The Cabin serves plenty of not-so-Cajun lunches every day, including fried chicken we can definitely recommend and a memorable meal of pork chops with smothered cabbage and rice. And if you don't want bread pudding for dessert (you do!), they make a tender-souled buttermilk pie.

To accompany these good meals, whether modern or antique, The Cabin offers all the right beverages—from long-neck beers and iced tea to hot toddies and mint juleps.

CASAMENTO'S
4330 MAGAZINE, NEW ORLEANS, LA (504) 895-9761

Casamento's is a neighborhood oyster bar, a local favorite for nearly fifty years. It closes for a long vacation every year between June and September, but when it is open, there's hardly any room for customers. Casamento's is tiny, two small dining rooms with maybe a few dozen chairs, plus room for a couple of stand-up oyster eaters at the bar. Floors and counters are decorated with lovely flower and scroll tiles like a pretty—but modest—home kitchen. The oyster bar is worn from years of use. A few plants soften the hard-edge look.

Despite its modest appearance, Casamento's is one of the great New Orleans restaurants—a landmark of Creole cooking where customers come to feast on raw or fried oysters, fish or shrimp, or soft-shell crabs in the spring.

Casamento's reputation is for seafood, but many regular customers come for its excellent spaghetti, or for the fascinating sweet-and-savory pot roast that has played a definitive role in the shaping of Creole cookery—the meaty, gravy-laden platter of long-cooked goodness known as daube.

The most famous dish in the house is an oyster loaf. It's like a po' boy sandwich—New Orleans' version of a hero, sub, grinder, hoagie—but even bigger. To make an oyster loaf, first they fry the oysters. And let us tell you, you have never known an oyster quite so delicious, so briny-sweet, so crackle-crusted. To eat one is an epiphany. The brittle skin shatters at the slightest pressure, giving way to a wave of melting warm, briny oyster meat across the tongue. When we asked Mr. Gerdes what made them special, he told us that the method was "too simple to call a recipe." They are freshly shucked, dipped in corn flour, then dropped into open iron pots of pure hot lard. "Everything is fried by feel and sound," he said. "It requires a lot of personal attention and experience."

Casamento's improves on these nuggets of excellence by loading them into an entire loaf of bread. It is unsliced white, cut lengthwise, scooped out, and toasted, its bland yeasty tenderness a perfect foil for the sharp oceanic bite of the oysters. A feast for two.

CENTRAL GROCERY
923 DECATUR ST., NEW ORLEANS, LA (504) 523-1620

Among the many things that make New Orleans a good place to eat are the sandwiches: po' boys, oyster boats, pirogues, and a doozy called the muffuletta. "Muffuletta" is a name that once referred only to the kind of bread used for the sandwich: a chewy round loaf turned out by local bakers. A few grocery stores that sold the loaf got the idea to slice it horizontally and stuff it with cold cuts and olive salad. The muffuletta sandwich was born. The place that claims to have done it first is the Central Grocery on Decatur Street.

The Central is still a neighborhood store, its yellowed walls decorated with travel posters, the air inside smelling of garlic and sausage and provolone cheese. Shelves are stocked with imported olive oils, sauces, and pasta. There is no place to sit down. Give your order to the man behind the counter, who goes to work assembling the sandwich—an exacting process visible in a small mirror installed above his work space. The big round loaf, its top spangled with a few sesame seeds, is cut so its insides can be drizzled with oil. Onto the bottom half goes a load of salami, ham, provolone cheese, and the garnish known as olive salad.

It's the olive salad that makes a muffuletta unique: broken pieces of black and green olives, garlic and herbs, a dash of anchovy, and plenty of fragrant olive oil. Originally made from the pieces at the bottom of the barrel, good muffuletta olive salad is briny and killer-strong—*too strong* without the cushioning effect of the bread.

The muffuletta is served wrapped in paper. It's up to you to find a place to eat it. No problem. Grab a bottle of Barq's root beer, stroll into Jackson Square, find a bench where you can watch the goings-on in the French Market, unhinge your jaw, and plow in. Although muffulettas are cut in quarters by the sandwich maker, the segments are impossible to eat with any sort of propriety. That's the fun of it. Olive salad stains on the lap mark a person who has eaten well in New Orleans.

CHEZ MARCEAUX
HIGHWAY 90 EAST OF AMELIA, LA (504) 631-9843

C hez Marceaux is a pretty darn ugly restaurant and lounge—cinderblock walls, bright Formica tables, and molded plastic chairs. In any other part of the country, you'd be correct to drive right past it, assuming the cuisine was, at best, ordinary blue-collar grub.

What's to eat? How about crawfish étouffée, a masterful stew of herbed crawdads in their own ambrosial fat; or a full-size dinner plate heaped high with boiled crawfish or shrimp; or shrimp gumbo, thick and meaty, suffused with a giddy kaleidoscope of spices? Or what about a po' boy? Chez Marceaux's sandwiches are impressive, made on long, lovely loaves of bread, filled with decent cold cuts and excellent (if somewhat parsimoniously allotted) fried oysters or shrimp.

Where we come from, this is not blue-collar lunch. But in Amelia, it is. You eat this eloquent food, which is accompanied by plastic baskets of pre-wrapped white bread, in the humblest surroundings. The lower Atchafalaya River is oil country, and this cafe—whose wall clock is a twinkle-light tableau of oil rigs at sunset—is where oil workers come to eat, with their hard hats set on the table alongside their bowls of turtle piquant and plates of delicately breaded crawfish.

EDDIE'S
2119 LAW ST., NEW ORLEANS, LA (504) 945-2207

E ddie's is a hole-in-the-wall with some of the best food in New Orleans. Two blocks from Elysian Fields, on a tucked-away side street, with a small sign announcing "Eddie's: Home of New Orleans Cooking," this unpretentious dining room has drawn raves from hard-to-please local food critics for years. If you are a traveler in search of authentic New Orleans food, you won't find better.

Eddie Baquet's cooking reveals the connection between the southern soul-food kitchen and Creole cuisine. Taste his fried chicken with its garlic and onion imprint, or catfish with its peppery crust, or the big sizzling pork chop, sweet and smoky, with greens on the side, and you understand why such lip-smacking eats are called *soul* food. Every plate that issues forth from this stove or oven is seasoned with brio. It's the kind of food that makes you want to throw away utensils, roll up your sleeves, and eat with abandon.

We nearly fainted from the roundhouse punch of Eddie's gumbo, which he cooks entirely by taste, adding rainbows of spices as he goes. Extraordinarily smoky, thick with shrimp, oysters, chicken, ham, hot sausage, beef, and pork, it comes to the table trailing a fragrant cloud of steam that smells like swamps and garlic and fire and ocean. Inhale that perfume, then tear off a hunk of French bread and dip it in the murky brew: what good eating!

New Orleans is one of the few cities where frying seafood is an art; but not all of Eddie's fish specialties are fried. In fact, contrary to the exuberant techniques of so much Louisiana cooking, one of the most delicious meals he makes is hardly seasoned at all. Trout Baquet, a happy combination of fresh trout and lump crabmeat, gets a Creole-sized dose of garlic; but other than that, what you taste is crabmeat coddled in butter and the sweet simplicity of broiled trout.

Another of Eddie's renowned specialties is oyster stuffing, a tender mélange of ground beef, chopped oysters, gobs of garlic, pepper, oregano, and thyme, all gently simmered until moist and funky-flavored. It comes on the side of pork chops or fried chicken, or it serves perfectly well as a meal unto itself.

No Creole-soul-blue-plate-special menu would be complete without a few genuine New Orleans sandwiches, made possible only because the restaurateurs who construct them demand the best, freshest, crustiest French bread. Eddie's po' boys earned him a "Golden Poor Boy Best Bet"

Award in 1983 from the *New Orleans Restaurant Guide Newsletter*. Although he makes po' boys on French bread out of any cold cuts you desire, the infallible *Newsletter* liked grilled ham and cheese best.

The sandwich we can never resist at Eddie's is an oyster loaf, for which a long length of bread is toasted, scooped out, and stuffed with fried oysters. Its goodness depends entirely on fresh oysters, fried to order, so that when your jaws clamp down through the bread's crust, through its fluffy white insides, then into the crunch of cornmeal breading, you are finally rewarded with soft, briny-sweet pockets of the oysters' oceanic tang.

Did you ever wonder why New Orleaneans make such a fuss over a dish as simple as red beans and rice? Taste Eddie's: now you know. These silky beans, dished out in mountain-size proportions, have a sumptuous ham and garlic smack that transcends their essential plainness, elevating the humble legume into the realm of elegance. After dispatching a bean-centered meal made with such prodigious yet unaffected cooking skill, you can appreciate why Louis Armstrong always signed his letters, "Red beans and ricely yours."

LASYONE'S MEAT PIE KITCHEN
622 SECOND ST., NATCHITOCHES, LA (318) 352-3353

When he was a boy growing up in the city of Natchitoches, the oldest settlement in Louisiana, James Lasyone used to buy meat pies from street vendors and eat them out of hand. Meat pies have been a popular food in these parts since the eighteenth century, sold on the street and eaten for lunch in private homes. But by the time Mr. Lasyone opened his own bakery in town, all the meat-pie vendors were gone. So he rescued the idea and began making and selling his own meat pies, using a recipe that took him two years of experimentation to develop.

Lasyone's meat pie, now the renowned *spécialité* of Lasyone's Meat Pie Kitchen, a casual storefront cafe with a huge papier-mâché pie hanging in its window, is a brightly seasoned mash of pork and beef, onions and parsley, enclosed in a deep-fried half-moon pastry. Like a piquant Cornish pasty, it is practically a meal unto itself.

But don't stop with a meat pie. There is plenty more good stuff to eat at Lasyone's. A real Louisiana menu provides the opportunity to accompany a meat pie with crisp fried seafood (shrimp, oysters), Cajun specialties (superb red beans, sausage, and dirty rice), and Dixie classics from catfish platters to chicken and dumplings with cornbread and black-eyed peas.

We have eaten first-rate banana pudding for dessert, but the sweet tour de force here is a dish invented by Mrs. Lasyone called Cane River cream pie—a variant of Boston cream pie, but with gingerbread instead of white cake.

MIDDENDORF'S
U.S. 55 IN PASS MANCHAC, LA (504) 386-6666

Catfish is the reason to eat at Middendorf's. There is none this good in New Orleans; and there are times, when we crunch into a thin catfish fillet at a Middendorf's table after a long spell away from Louisiana, that we are willing to say there is none this good anywhere in America.

It is sold thick or thin. Thick catfish is a meaty cross-section of fish, similar to a steak wrapped in breading. It is sweet-smelling and has resounding vim that is unlike any seawater fish. Thin catfish is more elegant than thick. Sliced into a diaphanous strip that is sharply seasoned, lightly breaded, and quickly fried, a thin cat fillet crunches loudly when you sink your teeth into its brittle crust, which is sheer enough to let the rich flavor of the fish resonate. With the catfish, thick or thin, there are perfectly good and unsurprising companions: French fries, hushpuppies, and cole slaw.

After catfish, just about any seafood on the menu is well worth eating. We have had some great gumbo here, made with shrimp and crabmeat, which was surprisingly delicate compared to the more overpowering versions sold in the city's best gumbo houses. There are sautéed soft-shell crabs, po' boy sandwiches, and Italian salads loaded with olives and spice. And there is fried seafood of all kinds. In most other parts of the country it is easy to come to believe that fried seafood is bad; Middendorf's will restore your faith in just how scrumptious it can be—not only when it is freshwater catfish that are fried, but oysters and shrimp as well. Fried oysters are butter-rich with a marine tang; the fried shrimp are sweet, brittle-crusted wonders. And, too, there are good oysters on the half shell for appetizers, and lengths of French bread to accompany any seafood dinner.

As you might expect at a Tangipahoa Parish seafood house situated among a string of bait shops and take-out stands, Middendorf's is extremely casual, noisy, and fun. Even with more space added next door to the original restaurant, a wait can be expected at suppertime, especially on weekends. This has long been the great country catfish restaurant of New Orleans, favored by the city's fried seafood connoisseurs, and reason enough to drive forty-five minutes north of town, then stand in line waiting to eat.

MOSCA'S
HIGHWAY 90, WAGGAMAN, LA (4 MILES BEYOND THE HUEY P. LONG BRIDGE)
(504) 436-9942

About a half-hour's drive southwest of New Orleans in surroundings only a little more inviting than a swamp, you will find Mosca's—a dilapidated roadhouse by the side of U.S. 90. Inside this big white wooden shack, you will probably wait quite a good long time for a table and you will experience service that while seldom actually impolite, is not what you would ever call refined. Throngs of passionate eaters put up with whatever inconvenience is involved because Mosca's serves what nearly every traveling gourmet acknowledges as the finest Creole-Italian food in Louisiana.

New Orleans is best-known for French-accented soul food, as well as for oysters on the half shell, po' boy sandwiches, breakfast at Brennan's, and the grandiose Creole cuisine of Antoine's. What few outsiders know is that it is a city with superb Italian-accented restaurants, too. You enjoy unique Creole-style Italian food in the form of muffaletta sandwiches (cold cuts and olive salad on great rounds of crusty bread), or in the familiar Italian salad served by so many restaurants, for which greens are heaped with chopped pickled vegetables and olives. But the best place to eat Italian in New Orleans is out at Mosca's.

Tradition demands going to Mosca's as a group of at least four but preferably six or eight people so you can order lots of different dishes and taste some of everything. (Warning: most portions for one are actually big enough for two.) Whet your whistle with marinated crabmeat, available in or out of the shell, and always utterly fresh. Then move on to one of several pastas, which include homemade ravioli, meatballs and spaghetti that transcend the cliché, and the dish that many consider Mosca's best—spaghetti bordelaise, which is an elegant, dizzyingly aromatic, and unimprovable combination of noodles, butter, oil, and garlic.

After pasta, you are ready for Mosca's big-gun main courses. There are a couple of luxuriously rich seafood casseroles, known by the simple names "baked oysters" and "baked shrimp." The shrimp or oysters are cooked with massive amounts of garlic and seasoned bread crumbs—a preparation so perfect that dozens of restaurants throughout Creole country refer to similar dishes as "shrimps Mosca" or "oysters Mosca"; there is succulent chicken cacciatore; there are steaks and chops cut to order and homemade Italian sausage served with big buttered mushrooms; even a dish as simple as roasted chicken somehow tastes better than it ought to, considering its simple-seeming ingredients.

Yes, Mosca's is a dilapidated-looking place, but as soon as you twirl your fork into the spaghetti bordelaise and inhale its garlicky bouquet, you realize that this restaurant by the side of the long, lonely highway is one good reason New Orleans is famous as a food town.

MOTHER'S
401 POYDRAS, NEW ORLEANS, LA (504) 523-9656

Mother's is reason enough to visit New Orleans. The place remains what it has been since the 1930s—a blue-plate lunchroom where, for a few dollars, locals from every rung of the social ladder come to feast. In the morning, there are grits, which are available with debris (the local term for shreds of beef that enrich the gravy) and biscuits. At lunch, in addition to po' boy sandwiches, they serve gumbo (Wednesday), red beans and rice (Tuesday), and bread pudding with brown brandy sauce for dessert.

It's an everyday place where everybody waits in line. Come early, not only because you will get your sandwich sooner. The first lunchtime customers have the opportunity to avail themselves of a lagniappe—cracklin's from the baked ham. These are the little amber squiggles and crusty sweet chunks from the outside of the roast, which connoisseurs use to gild their po' boy.

The most famous of Mother's po' boys is a Ferdi's special: roast beef and beef gravy, plus a pile of ham and (if you get it "dressed," which you should) pickle slices, lettuce, mustard, and—as they say in New Orleans— my'nez. All these things are contained inside a length of crackle-crusted bread only a few hours fresh out of the baker's oven.

Rugged as it is, the bread is fleecy-soft inside, and cannot stave off the inevitable escape of all the sloppy things it holds. Mayo leaks, then some tomato slithers out, and gravy drips. You eat fast, and try to catch falling debris, and although the bread stays intact, the table over which you have ingested this majestic work of culinary art looks like the aftermath of a world-class food fight.

ROBIN'S
HIGHWAY 352, HENDERSON, LA (318) 228-7594

We had a heck of a time getting to Robin's the first time we ate there. A tipster had written the name down on a piece of paper, and as we drove through Breaux Bridge and up to the edge of the Atchafalaya Basin, we asked a lot of people to direct us to Robin's, pronouncing it just like the name of the red-breasted bird. It wasn't until we met Lionel Robin, the proprietor, that we realized why everyone we asked had seem perplexed when we told them where we were going. The accent in Robin's name is on the second syllable—it is pronounced Ro-*ban*, in French, as in superb Cajun cooking.

Here are some of the most distinctive restaurant meals in swamp country. When it's crawfish season, this is the place to eat it: any one of ten different ways: Étouffé, fried, boiled, stewed, stuffed into green peppers, rolled into boulettes, made into meatballs, cooked in a pastry crust, in gumbo, and in bisque. A crawfish dinner gets you the best of these, starting with the bisque, which is smoky, complex, and rich with the essence of crawdads. Dinner then moves on to a few boiled and fried ones, étouffé served over rice, boulettes (a boulette is like a meatball), stuffed pepper, and a superior pie in which the little crustaceans share space with vegetables and plenty of garlic in a translucent-thin crust.

The only crawfish dish we don't particularly recommend at Robin's is gumbo—not because it isn't good (it is), but because the shrimp and okra gumbo is even better. And chicken and sausage gumbo, while containing none of the seafood for which Robin's is renowned, is wonderful—brilliantly spiced, thick with sausage you will remember for a long time.

Although Henderson is out in the cane fields pretty far from civilization as we know it, Robin's is a polite and sophisticated restaurant: white cloths on the tables, double digit prices, credit cards accepted. This notation on the menu, however, is no affectation: *"Ici nous parlons français." Et nous bien mangons!*

SCHNELL'S
5501 FOURTH ST., MARRERO (NEW ORLEANS), LA (504) 347-7518

One of our most trusted *Roadfood* tipsters, Dave Kershaw of the Kershaw Ready-Mix Concrete and Sand Company of Kansas, returned home from a trip to New Orleans and wrote to us to say, "Schnell's on the

West Bank: a joint. Roast beef sandwich out of this world. Very messy, needed to clean my beard between each bite." Bull's-eye! Any time of day you want a fistful of messy po' boy sandwich, a Creole blue-plate lunch, or sleeves-up Gulf Coast seafood, this functional eating hall with its condiment-stocked tables fills the bill just about perfectly.

The sandwiches are oozy ones made using superior French bread and loaded with ingredients. In addition to Kershaw's choice of gravy-dripping, pot roast–tender beef there are good cold cuts (ham especially stands out), fried oysters, and even really good hamburgers and cheeseburgers (this kitchen grinds its own beef).

Every day Schnell's offers a couple of old-fashioned, New Orleans lunches: white beans and rice with smoked sausage or baked macaroni and sausage on Monday; highly seasoned red beans and rice or chewy pork chops on Wednesday; fried chicken on Thursday, available with stupefyingly tasty "cream potatoes and gravy" or lima beans and rice; shrimp stew or seafood gumbo on Friday. On Sunday, the specialty of the house has long been chicken, baked or stewed, accompanied by oyster dressing, rice and gravy, peas, or potato salad. Every day of the week there is a roster of boiled or fried seafood, including trout, shrimp, catfish, and local crabs and crawfish when they are in season.

Don't come to Schnell's for suave service or elegant cuisine or romantic atmosphere. Come to eat well and cheap.

MAINE

BEAL'S LOBSTER PIER
CLARK POINT RD., SOUTHWEST HARBOR, ME (207) 244-3202

B eal's gives out a small map showing how to find Southwest Harbor, along with a drawing of a lobster and a slogan: "Dine on the dock in a lovely Maine fishing village." It doesn't get much lovelier than this. You sit at picnic tables on a pier over the water, with lobster traps for decoration and fishing boats for scenery. There is a shed where you pick your live lobster by size and choose raw or steamed clams, shrimp or crabmeat for an appetizer. The lobsters are steamed for about twenty minutes and are served piping hot, their shells packed with a wealth of firm sweet, pink meat.

Near the shed where you get the lobster is another, smaller shed that sells quahog chowder, which makes a great first course, and engagingly homemade blueberry cake or pie for dessert. Carry all your own food to a table and, with the mountains of Acadia National Park for scenery, and the sound of the lobstermen's boats rocking in their berths for background music, dig into one of this land's finest sleeves-up meals.

CHAUNCEY CREEK LOBSTER PIER
CHAUNCEY CREEK RD., KITTERY POINT, ME (207) 439-1030

Would you like some good Down East blueberry pie or crusty French bread or fresh garden salad with your meal? If so, you will have to bring them yourself to the Chauncey Creek Lobster Pier. Bring your own beer or wine, too, if you want some, because the menu here is short and true to shoreline tradition. No frills . . . and no disappointments.

There are a few nice things to eat other than lobster. A chowder of the day is always on the menu, as are peel-and-eat shrimp, shrimp cocktails, and lobster rolls. You can get oysters on the half shell, mussels steamed in wine with garlic; and to accompany the lobster there are cole slaw and potato salad and bags of potato chips. To drink, there is coffee, tea, or soda pop. The dessert selection is limited to frozen ice cream on a stick.

Pick a live lobster and they boil it for you. It comes with butter for dipping and a nutcracker for cracking, and you can eat outdoors (bring a sweater at night) or under a roof. It is a simple meal, and a relatively cheap one (depending on the current price of lobsters, which seems headed downwards these days), but ambience like this cannot be bought at any price.

COLE FARMS
ROUTE 100, GRAY, ME (207) 657-4714

Inland Maine is an interesting place to eat, where the cafes, diners, and lunchrooms are a treasury of true New England cookery, with little shoreline compromise to please out-of-towner tastes. Coming from the south up the Maine Turnpike, the first such place to savor is Cole Farms in the village of Gray. Here is an honest menu, listing, for example, two kinds of soup: Campbell's or Cole Farms', the latter selling for ten cents more per cup. It also lists "Mashed Potatoes—When Available." The waitress explained that Cole Farms does not use instant spuds, so when one batch of real mashed potatoes is gone, customers must wait until more are mashed. Lemonade is freshly squeezed; can it be that the mayonnaise on the BLT is homemade?

It isn't just authenticity that makes Cole Farms' food special. It has uncommon character. Many house specialties are stubbornly regional. The menu lists five kinds of pudding, including odd New England favorites like Indian (cornmeal) and Grape-Nuts. (There is Grape-Nuts ice cream, too.) You can make a meal of baked beans, with or without hot dogs, or of American chop suey, the dowdy combination of ground beef, overcooked vegetables, and elbow macaroni that some New England boarding school alumni may remember with horror. Corn or fish chowder is always on the menu, as are super-clammy, crunchy clam cakes.

When Cole Farms opens at five in the morning, most customers come for muffins. A list of the day's repertoire is posted by the door. They are available with fillings such as blueberry, apple, bran, even oatmeal; or you can get them absolutely plain—a purposeful breakfast breadstuff that Warren Cole told us is known simply as "old-fashioned egg muffins." These are truly wonderful, and the kind of ordinary food no tourist restaurant would ever dream of serving. They are warm and eggy, served hot directly from the oven, augmented with a pat of butter and a blob of honey.

Cole Farms is a big cafe, four or five rooms strung together, then partitioned with a kind of chicken-wire fence, so that even though the space is sprawling, each booth seems cozy. Pleasant as it is, you would never call it picturesque. Decor is a cavalier mix of varnished pine with Formica. Place settings are marked by paper mats that ask *Did You Know?* and feature trivia questions.

EATON'S LOBSTER POOL
LITTLE DEER ISLE, ME (207) 348-2383

A simple restaurant with an indoor dining room and a short menu, Eaton's Lobster Pool affords a lovely view of water all around. Steaks, seafood, and sandwiches are available ("for children," our waitress explained), but the reason you want to come here is seafood, lobster in particular, which is perfectly steamed and served whole with all the necessary tools for extracting its sweet meat. Get it accompanied by steamers and sweet corn (late summer). Bring your own beer or wine, and reservations are advised.

THE ENTERPRISE
ROUTE 25, CORNISH, ME (207) 625-4452

Mel Allen of *Yankee* magazine once called the pies baked by Elaine Noyes of The Enterprise "perfect." She makes three or four dozen every day, about ten or twelve varieties. There are the usual fruits and berries (raspberry pie is made using berries from her own bushes), lemon meringue, pumpkin, peanut butter cream, custard, and chocolate cream;

and there are some wild-and-crazy, brightly colored ones like gelatinized grasshopper pie (crème-de-menthe green). Some are the soul of tradition: apple pie is little more than Granny Smiths, sugar, cinnamon, nutmeg, a dash of vanilla, and butter inside a double crust. Some of the wilder variations are insouciantly modern: cherry brandy pie combines a whole jar of Marshmallow Fluff with whipped cream, cherry juice, brandy, and chopped Maraschinos.

People from Portland, an hour away, regularly take Sunday drives up Route 25 to the foothills of the White Mountains so they can come to The Enterprise and eat a slice or two of Mrs. Noyes's pie. Travelers serious about their *Roadfood* do not want to head up into Maine without one.

One important thing to know about The Enterprise is that the food served before the pie is excellent. It is not fancy, certainly not as dazzling as pumpkin walnut pie or any of the pumped-up meringue beauties always available; but it is real (as in *real* mashed potatoes, with occasional lumps and flecks of skin) and it is satisfying (as in tender Yankee pot roast with natural gravy). There are steaks and chops, seafood of all kinds, sandwiches and hamburgers, hot breads with dinner, and blueberry, sunrise, and honey-bran muffins every morning. Whatever you order, be assured that it will be good and homey. What Elaine Noyes doesn't make, her sisters and her daughter do.

HARRASEEKET LUNCH & LOBSTER COMPANY
AT THE TOWN LANDING, FREEPORT, ME (207) 865-3535

The specialty of Harraseeket Lunch and Lobster Company, other than lobsters (live, to go; or boiled, to eat here) is a fried seafood basket. Don't let that scare you away if you are a fried-food frowner: the boiled lobsters are delicious, and Harraseeket serves steamers and hot buttered clam rolls and lobster rolls, too; all are just fine. But when we dine here, it is on fried seafoods—fish, oysters, and clams. The clams are giants, hefty gnarled spheres of golden crust enveloping mouthfuls of ocean nectar. On the side, you want onion rings: puffy circles of brittle sweet batter around a hoop of onion that still has crunch. Clam cakes are good, too, their puffy dough holding dozens of little nuggets of marine goodness.

Now that the management has put an awning up over the picnic tables, you can dine outdoors even when it rains. They tell us that it does rain in Freeport, but every visit we have made to town in search of our favorite clam baskets and onion rings, the sun was shining brightly and gulls were

swooping overhead through the blue, blue sky. It is almost painfully picturesque, this eat-in-the-rough jewel of a clam shack overlooking the South
Freeport Harbor. But even if it were ugly, we would recommend it for the
seafood baskets.

LINE HOUSE RESTAURANT
ROUTE 1, YORK, ME (207) 439-3401

The Line House has been selling clams and more here on the Kittery
border for half a century. It began as a small seafood shack, and the
basic shoreline eat-in-the-rough plates featuring seafood and fried potatoes
are still delightful; but now there is so much else to eat.

Breakfast, for example: hot corned-beef hash with a butter-burnished
fried egg on top; warm blueberry muffins that fall into fluffy tufts of indigo-
streaked cake when pulled apart to receive a pat of butter; good, strong
coffee served with real cream.

The meal we like best in this comfortable roadside eatery is lunch. We
start with oyster stew, which is in fact little more than milk, oysters, oyster
liquor, and a surface slick of butter dotted with paprika. Then we move on
to either fried seafood or clam cakes (both highly recommended) or such
habitual blue-plate delights as hot turkey sandwiches, meat loaf and potatoes, or franks and really fine homemade baked beans. Frequently, the
daily specials include that dowdy Down East delight, American chop
suey—a bit like a superior homemade Hamburger Helper—or simple and
tasty macaroni and cheese. For dessert there are, of course, puddings. Or
strawberry shortcake, served on a flaky baking powder biscuit.

MAINE DINER
ROUTE 1, WELLS, ME (207) 646-4441

Years ago, we used to pass the Maine Diner while motoring up Route 1,
but never stopped to eat. Any normal traveling time of year, it was
closed. In fact, a native of the town of Wells informed us that the owner, a
Down East coot whose pleasure was to serve only neighbors and friends,
locked the door as soon as tourists started coming. Each winter, after all
the meddlesome interlopers disappeared, he opened up once again. It was
a curious little place, a north country diner made entirely of wood, painted
white with crisp blue trim. Its local look, and the legendary inhospitality of
the owner, made it all the more intriguing.

In the mid-eighties, Bruce and Myles Henry of Drake's Island bought the place, spiffed it up, and changed its policy. They decided to keep the diner open during normal business hours, they told us, because they actually are interested in attracting customers, even ones who aren't natives. The Henry Brothers devised a menu of sleeves-up Yankee shoreline cooking, the kind of food we tourists crave when we hit the road north.

Fried clams, for instance: vigorously oceanic, just a wee bit oily, so fragile the crust seems to melt away as your teeth sink into them. And lobster, most especially a hot lobster roll that the menu immodestly describes as "FANTASTIC!" The menu is not exaggerating. It is what we have always thought of as a Connecticut-style roll, meaning that it is *hot*, as opposed to a lobster-*salad* roll, which is served cold, with mayonnaise. You get nothing but plump chunks of resilient, buttery lobster meat spilling out of a grilled wiener bun. It is impossible to eat with one's hands like a sandwich, because the bun is soaked with butter and disintegrates under the weight of its filling. But you *do* eat it with your hands, and fingers glisten as they pick smooth strips of claw and knobby knuckle meat, and occasional shreds of butter-sopped bread.

The lobster roll is glorious, but we have saved the best for last: the Henry brothers' grandmother's lobster pie. Of all the good Down East things you can eat along the coast, this casserole, elegant yet elementary, is one that mustn't be missed. Your ceramic dish contains plump sections of lobster—soft claw and chewy tail meat—drenched in butter, topped with a mixture of cracker crumbs and tomalley. It is a strange, punk-colored dish, monstrous green and brown and pink, shockingly rich.

Each patron who orders lobster pie is awarded a bumper sticker that tells the world all about it.

MOODY'S DINER
ROUTE 1, WALDOBORO, ME (207) 832-7468

The introduction to the little book *What's Cooking at Moody's Diner* notes that the Moody family runs its diner "like a restaurant, not a museum." This is an important point to make because Moody's is such an antique you could mistake it for an exhibit at the Smithsonian: a half-century-old green and white diner by the side of the road with a neon sign outside heralding "EAT," an interior of worn-smooth pine booths and green-upholstered chrome counter stools, and a staff of waitresses who gab with the regulars in Maine accents so thick you can hardly understand them.

Hungry travelers will find just about anything they crave on Moody's big menu, but we like it for its repertoire of such culinary curios as New England boiled dinner (on Thursday), red flannel hash, haddock in egg sauce, a full array of seafood stews, butterscotch pudding, Grape-Nuts custard pudding, and steamed Boston brown bread to accompany plates of baked beans.

Alvah Moody attributes the success of the diner to the fact that it was the only place open round-the-clock between Bangor and Portland before the interstate highway was built; but that's just typical Down East understatement. Moody's has thrived since the 1930s because it serves good food at low prices and is as comfortable as an old slipper. Although it has changed over the years, evolving from a lunchwagon to a full-kitchen diner with counter, stools, and booths, the food has remained constant: unadulterated Yankee cooking.

For breakfast there are blueberry muffins that are gorgeous when pulled in half and dolloped with butter: watch the butter melt into the lacy-textured purple- and cream-colored cake. Or choose a molasses doughnut, which is great for dunking; or a hermit, which is a simple square of glazed crust filled with jam. At lunch and dinner there are meals of meat loaf, corned beef, and pork chops with potatoes as well as sandwiches, hearty chowders, and such local favorites as fried tripe, franks 'n' beans (great beans!), and subtly spiced Indian pudding for dessert. Of course, there are plenty of pies, including a nursery-nice custard pie dusted with nutmeg and a wickedly sweet walnut cream pie.

To accompany your meal, there is a soda fountain repertoire of beverages with names that will make no sense whatsoever to an out-of-stater. A "milk shake," for instance, is milk and flavoring, whereas a "velvet" is what most of the rest of the world knows as a milk shake (except in Rhode Island, where it is called a "cabinet"): milk, flavoring, and ice cream.

NUNAN'S LOBSTER HUT
CAPE PORPOISE, ME (207) 967-4362
(SUPPER ONLY, STARTING AT 5:00 P.M.)

The best thing about Nunan's Lobster Hut, other than the lobster, is the plumbing. In particular, the sinks. Should you desire to wash your hands before, during, or after eating, the sinks are right there, out in the open dining room, ready for immediate action. They are serious, proletarian sinks, like you'd want to have next to your workbench in the basement.

For drying hands, Nunan's supplies rolls of paper towels.

In some restaurants, this arrangement might not be so appealing, but at Nunan's Lobster Hut—which really is a hut—the sanitary accommodations are exactly right because this place is designed for serious lobster eating. Tables have easy-wipe surfaces with ribs around the edge to keep the inevitable mess from falling to the floor. The floor is painted battleship gray, which makes it easy to swab at the end of the day. Overhead lights are unadorned tubes. A touch of romance is provided in the form of a utility candle stuck in a thick cork on every table.

Lobsters are brought to tables on pizza pans, accompanied by bags of potato chips and store-bought rolls. Coffee is served in mugs. Water comes in paper cups. Bring your own wine or beer.

No frills at Nunan's will distract you from the perfection of the lobster (except maybe the view, when the panels on the sides of the dining room are raised and reveal a pleasant vista of Cape Porpoise marshlands). Each lobster is steamed to order in several inches of salty water for exactly twenty minutes, emerging with silky tender claw meat, its knuckles and tail succulent and chewy. The only secrets to her lobsters' deliciousness, Bertha Nunan told Mel Allen of *Yankee* magazine, are that the water must be *fresh* for each batch, and the lobster must be cooked immediately before serving.

The Nunan family has been lobstering for three generations, so by now they have the process of enjoying their catch down to its essence. After you've polished off the lobster, there are homemade brownies or a slice of one of Bertha Nunan's pies, the recipes for which have been perfected over the last thirty years. Blueberry and apple are memorable, their subtly sweetened fruits encased in sugar-dusted crusts.

ROBINSON'S WHARF
ROUTE 27, SOUTHPORT, ME (207) 633-3830

Most tourists, ourselves included, are attracted to the pier when they first dine at Robinson's Wharf. Here one sits at picnic tables overlooking lobster boats in Townsend Gut, inhaling the scents of cold seawater, hot lobster meat, and buttered corn-on-the-cob. It is a stirringly appetizing place to eat. But indoors at Robinson's Wharf is nice, too. The big gray dining room is reminiscent of a mess hall in a battleship, with wood tables and iron chairs and a utility sink at one end for washing up.

Wherever you eat, Robinson's Wharf is an authentic Maine culinary event you will not soon forget. Operated by lobstermen (who sell live lobsters and clams by the pound or peck), this place is as casual as a meal can be . . . and as sublime. You pick your lobster, they weigh it, and they boil it. It is cooked an old-fashioned way, in a net along with ears of corn and steamers in a boiling tank of briny water. While you wait, you can avail yourself of fish chowder or milky lobster stew, a clam roll or a clam plate, or a bucket of steamers. When the lobster is ready it is served on a cardboard tray with a bag of chips and no utensil other than a nutcracker, which signs remind customers to return when they are finished eating.

Cakes, brownies, and ice cream are available for dessert: a sweet ending for a consummate culinary experience.

MARYLAND

BARBARA FRITCHIE CANDYSTICK RESTAURANT
ROUTE 40W, FREDERICK, MD (301) 662-2500

The Barbara Fritchie Candystick Restaurant was modern once. It reminds us of an extra-wide postcard or a CinemaScope movie from the 1950s: broad and enthusiastically styled, bright and pretty and proud of itself, now a relic of simpler times.

Come here to eat if you like things like triple-decker sandwiches and full-course roast turkey with potatoes, or if you seek such regional fare as baked crab imperial and butter-fried crab cakes. Barbara Fritchie's country ham is the real thing: crusty, salty, chewy, with an acute, complex flavor that makes it one of the South's most esteemed foods.

Baked things are a specialty ("Baked in our ultra-modern kitchen," according to the giddy menu). Mince pie, filled with dizzyingly rich mincemeat made on the premises, is sensational, as is the big, rugged-crusted apple dumpling loaded with supple spicy slivers of baked apple, and available for fifty-five cents extra with a half-pint carton of milk to pour on top (get the milk; it balances the somewhat dry, albeit delicious, crust).

Breakfast is served all day, and it is a satisfying roadside meal. We especially recommend the powerhouse ham, the good and greasy hash-brown potatoes, a slice of banana bread, or the apple dumpling. If you have a big appetite and want to savor a really fine, rib-sticker of a meal often served in cafes and restaurants along the Pennsylvania-Maryland border, but considered uncouth nearly everywhere else, try Barbara Fritchie's creamed chipped beef on toast. It is an agreeable plate of food—contrary to its ignominious reputation.

Waitresses at the Barbara Fritchie are good old (and good young) gals of the no-nonsense school of waitressing: uniformed and shod in fast, orthopedic shoes. The dining room is a capacious place with long, long counters and comfortable booths lined up alongside picture windows. It is all done up in candy-colored upholstery and bright "candystick chandeliers" (a product of Denmark, the menu advises, further boasting that they are made of a material named Rotoflex) in shades of yellow, orange, green, and red. A small array of souvenirs is available near the cash register, including boxes of Barbara Fritchie candies.

It is amazing to come across this place if you are traveling from east to west. The trip through Frederick goes past every brand of fast food known to humankind, plus all the usual mini-malls, billboards, and gas stations that are a familiar part of urban sprawl. Then at the far end of town, just as the road returns to its lovely bucolic rhythms of hills and greenery, you spot this fine old restaurant that isn't like any of the others. You cannot miss finding it if you are traveling along I-40. Its sign is a giant red-and-white-striped candy cane.

CAPTAIN'S GALLEY
MAIN ST., CRISFIELD, MD (301) 968-1636

Crab cakes, like barbecue and Chicago-style pizza, never seem to taste quite as good when you eat them in restaurants outside their natural habitat. They belong to the Chesapeake Bay; it is here they are in their glory, and it is practically impossible to find a bad one. Crab cakes are served at every level of the socio-gastronomic ladder—from the cheap (and delicious) ones you will have on paper plates in funky waterside crab houses along the shore in St. Mary's County to elegant ones dished out on fine china in D.C.'s swankiest restaurants.

Perhaps it is the perfume of the nearby water that makes the pearly white meat taste so especially right, or the tart mid-Atlantic accents of the waitresses, or the cold beer that is almost always served alongside; most likely, it is the utter freshness of the crabmeat that makes the difference. This is where crabs are harvested, and where restaurant chefs as well as home cooks have devised dozens of ways to take advantage of the local crop.

There is no place to find crabs fresher than on the tables of the Captain's Galley, a wood-paneled, family-style dining room in Crisfield perched above Chesapeake Bay. The Galley is a polite place with a decoy display on one wall and a gift shop next door, and a menu of dinners that come on plates, designed to be eaten with utensils (no sleeves-up crab feasts here).

There really is a captain running the Galley; his name is James Dodson; he is a crabber who makes his living not only at the restaurant, but also by going into the bay, which he claims supplies his kitchen with "ninety-eight percent of the seafood we serve." He explained to us that crab cakes are so good in these parts because Maryland backfin crab is sweeter and lumpier than crab from anywhere else; and we were convinced of that fact as soon as we dug into a pair of his crab cakes. They were beauties: golden-crusted with buttery fissures exposing the creamy crabmeat inside, so tender you want to call it fluffy. We have also relished Captain's Galley soft-shell crabs—lightly battered and sautéed in butter, as well as hefty oyster fritters and a luxurious crab imperial. But it's those big, sweet crab cakes that will keep us coming back to the Captain's Galley.

COPSEY'S SEAFOOD RESTAURANT
ROUTE 5, MECHANICSVILLE, MD (301) 884-4235

Seafood is Copsey's specialty; in fact, we believe this squat roadside eatery serves some of the best crab cakes in all of St. Mary's County, as well as freshly shucked oysters on the half shell, naughty but delicious fried seafood, smoky-flavored crab soup loaded with shreds of meat and vegetables, and full-blown crab feasts. We will tell you about those glorious crab cakes forthwith, but first, a word about stuffed ham.

A Maryland rarity that goes back to Colonial times, ham-stuffing is a strategy of embellishment that started as a way of dressing up lowly pig parts with a "stuffing" of greens, kale, and spice. Somehow it moved up the food chain to the finest of pig parts, the ham. On the one hand, this is the most deluxe way of serving ham, primarily the province of classical and accomplished mid-Atlantic home cooks; but, strangely, it is also the work of chefs in taverns, ham houses, and casual cafes along Route 5 south of Baltimore.

Copsey's serves tender slices of pink, not-too-salty ham augmented by a mellow mixture of cabbage, onions, and kale. Hot sauce is provided if you want to spice it up (many people prefer their stuffed ham highly seasoned), but we like it just the way it is, with some bread and beer on the side.

Now, about the crab cakes. Tidy little ovals of pearl white meat enveloped in a faintly crunchy crust, infused with pepper: a simple and divine dish, served here in a dining room adjacent to a little shop, on tables covered with brown paper for crab feasting. The experience of eating these cakes, or the ham, is a strange one: truly elegant food in the down-homiest surroundings. Just the way we like it.

COURTNEY'S
WATER'S EDGE AT THE END OF 252, RIDGE, MD (301) 872-4403

For shoreline eats of all kinds, crabs in particular, this is a place you want to be. Courtney's specializes in all-you-can-eat steamed hot crabs and beer, served on paper-covered tables, every weekend (or during the week if you call ahead).

Crab cakes are on the menu every day, and they are an only-in-Maryland treat. Loosely packed chunks of meat, gently spiced with pepper, bound inside a fairly rugged red-brown skin, these savory rounds are more crab than cake, and tend to fall apart as soon as they are prodded.

Courtney's soups are extraordinarily good. Hot, bright orange crab soup is packed with shreds of meat. Oyster stew is insinuated with a smoky zest, sprinkled with pepper and with a pool of melted butter atop its milky surface. Underneath are oodles of oysters and tiny bits of onion. Every spoonful lifted from the bowl gets gilded by the butter slick that floats on top.

Courtney's is a place of simple pleasures, located by a marina. The dining room is wood-paneled; silverware comes wrapped in a paper napkin. The view out the big red-curtained windows is of the Maryland shoreline stretching away toward the horizon.

THE CRAB CLAW
NAVY POINT AT THE END OF MILL ST., ST. MICHAELS, MD
(301) 745-2900

Hot spiced Maryland blue crabs from the Chesapeake Bay are an obsession on Maryland's Eastern Shore. The most adventurous way to eat them is at a "crab feast." Heaps of cooked crabs are dumped onto your table and you go after their pearl-white spiced meat armed with pick and mallet, piles of napkins, and pitchers of beer. The Crab Claw provides all the fixings for just such a banquet. High on a pier overlooking the Miles River, its dining room clatters with all the sounds of hammering, cracking, and slurping that are a crab feast's happy tune. A sign above the tables strewn with emptied shells proclaims "BLUE CRABS REIGN SUPREME."

Placemats provide instructions about how to extract meat from a cooked hard-shell crab; but unless you are experienced in crustacean gastronomy, you will work hard to get those big, silky hunks of sweet spiced meat that veteran crab feasters manage to extricate with aplomb. Ourselves, we are all thumbs when it comes to crab-eating, and too often seem to be able to salvage only strings and shreds of meat from even the largest crabs. That is why we frequently forgo crab feasts at the Crab Claw and indulge in the rest of their menu, which promises "Crabs—All Ways."

Crab fluff, for example: here is a dish for those of us who lack the manual dexterity serious crab-eating requires. A fluff is a sphere of crabmeat dipped in spicy batter and deep-fried: like a crab cake, but brittle-skinned and with the added naughty smack of lusciousness that only a fry basket can impart. The crab cakes are good, too. There are soft-shell crabs with parchment-crisp exteriors holding the sweetest (and delightfully accessible) meat; there is crab imperial; and there are roes of assorted fish in the spring. The Crab Claw even makes a fried hard-shell crab, which is a strange concept indeed. A whole crab, in its shell, is blanketed with batter and fried until golden brown, then served with a knife and a mallet. The idea is to pick some of the batter off the exterior, then crack the shell and retrieve the meat inside. It's as much work as a crab feast; and in our opinion, the bonus of all that good fried batter doesn't compensate for the relatively small amount of meat a single specimen contains.

The Crab Claw sells crabs by the dozen, to go, for picnickers; it also provides a dinghy to accommodate customers who arrive by boat and cannot find a berth within convenient walking distance.

GUNNING'S CRAB HOUSE
3901 S. HANOVER ST., BALTIMORE, MD (301) 354-0085

For good eats and good times, go to south Baltimore and find the neighborhood known as Brooklyn. This working-class part of town is famous for its crab houses: big, bare eateries where people go to drink beer by the pitcher and eat steamed, spiced hard-shell crabs by the dozen.

You will have an abundant choice of crab houses in Brooklyn, and we can practically guarantee they're all good. Steaming crabs is a talent bred in the bone of Chesapeake Bay cooks; crab feasts are to this part of the country what barbecue is to Memphis and clam bakes are to Cape Cod. Served the old-fashioned way, preferably in a neighborhood tavern, this is the single distinctive regional meal that all visitors to Baltimore really ought to try.

When the urge for serious crab-eating strikes, and we are anywhere near the Chesapeake Bay, the place we like to go is Gunning's Crab House.

Gunning's is designed to maximize the pleasure of crab eating. The crabs are served as a classic crab house feast, with all the informality the ritual demands. Groups of people buy them by the dozen—jumbo crabs preferred. (Jumbo means more meat for less work.) Instead of being served on plates or platters, they get strewn by the bushelful onto Gunning's Formica tables, which are covered inelegantly with sheets of butcher's wrapping paper. Now it is up to customers to get their meat. Using wooden mallets, plus assorted nut crackers and picks, most people fall into a state of monomaniacal ecstasy as they excavate sweet, lush hunks of pearly white crab from within spice-encrusted shells the color of Mars. The sound of a crowded Gunning's dining room is like some wild jungle filled with monstrous animals busy cracking, breaking, tearing, and slurping at their feed. Eating crabs is not a pretty sight! But it sure tastes good.

Gunning's creates these delectable creatures by steaming them in a big cooker that resembles a gigantic double boiler. This system allows the crabs to suck in vast amounts of the peppery seasonings that simmer in the water below.

To go with the crabs you'll want French-fried onion rings and plenty of beer and maybe, for a change of pace, one of Gunning's succulent deep-fried soft-shell crab sandwiches, or a few of the fragile broiled (not fried) crab cakes. And to put a point on this distinctive feast, you will want an order of deep-fried green pepper rings. They are not dessert, not like chocolate cake or a hot fudge sundae, but these weird, wonderful rings of battered vegetable, lightly dusted with powdered sugar, do make a perfect accompaniment to—or conclusion of—a crab feast; and they are, as far as we know, a Gunning's exclusive.

All this hale-and-hearty food is served in one of two dining rooms adjacent to the bar, or (weather permitting) in an open-air "crab garden" out back. The only other thing you need to know about is Gunning's dress code: it is essential that you wear sloppy clothes. Eating crabs is a wipe-your-hands-on-your-jeans jubilee.

LEXINGTON MARKET
EUTAW AND LEXINGTON STS., BALTIMORE, MD (301) 685-6169

Although touched by the sanitizing brush of urban renewal, the Lexington Market remains triumphantly funky. Stall merchants hawk shellfish, fresh-killed chickens (feet attached), dead rabbits, grated horseradish, and the favorite snack foods of the mid-Atlantic coast amidst a marketplace confusion that teems with streetwise characters who make you want to hold tight to your wallet. But hey, loosen up, put on some blue jeans (where you don't mind wiping your hands between rounds of seafood, fast food, street food, and junk food), and bring a big appetite to this merry place.

Stroll from dozens of freshly opened oysters on the half shell at Faidley's to a hot spiced hard crab, to a paper plate full of crab cakes, to a hoagie or a Mount Olympus gyro, and then to the tubby porcine franks known in these parts as half-smokes, and finally to a teetering cone loaded with your favorite ice cream. Long before the 1980s, when the term "grazing" was popularized to describe the culinary habits of ants-in-the-pants yuppies, markets such as this provided eastern city dwellers the opportunity to feast forever.

OLDE OBRYCKI'S
1729 E. PRATT ST., BALTIMORE, MD (301) 732-6399

Here is why people who live around the Chesapeake Bay call a meal of crabs a crab feast. Spiced hard-shell crabs are dumped by the basketful onto plain tables, accompanied by pitchers of beer. It is an unholy mess, and when the tables are crowded, all the cracking and hammering make the dining room sound like a convention of orthopedic surgeons. It is a feast indeed, the ultimate indulgence for crab lovers, who always accompany the sweet, spicy meat they extract from these big beauties by great, cold pitchers of beer. After eating here in 1981, Craig Claiborne proclaimed Olde Obrycki's "the finest crabmeat feast I have ever been witness to or participated in."

Crab feasting is hard work; if you want to relax and let the kitchen get the meat out of the exoskeletons, Olde Obrycki's also happens to be a fantastic lazy person's seafood restaurant. Try the gossamer-textured crabcakes, or the deep-fried deviled crab, or sauteed soft crabs, on a plate or in a truly luscious sandwich. Or crab imperial—a dish that is so awful everywhere else that it ought to be outlawed; at Olde Obrycki's, it's a creamy revelation. The other good thing is the place itself—formerly a weather-beaten tavern in an old row house. Its dining rooms have been spruced up, and the staff tends to be more obsequious than the rough-and-tumble characters who dish out the chow in most other crab houses. There is even candlelight to crack crabs by, but the neighborhood all around Obrycki's still has the salty smack of a seaboard city not yet "saved" by progress.

WOMAN'S INDUSTRIAL EXCHANGE RESTAURANT
333 N. CHARLES ST., BALTIMORE, MD (301) 685-4388

B ack in the roaring 1980s when eating was fashionable and trend-watchers got all agitated about hip styles of cookery, an editor of a cooking magazine predicted to us that gelatin was "coming back."

"Jell-O?" we questioned with glee, being devotees of elaborate, ultra-customized gelatin salads festooned with coconut, marshmallows, mandarin oranges, nuts, seeds, cheese, etc.

"No, not Jell-O," she explained, reminding us that "Jell-O," like "Kleenex" and "Band-Aid," is a trademarked brand name. "Not bright-colored, sticky-sweet desserts. I mean subtle-flavored aspics, made from scratch, with plain gelatin and interesting stock."

Her prediction never came to pass, and the bubble of fascination for trendy food burst with so many other affectations of the upscale decade; but even if nouvelle gelatin is an idea whose time will never come, we know just the place to go to enjoy a taste of it. And it is hardly an avant-garde restaurant.

The Woman's Industrial Exchange Restaurant in Baltimore is so far out of fashion, it's cool. Aspic never lost favor in this downtown lunchroom that first opened for business back in 1882. The last time we were there, we had an inspired lunch of what the menu called "chicken jelly" (a.k.a. chicken aspic), accompanied by deviled eggs and freshly made mayonnaise, and a plate of oven-warm baking powder biscuits.

The front room of the Woman's Exchange is an outlet for ladies' handwork such as shawls, embroidered pillows, doll clothes, and hand-knit sweaters (at low, low prices). "Whenever you purchase any of the merchandise," a sign advises, "you receive good value and are aiding a very deserving woman."

The dining room in back is a time machine into the genteel past: black-and-white tile floor, long red banquette, cream-colored walls hung with soothing pictures of birds and flowers. Waitresses, in their crisp blue uniforms, are the type who fret if you don't clean the plate. When we left half of a deviled egg, our waitress insisted on wrapping it up so we could have it with us later, for an afternoon snack.

The menu is from-scratch good food, some of it as nostalgic as the chicken jelly. Croquettes are a frequent lunch special, as is floating island dessert. There are regional meals, too, such as Baltimore crab cakes, made with great hunks of sweet meat; and breakfast of biscuits and country ham. The dessert list features towering meringue pies, mocha cake, yellow cake, and devil's food cake (with white icing).

When you leave, you will notice a wide variety of jams, jellies, and preserves for sale by the cash register. They are the work of deserving women, too, packed in mismatched, miscellaneous jars the way Grandma used to do it.

MASSACHUSETTS

ANN'S CAFETERIA
250 HUNTINGTON AVE., BOSTON, MA (617) 266-1980

Ann's announces itself to passers-by with a sign of handsome neon let-ters that spell out "SELF-SERVICE—CHARCOAL BROILED." Below these durable boasts the restaurant's storefront window is filled with messages on semi-permanent placards, including "Breakfast All Day," "Roast Beef on a Roll," and "No. 1 Special Cheeseburger Sandwich." Blue-plate specials are alive and well at Ann's, and some of them are mighty good.

The interior is bathed in the greenish glow of overhead fluorescent lights. Tables, topped with boomerang-pattern Formica, are lined up in rows, like prison or school lunch; and the big ones down the center of the room, with six chairs each, are often shared by strangers. There are no waiters or waitresses and no printed menus. When you enter Ann's you proceed to the back of the room to the service counter, behind which are posted at least a dozen menu boards on which movable white letters on a black background list everything the kitchen is currently producing.

The range of food is immense, almost all of it comfortably homespun, from griddle cakes (all day) to such not-unfamiliar exotica as shishkebab with rice pilaf, meat cakes with spaghetti, and Greek sausage served with Greek salad. There is a luncheon special (baked chicken pie with mashed potatoes), a dinner special (soup, roast stuffed turkey, mashed potatoes, and butternut squash), and a breakfast special (eggs and corned-beef hash) as well as several "today's specials" (liver and onions, chicken croquettes, salisbury steak, macaroni and cheese), and a list of nearly a dozen vegetables *du jour* (all unabashedly overcooked and steam-table limp).

Service is close to instantaneous. Within a minute or so of taking your order, the lady behind the counter will have started piling an orange plastic tray with loaded dishes. Pay for the meal, then carry the tray to a table and dig in. None of what you eat at Ann's will awe a fussy gourmet; and frankly, we weren't impressed by either the cheeseburger (nicely greasy-gray, but without the zest of a well-seasoned griddle) or the rice pudding (pasty)—both of which *should* be excellent in this sort of establishment. On the other hand, the French fries are superb in their wanton way—crisp, greasy, fresh out of hot oil. The butternut squash, nearly decomposed from its long tenure behind the counter, is deliciously déclassé. Egg breakfasts with spicy corned-beef hash are jim-dandy; and there's always Jell-O for dessert. In short, we find Ann's exhilaratingly inelegant.

Perhaps the most arresting single charm of this joint, even before you get to the food, is its aromas. A few steps in the door and you begin to inhale the sentimental smells of kitchen history, from an era before food's ascension to high fashion: steam-table string beans venting their well-cooked essence into the air; hot roasted potatoes so soft they are falling apart in their pan, sending forth clouds of starchy perfume; heaps of beef stew; frying beef patties; sizzling hunks of well-cooked skewered lamb; Fryolators bubbling with batches of French fries turning amber in their oily depths; split pea soup as thick as lava, laced with the porcine sweetness of a hambone. If such vintage fragrances pique your enthusiasm and appetite, you will be ravenous by the time you present yourself at Ann's counter to place an order.

BAXTER'S FISH N CHIPS
177 PLEASANT ST., HYANNIS, MA (508) 775-4490

E at in the rough: that's the *Roadfood* way along the shore in New England. Stand in line and study the menu up above. When your turn comes, tell the server what you want. If you are like everybody else, you want fried food and maybe some clam chowder; if you don't want fried food, you are at the wrong restaurant.

When your clam, shrimp, oyster, or scallop plate is ready, it is presented to you on a tray and it is your job to find a place to put this tray so you can eat your meal. Baxter's provides seating at varnished tables in a nautically decorated dining room overlooking Hyannis Harbor, outdoors at picnic tables on the pier, or on the *Governor Brann*, an old ship docked alongside the restaurant.

Crisp, brisk food. The nuggets of clam are meltingly savory, and their sandy-textured, honey-colored crust has a fine, salty smack to it. Scallops and shrimp are good, too; but it's clams that are the *pièces de résistance* from this kitchen. On the side there are the usual fries; but you can also order clam fritters, which are a delightfully doughy variation of the fried-food theme. Red-gold globes of sweet, soft bread, their exteriors more tough than crisp, are dotted with little bits of oceanic clam and served with packs of honey for dipping. For those of us whose appetite for fried things grows insatiable when we are exposed to brisk sea breezes, the fried spheres of clammy bread are a great idea—the perfect companion to a plate of fried clams and fried potatoes.

BRANDY PETE'S
267 FRANKLIN ST., BOSTON, MA (617) 439-4165

Most Bostonians who eat at Brandy Pete's come to have the usual: all-American vittles such as turkey with mashed potatoes and cranberry sauce, pork chops, lamb chops, broiled chicken, and sirloin steak. They come for sole, scrod, or scallops—fried, broiled, or baked-stuffed. Or maybe just for tuna salad sandwiches or BLTs. It is a likable menu, with good chowder to start, and man-sized slabs of pie to top things off.

We like to eat square meals at Brandy Pete's: they make a dandy Welsh rarebit "en casserole" with toast and (optionally) bacon. There are turkey croquettes with "supreme sauce" (a.k.a. white sauce); there are stuffed peppers, old-fashioned spaghetti, and a fine plate of juicy meat loaf. In addition to these everyday delights, Brandy Pete's distinguishes itself as one of New England's pudding bastions, with at least one or two always on the menu, including puddings made from Grape-Nuts, bread, tapioca, and rice.

Favored equally by men in pinstripes or blue collars, as well as ladies in pantyhose or overalls, Pete's has moved from its original location in a yellow-walled pool hall, but it remains a true taste of Beantown in the raw.

BUTLER'S COLONIAL DONUT HOUSE
461 SANFORD RD., WESTPORT, MA (508) 672-4600

B utler's is a little house on the road to Horseneck Beach that serves doughnuts only on the weekends—Friday, Saturday, and Sunday, starting at seven and going until five in the afternoon, or until the supply runs out. They are made by hand, about three hundred dozen each day, starting at two in the morning.

Gosh, they're good. Light and glazed or raised and honey-dipped, these are classic breakfast pastries the likes of which you will find only in New England where, despite the supposed hegemony of muffins, the doughnuts are the best in the land.

The choicest time to come is in the cool weather months, when whipped-cream doughnuts are available. There are long johns filled with sweet red jam and whipped cream, round tan donuts without holes filled with whipped cream and sprinkled with powdered sugar, and the greatest doughnut of them all—a hefty circle of pitch-dark chocolate cake loaded with thick whipped cream.

DURGIN-PARK
30 N. MARKET ST., BOSTON, MA (617) 227-2038

N o reservations are accepted at Durgin-Park, so at any ordinary mealtime, you will likely wait, standing up in line on a creaky wooden staircase. You will be seated at a communal table, where strangers are midway through their dinners, in a garish eating hall that sounds like a gymnasium at half-time and was once described as a cross between Pilgrim dinner and boot camp mess. Like the the Old North Church or the swan boats in the Public Garden, Durgin-Park is a landmark; no other restaurant is truer to the spirit of New England cookery gastronomy yet so exceptional.

Twice a day the open kitchen clatters out good food in large portions at reasonable prices. Every customer begins with a square of grainy yellow cornbread. Then you can move on to such old favorites as lobster stew or Boston scrod, or pot roast or pork loin. The house specialty is prime rib, a gargantuan cut that overhangs its plate. Side that with a mountain of mashed potatoes (into which the kitchen indelicately slides pats of butter, still in paper wrappers) and a scoop of fresh applesauce, and you've got a mighty meal.

What could be more all-American than roast turkey with sage dressing

. . . or New England boiled dinner of corned beef and cabbage? The beans Durgin-Park serves are real Boston baked beans, firm and silky, not too sweet, with a whiplash of molasses. This frumpy food traces its genealogy back to 1742, when the Faneuil Market was opened and a second-story eatery was established to serve the produce vendors. About a century later, it was named for its proprietors John Durgin and Eldridge Park, whose idea was to put heaps of good food on the table at the lowest possible price—amenities and frills be damned.

Although the Faneuil Hall Market has been renovated into a modern urban grazing emporium around the restaurant, and there is even a branch of Durgin-Park at Copley Place, the wide-open dining room, with its red-checked cloths and tables for twenty, is as rude and idiosyncratic as it ever was.

Nobody gets celebrity treatment; nobody is even treated nicely—and that's the fun of it. You'd better know what you want when the waitress comes around, because these gruff old birds give no quarter. They serve meals with all the grace and charm of a hockey player. And the food itself, slapped onto plates in the kitchen, comes in portions suitable for Elmer the Elephant. When you are finished, you pay the lady with dollars. No checks or credit cards, bub.

The Durgin-Park dessert list is tradition itself, featuring hot mince pie in the autumn, apple pan dowdy, deep-dish apple pie, strawberry shortcake on a biscuit, and the quintessential Yankee dessert—Indian pudding. We remember one evening meal at Durgin-Park when we were seated along-side a couple from Alabama who were tasting New England food for the first time. They asked what Indian pudding was. We described the steam-ing cornmeal gruel sweetened with molasses, and these good folks—whose idea of proper dessert was coconut layer cake and divinity fudge—thought we were joking. Cereal for dessert seemed as weird to them as Eskimos eating blubber. But they were brave, and they ordered a dish. The pasty autumn-colored samp arrived hot, with vanilla ice cream melting on top. Their first taste was tentative, but they quickly learned to spoon up some ice cream with the pudding, for a confluence of smooth sweet cream and spicy grain. "It's good," they declared, still not fully convinced, "like sug-ared grits."

FARNHAM'S
88 EASTERN AVE. (RT. 133), ESSEX, MA (508) 768-6643

"Here's your blues," said the waitress as she presented us with a couple of gorgeous blueberry muffins for breakfast at Farnham's. These were delicious muffins, the kind of simple but utterly satisfying cakelike wonders only served in diners and town cafes north of Boston, mostly along the shore, up into Maine. We were amazed at the excellence of the muffins in this adorable little wooden diner by the side of the road because we had always thought of Farnham's strictly as a clam stop.

Clams are Farnham's glory; and as a waitress said to us on an earlier occasion as we tucked into a couple of clam boats (half clams, half French fries), "We are a clam-eating institution." These clams are golden brown, so faintly crisp they taste *delicate*; and their insides, while full and juicy, are never grossly so. Nearly every clam in the boat (or in a box, or on a plate, which also includes superb onion rings) seems to be a perfect balance of crust and crustacean meat—toasty, clean, and ocean-flavored.

On the side, to wash down clams, Farnham's sells Moxie and sarsaparilla.

MA GLOCKNER'S
151 MAPLE, BELLINGHAM, MA (508) 966-1085

Since it opened on Thanksgiving Day in 1937, Ma Glockner's has been endorsed by many, including Arthur Godfrey and Michael Dukakis. Even if celebrity stardust of such magnitude fails to impress you, you will be kind to your tongue if you make it your business to find Maple Street in North Bellingham (you will likely get lost) and feast on chicken dinner at Ma Glockner's.

Specifically, what Messrs. Godfrey and Dukakis liked most about Ma Glockner's were the Swedish rolls—hefty, hot cinnamon buns swirled with spice and sugar. It seems strange to us out-of-towners, but there is an undeniable culinary logic to serving big, tear-apart sweet rolls with chicken dinners. Some of the best-respected chicken dinner halls in and around Rhode Island do it; but Ma Glockner's rolls are definitely the cream of the crop. "People kill for our rolls," a waiter once told us.

Her chicken is superb, too. It is called "berched" chicken, a made-up term for a process that involves deep-frying, steaming, then grilling. The result is a flattened bird with meat that fairly falls off its bones and buttery crisp skin. It is served along with French fries, jellied cranberry sauce, salad with Ma Glockner's "deluxe dressing" (available to take home), and the famous rolls. It is a meal close to perfection, and it is the only thing Ma Glockner's serves (except on Friday night, when baked stuffed shrimp are available). Oh, yes, there is dessert, too: coconut cream pie, ice cream, sherbet, or Jell-O.

Despite having expanded from a twenty-four seat cafe into a multi-room roadhouse that holds five hundred customers at a time (and sometimes has long lines of people outside waiting to get in), Ma Glockner's is a homespun kind of place with varnished pine-paneled walls and the happy ambience that comes from crowds of people all plowing into the same satisfying meal. It's easy to spot once you're on Maple Street: just look for the building with the large neon hen roosting on top.

MIKE'S DONUT SHOP
127 BROADWAY, EVERETT (BOSTON), MA (617) 389-9415

We discovered Mike's doughnuts thanks to Arlene the cab driver, a regular character on Boston's WZLX radio, for which she provides daily morning on-the-road commentary (via cellular telephone) about the underbelly of Beantown life. One chilly November day at dawn Arlene put us in the back of her taxicab and took us on a high-speed tour of Boston's tackiest and wackiest locations. The excursion included gazing upon a "leaning tower of pizza" restaurant, a tour of the Hilltop Steak House (surrounded by a herd of fiberglass cows), a few rounds of Putt-Putt at a dinosaur-themed miniature golf course, a backwards dash the wrong way up Route 1 in Arlene's yellow Chevrolet, bloody Marys in a tavern with walls decorated by its patrons' bounced checks, and the observation of several hideous crime scenes and murder houses for which Arlene provided blow-by-blow forensic details.

As we careened through the produce market, Arlene asked if we were hungry for a Boston cream doughnut. If we were, she advised, she knew where to get the city's best. And before we could blurt out a reply, Arlene's taxi lurched into Mike's parking lot among a swarm of early-morning pick-up trucks, delivery vans, and other cabs. The motto of Mike's, emblazoned on all take-out coffee cups and bags, is "Fresh Cut Donuts."

The joint was crowded, noisy, and confusing, its air thick with the aroma of strong coffee, hot pastries, and sugar glaze. Because she was the expert, we let Arlene order for us. The muffins looked mighty good, but she would have none of them. Donuts are Mike's *spécialité,* and it was donuts we ate: jelly-filled, cinnamon-dusted, chocolate frosted, and plain. All were excellent; and although New England's best breakfast breadstuffs are generally considered to be its muffins, these doughnuts deserve a place on the morning honor roll. We love the plain doughnuts here—with just the right crunch to their crust and a steamy, lightly spiced fluff inside; and we *really* like Mike's French crullers—gossamer twisted circles of eggy batter with a faint sugar coating. Arlene's favorite, the Boston cream doughnut, was a paradigm of its type, a big tan sweet bun loaded with silky cool goo and blanketed on top with a thick sheath of dark chocolate.

Mike's is way off the beaten path, nowhere near any of the city's usual tourist attractions. But if it is good food that attracts you, take a tip from us and Arlene: forget that Old North Church and check out these Boston cream sinkers.

MILDRED'S CHOWDER HOUSE
290 IYANOUGH RD., HYANNIS, MA (508) 775-1045

Chowder isn't the only good thing about Mildred's, but no one should eat here without at least a cup. It is an exquisite soup, its porky pungency rounded by the gentleness of cream, loaded with bits of clam and tender little chunks of potato. This is the paradigm for Cape Cod clam chowder; Mildred's has built a reputation on it since 1949. The little roadside shanty grew into a big eating hall in which uniformed waitresses now wear electronic paging devices so they can be summoned to the kitchen from the far reaches of the dining room, and the menu has expanded to include the likes of seafood Newburg *en casserole* and steaks for fish frowners. But it is the shoreline basics that put Mildred's on America's food map.

In addition to exquisite chowder, there are grand seafood stews, which are svelte bowls filled with little more than warm cream and melted butter combined with big chunks of lobster or scallops. There is fine broiled fish—scrod, sole, haddock; and to end a meal, the menu lists classic Yankee comfort-food desserts, including ginger-spiced Indian pudding, a big heap of Grape Nuts custard, and deep-dish apple pie with ice cream on top.

NO NAME RESTAURANT
15-1/2 FISH PIER, BOSTON, MA (617) 338-7539

You ou want atmosphere? Go to Boston's Fish Pier and inhale. That's fish you smell, on their way from fishing boats to packinghouses. Listen up above. Those are gulls you hear, swooping low, fighting it out with fishermen unloading their catch. (Yes, those are jet planes you hear, too, zeroing in on Boston's Logan Airport: Fish Pier is below their flyway.)

Now look for this address: number 15-1/2. Anywhere near lunch or dinner time, you will have no trouble locating it. Just find the line of people waiting to get in and eat. They are a jumbled complement of tourists, frugal locals, uncompromising seafood fanatics, and *Roadfood* adventurers marking time outside Boston's worst-kept culinary secret: the No Name Restaurant.

No Name is its name. There is no sign outside; none is needed; every Bostonian who knows anything about good eating knows exactly where No Name is. It started many years ago as a luncheonette with a counter and a few tables, strictly for wharf workers. But word got out about its inexpensive, simple, and fresh seafood, and No Name expanded. There is still a dingy luncheonette counter for single diners. But most sightseers get seated in the new-and-improved paneled dining room with its nautical decor and picture-window view of the harbor.

The scene is energetic. Tables are communal and crowded. Customers holler out their orders; waiters holler back, then practically toss the food at you from the kitchen. Help yourself to a paper cup from the stack on the table and pour your own water from the pitcher. Service is fast, prices are low, and the menu is minimal.

You will want to start with fish chowder. It is New England style chowder: milky white but not too creamy rich, weighted with chunky spoonfuls of sweet-fleshed fish. There are not even any potatoes to impugn its purity. It's just fish, the snap of a salt pork base, and the sweet complementary dairy flavors of butter and milk, tingling with paprika.

Scrod, sole, bluefish, scallops, clams, or salmon are your choices for a main course. Get the scrod broiled. It comes dusted with paprika on a faintly charred crust, in a pool of butter on a silver plate. The fish falls into great luscious hunks at the slightest prodding of a fork. Fried clams positively burst with marine sweetness. Portions are immense. An order of scallops yields three dozen. The clam roll sandwich spills over like a cornucopia. A salmon steak stretches toward the edges of its plate.

On the side come pickly homemade tartar sauce and a fresh-cut slaw with a light, milky dressing. For dessert, No Name offers pie: inelegant wedges of strawberry-rhubarb or blueberry. Get your pie à la mode: a fitting finale to a seafood feast, Yankee-style.

SANTARPIO'S
113 CHELSEA, BOSTON, MA (617) 567-9871

In the front room, they are charcoal-grilling *spiedies* (Italianate shishkebab) that perfume the air with deliciously garlicky aromas. When you head toward the back, the smell of spiedies begins to mingle with the heady aroma of hot crusts from pizzas still smoking from their time in the oven. In this back room of Santarpio's, an inconspicuous neighborhood joint just off the road that takes you to the airport, they serve authentic East Coast neighborhood pizza reminiscent of the way American pizza was born nearly a century ago—as a bakery sideline to keep the bread ovens busy all day long.

This is crust-lover's pizza. The toppings are just fine—alluringly aromatic tomato sauce, rough-textured sausage, and all the usual things. But it is the bread below them that sings—a thin, yeasty crust poised on the cusp of perfection between chewy and brittle. If this is what you like, tell them you want your pizza "dry," which means sprinkled with nothing but oil and a dusting of grated cheese. Like Santarpio's itself, this combination is primitive and unimprovable.

WOODMAN'S OF ESSEX
121 MAIN ST., ESSEX, MA (508) 768-6451

Woodman's claims to be the place where the fried clam was invented —on July 3, 1916, when Lawrence Woodman tried to drum up business by tossing clams into the deep fryer along with the Saratoga chips he was selling at his clam bar. Who knows if the story is true? Who cares? The fact is that Woodman's is today the *ne plus ultra* of North Shore clam shacks.

Overlooking a scenic marsh in the heart of the clam belt, where towns have bivalvular names like Ipswich and Little Neck, Woodman's defines a whole style of informal Yankee gastronomy. They call it "eat in the rough" around here, which means you stand at a counter, yell your order through the commotion, then wait for your number to be called. The food is served on cardboard plates with plastic forks. Carry it yourself to a table (if you can find a table that isn't occupied) or go out to your car and eat in the front seat or *al fresco,* off the hood.

You never knew fried clams (or any fried shellfish) could be so good. The nectarous, whole-bellied clams are sheathed in a shatteringly brittle honeytone crust, ideally accompanied by onion rings that wrap each sweet hoop in a halo of lush crunchyness. Once you have plowed into a Woodman's platter, no other plate of seafood will ever fully satisfy. Clams are the magnum opi, but you can also get shrimp, scallops, fish, and even nonfried lobsters.

MICHIGAN

CORNWELL'S TURKEY HOUSE
18935 15-1/2 MILE RD., MARSHALL, MI (616) 781-4293

Guess what's on the menu at Cornwell's Turkey House, also known as Turkeyville, U.S.A. Actually, there are all kinds of ways to eat the Cornwell family's turkeys at this single-minded restaurant, from complete dinners with all the fixin's, to turkey salad, turkey steaks, barbecued turkey, "sloppy Tom," and turkey-Reuben sandwiches.

Our recommendation when you go through the cafeteria line in this jumbo, country-craftsy restaurant (complete with ice cream parlor, butcher shop, attached souvenir store, adjacent antiques barn, and facilities for *al fresco* dining) is to get a sandwich. Their other ways with turkey are quite all right, and you can see them slice it right before your eyes on weekend nights when the all-you-can-eat turkey buffet precedes—are you ready?—dinner theater. But for the traveler in search of something good to eat, all the window dressing doesn't mean much. Cornwell's white meat turkey sandwich on a buttered bun is what counts. The turkey is piled high, and has that ineffable bland, comfy flavor that only a plump, freshly roasted, farm-raised gobbler can deliver, and that tastes so right in concert with the simplest things like butter and bread. Eat your sandwich, buy some hot caramel corn for dessert, and this grandiose restaurant will leave a fine taste in your mouth.

DRAKE'S SANDWICH SHOP
709 N. UNIVERSITY, ANN ARBOR, MI (313) 668-8853

S ixty-seven years in business has hardly changed Drake's Sandwich Shop. The 1920s marble soda fountain still has all the proper malt dispensers, milk shake mixers, syrup taps, and soda squirters. Booths in back are still high-backed wood, now aged to a lustrous dark patina. Upstairs, there's an annex one is tempted to call newfangled: it's the "Martian Room," decorated during that mid-century era when Formica and boomerangs were the height of fashion.

The menu is a journey back to days of sweet-shop innocence. Of course there is an array of soda fountain specialties: malts, shakes, sundaes, and banana splits. And because Ann Arbor is a college town, the Dagwood sandwiches have collegiate names: the "Cornell" (tuna and tomatoes), the "Northwestern" (ham and Swiss), and the hometown favorite, "Michigan" (chicken and tomatoes). Study the menu, decide what you like, write it on a small pad provided by the management, and bring your order up to the counter.

The thing we like best at Drake's is the pecan roll, Ann Arbor's favorite mid-morning (or mid-afternoon, or late-night) snack. It is a sticky swirling bun that aficionados ask for "twice cooked," which means it gets buttered and toasted on a grill. Then there is the day's cake, gloriously displayed in a cake tray on a pedestal on the soda fountain counter. There is a different one every other day. These are double-layer cakes, moist and fragile, lathered with appropriate frosting. Spice cake is our favorite, followed closely by banana, peanut butter, then double chocolate.

Many Drake's aficionados contend that the best things to eat, other than the glorious grilled pecan rolls and layer cakes, are the dainty ones: cucumber sandwiches on buttered white bread, accompanied by freshly squeezed limeade. Or cream cheese and jelly. Or ordinary grilled cheese.

Or—we have saved the best for last—you can order milk toast. Milk toast, that great antique dish of nursery comfort food, is nowhere more at home than in this venerable 1920s eatery. In fact, we cannot think of another restaurant, anywhere other than a few old hotels in the East, that even offers milk toast any more. It's so passé, so prim. But for a quiet breakfast, or a midnight snack after a long, hard day, no meal on earth is as kind and tender.

In addition to its antiquated menu, Drake's is known for candies. The shelves all around the front of the dining room are lined with jars full of licorice whips, jelly beans, caramels and kisses, nougats, lozenges, and lollipops: a confectionery dream. Buy them boxed, or weigh out bagsful according to your passion of the moment.

GRACIE'S COUNTRY INN
9483 GENESEE ST., NEW LOTHROP, MI (313) 638-5731

"Country Inn" is not the way we would describe Gracie Yott's restaurant in an old bank building on the other side of Flint. "Chow house" is more like it. Oh, it's a perfectly pleasant place to sit and eat; you could take your grandmother here. They serve nice fried-chicken dinners, excellent tenderloins and T-bones with hash-brown potatoes on the side; but the reason many people come here is, frankly, to pig out.

The salad bar at Gracie's Country Inn is its *raison d'être*. There are about four dozen things to choose from, including an array of only-in-the-Midwest salads: macaroni salad; potato salad; plain and fruited, clear and opaque Jell-Os; multiple bean salads; pea 'n' nut salad; slaws of all kinds; marshmallow ambrosias; relishes; pickled vegetables; etc. And desserts: cakes, brownies, cobblers, puddings. And breads: there are many kinds of very good, baked-here bread available at Gracie's, but the one that will slay you, the one item that makes a visit here a must for all touring trenchermen, is the cinnamon roll. It is not an especially handsome roll (very handmade), nor is it particularly large (about the size of a baseball), but observe all its uneven convolutions, and how they hold glistening brown veins of cinnamon sugar and melted butter. What fun it is to eat this roll—or half a dozen of them. Beyond its sweet amber glaze, it is substantial breadstuff, yeasty and flavorful, and the worthy highlight of any meal at Gracie's Country Inn.

HAAB'S
18 W. MICHIGAN, YPSILANTI, MI (313) 483-8200

One of the few remaining restaurants in America officially licensed to serve Chicken-in-the-Rough (and with the unusual pan-frying appliance to prove it), Haab's is a satisfying slice of bygone good eats. In a century-old building, you dine at bare wooden tables surrounded by Americana. There is a rustic quality to the setting, with its cottage curtains and capacious, wood-beamed ceiling. Drinks, served at the bar or at tables, are big and strong. Meals are big and tasty.

After homemade onion or vegetable soup (served in a pewter bowl), we like to savor that once-popular predecessor of Colonel Sanders and his franchised bucket brigade, Chicken-in-the-Rough, which really is a swell idea. Each piece is batter-dipped and pan-fried, turned only once as it cooks. The result is a great knobby hunk of food with juicy meat beneath its thick, well-seasoned envelope of crust. To go with this chicken, there are exemplary potatoes, baked or fried, actually tasty vegetables, and a warm loaf of bread.

If chicken is not your dish, Haab's is famous for beef—steaks and big hunks of prime rib, and an especially comely filet mignon served the swanky way, wrapped in bacon. Even the low-priced meat we have eaten here, meat loaf, is fascinatingly spiced and somehow virtuous-tasting.

You know a place as nice as Haab's isn't going to let you down at dessert. They make beautiful pies (pumpkin is a specialty), as well as sundaes and shortcakes and warm apple strudel served with vanilla ice cream.

HAM HEAVEN
70 CADILLAC SQUARE AT RANDOLPH, DETROIT, MI (313) 961-8818

Welcome to the wonderful world of pigs. Pictures, cartoons, statuary, piggy banks, and memorabilia in this downtown Detroit sandwich shop on Cadillac Square are all of the porcine persuasion (there is even a small toy pig in a bird cage); and in case you didn't guess, the specialty of the house is pig meat—ham in particular, in every cut, shape, and size a chef can imagine.

Get your ham sliced and baked or fried; get ham and eggs or get it folded in an omelette or strewn atop a salad; get it ground into hash and served on a plate with some of the most luscious scalloped potatoes you ever ate (Thursday only). Have some split pea soup, redolent of hambone and with big, fork-size hunks of ham floating in the wondrous opaque brew. Bean soup is another favorite, enriched with pieces of ham, of course. Or if you are a real contrary type, you can get a turkey sandwich made without ham.

The best dish of all, and one we have never seen on another menu, is known as a hamlet. A hamlet is a fistful of ground-up butt and shoulder meat laced with just enough moist vegetables to hold it together, flattened into a patty, and fried. The result is similar to a hamburger (the name of which suddenly seems wrong in the context of this restaurant) but ever so much more sweet and luscious. Because it is ham and more naturally unctuous, a hamlet gets crustier than a beef patty; and because it is quickly fried from already-cooked meat, it is succulent. Hamlets are served as sandwiches on buns, with perhaps some lettuce as a garnish and a squirt of mustard as their only proper condiment.

Ham Heaven is as informal as a restaurant can be, with a fast pace, low-low prices (under five dollars for any meal in the house), and a snappy attitude to match. They take no credit cards or reservations, and little guff from their loyal legions of customers. They open at six in the morning (eight on Saturday) for breakfast; at lunch the joint is jammed, and you may have to wait a few minutes before availing yourself of the otherwise lightning-fast service. Our favorite time to dine here is the end of the lunch hour when things quiet down, before Ham Heaven closes for the day (no dinner is served). Most of the rushed noontime crowd has cleared out, and the seductive perfume of sizzling ham lingers in the air.

JUILLERET'S
130 STATE, HARBOR SPRINGS, MI (616) 526-2821

A big meal at Juilleret's is one of the gastronomic wonders of the Great Lakes. The specialty of the house is whitefish, brought forth from the kitchen on a seasoned hardwood plank, where milky-white fillets, glistening with rivulets of butter, their edges crisped to a luscious brown, are heaped in a pile and strewn with slices of lemon and tomato. Encircling the sweet mound of fish, shoring in juices around the circumference of the platter, is a mighty wall of piped-on mashed potatoes. What a feast!

Planked whitefish is available after five in the afternoon for any number of people from two to ten—the size of the plank and the number of fillets are adjusted accordingly. With it comes a loaf of warm bread and access to a superb, only-in-the-heartland salad bar where you can help yourself to the likes of spinach salad (dressed with sweet-and-sour vinaigrette and sprinkled with bacon), pea and walnut salad, carrot slaw, and marshmallow ambrosia.

You don't have to eat planked whitefish at Juilleret's. On weekend nights, they have planked prime rib, too. Many customers come only for sandwiches or burgers; and some come just to hang out. Juilleret's is a town lunchroom, favored by generations of vacationing Michiganders for the last ninety-some years; and its ambience is boisterous, extremely casual, and loads of fun. It is a place to table-hop, carry on across-the-room conversations, flirt, and banter.

The merry nature of Juilleret's is abetted by its other special gastronomic drawing card, the soda fountain. Ice cream is homemade, and the soda jerks are proficient at sodas, sundaes, banana splits, tin roofs, cream puffs, coolers, rainbows, and a couple of Juilleret's exclusives, the "velvet" and the "thundercloud." For the former, vanilla ice cream is blended with bittersweet chocolate sauce and marshmallow cream to create something akin to what St. Louis custard aficionados know as a "concrete"—a milk shake so thick it must be eaten with a spoon. A thundercloud uses the same ingredients, but layered and topped with chopped nuts.

A historical note: the fox trot "Sleepy Time Gal" was written in Juilleret's dining room in 1923.

LAFAYETTE CONEY ISLAND
118 W. LAFAYETTE, DETROIT, MI (313) 964-8198

If you drew a map of America and stuck pins in all the places with great wieners, Lake Erie would be surrounded: Buffalo's charcoaled red-hots and Rochester white hots to the east, Cleveland Coneys on the southern shore, and Lafayette Coney Islands in Detroit. As in most of Michigan and Ohio, the hot dogs sold in this hoary dog house are known as Coneys, and few customers ingest them plain. Lafayette devotees like their tube steaks smothered with chili (a.k.a. Coney sauce) and raw onions. It's go-down-easy greasy chili; the dog is good and awful, and awfully good. This is an authentic albeit ignoble midwestern urban eating experience, at your service twenty-four hours a day, where fluorescent lights may flicker but never cease to shine.

STEVE'S SOUL FOOD
8443 GRAND RIVER, DETROIT, MI (313) 894-3464

Steve's is a modern serve-yourself cafeteria where the prices are ridiculously low and the food is astonishingly good. Leave your calorie counter at home, because Steve's meals are hearty ones. Chicken, fried, and pork chops, smothered, are our favorite things to eat; although sometimes we switch things around and order smothered chicken and fried pork chops. Any which way, these are delectable dinners: the fried chicken tears into big, dripping shreds of meat and crust; the pork chops ooze juice if you simply press them with a fork. Other notable entrées include meat loaf, steak and gravy, barbecued ribs, pig's feet, and chitterlings.

Dinner always comes with a couple of good things on the side, which are such soul-food classics as collard greens, candied yams, macaroni and cheese that tastes richer than any macaroni and cheese has a right to taste, "dirty" rice, peas, beans, and sweet corn muffins that go well with everything. For dessert there is achingly sweet peach cobbler, cheesecake, an endearing banana pudding, and all kinds of cake. It isn't gourmet cake; in fact, it reminded us of cakes from school lunch when we were children. That's the kind of effect Steve's has on us: it is a restaurant so square and upright that a meal here results not only in satisfaction but nostalgia for the days when food was a simple (and supreme) source of happiness.

MINNESOTA

AL'S BREAKFAST
413 14TH AVE., S.E., MINNEAPOLIS, MN (612) 331-9991

You can literally see this eatery's atmosphere—a cloud of tantalizing scents from bacon and corned-beef hash sizzling on the griddle alongside hash-brown potatoes, buttermilk pancakes, and furiously frying eggs, the savory haze laced with the perfume of coffee, served in heavy mugs that appear to have tendered oceans of potent java in their time. Welcome to Al's—happy hunting grounds for those who spend their lives in search of great diner breakfasts.

Al's is a cubbyhole of a diner wedged perpendicular to 14th Avenue among the shops of Dinkytown, near the University of Minnesota. It doesn't seem even as large as a SceniCruiser inside; and customers waiting for a stool stand hovering just above and behind those who are seated and eating. On a shelf underneath the aged yellow counter are accumulations of newspapers to read. Behind the counter, where the hash slingers race with seasoned aplomb, decor consists of pictures of Elvis and Wayne Newton, foreign currency, and a sign that advises customers "TIPPING IS NOT A CITY IN CHINA." Also behind the counter is a pile of twenty dollar meal-ticket books, each inscribed with someone's name. Many of Al's customers buy these books and keep them here, so they know they can come eat, using coupons instead of dollars, even when their wallet is empty.

The specialty of the house is blueberry pancakes, which are made with either a whole-wheat or buttermilk batter, and are also available studded with walnuts or corn kernels. We chose blueberries and buttermilk—an enchanting balance of sweet fruit poised in their faintly sour medium, infused with butter. They were just barely sticky, delicate-textured, and profoundly satisfying, especially when lightly drizzled with maple syrup. Al's flapjacks are sold as a short stack (two), regular (three), or long (four); and you can also have your waitress garnish them with sour cream and/or strawberries.

The short-order chef up front spends a lot of his time making eggs, omelettes, and truly excellent corned-beef hash, as well as exorbitantly luscious hash browns, which he drenches as they turn crisp and brown on the grill with seasoned oil from a small pitcher. It is an old-fashioned plea-sure to watch this guy work, handling about a dozen orders at a time, always snatching whatever he is frying, poaching, or grilling away from the heat at the peak of its perfection.

LINDEY'S PRIME STEAK HOUSE
3610 N. SNELLING, ARDEN HILLS, MN (612) 633-9813

"You *must* listen to us," implored *Roadfood*ers Wilson and Ann Robin-son in their letter recommending Lindey's. "We *know* what's unique and delicious, and Lindey's serves the best steaks and the best hash-brown potatoes in town."

Amen.

There is a menu at Lindey's, and you want to see it just because it's fun to look at. It is toted to the table by the waitress. Printed on a slab of var-nished plywood, about two by three feet, it lists everything the kitchen makes, which isn't much. There are three entrées: special sirloin, prime sirloin (smaller), and chopped sirloin. Choose one, and about the only other choice you have to make is whether you want coffee or tea. The rest of your meal is ordained.

First, about that special prime steak: It is nearly two inches thick and arrives at the table sizzling furiously on its platter. A knife slices through it easily, triggering a gushing river of natural juice. It chews well: tender but in no way mushy; and its flavor resonates with beefy authority.

The spuds recommended by the Robinsons are indeed world-class. The menu touts them as greaseless, and they seem to be. But don't worry: the big platter has the savory crunch that only well-lubricated potatoes develop when they are fried, and there is enough tender pulp to make them ideal for soaking up sirloin juices. Another great side dish is Lindey's garlic toast—served in a basket and cut into pieces sized for popping into your mouth. Also on the roster are chunks of sweet watermelon rind and a big chef's salad for starters.

That's all you need to know about Lindey's, except that they don't take reservations; so be prepared to wait. It's worth it.

MURRAY'S
26 S. SIXTH ST., MINNEAPOLIS, MN (612) 339-0909

If you like meat and potatoes and old-fashioned luxury, and if you are in the mood to splurge, go to Murray's in Minneapolis, where steaks are still the Cadillac of meals. Murray's is now run by Patrick and Tim Murray, son and grandson of Art and Marie Murray, who opened the Red Feather Restaurant in north Minneapolis in 1933 and became locally famous for their good beef. Thirteen years later, the Murrays moved their business downtown, and it has since become a beacon for meat-eaters throughout the Midwest. They serve all the usual shapes and sizes of steak at Murray's, most of them simply cooked but seasoned with a special blend of spices, ranging up to the top-of-the-line cuts, which include a nearly two-pound strip steak (for two) and a behemoth known as the "golden butter knife steak," costing over one hundred dollars, serving three to four hungry carnivores.

What we like about Murray's, in addition to the meat, is how retro epicurean it is. Ornate iron chandeliers hang above the tables and drapery bunting festoons the walls and windows. Table linen is rosy pink. It is a dining room that is supremely comfortable, a suitable location for an evening of soul-satisfying, semi-classical mid-American gastronomy. Start with a well-mixed cocktail, then slice into a juicy slab of beef with a heap of luscious au gratin potatoes on the side, and finish off with a wedge of lemon ice box pie for dessert. God bless America!

SRI LANKA CURRY HOUSE
2821 HENNEPIN AVE., MINNEAPOLIS, MN (612) 871-2400

When you order your food at the Sri Lanka Curry House, the waitress will likely give you a warning. The menu says that most dishes are available medium, hot, and very hot. "Medium," she says, "is like the hottest Szechuan food you ever ate." If you like mild meals, we suggest you find another place to eat in Minneapolis. Sri Lankan food is known as the cuisine of fire and spice.

The Curry House is easy to find along Hennepin Avenue. Look for the set of mammoth wooden doors, each bedecked with an enormous round gargoyle-faced handle so elaborate you don't really know where to grab and pull. The inside is less like an exotic Ceylonese temple than a basic Oriental-American storefront restaurant, staffed mostly by local Caucasian youths who are contagiously enthusiastic about the hot food they serve. Travel posters hung on black burlap walls show pictures of Sri Lanka—leopards, scenery, and ancient temples. On weekends, there is a small stage where live entertainers provide the clientele of Minneapolis epicures a taste of Sri Lankan music to accompany their food. On quieter weekday nights, in addition to recorded mood music in the background, the ambience of the dining room is enhanced by the sound of diners sniffling, as the curries they eat cause their sinuses to drain.

Swell appetizers: chutney chicken wings, served hot and sticky; or lentil pancakes cooked brittle crisp, yet still moist inside, served with a syrup that sets your mouth on fire. The rest of the menu is big, and obscure if you aren't familiar with Sri Lankan cuisine (who is?); so waitresses spend plenty of time patiently explaining what is what and recommending, for example, Curry Number Two, available with shrimp, lamb, beef, or chicken, as a good introduction. It comes with your meat of choice swathed in big oily green leaves that seem to be spinach but are somehow infinitely zestier than any spinach we have ever tasted. Also on the plate are potatoes, mashed chick peas, tomato-and-onion salad, and two or three unidentifiable, highly spiced vegetable things. It is all powerfully seasoned, strange, and dizzyingly complex.

Advanced customers who go beyond the combination plates order just those things they like best—such exotica as prawn *mallung* (with coconut), whole curried lobsters, and vegetable *roti*. Some day, we would like to come in and order a dish of the lamb curry extra hot, just to test the outer limits of this blazing cuisine. All full meals come with a three-cup condiment tray loaded up with coconut, parsley, and a wondrous onion-tomato relish that tastes good on just about everything.

After a meal like this you want something soothing; and chef Heather Balasuriya of the Curry House provides it: cool passion fruit shakes made with Häagen-Dazs or a dish of plain vanilla ice cream topped with mango pulp. Your exhausted and utterly satisfied taste buds will thank you.

MISSISSIPPI

ABE'S
616 STATE ST., CLARKSDALE, MS (601) 624-9211

Abe's reputation as a bulwark of great barbecue goes back to 1924, when Abe Davis opened a snack stall on the street in Clarksdale. Today his progeny maintains the name and the high-quality cooking, which includes not only mighty fine barbecued pork but that incongruous Mississippi Delta specialty, the hot tamale.

Order your tamales three at a time, with or without chili on top. They are a steamy plate of food, redolent of coarse-grain yellow cornmeal and lots of hot sauce.

Abe's barbecue is hickory-cooked, then cut and cooked a second time on the grill—a peculiar process Abe's shares with the Ridgewood of Tennessee. The result is lean meat with lots of juicy buzz in its pale inside fibers and plenty of crusty parts where it has sizzled on the grill. When the pork is brought to your table, along with a toasted burger bun, it is accompanied by two bottles of sauce—hot and mild. Dark red, tangy, with the resonance of pepper and spice, the hot version is dynamite and, used judiciously, it is a sublime companion for the meat.

Despite its venerable history, Abe's is now a modern and fairly nondescript establishment, with only a single work of art hinting at its distinction. On one Formica wall, a mural shows an old smoke shack (Abe's) and a merry pig playing a violin.

234

DINNER BELL
229 5TH AVE., MC COMB, MS (601) 684-4883

We could never sympathize with epicures whose gripe about a restaurant is that the food arrived too quickly, or that a meal was hurried along by the staff. As far as we're concerned, that is an impossibility. Food cannot arrive too quickly. Nor is it possible to eat it too fast.

That is why we like eating at the Dinner Bell so much.

Don't get us wrong. There is nothing uncouth about a Dinner Bell meal. On the contrary. It is a genteel restaurant, in a refined Colonial home. Its reputation as a standard of good eating has unfurled ever since it opened in 1945. It moved in 1959 due to a fire, and in 1978, to the horror of its fans, the Dinner Bell closed. Then, in 1980 the Lopinto family came along and opened it again, for which they were selected "Family of the Month" by the local Chamber of Commerce Howdycrat Board.

The Lopintos' goal was to preserve a great and unusual dining tradition. The tables at the Dinner Bell have always been known for the country-fried chicken and vegetable casseroles they hold, as well as for the fact that they spin in circles.

Yes, the tables revolve. They are round, and in the center of each is a lavish lazy Susan. Service is boardinghouse style: spin the lazy Susan and take what you want. When any serving tray starts getting empty, out comes a full one from the kitchen. Grab as much as you want. Eat at your own speed: our kind of meal!

It isn't only speed and convenience and abundance that make Dinner Bell meals notable. This is some mighty marvelous southern-style food: chicken and dumplings, catfish, ham, corn sticks, sweet potato casseroles, black-eyed peas, fried eggplant, and fried okra. The dishes that most travelers remember best are vegetables. They are deep southern style: prepared as flamboyant casseroles enriched with canned soups and/or cheese and/or cracker crumbs and always lots of margarine. They are—need we say it?—different from the kind of vegetables that health food advocates prescribe. We, on the other hand, *do* prescribe them; we firmly believe that a down-home Dixie dish such as spinach casserole enriched with cream cheese and margarine and bread crumbs and cans of artichoke hearts is good for the soul . . . not to mention the fact that it is scrumptious.

For dessert, the Dinner Bell lazy Susans hold shortcakes, fruit pies, and a classic whipping cream pound cake; as well as not-so-classic but delectably wanton "banana breeze pie" and pistachio nut cake.

DOE'S EAT PLACE
502 NELSON, GREENVILLE, MS (601) 334-3315

Only in the Deep South, perhaps only in the Mississippi Delta, would a place like Doe's keep on going, and going strong. Honestly, it is a dump: the back rooms of a crumbling old grocery store with dining tables spread helter-skelter among kitchen equipment. Plates, flatware, and tablecloths are all mismatched. It is noisy and inelegant, and service—while perfectly polite—is rough and tumble.

Doe's fans, ourselves included, love it just the way it is. The ambience, which is at least a few degrees this side of "casual," is part of what makes eating here such a kick. This place is *real*—ragged-edged, defiantly odd, and downright proud of being absolutely unfashionable. Mississippians have eaten here for generations now; for regular patrons the eccentricity makes the experience as comfortable as an old shoe. Newcomers may be shocked by the ramshackle surroundings, but Doe's is easy to like once the food starts coming.

Start with tamales. They make them here, and sell them to go by the dozen in coffee cans. Peel away the corn husk and the peppery, steamy meal inside is positively luscious, messy enough to eat with a fork unless you are a tamale-eating expert and can eat it straight from the husk. Now you want steak. Doe's is famous for its meat, and serves what many knowledgeable travelers consider to be some of the best steaks in America, expensive, well-marbled beef. Describe the cut and size you like, and a few raw ones are brought from Doe's locker for your selection and approval. The one you choose is carried out to the grill in the front room; and while it cooks, you eat some salad, which the waitresses fetch from a big bowlful they are constantly mixing and dressing (with lemon and olive oil) throughout the dinner hour.

Now comes the steak, a T-bone, let's say, sided by a mound of golden French-fried potatoes (they, too, are made in the middle of one of the dining rooms, on a stove in a big skillet). Slice a knife through the meat's charred-black crust and inhale its profound beef aroma as you fork up a juice-heavy triangle of the most luscious protein money can buy.

Doe's is not cheap; but it shouldn't be. This unique combination of top-drawer steak and downscale atmosphere is priceless Americana.

GOLDIE'S TRAIL BAR-B-QUE
4127 S. WASHINGTON, VICKSBURG, MS (601) 636-9839

Goldie has been gone about ten years now, but people who remember this place from the 1960s tell us that nothing has changed. A snug cafe by the river, it is still the finest smoke pit in town, using recipes developed by Gola "Goldie" Marshall, who started in the barbecue business in Arkansas in the fifties.

The specialty of the house is pork, hickory-smoked and sliced extraordinarily thin, and yet, almost magically, still succulent and heavy with natural juices. It is served with a thick, nearly copper-colored sauce that electrifies the flavor of the meat. To balance this keen-flavored dish, Goldie's makes a cool, chunky potato salad.

The brisket here is wonderful—about as good as you will find this far east. It is mildly smoky, relatively lean (for brisket), but striated with enough veins of fat to lubricate every mouthful and make chewing it sinful gluttony. Even with its smoke flavor and some sauce, brisket is quite mild, so to complement it there are sausage links—zesty tubes of coarse-ground, well-peppered pork. Brisket, links, and potato salad, with sweet iced tea on the side: a meal in perfect equilibrium.

JOCELYN'S
HIGHWAY 90, OCEAN SPRINGS, MS (601) 875-1925

Having written *A Cook's Tour of Mississippi*, Susan Puckett knows the ins and outs of good eating in these parts, so when she recommended Jocelyn's, we were on our way. She said that Jocelyn Mayfield used to be a cook at the legendary Trilby's of Ocean Springs; and now, in a restaurant she runs with her husband Harold, she is continuing the tradition of Gulf seafood with a New Orleans accent.

You wouldn't call Jocelyn's a fancy restaurant, but neither is it nonchalant. Clearly, it is serious about the business of preparing and serving fine food. It's a tropical orange home with lace curtains in the windows; the tables inside are tidy and service is suave, but the dining room is unpretentious and prices are half of what you pay in the gastronomic temples of New Orleans .

As for the food you will eat at Jocelyn's, it is a match for New Orleans's best, the kind of urbane, elegant fare that in most cities you expect—no, *hope,* in vain, to get—from the conspicuous and exalted four-star kitchens.

Out of Jocelyn's tiny kitchen come dishes that are beautiful on their plates; more important, they are brilliantly prepared. There are oysters, shrimp, and crabmeat galore—raw, stuffed, broiled, en brochette, au gratin, or in marvelous casseroles that drip garlic, crumbs, and cheese. Local fish like pompano, trout, and redfish are impeccably fresh, available simply broiled or stuffed. On rare occasions we have sampled nonseafood dishes, and weren't disappointed: the fried chicken is crusty and delicious, the calf's liver is elegant.

Fabulous desserts: Creole bread pudding with whiskey sauce, English trifles, sophisticated layered tortes, and the house specialty—pecan pie the likes of which you won't find for miles.

Awhile ago when we left Jocelyn's after a seriously satisfying dinner we were thinking that there is nothing at all like this wonderful restaurant's blend of informality of elegance where we live; nor, for that matter, is there anything like it anywhere else. Obviously, we are not the only people to have had that thought. Outside Jocelyn's a sign was posted: *Aucune place comme ça.*

LUSCO'S
722 CARROLLTON, GREENWOOD, MS (601) 453-5365; RESERVATIONS REQUIRED

Drive into the Mississippi Delta through time-weathered hamlets like Panther Burn and Alligator, past tin-roof cabins and columned plantation homes, and find the wrong side of the tracks in a dusty Zion named Greenwood—"the cotton capital of the world." Here, in a dilapidated ex-grocery store, with paint peeling off the tin ceiling and bathrooms out the back door, is Lusco's, which is one of the weirdest, and most wonderful, restaurants in America.

When you arrive (after five, Tuesday through Saturday only) you may have to loiter in the front room, which is the remnants of the grocery, now a display for taxidermized ducks and dusty provisions on shelves. There is a telephone, too—in a self-contained all-weather booth inside the room. When a table is ready a waiter will come get you and lead the way back down a hall until your sanctum is reached. Constructed during the 1930s to provide cotton planters a place to drink home brew with their meal, Lusco's dining area provides everybody with a private room. As in a jerry-built bordello, every customer (or in this case, every party) gets his or her own cubicle of Faulknerian hoar and secrecy, veiled from the hall and from other rooms by a grimy chintz curtain. The paint in the room has faded to no-color green; but the table is graciously set, covered with a soft, cotton cloth and generous napkins (this *is* cotton country); and each table is equipped with a discreet button for summoning the serving staff when you want them.

Regulars come to Lusco's for pompano, broiled in lemon butter sauce, which is truly an aristocratic plate of food, or for sirloin steak (once described to us by a Lusco's waiter as "tender as a mother's love"). On the side you want freshly cut French fries or battered onion rings, served on plates ringed with a Mississippi magnolia pattern. These meals are expensive, and they are as luxurious-tasting as any four-star city dining room; but eating them in one of these secret booths is ever so much more fun.

Other than steak and pompano, Lusco's menu is small, limited to shrimp, oysters, chicken, or spaghetti, the latter a reminder of the restaurant's beginnings, when Papa Lusco served local cotton kings homemade wine in his backroom booths.

Lusco's is a taste of history, and a delicious one at that. People who live in the Mississippi Delta cherish it because everything about this peculiar place, from its first-class food to the sickly green walls, drips tradition, and in this part of the world, tradition is hallowed.

MACK'S FISH CAMP
OFF HIGHWAY 49, 6 MILES N. OF HATTIESBURG, MS (601) 582-5101

In the little black book of every catfish aficionado is the name Mack's Fish Camp, a rustic eating hall deep in the woods outside Hattiesburg. Wide communal tables covered with blue-checked cloths, broad-beamed ladder-back chairs, overhead fans to cool things down: everything about this capacious place is designed for eating in bulk; and as long as you keep eating, Mack's keeps bringing platters piled with whole (but headless) farm-raised catfish, their lean and clean flesh encased in brittle gold envelopes of sandy crust. (Timid eaters can pay extra for catfish fillets and avoid dealing with bones.) With the fish come mountains of steamy, onion-flecked hushpuppies, as well as French fries and cole slaw. Pay one price and eat 'til you drop your fork. The delicious vittles are accompanied by iced tea served in titanic glasses, about a quart's worth, barely graspable in one normal-size hand. "Did you have plenty to eat?" asks the lady at Mack's cash register. How could anyone say no?

MENDENHALL HOTEL REVOLVING TABLES
MENDENHALL, MS (601) 847-3113

A meal at the Mendenhall hotel is an inspiring reminder of how the word "restaurant" originated: as a place to restore strength and good spirits when far away from home.

The main thing that inscribes the Mendenhall in the *Roadfood* Hall of Fame is the amount of food it tenders. If you have not personally luxuriated in any of Dixie's classic communal dining rooms, such as Mrs. Wilkes's in Savannah, or the Hopkins Boarding House in Pensacola, you can hardly imagine how much there is to eat. A vista of vittles is spread before you: baskets of steaming hot biscuits, cracklin' cornbread, yeast rolls, and sweet muffins; a dozen or more vegetables and ultra-customized vegetable casseroles, fried chicken (*de rigueur* at any good boarding house meal), ham and pork chops and barbecued beef and Brunswick stew, and peach cobbler and icy pitchers of pour-it-yourself pre-sweetened iced tea.

Pay one price (under ten dollars) and eat all you want; and when you are done, find a rocking chair on the front porch and snooze a spell. It is not exactly power lunch, and gourmets won't find the latest trendy food on the table; but for those in search of authentic American cooking, there is no restaurant experience that can compare to this grand old hotel in the small town that was once a stop on the rail line between Jackson and Hattiesburg.

It was back in 1915 that Mrs. Annie Heil, owner of what was then called the Heil Hotel, started serving meals to trainmen and travelers who stopped for a quick half-hour lunch on their way north or south. Because they had no time to dally over a menu or a course-by-course meal, Mrs. Heil came up with a system to serve them fast: round-table dining, for which she sat everyone at a big round table with a lazy Susan in the center where the whole meal was unfurled and ready for fast eating action. The wheels of good food have been spinning ever since, at the Mendenhall Hotel and at a few other citadels of Dixie cooking in this part of Mississippi.

What fun it is to eat this way! It's practical, too. Cuts down on the reaching, stretching, and pass-it-to-me's that obstruct ordinary boarding-house meals. All the platters, bowls, casseroles, bread baskets, pitchers, and condiment jars are within easy reach. When you want something, spin it and grab. Whenever a serving tray on the lazy Susan starts looking empty, a member of the staff snatches it back to the kitchen and returns with a full one.

What most visitors remember best about a visit to the Mendenhall Hotel are the arrays of vegetables—perhaps a dozen different kinds at every meal, ranging from locally grown, garden-fresh tomatoes (yes, we know; technically, tomatoes are a fruit) to legendary southern-style whipped yams, streaked with marshmallows and scented with vanilla; creamed corn; mighty bowls of butter-rich squash and luscious creamed spinach.

As for *how much* it is polite and proper to eat at such a meal, take a hint from the house motto displayed in a pretty needlepoint sampler on the wall of the Mendenhall Hotel dining room: "EAT 'TIL IT OUCHES."

OLD SOUTHERN TEA ROOM
801 CLAY ST. IN THE HOTEL VICKSBURG, VICKSBURG, MS
(601) 636-4146

The Old Southern Tea Room has returned. For years a bastion of plantation cookery such as fried chicken and country ham and corn pudding and sweet potato pie, the grande dame of Mississippi River restaurants suffered through some hard times, sputtered through the eighties as a ghost of its former self in a motel's dining room, then vanished when the motel had a bad fire in April 1987. A tradition that connoisseurs of regional Americana had enjoyed since 1941 was gone.

Then George P. Mayer did the nearly impossible. He made the South rise again, at least gastronomically. He reopened the Old Southern Tea Room in 1989, this time in the stately two-story dining room of the Hotel Vicksburg, which was itself built in 1928 and is listed on the National Register of Historical Places. Mayer found and rehired many of the old cooks and waitresses, some of whom had worked for Mrs. Mary McKay, the original owner, for decades; and he got out the tried-and-true McKay family recipes for plantation kitchen favorites ranging from Creole gumbo by the cup (for starting a meal) to tipsy pudding, down-in-Dixie bourbon pie, and chocolate-sherry-sauced ice cream for dessert.

Today's Old Southern Tea Room offers such all-American modern foodstuffs as soup and salad bar or cheeseburger and French fries (known here as "the Vicksburger"), as well as familiar regional specialties, from catfish and hushpuppies to old-fashioned fried chicken. But adventurous eaters will direct their attention to the haute Dixie specialties, which represent a kind of deluxe southern cooking that scarcely exists anymore in homes or restaurants: stuffed baked ham made from a recipe the menu advises is over 150 years old, or a swanky mushroom-sauced fried chicken dish known as Old Plantation chicken.

All dinners come with little hot biscuits and corn muffins; and the choice of vegetables includes turnip greens, black-eyed peas, princess potatoes, and sweet potato pone that is custard-rich and dotted with raisins. It was vegetables that endeared the Old Southern Tea Room to America's original traveling gourmet, Duncan Hines, who once said that the first thing he wanted to do upon returning to America from Europe was go to the Tea Room and eat stuffed eggplant and corn pudding.

RUTH & JIMMIE'S
ROUTE 7, ABBEVILLE, MS (601) 234-4312

The formal name of the restaurant we are about to describe is Ruth & Jimmie's Sporting Goods & Cafe. You come here to buy a rod and reel, hip boots, or shells for your shotgun. You stock up on live bait from the buckets on the porch. You gas up at the pumps out front. You buy a pair of pantyhose, a Hav-A-Hank for your breast pocket, or sack of White Lily flour for making biscuits.

The main reason we recommend a visit to Ruth & Jimmie's is lunch. Toward the back of the store, beyond the dry goods and hardware, past ammo and groceries, is a counter with twelve stools. It opens at five-thirty in the morning, and serves food until seven-thirty at night. Midday is the choice time to come, when a short list of the day's meals is chalked on the blackboard.

The cuisine is country-style: fried steak smothered with gravy, ham and cooked apples, roast beef and creamed potatoes. There is always a big selection of vegetables such as black-eyed peas, squash casseroles, collard greens, and fried okra: choose three to accompany any main course. There is cornbread for mopping up gravy, and fruit cobbler or mud-thick fudge pie for dessert.

The food is good. Honest vittles. Soul-satisfying in a way few hifalutin' dinners ever are. But it is not the food that makes a Ruth & Jimmie's meal extraordinary. It is the ambience. It is the pronounced tilt of the old wood frame "shotgun" building, its creaky floor, and the complex aroma of steak gravy mixed with the good smell of a hardware store that wafts across the ancient lunch counter.

The experience of eating here is unique to the Deep South, to Mississippi in particular—where tradition reigns supreme. As you plow into a plate of smothered chicken and dressing at the back of this old country store, it is hard to believe that outside, the twentieth century is nearly over. Conversely, when you leave Ruth & Jimmie's, get back on the main road, and reenter a world of fast-food franchises, you might begin to wonder if this colorful legacy of rural life wasn't some Brigadoon-like fantasy.

It is real, we assure you. And Abbeville is a real town, with a population of 450. Ruth & Jimmie's, at the crossroads that constitutes the "business district," was built in the 1930s and started serving meals in 1973. Most of the lunch traffic is local folks, supplemented by a loyal contingent from the University of Mississippi in nearby Oxford, as well as hunters in season, and occasional tourists visiting Ole Miss for events such as the annual William Faulkner Conference.

You won't spend more than a few dollars to eat here, but there are few culinary experiences anywhere in America as rich.

SMITTY'S
208 S. LAMAR, OXFORD, MS (601) 234-9111

A two-room cafe with red-checked curtains, its counter stools and tables fully occupied every morning by citizens of Oxford drinking coffee and eating biscuits: Smitty's is a real taste of small-town good food.

Come early and smell the coffee and grits and biscuits in the air. You can get smoked sausage with biscuits and grits, steak with biscuits and grits, ham with biscuits and grits, or just biscuits and grits with sawmill gravy (creamy-thick) and/or red-eye gravy (dark and porky). There is dark red country ham (salty and distinguished) and pink city ham (blubbery and bland). And to spread on the large, irregularly shaped oval biscuits, there are homemade jams, pear jelly, and muscadine preserves. This is good eating in a big way—all the more fun for the hometown atmosphere of Smitty's, which is patronized every morning by a happy contingent of townsfolk, Ol' Miss students, and traveling trenchermen who consider it a biscuit beacon in the Deep South.

Breakfast is the great meal of the day, but if you happen to pass through Oxford at lunch, Smitty's is a fine place to go. Eat a catfish supper (whole or filleted), a country-fried steak, or a simple meal of greens and hog jowl with a piece of oven-hot cornbread. There is even a salad bar if you want to eat more modern food. But our favorite midday meals at Smitty's are the genuine antiques, in particular the southern-style plowman's lunch: a bowl of beans cooked with a ham hock, served with cornbread, onions, pickle relish, and hot sauce.

STUB'S
HIGHWAY 49E, YAZOO CITY, MS (601) 746-1204

This two-room roadhouse is the nice place in town, where nice people come to eat hot lunch. Gentlemen are mostly white-collar types who wash their hands before they eat and know how to use silverware; ladies have neatly sculpted hairdos and purses that match their shoes. Waitresses introduce themselves by putting a little card down on your table that says, "Hello, my name is . . ."

Hot lunch means meat and vegetables with freshly baked bread on the side and homemade pie for dessert: food that cannot be eaten by hand or from a lunch pail. Last time through, we ate catfish fillets with hushpuppies and a side order of field peas and roast beef with dressing, accompanied by new potatoes in cream sauce and a bowl of pungent collard greens sopped in pot likker. These satisfying lunches were accompanied by glasses of pre-sweetened iced tea (unsweetened is also available), hot rolls, and crunch-crusted corn muffins. Other frequent daily specials at Stub's include a wonderful chicken pot pie in peppery gravy, barbecued ribs, and fried chicken (whole pieces and strips); side dishes we remember kindly are yams in sweet syrup, English peas in cream sauce, and a charmingly out-of-fashion pear salad composed of half a canned pear with a dab of mayonnaise on top.

Stub's is so proud of its pies that it displays the best of them—chocolate chess pie—in a small case next to the cash register, bathed in the heat of a sunlamp. A slice of this famous pie arrives at the table warm, like heavy cocoa pudding with a pale sheet of dry chocolate crust on top. An excellent contrast to this masterpiece, if you can handle two pieces of pie, is a slice of Stub's lemon ice box pie, served cool and frosty, white as snow.

TAYLOR GRO. & RESTAURANT
TAYLOR, MS (NEXT TO THE POST OFFICE) (601) 236-1716

West of Tupelo, where Elvis was born, and south of Oxford, William Faulkner's home, is a speck on the map known as Taylor, Mississippi: four tin-awning buildings lined up on a skinny country road. One of the buildings, open only at night, Thursday through Sunday, is the Taylor Grocery—Mississippi's premier catfish parlor.

While you munch hushpuppies and pluck big, meaty hunks of fried catfish off the bone at a table in the back of this grocery store, you have a nice view of the shelf of Lady Beverly one-size-fits-all pantyhose, as well as years' worth of graffiti inscribed on the lumpy plaster walls. Scribblings about Yoknapatawpha County and names of Faulkner's characters are intertwined with proclamations of love and fidelity written by Ol' Miss students, who have made a ritual of coming for catfish on the night before a big football game. You want atmosphere? Observe the broken-down gas pumps out front, the torn screen door, the naked bulbs hanging above Formica tables and their mismatched vinyl-seated kitchen chairs.

Of course, all such folderol would be worthless if the cuisine were not superb. The specialty is whole country catfish, sweet and luscious in its golden crust. On the side come hushpuppies, French fries, and slaw, and a basket of saltines. Table service is a single fork, wrapped in a paper napkin. Feel free to bring your own wine or hard liquor but, strangely, beer is forbidden by local ordinance.

WEIDMANN'S RESTAURANT
208 22ND AVE., MERIDIAN, MS (601) 693-1751

L et us start with dessert. For at least a few decades now, Weidmann's has been known for black-bottom pie. This dark cocoa creation, laced with bourbon, is an ethereal chiffon perched atop a sharply flavored gingersnap crust, with a thin vein of intense, bittersweet chocolate to separate the elements. You will not forget this pie once you taste it; there are imitators galore throughout the South and the whole country, but Weidmann's pie is unique: the paradigm.

Even besides the pie, there is no restaurant like this anywhere. Founded by Felix Weidmann and his wife Clara in 1870, and dripping with history and tradition, it is a living museum of Mississippi foodways. There are many rooms that have been added over the years, but the place you want to be is the front dining room with its brass rail separating the counter from the tables, its high ceiling with slow-spinning fans, its dark aged wood walls festooned with pictures of celebrities from Meridian's own Jimmie Rodgers and Miss Orange Bowl of 1935 to Babe Ruth and Dizzy Dean. Here, too, are lots of stuffed gamefish and glass-eyed heads of animals, an ornate Bavarian cuckoo clock, a display of vintage beer steins, and a sign announcing, "It's the food that counts."

The menu is enormous—good reading for days, including such curious sections as "kosher sandwiches" (pastrami, corned beef, and—inexplicably—fried oysters on a bun) and "Ember-Glo-Char Broiled" steaks, as well as plenty of items that we would classify as polite tea-room fare ("half grapefruit, maraschino," strawberry parfaits). The great specialties of the house are seafood. In particular, we love the shrimp broiled in butter and garlic, the hefty slab of flounder topped with cheese-enriched potatoes, the classic trout amandine, and the crab Belvedere, which the menu declares "a delicious way to treat our wonderful southern Gulf crab lumps, delicately seasoned and stuffed in a shell." Every Friday, Creole gumbo is served; and you can always get oysters—chilled on the half shell, in a milk stew, fried (for those "kosher" sandwiches), or broiled with bacon en brochette.

Oh, dear, there is so much to eat at Weidmann's. We have never even tried the sautéed half chicken in wine sauce, which locals tell us is one of the hidden treasures of the kitchen. Nor can we tell you much about Weidmann's southern-style vegetables (turnip greens, sautéed corn kernels, steamed okra), except to say that we always forget to taste them because we are so mesmerized by everything else on the table.

As for dessert, the long menu is a cafe aficionado's dream, from the utter simplicity of a sliced banana with cream to the glory of the famous black-bottom pie. Other notable items include silk-smooth caramel cup custard, bourbon pie and egg custard pie, and coconut custard pie to make you swoon. Then there are the oddities we have yet to order, but crave to sample some day when we have the gumption (and a shred of appetite remaining): there on the dessert list, right after the parfaits and sherbets, are listed cream cheese with jelly, blue cheese with jelly, and Swiss cheese with jelly. The waitress told us they are served with hot rolls and butter and a knife for spreading. It sounded rather weird to us, but who are we to question the ways of a 122-year-old kitchen?

MISSOURI

ARTHUR BRYANT'S
1727 BROOKLYN, KANSAS CITY, MO (816) 231-1123

Although Arthur Bryant really did die in 1982 (an event marked by an obituary in *The New York Times* headlined "Arthur Bryant, Barbecue Man"), reports of the death of what he called the House of Good Eats are greatly exaggerated. As far as we can tell, the brisket is still as lusciously tender and adipose as ever, and still served mounded into sandwiches so tall they stretch your jaw to eat; the pork ribs are still gorgeously glazed with blackened burned edges and lodes of meat below their spicy crust. The skin-on French fries are bronze beauties, as ever. The goopy barbecue beans are some of Kansas City's best. Most important, the sauce—that gritty red-orange blend of spice and sorcery—packs the same wallop it always has, adding glow to meat without overpowering it with heat.

The place is the same, too: a go-to-hell mess with oil-slick floors and plenty of dropped shreds of meat all around the tables (resulting from sandwiches impossible to raft from plate to mouth without major spillage), and brusque cafeteria-style service by barbecue professionals who, while seldom actually rude, wield their cleavers with the hauteur of blasé master chefs.

BUSCH'S GROVE
9160 CLAYTON RD., ST. LOUIS, MO (314) 993-0011

"The Grove," as friends of Busch's Grove Restaurant know it, has been around for over a century. John Busch started it in 1890 when he turned a general store called the Woodland Grove into a restaurant. His son, along with Paul Kammerer, took over twenty-eight years later; and the rest is St. Louis culinary history. (For further historical information, look at the carving in Busch's Grove's men's bar, where the founders are pictured in bas-relief.)

There is an old-fashioned, country-club feel about this venerable restaurant, some of whose tables have been engaged by the same families for generations. The dining room is wood-paneled with a fireplace; and when we have sat inside, there was so much table-hopping it seemed that nearly everybody who comes to eat here knows everybody else. In the summer, regulars frequently have themselves seated out back in the "cages"— screened grass-hut gazebos that make dinner into a tropical party.

Salads are the dishes that best capture the spirit of this tradition-loving place. They are old-time classics, made using familiar, nonintimidating greens (iceberg and romaine lettuce), and dressings made from good ol' mayonnaise and familiar oils (no raspberry-flavored vinegar or other such nouvelle affectations), and they are served in big, happy mounds. There is a spinach salad, lavishly adorned with bacon and eggs and delicious sweet-and-sour dressing; and there is Russ's salad—a customers' favorite for many years. It is like a chef's salad, but made even richer and more luxurious by the application of "Bellevue" dressing made with hard-cooked eggs and a dusting of garlic flavor.

The main thing to eat at Busch's Grove is meat: steaks and chops with au gratin potatoes on the side, prime rib, and good, expensive shrimp. There is one peculiar local oddity, usually served in Italian restaurants on "the Hill"—toasted ravioli, which is the uniquely St. Louisian way of serving the familiar Italian dumplings: deep-fried, sprinkled with sharp cheese, tomato sauce on the side. Split it as an appetizer.

Whether you are seated outdoors in a grass hut or inside the clubhouse/dining room, the traditional libation to accompany a Busch's Grove meal is a mint julep. It arrives topped with a paper parasol, an orange slice, a maraschino cherry, and fresh mint leaves; and it is served in the classic julep manner—inside a big silver tumbler filled with shaved ice and oceans of bourbon. We will never forget our waiter's proclamation the first time we ordered juleps at the Grove. As he set the regal drinks before us, he intoned, "From a man's bar—Butch's Grove."

C & K BARBECUE
4390 JENNINGS STATION RD., ST. LOUIS, MO (314) 385-8100

Some people actually come to C & K to eat ribs, and good ribs they are; but to walk out the door without a mouthful of snoots would be like visiting San Francisco and ignoring the sourdough. Snoots are a St. Louis soul-food passion, and what they are, are snouts: pig snouts, sliced and fried and sauced and served in cumbersome sandwiches that cannot be eaten without scattering globules of sauce and snoot pieces all over your lap.

Other than the concept, there is nothing intrinsically hideous about snoots, and they are not nearly as visceral in taste or texture as some of the more awful offal. In fact, they are a rather refined-tasting foodstuff once they have been fried: crisp, porous, lightweight, like the strips of pigskin one sometimes finds along the buffet at a traditional Deep South pig pickin'. When glazed with C & K's dynamite dark orange-pepper sauce, snoots sing, and there is nothing nasal about their tune.

Now, ribs: we don't want to give them short shrift, because they are some of the best in St. Louis. They are long-cooked and packed with smoke flavor and a real joy to chew. In fact they are more chewy than tender, but that's all right because the flavor that develops as you chew is symphonic. Like snoots, ribs are mostly sold as sandwiches—an incongruous presentation, but nonetheless a traditional one, requiring you to do a lot of picking, rearranging, bread-tearing, sauce-dipping, mopping, and lip-smacking— all of which are reasons eating barbecue can be so much fun. This kitchen adds its own eccentric touch to its rib, snoot, and sausage sandwiches—a scoop of potato salad heaped on top of the meat before the top slice of bread is flattened down. What a righteous mess!

C & K desserts are well worth ordering. There are various homey layer cakes and miniature sweet potato pies, sized for one or two. The pies are deep amber color, supersweet, and just the ticket after a hot and spicy pig-part meal.

The one problem about eating at C & K is that you cannot eat at C & K. Business is strictly take-out. If you value your car's upholstery, you will find some other place to eat.

CROWN CANDY KITCHEN
1401 ST. LOUIS AVE., ST. LOUIS, MO (314) 621-9650

The Crown Candy Kitchen makes all its own ice cream and sauce, and still practices the venerable art of confectionery. Every holiday is cause for chocolate figurines, including Santas, turkeys, Valentine's Day hearts, and forty-five different sizes and varieties of Easter bunny. In addition to molded chocolates, there are nougats, peanut brittle, cream centers, and heavenly hash.

Opened in 1913 by Harry Karandzieff and Pete Jugaloff, who brought their confectionery skills from Greece, the shop is now run by Harry's descendants, who maintain its historical ambience and boast that it is the oldest soda fountain in St. Louis. The walls are packed with turn-of-the-century memorabilia, including an impressive collection of Coca-Cola advertising trays. For a nickel, a rickety machine will tell your weight and read your horoscope. Overhead, hanging from the tin ceiling, fans spin slowly.

It is possible to have lunch here. They make all kinds of sandwiches, including some mighty zesty chili dogs. But the reason to seek out this place is not the sandwich menu. It is the soda fountain.

Punch up a tune on the jukebox in your booth, order a mile-high "Lover's Delight" or a strawberry-pineapple-marshmallow-sauced French sundae studded with toasted cashews and chocolate sprinkles, or a fruit salad sundae topped with fresh and frozen fruit ("It's good for you!" promises the menu). The Crown Candy Kitchen's turtle sundae is exemplary. Silken vanilla ice cream is shrouded with hot fudge, the fudge covered with caramel sauce, and the caramel sauce mounded with buttered and toasted pecans. Everything is served in its proper soda fountain serving glass, accompanied by a long-handled spoon.

The specialty of the house, and the taste sensation that earned the Crown Candy Kitchen a permanent place in our Pantheon of good eats, is the malted milk shake. They make malteds here the old-fashioned way, using malt powder, ice-cold milk, their own ice cream (not too rich, not too sweet), and the full repertoire of soda fountain syrups, including cherry, pineapple, marshmallow, strawberry, and, of course, vanilla and chocolate. They serve them the old-fashioned way, too—in twenty-four-ounce silver beakers, filled nearly to the top. Drink five such malteds in thirty minutes (that's approximately one gallon) and you get them free!

The most unusual of the malted flavors is banana, for which a fresh banana is pulverized along with the ice cream and milk. They serve it topped with a dusting of nutmeg. Or if you really want to gild this lily (you do!), have them add chocolate syrup to the brew. They will also dollop a blob of whipped cream on top and sprinkle that with chopped nuts, for an item known as the "Johnny Rabbit Special." Actually, we find the whipped cream and nuts superfluous. The combination of banana and chocolate and vanilla ice cream and malt powder, however, is irresistible—a kind of supercharged banana split in a glass.

DOGWOOD TRAILS
JUNCTION OF ROUTES 63 & 142, THAYER, MO (417) 264-7900

A t Dogwood Trails (formerly Nettie's), the dinner bell resounds every day at 11:00 A.M. Hungry customers grab trays and begin their expedition along the line of good food.

We can never resist baked chicken when it is available in the cafeteria line. It is so limber it cannot be lifted from the plate without all the meat sliding off its bones. To accompany this sunny plate of food, we like dumplings in chicken broth. For dipping in the broth, a pair of warm dinner rolls exactly fill the bill.

But Dogwood Trails is not all gentleness and soft things to eat. Fried chicken is a handful and a mouthful—brittle-crusted, meaty, saturated with the punch of black pepper. There is spicy spinach, too, cooked the way collard greens are cooked in a traditional southern kitchen, served wallowing in a pool of potent pot likker.

As in so many good cafeterias, the choice of salads is extensive. There are leafy things, creamy slaws, multi-colored gelatins, marinated vegetables, and cool, sweet macaroni. The one we like best is a wide-awake combination of black-eyed peas, chopped scallions, and diced red peppers in a sugary marinade. It is tart, sweet, sour, and—because of the peas—substantial.

As for dessert, if you're here early in the dinner hour, it is likely the excellent coconut meringue pie will still be warm when you put it on your tray.

Getting to Dogwood Trails can be half the fun. The prettiest way to find it is to head down Route 19 through the Mark Twain National Forest toward the Ozarks. Just before crossing into Arkansas, you come upon a small shopping center. And there it is. If it's just before eleven o'clock, there will likely be a group of townspeople outside marking time until the bell rings.

JESS & JIM'S STEAK HOUSE
517 E. 135TH ST., KANSAS CITY, MO (816) 942-9909
(JESS & JIM'S ANNEX IS AT 13035 HOLMES RD.)

No steak makes a grander entrance than the "Playboy Strip," carried from Jess & Jim's kitchen on a metal tray—a furiously sizzling pound-and-a-half sirloin, its outer band of amber fat sputtering, juices oozing from fissures in the darkened crust. Ease a knife down into it and sever a piece, but before you put it in your mouth, admire its roseate lusciousness, watch the fibers glisten, and smell the acute perfume of well-cooked protein. This piece of meat is why Kansas City is famous for its steaks.

To accompany the heroic mesa of meat, Jess & Jim's sells either a gargantuan twice-baked potato, fluffed up and sopped with margarine, or the K.C. favorite, cottage fries—cross sections of potato cooked in a motley heap so that some are soft as mashed, others crisp as chips.

Salad is head lettuce (that's midwesternese for iceberg) with bottled dressings martialed on every table; there are no desserts whatsoever; and the wine list is red, white, or pink. Meat and potatoes: that's the ticket at Jess & Jim's.

JUST COATES RESTAURANT & BAR
9922 HOLMES, KANSAS CITY, MO (816) 941-0399

Kansas City fried chicken: the meal is a ritual. It begins with salad. It is a nice, ordinary salad unless you pay extra for bleu cheese dressing, in which case it is fantastic. The dressing comes in its own little bowl—a mountain of cheese. Now comes dinner: platters of chicken that has been fried slowly in a skillet until its thin coating turns dark and hardens into a wicked crust, faintly tweaked with pepper. Inside this crust is dewy white meat or even more succulent dark meat with a real chicken flavor that cannot fail to convince you of the unrivaled glory of Chicken Betty, Kansas City's legendary chicken chef who long ago showed Al Coates's kitchen how to do it right.

With the chicken come superior side dishes—mashed potatoes (real ones, of course) and cottage fries of nearly infinite variety, fluffy white biscuits, and cream gravy. That's all you need to know. There are other things on the menu—chicken-fried steak, gizzards and livers, catfish, and steak; but if you are coming here only once, fried chicken is what you want.

Just Coates is a descendant of Boots and Coates, which was for many years one of Kansas City's premier fried-chicken houses. The original is gone, and the place where it used to be is an auto showroom. We miss its dark, clubby atmosphere and could do without the Kansas City Royal blue motif of Al Coates's new place. However, Just Coates is much more comfortable to sit in, you don't have to wait in line as long, and it's easier to find a place to park outside. More important, the fried-chicken dinners are as magnificent as ever.

LAMBERT'S CAFE
2515 E. MALONE, SIKESTON, MO (314) 471-4261

Motoring south along the Mississippi River out of St. Louis, you will see a billboard advertising Lambert's Cafe, "home of the throwed roll." From the outside, the restaurant looks fairly ordinary. Inside, hot rolls are sailing across the dining room, "throwed" by waiters from the kitchen to customers at tables, who gingerly split them open to let steam escape, then dip them into puddles of sweet sorghum molasses oozing all over the oilcloth-covered tables. Other eaters will be popping nuggets of crisp fried okra down the hatch, spooning up heaps of beans and pepper relish, and drinking iced tea from one-quart Mason jars.

Lambert's is one-of-a-kind, and not just because it looks like a food fight is in progress. Even if the rolls weren't "throwed" and everybody's table weren't an awful mess of spilled and dripped food and Norm Lambert didn't keep coming around with his sorghum bucket and ladling more of the sticky stuff all over your table, this would be a unique and worthwhile *Roadfood* landmark. First of all, those rolls are *good*—warm and fluffy; and Lambert's country ham with white beans and turnip greens is Ozark country cooking at its most toothsome. In fact, the whole menu is a sampler of authentic, downhome vittles, all expertly prepared, including catfish and smothered steaks, fried chicken and country ham, and a dish listed on the menu as "pie pan of beans," for which the beans are accompanied by fried bologna, cornbread, a King Edward cigar and a stick of Big Red chewing gum. For dessert, choose cobbler or coconut cream pie. The menu says, "We serve the largest slab of pie in the United States."

What else can you possibly want to know about Lambert's Cafe, "Home of the Throwed Roll"? Well, you probably ought to be aware that if the 924,180 rolls that Lambert's bakes every year were laid side by side, they would be seventy-three miles long.

MCDONALD TEA ROOM
GALLATIN, MO (816) 663-2021

"I am confident you will like your visit here," wrote America's first motoring gourmet, Duncan Hines, back in 1936. "The McDonald Tea Room is amazing. Whenever I am in this section of the country, I always make a point of going here for dinner."

We do likewise, and suggest that travelers in search of genuine Americana follow Mr. Hines's lead. Virginia Rowell McDonald died in 1969, but her personality informs this oasis of ladylike cuisine in the farmland east of St. Joseph, Missouri.

Her hats—wide, flamboyant, feathery creations—are hung on the wall as decoration. Her china collection fills one of the back rooms. The color scheme is pink and black; the chairs are elegant wrought iron; the whole frills-and-flowers style of the place is feminine in a way that has long since vanished from the American restaurant scene.

"A love of the beautiful, cleanliness, and order are the dominant passions of my life," Mrs. McDonald once explained. "All three are very necessary attributes of a successful cook." Even today, more than twenty years since she died, you get a feeling for her sense of propriety when you arrive. The Tea Room is a clean white building, virtually gleaming in the sun, with flowers in the windows and a cozy little pathway leading to the front door.

When we walked in for lunch, the first thing we noticed was the smell: a yeasty, come-hither aroma of rolls fresh out of the oven. "Bread is the most important part of any meal," Mrs. McDonald wrote in a small pamphlet of recipes she printed in 1937. "Being southern, I like hot bread."

Beyond the fresh-baked rolls that come with every meal, the menu is small and simple—southern-accented classics such as country ham, fried chicken, tenderloin, and roast beef. If you don't want a hot meal, there are sandwiches; and there is a salad bar set up with greens, garnishes, and composed salads to heap on a plate.

We had fried chicken and ham, both of which were quite all right, but what we remember best are the rolls, the side dishes, and dessert. Along with each main course, we received a bowl full of buttered potatoes—plain boiled potatoes, glistening hot and fork-tender. And there was another bowl of what the waitress referred to as spinach delight—a heap of limp green leaves enriched with bite-size pieces of bacon and sautéed onions. The spinach was an invigorating combination of ingredients with nostalgic appeal—the kind of decent yet rather luscious dish for which tea-room proprietors like Mrs. McDonald were once renowned. Each customer received a silly salad, too: a scoop of cottage cheese set atop a pineapple ring, crowned with a maraschino cherry.

It has always been customary at the McDonald Tea Room to follow a meal with pie. "Men prefer this form of dessert," Mrs. McDonald wrote, explaining that the three necessary ingredients to a good pie were a flaky crust, smooth insides, and a stiff-standing meringue. All three were in resounding evidence in the slices of peanut butter cream pie we got at the climax of our lunch.

MISS HULLING'S CAFETERIA
11TH & LOCUST ST., ST. LOUIS, MO (314) 436-0840

You can believe St. Louis's claims to have invented angel food cake when you see the variety presented at Miss Hulling's Cafeteria: angel food swirl, mocha angel food, angel food with strawberries on top. Our personal favorite is the one called ribbon cake—layers of pink, white, and chocolate separated by dark red jam, the whole shebang spread with blushing pink frosting.

The livery of the restaurant matches the pretty cakes. It is a festival of peppermint pink—pink napkins, pink uniforms for the staff, pink walls, pink tables, and pink awning stripes. The point of all the pink is nostalgia, for Miss Hulling's is not only a genuinely old restaurant (since the thirties); it is a restaurant that likes being old-fashioned. Attached to the full-meal cafeteria is an ice cream shop and pastry shop serving swell old-tyme soda fountain treats and cakes, and on one wall there is a wistful mural that depicts hobnobbing ladies and gentlemen of the Mississippi River's belle epoch. The entryway is watched over by very proper portraits of Miss Hulling and her family.

We're in seventh heaven when we see a spread like the one in Miss Hulling's cafeteria line. There are individual Jell-O molds, salads and slaws galore, such comfort-food meals as chicken fricassee with creamy, four-star mashed potatoes, cut-to-order roast beef, chicken pot pie, and lovely pink ham. From a roster of about twenty side dishes you can choose buttermilk squash with corn flakes and apple chunks—a sweet, crunchy sensation; twice-baked potatoes, beans and peas and carrots and rice of every stripe; and there is always a great daily selection of homemade biscuits, muffins, rolls, and fritters.

As for dessert, that is a crowning glory of this venerated landmark of culinary Americana. In addition to all those beautiful angel (and layer) cakes, there are puddings and custards; pies, tortes, crisps, and dumplings; oodles of ice cream and sherbet flavors available with hot fudge, caramel, butterscotch, or rummy pineapple sauce; and from the bakery there are cookies, chews, kisses, gems, bars, brittles, squares, babas, and divinity.

SMOKESTACK BAR-B-QUE
135TH & HOLMES, KANSAS CITY, MO (IN MARTIN CITY) (816) 942-9141

If it moves or even if it doesn't, they likely smoke it at the Smokestack. The mighty brick ovens that you see when you enter the restaurant, and whose hickory scent suffuses all the dining rooms, contain not only all the expected and a few unusual K.C. meats—brisket, pork loins, lamb ribs, chicken, turkey, and sausage—but also some items not found anywhere else.

Barbecued trout, for example: succulent beyond belief. Catfish, grilled over hickory: you never knew the cat could taste so deluxe. Why, there are even hickory-grilled tuna, salmon, and—are you ready—vegetables. For dieters! No, the Smokestack is not your typical Kansas City high-fat, low-comfort barbecue parlor; but if good eats are what you crave, you shouldn't be dissuaded by all the amenities and fancy stuff on the menu.

In no way is the Smokestack swank. Out in the country south of Kansas City, it is a roadhouse with comfortable tables and chairs, plenty of interior decor (Old West bric-a-brac, hanging plants, stained-glass windows, a stone fireplace), and a menu that, although more eclectic than a single-purpose pit, does indeed have some terrific, down-home things to eat.

The meats themselves are beyond reproach. Butter-tender brisket, succulent pork ribs, even more succulent and more tender lamb ribs: cooked long and slow, impregnated with just enough flavor of the fire, these are our stars from the menu (other than that sensational trout), so good that we apply hardly any of the Smokestack's powerhouse hot sauce. Among the side dishes, pit beans, threaded with oodles of well-cooked barbecued pork, are not to be missed. Ditto the curlicue French fries. Ditto onion rings.

One favorite item we can never resist here is "burnt ends." These are all the crisp and crunchy, overcooked shreds from the outside of the beef, pork, and ham that are left over once the tender pieces have been cut away for more expensive dinners. "Burnt ends" (known elsewhere around town as "brownies") are cutting-board scraps; but if you love the taste of smoke and sauce and the lusciousness of a serious chaw of meat that fairly explodes with flavor, they are nothing less than the essence of the smoke pit, like barbecue bouillon. They are served drizzled with sauce, for picking as an appetizer, or as a low-cost sandwich. The sandwich, which is immense, is made not on the blah white bread that is expected and perfectly acceptable in all other blue-ribbon barbecue restaurants. It is made on high-quality French bread—yet another refinement we are only too happy to forgive. That sturdy bread soaks up Smokestack hot sauce like nobody's business.

SNEAD'S BARBECUE
171ST AND HOLMES IN BELTON (KANSAS CITY), MO (816) 331-7979

Warning: we are about to blither. Snead's does that to us. There are many fine barbecue restaurants in and around Kansas City, but this place—way, way out of town—sends our heads spinning with delight.

There are so many good things to eat, you cannot possibly sample all of them in one visit. To wit: beef and/or ham brownies, which are the crusty, smoky chunks stripped from the ends and tips of the meat. Order a plateful. They aren't as soft as the ordinary barbecue, but they fairly explode with the flavor of meat, smoke, and sauce.

Regular pork barbecue, cooked over hickory wood, is sweet and tender, without the punch of brownies but with satisfying heft. The beef brisket is shockingly fatless, and yet somehow supple and dizzyingly luscious. *People* magazine once referred to it as the leanest (but among the best) barbecues in America.

Then there are log sandwiches, named for their shape: big tubular mixtures of finely ground barbecued beef, pork, and ham, all minced together and wedged into a long bun. The result is a salty, powerful mélange reminiscent of a Maid-Rite sandwich—not as potent as the brownies, but in some long-term satisfying way even more complex.

And did we mention the sensational, hand-cut, freshly made French fries? And the sweet, saucy barbecued beans? And finely chopped cole slaw, perfectly suited to salving a sauce-fatigued tongue? Oh, yes, about that sauce: there are two kinds, and you add it yourself (all meat is served dry). The dark sauce is mild and molasses sweet—easy to eat. The brighter one is fiery red-orange, flecked with pepper, and dangerous. It doesn't seem too hot, but after half a sandwich's worth, you will feel the incandescence on your tongue.

Snead's is a wood-paneled roadhouse with laminated tables and assorted dead animal heads on the walls, and one room with big windows that look out onto the countryside. It is a long drive from downtown Kansas City, but anyone who wants to savor pit-cooked greatness cannot ignore it.

STROUD'S
1015 E. 85TH ST., KANSAS CITY, MO (816) 333-2132

Stroud's makes the most delicious fried chicken in America, and accompanies it with potatoes, pepper gravy, and cinnamon rolls to match.

It is fried in a heavy iron skillet and arrives at the table a shade of gold that is breathtakingly beautiful. Each piece is audibly crusty, but not the least bit bready; there is just enough of an envelope of crust to shore in all the chicken juices. Once you crunch through it, though, the juices flow down your chin and fingers and forearm: you are an unsightly mess, but you don't care because the juices are ambrosia.

Superb mashed potatoes: nearly fluffy-textured, with an intense flavor of . . . *potato!* As you fork up big mouthfuls of these spuds you learn new respect for real mashed potatoes and new intolerance for bogus ones. The only way these lovelies can be improved is if you ladle some of Stroud's gravy on them. It is zesty, pan-dripping gravy, redolent of chicken and powerfully peppered.

At the risk of sounding hysterical, we must tell you that the cinnamon rolls that accompany this meal are fantastic, too. Tasting more of yeast and cinnamon than sugar, they are big, swirly things with only the faintest hint of caramelized cinnamon butter around the base.

As is true of many of the world's great restaurants, Stroud's ambience perfectly complements the food. It is a wood-floored roadhouse that was at the edge of the city when Mrs. Stroud opened it in 1933 (but is now on a busy road where parking is a problem). There are bright yellow curtains on the windows and red-checked cloths on the tables. Above the bar at one end of the dining room, a taxidermized deer head wears a bandanna and looks out over the partying chicken-eaters through 3-D viewing glasses.

STROUD'S OAK RIDGE MANOR
5410 N.E. OAK RIDGE RD., KANSAS CITY, MO (816) 454-9600

This upscale branch of Stroud's serves the same superior fried-chicken dinners with all the proper fixin's—including potatoes, gravy, and cinnamon rolls; it also cooks steaks, pork chops, chicken-fried steak, ribs, shrimp, and catfish. And instead of being a rowdy roadhouse, the Oak Ridge Manor, also known as Stroud's North, is an antique home with valuable furniture including a walnut cabinet that once belonged to a relative of Daniel Boone. But don't let Aunt Emma's grand piano and the original land deed signed by John Q. Adams inhibit you from rolling up your sleeves, digging in, and letting the chicken juices run down your chin.

This is supreme four-star chicken, skillet-fried until shatteringly crisp, with more nectarous juices in the meat than any chicken has a right to have. A "regular" dinner consists of a leg, a thigh, a wing, and a breast, each of which is swell in its own way—the breast steamy and cream-tender, the thigh so succulent it feels naughty to eat. If you wish, you can choose dinners that are all white, all dark, even all gizzards. The cinnamon rolls are wonderful—a perfect bready companion to the moist birds; the cottage fries are among the very best in a city where cottage-fried potatoes reign (the mashed potatoes are wonderful, too!); the gravy for the chicken is powerfully peppered. There isn't anyplace in America that serves a chicken dinner this good, except maybe Stroud's other restaurant on 85th Street.

TED DREWES
6726 CHIPPEWA, ST. LOUIS, MO (314) 481-2652;
OTHER LOCATION: 4224 S. GRAND

If you are searching for the ultimate milk shake (who is not?), there is one place in St. Louis that you've got to try: Ted Drewes Frozen Custard (actually, two places if you consider both locations). Drewes, which makes true, pure soft ice cream custard from whole eggs, real vanilla, and a touch of honey, specializes in a monumental milk shake known as—are you ready?—a *concrete*. "Why is it called a concrete?" we ask our server, who wears a plastic hard hat. And without a word of explanation, he hands us our strawberry–chocolate chip concrete *upside-down*, with the spoon and straw stuck in it. Nothing falls out, not a drip. Once you turn it right side up, the straw is useless. Even the plastic spoon hardly seems sturdy enough to plow into this luxuriant adiposity.

There are dishes other than a concrete at Ted Drewes: you can get your custard in a cone or cup, too; and the flavors include immaculate vanilla as well as hot fudge, strawberry, and chocolate chip. However you eat this stuff, with a spoon or straight from a cone, it is Grade-A heifer heaven, richer and sweeter and more sumptuous than a draft of pure cream.

WINSTEAD'S
101 BRUSH CREEK BLVD., KANSAS CITY, MO (816) 753-2244
(FOUR OTHER LOCATIONS IN AND AROUND KANSAS CITY)

W instead's steakburgers are broiled on a greaseless griddle, according to a boast on the plastic laminated menu; but don't worry, they aren't really greaseless. They are just as savory as you want when you go to a drive-in for a burger. Served in a paper pocket in configurations of a single patty, a double, or a triple, these are classic (since 1940) fast-food burgers, gray through-and-through, flavored with the luscious perfume of a well-seasoned griddle. Order it with the works and you get pickle, onion, ketchup, mustard, and sauce. Cheese and lettuce cost extra.

On the side with a steakburger, one wants French fries or onion rings. The fries are fine, although not really memorable; we recommend the onion rings. All the grease from the greaseless grill seems to go into these crusty dark rings, so that the bottommost ones fairly glisten with it. Delish.

Winstead's is famous for its soda fountain treats: limeade, lemonade, orangeade, masterfully mixed milk shakes and malts, handsome sodas and sundaes, and a deluxe concoction known as the "special chocolate malt," so thick that it is served with a spoon, the only utensil that will get it from its glass to your mouth.

About the waitresses: they wear nurse-like white caps and have big, starchy hankies pinned to their green uniforms, and like the menu at Winstead's, they suggest an earlier, pre-corporate era of quick eats. When ours saw us spooning up our special chocolate malt with glee, she asked, "Don't you just love it? Isn't it the coup de goo?"

NEBRASKA

CONEY ISLAND LUNCH ROOM
104 E. 3RD ST., GRAND ISLAND, NE (308) 382-7155

S trange: throughout America there are restaurants that sell "Coney Islands" but if you go to Coney Island in New York, to Nathan's on the boardwalk, and ask for a Coney Island, the man behind the counter won't know what you are talking about. Coney Island calls its tube steaks frankfurters. Nearly everywhere else they are Coneys.

What happened is that back in the twenties and thirties, dozens—maybe hundreds, maybe thousands—of Greeks who worked at New York hot dog stands moved west (and a few moved east, to Rhode Island). They came to Cincinnati and invented five-way chili. They opened wiener stands, which were sometimes enhanced by soda fountains and short-order kitchens, in Cleveland, Detroit, Chicago, and smaller towns all over the heartland. Many are still around, and still serve hot dogs, which are known as Coney Islands, because that is where they came from.

The Coney Island Lunch Room of Grand Island opened in 1933, and it has hardly changed since. Behind the glass brick front of the narrow storefront eatery are a counter and a row of booths and an open kitchen where hot dogs, along with hamburgers and French fries, are cooked. The dogs are just fine: cute, beefy ones tucked into steamy soft buns and covered with the unique kind of chili sauce found only in Greek-run wiener shops. Reminiscent of five-way chili, the sauce is spicy, almost sweet, rich red, and an ideal wiener companion. For lunch you want at least two chili-topped Coneys, three or four plus fries if you are hungry.

To wash them down: genuine chocolate malts, made from scratch using ice cream, flavorings, and chilled milk. It is a formula for excellence, and these shakes are four-star soda fountain fun. The server pours some into a glass and presents it along with the tall silver beaker in which it was made. Inside the beaker is at least another glassful.

DREISBACH'S
1137 S. LOCUST, GRAND ISLAND, NE (308) 382-5450

It has been nearly ten years since Dreisbach's burned to the ground and beef eaters all across America wept. This venerable eatery had become one of the most cherished steak houses in the Midwest since it opened in 1932. People came for T-bones and tenderloins surrounded by terrific fixin's served family-style to groups of four or more people. For us *Roadfood*ers, always on the prowl for meals with powerful regional flavor, it was hard to imagine a trip west along Route 80 without planning the itinerary around a major feed at Dreisbach's. Lucky us, we didn't have to wait long for Nebraska's king of beef to return. Dreisbach's was rebuilt and going strong by mid-1988.

Beef is the only thing you want to consider eating: T-bones, sirloins, New York strips, and filet mignons at least three inches tall. This is blue-ribbon meat, char-broiled so it has a savory, blackened crust and tender pink insides that pocket loads of juice, ready to spurt at the first incision of a sharp knife. Along with the beef, there are excellent biscuits: air-light, served by the basketful. And potatoes: real mashed with good gravy, crusty hash browns, or the specialty of the house, sunflower potatoes.

Sunflower potatoes have been the hallmark of Dreisbach's meals since the 1940s, when owner Frank Dowd (who bought the steak house from Fred Dreisbach in 1944) invented them. They are designed to actually look like a Great Plains sunflower, with a sunny yellow center (melted cheddar cheese) surrounded by a burst of petals (crisp cuts of cottage fried potatoes). You can use a fork to eat them if you want to be polite, or you can pick up the hunks of spud by hand and scoop them through the cheese. A memorable eating experience!

Alas, the new Dreisbach's is all clean and sanitary, nearly as tidy as a franchised food restaurant; and it has none of the ramshackle charm of the original eatery, which was a windowless bunker with cow's-face crests on the outside. But who cares about decor? Despite the makeover, the food is exactly the same, which means it is inspired.

FAIRVIEW CAFE
1201 N. CHESTNUT, WAHOO, NE (402) 443-9941

The place to see and be seen in Wahoo is the Fairview. We have never been here to eat dinner, when they open up the fancier room (with blue cloth napery) and purport to serve "Wahoo's biggest steak dinner"; but the cafe with its worn pink Formica counter and booths suits us fine. We especially like the ambience at breakfast, when the overall set from the farms commingles with white-collar townsfolk over coffee and jumbo cinnamon rolls.

The Fairview is especially proud of its bakery. The Nebraska Department of Agriculture has awarded it honorable mention in bread and rolls, a fact commemorated with a plaque across from the cash register. We like the plain dinner rolls we got with lunch best of all, better even than the morning cinnamon buns (which, to our tongues, seemed less than hot-from-the-oven fresh). And pies. Wow, what pies! They are displayed behind the counter: hefty, creamy ones under towering halos of meringue. The raisin cream (a flavor we can never resist) was good and chock-a-block with sweet, bloated raisins, albeit strange-textured, with an unusual grit in the cream. First time through Wahoo, we were disappointed by the butterscotch pie—too bland. A second taste showed marked improvement.

Other than hot rolls and sky-high pies, the menu at the Fairview is mostly meat-and-potatoes classics (although we have eaten a relatively nouvelle taco salad). There are roast beef dinners, of course, and some very good corned beef (both served, alas, with second-rate mashed potatoes), pork chops and ham steaks accompanied by nicely flavored sweet potatoes. Our fondest thoughts are of the Fairview's sunny-colored chicken soup thick with homemade noodles and an aromatic lunch of creamed chicken on a biscuit—true Nebraska comfort food.

JOHNNY'S CAFE
4702 S. 27TH ST., OMAHA, NE (402) 731-4774

Johnny's is no more a "cafe" than a porterhouse steak is a beef patty. Years ago, it was a little place that catered to the men who worked in Omaha's stockyards; now it is a large-scale restaurant, a majestic monument to meat—still in the stockyards area, but now catering more to beef barons than to bull shippers. You could fit a whole cafe in the vestibule, which includes not only a photo gallery of Johnny's employee Hall of Fame, but various oil portraits and newspaper testimonials to Johnny's greatness.

Through the dimly lit entryway, you will be guided by a host into a fabulous, multi-leveled dining room that feels like a stage set with dramatic lighting (dig the cascading ultra-moderne chandeliers!) and you will be seated in great upholstered rolling chairs at tables big enough to hold plenty of grub. Service is indeed cafe-speedy; and despite Johnny's airs of grandiosity, waitresses are friendly, no-nonsense ladies in uniforms who will see to it you are happy.

Steaks, chops, ribs, liver, even, on occasion, tongue or ox tail are the things to order. You can splurge at dinner and eat the finest filet mignon or chateaubriand for miles around, and pay accordingly; or at lunch, for well under ten dollars, you can have yourself a superb downsized slab of prime rib. Alas, the mashed potatoes to accompany the fine meats are bogus; but the green blocks of fruited Jell-O we ordered as hors d'oeuvres were expertly molded; the rolls, although homemade, were not particularly interesting.

You don't want to miss dessert. For the ladies, we recommend the lovely, pastel-hued crème de menthe sundae. For menfolk, there is a more weighty turtle pie—a frozen block of the same ingredients used in Turtles candy, with the addition of ice cream: chocolate, nuts, and caramel. Johnny's serves it still fairly well frozen, so you will have all sorts of merry fun trying to fork off a piece. It is gooey, sweet, and—like Johnny's Cafe—ingratiatingly blunt.

LITTLE PARIS CAFE
201 E. 5TH ST., LEXINGTON, NE (308) 324-5887

West of Grand Island, the culinary pickin's get mighty slim as you travel I-80 along what used to be the Oregon Trail. But for anyone hungry for breakfast or lunch, we've got just the place. A hop off the inter-state in Dawson County is the town of Lexington (formerly Plum Creek, for you western history buffs) and some of the handsomest breakfast buns in the West. Big, sticky, caramelized puffs of yeasty dough—served every morning, with coffee and a full array of egg-and-pig-meat breakfasts, in a jim-dandy cafe called Little Paris, situated in a red brick building that used to be an automobile dealership.

In this region of the country all self-respecting cafes have a salad bar set out for lunch and supper, and Little Paris's is a doozy: all the leafy com-ponents to create your own, plus an array of at least half a dozen composed salads made with macaroni, ambrosia, even taco ingredients, and Jell-O. As for main courses, they are Great Plains paradigms. Meat loaf, roast beef, liver (beef liver, that is) with onions, ham steaks, fried chicken, or chicken-fried steak, accompanied by mountains of mashed potatoes and gravy and green beans that (honest) didn't taste like they had been poured out of a can. The kitchen often serves pot roast, and it will be your lucky day if it is on the menu when you stop by, for it is memorable—gentle-fibered, rich-flavored in a thick gravy.

To match the hearty meals that come before, desserts at Little Paris are big and beautiful. The pies, always nearly a dozen varieties available, are the real thing in a real flaky crust: strawberry-rhubarb, apple, cherry, peach, etc. Cream pies are even better than the fruit-filled ones. There are lemon meringue, banana cream, and such, plus that irresistible specialty found only in this region, raisin cream. That's the one we go for every time.

By the way, Paris is the owners' name, so expect nothing French on the menu. In fact, Little Paris is as all-American as can be.

RUNZA DRIVE-INNS
LOCATIONS THROUGHOUT EASTERN NEBRASKA,
AS WELL AS SOME IN KANSAS AND IOWA

Runzas are spreading. When we first ate one back in the late seventies, there were maybe a half-dozen Runza Drive-Inns around Lincoln. Now there are dozens. They are all pretty much the same—clean, innocuous, plastic-seat franchised-food restaurants. Still, we recommend them because the food they serve is a genuine regional specialty of this part of the world; and more important, it is really very good.

Similar to a pasty, a Runza is a big pocket of dough filled with ground beef, cabbage, onions, and spice and baked until light tan and steamy hot.

The concept was developed by pioneer cooks here in Nebraska who came to America from Germany, after first spending time in Russia. Exactly how these peregrinations led to the invention of a portable, mildly spiced, meal-in-a-breadloaf is a question we will leave to culinary historians. Suffice it to say that if you find yourself in the vicinity of a Runza Drive-Inn, and you are hungry, you will do well to give it a try.

The first Runza Drive-Inn opened back in 1950 when a Lincoln woman named Sally Everett opened up shop in an old corn dog stand, basing the house specialty on her mother's recipe for the pocket sandwich she called a Runza (a word Sally says she invented and that is now trademarked). The menu at modern Runza shops has expanded, but only a little. There are some highly praised hamburgers available, good onion rings, French fries, and brownies for dessert; there are even cheese Runzas and Italian Runzas (with mozzarella and tomato sauce). We recommend the regular Runza.

ULBRICK'S
ROUTE 75, NEBRASKA CITY, NE (402) 873-5458

On Route 75 just east of Nebraska City, heading into town, look carefully on your right. See that old gray gas station? It isn't a gas station any more. It is Ulbrick's, home of midlands fried-chicken dinners extraordinaire. Yes, it looks like a dump. Even when you enter, you don't see much in the way of linen napery or lovely table settings, fine art on the walls, or gleaming crystal. What you do see is a counter in what used to be the front of the gas station, and a rather cozy room in back, set up with oil-cloth-covered tables in rows: that's the main dining room. It is done up in what one woman we know, a very proper and polite sort of midwestern lady, described as "clutter decor." Does that dissuade that polite lady from eating at Ulbrick's? Not on your life. She, like so many folks along the Iowa-Nebraska border, have fallen in love with this place just the way it is, mismatched chairs and all.

The cause for regular customers' affection is simple, and can be expressed in three words: *fried-chicken dinner.* We thought about shortening it to two words—*fried chicken*—which is moist and succulent inside its shockingly crisp, well-seasoned golden crust; but that would have left out a lot of the reasons people love to come to Ulbrick's and put on the feedbag: the vegetables and salads that come alongside.

First, let's deal with potatoes. Years ago, Ulbrick's was known for mashed potatoes, and the first person who told us about this out-of-the-way eatery sang praises of those spuds. Alas, he said, they stopped serving mashed potatoes, except on Sunday, and they now serve fairly uninteresting accordion-shaped French fries. What a tragedy, we thought; but when we asked our waitress about this loss, she said in no uncertain terms—and we quote precisely: "Potatoes are immaterial to us. What we care about are vegetables." These fried spuds are fine, but you won't think about them much once you begin digging into all the other stuff.

The meal starts with salads that bear no resemblance to the boring bowls of lettuce and rabbit food that go by the name of salad in other restaurants. These are dazzling sweet, goopy salads, like macaroni mixed with mandarin orange segments, pineapple, marshmallows, and Cool Whip; or sweet pickled kraut; or the *pièce de résistance*, known hereabouts as "frog-eye salad," a saccharine amalgam made with tapioca and multicolored, bite-size Funmallows. Salads are accompanied by rolls that are homemade but undistinguished.

Now come vegetables—oh, such vegetables, the likes of which our moms never made! Nearly everything is creamed to a fare-thee-well, every bit as luscious as mashed potatoes could ever be, and glorious companions for the brittle-skinned chicken. You can get creamed corn, creamed cabbage, and a redundant-sounding (but essential) chicken and noodles, as well as ridiculously limp and totally uninteresting (uncreamed) green beans. Every table is allotted about two pieces of chicken per person, and all the vegetables and salad you want, served in family-style bowls. There is no dessert, but to be honest, after all those salads, our sweet tooth was satiated.

Note: Ulbrick's is small and can get crowded; and as the chicken takes forty-five minutes to prepare, reservations in advance are highly recommended.

NEVADA

THE GREEN SHACK
2504 E. FREMONT ST., LAS VEGAS, NV (702) 383-0007

We cannot tell a lie. When we are in Las Vegas we love to eat $3.98 prime rib and free shrimp cocktails and to stuff ourselves on tons of lousy food at the casino buffets. But there are occasions when the ersatz glories of Vegas begin to wear thin and we crave actual food in a normal restaurant. Those times, the only place to go is The Green Shack.

Southern fried chicken, steaks and chops, and thickly battered shrimp, accompanied by a relish tray, green salad, biscuits, and potatoes, are the specialties of the house, as they have been since the thirties when The Green Shack opened on the outskirts of town on the road to what would soon be Hoover Dam. The chicken is good eating, especially with the biscuits; if you don't like ordinary white meat or dark, livers and gizzards are still on the menu, too.

The Green Shack is filled with Old West memorabilia and Indian relics, and is staffed by people who don't seem to have their palms up most of the time in search of green grease (tips). The dining room can get mighty crowded around dinnertime, so you may have to wait for a table. We suspect that a lot of Vegas visitors share our ambivalence about the neon city. Much as we relish the pomp and impudence of its majestic edifices, it is awfully nice now and then to sit down to a plate of chicken and biscuits in a restaurant that calls itself a shack.

LOUIS' BASQUE CORNER
301 E. FOURTH ST., RENO, NV (702) 323-7203

W hen you travel around in search of good things to eat, some places are treasure troves; others are barren. Nearly every city is fun because it will at least have interesting ethnic food, or a diner, or an old, picturesque lunchroom. And most small towns have a cafe where local people gather for an honest meal.

But there are huge parts of this land, especially in the West and Great Plains, where there are no cities, no towns, and therefore almost nothing good to eat. That is why we like Route 80 through Nevada. The oases of civilization on this scenic highway are far apart, but nearly every one has a good restaurant. Thanks to the Basques.

Three-quarters of a century ago, Basque shepherds from the French and Spanish Pyrenees immigrated to the West—to Idaho, Nevada, and the California hills—where the high mountain pastures were ideal grazing land for sheep. They were men who lived solitary lives for months, coming to town only two or three times a year. When they came—to Elko, Winnemucca, Tuscarora, or Reno—the town's hotels sought their business by serving familiar Basque food. And to this day, the best—the only—places to eat are those that are descended from the shepherds' boardinghouses and hotels.

Basque cuisine, like their language, is unique. Although many of its dishes are similar to French and Spanish cooking, it has a high-spirited style all its own, well exemplified by the spread on the tables of Louis' Basque Corner, just a few blocks from the lights of downtown Reno.

Louis' has a frontier feel about it—transplanted Old World memorabilia in a rough-and-ready western setting. On the walls are Basque proverbs and pictures of the Pyrenees. Tables, covered with bright red cloths, are designed for twenty people at a time. And meals are served in chuckwagon abundance—great family-style bowls and platters carried to the table by waitresses in Basque costumes.

A meal at Louis' is six or seven courses, starting with a tureen of soup—usually a hearty one, stocked with barley, lentils, or noodles, or on some occasions with chunks of garlic bread (known as "Drunkard's soup"). Then comes salad, bread and butter, and a dish of Basque beans.

All of that is the prelude to "the first entrée." This is always a vigorously seasoned casserole such as paella or tripe stew or chicken Basquaise. It would be a meal anywhere else, but with typical boardinghouse abundance, it is always followed by a meaty western-style entrée such as steak, pork chops, or leg of lamb. Then comes a small dessert, either ice cream or a plate of cheese.

After plowing through so formidable a meal, many of Louis' customers put a point on things with a cup of brandy-laced café royale or the bittersweet Basque *digestif* known as picon punch. Having shared one's feast with strangers, it is natural to linger and chat in the afterglow.

Louis Erreguible, who came to Reno from southern France in 1948, opened the Basque Corner more than twenty years ago; and in that time it has become a beacon for cross-country travelers, as well as local folks from all walks of life, including ranchers, sheep herders, and even a few Reno entertainers. Louis' wife, who manages the restaurant, explained the appeal of Louis' Basque cuisine as "simple food cooked to perfection."

NEW HAMPSHIRE

S & S LANCASTER DINER
ROUTE 2, LANCASTER, NH (603) 788-2802

E ven if it didn't serve hot cinnamon rolls every morning and swell chicken pot pie, we would have a soft spot in our hearts for the S & S Lancaster Diner. It is gorgeous. A storefront rather than a free-standing diner, its interior is gleaming silver and well-aged wood, with a vaulted ceiling and upholstery on counter stools and booths in luxurious shades of red and yellow reminiscent of a Buick convertible from 1946. The sign in the oval windows is a neon dazzler.

Now, about those rolls. They are yeasty jumbos swirled with cinnamon; one is a good breakfast with a couple of cups of coffee. For lunch, the menu is pure diner chow—nothing elegant or expensive, all comfort food. There is usually a meat pie—chicken, beef, or turkey; if it's poultry, cranberry sauce comes alongside, as well as the vegetables *du jour*, which are such well-cooked familiars as buttered beets, green beans, and succotash. One homemade soup is available every day, offered as a lunch special with a sandwich. Last time we passed through town it was hearty tomato vegetable, and the featured sandwich on the side was grilled cheese.

Pies and Jell-O are available for dessert, and we have fond memories of lemon meringue pie and hot mince pie from a few years ago, but neither has been available on recent visits. That was okay, because we did manage to polish off a couple of bowls of jim-dandy Grape-Nuts custard pudding. Other notable puddings we have eaten at the Lancaster include tapioca and chocolate. Lunch doesn't get any squarer.

POLLY'S PANCAKE PARLOR
ROUTE 117, SUGAR HILL, NH (603) 823-5575

Polly's is like fancy-grade maple syrup: sweet and rare, rustic and deliciously old-fashioned. It began in 1938 when "Sugar Bill" Dexter and his wife Polly converted the carriage shed of their farm into a tea room in order to showcase all the good things that could be made from the sap gathered from Dexter's sugarbush. They served pancakes, waffles, and French toast as well as white bread laced with maple syrup and even something called "Hurricane Sauce" for ice cream (created by boiling syrup with the apple windfall on the ground after the hurricane of '38).

Today, Sugar Bill's descendants continue serving good, simple food with an array of maple products to pour, spread, and sprinkle on it. Pancakes are the specialty of the house; they are made from stone-ground flours or cornmeal, either plain or with their batter upgraded with shreds of coconut, walnuts, or blueberries. One order consists of half a dozen three-inchers; and it is possible to get a sampler of several different kinds. There is a remarkable range from, say, blueberry-cornmeal to buckwheat-walnut to plain; but they all share the wondrous delicacy that only expertly made pancakes offer. They come with the clearest and most elegant maple syrup, as well as maple sugar and a luxuriously unctuous maple spread. You can also get maple muffins, sandwiches made with maple white bread, an ambrosial gelatinized dessert called maple Bavarian cream, and all sorts of maple candies to take home.

What a visual feast it is to come eat at Polly's. It opens after mud season in the spring, when many of the surrounding maple trees are hung with taps and buckets; the spectacular time to visit is autumn, during the sugarbush's chromatic climax. The dining room has a glass-walled porch that overlooks fields where horses graze; and its inside walls are decorated with antiques and tools that have been in the family since the late eighteenth century, when Sugar Bill's ancestors began farming this land.

SUGAR HOUSE AT MT. CUBE FARM
ROUTE 25A, ORFORD, NH (603) 353-4814
(OPEN FOR BREAKFAST AROUND MEMORIAL DAY
FOR THE SUMMER ONLY)

Sugaring season begins when the weather is still bitter-cold. Sugar men and their families snowshoe into the forest and sink tapholes into each mature rock maple tree. It is an exacting process. If the holes are too deep, the bark will split and the sap will trickle down the trunk. Into each hole they insert a spout at a slight downward angle so the sap runs free. Buckets are hung on the spouts, then covered, so they don't also collect rain, twigs, and bugs.

If the weather is exactly right—a succession of freezing nights and warm days—the tree roots absorb moisture, building pressure inside the tree that pushes sap out the holes. During the days, when the sun thaws the sugarbush, you can stand among the trees and listen to sap begin to flow—a rushing ping that rouses Yankee appetites.

Once the sap is flowing, the hard work begins. Full buckets are emptied into barrels that are ferried back to the sugar house by horse-drawn cart or tractor. Forty gallons of the nearly tasteless sap are needed to make one gallon of syrup, and there is no way to predict the quality each year. The first run is invariably considered the best, producing the most delicately flavored nectar; by the fifth week, the yield turns coarse and dark. By now, the croaking of the newborn tree frogs will have signaled the end of the sugaring season. The spouts will be pulled, and the trees will scar up around the tap holes.

In Orford, New Hampshire, at Mt. Cube Farm, the Thomson family works a sugarbush that has been tapped annually since before the Civil War. To supplement the sap collected in the woods by tractor-drawn cart, they run plastic tubing from nearby tree spouts directly to the sugar house. Mt. Cube syrup is made in a modern arch that burns four gallons of oil for each gallon of syrup it produces. Yet for all the labor-saving equipment, the Thomsons' production is limited by what the trees produce—about a thousand gallons in a good year.

Mt. Cube is the nicest place we know to learn about—and savor—the slow and steady process of maple sugaring. In the front room there are a few tables set up with folding chairs around them: a unique breakfast restaurant, with a minimal menu of either pancakes or doughnuts, maple syrup on the side. The pancakes are made according to Mrs. Thomson's recipe, which is equal thirds cornmeal, whole wheat flour, and white flour. Each weekend morning, they are enjoyed by neighbors, passers-by, and cross-country hikers who avail themselves of the trails around Mooselauke Mountain and the sugar house. If you don't want pancakes, the other choice is doughnuts—plain yeast-leavened doughnuts, made by a lady down the road. They are served with disposable cups full of syrup, suitable for dunking. It is the humblest and happiest of meals, on paper plates with plastic utensils, with no music other than the hum of the evaporator boiling syrup in the back room.

NEW JERSEY

BROWN'S STOP IN
RT. 130, COLLINGSWOOD HEIGHTS, NJ (609) 456-4535

Camden County's oldest drive-in restaurant (since 1948) has been a favorite cheese-steak and milk shake stop for us from the time we first hit the road looking for good eats (1973). The management has changed, the strip of road has had some ups and downs, but we have always been able to rely on those great mounds of shredded, aromatic, oily beef and onions and plenty of melting cheese in a crisp, hot roll. This is one fine steak sandwich, different from Philly's best in that the bread is toasted; but we accept that because, to be honest, the bread here is not the four-star loaf used by the great cheese-steak shops to the west or over in Atlantic City. But the meat tastes great, and combines flawlessly with limp onions.

In addition to the classic sandwich, Brown's dishes out such layered lovelies as a Brownie special (a cheese steak with onions and ham!) and a Texas Tommie (a hot dog with bacon and cheese). Soda is served in frosted mugs; and milk shakes are made from scratch, with malt powder added if you wish. Our kind of place.

LIBBY'S LUNCH
98 MC BRIDE AVE., PATERSON, NJ (201) 278-8718

We had always thought it curious that there were so many good hot dogs in New Jersey (see also Rutt's Hutt, page 277, and Brown's Stop In, p. 275), many of them going by the name of "Texas weiners," with "weiner" spelled *e-i* instead of *i-e*. Our curiosity was requited when we got a letter from Robert C. Gamer of Wyckoff, in which Mr. Gamer included a treatise he had written for *New Jersey Monthly* titled "The Texas Weiner: Take a Bite of Our State Dog."

Gamer's chronicle tracked the origin of the Texas weiner to John Patrellis, a Greek immigrant who worked at his father's hot dog stand at the Manhattan Hotel in Paterson and devised the formulation that makes Texas weiners different from all others: a long, deep-fried frankfurter in a too-short bun topped with mustard, onions, and spicy chili sauce, traditionally accompanied by French fries and a mug of root beer. In 1920 the hot dog stand was renamed the Original Hot Texas Weiner. And thus a new dish was born: move over, Monsieur Brillat-Savarin, and make way for John Patrellis in gastronomy's Olympus. Today, Mr. Gamer observed, "Paterson almost certainly has more Texas weiner stands than any other town in the Garden State (or, for that matter, in the world)."

We followed his tip out along the Passaic River to the Texas weiner stand he believed—after sampling nearly four dozen different local dog houses—was the best of the best: Libby's Lunch, specializing in Texas weiners since 1936. Here in a sassy shack without a jot of pretense but with unimpeachable pedigree, the countermen were dishing out "dogs all the way," meaning topped by mustard, onions, and chili, sided by French fries. You have your choice when it comes to fries: plain, topped with dark, beefy gravy, or topped with more of the spicy red chili sauce. In addition to root beer, Libby's sells draft beer, as well as all other kinds of juice and soda. The fries smothered with beef gravy (which we like better than fries with chili sauce) are crisp, luscious, and salty as well they should be; and the hot dog is a real beaut: tough-skinned with tender, succulent insides. It's a swell plate of food; and a genuine New Jersey, and uniquely American, feast.

RUTT'S HUT
417 RIVER ROAD, CLIFTON, NJ (201) 779-8615

There is a sit-down side of Rutt's: a big easygoing taproom with wood-panel decor and a long menu of stalwart hot meals. Here customers quaff their beer with platters of chow such as chicken croquettes, stuffed cabbage, Jersey pork chops, and bean-heavy chili by the cup or bowl. Prices are low, and the food we have tasted, although far from hifalutin', is satisfying in a blue-plate way.

It's the open half of Rutt's Hut that's really fun. There are no seats, just high counters with a view of the parking lot and Highway 21. A couple of scrawny potted plants are the only interior decoration. Customers stand and scarf their food while reading journals of classified auto ads that are strewn about. Signs ask "PLEASE DO NOT SIT ON COUNTER" and "PLEASE PAY WHEN SERVED." Although there is no background music *per se,* one's ears are serenaded by the repartée of the countermen, hollering out the euphonic language of the greasy spoon.

"Cheeseburger—dipped!" they call out, meaning that the bun gets sopped with gravy. "I got a dog working!" is the cry to hustle things along. "Twins!" seemed to be another frequent call, which we assume referred to a pair of hot dogs on a single plate.

The menu in this part of Rutt's is limited to only a few weekend special sandwiches, plus the people's choice: hot dogs and hamburgers. The burgers are regular lunch-counter patties: thin, chewy, slick enough to moisten the bun even if you don't get it dipped. Onion rings are excellent—fat hoops of sweet, crisp onion barely sheathed in brittle batter. You'd almost call them couth.

Hot dogs are the *pièces de résistance.* There is nothing intrinsically wonderful about the meat of the dogs themselves; they appear to be your basic tubes of mild pork and beef. But Rutt's trick is to deep-fry them, then serve them forth with sweet yellow mustard and a good onion condiment. Their skin is fissured by the high heat and gets all crackly and chewy, but the inside stays soft. So it's the wieners' texture that's the kick. They are a splendid highway chew.

(For tipping us off to this four-star dog house, we thank New Jersey native Martha Stewart. Really.)

SHORT STOP DINER
315 FRANKLIN ST., BLOOMFIELD, NJ
(EXIT 148 OFF THE GARDEN STATE PARKWAY) (201) 429-1591

"What's good today?" We asked the waitress the first time we visited the Short Stop, at eight in the morning. "Eggs," she answered. Next time through New Jersey, about noon, we asked the same waitress what was good for lunch. Her answer: "Eggs." She seems to be gone now, but we don't bother to ask the new waitress for her suggestion. We know what to eat here, and we hereby pass the word to you: eggs.

Not just any hen fruit, these. These are ova with a title, which is "Eggs in the Skillet." What this means is that if you order a pair for breakfast (or lunch or dinner), they are cooked in butter in a small silver skillet and served to you still bubbling in their butter, still in their skillet, along with bacon, sausage, even steak, and whatever else you want. The skillet is set on a wooden trivet, and it keeps the eggs nice and warm while you eat. Sunny-side up, over easy, scrambled, or as a "he-man omelette" (that's a trio with cheese, hash browns, lettuce, tomato, toast, and jelly), eggs served this way look especially appetizing; the fluorescent-and-Formica ambience of the Short Stop (where a sign near the telephone advises "Do not answer phone unless you are dumb enough to work here"), adds hash-house panache to their farm charm.

Outside in the lot, another sign warns of "15-Minute Patron Parking"; but that won't be a problem in this restaurant, which is designed for travelers who want to eat it and beat it. Everything comes quickly. Beyond eggs, the menu is limited to hamburgers and sandwiches, pie, and good, rich coffee. You wouldn't want any more at the Short Stop, where the skillet meals are a kind of apotheosis of vintage diner breakfast—served, natch, all day.

TICK TOCK DINER
ROUTE 3, CLIFTON, NJ (201) 777-0511

The motto of the Tick Tock, displayed in large letters on the clock above the sign outside, reads "EAT HEAVY." The planet's most extravagant diner has a menu a yard wide, ranging from a dozen omelettes to a seafood catalogue that includes virtually every species of edible fish available in the Northeast (albacore tuna to sole and smelts to lox on bagels), broilings (steaks and chops; kidneys and liver), scores of sandwiches, forty-two different listed desserts, plus dozens more mile-high pies and sculpted pastries in a spinning display case, and a soda fountain repertoire of milk shakes, sundaes, and ice cream sodas.

When it opened in 1949, Tick Tock was a good-size, albeit modest diner. Now the word "diner" hardly does justice to a colossus whose pituitary enormousness comprises impressionistic paintings (of horse racing), electrical fireplaces, mirrored walls, gold curtains, and antique-like chandeliers.

What to eat? We have had some good sandwiches, a glorious Greek salad, and some not-so-glorious chicken croquettes with gravy. Breakfast is the meal we would recommend without hesitation. There are hefty muffins of all kinds, apple turnovers and cinnamon horns, Danish pastries and strudels, bagels with cream cheese or with a smoked-fish plate, blintzes (cheese or blueberry) with heavy sour cream, biscuits, sticky buns, French toast made with egg-rich diner bread, and an array of excellent omelettes, available plain with whatever you like in them, or "unflipped"—cooked pancake-style with salami, corned beef, or pastrami.

WHITE HOUSE SUB SHOP
2301 ARCTIC AVE., ATLANTIC CITY, NJ (609) 345-1564

What do you call a long tube of crusty bread stuffed with cold cuts or meatballs? In many parts of the country it is known as a "hero." In New Orleans, it's a "po' boy." In Miami, they call it a "Cuban"; in the southern Midwest, it's an "Italian." In upstate New York, it's a "bomber"; downstate, a "wedge." In Connecticut, it's a "grinder." We've seen menus listing "rockets," "Garibaldis," "zeps" (short for "zeppelins"), "spukkies," and torpedoes."

In the Delaware Valley, where behemoth sandwiches are a passion, the most common nicknames are "hoagie" and "sub." You don't have to be an etymologist to figure out that "sub" is short for "submarine," a moniker that some culinary historians trace to the White House Sub Shop of Atlantic City, which has launched approximately ten million of the mighty pigboats since it opened for business in 1946. Until that time, the term hereabouts was "hero"; but according to this culinary tale, to honor the silent service of World War II, Tony Basile of the White House started calling his heros "subs."

In keeping with its seminal importance in the history of American rude food, the White House is a humble Naugahyde-and-neon eatery with a row of booths along the wall and a six-stool counter up front. The lighting is harsh, the napkins are paper, and the service is lightning fast: it would be a sin to sell subs any other way.

These sandwiches, let us tell you, are elite eats. Each is about two feet long, loaded with ingredients that range from fancy white tuna fish to meatballs that are made right behind the counter while you watch. The "White House Special" is a tide of cold cuts—Genoa salami, ham, capicola, and provolone cheese—all tightly packed inside the loaf, lubricated with olive oil, decorated with lettuce and bits of sweet pepper.

The ingredients are excellent, but submarine connoisseurs will tell you that it's what's outside that counts. The White House gets its bread from nearby bakeries, and it is impeccably fresh whenever you eat here—elegant-textured inside but with enough muscle so it doesn't fall apart even when loaded with hot-sauced meatballs. And it has a wickedly brittle crust that stays crisp no matter what's inside.

The White House is a landmark for sandwich connoisseurs; and like the cheese-steak shops of Philadelphia, it boasts a stellar clientele. Pictures of celebrity customers line the walls, inscribed with praise for the excellence of the cuisine. News clippings tell of the time the astronauts came to scarf down subs, and of Frank Sinatra craving them so much that he once had a mess of them shipped from New Jersey across the world to a movie location. Jerry Lewis, Joan Rivers, Joe Frazier, Ray Charles: all have ingested subs from the White House.

NEW MEXICO

ABEYTA'S MEXICAN KITCHEN
2805 SAN MATEO NE, ALBUQUERQUE, NM (505) 881-5314

A beans-and-chicharrones burrito: There isn't a plusher and more pin-
guid dish anywhere in the Southwest. Chicharrones are little cubes of
lardaceous pork, fried until crisp, similar in taste and texture to the Jewish
delicacy known as gribenes (made by frying chicken skin in chicken fat).
They are an extreme food—extremely luscious, piggy, and wonderful. Perhaps the best way to really savor them is simply, as an appetizer, accompanied by corn tortillas and salsa. But let us tell you, they go so well with
well-seasoned beans, wrapped inside a freshly made tortilla, covered with
hot green chili: that is an Abeyta's burrito, and it is one of the splendors of
Albuquerque's *los de abajo* cuisine.

Abeyta's is an unvarnished place. Last time we visited, it was a little
hard to get inside because someone (apparently an employee) had parked
his big, snazzy motorcycle so close to the front door. The dining room
beyond the front desk (a lot of business is carry-out), with local radio playing a little too loud, is—let us be kind—disheveled. But the people who
work here are nice, and the food is exemplary.

Fierce *carne adovada* (red chili-soaked hunks of pork) is accompanied
by beans, fried potatoes, and a warm, flavorful flour tortilla. There is "diet"

carne adovada, too, prepared with chicken breast and served with whole beans rather than *refritos*. Abeyta's makes really fine menudo—a long-simmered comfort stew of tripe and big, puffy nuggets of posole, seasoned with your choice of lemon, onions, or oregano and accompanied by a soft tortilla. Tamales are homemade, fragrant with the perfume of hot corn and highly spiced pork. You can eat blue-corn enchiladas, chili rellenos, *huevos rancheros* (excellent with chicharrones), even fajitas (made with sautéed rather than grilled meat), and an amiably bland natilla pudding for dessert.

We don't recommend Abeyta's to everyone. There are more genteel restaurants in town for those of delicate sensibility. But for real New Mexican food in real neighborhood surroundings, this is the place.

BIEN MUR INDIAN MARKET
EXIT 234 OFF I-25 (TRAMWAY RD.), ALBUQUERQUE, NM (505) 821-5400

"Cigarettes are back!" trumpeted the Bien Mur billboard along I-25, but it is not for cheap cigarettes, or for crafts and jewelry, that we recommend a visit to this Indian-run tourist attraction. It is for cookies and fry bread. Across the driveway from the big round gallery where smokes and sundries are sold is a beehive-shaped adobe brick oven, called a *horno*, in which bread and cookies are baked, and a skillet full of hot oil in which rounds of bread are fried to order. The *al fresco* cookshop is not actually part of the bargain-hunter's headquarters, but it is staffed by local Indian women. Their bread is beautiful: puffy golden disks as light as air, accompanied by a squirt of honey if you wish. The bread is good, but the bags of cookies they sell are even better. They are a half-inch thick, shaped like clubs (the playing-card suit, not the weapon), and they have an elegant crumbly texture and a faintly caramelized taste. Only barely sweet, they are subtle in their appeal; it was about twenty-five miles down the road, when our bag was emptied, that we sorely wished we had bought more.

Oh, yes, one more culinary tip: across from the cookie-and-bread lady is another lady at a folding table set with Crockpots full of green chili, red chili, and beans, as well as a tub of grated yellow cheese and a pile of tortillas. We didn't try any of this food, but we did notice that the table was surrounded by local Indians eating plates full of it with gusto.

(No one here has ever given us a straight answer as to when the cookies and chili are available. We take our chances, and you will have to also. No problem, though—Bien Mur is just off the highway.)

CHOPE'S
RT. 28, LA MESA, NM (505) 233-3420

Chope's is two places to eat: a bar and a house, about fifty yards apart. Both have their charms, but we like the house better because if you sit at the right table, the one nearest the Coke machine, you look into the back room kitchen while you eat. You can watch the staff carry skillets full of lard to the stove for deep-frying sopaipillas, see them count out the warm flour tortillas that are allotted to every table, and gasp at the beauty of the huge tray of big green roasted chili peppers carried in from another room, ready to be battered.

The chilies are the basis for Chope's chile rellenos. They are quick-fried and served three to an order, or singly alongside any of the combination plates. They are some of the finest you will find here in the heart of chili country: bright-flavored but not overwhelmingly hot, glowing with the sunny taste of the native pods, encased in a crisp coat with a few flecks of melted cheese on top. Also terrific, and milder than the rellenos, are Chope's red enchiladas. Green enchiladas are available, too, and they are hotter; but the man who took us to Chope's insisted we get red. Since this man was Dr. Paul Bosland, America's foremost chili breeder, we took his advice. We were not sorry. These enchiladas sing of chili flavor and have only enough heat to set your tastebuds glowing pleasantly. Get a stack, with a fried egg on the top.

Meaty, gritty tamales are available by threes or as part of combination #1, which also includes an enchilada, a soft (and tasty) taco, rice, and beans. The menu is a typical one for this part of the country, featuring bowls of chili with or without beans or *con queso* (with cheese), as well as light-as-air sopaipillas for dessert. Nothing we have sampled is less than exemplary.

A word of warning: although Chope's is in the middle of nowhere in a one-horse town, it gets crowded at lunch with chowhounds from Las Cruces, local chili planters carrying their cellular telephones, and hot food pilgrims from throughout the state. By 11:45 in the morning, customers are lined up outside the house waiting for the dining room to open. The turnover is fast, but it is likely you will have to put your name on the waiting list if you arrive much after noon.

DON JOSE'S COCINA
ROUTE 279, BIBO, NM (505) 552-6726

"World Has Retreated from Bibo" was the headline of an article Bart Ripp wrote about Don Jose's Cocina for the *Albuquerque Tribune* in 1986. He described a quiet village in the shadow of Mount Taylor "far from Interstate 40 and eons from Albuquerque" where horses roamed the empty streets and where life had come to a near-standstill after the nearby Jackpile Mine (once the world's biggest source of uranium) was closed.

Bart has always been a source of great *Roadfood* tips, so we kept his article because he had described an eatery in Bibo named Don Jose's Cantina; and five years later, on a drive west along old Route 66, we detoured up into the mountains to see if there was anything left of the town that time forgot, and if it was possible that Don Jose's was still in business. Other than half a dozen horses wandering freely down the main street, we saw no signs of life. The town's few businesses, lined up along a raised walkway under awnings to protect them from the western sun, seemed long-closed, and that included the one with "Don Jose" etched into the sidewalk out front.

We pushed on the door . . . and it opened! There inside was Pauline Michael talking on the phone and sipping coffee. She gestured for us to sit down at one of the red-checked-oilcloth-covered tables in the dimly lit eating hall (which is in fact the room where she was born in 1920, when this place was the family home). We signed the guest register, and as soon as she was off the phone Mrs. Michael—owner, cook, waitress, and cashier at Don Jose's Cocina—brought us coffee (for hospitality's sake), then prepared a couple of plates of food: roast beef burritos topped with hot green chili, accompanied by beans, chips, and salsa, and freshly fried sopaipillas, as well as a platter of enchiladas rolled around cheese, onions, and rice. It was exemplary local vittles, and as we ate, Mrs. Michael told us about her homemade blue-corn tamales topped with chili, which we promised to try the next time we passed through town.

You will never accidentally get to Bibo; but for a true taste of old New Mexico and a visit with a nice lady who happens to be a very good cook, this detour off the highway is a *Roadfood* bonanza.

DORA'S
401 E. HALL ST. (HIGHWAY 85), HATCH, NM (505) 267-9294

Don't be surprised when you arrive in Hatch to find there is no restaurant in town named Dora's. It might be called "El 85 Chile Capital Cafe," or possibly "Dora's Chile Capital Cafe," because the owner, Alex Martinez, has been trying to change the name ever since his wife Dora divorced him seven years ago. But each time he comes up with a new one, no one pays any attention. "'I don't give a damn what you call it,' Mr. Martinez told us one local customer informed him. 'It will always be Dora's.'" So if you get lost, just ask anyone in town for Dora's. They all know where it is, and an awful lot of them eat here. If you are traveling north of Las Cruces, you must eat here, too. There isn't another cafe in chile country that is as real and as good.

It is a minuscule place, with about eight tables, a few of them with vinyl cloths, and no decor whatsover. The regulars seem to occupy the two tables up front during breakfast, coming and going and talking about such subjects as tractors, crops, hunting, mud, and irrigation. The walls of the two-part dining room are painted wood paneling, resembling the interior of a deluxe manufactured home. The menu is basic: enchiladas, burritos, flautas, *tostadas compuestas,* red or green chile by the bowl, and *huevos rancheros* for breakfast.

Nearly everything is made with chili (or as they like to spell it here, chile), which is available red or green and in three degrees of hotness. Even the hottest isn't unbearable, although our waiters informed us that it was running a little mild these days—a function of horticultural fluctuations over which the kitchen has no control. The most amazing thing about this chili is not the heat, but the flavor. The red chili has an earthy, almost sweet vegetable perfume about it. The green seems more viscous, sneakier, maybe more complex—although not nearly as pretty. Spread across *huevos rancheros* with chunks of fallapart-tender beef, or in a bowl all by itself, or maybe con *queso,* sided by warm flour tortillas, it is chili-lover's manna. Unlike Texas, where chili is always *con carne,* or other places where it has beans or macaroni or what-have-you, this chili is pure and elemental. It is a bowl of roasted, cooked and seasoned vegetable pods picked off plants from nearby fields. Once you have tasted this potion, all other chilies—no matter how excellent they may be—will only remind you of Dora's greatness.

As much as we relish the hearty lunches of chunky red and green chili piled into burritos or served in a bowl at lunch, breakfast is the meal we like best in this place, not only because those *huevos rancheros* are so fine (with stupendously good fried rice and refried beans), but also for the menudo. It is sold by the bowl, with one complimentary refill if you want it. That first morning we ate at Dora's, while most of the anglos in cowboy hats were plowing *huevos,* the Mexican-looking customers all sat before big steaming bowls of menudo. This renowned dish of long-simmered tripe and hominy stew has legendary powers of revification; and when you spoon into a bowl, you can see why. It comes with a heap of raw onions (sprinkle them on), lemon wedges (for squeezing), oregano, garlic salt, and pulverized dry red chili for adding heat. The nice chew of the puffed hominy combines with the slick, tender tripe to make a startling and perhaps even off-putting bowl of food. It is definitely not your basic warm oatmeal. But if you are an adventurer in search of genuine American vittles, you must try it.

Dora's is worth visiting for more than cuisine. The ambience of the place and its agrarian surroundings are exquisite *Roadfood.* Hatch is the heart of chili country, in the midst of acres of chili fields, and dozens of roadside stands that sell pods by the forty-pound bag (to take home, roast, and store for the winter), by the ristra, and as powder, sauce, and salsa. We spent time at Dora's in the mornings at the peak of the harvest, in September, and the tables were occupied by growers, pickers, roasters, and packers; the air was perfumed with the tantalizing smell of fresh chili—which could have come either from the customers' well-worn work clothes or from the kitchen. Most conversations hopped from table to table as the gentlemen in baseball caps or cowboy hats sipped coffee, spooned into their bowls, and shot the breeze in a kind of informal town meeting. When Dora's ex-husband, Mr. Martinez, saw that we showed a special interest in his chilies, he took time to explain the differences between red and green, and the variations of flavor and heat. And he assured us that when we returned, Dora's would be called something else.

DOUBLE RAINBOW
3416 CENTRAL, S.E., ALBUQUERQUE, NM (505) 255-6633

We are coffee hounds. Probably the thing we like least about traveling around eating all the great food we can find is how little good coffee there is. Along the West Coast and East Coast, coffee is not a problem; and in some Midwestern cities, Minneapolis and Chicago in particular, there is great, strong java to be drunk. However, throughout many of the smaller, and even larger, cities of the heartland, it seems impossible to get a rich, freshly brewed cup of coffee. The problem is especially severe in the Southwest, along Route 66, where most coffee is what truckdrivers call "western style," meaning it tastes like it has been on the range all day. That is why we were delighted to discover Double Rainbow on Central Avenue, a.k.a. Route 66, in Albuquerque.

Our first few visits to this coffee shop near the University of New Mexico, all we had was coffee: double expressos, lattes, cappuccinos, and espresso à la mode. But then we began to notice that the edibles in the bakery case up front looked mighty good, so we ate croissants, pecan rolls, almond cakes, and chocolate cakes, and you know what? These pastries are sensational—high-quality, sophisticated breadstuffs (especially the *pain chocolate!*).

Last time through town, we branched out and had a few lunches at Double Rainbow, too; and they were grand. Zuni stew, East Indian pot pie, big sourdough bread sandwiches filled with smoked turkey: after a week eating our way up through chili country, these modern urban meals were a tasty change of pace (although the chili here was fine, as well—and *hot)*; and the powerhouse coffee served with our after-meal cakes was such a welcome pleasure.

Double Rainbow, which is a branch of a business that began in San Francisco, is a student hangout staffed mostly by young men and women with postmodern hairdos, and you can always count on a hip CD to be playing for background music. The walls are lined with one of the most eclectic selections of periodicals in the West (including British biker magazines, political and poetical journals, and more photography magazines than we ever knew existed), and it is common for customers (ourselves included) to linger at a table, indoors or out on the sidewalk, for hours, sipping coffee, conversing, and reading.

One more thing: ice cream. Double Rainbow makes its own, and it is swell.

DURAN CENTRAL PHARMACY
1815 CENTRAL, N.W., ALBUQUERQUE, NM (505) 247-4141

To get to a seat in this distinctive eating establishment, you have to walk past counter displays of Dr. Scholl's foot remedies, calamine lotion, headache cures, and Vaseline. No, it is not a theme restaurant specializing in hypochondriac cookery; it is the Duran Central Pharmacy cafe, an alcove on the side of a working drugstore. Enjoy delicious southwestern food and have your prescriptions filled at the same time.

A low-slung, sand-colored building along a thoroughfare not far from Albuquerque's Old Town, Duran is a breakfast and lunch place with a counter, a scattering of tables, and a sunny patio where customers enjoy low-priced, short-order, genuine New Mexican cuisine. Enchiladas come topped with red or green chili, and for about four bits extra, with a single fried egg. You can get a beef taco plate or a burrito, and on Wednesday and Friday you can get sopaipillas—puffy, fist-size fry breads served two at a time, stuffed with green chili, beans, and cheese. Thursday, the specialty of the house is *carne adovada*—pork marinated in a keen purée of red chilies.

A batch of ladies behind the counter do the cooking. One of them seems to have a single task, central to nearly all the good things the lunch counter serves. She makes tortillas. On a two-by-two-foot counter with nothing more elaborate than a short wooden dowel, she rolls out a ball of flour into a flat, eight-inch circle. Her work is swift and effortless, with an economy of motion that bespeaks cooking skills practiced over time. After rolling each tortilla, she picks it up and walks it toward the grill, tossing it back and forth between her hands with a gesture that looks like clapping. This makes each round more supple, until it is slapped down on a nearly greaseless griddle.

Like flattened scones, the tortillas bake more than they fry on the hot iron surface. There is room for two at a time, and people eat fast at the Duran Central Pharmacy, so during busy mealtimes the tortilla lady might never have the chance to build up a stockpile. Even an hour or so old, these tortillas are delicious: wide, tawny circles, mottled brown from the grill.

We like ours on the side of a bowl of red chili—an opaque orange brew heavy with ground meat and beans, with a strong earthy odor and a pepper kick. At breakfast, the Duran Pharmacy way with tortillas is to use them as the foundation for a plate of *huevos rancheros*—eggs, potatoes, beans, and a ladle full of chili. At lunch, they are made into "torpedoes"—huge, drippy, wrappings for soft cooked potato chunks, chili (red or green), and cheese. You can even order a hamburger with a tortilla instead of a bun.

FRONTIER
2400 CENTRAL, SE, ALBUQUERQUE, NM (505) 266-0550

The printed menu of the Frontier restaurant is emblazoned with this boast: "Home of the latest in broiled food and the homemade sweet roll." Culinarily speaking, we are incurably out of fashion, and therefore haven't the vaguest idea what the "latest" broiled foods are (the menu lists hamburgers, cheeseburgers, bonanza double burgers, hickory-flavored flameburgers, as well as chopped steaks and sirloin steaks), but we sure can tell you about the Frontier sweet roll. It is a bulky beige swirl blanketed with a buttery sugar glaze, and it makes one heck of a good companion for a cup of coffee. You see dozens of these rolls by the panful behind the counter of the Frontier; at least half the breakfast crowd orders one or two, and dozens of shoppers come for six-packs of the famous rolls to go.

Most customers never see a printed menu. Service in this gargantuan barn-shaped beanery across the street from the University of New Mexico is stand-up-and-holler style. Present yourself at the order counter, above which is a list of all the things the kitchen makes: broiled foods, Mexican classics, and breakfast. Pay for what you want, at which point you will be assigned a number; then find a seat in one of the five (count 'em!) connected storefront dining rooms, most of which are decorated with primitive south-western art (including wagon-wheel chandeliers and a couple of magnifi-cent portraits of John Wayne). There are tables surrounded by short stools permanently attached to the floor and there are booths with orange Nau-gahyde seats; and throughout the day, from six-thirty in the morning to midnight, these seats are occupied by a changing (and in a few cases unchanging) roster of students, street people, cops, and robbers. When your order is ready, your number will be called over a loudspeaker system.

Celebrated as the rolls and broiled foods may be, neither is our favorite thing to eat at the Frontier. What we like best is the breakfast bur-rito—a big (made here) tortilla wrapped around a mess of shredded hash-brown potatoes, grated cheese, scrambled eggs, and hot green chili. It is a beautiful package, lacking only some salsa on top; but that's easy. Across from the counter where you get your food there is a big pot of freshly made green chili salsa. Ladle on as much as you want, but beware: it is for hot-food aficionados only.

Other good stuff to eat includes just about anything from the Mexican part of the menu, especially soft tacos and wonderful vegetarian green chili enchiladas, as well as tortillas by the dozen. One more tip, and it's a rarity in this part of the world, especially in a cheap-eats haven such as this: orange juice, served in giant paper cups, is freshly squeezed.

THE HACIENDA
2605 S. ESPINA, LAS CRUCES, NM (505) 522-6380

When the sun sets in the Mesilla Valley, its last rays gleam gold. Indigo mountains rise in jagged relief above the earth-tone adobe city of Las Cruces. The first time we saw it, the sight was so dazzling that we screeched to a stop and got out of the car to gape. By the side of the highway on a cool June evening, we understood for the first time a line we have sung and heard a thousand times about "purple mountains' majesty."

It was a soul-stirring spectacle that inspired all kinds of feelings . . . not the least of which was a big appetite for southwestern food. So we went to The Hacienda and feasted on blue-corn enchiladas and tacos in blue-corn shells with hot green chili on the side. We ate chili Colorado (cubed beef and red chili) and double whammy chili rellenos made with locally grown "big Jim" pepper pods, each eight inches long, stuffed with yellow cheese and asadero cheese (made from goat's milk), batter-dipped and fried.

Hot stuff! To salve the tongue, traditional New Mexican meals include sopaipillas, triangles of deep fried bread that are air-light with a golden flaky skin. Tear one open, pour in a dab of honey, and it's like eating sweetened puffs of crisp-edged cloud. At The Hacienda, they have even found a way to serve sopapaillas for dessert, cut in strips and drizzled with spicy hot chocolate sauce: a wonderment known as *sopaipillas y champura.*

JOSIE'S CASA DE COMIDA
225 E. MARCY, SANTA FE, NM (505) 983-5311

Santa Feans relish Josie's. If you are looking for red or green chili, blue-plate specials, and spectacular desserts, you will, too. It is hard not to fall for this little whitewashed house on a side street off the square, with a broad front porch decorated by chili ristras.

There is a menu that lists the New Mexican meals that are always available: plates or bowls of chili, tamales, enchiladas, and tacos. Before lunch, there are chips with some nice, salty, hot red sauce for munching. We especially like Josie's way of serving chili in a bowl, accompanied by posole (hominy corn) to soften the peppers' bite. The rolled enchiladas are swell, too; and the tamales are big (unwrapped) mounds of grainy corn with lots of shredded meat inside, served on a plate surrounded by chile sauce and beans.

Beyond the menu, a blackboard lists at least half a dozen other dishes every day; and these tend to be less distinctly New Mexican and more what you'd expect in an exemplary southwestern town cafe. Chicken-fried steak is sometimes available, and we love the chewy, high-flavored slab of meat, even if the potatoes that accompany it are made from flakes instead of spuds (Josie really does know how to doctor them up to nearly authentic level). We also like Josie's liver and onions, accompanied by biscuits; and you will go a long way to find a better hamburger.

What is truly amazing about Josie's is dessert. The number of choices is mind-boggling: there are always at least a dozen different signs posted on the walls of the dining room listing pies, cakes, puddings, cobblers, and cookies from which to choose. They are all unmistakably handmade—big, sweet, and monumentally satisfying. Pear pie, made with fresh pears, is a giant, crumb-topped wedge—inelegant, perhaps, but oh, how good it tastes, especially when served under a big spill of sour cream, the tang of which brilliantly offsets the sugary sweetness of the pie and silky smoothness of which is a perfect foil for the granular texture of the big chunks of pear. Josie's mocha cake is famous, rightfully so; her baked apple is a plump, falling-apart paradigm. Apples are big on the dessert menu: Dutch apple pie (with a crumb top), French apple pie (with raisins and walnuts), apple cobbler. Let us just mention a few other things posted around us the last time we ate at Josie's: Boston cream cake (like Boston cream pie, but made with chocolate cake), Russian cream pie, pumpkin pie, cherry pie, fresh strawberry shortcake, and boscochitos (peanut butter cookies).

Josie's is fun. Not soigné, but real. The booths are small, cramped, hardwood. The tables are wobbly. The room tone is noisy with the sounds of people enjoying themselves as they eat; and there is much kibitzing back and forth between regulars and the staff. On the walls, there is some handsome local art, including one beautiful painting of the exterior of Josie's—a soft-focus, impressionistic image of the little whitewashed cottage, with its chili ristras on the porch and a long line of people waiting patiently to get in and eat.

LA TERTULIA
416 AGUA FRIA, SANTA FE, NM (505) 988-2769

The food at La Tertulia isn't as spectacular and hot as it used to be, but it still tastes good; and if you are looking for a restaurant in Santa Fe that serves all the traditional local fare in the politest and pleasantest surroundings, this is it. Don't be scared by some local guidebooks that describe it as "formal." What formal means, in this laid-back city, is that waiters wear clean white shirts, tables are covered with lace, napkins are cloth instead of paper, and the check comes when you request it, not with the meal. A dress code posted on the door of the restaurant advises that all men must have shirts with "at least" short sleeves; tank tops, muscle shirts, and net shirts are forbidden; and "hats or caps must be removed before service is rendered." The people who come to eat at La Tertulia (which is situated in a handsome old convent) are a mannerly bunch; there were plenty of blue jeans evident, but none were ripped.

So, none of the food will burn your tongue (unless you gobble too much of that very hot sauce that comes with chips at the beginning of the meal); but it can make you glow. Chili rellenos, about the hottest dish on the menu now, has a good, intermittent nip (depending on whether a particular forkful has many seeds from the big green chili pepper), but the most important thing about it is flavor, not heat. You really taste the vegetableness of the pepper pod; and it is delicious, unlike any other vegetable: earthy, almost sweet underneath its heat, and invigorating. All the usual native dishes are available, including very good enchiladas, but the one we like best is *carne adovada.* It is a sort of New Mexican pot roast, cooked to a state of fall-apart tenderness, infused with the flavor of chili (but not its heat). To precede your meal, there is perfunctory guacamole or jalapeño bean soup (good, but awfully filling); and to accompany it, there are sopaipillas. La Tertulia's sopas are large, square fried breads—not exactly elegant, but perfectly tasty and a great mop for *carne adovada* sauce. They are served with a little bowl of honey butter; and when you have eaten your allotted amount, you will be brought more, hot from the fry kettle.

M & J RESTAURANT
403 SECOND, SW, ALBUQUERQUE, NM (505) 242-4890

Since 1974, Beatrice and Jake Montoya have operated an eatery in downtown Albuquerque that has caused thousands of people to fall in love—with chili and tortillas. The M & J Restaurant, which is also the M & J Sanitary Tortilla Factory, serves not only fresh, crisp corn chips with fiery salsa on the side, but gorgeous blue-corn enchilada plates, and a burrito stuffed with *carne adovada* that just might be the best version anywhere of the ultimate New Mexican dish. The *carne* in the *adovada* is pork, and it is saturated with a pepper flavor that simply does not exist anywhere outside of true southwestern kitchens: profound and earthy, radiant with a hot taste that makes us think of blazing sunlight. The enchilada plate is a trio of them (blue or regular yellow cornmeal) smothered with chili (red or green), melted cheese and onions, with superb, lard-luscious beans on the side. Only the regular yellow-corn enchilada plate comes with sour cream, but it is worth seventy-five cents extra to get a side of it with blue-corn enchiladas. The cool, silky white stuff is a perfect complement for the grainy texture of blue corn, and it does help tamp down the fire of this very spicy food.

All dinners come with a basket of sopaipillas. Terrific sopaipillas: big, golden triangles puffed up with air and too hot to handle when they arrive at the table. They might not be the most delicate ones you will find in New Mexico, but they are definitely the best-tasting, with a real bready goodness. Squeeze-packs of honey are provided to sweeten them up, but we prefer to use them as mops for all the chili, beans, and cheese on our plates.

In addition to its repertoire of classic southwestern food, what makes M & J so much fun is its atmosphere. It has expanded over the years, but it still has the folksy feel of a mom-and-pop cafe. Bea bustles about behind the counter and among the booths and tables like a mother hen; and it seems that well over half the customers are regulars: cops, business people, culinary bargain hunters, and seekers of fine home cooking. For many years, a lot of M & J business has come from the Greyhound station, which is just down Second Street; and the rough white walls of the big dining room are covered with business cards and handwritten testimonials from wayfarers who accidentally stepped into the simple cafe and discovered the anything-but-simple glories of New Mexican cooking.

NELLIE'S
1226 W. HADLEY, LAS CRUCES, NM (505) 524-9982

 whitewashed bunker on a side street in Las Cruces, with the jagged Organ Mountains rising up in the background above a parking lot full of pickup trucks and muscle cars, Nellie's is a jewel in the rough—in the very, very rough. It is not a pretty restaurant, that's for sure, at least not pretty by standards customarily used to size up a public dining room. But if you are a fan of sleeves-up neighborhood cafes, it is a taste of heaven. We especially like the humming Dr. Pepper cooler in the second dining room, and the way the overhead fluorescent tube lights illuminate the cinderblock walls and the bare Formica tables and the sickly yellow paint job. It's all just perfect for savoring utterly authentic meals that are cheap, down-home, and, in some cases, ferociously hot.

This is the cuisine of the Mesilla Valley. What they grow in this valley are chilies: big and small ones, sweet and hot ones. It is from here that New Mexican cooking derives its soul. You know you are in for a wild ride as soon as you dip a chip into the salsa carried to the table at the beginning of the meal. It is a clay-dirt red, delicious, spicy, and so addictive that it is possible to scoop out an entire bowlful before the meal arrives: some feat, considering that service out of this kitchen is nearly instantaneous.

The menu is standard, but the food is not: the combo plates, enchiladas, burritos, tacos, etc. are paragons, especially any of them made with Nellie's transcendent, semi-incendiary green chili (milder red is also available). One of the most delicious dishes you can eat here is the chili rellenos, for which two substantial sweet-fleshed green pepper pods are battered and fried, creating a harmony out of the vegetable's verve and its luscious, bready jacket. You can hardly believe the sopaipilla compuesta when it gets toted from the kitchen: a plate-sized round of puffy, fragile-textured fry bread is heaped with beans, chili, meat, lettuce, tomatoes, and two kinds of cheese. Sensational!

One other rave is necessary, about the refried beans that accompany nearly all of Nellie's dinners. These beans are the real thing, rich and lardy and flavorful; and for us, whose last meal at Nellie's was after months of Mexican food deprivation in the East, it was the beans—so primitive and so good to eat—that made us weep for joy.

Nellie's is open for three meals a day. We haven't had breakfast here, but some day we would like to return for the eggs and chorizo sausage, a breakfast burrito, or menudo—the traditional hangover-cure soup made from beef tribe and hominy simmered in red chili—listed on Nellie's menu as "The Breakfast of Champions."

OJ SARAH'S
106 GUADALUPE ST., SANTA FE, NM (505) 984-1675

T-shirts available at OJ Sarah's say "Great Buns and No Coyote Art," the idea being that this is a place for people who like to eat good local food rather than buy bad local souvenirs. OJ's hours of operation are seven to two in the afternoon, and although there are plenty of hamburgers, vegetarian hot plates, and traditional Santa Fe lunches on the menu (including excellent cheese enchiladas topped with ultra-hot chicken chili and accompanied by whole-wheat or blue-corn tortillas), breakfast is the right thing to eat.

Start with fresh—really freshly squeezed—orange juice or carrot juice (listen to the juicer whir when you order the latter). Then you will have some hard choices to make: cottage cakes or blue-corn pancakes, a giant cinnamon bun or a blue-corn muffin, OJ Benedict (served with your choice of bacon, ham, corned beef, or chili) or an omelette filled with apple-cinnamon relish. There is sensational corned-beef hash served on a bed of hash browns; there are breakfast burritos, *huevos rancheros*, and chili-and-cheese-topped hash browns.

Cottage pancakes are what we like best. Their batter is made with cottage cheese, so they are moist and silky-rich with a vaguely sour flavor that teases the tongue. To balance their tart kick, OJ serves a little dish of raspberry purée, which is fine, but our recommendation is to spring for the ($1.25 extra) pure maple syrup (otherwise the syrup you get is cane); the maple and cheese create a complex and memorable flavor chord. Each cottage cake, by the way, is as wide as a dinner plate and about as thin as a nickel. Blue-corn pancakes are thicker, grittier, not nearly as sophisticated-seeming as the cottage cakes; but that is their charm: they are rugged, made from coarser meal, and they are swell.

The menu says the cinnamon bun is "legendary." Bunyanesque in size, it is a full meal and then some, about six inches in diameter and at least two inches high. It is served with a cup of whipped butter and utensils, but who can resist tearing at this chewy ring of sweet dough with fingers? Raisins spill out, veins of cinnamon sugar are revealed, butter drips into crevices and turns the cinnamon into syrup.

OJ Sarah's is a relaxed and relaxing place to eat. There are two airy dining rooms and walls painted with big pictures of fruit. Up front is a short counter with four stools, where in our experience, at least one local character usually hangs out gabbing endlessly with the staff. Last time we smacked our lips over glasses of sweet, invigorating carrot juice our waiter advised us that if we really wanted a treat, we ought to some day try drinking his personal favorite, alfalfa juice (alas, not available at OJ Sarah's).

POWDRELL'S BARBEQUE
11309 CENTRAL AVE., N.E., ALBUQUERQUE, NM (505) 298-6766

There are three Powdrell's Barbeques around Albuquerque, and we are fans of all of them; we even like the sandwiches and platters Powdrell's dishes out along the Midway of the New Mexico State Fair every September. But the best location is east of the city, way out on Central Avenue. There is a special pleasure driving to the edge of the city around sunset, when the southwestern sky turns gold and the neon signs of the ancient motels begin to glow and flicker. It feels especially right to saunter into the low ranch building, then into one of the paneled dining rooms (smokers to the right, nons to the left) and inhale the aroma of slow-smoked meats.

Cooked at less than 200 degrees for about eighteen hours, Powdrell's beef is the kitchen's masterpiece. When it is done it is refrigerated, then heated again—a process the menu says helps it become even more tender. But it isn't extraordinary tenderness that will make you happy; it is this meat's flavor. Each handsome strip is saturated with smoke and oozes with natural beef juice; a pile of them is spread with an explosive cinnabar-red sauce. Served on a platter with Texas toast and a basket of steamy yellow corn cakes and your choice of two side dishes (including corn on the cob, potato salad, French fries, beans, and cole slaw), and with maybe a dab of hot green roasted chilies on the side to spice it up, this is one of the significant Route 66 eating experiences.

There are plenty of other good meals to eat at Powdrell's, all of them (except Friday catfish) from the smoker: pork ribs, hot sausage links, chicken, and sliced pork. The beef is best, but if you simply must try some of everything, you can order a combination plate, which is a pound of assorted meats with all the fixin's. There is also a family meal for four built around two pounds of pork ribs, sided by fries, corn, and toast.

Desserts are smokehouse classics: peach cobbler (super sweet) and sweet potato pie (super mellow).

RANCHO DE CHIMAYO
RTE. 520 (OFF RTE. 76), CHIMAYO, NM (505) 351-4444

N orth of Santa Fe, through the foothills of the Sangre de Cristo Mountains, a two-lane road leads toward the ancient village of Chimayo. It
is a stunning journey, past apple stands and adobe homes draped with
bright red chili ristras hung out to dry.

Chimayo is a town as wondrous as any in North America, settled in the
eleventh century by Tewa Indians and long known for the skills of its
weavers, whose signature is a distinct diamond-and-stripe-pattern cloth.
The town is built around the Santuario, a tiny chapel erected on a plot of
earth alleged to have miraculous curative powers, and today the town is
still a mecca for pilgrims who come to apply the healing dirt to their bod-
ies, as well as for tourists, low-riders in dazzling early-1950s Fords and
Mercuries, and hungry people in search of what many consider to be the
Land of Enchantment's most exquisite dining experience—at Rancho de
Chimayo.

Built a century ago by the Jaramillo family, whose ancestors arrived in
the 1600s, Rancho de Chimayo is a spacious home of wide wood planks
and low-beamed ceilings, hammered tin chandeliers, and a capacious fireplace. It became a restaurant in 1965, and since then has gained fame not
only for its charm and ambience, but for a kitchen that exalts the cuisine of
New Mexico.

Native New Mexicans seldom sit down for a "bowl of chili." In fact,
chili as a meal isn't even listed on the Rancho de Chimayo menu. But
there are few dishes this kitchen makes in which the chili pepper doesn't
play a vital role. New Mexican cooks use their native pod in stews and
omelettes, on top of steaks, stuffed into sopaipillas, and as a marinade for
the fire-breathing native specialty known as *carne adovada*—pork infused
with a fierce pepper bite. If you are coming to Rancho de Chimayo only
once, and if you like hot food, carne adovada is the dish to order. The pork
glistens red, and has turned shockingly tender from its long marinade in a
sauce made from hot red chili pods. The amazing thing about it is the
earthy, complex flavor of the chili—yes, *flavor*, beyond its eye-popping
heat. On the side of this fiery pork the kitchen provides a mound of posole
(hominy corn)—nice, mild little pillows of tenderness to soothe the tongue.

For those who want something a little less incendiary, Rancho de Chimayo's menu also offers sopaipillas rellenos, in which the triangular fried
hot breads are stuffed with beef, beans, tomatoes, and Spanish rice, and

topped with red or green chili sauce. There are flautas, too—rolled corn tortillas filled with chicken or pork and fried crisp, topped with cool sour cream.

To drink, you want frozen margaritas or Chimayo cocktails, the latter made from tequila and native Chimayo apple juice.

On a warm evening, the place to enjoy this great American feast is outdoors at a candlelit table. Strolling guitarists strum southwestern tunes, and the air is perfumed by sagebrush and the fiery spice of native cooking.

ROQUE'S CARNITAS
AT THE CORNER OF PALACE AND WASHINGTON, SANTA FE, NM
(NO PHONE)

"Take a napkin," says Mona when she hands you your carnitas. "Take three. Take half a dozen. You'll need them." You *will* need them, unless, like so many regular customers of Roque's Carnitas just off the square in Santa Fe, you have perfected the technique of eating your fistful of food while bending over at the waist, leaning forward so all the oozy juices and stray chunks of tomato and pepper and beef cascade out beyond the tips of your shoes. There is a large public trash can adjacent to the carnitas wagon, and it is not uncommon at lunchtime to see three or four neatly attired carnitas-hounds gathered around the can, each of them inclined so the debris falls right into the can as they eat.

Here is Santa Fe's sloppiest and most delicious quick meal. Carnitas, which in this case are strips of lean beef (in Los Angeles, "carnitas" customarily refers to pork), are sizzled on a grate over an open fire along with hot green peppers and onions and spice. When the meat's edges begin to blacken and it has sucked in the flavor of the fire, a huge mound of it is hefted off the hot grate and wrapped inside a flour tortilla (also warmed on the grate). The meat is topped with a green chili salsa thick with tomato chunks and some mighty, mighty hot spices. The package is wrapped in aluminum foil. That is the only food served at this street-corner cart, and you have your choice of lemonade in a cup or soda in a can to accompany it.

Eat hanging over the garbage can or leaning against the nearby wall of the Museum of New Mexico, where Roque's cassette player broadcasts a tape of merry Mexican tunes to put you in the mood for munching; or find a bench in the square, where flocks of well-fed pigeons will very much appreciate all the good stuff that falls out of this superb street-food sandwich.

STOP AND EAT DRIVE IN
110 S. PASEO DE ONATE, ESPAÑOLA, NM (505) 753-7400

*S*top and Eat celebrated its twenty-fifth anniversary in 1991; but we would have guessed it to be at least a decade older than that. This vintage drive-in at the crossroads across from the Chimayo Trading Post is an adorable taste of vintage American road culture. A huge sign above the brightly painted red-and-white building boasts of "JUMBO BURGERS" (in fact, we thought Jumbo Burger was the name of the business for two years); and although there is an interior dining room with three short counters and sixteen low stools, most business is done at the walk-up window. Place your order and you are given a number. Return to your car in the broad gravel lot and listen to the radio or make out with your date; in a few minutes a voice on a loudspeaker blasts your number into the New Mexican night.

To be honest, the jumbo burger isn't all that huge. It is good-sized and it is, as advertised, "no-grease-broiled" on a grate that allows the fat to drip away. It is served on a big spongy bun with shredded lettuce and pickle chips. It is a pre-franchise classic. If you want more meat, you can get a "jumbo twin" (two patties); and if you want less, there is a baby version, too. Onion rings make an excellent companion.

Here's a good place to eat local food the way ordinary local people like it (as opposed to the way hifalutin' chefs "interpret" it). Burritos, for a little less than a dollar apiece, are appealing little packets of meat, beans, chili, and cheese, so neatly wrapped that not a drop of the oozy ingredients will likely fall out onto your upholstery. That well-liked plebeian meal in these parts, Frito pie, is served in all its glory, in a cardboard boat. Prepared to order, of course (Frito pie can never be made in advance because the chips turn soggy), there are enough Fritos still on top of the soupy hot red chili to provide real crunch if you want it, and enough buried down below to give just the right amount of corn-flavored chew.

There is a long beverage list, including all the usual soda pops and milk shakes as well as the ideal libation to accompany Frito pie, as right with it as white wine is with fish: Hawaiian Punch. The heat of the peppers in the chili, the viscous luxury of the meat, and the snap of the salty Frito chips are all brought to a kind of *Roadfood* epiphany by a tall, icy cup full of bright red bug juice.

TECOLOTE CAFE
1203 CERRILLOS RD., SANTA FE, NM (505) 988-1362

When Bill and Alice Jennison opened Tecolote in 1980, they did so with a sense of mission. Their goal, stated on the back of the menu, was "to serve a wholesome, tasty meal, at a reasonable price, in a comfortable and cheerful environment." On occasion they have opened up for evening meals, but the Jennisons' specialty, and the distinction of Tecolote, is breakfast. Lines of morning customers waiting to get in are testimony to their fulfillment of the mission. This sprawling roadhouse serves some of the tastiest breakfast in the Southwest.

Personally, we like Tecolote's *atole piñon* hotcakes best of all. Made with blue cornmeal and studded with roasted piñon nuts, they actually resemble wide, low-rise cakes more than ordinary flattened-out flapjacks. Pale blue inside with a faintly crusty exterior from the grill, each cake is ethereally fluffy; and gosh, what joy it is to bite into a little lode of those roasty-rich nuts! There are blueberry hotcakes, too, made with a similar, from-scratch batter, and plain ones—each available singly, as a short stack (two), or a full stack (three).

Sometimes we don't eat pancakes at Tecolote because the roster of breads available for French toast is just too alluring. Last time we came through town, there were cinnamon-raisin, molasses-oatmeal, honey-wheat, and orange–poppy seed. We chose the last, made with freshly squeezed orange juice (you can actually feel a bit of pulp as you bite into the puffy triangles of batter-dipped and butter-grilled toast).

Of course, there are omelettes galore and eggs of every kind, including shirred on a bed of chicken livers; as the crown of corned-beef hash; and *rancheros* style—fried on a corn tortilla smothered in red or green chili and topped (at your request) with cheese. Tecolote even offers low-cholesterol breakfast burritos made with Egg Beaters. To go with eggs, hotcakes, French toast, or waffles, the meat list offers bacon or link sausage, ham, hash, pork chops, a New York strip steak, a hamburger patty, or Morningstar strips and links made from soy protein rather than pig.

Now a few short words about one nontraditional meal we hold dear at Tecolote. It is a gallimaufry called "sheep herder's breakfast"—new potatoes boiled with jalapeño peppers and onion, cooked on a grill until crusty brown, then topped with two kinds of chili and melted cheddar cheese. On the side come hot flour tortillas. Mighty good, mighty good.

They serve lunch at Tecolote: enchiladas, tacos, and chili, as well as hamburgers accompanied by those great breakfast potatoes. And if you want a truly local meal, we recommend Tecolote's superior *carne adovada,* for which lean pork, marinated in chili sauce, is cubed and stuffed into a flour tortilla and topped with cheese, then served along with beans, posole (hominy corn), or potatoes.

One of the perks of eating Tecolote's good food is its good spirits. The staff is young, hip, and friendly. The art on the walls ranges from a collection of unicorn needlepoints to serious works by local artists (for sale). The dining rooms are wide and comfy, mellow and informal (paper napkins, bare tables, yellow-checked tablecloths). The coffee is good, and served with real cream.

"*Tecolote,*" by the way, is an Aztec word that means owl, chosen by the Jennisons because Bill had been fascinated by a nearly deserted village by that name in northern New Mexico. "We like to think of him as our 'wise friend,'" says the Tecolote menu, "and hope that you will think of those of us at Tecolote Cafe that way."

TRUCHAS MOUNTAIN CAFE
TRUCHAS, NM (505) 689-2444

We are worried about the Truchas Mountain Cafe. Among the small selection of crafts and jewelry on display in the dining room are some brochures plugging local sites of interest. One of these brochures is a real estate company flyer advertising the Truchas Mountain Cafe: "This charming restaurant in the historic village of Truchas . . . truly one of the most beautiful in New Mexico." As of the summer of 1991, the restaurant and cafe were on the market for $150,000. We asked the family in the kitchen why they were selling, and they reassured us that it was only to find a bigger place, to which they hoped to move sometime early in 1992. This minuscule treasure, on a street barely more than an alley in the vest-pocket village of Truchas, deserves more space, and we suspect it will remain a *Roadfood* treasure wherever it relocates; but to be honest, we adore it as it is.

There are two dining rooms: a sunny alcove with blue hardwood tables and chairs and an interior room that is dark and almost monastic in tone: bare wood tables, hard cushionless chairs, a few spare *objets d'art* around for sale (ranging from high-quality jewelry to a delightfully silly "tortilla clock" with red-and-green-pepper hands), and background music provided by a CD with Mexican guitar classics playing low.

Our waitress, the owner's daughter, was about nine years old and painstakingly serious in her work, which she performed flawlessly. And it is hard work. Nearly everything you can order at the Truchas Mountain Cafe involves many different choices: red or green chili, sopaipillas or tortillas, roast beef or ground beef?

What we like best is the stuffed sopaipilla, filled with roast beef and green chili. The big fry bread is split open like a clam shell and loaded with chunks and shreds of utterly scrumptious, deeply seasoned roast beef as tender as mom's pot roast plus a load of zesty green chili and some cheese, too. Like all other meals in this humble place, it is served on a Styrofoam plate and accompanied by plastic utensils that bend treacherously if you try to cut anything with them. About the sopaipillas, baskets of which accompany most meals: they are puffy beauties with a unique—is it yeasty?—flavor and a nearly brittle crisp skin. They are served with plastic packs of honey for squeezing inside, but as good as honey is with fry bread, we like these elegant pillows plain, or as mops for chili. The rest of the menu is a fine roster of native New Mexican food, including wonderful blue-corn enchiladas, tostadas, even a "tortilla burger." All items are available as whole meals, with the works (beans, sopaipillas or tortillas, chili on the side) or as side orders to accompany something else.

Astonishing desserts. There is one called panocha, which reminded us of Indian pudding, only infinitely sweeter, almost caramelized. Accompanied by a scoop of vanilla ice cream, it was a sugar-lover's dream. Less saccharine but even richer, the pumpkin nut roll is an imposing orange cake reminiscent of carrot cake, layered with thick ribbons of cream cheese and topped with a spill of slivered almonds. It too is available with ice cream or with whipped cream.

This high-mountain cafe also serves breakfast: scrambled eggs stuffed into a sopaipilla, *huevos rancheros,* or egg-and-cheese-filled burritos topped with red or green chili. We have never eaten breakfast here; but we sincerely hope we get the chance to do so.

Note: As of our last visit, in September 1991, the cafe was still in the same place (and still a treasure); but our waiter said that construction had begun on a new restaurant, out on the main road, and that he expected it to open in the spring.

WOOLWORTH'S
58 E. SAN FRANCISCO, SANTA FE, NM (505) 982-1062

We confess to loving all Woolworth's snack counters, whevever they may be, and however mundane their food. Eating in a variety store is a special treat, as much fun as eating at a pharmacy soda fountain counter or in the back room of a grocery. Dime-store lunch is especially fun because most of the places that serve it have a menu of such delightfully antediluvian cuisine as tuna casserole, ham-on-white, and turkey club sandwiches stuck together with toothpicks.

The adobe Woolworth's on the square in Santa Fe serves just such retro food, but it goes all other dime store eateries we know one better: it serves Frito pie. Although the fine and sophisticated cuisine of Santa Fe has been discovered in the last several years by upwardly mobile chefs in cities all over America, none of the fancy-pants guys have elevated Frito pie into the repertoire of acceptably polite Americana. Nonetheless, Frito pie (known among local connoisseurs as a "stomach grenade") is one of the most beloved dishes of the real people in and around Santa Fe, and it is served by hash houses and drive-in restaurants throughout northern New Mexico. No one dishes it out with the panache of Woolworth's.

There are two sizes of Frito pie available: regular or jumbo. Give your order to the lady behind the take-out snack bar (there is a counter with stools, too, but most people like to take their pie out and eat it on the stroll in the square). She hollers out which size you want, and a lady behind her nabs an appropriately sized bag of Fritos that has been neatly torn open along its side. She gingerly squeezes the top and bottom of the bag, turning the torn-open side into a gaping maw, into which she ladles a cascade of hot red chili. The chili is then blanketed with a fistful or two of shredded yellow cheese, and the now-loaded Frito bag gets wrapped in napkins, a plastic spoon is planted in it, and, in exchange for about three dollars, it is handed over to you. If you want to add onions, there is a panful on the counter: spoon them on top of the cheese.

What a pleasure this pie-in-a-bag is to eat! At first, the Fritos at the bottom are still brittle crisp; so as you spoon down through the chili, you can retrieve hard, crusty chips to go with the meaty brew. Gradually, the chili seeps down to the bottom and the remaining chips begin to soften, turning semi-crisp, then totally limp. Even then, when you are spooning out the last of your pie, those pliable ribbons of corn are an inspired foil for the peppery hamburger meat and rich cheese.

If, for some reason, a Frito pie is not a balanced-enough meal for you, the Woolworth's take-out counter has another specialty that goes well with the pie; and it, too, is a favorite among regular customers and a real street-food archetype: a deep-fried corn dog on a stick.

NEW YORK

ANCHOR BAR
1047 MAIN ST., BUFFALO, NY (716) 886-8920

The Anchor Bar was established in 1935, but it wasn't until July 29, 1977, officially proclaimed by the city of Buffalo to be Chicken Wing Day, that anyone other than its loyal local clientele gave a hoot about it. In the last fifteen years chicken wings, as well as the Anchor Bar where they were invented, have become something of a culinary obsession all over America.

Teresa Bellisimo, who ran the bar with her husband, Frank, invented wings in 1964. Of course, chicken wings existed before this date; Buffalonians seem to have been quite fond of them as hors d'oeuvres; indeed Calvin Trillin uncovered a man named John Young who claims to have invented wings himself long before the Anchor Bar. Mrs. Bellisimo's genius was to cut the wings into two wieldy sections (drumettes and bows) and, after deep-frying them, stir them up in buttery hot sauce. She then served the peppery little morsels along with celery stalks and a bowl of blue cheese dressing to help tamp down the wings' heat. It was, and is, a sublime combination of tastes and textures—easy to munch, an ideal food to accompany drinks, and lots of lip-licking fun.

Much to the credit of Mrs. Bellisimo's descendants, the Anchor Bar is still the same joint it was nearly thirty years ago when the wing concept took off. There are press clippings and proclamations on the walls, but the ambience is still strictly corner tavern. The menu includes lots of fried seafoods, red-sauced noodles, potato skins, hamburgers, and an item listed as "chicken lips"—which are unlikely to give wings a run for their money.

It is certainly not for the other food we recommend lunch or supper at the Anchor Bar; nor would we send you here for a lesson in the history of hors d'oeuvres. The reason to come is for those wings, which are served exactly as they were in the beginning, and are still the best you will eat anywhere. The presentation is now classic: under an upside-down bowl (for bones) with a few stalks of celery (we usually ask for more) and a bowl of creamy blue cheese dressing. The wings are crisp, a lovely orange-yellow, not dripping sauce, but imprinted with it. They are available hot or mild. Hot is fiery and will burn your lips; mild is more butter-flavored. They are addictive.

BARNEY GREENGRASS

541 AMSTERDAM AVE., NEW YORK, NY (BETWEEN 86TH & 87TH STS.)
(212) 724-4707

Barney Greengrass has been serving lox and bagels to New Yorkers since the twenties. Food trends come and go, the West Side's fortunes rise and fall, but the smoked fish in this archetypal delicatessen-restaurant, a place known to its fans by Mr. Greengrass's self-anointed title, "the Sturgeon King," is unvaryingly excellent. Sturgeon (lean, silky), lox (salty cured salmon), Nova Scotia (glistening pink slices), whitefish (snowy-fleshed), and sable (rich and garlicky) are available on platters, with fine, fresh bagels and bialys, cream cheese, onions, tomatoes, and olives. It is the classic Jewish breakfast, and there isn't a restaurant in town that does it with the aplomb of bare-tabled Barney Greengrass.

Good as the smoked-fish platters are, the single best dish in the house is the one known as eggs-and-Novie. If you come in the morning, especially on a weekend, you will smell plates of it being carried from the kitchen to customers as soon as you enter. It is eggs scrambled with plush morsels of Nova Scotia salmon and onions nearly caramelized by frying. The combination tastes opulent; the textural range from the eggs' soft curds to the firm nuggets of fish they enfold to the slippery web of onions is a tongue's delight; and the aroma of these ingredients, as well as the smells of freshly toasted bagels and of cold cuts, salamis, and garlic pickles from the take-out side of the restaurant, makes walking into Barney Greengrass one of the most dizzyingly appetizing experiences New York City has to offer.

BENNY'S BURRITOS
113 GREENWICH AVE., NEW YORK, NY (212) 633-9210

B enny's burrito is the size of a dinner plate, a foot-wide flour tortilla bundled around beans, rice, guacamole, gobs of sour cream, and chunks of fall-apart tender beef (or chicken). The fillings are real food: ample pieces of meat delicately seasoned—nothing like the pulverized dog chow that passes for Tex-Mex in so many north-of-the-border restaurants. On top of this Mexican magnum opus, you get your choice of salsas: verdes (green), rojas (red), or mole. Beg your waiter for some of each; or if you're a group of people, each get a different one. They all demand attention. The green is brilliant with the tang of tomatillos. Red is the color of cinnabar— grainy, complex, with a real chili pepper flavor. Mole is the strangest. Yes, you really taste chocolate, but isn't it exotic to have it without candy's sweetness? The profundity of cocoa is blended with the adult pleasure of toasted almonds, and the punch of three kinds of hot pepper. It is deep, deep red, darker than mahogany.

The beans that come with the burrito—black or pinto—are exquisite. They haven't turned to mush, yet they are fragile enough to yield a flood of vegetable vim at first bite. The rice you would happily eat by itself—a vegetarian meal. It is infused with tomato purée, onions, chili powder, and a jolt of this kitchen's favorite herb, cilantro.

Benny's is cheap, delectable, and fun: a street-corner shop in Greenwich Village, with pink Formica luncheonette tables and a collection of way-out 1950s lamps. Of course you can drink margaritas or Mexican beer, as well as such Benny's originals as a Red Hot (Tabasco-tinged peppermint schnapps) and a La Boca de Fuego (pepper vodka). Merry as it is, good food is what makes this restaurant (now in a second location at 93 Avenue A) a small miracle. Except for the fact that parking is impossible (and the line waiting for a table can stretch into the street), Benny's Burrito's is *Roadfood* deluxe.

CONDRELL'S CANDIES AND ICE CREAM PARLOR
2805 DELAWARE AVENUE, KENMORE, NY (716) 877-4485

Among traveling gourmets, the Nickel City is best known for spicy hot chicken wings and roast beef sandwiches on caraway-seed hard rolls, both of which are terrific; but it is impossible to eat one's way around town without noticing that nearly everywhere you go there are stands, stores, shops, and parlors touting their ice cream specialties and hand-dipped candies.

The candy selection, at its best purveyors, is nothing less than spectacular. For instance, drive north to the section of Buffalo known as Kenmore and look for the avocado-green façade of a place called Condrell's. Step inside; eyes right: it is an amazing sight. Case after case is filled with candy, nearly all of it made on the premises, hand-dipped and delicious-looking. Choose from among molasses paddles and chips enrobed in dark or light chocolate; cashew or pecan turtles; chocolate-covered chunks of candied orange, pineapple, and ginger; dozens of varieties of cream centers, almond bark, truffles, chocolate-covered pretzels, and malted milk balls. The array of sweet things to eat makes a customer truly feel like a kid in a candy store.

The rest of Condrell's is an ice cream parlor with small tables surrounded by plush upholstered (in that avocado green again!) chairs. The menu is small and to the point: ice cream, ice cream, and ice cream. There are regular sundaes and sodas, of course, as well as various troughs of giant-size specialties including the Fudgana (four scoops, hot fudge, whipped cream, and nuts), banana boats, and assorted pigs' dinners for two or four ice cream gluttons.

The sundaes are beauties, although we found the hot fudge to be fairly wan, without the kind of chocolate wallop we like on a sundae. We recommend that serious cocoa-heads choose semi-sweet chocolate sauce instead of hot fudge, and perhaps pay thirty-five cents extra to get a double portion on their sundae. The other alternative that will satisfy a serious chocolate craving is a Condrell's creation listed as *French* chocolate sauce. Now this is an inspired idea: ultra-thick, pitch-dark topping that is in fact warm chocolate pudding. A stroke of genius! Heaped upon a quartet of scoops of vanilla ice cream and topped with real whipped cream and plenty of toasted nuts, its avoirdupois and warmth are a perfect foil for the cold luxury of the ice cream underneath.

The intensity of such ice cream spectaculars makes one crave water;

and that is an odd thing about Condrell's. Water is served in tiny glasses barely bigger than a jigger. We went through a half-dozen refills before our French chocolate sauce-induced thirst was finally slaked.

COPELAND'S RELIABLE CAFETERIA
547 W. 145TH ST., NEW YORK, NY (212) 234-2356

Copeland's serves the cuisine of Harlem: soul food with an uptown twist. The twist is in the form of a deluxe restaurant with linen tablecloths, suave waiters, and a repertoire of such hifalutin' fare as shrimp scampi Provençal and cherries jubilee as well as proverbial Beulahland cuisine including peanut soup, fried chicken with corn fritters, Maryland crab cakes, Creole gumbo, and—are you ready?—chitterlings in champagne. We have never eaten Copeland's *haute* chitterlings; in fact we have never eaten in the deluxe half of Copeland's at all, because we are smitten with the other half—the cafeteria.

Here are molded plastic bench seats and laminate tables and positively awful lighting . . . and a cafeteria line to cause far-from-home fans of southern-style cooking to weep for joy. Crowds of plain and fancy customers line up every day of the week, but especially on Sunday after church, to fill their trays with such Dixie delectables as falling-off-the-bone smothered chicken with elegantly textured stuffing, meat loaf with luscious ox tail gravy, porcelain-pink baked Virginia ham, glazed spare ribs, short ribs, and even pretty good, albeit tame, barbecue. The array of side dishes includes whipped potatoes, candied yams, unctuous collard greens, red rice, white rice, macaroni and cheese, and always casseroles of vegetables baked with plenty of spicy, cheesy, buttery, ennoblements. On the side there are whole-wheat dinner rolls and cornbread mini-loaves; and for dessert, choose from among pies, cobbler, pound cake, and silk-sweet, soft-souled, meringue-topped banana pudding.

It is a long way to West 145th Street from midtown Manhattan; but there is simply no restaurant down there that serves anything remotely like the true American feast carried forth on the trays of Copeland's Reliable.

CROMPOND DINER
U.S. 202 W, PEEKSKILL, NY (914) 737-1562

The Crompond Diner serves three squares a day, but breakfast is the meal you want to eat. Bacon and eggs, fried potatoes, toast and coffee are dished out faster than you can read through the menu in this comely stainless-steel diner with its purple window shades and arched pink-and-white monitor roof. Biscuits come hot from the oven, as do jumbo muffins (blueberry, corn, bran). You can even eat Nova Scotia lox (smoked salmon) and cream cheese on a bagel, or an omelette made with the traditional Jewish delicatessen ingredients of sweet onions and small bits of lox.

One of the reasons breakfast is so good is that the ambience broadcast from behind the counter suits a brisk and efficient morning meal. There is a rousing bustle to this place, and a workmanlike efficiency that has made it a favorite among locals (who have known it as "Pete and Ray's") since the fifties. For travelers along the Taconic Parkway, the Crompond is a beacon of low-priced breakfast specials, fast service, hot coffee, and pure, mid-century American diner pizzazz that is hard to match.

Don't get us wrong: as good as breakfast is, lunch and dinner at Pete and Ray's are fine meals, too, especially the fried chicken in a basket with French fries and salad, which is available in a take-out box because so many customers like to bring their chicken home. In fact it was at dinner that we discovered what turned out to be our favorite breakfast item at the Crompond Diner: the hot apple dumpling. It is served as dessert, which is probably what it ought to be; but to our taste, there is something irresistibly luxurious about an apple dumpling for breakfast. And the Crompond Diner's apple dumpling, made daily and served piping hot under a drizzle of rum sauce, is one of the best.

ECKL'S
4936 ELLICOTT RD., ORCHARD PARK, NY (716) 662-2262

A locally favored eatery since 1934, Eckl's is an excellent place to taste Buffalo beef on weck. This is a sandwich of thin-sliced roast beef on a salt-crusted hard roll. "Weck" is short for *Kummelweck*, the German word for caraway seed, with which the salt-spangled, hard-crusted sandwich bun is liberally infused. It pockets velvety slices of thin-sliced, blushing pink, juice-heavy meat. Some beef-on-weck fanciers prefer a sandwich of only beef and weck. Others request that each half of the sliced roll be dipped momentarily in a puddle of natural gravy, adding even more savor to the sandwich. All insist that the beef be sliced as thin as possible—nearly shaved, preferably by hand.

Eckl's does it right. "We simply endeavor to bring you the finest flavor possible in steaks, prime rib, and roast beef," the menu says. "We refuse to succumb to the so-called advances of portion control, blast freezing, and chemical tenderizers." When you order a sandwich Eckl's hand-slices its beef from a great haunch of cow that has been slow-roasted to perfection and trimmed of fat. Eckl's rolls, baked each morning, are crusted with a heavy measure of pretzel salt and enough caraway seeds to give the dough a real personality. Sandiches are available with or without gravy, with or without slaw, and French fries on the side. Visitors who want to experience an all-upstate meal can also get a plate of fiery hot chicken wings in their classic configuration—with bleu cheese dressing, celery, carrots, and a moist towelette.

Eckl's atmosphere is a stalwart pleasure. Here is an honest, old-fashioned supper club (open only in the evening) lit with wall sconces and decorated with pictures of leaping deers, where customers come to eat something fancier than home cooking. Couples sit at tables sipping sweet Manhattans and spooning up great wads of goo from their crocked onion soup. Ever-present in the dining room, watching the roast get sliced and shepherding it on its way to the tables, is Dale Eckl himself, nattily uniformed in a short blue coat. Mr. Eckl is the soul of efficiency, an upstate beef man extraordinaire.

EISENBERG'S SANDWICH
174 FIFTH AVE., NEW YORK, NY (212) 675-5096

We were led to Eisenberg's Sandwich by Rozanne Gold, who is employed by Joseph Baum and Michael Whiteman Associates, an organization run by guys who have been responsible for creating some of New York City's swankiest restaurants, from the original Four Seasons to the modern resurrection of the Rainbow Room. The only problem was that we and Rozanne couldn't sit together. None of the tables at Eisenberg's Sandwich have room for more than two people. So she sat at one and we sat at another just behind it, and we called back and forth over our sandwiches. It was wonderful—perhaps not quite as wonderful as dinner at the Rainbow Room, but every bit as true a taste of New York, and considerably less expensive.

Eisenberg's Sandwich is arranged in the time-honored delicatessen-restaurant configuration, only it is thinner. On the left as you enter there is a counter behind which meals are made. Dead-ahead is an aisle so skinny that wide-hipped people will have to move sideways; and on the right of the aisle, squeezed up against the rough plaster wall, is a bank of tables for two.

Each table is set with a silver tray of briny pickles: good munching as you wait for your meal. The menu is simple, pared to what a deli does well, from matzoh balls to terrific spiced hot meats. Lean, brick-colored corned beef or fattier and pepper-rimmed pastrami is piled high on sour rye bread; each is a paragon. Tuna salad is extravagantly mayonnaisey. If you want more than a sandwich, Eisenberg's offers one hot meal selection each day: either franks and beans or a tasty meat loaf with potato salad. Whatever you get, you cannot go wrong. Thanks, Rozanne.

FRANK'S
431 W. 14TH ST., NEW YORK, NY (212) 243-1349

There is still sawdust on Frank's floors, but carcass haulers and cutters from the meat market on 14th Street no longer come in for coffee at 3:00 A.M. Frank's is now strictly for the lunch and dinner crowd; don't come to dine wearing your blood-splattered apron. The swank Frank's is nearly as expensive as any steak house in New York. The sawdust is clean and tables are covered with soft linen; but such niceties do not diminish the carnivorous authority of this restaurant originally made famous because it was where local butchers came to eat.

Here are some of the city's finest steaks and chops, selected with market-honed experience by proprietor George Molinari (Frank's son-in-law). The shell steak, a boneless behemoth oozing savory juices from fissures in its well-charred crust, is the most succulently beefy you will taste in any restaurant; skirt steak overhangs a dinner plate in all directions; prime rib and rack of lamb are meat monuments. For those who enjoy animals' other parts, euphemistically named "variety cuts" and including liver, sweetbreads, kidneys, and tripe, Frank's is a unique culinary mecca. Especially wonderful is a dish called tripe Florentine, sold as an appetizer or entrée, in which the ignominious innards are cooked to fall-apart tenderness and cosseted in a zesty tomato and wine sauce.

Getting to Frank's is half the fun. Once, as our cab headed west on 14th Street, the driver screeched to a stop and accused us of directing him to a deserted location so we could mug him. This is indeed a weird neighborhood, virtually abandoned after nightfall. But the amazing news is that if you drive, it is likely you can find a place to park just outside.

GRAND DAIRY RESTAURANT
341 GRAND ST., NEW YORK, NY (212) 673-1904

The waiters wear white shirts and black bow ties, but the fancy dress doesn't mean they won't give you a hard time if you don't finish all your lentil soup. They aren't the crabbiest Jewish waiters in town (for that, the staff of the 2nd Avenue Deli, p. 323, takes the prize), but the folks at Grand Dairy Restaurant have developed the exquisite, usually intra-family, talent of making guests feel at once appreciated and a bother.

However this peculiar treatment affects you, brave it for the food. At Grand Dairy Restaurant, which is kosher, you will get no meat; but oh, what bread! The basket that comes to the table contains chewy pumpernickel rolls and midnight-black pumpernickel bread, eggy dinner rolls, onion bread, and shiny-crusted rye. You could make a meal of Grand Dairy's bread basket along with a bowl of homemade soup—mushroom-barley, lima bean, borscht.

Appetizers include mock chopped liver made with vegetables, gefilte fish, and tangy sweet-and-sour pickled herring. There are kasha varnishkes (bow-tie noodles and buckwheat groats), indelicate blintzes stuffed with cheese or fruits, and even a "roast" made of mushrooms and ground-up vegetables. There are usually a few kinds of cake for dessert, but the great thing to finish off a dairy meal in this place is the dish they call banana fritters—nothing but chunks of banana sautéed in butter and gobbed with sour cream. Many customers drink coffee or tea, but the beverage list also includes sweet cream by the glass.

HOFT'S LUNCHEONETTE
3200 WHITE PLAINS ROAD, BRONX, NY (212) 654-5291

What a relic this store is, complete with stamped tin ceiling, mahogany booths, and honeycomb tile floor. It's a corner candy store where you can go for an ice cream soda, a chocolate-dipped graham cracker, and, most famously, an egg cream. Places like Hoft's used to be all over New York, the boroughs, and in cities throughout the Northeast. Now they are rare, so Hoft's—looking the way it did when it opened in 1949—is well worth inscribing in the book of American classics.

Superior egg creams are what first drew us here, and they are beauts. The soda jerk grabs a buxom soda fountain glass (never a paper cup!). He leans once, hard, on the chocolate syrup dispenser, squirting out approximately three-quarters of an inch of syrup into the glass. He doesn't seem very neat about it; a streak of syrup slashes along the inside of the glass, nearly to the rim. But that streak was no accident. Now he grabs a carton of milk from the refrigerator case; but not just any carton. The *coldest* one is essential, so the icy milk is on the verge of crystallizing. The milk is splashed in atop the syrup. Without a second wasted, a spoon is plunged into the yet-unmixed milk and syrup, twirled once or twice, and the glass is set beneath the high-velocity soda dispenser. A furious stream hits the back of the spoon at the bottom of the glass, spraying down at just the right angle, plowing into the milk and syrup, mixing them without any stirring. Then, as quickly as it started, the fast stream is cut off, the handle flipped the other way, and the seltzer pours out easily. As it pours, a foamy head builds, rising faster than the liquid down below. It reaches the rim of the glass and continues up. The soda jerk slides it off like a bartender cutting the head off a quickly poured beer, and the soda continues into the glass until the head is approximately the top one-third, and the bottom two-thirds are well-blended, pale cocoa colored. If the soda was squirted in just right, no further mixing is necessary. But that one "sloppy" streak of chocolate syrup remains in the glass—like a painter's signature, symbol of a perfectly made egg cream.

Now, the good part: drinking it. Egg cream magic does not last long. Egg creams must be dispatched with utmost speed, within three minutes of their being made. If not consumed immediately, they loose their head; they turn flat; they go from the champagne of soda fountain drinks to watery chocolate milk. That is why egg creams are seldom served to accompany a meal. They are a snack unto themselves, worthy of contemplation. The only proper companion for an egg cream is a pretzel rod.

Other than egg creams, Hoft's is soda fountain paradise. Its menu includes such nostalgic ice cream concoctions as a Broadway Flip and a real banana split, served in the proper boat-shaped bowl with lengthwise-sliced bananas. There are hamburgers and cheese sandwiches, and a full array of old-fashioned candies: chocolate bunnies around Easter time, chocolate cigars (with pink or blue bands) any time of year.

KATZ'S DELICATESSEN
205 E. HOUSTON ST., NEW YORK, NY (212) 254-2246

Katz's celebrated its hundredth birthday a few years ago, but the interior doesn't look a day over sixty. It is a vintage, fluorescent-lit lunchroom that feels like old New York. You get a ticket when you walk in, and as you order food at the counter, the men who make the food punch the ticket; then you eat, and on the way out, you pay according to the holes in the ticket. Having eaten at Katz's only about a hundred times, we haven't yet figured out the punch-hole system. But we don't mind—the cost seems fair enough; nor are we dissuaded by the fact that the streets around Katz's are an appalling vista of urban blight (if coming by cab, we have the driver wait). The reason we continue to love this place is that there are some foods here that are simply the best anywhere.

French fries, to start with a not-so-minor example. Katz's fries are big rectangular chunks of potato, cooked golden yellow, big enough so their faintly leathery crust contains great, steamy lodes of fluffy white spud. We have been told that they use schmaltz (chicken fat) in the cooking oil, which is what gives these potatoes a richly seasoned flavor even before they are salted. Whatever. It doesn't matter to us how they do it; these are simply the best French fried potatoes in the world, all the more charming because they are served in brown paper bags that quickly disintegrate if you don't dump them out on the table pretty quickly.

Hot dogs: we wouldn't necessarily say Katz's are the best in the world; but they are way up there in the all-beef kosher dog pantheon. They are hefty tubes with a crackly skin and a basso profundo garlic taste, served in nice, steamy-soft buns.

Pastrami and corned beef: here you've got to do some work to get what you want; and if you do, this can be the best corned-beef or pastrami sandwich you will ever eat. When you order it, the man behind the counter forks a roast from out of its metal box and slaps it down on the ancient cutting board. Now is your opportunity to try to convince him you want lean or fatty, this piece or that. If he's nice, or if you tip him well, he will oblige: he goes to work and slices out a sandwich's worth (by hand, of course), and sometimes—if he's feeling generous—offers you a slice or two across the counter as you watch. The sandwiches are always piled high (on good rye bread), and whether the slices you get are fat or lean, they are deeply seasoned, smoky, and ridged with a band of blackened pepper and spice.

There are dozens of other kinds of exemplary deli sandwiches (salami, bologna, tongue, brisket), as well as luxurious salami omelettes, fried pancake-style. For drinks there are beers, hot tea served Russian-style, in glasses, and—the deli sandwich connoisseur's choice—Dr. Brown's Cel-Ray celery-flavored soda pop.

KNISH NOSH

101-02 QUEENS BLVD., FOREST HILLS, NY (718) 897-5554
(ALSO AT 145 FOURTH AVE., BETWEEN 13TH & 14TH ST.,
NEW YORK, NY)

K nish Nosh is a corner store that does mostly take-out business, although three window tables, each with a maximum seating capacity of two, allow for eating-in. A soft drink cooler hums loudly to the left, and when you step to the worn Formica counter to place your order, you are asked if you want it hot (for eating here) or cold (for taking home). The menu is limited to knishes, although in recent years the basic repertoire of potato, kasha, or liver knishes has been supplemented by carrot, broccoli, or spinach-stuffed ones.

These are all orthodox knishes, round and firm and fully packed, not the reformed rectangular impostors. Each is three inches in diameter, a little over an inch tall, and approximately one pound. They smell *good,* especially the liver knish, which is reminiscent of the pot roast perfume in grandmothers' apartment building hallways. Kasha (buckwheat groat) knishes are mealy, cereal-textured, and satisfying—nearly all filling, with a papery tan crust wrapped around the outside. Potato knishes are the spiciest, the lumpy filling nearly viscous in texture, dotted with onion and infused with plenty of savory seasonings.

One knish is a meal. But for taking home, Knish Nosh also sells cocktail knishes, downscale doots that we find completely unsatisfying, without the va-va-voom that gives full-size dumplings their whole hog authority.

Aside from superior knishes, the original Knish Nosh offers a fascinating taste of Queens Boulevard's cultural reach. Although the knishes taste straight from an Eastern European kitchen, the staff is American urban black; and what a weird experience it is to hear them call out words like "kasha" and "schmaltz," words you have formerly heard spoken only with heavy Jewish accents.

NICK TAHOU

2260 LYELL, ROCHESTER, NY (716) 429-6388

N ick Tahou is unchallenged as home of the garbage plate. To our knowledge, no other restaurant has even tried to imitate or better it. What it is: separate piles of baked beans and home-fried potatoes topped with a spoonful of raw onions and a couple of split grilled hot dogs, the hot dogs crowned with mustard and spicy chili sauce and the whole shebang sided by a big scoop of cool macaroni salad and accompanied by a couple of slices of bread for mopping up. All these ingredients are marshaled on a thick cardboard plate that lasts about fifteen or twenty minutes before it starts to disintegrate.

What a wanton, disrespectful, and delicious mess! Especially noteworthy is the sauce atop the hot dogs, a fine-grained, Greek-accented brew that is also available on such lesser variants of frankfurter cookery as Nick Tahou's peppery pork hots and garlic-packed Texas hots, as well as on grilled hamburgers.

Forget burgers. This is hot dog country; and Nick's are exemplary, if not epicurean. They are split and fried, which gives them a nice, chewy exterior and hash-house raunch that boiled or even charcoal-grilled wienies do not offer.

As befits its menu, Nick Tahou is a raffish dog house, with chairs and tables scattered around its cramped interior, and plenty of noise as customers at the order counter call out for red hots and white hots with the works and waitresses assemble them with lightning speed. Of course Nick Tahou is open all night. You never know when the craving for a garbage plate will strike.

PARKSIDE CANDY
3208 MAIN ST., BUFFALO, NY (716) 833-7540

B uilt in 1927, Parkside Candy of Buffalo is one of the prettiest ice cream parlors on this earth. It is an old-fashioned candy factory specializing in saltwater taffy, all-day suckers, bon-bons of every size and shape, and a spun molasses specialty known as sponge candy (or honeycombs), as well as a full repertoire of soda fountain specialties including dusty roads, rocky roads, tin roofs, egg creams, and peanut butter fudge banana splits.

Walk into this place and your nose fills with a liquorish cocoa butter aroma even before your eyes can focus on the stunning interior decor. In a grandiose oval room lined with classic columns and umbrellaed by a domed ceiling, candies are sold from a series of vending stations around the circumference. Soft background music and subtle indirect light create the reverential atmosphere of a fine art museum. In the center of the room, on a checked tiled floor, are a group of wooden tables and chairs where customers peacefully contemplate the fine gastronomic artistry of their

Creamsicle frappes, root beer floats, and maple nut sundaes.

You can even eat a meal. Breakfast on homemade muffins, stuffed croissants, French toast, or a Belgian waffle. At lunch, the sandwich list includes the unique combo known around here as "beef on weck"—thin-sliced roast beef *au jus* on a hard roll crusted with salt and caraway seeds—as well as sentimentally named sandwiches from days of yore such as "The Windemere" (roast beef and cheddar cheese) and "The University" (*More than a meal:* ham, turkey, salami, Swiss cheese, American cheese, lettuce, tomato, cucumber slices").

Very nice eats, but the really good part is what comes from the soda fountain: floats, shakes, sodas, and coolers. The menu lists more than a dozen different sundaes, including "Mexican" (made with little peanuts) and out-of-this-world bittersweet chocolate. Frappes, which in this case are simply complex sundaes, come in twenty-four different varieties, from classic hot fudge and a triple-tiered banana split to new-wave cookie crunch and cocoa-kill triple chocolate.

If the Parkside fountainmaster will pardon our impertinence, we must say that some of these frappes seem quite iconoclastic. Rocky road, for instance, is made with heavenly hash ice cream, instead of ice cream with mini-marshmallows on top. The pecan turtle is served underneath an actual candy Turtle. We love the Creamsicle frappe, made with vanilla ice cream and orange sherbet, but the candy mountain frappe, heaped with chocolate candies, is too too much. Parkside's dusty road is vanilla and chocolate ice cream topped with marshmallow goo, then whipped cream and malt powder. The supreme sundae, which we have read about on the menu but never dared to sample, is "The Old Granada Special," which customers are invited to design themselves using eight flavors of ice cream, four toppings, two types of nuts, and "a mountain of whipped cream."

PASTRAMI KING
124-24 QUEENS BOULEVARD, KEW GARDENS, NY (718) 263-1717

D o not take the name of this restaurant casually. It *is* the Pastrami King, a fact of which you will be convinced as soon as you sink your teeth into a sandwich and suddenly your tongue floods with garlic and pepper zest. The flaps of cured meat are piled high on rye; each one is sultry red, lean except for a glistening halo of fat and an edge black with spice. It is profound pastrami, firm and muscular, with character that develops during a long dry cure when it sucks in the smoldering flavor of cedar smoke.

Slather on the grainy mustard, heft the half-sandwich (two hands are required), and inhale: the meaty pungency sets your head spinning. Regain your sanity by crunching into a sea-green dill pickle, set upon the table in a silver bowl.

"I want you to eat slower," says the waitress. "You eat too fast." Then she stumbles as she sets a plate of rugged-crusted potato latkes on the table next to us. We apologize for being in her way. "I knew it would happen," she calls back over her shoulder as she glides away. "You got big feet."

Throughout the meal, this old bird abuses us and every other customer she waits on. And nobody would want it any other way. This is how it must be at Pastrami King, the definitive delicatessen, where a grumpy staff is every bit as crucial as schmaltz in chopped liver.

Pastrami King is not pretty. The floor is slick, the tables wobble, rock music blares too loud on the radio. For decor, it's got some pictures of rabbis, one looking sad at the wailing wall, another blowing a shofar. And there are life-size bas-reliefs of Judaic-looking sovereigns. (Could they be the original pastrami kings?) At lunch, the place is crowded with lawyers and judges from the Queens County courthouse across the street; even the most eminent of them are verbally assaulted by sandwich shleppers who are experts in *angst*.

In addition to the nagging and the nudging and the ultimate pastrami, people come to Pastrami King for pickly corned beef and steamy-textured fall-apart brisket; for real French fries oddly cut into fat bricks and frizzled sticks; for potato pancakes, kasha varnishke, and chicken in the pot.

Pastrami King is a bastion of Jewish deli food (and service) *par excellence*, and therefore an important citadel of old New York cuisine. Like the pork parlors of Memphis and the barbecues of Texas, Manhattan's delis are widely imitated all around the country; but there can be no substitute for the real thing, dished out by crabby waitresses in this very real place along Queens Boulevard.

PETER LUGER STEAKHOUSE
178 BROADWAY, BROOKLYN, NY (718) 387-7400

You have to cross to the far end of the Williamsburg Bridge to get to Peter Luger; the tables are bare oak and utensils have wooden handles; the waiters can be impatient; the menu is short (recited, not written) and not much fun; and the prices are probably higher than those of any restaurant in this book. Still, *Roadfood* would not be complete without paying homage to what is one of America's classic dinners—meat and potatoes in a grand, 105-year-old New York steak house.

Peter Luger serves stupendous-looking lamb chops and big slabs of prime rib, but the meal of choice—and the only thing first-timers should consider—is steak, sized to fit from one to six eaters, and always more than you anticipate. They call it a porterhouse, which here means an extra-heavy cut T-bone with a wide, soft fillet on one side of the bone and a long, juice-heavy sirloin strip on the other. This massive cut, served already sliced on a plate that the waiter balances on a little dish so all the juices puddle up at one end (easier to spoon out that way) can take a ferocious charring outside but stay bright pink and swoonfully tender underneath its crust. Get a sliced-tomato-and-onion salad (in season) to start, and be sure to sample the great onion bread in the basket; then order hash browns or a baked potato (at dinner) or terrific French fries at lunch, with maybe creamed spinach on the side; finally, top it all off with a beautiful block of cheesecake to send the meal's calorie count into quadruple digits.

POPOVER CAFE
551 AMSTERDAM AVE., NEW YORK, NY (AT 87TH ST.) (212) 595-8555

Popover Cafe serves three good meals a day, seven days a week, but we suggest you come for breakfast on a weekday. That's when you can luxuriate in the house specialty, cappuccino eggs (not available on weekends). They are like scrambled, but instead of being merely stirred, they are steamed using a cappuccino jet. The result: eggs that are unbelievably tender, puffy and aerated, yet lusciously moist. A brilliant idea. And what a gentle companion these eggs have in one of the high-rise popovers that are the house specialty here, their exterior golden brown and brittle, their insides tender yellow fluff. With a good cup of coffee, those are the makings of a sublime morning meal in our book. But there is more.

Handmade sausage patties, deftly seasoned and grilled to crusty succulence; cheese grits with a real snap of flavor; expertly made omelettes filled with cheese, mushrooms, peppers, horseradish, even Basque vegetable piperade; skillet-fried potatoes to accompany eggs; freshly squeezed fruit juices: whatever you order for breakfast, it is excellent.

Lunch is good, too. Popover specializes in big combo sandwiches of multiple meats, cheese, and dressings, as well as half-pound hamburgers, huge salads, and homemade soup (accompanied by popovers, of course); and there is always an ambitious hot dish *du jour.* Desserts include lovely plump bundt cakes, ordinary brownies, and an extraordinary brownie cherry cake.

Fair prices, homey food, friendly help: an urban rarity.

QUINN'S RESTAURANT
330 MAIN STREET, BEACON, NY (914) 831-8065

Quinn's is a town cafe with a big American flag flying out front. It is staffed by experienced, professional waitresses who volunteer their opinions freely, even when not asked, about the banana cream pie ("It's a sin!"), the rice pudding ("Not today, hon"), the cream of potato soup ("A winner!"). Our waitress managed to provide a steady commentary, approximately every thirty seconds, on the progress of our order on its way from the grill to the counter to our table—this during an extraordinarily busy lunch hour.

Place mats are paper, with advertisements for local businesses surrounding this motto: "THE MEETING AND EATING SPOT OF BEACON." One time we ate at Quinn's there was a gallon jar next to the cash register serving as the town collection tray for a two-and-one-half-year-old local boy who needed an operation his parents could not afford. What mean person wouldn't like a cafe like this?

Now, here is the really good part: the bread. It is famous, and it is what puts Quinn's on the map of good eating places in the Northeast. It's white bread, baked in a squat oval loaf, with a rather tough, flavorful crust and substantial insides with powerful yeast flavor. For French toast, for sandwiches at lunch, to accompany meat loaf or a cup of homemade turkey noodle soup, this bread makes nearly every meal at Quinn's something special. It is cut into brawny slices—delicious buttered, but you don't even need that to make it something good to eat.

The day we first sampled this bread, the list of specials—handwritten on a piece of notebook paper—included a bacon, cheese, and tomato sandwich. No big deal, you say? It *was* a big deal, because the ingredients were sandwiched between two broad slices of the bread, which were buttered and set on a griddle until they turned all crusty brown and luscious, the grilling perfectly bringing out its natural wheaty flavor.

Also on the list of daily specials were macaroni and cheese, hot roast beef with gravy and French fries, and a turkey club sandwich (on *the* bread). Familiar food, yes, indeed; that's why Quinn's is such a nice place to eat.

Then, too, there is dessert. You don't want to miss that, not when the roster of pies—big homemade beauties in rugged crusts—includes a thick sun-colored custard with a ribbon of chewy sweet coconut on top, and banana cream, and spiced apple. The apples, by the way are also available atop ice cream, as one of Quinn's sundaes. That list also includes hot fudge, mixed fruit, marshmallow, strawberry, and a classic banana split.

Longtime fans of Quinn's tell us that it used to be a gorgeous place, complete with mahogany booths. Now the interior has been modernized with country-style barnboard wallpaper and decorator Coke trays. We are sorry to have missed the good old days, but we are mighty happy, we assure you, to know about Quinn's today. It is a rare beacon of good food along the Hudson River.

SARABETH'S KITCHEN
412 AMSTERDAM AVE., NEW YORK, NY (212) 496-6280; AND
1295 MADISON AVE., NEW YORK, NY (212) 410-7335;
ALSO AT THE WHITNEY MUSEUM

Sarabeth's Kitchens are small and cozy, with friendly food to match. The original location on the West Side is always thronged with eager eaters; but the close-together tables can add to the genuine neighborhood feel of the storefront nook. Mid-morning or afternoon on a weekday, when the crowds thin out, it is a delightful place to linger over the daily paper and coffee and scones served with a selection of marmalades and jams. The East Side Sarabeth's, in an old hotel, is roomier but not as neighborly feeling; however, the eating is every bit as good.

The kitchen's repertoire is simple, homey, and rather unusual for a city restaurant. Here are real porridge and hot cereals, potato and cheese blintzes as good as any Jewish mom's, biscuits and muffins hot from the oven. Don't be so enraptured by the morning-glorious selection of coffee cakes, rolls, short breads, pumpkin waffles (best dish!), and Linzer torte that you forget to order eggs: Sarabeth's omelettes are gorgeous.

Breakfast (okay, you can call it brunch if you wish) is served all day and is the only meal to eat at Sarabeth's Kitchen. We haven't yet tried the newest Sarabeth's, at the Whitney Museum.

SCHWABL'S
789 CENTER RD., WEST SENECA, NY (716) 674-9821

S chwabl's serves the best beef-on-weck sandwich in Buffalo, therefore the best in the world. Their hard rolls are heavily crusted with coarse grains of salt and infused with caraway seeds (a.k.a. *Kummelweck*; hence the sandwich's name), rugged enough to hold up well when sliced in half and dunked in natural beef gravy until the insides soften and are ready to receive the meat. Schwabl's beef is superb: thin, rare slices severed from the roast just before the sandwich is assembled. It is piled high inside each sandwich, a tender and luxurious pillow of protein. The only thing this sandwich could possibly want is a schmear of horseradish, which is supplied on each table and along the bar.

That is all you need to know about Schwabl's, except for the nice hot ham sandwich on white bread in a pool of tomato-clove gravy, served with warm potato salad. The ham is an interesting alternative to the beef, although it has none of the famous local sandwich's authority.

Schwabl's is a casual, well-aged beef house, attended by business people at noon and families at suppertime. Tables are covered with heavy-textured imitation leather, easy to wipe clean of gravy stains. Waitresses are fast and professional, outfitted in nurse-like uniforms, and refreshingly blunt. "You don't want the haddock," one advised us at the beginning of a recent Friday night meal; and by golly, she was right. Beef is what you want at Schwabl's, beef on weck.

SECOND AVENUE DELI
156 SECOND AVE., NEW YORK, NY (212) 677-0606

T he Second Avenue Deli is a stronghold of the kind of cooking for which Jewish mothers are famous, heavy on the schmaltz (chicken fat) and free advice. Located in a teeming ethnic neighborhood, it is a real taste of modern Manhattan, and a good place to eat such stalwart classics of the Old World kitchen as schmaltzy chopped liver, kasha (buckwheat groats) and kugel (noodle pudding), mushroom barley soup, matzoh balls, and kasha varnishkes (those groats with bow-tie noodles), as well as New York City's own favorite sandwiches, corned beef and hot pastrami on excellent rye bread.

Waiters trudge among the tables carrying soup and sandwiches, silver bowls of sea-green dill pickles, and vast tureens containing a soothing stew called chicken-in-the-pot. They've got a distinctive shuffle, these old men in their rumpled mustard-colored jackets, an orthopedic two-step perfected through years of dishing out the cold cuts and complaining all the while. Whatever you order from them, it always comes with pearls of world-weary wisdom on the side. These hang-dog men have seen it all. You want to really make them groan? Ask for corned beef on white with mayonnaise (instead of the proper way, on rye with mustard). *Oy vay!*

SHARKEY'S
56 GLENWOOD AVE., BINGHAMTON, NY (607) 729-9201

Bob Sharak told us that his father, who opened Sharkey's tavern over forty years ago, was the first man in Binghamton to sell spiedi meat for cooking at home. Well before Mr. Sharak's innovation, spiedies were a popular food in these parts, cooked and served in taprooms and on backyard patios. Strangely, they seem never to have traveled beyond the Binghamton environs, and even more strangely, although the name "*spiedi*" is Italian (for shishkebab), the best spiedi parlors are in Polish and Ukrainian parts of town.

"The secret is in the marination," Mr. Sharak told us the first time we sat at a table in this dark, neighborhood tavern and ordered a couple of sticks. In fact, the secret seems to be not too much marination, for the excellent lamb spiedies that came to our table along with paper plates and stacks of thin-sliced French bread were mild-flavored, rich, and juicy. Spiedies ought to be eaten straight from the grill, and at Sharkey's they arrive from their spell over a high-temperature charcoal fire (in the adjacent room) still sizzling with faintly blackened edges but pink, juicy insides. The way to eat them is to grab a piece of bread in one hand and use it like a mitt to pull off a couple of hot hunks, thereby making an instant sandwich. The simple flavors of the charcoaled meat with its shot of tangy marinade combined with the soft bread that holds it make an ideal sandwich that needs no condiments or companions. There are nonetheless French fries and onion rings for side dishes, as well as good, creamy slaw.

Sharkey's menu goes beyond spiedies, although we have never been much interested in trying anything else: there are chilled shrimp, steamed clams, Buffalo chicken wings, and kielbasa. The place has a supremely comfortable neighborhood feel about it; we've never eaten here when there weren't at least a few locals gathered around a table shooting the breeze and drinking coffee or mugs of beer from the tap. Last time we stopped by it was a Friday afternoon, and the Sharaks were doing a booming take-out business not only in already-marinated meat, but also in spiedi bread and spiedi skewers for weekend home cooking.

TED'S JUMBO RED HOTS
2312 SHERIDAN DR., TONAWANDA (BUFFALO), NY (716) 836-8986

Y ou cannot drive far in western New York without noticing that this is serious hot dog country. Not to slight the great wienies of Chicago or Detroit, or of New York City's street-corner peddlers and kosher delis, but the fact is that upstate New York is truly fanatical about frankfurters, from the pale "white-hots" of Rochester to the charcoal-grilled red-hots of Buffalo, the best of which are dealt out by Ted's of Tonawanda.

What makes these dogs great is less their ingredients and more the way they are cooked: over hot coals that infuse each link with pungent smoke flavor and burnish its taut skin with a seared crust. As they cook, the chef pokes them with a fork, slaps them, squeezes them, and otherwise abuses them, thus puncturing the skin and allowing the dog to suck in maximum smoke flavor.

As the dogs cook, you must make some decisions. In consultation with a person behind the counter known among aficionados as "the dresser," you decide how you want to garnish your tube steak. The condiment of choice is Ted's hot sauce, a peppery-hot concoction laced with bits of relish. You also want onion rings, sold in tangled webs of crisp fried batter and limp, slithery onion by the basket. To accompany a foot-long and a basket of O-rings, the beverage of choice in these parts is loganberry juice, which is like an exotic Kool-Aid.

THE TEXAS TACO
ROUTE 22, PATTERSON, NY (914) 878-9665

W e enjoy the grub at The Texas Taco very much, but the astonishing flavor of this place has less to do with hot tacos, soft burritos, and spicy chili dogs than it does with spray paint and eye-shadow. Are you confused? Good, because confusion is the proper state of mind for appreciating this off-the-wall hole-in-the-wall by the side of the road.

Exterior: A line of rusted tricycles circles around a tall sign on top of which a carousel horse rears skyward. The parking lot on the side of the low building, where the asphalt has been ornamented with freaky-colored swirls, holds two broken-down, festively painted Cadillac limousines. Behind the lot, a statue of Paul Bunyan, missing one arm and both feet, lies on its back staring up at the sky. Around front, the entryway is flanked by topiary shrubbery cut to resemble large lima beans.

In nice weather it is possible to eat outside, but the real fun begins when you walk into The Taco. On the left is a dining room with four tables, each covered with glass under which are accumulated piles of business cards and tattered leopardskin tablecloths. The chairs at these tables are made of iron, and are as rickety as a chair can be and still remain upright. The tiny place is crammed with junk: mannequins in thrift-shop attire, old magazines, flea-market curios, deflated balloons dangling from chandeliers, and walls plastered with sheaves of pictures of celebrities and friends of the management. Fragments of wall visible underneath the ephemera are smeared with metallic and nonmetallic ribbons of paint. On the other side of the building to the right is where you place your order, adjacent to a little pushcart (like on the street) from which proprietor Rosemary Jamison, whose magenta eye makeup beats anything ever worn by the late film actor Divine, prepares your meal. "I always wanted to be in the spotlight," she told one reporter, who noted, "Half of her head is shaved, the other half worn a style reminiscent of Veronica Lake." (The hair had grown in the last time we ate at The Taco.)

Miss Jamison's menu is short and to the point, with nearly everything she serves based on the chili she brews. It is tasty stuff—lumps of ground meat in a viscous red emulsion with a diplomatic nip (the temperature has waned over the years; now, big bottles of hot sauce are provided to each table). Already-bent, bland tortilla shells are loaded with this chili meat, and with cheese and onions. Soft wheat tortillas are wrapped around the chili with cheese and onions to make burritos. Hot dogs are topped with the chili, cheese, and onions. It is a monomaniacal menu (you can also get chili by the bowl, supplemented by beans, or guacamole), but each of the configurations of chili, cheese, and onions has a different character because of what it is on or in. The burrito is a neat package—good-tasting and so soft it is nearly sticky; but personally we like hot dogs best. They are served in warm, steamed-tender buns, and have just the right pulchritude and a garlic flavor that the other ingredients complement so well. Each item is brought to the table on a wood-grain paper plate.

At one time, Miss Jamison opened a second Texas Taco in Danbury, Connecticut, and had plans to franchise her hot, cheap eats all over America. Apparently, the plan never jelled; and as far as we know The Texas Taco remains unique. Totally unique.

TOTONNO'S
1524 NEPTUNE AVE., CONEY ISLAND, NY (718) 372-8606

A few blocks this side of Nathan's Famous hot dog stand on the board-walk of Coney Island, the honky-tonk end of Brooklyn disintegrates into a bleak landscape that looks like a city that has suffered from pro-longed bombing raids. Buildings have collapsed or have had their windows blocked with tin. Whole blocks have crumbled into piles of brick and refuse. In the midst of the appalling rubble is one short stretch of buildings and business that are still thriving. Here are an auto repair shop, a few weather-beaten but functioning storefronts, and a Caribbean-blue restau-rant without any sign outside. Somehow, this block has managed to survive the urban decay all around it: an oasis of civilization and a legacy of pizza-making craft that have all but disappeared everywhere else.

The restaurant is known as Totonno's and is run by Jerry Peno, whose father, Anthony ("Totonno") Peno, was a pizza-maker at America's original pizzeria, Lombardi's on Spring Street in Manhattan, which opened in 1895. Decor is vintage neighborhood eatery: pressed-tin ceiling, old framed newspapers on the wall, tables, and booths. Behind the counter is where the pizzas are made—in a coal-fired oven that turns out broad pies with terrific crust.

Mr. Peno uses only handmade, hand-sliced, fresh mozzarella on his pies because, he says, hand-slicing keeps the savor in the cheese. The fresh mozzarella gives the topping on his pizzas a lush, sweet flavor that makes ordinary pies made with shredded cheese taste petrified by compar-ison.

You can get all the usual ingredients on a Totonno's pie. The variety we like best is pizza bianca—pure cheesy white except for garlic (freshly chopped) and oregano sprinkled on top. Pizza with tomato sauce is good, and the anchovies are fine, but forget the watery sausage. Whatever kind of pizza you get, come and get it early. Totonno's opens at 4:00 P.M.—only on Friday, Saturday, and Sunday—and when that day's freshly risen dough runs out (usually between 7:00 P.M. and 8:00 P.M.), the kitchen closes.

ZAB'S BACKYARD HOTS
365 PARK AVE., ROCHESTER, NY (716) 473-4510

W e saved the paper placemat from our first visit to Zab's because it was so educational. "Whenever a meat is low in fat," the mat advises, "we have a tendency to add fat to it before it is consumed. For instance: we add gravy to lean white turkey meat and mix tuna with mayonnaise to make tuna salad. But the Zab's Premium Red Hot Dog needs only to be eaten!" Next to these encouraging words is a chart showing how much fat there is in a serving of some popular foods including sirloin steak, macaroni and cheese, chicken pot pie, potato chips, chili, and Zab's hot dogs. Amazingly, Zab's dogs are the leanest thing on the list!

You'd never know you were eating health food when you sink your teeth into a porky red hot dog and the taut skin splits and lush, spicy juices flood out. White-hots, which are a wee bit fatter, actually taste leaner. They are packed with a mildly spiced mélange of veal, ham, and beef, and because they are cooked over coals (the preferred way of cooking in all good upstate wienie parlors), they absorb a sizzly charcoal taste. Both red and white dogs are available normal-size or jumbo. The menu also includes Italian sausage, hamburgers, and chicken; but red- and white-hots are best. To complete these fine charcoaled franks, Zab's dishes out a powerful hot sauce—with all the punch of incendiary taco sauce but with a fetching tang well suited to dress an upstate tube steak.

NORTH CAROLINA

ALLEN & SON BAR-B-QUE
ROUTE 54 JUST SOUTH OF I-85, GRAHAM, NC (919) 578-5270 (ALLEN'S HAS TWO OTHER LOCATIONS: IN PITTSBORO AND CHAPEL HILL)

Feast on heaps of pork at Allen & Son. It is hacked into shreds, limp and tender with crusty, charred tips and edges, imbued with the tangy perfume of wood smoke from the pit, served unadorned by sauce. Here is authoritative North Carolina style Q, different than slow-smoked pig meat just about everywhere else in America.

Should you wish to spice up this elegant-tasting but casually served meal, there is a catsup bottle on the table. It does not contain catsup. It contains thin, powerful, vinegar-based hot sauce loaded with spice and cracked pepper. Just a sprinkle is all you will want to make this pork sing. In fact, you may not want any sauce at all. The meat is that good.

We recommend getting Allen's meat on a plate (rather than a sandwich), which includes a pile of sparkling cole slaw and about a half-dozen crisp-skinned hushpuppies. The hushpups are arranged like a sculptor's work, *on top* of the pork. It is a field of spheres atop a heap of meat: a lovely, aromatic, and absolutely mouth-watering sight.

If you get the combination plate known to some locals as "stew and que" (highly recommended), the pile of good smoked meat is supplemented

329

by a bowl of Brunswick stew, another traditional companion to smoked pork in these parts. Unlike the meatier Brunswick stews of southern Virginia, this luscious stuff is mostly vegetables with a few shreds of meat, all cosseted in a tomato-rich sauce. It is a hearty, rib-sticking food that makes a wonderful contrast to the exquisite pork.

Dessert isn't usually a big deal after barbecue for the simple reason that most good barbecue meals are completely and thoroughly satisfying. At Allen's, cobbler is a specialty. In fact, Allen & Son is so proud of it, they display a panful right near the entryway under a heat lamp, and it is nearly as arresting as the restaurant's collection of taxidermy, which includes the entire front third of a deer, appearing to bust through the back wall, as well as a whole small fox standing atop the wood-burning stove. Allen's cobbler *is* gorgeous: golden crusted, glistening sweet. The menu says it is apple, but it was peach the day we dined at Allen's #3 in Graham, just off I-85, and it was delectable, even sweeter than the pre-sweetened iced tea that is the beverage of choice with so many casual southern meals.

BIG NELL'S PIT STOP
HIGHWAY 179 BETWEEN OCEAN ISLE BEACH AND SUNSET BEACH, NC
(919) 579-6461

"Thank you for stopping at Big Nell's Pit Stop," says the menu. "We hope you will enjoy the food, fellowship, and B-S." On your way to or from Myrtle Beach, this all-purpose roadside eatery will provide you with plenty of all three any day until mid-afternoon; but it was the food most of all that inspired our Connecticut friend Mary Ellen Peterson to recommend it. She called the barbecue "elegant," which seemed to be a pretty high-flown word considering Big Nell's "casual" ambience (house logo: a pig) and informal menu (the one-item wine list consists of "By the Glass: $1.50"). But *elegant* is a good word to describe this Q. It is essence of sweet, smoky pig, sliced or chopped (the latter is better—more succulent), just barely touched with tangy sauce for accent. It isn't especially hot or complex or dazzling. It is food of the "less is more" philosophy: an opportunity to savor the pure flavor of the meat. Big Nell's dishes it out by the sandwich (with slaw), tray (with slaw and hushpuppies), or plate (with slaw, hushpuppies, and French fries), as well as by the pound (with hushpuppies by the dozen).

The barbecue is swell, but Nell's aims to please everyone, so the kitchen turns out lots more. Brunswick stew, for example, despite its cutesy description on the menu ("Roadside Kill") is actually a fine version of barbecue's traditional companion stew, thick with vegetables and shreds of meat. It is served by the bowl (a meal) or cup (side dish). There are sandwiches of all kinds; fried seafood aplenty as well as deviled crabs and local spot in season, corn dogs, hamburgers, and something listed as "garbage soup."

We haven't tasted much in the way of lunch beyond Big Nell's fine barbecue and Brunswick Stew, but we have had breakfast, and recommend it highly. Big Nell's is a breakfast kind of place. Eggs are available any style ("We do know how to poach an egg," the menu boasts) and are served with sausage, city ham or country ham, grits or hash-brown potatoes, toast or knobby-surfaced "cat head" biscuits. If you want to skip eggs altogether, the kitchen offers breakfast sandwiches of ham, bacon, sausage, pork tenderloin, scrapple, or even barbecue on bread or biscuits.

Among the locals who dine at Big Nell's, Fred likes the bacon biscuit; Steve prefers city ham with grits; Robert gets Egg Beaters; Paul chooses eggs, over light with sliced tomatoes, grits, and link sausage. How do we know what they eat? Their names, along with their favorite meals, are listed on the menu of Big Nell's Pit Stop, under a headline proclaiming, "WE ARE VERY PROUD OF OUR CUSTOMERS!!!"

BLUE MIST BARBECUE
HIGHWAY 64 EAST OF ASHEBORO, NC (919) 625-3980

The Blue Mist doesn't look like much of a find as you approach it from the highway—a modern, sanitary edifice with blue booths inside and none of the funky character one expects from a memorable pit; but it smells great. Long before you pass through the front door, you will get a noseful of why this place is on the map of major American eats: hickory smoke used to slow-cook pork until it attains maximum succulence.

Order a tray. The meat comes heaped in a pile with only a faint infusion of tangy, barely sweet, judiciously peppered, pale tomato sauce—just enough to moisten it. The meat is wondrous: flakes and shreds and fibers and little chunks of nut-sweet porky tenderness, gently glowing with the whisper of smoke, along with chewy bits of crust and a few crackle-crisp edges where the slow-burning wood has charred it. This is food that invites long, philosophic contemplation as you savor its variety and complex character.

As a breather from your pensive pork appreciation, have a chaw of a hushpuppy. They are nice knobby companions to the meat, but like the cole slaw that also comes with a tray of barbecue, strictly second fiddle. It's the Blue Mist meat that sings.

LEXINGTON BARBECUE #1
HIGHWAY 29-70 SOUTH, LEXINGTON, NC (704) 249-9814

P ork shoulder, cooked over burning hickory logs for ten full hours, is shredded into piquant fibers that vary from moist, melting soft to burned crisp. It is as fine as hash, with a peppery piquancy that is a consummate blend of smoke and spice. The hacked meat is sold in a sandwich, on a bun with finely chopped slaw and a mild, vinegar-thin red sauce, or as part of a platter, on which it occupies half a small yellow cardboard boat, with slaw in the other half. As part of the platter with the meat and slaw, you get terrific, crunch-crusted hushpuppies.

"Monk's Place," as locals know it (in deference to owner Wayne "Honey" Monk), is an undistinguished building with booths and tables inside and drive-in service for eating in your car. It is easy to spot by the sign outside proclaiming it to be the "National Outlet" of Monk's dynamite sweet-hot sauce, marketed as Smokehouse brand.

By the way, in 1983 the North Carolina General Assembly designated Lexington as the "Hickory-Cooked Barbecue Capital of Piedmont, North Carolina"; and that same year the White House asked Mr. Monk to cook barbecue for President Reagan and other heads of state at the Williamsburg International Economic Summit.

MCDONALD'S
I-85 & BEATTIES FORD RD., CHARLOTTE, NC (704) 393-8823

M cDonald's is a soul-food cafeteria in a modern shopping center. It is a place to feast, but we have a hard time recommending exactly what to eat because everything we sampled was so delicious. We mean everything, even the simplest side dishes like carrots. They appear to be plain, boiled carrots, but they are transcendent: enriched probably by margarine, possibly by sugar, too. Not that they are unctuous or sweet-tasting; they are simply the best-tasting carrots you could possibly imagine. Macaroni and cheese is like that, too: cheesier and richer and more flavorful than such a plebeian dish has any right to be. And the au gratin potatoes, also rich with cheese and cream, are just tender enough to bend rather than break when hefted with a fork, but still have enough stout spuddy body to give you that satisfying feeling you get only from biting into a piece of properly cooked potato.

And there are turnip greens lolling in pungent pot likker, and lush squash casserole, and an unbelievably complex chicken stuffing that goes with just about any of the half dozen or more main courses available in line. The stuffing is loaded with unidentifiable rainbows of spices, rice, and big chunky giblets. It is stupendously lush, a meal unto itself.

To accompany these stellar vegetables, you probably want a main course, although it is not necessary. Many customers exit the food line with nothing but a tray full of vegetables. Don't do that, because McDonald's meat loaf is some of the best you will eat anywhere: moist, rich, veined with spices that reminded us of Indian and Oriental delicacies as much as the stalwart American kitchen classic. The loaf is served under a blanket of rich brown gravy dotted with peas. The other great main course we sampled was fried chicken: crusty golden brown, without batter but with a wicked crunch. The breast was served hacked in half by the server for easy picking at the steamy white meat below the crust with hand or fork.

McDonald's bread selection includes pull-apart dinner rolls with three big domes on their top, and squares of cornbread: both are excellent for mopping up gravies and drippings. And desserts are a fitting climax. We swooned over banana pudding, chunky with vanilla wafers, and bread pudding as rich as mince pie filled with raisins and nuts, each serving dolloped with a big spoonful of sweet lemon sauce.

Service at McDonald's is old-fashioned cafeteria-style, meaning you do not help yourself. As you proceed through the line, admiring pans and trays of food the kitchen has made, you discuss your wants and selections with a team of serving ladies behind the food. Tell them what you want and they dish it out, always with a generous hand.

MELTON'S BARBECUE
631 RIDGE ST., ROCKY MOUNT, NC (919) 446-8513

Colonel Bob Melton is to North Carolina barbecue what Escoffier is to chaud-froid: Zeus, from whom all else has descended. Known for years as the Barbecue King of the South, he is now with Monsieur Escoffier in the culinary firmament, but his legacy lives on in this quintessential Tarheel barbecue parlor on a tree-shaded street in Rocky Mount.

The barbecue Melton's serves is unlike barbecue in Tennessee or

Georgia, and extremely unlike the food that goes by the same name in Texas. First off, it is pork—simple, elegant, and ambrosial, served without getting clobbered by the taste of sauce. Second, it is not sliced; it is hacked to smithereens. A Melton's "pig pickin'" begins with a palate-teaser of tart mustard slaw, then moves directly to heaps of barbecued meat that is amazing for its textural variety: moist, motley shreds, velvet-soft chunks, and succulent "outside" nuggets crusted with basting juice. The pork arrives with hushpuppies, Brunswick stew, and potatoes, but it is utterly unsauced—all the better to savor its luscious, porcine subtleties. Those who want to gild it are free to concoct their own sauce from an assortment of Tabasco, pickled peppers, vinegar, and hot condiments set at every place.

Despite a picturesque view of the Tar River below, the ambience at Melton's is austere, suitable more for focused contemplation of food on the plate than idle sightseeing out the window. Everything is weathered wood—walls, floor and ceiling, tables and chairs. The oak-topped communal tables are lined up in perfect rows, every one set with identical sets of extra hot sauce, peppers, and vinegar. Chairs are uniformly spaced, as serious as prie-dieux.

During one crowded dinner we sensed a hush fall over Melton's dining room. Conversation simply wasted away as everyone chowed down with gusto and the Carolinians around us seemed suddenly to be overwhelmed with an emotional fervor akin to patriotism as they ate their barbecue and continued the hallowed tradition begun so many years ago by Colonel Bob.

PARKER'S BARBECUE
U.S. 301, WILSON, NC (919) 237-0972

At Parker's in Wilson, not far from Interstate 95 (and in the heart of America's largest antique-furniture marts), throngs of customers pack the capacious dining rooms for feasts of chopped and minced pork with a luscious, tender texture and a sharp vinegar tang. There is no sauce at all poured onto it; and the meat has none of the smoky pungency of that which gets slow-cooked over smoldering oak or hickory for hours. Instead, it is subtle-flavored, its chunks and shreds so pale and delicate that your tongue can savor the true flavors of the butter-tender pork. The vinegar sauce used to accent it is not at all like the catsupy red stuff used on other kinds of barbecue. It is a subtle dressing designed to add merely a tangy halo of spice to the pork-focused taste experience.

The chopped meat is heaped on a plate along with boiled potatoes, corn sticks, slaw, and iced tea: a true Tarheel banquet, sold by the plate or family-style to groups who want seconds and thirds. We will warn you that Parker's-style barbecue is not for everyone, especially not for those who actually like the sweet, red sauce more than they like the meat itself. In this part of North Carolina, the pork's the thing.

SKYLIGHT INN (JONES' BARBECUE)
SOUTH LEE ST., AYDEN, NC (919) 746-4113

"The best I ever tasted," proclaimed eater extraordinaire Alan Richman after polishing off a Skylight Inn sandwich while on a cross-country smoke pit pilgrimage. It is aristocratic food, coarsely served—pork shredded with a heavy cleaver into vittles of nearly infinite variety, including pillowy pale little fibers and brittle shreds from the outside of the pit-cooked meat, all tossed together and accurately dressed with just enough hot sauce to make its natural sweetness blossom. Compared to the heavily sauced and sweetened barbecue popular in most other parts of the country, this style of Q, unique to eastern North Carolina, is almost ascetic in nature. It encourages connoisseurship, so much so that if you get a tray (as opposed to a sandwich), you will likely want to use a fork rather than fingers to eat it.

Barbecue is all that's served at the Skylight Inn. Get it on a bun, or in one of three sizes of cardboard tray with cornbread and a mound of cole slaw, or by the pound. Have a Coke to go with it, then quit at the peak of perfection. Alan Richman made the mistake of trying to top off his magic meal with pastry selected from the Skylight Inn's dessert rack: a moon pie that he said "tasted as though it had been around since 1830."

Although there was no sign outside that we could see, the Skylight Inn (which all the employees know as Jones' Barbecue, after the pitmaster) is easy to find. Look for the place with the white dome on top.

STAYMEY'S
2206 HIGH POINT RD., GREENSBORO, NC (919) 299-9888

Staymey's is a big modern restaurant on the outside of town, built in a barnboard-rustic style. It looks brand-new, and the building is; but the food served in this place comes from venerable recipes that go back to

1930, when Charles Staymey started smoking pigs under a tent in the town of Shelby. In 1953 he moved to Greensboro, and Staymey's is still run by his family. The history is depicted on the wall of the vestibule as you enter the spanking-new dining room, in pictures that show a simple wood-frame shack in a rustic part of town, surrounded by a haze of the same smoke that perfumes the air around Staymey's today. Alongside the historical images is an oil portrait of Mr. Staymey himself.

No longer are the hogs cooked in an open pit dug in the earth. Behind the part of Staymey's where you eat, there is a modern pit that could only rightfully be called a factory. It is a building as big as the restaurant with three or four separate pits that look like huge coal-burning furnaces from a steel mill. For blocks around in Greensboro, the air smells of burning wood and sizzling pork.

At the entrance of the great pit sits a man in a chair. He is the pit-master. And although he looks like he is just loafing and occasionally spitting tobacco out onto the lawn, he is in fact performing the ritualistic mysteries that make barbecued pork such a hallowed special meal in North Carolina.

We came to dine at Staymey's at ten o'clock one Friday morning. Four waitresses were sitting at the counter eating barbecued chicken. One named Whitey came to our booth and apologized for taking longer than sixty seconds to attend to us. "We're getting our strength for the day," she explained. "We need it; it's Friday, and we'll be flying low all day." Like all the waitresses, Whitey wore a white uniform and speedy white shoes. Our barbecue arrived within three minutes of her taking our order.

Staymey's menu is absolutely minimal, all business. There are no unnecessary adjectives, no mouth-watering descriptions or cute pictures of dancing pigs. It lists the basics: pork, large or small, chopped or sliced, baked beans or hushpuppies. Nor is there any folderol in the presentation. The food comes on partitioned paper plates, which tend to disintegrate underneath the moist food unless you eat fast.

The food is superb. Interesting hushpuppies: they aren't the usual round shape; instead, they are tubular squiggles. The beans were lush and hammy; and the cole slaw was HOT! Mixed into the basic sugar and vine-gar dressing was a dose of Staymey's barbecue sauce, giving it a zing that made it a fascinating companion flavor to the mild sliced pork.

The pork itself had two natures, depending on whether it was ordered chopped or sliced. Chopped, the pulverized meat seemed complex and zesty, especially if sprinkled with some of the peppery barbecue sauce on the table. Sliced, it was tender and mild: big, thick pieces of gentle-flavored pig meat, really quite an elegant food.

To be honest, we were too happy wallowing in the afterglow of good Carolina pig meat to bother with dessert. There were three choices: cobbler, ice cream, or ice cream and cobbler together.

NORTH DAKOTA

FARMERS INN
MAIN ST., HAVANA, ND (701) 724-3849

We cannot suggest what you ought to order if you come to eat breakfast or lunch at the Farmers Inn; in fact, we cannot promise that it
will taste good. We can assure you that what you eat will be genuine western farm-wife cooking.

Operated by the Havana Community Club and staffed by a rotating
group of local women, the Farmers Inn has a menu that depends entirely
on who's cooking that day. We hear breakfast is usually pretty much the
same—eggs, toast, bacon or sausage patties, and pancakes—unless the
chef *du jour* happens to be a whiz-bang biscuit maker or specializes in cinnamon rolls. Lunch, which is called "dinner" in this part of the country,
can range from roast turkey with all the fixings to pigs in blankets with
Tater Tots on the side.

Our single experience was dinner, in the late spring, and whoever had
drawn kitchen duty that day made hamburger steaks and pepper steaks;
and we were also told that we could have chicken strips if we wanted. The
meat was fine, but what we remember best was the soup—real comfort
food, made by a person who, if not a pro, was certainly an expert. There is
always a soup on the menu; it was chicken, loaded with shreds of meat and

silky, handmade dumplings. We were told that other frequently made soups include corn chowder, hamburger soup made with V-8 juice, vegetable-beef soup, and goulash.

The after-dinner sweet of the day was what one of the ladies called "rhubarb dessert," a sort of cobbler served in a dish with syrupy sweet shreds of rhubarb and a nice flaky pastry. We were told by a gentleman who shared our table that the rhubarb was some of the season's first, just picked by one of his friends from a backyard garden.

SMOKY'S
U.S. 81, ARDOCH, ND (701) 248-3634

"Only a Dakota wheat farmer with a harvest-size appetite dares dig into a 'French-baked' spud and a 52-ouncer at the same sitting," *Midwest Living* proclaimed in its mouth-watering roundup of the heartland's great steak houses back in 1988. The spud and the 52-ounce steak are the specialties of Smoky's, a vintage restaurant and tavern in grain-elevator country north of Grand Forks. We didn't even try to eat one of the big steaks, thus forsaking our legitimate claim to the T-shirt that says "I ate a 52-ounce steak at Smoky's," as well as the one that says "I almost ate a 52-ounce steak at Smoky's." We wimped out and ate steaks that were only a pound and a half each, and they were terrific: juicy, tender enough to slice easily but with enough resistance to provide a satisfying chew, heavy with juice inside their crusty, glistening surface.

As for the "French-baked" potato, that is a big one that is baked, then peeled and fried whole in deep fat until it turns golden brown and develops a new, crisp skin that is a wickedly savory blend of seasoned oil and potato pulp. It's the kind of delirious dish that seems insane when we are back home among right-thinking, nutrition-minded pals. But in Ardoch, alongside our steaks, it tasted great and we each ate one up without a second thought. (American fries, hash browns, and French fries are also available.)

At the end of the meal, when our waitress suggested chocolate cheese-cake, strawberry shortcake, or a slab of cream pie for dessert, we couldn't in good conscience order even one of them for a taste. So we cannot tell you about desserts. But we can say with assurance that even if your appetite isn't wheat-farmer-at-harvest size, Smoky's is a tremendous place to plow into the kind of monumental meat-and-potatoes meal rarely found in restaurants on either coast.

OHIO

BALATON
12523 BUCKEYE ROAD, CLEVELAND, OH (216) 921-9691

The Balaton, with its easy-wipe paneling and plain paper placemats, is a diamond in the rough that all hungry visitors to Cleveland ought to know about. The specialty of the house is Hungarian cooking. Like the best of the melting pot Midwest's neighborhood restaurants, the meal is all the more fun because the place is so real.

It is a friendly neighborhood cafe with brisk, uniformed waitresses and a menu of honest blue-plate food. Local workers sit side by side with culinary connoisseurs eating lunch of chicken paprikash, served "disjointed," with nockerli—squiggly little dumplings—in a cream gravy faintly pink with paprika. Or goulash, made with chunks of tender pork. Or stuffed cabbage—a spiced mélange of beef, pork, and rice, wrapped inside a tender sheaf of steamed translucent leaves, accompanied by sauerkraut.

Dessert is the Hungarian cook's tour de force. Look, for example, at the dobos torte, a multi-tiered extravaganza known as "the queen of pastries"—eight layers of moist sponge cake separated by seven velvety ribbons of cream filling, haloed by a thin sheen of slick chocolate glaze. There are strudels and chestnut cakes, mocha rolls and palacinke, a pancake stuffed with apricots and poppy seeds. On the side, to put a point on this fine meal, have a cup of powerhouse espresso coffee, served in an elegant gold-rimmed glass.

BUN'S
10 W. WINTER ST., DELAWARE, OH (614) 363-3731

B un's has been baking cakes, rolls, and breads since it opened on Winter Street in 1863. Now run by a fifth generation of the Hoffman family, who founded it upon arriving from Germany, it long ago expanded its operations beyond the bakery to become a restaurant specializing in such vittles as roast pork and real lumpy mashed potatoes, turkey with dressing made from bakery bread, and ham in every shape, form, and size you can think of, including superb ham loaf, ham salad, and something known as a "bunwich" ("Bun" was the nickname of founder George Hoffman's son), which is ham and cheese grilled on whole wheat.

On a recent trip through Delaware, we stopped at Bun's for lunch. The daily-printed menu listed plenty of the usual cafe hot plates and sandwiches as well as some frightfully healthy-sounding dishes including sesame chicken strips and an all-vegetable plate. The soups of the day were black bean and cheddar. With a couple of slabs of Bun's freshly baked and freshly toasted white bread, the cheddar soup was a simple and satisfying meal, although not nearly as satisfying as our other meal of crusty, dark-sauced spare ribs, accompanied by aromatic rye rolls and a pile of scalloped corn.

You can have Jell-O for dessert, but the only proper way to end a Bun's meal is with a dessert from the bakery case up front. In particular you want fudge cake. The cake is a nearly black brick of fudgy moistness—nostalgically old-fashioned chocolate fun that is excellent all alone with a cup of coffee, even better à la mode.

Bun's serves lunch and dinner, but if you happen by in the morning, it is possible you can join the townsfolk who come here for a kind of informal coffee-klatch breakfast: help yourself to coffee, choose a Danish pull-apart, pecan loaf, or butterscotch twist from the bakery case, and carry your own freshly baked breakfast to a table. Bun's is easy to find once you are on Winter Street. Look for the cafe sign dangling high over the pavement, pointing the way to the second-oldest family-owned business in Delaware, Ohio.

CAMP WASHINGTON CHILI, INC.
COLERAIN & HOPPLE, CINCINNATI, OH (513) 541-0061

You could start another Civil War debating which state has the best chili in America. New Mexico? It serves the hottest. Texas? Chili con carne was invented in the Lone Star State about a hundred years ago, and sold all over San Antonio by street corner cooks known as "chili queens." We've eaten mighty fine "chili mac" and Green Bay–style chili on the western shore of Lake Michigan. But if you are looking for the chili capital of America, Cincinnati is it.

Cincinnati is a city in love with chili. It is easier to find a good plate of chili here than a hamburger. There are approximately 100 chili parlors in town, each of them dishing out their own version of the unique regional specialty called "five-way." What a melting pot extravaganza! It is finely ground, nearly pulverized beef spiked with cinnamon served on top of spaghetti noodles, layered with kidney beans, raw onions, and Wisconsin cheddar cheese. Only in America!

Cincinnati's chili passion goes back to 1920, when Athanas Kiradjieff arrived in New York City from Greece and got a job in a storefront eatery selling those relatively new German-accented sausages that people were starting to call "hot dogs." He moved to Cincinnati and opened a stand called The Empress, specializing in wieners that were named "Coney Islands" in deference to their New York origins. Using an array of Balkan seasonings that included cinnamon and allspice, he soon perfected a special chili sauce to ladle on the "Coneys."

But chili dogs weren't enough for this gastronomic Zeus. Taking a cue from traditional Greek pastitsio, he decided to eliminate the hot dog altogether and mix his sauce with noodles. A customer—we guess an Italian customer—suggested he use spaghetti noodles as a base for the chili mixture. Nobody knows how or why Mr. Kiradjieff was inspired to add the beans, the onions, and the cheese.

Now Cincinnatians will have their chili no other way. They're hooked. Serious chiliheads can tell you the exact hour of the day when their favorite brew is at its peak; and they will endlessly debate whether Skyline chili is spicier than what's served at The Empress, or if Park Chili is more atomic than Blue Ash brand. We like Skyline and Empress (both big chains) and Park Chili and Blue Ash, but if you want to share a plate of Cincinnati's premier five-way with us, come to the counter of Camp Washington Chili, which we say serves the very best.

Camp Washington's chili is meaty, dark red, and seductively aromatic, made in sixty-gallon batches every day from freshly ground lean bull meat using a recipe known only to proprietor John Johnson and his wife, who blend the spices once every two weeks from a formula they keep locked inside a vault. It is served piled high on beds of thick spaghetti noodles on plates in the traditional deluxe five-way configuration; or you can get it three-way or four-way, without the beans or onions (known to connoisseurs as a "haywagon" because of the fluffy grated yellow cheese that dominates the mise-en-plate). Five-way is the way to go, as far as we are concerned: it is an astounding combination of exotic spices, textures, and aromas, as fun to eat as it is delicious. It is nothing like all-meat cowboy chili, which seems nearly Bauhaus-spare by comparison; but once you've savored a few plates of this wacky Cincinnati stuff, you'll wonder how you ever lived without it.

Camp Washington is a chili lover's mecca: Formica tables and booths, a well-worn counter, baseball trophies displayed up behind the open kitchen area, all lit by fluorescent lights that make human complexions look ghastly but lend a magic, glistening aura to the chili on plates and smothering the Coney Island chili dogs. Camp Washington has been open twenty-four hours a day, every day but Sundays, since 1940.

CHILI TIME
4720 VINE, ST. BERNARD, OH (513) 641-1130

A luncheonette with a counter and Naugahyde booths, Chili Time serves fine chili—the familiar local configuration on top of noodles with an especially meaty (albeit quite mild) sauce and firm, big beans; but we like it for its Coneys and double-decker sandwiches. The Coneys—small hot dogs—are not intrinsically different from other Cincinnati chili parlor dogs; but they are beautifully dressed. Order a chili-cheese Coney and you are served a fluffy mound of grated cheese that nearly covers the bun below. Buried underneath the bright orange mow are the hot dog and a spill of chunky chili sauce. Double-deckers, a specialty of many local chili parlors, are also impressive. Nearly all are made with ham and something else (beef, cheese, tomato). We ordered one listed on the menu as "ham and ham" and received a sandwich that was truly about a half-foot tall—three layers of bread (cottony soft white stuff) and approximately a pound of shaved ham.

Chili Time is a city neighborhood kind of place filled with eager eaters and staffed by take-no-prisoners waitresses ("Your tips are part of the employees' salary," the menu instructs). There is another branch on Reading Road that serves the same food, but is a wee bit more upscale in ambience. They have a shingle roof over the kitchen order window; and instead of pictures of baseball players, they display an autographed photo of actor Foster Brooks.

HENRY'S SOHIO
6275 U.S. 40, WEST JEFFERSON, OH (614) 879-9819

The gas pumps outside Henry's Sohio aren't working any more. There isn't much activity in the garage bays, either. The EAT sign by the side of U.S. 40 has turned to monotone rust, and the big blue clock above the doorway is stuck at 3. In fact, the door that leads into the cafe is permanently shut.

Don't let any of that stop you. Despite its forlorn appearance and its location on a stretch of highway that the Interstate (70) has made obsolete, Henry's Sohio is a bonanza for adventurous eaters in search of blue-ribbon *Roadfood*.

We mean that literally. When you enter the dining room (via the garage), you can see the blue ribbons pinned up on the wood-paneled walls, and strung in rows along the pie case on the counter. They aren't all blue: a few reds and yellows hang among the first prizes. Madge Knox, who bakes the pies at Henry's Sohio, sometimes takes the red, the white, *and* the blue ribbons when she enters baking contests in county fairs.

It isn't likely you will spend much time admiring the ribbons, because behind the colorful silk festoonery in that counter pie case are an array of the most lovely slices of pie a hungry traveler could ever hope to find. They are what's really beautiful . . . in a homespun sort of way. Deep dark blue and blackberry fillings, vivid red strawberries, dusty rose rhubarb, tan and tawny apple chunks: all these mouth-watering good things ooze from inside pale crusts that look ready to shatter into tender flakes as soon as you poke them with a fork.

Madge makes a dozen and a half such pies every day. Most are fruit-filled, although a few creams (chocolate, butterscotch, etc.) are available, too. She has been baking pies—and winning ribbons—for nearly twenty years. Although she doesn't remember exactly how she learned to do it, she recollects that the original recipes probably came from a local Mennonite cookbook, and were then adapted and elevated to blue-ribbon status.

It is the pies that inscribe Henry's Sohio on the *Roadfood* map, but you can precede them with some fine blue-plate meals. This is the place to chow down on skinny, griddle-sizzled hamburgers, bean-thick chili, diner-style meat loaf with mashed potatoes, and a rousingly megacaloric meal of ham and white beans served together in a trough, accompanied by a block of yellow cornbread—ploughman's lunch, midwestern-style.

KAUFMAN'S
1628 E. WOOSTER, BOWLING GREEN, OH (419) 354-2535;
DOWNTOWN LOCATION: 163 S. MAIN ST. 352-2595

We had checked into a motel on the strip leading into Bowling Green; and having no other hot leads, found ourselves at Kaufman's for dinner. The original Kaufman's restaurant was (and still is) downtown on Main Street. The new branch, on the strip, is what was once a Howard Johnson's. "The best food in town!" our motel clerk assured us. We were dubious. It looked so ordinary. Before going, we telephoned Kaufman's to investigate, quizzing them to find out if their mashed potatoes are handmade or instant. When they said they peeled and mashed spuds every day, we were on our way.

Inside the ex-HoJo's, what used to be the soda fountain is now a bar. The place is rather disheveled; the help is mostly young people, as in the average nobody-cares franchise . . . so you think. But you are wrong. The lad who brings the crock of cheddar cheese and crackers hors d'oeuvre takes an oath that the mashed potatoes are real. "Nothing we do here is phony," he assures you. And by golly, he is right.

Everything isn't necessarily wonderful. In this relatively *Roadfood*less region, however, we are grateful for apple sauce that is real, chunky, home-made—yes, homemade. And genuine mashed potatoes, even if the gravy is gluey. And real home-baked dinner rolls even if, at the end of a busy weekend, they have the dried consistency of yesterday's.

The pork chops are good: thick, juicy, satisfying. With those real spuds on the side and a heap of buttered corn kernels, this is a nice meal. The eight-ounce hamburger is ordinary and good. The onion rings that one can order with it are splendid—gigantic crunchy hoops of thick, sweet onion encased in brittle crust. Baby back ribs aren't the tender gentle ones you get in serious rib joints; they're bland; the sauce is no-account, without spark. But you can eat them and feel good.

Many surprises here, most of them pleasant: those Buckeye State favorites, sauerkraut balls, are on the menu as an appetizer. Slightly smaller than Ping-Pong balls, they come six to an order with a frilled toothpick stuck in each. They are sizzling hot, straight from the deep-fryer, with a tough golden crust around the moist mélange of kraut and pork inside. On the side you get a little bowl of hot horseradish dip. This is good food, and a real local specialty that has all but vanished in the wake of Ohio's occupation by the fast-food legions.

We enjoyed our meal at Kaufman's out on Bowling Green's motel strip so much we stuck around and had lunch in the downtown dining room the next day. It was gourmet chicken salad and a nice hot turkey sandwich, with those same kind of homemade but not quite fabulous potatoes we had had the night before. These are weird restaurants—not perfect by any means. But they do try hard. And like the man said, it's the best food in town.

MEHLMAN CAFETERIA
U.S. 40, ST. CLAIRSVILLE, OH (614) 695-1000

A quick tip for cafeteria hounds traveling I-70 west of West Virginia. Get off at Exit 220 or 218 and find the Ohio Valley Mall. Just east of it is Mehlman Cafeteria, a gymnasium-size eating establishment with at least three dining rooms, plenty of parking for cars and buses, and an infinite line of steam-table meals.

What's your pleasure? Turkey, ham, pork chops, sausage, chicken, prime rib, Salisbury steak? Baked, mashed, fried, sweet, or au gratin potatoes? Spinach, green beans, macaroni and cheese, rice and gravy, or stuffing? Plain Jell-O (red, orange, green, or yellow), tapioca pudding, three-bean salad, cole slaw, carrot slaw? These are some of the choices we have faced as we pushed loaded trays along the line; and most of what we have chosen has been good. Especially memorable are the ham, the cheesy potatoes that accompanied it, and a couple of fine desserts: walnut cake and pecan pie.

Mehlman is not a place for dainty eaters. It is big and noisy and most of what is served has—what shall we call it?—an institutional flair. That doesn't mean it tastes bad; just that it lacks the kind of personally tended chef's elegance that many connoisseurs of fine food seek. But if you appreciate vittles other than fine-and-fancy, if great, steaming vistas of such fare excite you more than a little doot of foie gras ever could, Mehlman is a rare thrill along the highway.

MILLER'S DINING ROOM
16707 DETROIT AVE., LAKEWOOD, OH (216) 221-5811

M iller's Dining Room has style. But it is not stylish. And we doubt if
its distinctive way of serving dinner will set any trends. It has been
doing things pretty much the same since 1949.

That was when fire destroyed Cleveland's old Central Market, and Mrs.
Ruby Miller, who had worked there in the family butcher shop, joined with
her husband, John, himself the son of a butcher at the West Side Market, to
open a restaurant on Detroit Avenue in Lakewood, just west of the city.
Their motto was "A Place for the Family." Those words are still inscribed
above the entryway to Miller's Dining Room, now run by the Millers'
daughter Doris Urbansky, with her husband, Tom, and their daughter
Carol.

If we had to be marooned on a desert island with only one restaurant,
Miller's Dining Room just might be the choice. We love this place, and
always plot any trip through northern Ohio so that we pass through Cleveland at lunch- or dinnertime.

No matter when we eat at Miller's, the experience reminds us of
Thanksgiving, as Norman Rockwell painted it. It *is* a place for families—
multigenerational groups skip, walk, and wheel their way inside. Wallpaper is muted blue; tables are set with fresh flowers and white linen; decor
is comfy Colonial.

The food is midwestern American. Chicken à la king—made from
cream and chicken and fresh green peppers and mushrooms—is served in
crunchy golden baskets of deep-fried potato shreds. Real roast turkey is
sided by fluffy hills of whipped potatoes, running rivulets of melting butter.
Ham puffs are accented by steaming heaps of spiced scalloped apples.

The only problem is that by the time these hearty entrées arrive, you
may be full. As soon as customers are seated, they are approached by one
of Miller's roll girls, carrying her battered metal tray heaped high with corn
sticks, cloverleaf rolls, and swirling cinnamon buns sticky with
caramelized sugar. Help yourself, and help yourself again the next time she
comes around. These rolls, always hot out of the oven, are nothing less than
sensational; and there are always more.

In addition to the roll girl, Miller's way of doing things includes a salad
girl. She approaches with a tray of only-in-Ohio variety, including carrot
slaw (its mayonnaise is freshly made), Waldorf salad sweetened with miniature marshmallows, Harvard beets, and snapping-fresh bean salad. Many

of the salads on the tray are gelatinized: fruits and nuts and cherries and coconut shreds suspended in jiggly Jell-O rainbows that would have done Busby Berkeley proud if he had been a salad-maker.

After the evening meal, which ought to conclude with dessert of sour cream apple pie topped with freshly whipped cream or crisscross lattice-topped cherry pie, or apple silk cheese pie, each customer is given a finger bowl. There is nothing pretentious about this little ritual. It is sincerely gracious—a civilized way to conclude a truly decent supper.

PUTZ'S CREAMY WHIP
2673 PUTZ'S AVENUE, CINCINNATI, OH (513) 681-8668

You might have a little trouble finding Putz's because the street it's on used to be called Baltimore Avenue (and still is, away from this location), but the girl handing us our shakes and splits explained that because Putz's has been here so long, the city changed the name of the street to match it. (If you are traveling west on I-74, get off at the Montana exit; if you are heading east, get off at Colerain, get back on the highway going east, then get off at Montana.)

As you might deduce from the name, Putz's specialty is soft-serve ice cream; but this is no franchised Carvel stand. It is an original, with 1940s-vintage machines that turn out silk-smooth, truly creamy stuff that sits high and neat atop a cone and has enough body to serve as the base for chocolate sauce, as well as bananas, nuts, and whipped cream. Creamy Whip, which is *not* custard, the management insists, is the *spécialité de la maison,* available only as vanilla or chocolate or a combination thereof, but if you are crazed to eat a hot meal first, these guys will set you up with a foot-long chili dog or a chili cheeseburger that is quite all right. Have a milk shake on the side (chocolate, strawberry, banana, caramel, or cherry) or a malted milk shake. They enrich malts here the old-fashioned way, with a hail of malt powder. Warning: be sure to grab a spoon. Creamy Whip shakes and malts defy straws.

(For this tip, we thank Joyce Miller and Mike Boylan, whose book, *Diving Out* [sic], published by Squish Press, is an indispensable guide to Cincinnati street food.)

RIVERSIDE RESTAURANT
WATER ST., STOCKPORT, OH (614) 559-2210

The Riverside Restaurant really is only eight feet from the bank of the Muskingum River, on Water Street at the foot of Main in the antique town of Stockport. Every seat in the house has a water view; the scene changes daily: boats under way, birds skimming through the air, solid ice in the coldest months of winter. "Like escaping from the world for a while," is the way it was described to us by Frances Brandum, who bought the building with her daughter Susan Moody at a sheriff's sale in 1980.

They gutted it down to its hickory beams and designed a restaurant to resemble a riverboat dining room of the mid-nineteenth century, which is when the building was constructed. It was originally a warehouse for goods traveling the waterways. "More turkeys and hogs were shipped east through here than from any place in the country," Frances told us.

When the railroad was built in the 1890s, river traffic slowed. The warehouse became a general store, then a feed mill. Since Frances and Susan turned it into a restaurant, it has gained a reputation far and wide as one of the prime *Roadfood* stops in southeastern Ohio. The guest book lists names from across the country and the world, including signatures of one couple who stopped in while traveling from New York to Denver on lightweight bicycles.

Many regular customers like to visit Stockport on Sunday, when Frances and Susan serve meals family-style, which means baked chicken and biscuits, four-star mashed potatoes and gravy, and all the fixin's served in big bowls. Other house specialties include royal roast beef served with mashed potatoes, barbecued ribs and pork chops, New England–style boiled dinner, dinner rolls and breads baked from old family recipes, and elderberry pie made the way Frances's Pennsylvania Dutch Great-aunt Ida used to do it.

SKYLINE CHILI
3083 MADISON RD., CINCINNATI, OH (513) 871-2930;
AND ABOUT SIXTY OTHER BRANCHES ALL AROUND THE CITY

We must tell you that *Roadfood* readers from the Cincinnati area have taken us to task for including—horrors!—*chain* five-way chili parlors in earlier editions of this book. When it comes to eating chili in Cincinnati, however, we gladly leave our culinary purism outside of town.

Chain or not, Skyline serves an exquisite brew, even if it is trucked to the sixty-some branches around the city from a central kitchen three times a week. Maybe the trip helps it age to perfection; it certainly doesn't hurt. Skyline's recipe, a closely guarded secret, is a taste of street-food excellence every serious eater ought to know, no matter how common it may be to Cincinnatians. (If you want to eat your five-way in a singular establishment, try Camp Washington Chili, p. 342.)

Cincinnati chili wasn't invented here. That claim is held by a competing chain, Empress, and its genius founder-chef-inventor, Athanas Kiradjieff, who first had the idea to combine spaghetti noodles, quirkily spiced meat, beans, onions, and grated cheese. (Empress chili parlors, also all over town, serve mighty fine chili, too.) Skyline was begun in 1949 by Nicholas Lambrinides. Today connoisseurs debate who makes the best, but take it from us: you won't go wrong sitting down at the Formica counter of any of the Skylines.

Spaghetti on the bottom. Soupy, nutmeggy chili sauce poured on the noodles. Then chopped onions. Then beans and cheese. Subtract beans and you get a "four-way," served in a broad bowl with oyster crackers on the side. The other item on the Skyline menu you ought to know about is a Coney Island: a tiny, four-inch hot dog served in an equally tiny bun and, like the architectonic chili, customarily topped with meat sauce, onions, and cheese, then usually a glob of bright yellow mustard. True aficionados frequently get a pair or trio of Coneys on the side to accompany their five-way.

YOUNG'S JERSEY DAIRY
6880 SPRINGFIELD-XENIA ROAD, YELLOW SPRINGS, OH (513) 325-0629

It was early spring the last time we stopped by Young's Jersey Dairy, and it was a little difficult getting service. Goats had just been born in the adjacent pens and it seemed that a good number of the staff as well as customers were outside kitchy-cooing with the baby Nubians. We didn't mind. Cute animals (and some not-so-cute ones, including some monstrous bulls) are one of the fringe benefits of a visit to this singular restaurant and working farm.

The main reason we like to stop here is the food. Young's is a bakery, with fresh breads available every day. It is a soda fountain, an ice cream store, and a sandwich shop, too. The menu is not exotic. It lists eggs, pancakes, and biscuits and gravy for breakfast; soup, sandwiches, and chili for lunch. But if the kitchen's repertoire is not original, its food sure is good. All the breadstuffs are homemade—white or whole-wheat toast, biscuits, or "English muffin bread." French toast is made from a loaf of sourdough. You can get bacon, egg, and cheese inside a Young's-made croissant. The double cheeseburger on a homemade bun, with bacon, lettuce, and tomato, French fries on the side, is a meal we'd be happy to eat nearly any day.

The best thing about eating at Young's is getting something from the dairy bar, whether it's a simple glass of pure "Jersey milk" or an ultra-thick, eat-it-with-a-spoon "cow shake." Even more luxurious than the cow shake is a "bull shake," which comes with a whole, unblended scoop of ice cream (pick your flavor) floating on top. And for real fanatics, Young's offers a monumental "King Kong sundae," which is a trough loaded with enough ice cream and syrup to feed a family of hungry gorillas.

OKLAHOMA

CLASSEN GRILL
5124 CLASSEN BLVD., OKLAHOMA CITY, OK (405) 842-0428

There is a perfectly satisfying lunch menu at the Classen Grill in the northwest part of Oklahoma City, which experts in such things tell us is the trendy part of town. You can eat hefty hamburgers (Oklahoma City is hamburger heaven) that are charcoal-grilled and served on onion rolls, available with everything from cheese to guacamole, bacon, or mushrooms and sour cream. There is a swell (albeit rather civilized, i.e., not too sloppy) chicken-fried steak and cream gravy served with home-fried potatoes. There are salads and omelettes and sandwiches. All very nice.

But the great meal of the day at the Classen Grill is breakfast. Whatever else you get, get cheese grits. They are mild, just faintly garlicky, pillowy-soft, and sunny yellow. Get them with tenderloin and eggs, pork chops and eggs, or eggs Benedict. Get them on the side of taquitas, which is eggs, sausage, potatoes, and tomatoes rolled up in flour tortillas and topped with green chili sauce and sour cream. The one breakfast with which you may not want to order cheese grits is the one they refer to here as "biscuit debris"—a colossal plate loaded with approximately 80,000 calories worth of biscuits and fried potatoes crowned with melted cheese and smothered with cream gravy loaded with hunks of ham and sausage. That, friends, is OK eating!

JAKE'S RIB
100 PONDEROSA, CHICKASHA, OK (405) 222-2825

The meal you want to see at Jake's Rib is the one listed on the menu as "House Special for ???" It consists of four meats and six side orders for $21.95 (as of summer '91). Sounds like a good deal, right? You have no idea how good a deal it is.

For a little more than two sawbucks, plus maybe a few extra dollars for iced tea or beer, Jake's kitchen sends forth enough vittles to feed an able-bodied foursome. The side dishes alone are a majestic sight: precarious piles of curlicue fried potatoes, at least a foot high; whopping heaps of "Okie-fried" spuds (cheese-encased potato skins); troughs of pinto beans and of sandy-crusted fried okra.

The meats, also served in unsparing portions, are as handsome as meats can be: mighty ribs, crusted with sizzling sauce the color of mahogany; heavy slices of smoke-scented, fall-apart pork; "sloppy Jake" (hacked pork) served like an enchanted potion, thick and glistening in a deep bowl; pepper-hot sausage links with crackling crisp skin and luscious insides. Even the bologna steak is big-time, sliced as thick as sirloin and charred on the grill. Iced tea is served in tumblers, beer in pitchers the size of a goldfish bowl.

We don't love Jake's Rib only because the meals are gigantic. They also happen to be delicious—powerful smoky southwestern good eats.

The meats themselves are excellent, but what puts them over the top is the sauce. It comes to the table before anything else, served warm in a pitcher, either hot or mild. Then you get some white bread: fresh, soft, good ol' American supermarket white bread—the classic and proper companion of barbecue. So you dip the bread in the pitcher of sauce, let it soak real good (but not so good it gets sauce-logged and falls into the pitcher), and slurp it up to your mouth.

The folks responsible for all this good stuff are a couple named Ron and Marianne Eaton. They've made Jake's Rib a notable culinary outpost along I-44. It is a modern ranch house with unclothed tables arranged around a big wood stove, and a large-screen television in the corner of the dining room. Nearly all the customers are locals who take Jake's for granted; but the waitresses were not surprised when we took pictures of the astounding portions of food they set down at our table. Newcomers, they explained, often take snapshots to amaze their friends back home with the wonders they have seen and eaten.

JIGGS SMOKE HOUSE
EXIT 62 OFF I-40, CLINTON, OK (405) 323-5641

We once convinced the folks at Jiggs Smoke House to send us a bunch of their beef jerky via the U.S. Postal Service. The package was too big to fit in our mailbox, so the postman left a note telling us to come to the post office and pick it up. As soon as we swung open the door of the post office, we smelled Jiggs's package. Clerks and customers were smelling it, too, commenting on its powerful, appetizing aroma—the pungent tang of well-cured beef that Jiggs's butcher paper wrapping did nothing to mask.

You may think you don't like beef jerky, but we urge you to withhold your opinion until you have tasted the stuff Jiggs makes. It is nothing at all like the puny strips of awful-tasting, rubber-textured, chemically enhanced meat food product sold in convenience stores. It is a chaw of urgent flavor: beef and smoke packed into great, ungainly flaps of mahogany-red rations that are utterly primitive and, for us, irresistible. Tear off a portion and bite down hard. It'll give your teeth a workout; but as you chew, the flavor blossoms and fills your mouth and satisfies your taste buds the way few foods ever do.

If jerked beef is just too scary, or if you do not share our fondness for it, Jiggs has much else to offer: bacon, hams, hog jowls, pork or beef sausages, an assortment of smoked cheeses, jars of hot chow-chow and tomato relish. All of this is sold in bulk, to take home; but for those who want a bite here, there are enticing chopped barbecue sandwiches served on giant hamburger buns. The shredded meat inside the buns is tender and moist, spiced with nuggets of blackened, crusty meat and tangy tomato-red sauce.

Other than for its fine, smoky vittles, we like Jiggs for its frontier character. It is a sweet-smelling cabin by the side of the access road along what used to be Route 66. On its walls are hundreds of customers' business cards; and whenever we have stopped by, there are always locals sitting at the construction spool table sipping coffee, eating barbecue, and offering gastronomic advice and suggestions to tourists. Last time through, we were engaged by them in a lively discussion of calf testicles versus turkey testicles: which were more tender, and which more flavorful. They suggested we settle the issue for ourselves by buying some of each from Jiggs's freezer and frying them up for dinner. We had to tell them that, alas, we were far from home; and there was no way the frozen gonads would last the trip.

LADY CLASSEN CAFETERIA
6903 N. MAY AVE., OKLAHOMA CITY, OK (405) 843-6459

L ady Classen is one of America's refined cafeterias. Located in a shopping center, it is decorated in a Colonial style complete with brass chandeliers (kept at candlelight level), mahogany and cherrywood china cupboards, and a serpentine red brick wall reminiscent of Jeffersonian architecture. Whether you come for Friday night leg o' lamb, Saturday night prime rib, a wonderfully dowdy lunchtime special called Austrian ravioli (similar to American chop suey), or a plain and tasty tuna skillet sandwich (Friday lunch), mealtime at the Lady Classen is always a civilized experience.

Most of the food presented in the cafeteria line is traditional southwestern fare: pan-fried catfish and hushpuppies, baked chicken and cornmeal mush, baked ham and potato royale. Entrées are complemented by homemade breads, individual Jell-O molds, vast varieties of vegetables, and shelves' worth of pies, cakes, cobblers, and puddings.

Weekday meals are just fine, but the really inspired time to dine at Lady Classen is Sunday. That's when the list of specials always includes turkey and dressing, available with more fixin's than will fit on a cafeteria tray; and it's when the after-church customers, mostly multi-generational family groups, are in full pastel regalia.

LEO'S BARBECUE
3631 N. KELLEY AVE., OKLAHOMA CITY, OK (405) 427-3254;
OTHER LOCATIONS AT 6816 N. WESTERN AND 5508 S. PENN.

W ill you think us perverse if we come to Leo's, Oklahoma City's premier barbecue parlor, and start with dessert? Leo's banana-strawberry cake is something to rave about. It isn't spectacular to look at, and in fact we bet its ingredients and techniques are hardly more complex than following some directions on a cake mix box; but there is something ingenuous about this bright yellow layer cake, iced with a thin sugar glaze and sandwiching slices of strawberries and bananas, that won our hearts in perpetuity. Leo sells it by the slice or whole cake.

Now, about the superior meats: ribs, beef, hot links, or bologna. That's the menu. Any one of them is available as a dinner (with macaroni salad and baked beans), plain, in a sandwich, or by the pound. Or you can order a "Leo's Special" and go around the world, getting a taste of some of everything, including baked beans and potato salad, for just under ten dollars.

The plainness of the menu in no way reveals the complexity of flavors each of these foods conveys. The beans, for instance, are a true pitmaster masterpiece, loaded with shreds and pieces of beef and pork. The plump hot links are explosively spiced. Sauce is available hot or mild, the former a potent, viscous brew for serious barbecue devotées only, the latter a pleasantly sweet concoction for beginners. And barbecued bologna? Yes, indeed: it is a favorite in this part of the country, sliced extra-thick, infused with flavor from the smoke pit, porky and lush.

Leo's is a barbecue shrine with atmosphere to spare. A former gas station with big brick pits smoking eighteen hours a day (starting at about five in the morning), it is packed with customers (three-piece suits as well as overalls) at lunch, and there is so little room inside that many simply eat their meals standing up outside in the parking lot. Hectic as it may seem during peak hours, order prevails. Maybe that has something to do with the fact that Leo's is staffed by men in sauce-splattered aprons wielding meat cleavers for hacking ribs.

MCGEHEE'S CATFISH RESTAURANT
OFF HIGHWAY 32, EAST OF MARIETTA, OK (405) 276-2751

On a bluff overlooking the Red River on the Oklahoma-Texas border, McGehee's is a far spell from anywhere and off the beaten path, so about ten years ago proprietor Rudolph McGehee built a landing strip out front. It is not unusual on a Saturday or Sunday night to arrive (by car—our preferred means of travel) and have to walk past a dozen private planes lined up by the side of the restaurant at the end of the strip.

Whatever their means of transportation, people *do* come to McGehee's; so many of them come that you probably ought to make a reservation beforehand (although on weekends, they don't accept them—everybody waits). The attraction is all-you-can-eat catfish dinners, sold with hushpuppies, French fries, and cole slaw. The catfish (steaks) are lovely— meaty steaks dredged in seasoned cornmeal and fried in hot peanut oil until they develop a crunch. Mr. McGehee, who has raised a few million catfish in his time, knows a thing or two about this creature, and the meat of the fish he serves in his restaurant is about as savory as catfish can be: firm, snowy white, heavy with juice, clean, and lean.

In addition to the good food, the reason people come a long way to McGehee's is the setting, which is just the kind of place in which a catfish feast seems right. It is a three-room cedar restaurant with frontier-implement decor (cross-saws, old phones, horse collars), a working fireplace, and a panoramic view of the Red River Valley and catfish ponds for nearly as far as you can see.

MURPHY'S STEAK HOUSE
1625 W. FRANK PHILLIPS BLVD., BARTLESVILLE, OK (918) 336-4789

A few years ago Laura Smith of Bartlesville wrote us a thirteen-page letter devoted mostly to raving about Murphy's Steak House. "Your *classic* Southwest eatery," she said. "Ugly exterior, vinyl booths, linoleum-topped tables, and a counter. If it was a flower, it would be artificial. The waitresses are mainly big, strong women, the older ones with beehive hair. One young one is a punk. It is called a steak house, but what they are famous for is French fries."

It took us some time to get to Bartlesville, but when we did, we found Murphy's exactly as Laura had described it, on a nondescript stretch of urban road behind a large sign shaped like a cow. There was even a punky-looking (but polite-acting) waitress. We came at high noon, and the counter stools were occupied by men in jeans and baseball caps; the cash register was manned by a gent in a soda jerk's cap. And nearly everyone was eating hamburgers or hot hamburgers.

Having been clued in by our *Roadfood* tipster, we recognized the "hot hamburgers" as an incognito version of the *spécialité du chef*; for a hot hamburger is not, in fact, a hamburger as we know it, served on a bun (that you can get, too). It is a plate covered with toast on top of which are French fries, a patty of ground beef that has been cooked then hacked up, sautéed minced onions, and torrents of dark, beefy gravy. The hamburger was fine, but it was the combination of the potatoes and gravy (and onions) that was truly excellent. Blanketed with gravy, the logs of fried potato had softened and sucked in lots of beef flavor on some in places, but had remained crisp in others. Even if you come to Murphy's for a big steak and a salad (served with squeeze bottles of Murphy's own dressing), be sure to get a plate of them. And when you leave happy, don't thank us; thank Laura Smith of Bartlesville.

SLEEPY HOLLOW
1101 N.E. 50TH ST., OKLAHOMA CITY, OK (405) 424-1614

There is no written menu at Sleepy Hollow; you choose one of three entrées: steak, chicken, or shrimp. We cannot tell you about the shrimp, but we highly recommend the steak, either a ten-ounce club steak or a one-pound Kansas City strip. This is superbly cooked beef with a blackened crust that yields readily to a sharp knife to reveal a great, juicy, blood-rare slab of protein that still has some good chew to it, and yields oceans of flavor as you eat it.

The chicken is terrific, too: fried to a golden crisp, with the kind of deep, nearly buttery flavor to its meat that somehow chickens in the North never have.

Steak or chicken is a fitting anchor for one of Sleepy Hollow's all-American meals, which always include substantial quantities of mashed potatoes served family-style in big bowls, buttered peas, hot little feather-weight biscuits as you need them, iceberg lettuce in sweet-and-sour dressing, and a tiny portion of pineapple sherbet for dessert—accompanied, of course, by all the iced tea you wish to drink. This feast is served at comfortable white linen tables in a romantic, low-light dining room. Sleepy Hollow is definitely *the* nice place in Oklahoma City.

SPLIT T BAR
57TH & N. WESTERN, OKLAHOMA CITY, OK (405) 842-0331

The Split T Bar is the home of the Caesarburger, a provocative combination of a hamburger and Caesar salad that has been a longtime favorite in Oklahoma City, where oddly dressed hamburgers of all kinds are beloved. This particular burger is a handful of edible chaos, which is why the Split T dishes them out wrapped inside an envelope of paper that cups all the ingredients until you are approximately halfway through the sandwich. By that time, so much of the Caesar dressing has oozed out, along with juices from the patty and shreds of lettuce, that the paper wrapper is disintegrating and the plate below becomes the receptacle for the spillage.

It is a sloppy sandwich all right, but what a winning combination of flavors! The hamburger is thick enough to ooze natural gravy, with a sharp, charred crust. The salad is a wild combination of garlic, pepper, and sharp cheese. In fact, the topping is considerably thicker than the kind of salad you'd serve in a bowl, actually closer to sauce than salad. With onion rings on the side, it is a grand feast.

The Split T is a fun place to eat: a big, happy tavern full of sports-and-burgers fans. Caesarburgers are available to take out for spilling on your lap in the car.

VAN'S PIG STAND
717 E. HIGHLAND, SHAWNEE, OK (405) 273-8704

There have been Pig Stands in Oklahoma since the twenties; in fact, some historians call Pig Stands America's original drive-ins. People in Shawnee recall this particular Van's going back at least to the thirties, when it was run by Jerry Vandegrift's father, who was always a stickler for using real hickory wood to cook his hogs. They still do it the old-fashioned way at this modern Van's, which is a nice brick building with a peaked roof and a tidy row of pine trees out back only occasionally obscured by smoke from the pit.

The menu can be confusing to newcomers because instead of the traditional taciturn listings in so many barbecues (if they have menus at all)—"pork," "beef," "ribs," "shoulder," etc.—Van's lists such puzzling items as "Van ribs," "Van pig," and "Vanized" potatoes in addition to just plain ribs, pork, and potatoes. It almost doesn't matter which you get, because this is first-class stuff, but if you are fussy and want to know exactly what you will be getting, here's the story. "Van," when applied to ribs or pork, means that the meat is served with curlicue French fries. They are very thin, light gold coils of spud—delish. When applied to a baked potato, "Van" means that the potato is opened and slathered with garlic spread—not as good as the curlicues, in our opinion.

Pork is what we recommend, either ribs or chopped shoulder. The ribs are sizzling with smoke flavor and peppery seasonings and they are loaded with meat; the shoulder chunks are big, tender ones. There is beef on the menu, too, and it is tender and moist, but somehow didn't harmonize quite as well with the sauce.

WILD HORSE MOUNTAIN BARBECUE
HIGHWAY 59, SOUTH OF SALLISAW, OK (918) 775-9960

Should you choose to dine out-of-doors at the Wild Horse Mountain Barbecue restaurant, a picnic table is provided. Entertainment is provided, too, in the form of crowing and cawing by a rooster and a flock of hens who peck around hoping for a scrap as you gobble down your pork and beef.

Need we tell you that Wild Horse Mountain does not require that men wear jackets and ties? In fact, you'd be a fool to wear anything finer than denim or sweat clothes to a meal in this down-to-earth restaurant. Although picnic-style utensils are provided to help scoop up the beans, most eating is done by hand. You'll disintegrate a good half-dozen paper napkins by the time dinner's through.

There are tables inside the cinderblock building, but they are no more civilized than the one outdoors. As for service, that is strictly do-it-your-self. There is a kitchen window inside where you give the man your order. While you wait, you can stake out a table and buy yourself some soda from one of Wild Horse Mountain's two coin-operated soda machines. Food comes out the window on partitioned plastic plates—barbecue and beans on one plate, pickles and jalapeño peppers on another; sandwiches are presented wrapped in yellow wax paper.

Barbecue aficionados wouldn't want it any fancier. The low-down ways of Wild Horse Mountain add a spice to the pleasure of a meal that no linen-tableclothed restaurant could ever hope to match. This is the way barbecue ought to be served.

And let us tell you, this is the way it ought to taste! Damn, this is good! Pork ribs or beef brisket is what we recommend. The ribs are the meatiest things you ever saw, more like pork chops than spare ribs, the bones weighted with lusciously tender rounds of fragile-flavored meat, each one haloed by a blackened rim of high-seasoned crust. Beef brisket is real southwestern-style, so tender it wants to fall apart when you heft a juicy piece off the plate, its meaty gravity insinuated with a skein of smoke fla-vor from the fire.

Along with the meat, you'll get beans. These are memorable beans, chock full of shreds of barbecued meat, and spiced hot enough to nearly scorch your tongue.

That's about all you need to know about Wild Horse Mountain Barbe-cue. It's a shack in the middle of nowhere, but it will be easy to find any time you're highballing along I-40 between Little Rock and Oklahoma City.

OREGON

ANDREA'S OLD TOWN CAFE
160 BALTIMORE, OLD TOWN, BANDON, OR (503) 347-3022

Breakfast is the first meal we ate at Andrea's, and still the one we like best. We wandered in early one morning and by the time we were on our fourth cup of Viennese coffee, we had managed to sample some of everything, and what a meal it was: oatmeal with grainy oomph, warm cinnamon rolls, flaky croissants accompanied by a crock of smoky-flavored pear butter, hefty bran muffins, blintzes with fruit sauce, and a couple of expertly made omelettes. Happy and bursting at the seams, we thought about returning for Sunday brunch, which is renowned in these parts for its ten-entrée menu that is a showcase for Andrea Gatov's expertise in the cuisines of the world, including Creole, African, Italian, French, Israeli, and new and old American.

It was dinner that lured us back, seafood in particular, including a garlicky fisherman's stew reminiscent of cioppino and a dish called gingersherry crab legs, which is nothing less than one of the most memorable ways with crab we have ever eaten. "I also raise my own lamb," Ms. Gatov told us. "And I have at least thirty cheesecake recipes."

Andrea's cafe is an appealing storefront in Bandon-by-the-Sea, a fishing and cranberry-growing village on the south coast between Port Orford and Coos Bay. Located in "Old Town," a neighborhood of crafts stores, art galleries, and book shops, it has an amiably eccentric character: lots of greenery on shelves and suspended from the ceiling and background music from a radio tuned to NPR.

BREAD AND INK CAFE
3610 S.E. HAWTHORNE BLVD., PORTLAND, OR (503) 239-4756

We'll warn you: Bread and Ink is not *Roadfood* in the raw. In fact, it is a fairly sophisticated urban eatery with a kitchen that knows its way around worldly exotica from Vietnamese spring rolls to Italian cassata. But if you are in the mood for a delicious, relatively inexpensive, and utterly unpretentious deluxe meal, this is the place to go in Portland.

The simplest dish on the menu, a hamburger, is first-rate: a hefty, one-third-pound patty grilled to crusty succulence, on a freshly baked onion bun, accompanied by ramekins of *homemade* mustard, catsup, and mayonnaise. It is available with cheddar or gruyère cheese, or accompanied by guacamole. The guacamole is not to be missed, with or without the burger. It is piercingly spiced, vibrant green, sold as a little dinner or big appetizer with a complex tomato salsa.

Most meals are fancier than burgers. You can begin dinner with hors d'oeuvres such as garlic and onion soup, garnished with parmesan croutons, or a silky sweet red pepper soup. Or there is a chewy pan bagna, a length of bread dolled up with anchovies, tomatoes, olive oil, and herbs. Even the regular bread set on the table is terrific—chewy and yeasty, with a brittle crust.

One of the really great items at Bread and Ink is cheese blintzes—served at lunch, dinner, and on Sunday, when the restaurant features a "Yiddish brunch," including chopped liver and scrambled eggs with lox and onions. The blintzes come as a threesome—tender crepe pillows filled with ricotta cheese, accompanied by sour cream and raspberry jam.

Bread and Ink is a nice place to sit. Its bright storefront window ledge is strewn with newspapers and magazines to read while you dine. White tablecloths are deformalized by a covering of butcher paper.

DAN & LOUIS OYSTER BAR
208 W. ANKENY ST., PORTLAND, OR (503) 227-5906

Warm milk, melted butter, and lots of briny oysters: this is Dan & Louis's oyster stew, the best dish in the house, and one of the fine, unaffected seafood specialties of the Northwest. According to the menu, it was invented by Louis Wachsmuth long ago on a cold, winter day. Its oysters are from the restaurant's own beds; and while they are not extraordinarily delicious on the half shell, they have just the right zest to give this stew panache. It is bracing food, an unimprovable combination of simple tastes. We recommend ordering it with a double dose of oysters for extra marine snap; otherwise, it's just too nursery-like.

Beyond the exalted stew, Dan & Louis sells plenty of raw oysters ("Eat 'em alive," says the menu), crab and shrimp cocktail with Thousand Island dressing or red sauce, pan-fried or deep-fried oysters, buttery stews of crab and shrimp, fish and chips, and a wonderfully dowdy "creamed crab" on toast (in winter months).

The restaurant's decor is eye-popping. Its handsome wood-paneled walls are arrayed floor to ceiling with an inexhaustible accumulation of nautical memorabilia.

FULLER'S RESTAURANT
136 N.W. 9TH ST., PORTLAND, OR (503) 222-5608

A couple of dozen stools are arrayed at the horseshoe counters, and the menu is coffee-shop simple; but people stand outside in the cold waiting for a place at Fuller's. It's that good.

Cinnamon rolls are yeasty and delectable; bread is homemade, too: white or cracked wheat. Many people come for French toast made from the good bread, dipped in eggs and cream and served six slices per order under a dainty cloud of powdered sugar. Other breakfast masterpieces include the folded-over German pancake, a "hotcake sandwich" of pancakes and eggs, a pig in a blanket (a sausage inside a German pancake), and the "famous omelette" made with onions, tomatoes, mushrooms, ham, and cheese. Egg orders are accompanied by excellent, made-from-scratch hash-brown potatoes.

Lunch is good at Fuller's, too. There are blue-plate specials every day such as creamed chicken on biscuits, meat loaf and mashed potatoes, and corned beef with cabbage. And there is always interesting seafood: salmon steaks in season, good batter-dipped fish and chips, fried shrimp with extra-hot sauce; and frequently you can order a pair of big, scary (but easy to eat) egg-battered, fried razor clams with French fries and cole slaw.

Off the tourist path but beloved by locals, Fuller's is not only prime Portland; it is a taste of a no-frills, high-quality style of urban hash house that has nearly vanished now from most American cities, whether they are on the skids or renovating.

HEBO INN
JUNCTION OF HIGHWAYS 101 & 22, HEBO, OR (503) 392-3445

If you are looking for the most calories for your money, we recommend coming to the Hebo Inn on Wednesday, when the kitchen makes chicken and dumplings. Here is a meal that native Oregonian Paul Pintarich once recommended to us as "designed for weight gain and to prevent hypothermia." The unsung specialty of so many rustic Oregon restaurants, chicken and dumplings is a swell, old-fashioned meal of tender things in creamy stuff: doughy dumplings, well-cooked chicken, and even better-cooked vegetables. It is pillowy food; and if you have a long way to go before your next meal, we recommend it.

Any day but Wednesday, three meals a day, there are plenty of other rib-stickers on the Hebo Inn menu. Creamy white chowder is nearly thick enough to eat with a fork; there are some tasty pancake-size clam fritters; and there is a full roadhouse menu of steaks, chops, and fried chicken.

Breakfast is an especially good time to eat hearty. Hot biscuits are served with a mantle of peppery gravy. Omelettes are made with three eggs, and pancakes are served in impressive stacks.

None of this is gourmet food, but it is satisfying; and if you have a hankering to eat where the locals eat, this is the place—frequented by fishermen and woodsy types who just wouldn't be happy if they were served a sissy's meal.

JAKE'S FAMOUS CRAWFISH
401 S.W. TWELFTH, PORTLAND, OR (503) 226-1419

You will know what Jake's is all about as soon as you set foot in the door. There in the front of the dining room is a blackboard with several dozen types of seafood chalked on. This is Jake's "fresh board," an inventory of which straight-from-the-market fish the kitchen has that particular day.

Many items will be familiar to any seafood dilettante: bay shrimp, littleneck clams, silver salmon, albacore tuna. Others are rare: kumamoto oysters, opaka, New Zealand pompano, broiled marlin. Nearly half the entries on the board are set apart with an asterisk, indicating they are local products. Among them are celebrated regional delicacies such as Dungeness crab, petrale sole, and chinook salmon. Here, too, are some surprises: Dover sole is listed as a local product, as are crawfish.

Although it has been called Jake's Famous Crawfish since 1920, when waiter Jake Freiman added the customarily Cajun (but in fact local) crustacean to the menu, crawfish pie and étouffée are not the great meals to eat at Jake's. Eat oysters on the half shell, crab any time it is listed on the fresh sheet, baked scallops, pan-fried petrale sole, or—most especially—salmon. Drink local wine, and top things off with a serving of Oregon "three-berry cobbler."

It isn't only the menu that makes Jake's a Northwest eating experience without peer. Look beyond the blackboard at the dining rooms. This is a grand place, about a century old, outfitted in Belle Époque gold-flocked wallpaper and antique chandeliers, its tables draped with thick white cloths, its high-backed wood booths dark with age. Above the booths and tables hang painted tableaux of Oregon scenery and wildlife, as well as moments of local history.

Although fine, Jake's is not fancy. Waiters in their white jackets are casual and efficient, without pomp. You can come to this restaurant for a quick business lunch as simple as a crab and cheddar sandwich or a hangtown fry (a fried oyster omelette). Many customers patronize Jake's for no reason other than to hang out at the bar, or to sip beer and fork down golden mantle oysters by the dozen.

For out-of-towners like ourselves, the most outstanding thing about Jake's is its character. The ancient wood booths, the daily printed "fresh sheet" (a reprise of the blackboard) enclosed in the regular menu, the loaf of hard-crusted sourdough bread set upon the table: these are a taste of Portland virtually unsullied by food trends and fashions. There are other restaurants in town that are very good, serve fresh fish, and offer innovative menus; but none resonates with the regional veracity of Jake's.

MO'S ANNEX
657 S.W. BAY BOULEVARD, NEWPORT, OR (503) 265-7512

There are branches of Mo's up and down the Oregon coast from Coos Bay to Lincoln City. All sorts of restaurants, stores, and food stands sell Mo's famous clam chowder. But to appreciate the full glory of Mo's, it is best to go to Newport, where Mo's was born half a century ago.

Mo's is on the Newport waterfront. Or perhaps we should say Mo's *are* on the waterfront, because there are two of them, across the street from each other—Mo's Restaurant and Mo's Annex. They are surrounded by a dockside sprawl of fish markets, seafood packing companies, piers where boats unload the day's catch, and stores that advertise they will smoke any fish, meat, or fowl you bring in.

Menus at both Mo's are similar, issued on disposable newsprint. The "Restaurant" tends to offer a slightly larger variety of dinners, including grilled things (oysters, salmon, halibut) and fried things (fish and chips, clam strips, onion rings); "Annex" offerings are limited to casseroles and stews. Both parcel out clam chowder by the individual cup or bowl or family-style for folks who like to serve themselves. No meal at either place costs more than $5.95, including chowder or salad and hot bread.

Although the menu at the Restaurant is bigger, we like eating at the Annex better. What a view! The bright red eating shed is perched above Yaquina Bay, allowing diners to look out over the water and the commercial fleet berthed at its dock, and to watch sport fishermen cleaning their day's catch. In the distance, sailboats skim across the bay.

The cuisine of Mo's (Annex and Restaurant) is traditional (as opposed to nouvelle) fish cookery. They serve none of the spartan, unadorned seafood dishes that seem to be fashionable these days; indeed, what we like best at the Annex are its defiantly old-fashioned luxury casseroles, in which fish gets cosseted in cheese, cream, sauce, crumbs, etc. Scalloped oysters, for instance, are a lavish baked-together comfort food combination of butter, cream, crackers, and oysters from Mo's own oyster beds. You can also get your oysters "barbecued"—shelled, sauced, smothered with cheese, and baked. They make prodigious cioppino (fisherman's stew) thick with tomato sauce; cheesy shrimp casserole; and a unique version of Hangtown fry, in which oysters or shrimp are combined with eggs, green onions, and bacon.

The chowder that made Mo's famous is not all that different from most clam chowders one finds along the Oregon coast—thick and creamy, stocked with pieces of clam, with a faint smoky taste. We like this chowder; but what we like even more is the oddly named variation that Mo's makes, listed on the menu in the category of seafood stews as "slumgullion." Slumgullion is clam chowder given a special marine sweetness by adding shrimp: a terrific combination, and with a salad and a hunk of bread, a royal supper.

MORGAN'S COUNTRY KITCHEN
85020 HIGHWAY 101, FLORENCE, OR (503) 997-6991

A portrait of John Wayne hangs on the wall of Morgan's Country Kitchen. It is captioned *Mr. America*. If the Duke is your kind of American, the Country Kitchen will likely be your kind of eatery. On the coast highway between Coos Bay and the Siuslaw River, this snug roadside cafe is a choice pie-and-coffee stop for truckers and tourists in search of red-white-and-blue cooking.

It is a new-looking place, all tidy with flower boxes outside and a greenhouse dining room out front, warmed by a woodstove. The inside is log-cabin rustic, with a counter for single diners to enjoy the view of pies in their case and tables where families and bunches of truck-driving men spread out and enjoy the hale rations that issue forth from the kitchen between seven in the morning and two in the afternoon.

Breakfast is the specialty of the house. Omelettes are cooked in individual skillets, heaped with ingredients such as bacon, mushrooms, and guacamole (all of which are included in one called "The Gringo"). Crisp waffles are available plain or packed with pecans. You can make a meal out of potatoes in the form of "California Chili Browns," which are hash browns mixed up with whole chili peppers (mild ones) and topped with melted Monterey jack cheese and spicy salsa.

Our favorite breakfast is the biscuit, which the waitress majestically transports to counter places and to tables like the monumental masterpiece it is. It is a single giant golden-topped rotunda smothered in spicy light brown gravy. It makes for a tender-spirited meal with inimitable rib-sticking satisfaction.

We had hit the Country Kitchen for breakfast on our way up the coast; heading south a few weeks later, we came by at noon; and lucky for us, we were very hungry. Do not come here for lunch without a sizable appetite.

The clam chowder, homemade daily, is a meal unto itself; follow it with meat and bean chili, or a chicken-fried steak with potatoes and gravy, or a meat loaf platter—accompanied by iced tea served in Mason jars.

Once you've mopped the last of the gravy off your plate, you are ready for dessert. Oregon is berry country, so it makes sense to finish things off with a piece of pie: blueberry, boysenberry, blackberry, or apple. They are handsome pastries, with sturdy thick crusts and mounds of filling. But after all the meat and potatoes we had for lunch, we've got to admit that the inelegant wedges we sampled were just too much—too heavy, too thick, too sweet. With John Wayne looking down from his picture on the wall, we felt like real wimps for having left half our desserts uneaten.

MORRIS' CAMP 18
MILE POST 18 ON HIGHWAY 26, ELSIE, OR (503) 755-0113

A magnificent log cabin restaurant that smells good—of cut wood, coffee, griddle cakes, and syrup. It is gigantic: the main room is supported by what the management believes to be the largest known ridge pole in the United States—twenty-five tons and 5,000 board-feet of lumber. On the walls are massive lumbering saws and old photographs of lumberjacks at work; deep-cushioned couches surround a walk-in fireplace; even most of the customers look like outdoor types, dressed in jeans and flannel; the rustic ambience is abetted by waiters in suspenders and waitresses in long skirts and aprons.

This is a theme restaurant, and the stage effects work. More important, the food delivers on the promise of the *mise en scène.* The kitchen's specialty is brawny northwestern cuisine, including family-style dinners of meat and potatoes or chicken and dumplings, big hamburgers and sandwiches for lunch, and proverbial lumberjack breakfasts.

You can order griddle cakes (here known as "flatcars") and blueberries, waffles ("corks") with slab ham and eggs, or four-egg omelettes ("bunkhouse" style) served with chunky, well-oiled fried potatoes and big powdery biscuits with melting butter shoved inside. Various flavors of jelly are served in a big carrier with wooden spoons as scoops; and plates are thick speckled dishware reminiscent of (but nicer than) tin. We especially enjoyed one breakfast of pan-fried razor clams, a regional specialty that is rare in roadside restaurants. The clams were huge, crunchy, sweet, and relatively tender, accompanied by spuds, eggs, and biscuits.

You will have no trouble spotting Morris' Camp 18 as you travel along Highway 26. It is surrounded for hundreds of yards by heavy tree-cutting equipment. It actually looks like it might be a lumber camp or, on closer inspection, a lumbering museum.

OTIS CAFE
HIGHWAY 18, OTIS JUNCTION, OR (503) 994-2813

E ver since the *New York Times* wrote that their food was the most fattening in the Northwest, Gail and Jim Powers of the Otis Cafe have been a little miffed when easterners come through with the newspaper clipping in their hand and seem to want to gawk at the meals they serve rather than eat them. Still, they haven't reduced the startling size of their hash-brown potato plate—an awesome heap of sizzled-crisp and cooked-tender spuds festooned with lush blanket of melted cheddar cheese.

Most regular customers (as opposed to tourists) get an order of potatoes to share, as a side dish to accompany excellent—and substantial—breakfasts of eggs with sausage, bacon, or a pork chop. There are also some fine sourdough pancakes and walnut waffles, and toast made with whole-wheat molasses bread or shockingly black bread as well as broad-beamed cinnamon rolls. Really serious eaters finish off breakfast with a piece of the cafe's renowned pie—strawberry-rhubarb, blueberry, apple or apple crunch, and sweet-sweet walnut. Most pie-eating takes place after lunch, which is a classic cafe repertoire of hamburgers, hot plates, soups, and chowder—frequently sent to tables accompanied by grade-A chocolate malts or milk shakes.

On a weekend morning, you will wait in line to eat at the Otis Cafe, and once inside, quarters are close indeed. Seating is limited to a mere four booths, two tables, and seven counter stools. The crowds are part of the fun; and on the last occasion that we stood in line in the parking lot, the wait went fast as we and others marking time reminisced and swapped stories about the greatest breakfasts we had eaten in the West.

ROAD'S END DORY COVE
LOGAN RD., LINCOLN CITY, OR (503) 994-5180

 bout a mile west of Highway 101, amidst marshlands near a clamming beach, this wood-shingled shack with fish net decor is a taste of

Pacific rim cookery without affectation. It is not for idealistic epicures who imagine Oregon cuisine to be a festival of fresh, lightly cooked local seafood and beautiful bowls of unadulterated wild berries—both of which are relatively uncommon in all but the fanciest Northwest restaurants. Dory Cove is more for people who like to eat well. Yes, there is seafood to be had here; and some of it is prepared simply enough to please a purist. There are local berries, too, although most of them are baked into super-sweet pies and cobblers. And honestly, the dish that most regular customers come to eat is a hamburger, the Dory Cove version of which is a half pound, topped with cheddar cheese and Canadian bacon, and served on an onion bun.

For us travelers who demand regional cuisine, there is some mighty fine Oregon-style (meaning ultra-thick) clam chowder as well as nutritionally reckless (but oh-so-good) baskets of fried shrimp, oysters, or scallops, accompanied by toasted garlic-parmesan French bread. Dory Cove's unfried fish is good—especially the char-broiled salmon and halibut steaks; and we must say that these fishes' flavor is all the more enjoyable because they are here usually accompanied by sweet soda pop served in Mason jars with handles.

For dessert, the thing to eat is pie, of which there are nearly a dozen homemade kinds every day, most of them available in a wonderful configuration known here as a "mini-pie," sized for two. The varieties include an array of chiffons, meringues, creams, and a substantial sour cream raisin. They are big, gooey things, not elegant but mighty satisfying.

TAD'S CHICKEN 'N' DUMPLINGS
HIGHWAY 30, ONE MILE EAST OF TROUTDALE, OR (503) 666-5337

Fair warning: we once sent a dainty friend to Tad's and he came back complaining that the food was "too heavy" and the atmosphere was "too rowdy." If you are looking to eat light in polite surroundings, go somewhere else. Tad's Chicken 'N' Dumplings is for chowhounds.

Whole families of them crowd this place Sunday afternoons to eat liberal quantities of hearty food at low prices, have drinks out on the back deck, and watch the sun set in the west through the picture windows in the dining room. Chicken dinner at Tad's—bring the kids!—has been a tradition in the Cascades for decades.

The house specialty comes to the table in a big tureen: chunks of chicken in a faintly seasoned creamed gravy, topped with a massive blanket of wide, biscuit-textured dumplings. Vegetables are served in bowls on the side. Eat 'til you drop, then have a piece of berry pie à la mode for dessert.

Warning no. 2: Tad's can be mighty crowded, and is open only for dinner during the week and starting at two in the afternoon on Sundays. Reservations are not accepted, so be prepared to wait.

PENNSYLVANIA

BROWNSTOWN RESTAURANT
ROUTE 772, BROWNSTOWN, PA (717) 656-9077

We don't often recommend eateries with outdoor toilets, but we promise you won't mind the facilities at the Brownstown Restaurant. Although outside, they are heated, and they have modern plumbing. Still, there is something undeniably antiquated about this former stage stop on Route 772 in Pennsylvania Dutch country.

It was morning when we first stopped in, The wooden building had a welcoming way station feel about it. The front room was occupied by locals sipping coffee and eating crumble-top brown sugar coffee cake. They sat at oilcloth tables beneath slowly spinning overhead fans. We ordered a few blocks of coffee cake, accompanied by slabs of scrapple, Pennsylvania's favorite breakfast meat. For those accustomed to bacon or ham or sausage, scrapple is something else: tender, griddle-fried slices from a loaf made of pork and cornmeal. "Don't you just love it?" asked Candy, our waitress. With mouths too full to answer, we nodded "*yes.*"

When Candy saw we were enjoying ourselves, she started to tell us about some of the Brownstown's other Pennsylvania Dutch specialties, including chicken and waffles, oyster pie, roast pork with filling (which is souped-up mashed potatoes), and beef rivel soup—a meaty broth thick with itty bitty dumplings.

She told us that the best time to eat at the Brownstown Restaurant is for dinner, especially on Sunday; so that is when we returned and ate in the back room. Here the inn has fancier wallpaper and wood paneling, and we sat among families gathered around for Olympic-class all-you-can-eat feasting. The tables groaned with bowls full of food from the robust local repertoire, including chicken corn soup, rivel soup, baked ham and roasted chicken, mashed potatoes, filling, buttered noodles, dried corn, baked beans, lettuce with mesmerizingly delicious hot bacon dressing, chow-chow, red beet eggs, apple sauce, and, of course, pies galore for dessert. Our favorites included raisin pie (known hereabouts as funeral pie, because that is when it was traditionally served) and a simple but swoonfully sweet buttermilk pie.

Culinary fussbudgets, go elsewhere. The Brownstown is a place to roll up your sleeves and plow into multi-course, multi-calorie meals designed for travelers with healthy appetites.

DUTCH KITCHEN RESTAURANT
ROUTE 61, FRACKVILLE, PA (717) 874-3265

The Dutch Kitchen calls itself a restaurant, but there is no disguising the diner it really is. Its exterior has been bricked over, and a wood-paneled room has been attached to one side, complete with such amenities as a salad bar and table service for families and genteel couples. But in the old room with the counter, booths, and cash register, where single drivers and assorted road people dine, the hash-house configuration is evident, reassuringly so. The well-worn counter affords stool-sitters a view of pie cases where meringues rise high and toasty, haloed by stainless-steel fixtures. Along the windows, red Naugahyde booths look out over the traffic on Route 61. The vaulted roof still shows pink Formica, and in the morning the smell of brewing coffee perfumes the air.

The most diner-like thing about the Dutch Kitchen is its menu of strapping things to eat such as meat loaf, giant sandwiches, and deep-dish apple pie. This is Pennsylvania coal mining country, where the cuisine is a mixture of Amish farm cooking and Polish pierogies. Whenever we are traveling along Interstate 81 north of Harrisburg and have an appetite for a roll-up-the-sleeves-and-dig-in blue-plate meal, we love to get off at Exit 36W and eat hearty.

Not everything is exemplary. Although the salad bar does have interesting pickled peppers, watermelon pickles, and relishes, it does not measure up to the spectacular arrays of "sweets and sours" you will find in diners closer to the heart of Pennsylvania Dutch country to the southeast. We are sorry to have to tell you that the mashed potatoes that come alongside the meat loaf seem to be made from a mix rather than freshly peeled potatoes (shame!).

However, the meat loaf, listed on the menu as Dutch meat loaf, is noteworthy, the kind of stout brown slab of comfort food that you find only in a good diner. It is served blanketed with a rich dark gravy and accompanied by huge disks of simple and delicious boiled carrots. Other good things to eat are the *real* not-from-a-loaf turkey and a tasty "Distleburger," which is a cheeseburger smothered with sautéed mushrooms.

The meal we recommend at the Dutch Kitchen is chicken pot pie. This is Pennsylvania-style pot pie, the words "pot pie" meaning pie that has been cooked in a pot, and is then served in a casserole dish. The whole casserole is a study in various tendernesses: faintly chewy dough dumplings, little fall-apart tender chunks of potato, well-cooked carrots, and big bite-size shreds of white chicken meat. All the ingredients are cosseted in a thick yellow gravy. To balance the rib-sticking goodness, the Dutch Kitchen serves a dish of apple sauce.

Finally, a souvenir suggestion: as you leave, buy a box of "Black Diamond" licorice candy, locally made in homage to the coal industry.

FARNSWORTH HOUSE
401 BALTIMORE ST., GETTYSBURG, PA (717) 334-8838

We cannot think of another restaurant that brags about the fact that it has a hundred bullet holes in the wall; but the Farnsworth House in Gettysburg aims to remind you in every way that it is a genuine Civil War–era relic—the town's only restaurant specializing in mid-nineteenth-century American food.

Waitresses wear long dresses and snoods. The walls are covered with artifacts from Union troops who headquartered here and Confederate sharpshooters who occupied the building, as well as paintings and photographs of the battle's heros and letters written by Generals Lee and Pickett. The sound system plays Civil War tunes (quietly); the candlelit tables are set with heavy Armateil service plates and water glasses; and a meal can cost twenty dollars.

We aren't usually big fans of such theme dining, because in so many restaurants that try hard to re-create another era, the theater seems more important than the food; but the Farnsworth House doesn't assault you with history. It is possible to think of it as simply a pleasant place to dine, with gracious service and some nice antiques.

Nor are customers forced to eat antique food. You can come for baked flounder, grilled chicken, Virginia ham, or surf-and-turf. Other than a few peculiar dishes from the past, most of what is on the menu is more regional than historical in character: the Farnsworth House is an excellent place to sample such still-surviving (albeit uncommon) Americana as southern spoon bread served in a crock, Georgia peanut soup, Chesapeake Bay crab imperial, and Pennsylvania Dutch relishes and apple butter.

The house specialty is a curio from another era: game pie, in this case made of pheasant, duck, and turkey. Big shreds of the various birds are mixed into a casserole with mushrooms, bacon, and wild rice and topped with a disk of egg-yellow crust. It is a smoky, robust meal, albeit surprisingly delicate in its harmony of flavors.

Along with every dinner, customers choose a vegetable. These include creamy cole slaw (ordinary), a potato of the day (the usual), sweet potato pudding (delicious), or pumpkin fritters (the single best thing on the menu). The fritters come three to an order. They are deep-fried, dark golden spheres with a crunchy crust and tender, nutmeggy pumpkin insides. Sweet but not cloying, they go well with any meal, especially salty, country-style ham.

The best dessert at the Farnsworth House is the opulent rum cream pie; there is also made-here black walnut ice cream that is not to be missed.

GROFF'S FARM
PINKERTON RD., MOUNT JOY, PA (717) 653-2048
(RESERVATIONS REQUIRED)

B etty Groff's family has had a lot of practice making good food. Ten generations ago, her ancestors settled in Lancaster County, Pennsylvania, which they thought was the next-best thing to heaven. They farmed the land and created an abundance of produce and good recipes that have been handed down through the years and have become one of this country's great troves of regional cuisine: Pennsylvania Dutch cookery.

Of the many restaurants that specialize in Lancaster County's let-out-your-belt-a-notch style of eating, one of our favorites has always been Groff's Farm Restaurant in Mount Joy. The menu at Betty Groff's place is a short one but the meals are huge. Everybody orders a main course such as home-cured ham, beef, or seafood; along with it comes a portion of the dish that has made Groff's Farm famous—a buttery chicken fricassee and dumpling dish Betty invented and named chicken Stoltzfus after her friends Elam and Hannah Stoltzfus.

It is a meal of countless side dishes, breads, soup, pies, cakes, and puddings that everyone is expected to pack away. Every dinner includes a choice from a bounty of relishes, pickled vegetables, gelatine salads (including a classic perfection salad), sauerkraut salad, dandelion greens salad with hot bacon dressing, and luscious German hot potato salad. For dessert there are pies galore as well as extra-creamy rice pudding and made-from-scratch caramel pudding.

The most unusual twist at Betty Groff's table is her customary selection of appetizers: cracker pudding served alongside small pieces of caramel-frosted buttermilk chocolate cake! She says she offers these little sweets before dinner just so everyone knows how good they are and leaves room for big portions of dessert after they've mopped their plates of chicken Stoltzfus.

THE HOAGIE EXPERIENCE
2532 WELSH RD., (NORTHEAST) PHILADELPHIA, PA (215) 552-9355 (THERE ARE TWO OTHER HOAGIE EXPERIENCES, ONE IN GLENSIDE AND ONE IN EAST NORRITON, PA.)

The Hoagie Experience takes its name seriously. No mere restaurant, it aims to be the ultimate hoagie experience—an ambitious claim in a city that prides itself on giant sandwiches. The restaurant seems to have two different mottos, both listed in quotation marks on the menu. Motto No.1: "Gourmet Hoagies & Steaks for the Connoisseur." Motto No.2: "We're Better Than We Have To Be." We would not argue with either one. The Hoagie Experience is indeed fit for a connoisseur of Philadelphia sandwiches, and the sandwiches are first-rate.

The first and foremost element in any hoagie is the bread. Hoagies are made on whole loaves or half-loaves of tubular Italian bread that must be freshly baked, crusty, hefty enough to hold together when loaded with sloppy ingredients, yet with a certain elegance of taste and texture. Hoagie Experience rolls definitely measure up. They are dandies—long, plump, and eager to be stuffed.

Among the good eats available between these beauteous buns are thin-sliced and nearly pulverized sirloin, combined with your choice of cheese (mozzarella, provolone, Cheese Whiz, or any desired combination thereof) along with optional fried onions and hot peppers or pizza sauce to make a fine, steamy-hot cheese steak sandwich. These are good cheese steak sandwiches, but they are not Philadelphia's finest. What puts The Hoagie Experience on the map are its hoagies.

Hoagies (a.k.a. heroes, grinders, submarines, spukkies) are like cheese steak sandwiches only in the fact that they consist of lots of different things piled into those long lengths of good bread. Unlike a cheese steak, a hoagie is customarily served cold rather than hot; and its ingredients are usually cold cuts: salami, ham, turkey, roast beef, cheeses, lettuce, and tomato. For nearly all top-notch Philadelphia-style hoagies, the sandwich-maker moistens the inside of the bread with a spritz of oil—olive oil or salad oil or, in the case of The Hoagie Experience, secret-formula "hoagie oil," redolent of spice.

At The Hoagie Experience, the variety of available combinations is nearly infinite, ranging from low-cal turkey and low-sodium lean ham to "The Great Italian Experience" (ham, capicola, cooked salami, Genoa salami, and provolone cheese) and the design-it-yourself "Great Experience" of any six meats and two cheeses you desire. There is a "Corned Beef Special Experience" (lean corned beef, cole slaw, Russian dressing), an "American Experience" (four assorted meats with provolone cheese), a "Tuna Experience", and a "Seafood Experience." There are even three-foot-long experiences for parties.

The fun of The Hoagie Experience isn't only the hefty sandwiches; it is the exorbitant interior decor. The dining room of the storefront shopping center restaurant at Welsh Road and Roosevelt Boulevard is done up in screaming chartreuse so bright you need sunglasses. There are signs every-where. Some are long, long lists of the various combination sandwiches available; others refer to diners' progress—from "This is the beginning of your experience" above the order window (everybody serves themselves) through "This is the end of your experience" above the trash cans.

JOE'S
7TH & LAUREL, READING, PA (215) 373-6794

Joe's of Reading is inscribed in the little black book of many a traveling epicure. It is a blue-ribbon restaurant in a most unlikely city, with a singularly focused menu. People come to Joe's from all around America to eat mushrooms.

When it opened for business in 1916, Joe's was a bar where workingmen came for mugs of beer and twenty-cent bowls of wild mushroom soup. The place was named for its owner, Joe Czarnecki; the soup was made by Joe's wife, Magdalena. Just as they had learned to do in Poland, Joe and Magdalena foraged for their mushrooms in pine forests and fields around Reading, then hung them on clotheslines behind the bar to dry.

Mushrooms have been a Czarnecki family obsession ever since. When Joe's son took over the business in 1947, he added tables and expanded the menu. By the late 1950s, word about Joe's had begun to spread, and connoisseurs made pilgrimages to Reading to taste not only the wild mushroom soup, but exotic dishes based on rare varieties such as cepes and morels, slippery jacks, woodblewits, and russulas. Now Joe's once-humble tavern is as swank an eatery as you will find in this city of railroads and heavy industry. Joe's son Jack, along with his wife, Heidi, have been running the restaurant since 1974; and despite its inconspicuous location, it is anything but a corner tavern. "Joe's?" said the local cop from whom we asked directions. "Joe's is gourmet dining." The focus of the menu, as ever, is mushrooms; and there are dozens of dishes created to celebrate their diversity and deliciousness.

The wine list is extensive (and expensive), meals are elegantly served from a rolling cart, fresh flowers decorate each table, and a chandelier glimmers overhead. This restaurant is fancy, but in a comfortable sort of way. It still has the feel of a family business—Jack and Heidi's place, where the proprietors stroll through the dining room, eager to share their love of mushrooms with customers.

Cream-sauced, marinated, stuffed, or paired with snails or quails or other such exotic viands, many of Joe's mushrooms come from the fungus-friendly soil of southeastern Pennsylvania. (There is a Mushroom Museum just south of Reading in Kennett Square.) Other, rarer varieties are imported from across the country and around the world. Jack and Heidi still enjoy foraging for oddities that never make it to the supermarket, such as "chicken of the woods," "puffballs," and "inky caps."

Befitting the luxurious spirit of the place, desserts are very, very rich, and one course into which the management hasn't yet figured out a way to inject its favorite kind of fungi. There are cheesecakes, tortes, and mousses; and when you are done with those, the house provides you with complimentary little truffles—the confectionery kind, made of minted chocolate.

Expect to spend fifty dollars for two.

MAMA'S PIZZERIA
426 BELMONT AVE., BALA-CYNWYD (PHILADELPHIA), PA
(215) 664-4757 OR 664-4758

Mama's is nothing like the famous city cheese steak shops of the Italian Market or Olivieri's in the Reading Terminal Market, where Philadelphia's hefty sandwiches are dished out with sass in rude surroundings amidst decor that consists of signed eight-by-ten photos on which celebrities declare their love of cheese steaks. Mama's is in the suburbs. It is clean and tidy and the staff is polite. It has no celebrity photos on the wall; in fact, it actually has interior decor, in the form of cartoon images of clowns doing amusing things.

You will forget all about the Formica tables and the clowns and the disquieting politeness of Mama's when you get a load of one of their cheese steak sandwiches. Here is true magnificence: a barge of glistening-crisp bread packed to a fare-thee-well with succulent heaps of beef and coarse-cut onions, the whole lovely mess blanketed with a barely melted layer of provolone. This is a cheese steak with breeding and class, which are qualities not normally associated with the sassy sandwich, but which make this one exquisite.

The single ingredient that makes Mama's sandwich truly wondrous is the bread, which is hefty, dainty-crusted, and with a scrumptious flavor all its own. You can relish this bread in many ways, not only wrapped around steak and cheese. Get a meatball sandwich or any one of a number of humongous hoagies (hot or cold), including one filled with nothing but vegetables and one called "steak cordon bleu."

It is cheese steak that puts Mama's on the map, but let it be said that the gourmet pizzas we have seen emerging from Mama's oven are tempting indeed. There are garlic and herb pizzas, pizzas made with freshly sliced tomatoes, wheat-crusted pizzas (which require a couple of hours' advance warning), pizzas topped with asparagus, broccoli, pineapples, mussels, shrimp, or zucchini. We have meant to sample one whenever we have returned to Mama's, but we never do. For us, it's cheese steak every time: how could we choose anything else when we know such perfect bliss is on the menu?

OAKHURST TEA ROOM
ROUTE 31, SOMERSET, PA (814) 445-5762

D on't let the "Tea Room" appellation give you the notion that this place is small and ladylike, or that the food is served in dainty portions. It *started* as a tea room back in 1933; since then the Oakhurst has grown into a gigantic restaurant, including a parking lot big enough for tour buses, Hans the organist playing favorite melodies every weekend, and roving musicians who surround tables of families and sing "Happy Birthday" or fiddle "The Anniversary Waltz."

There are three spacious dining rooms, seats for 450 guests, and a battery of buffet tables. Diners pig out on an unbelievable variety of hot and cold foods, from Jell-O and ambrosia salads to baked or fried chicken and country ham and roast beef to a galaxy of puddings, cakes, pies, and mousses. Each Friday night is the famous-for-miles-around surf 'n' turf smorgasbord: T-bone steaks, fried shrimp, stuffed flounder, lobster tails, and filet mignon, accompanied by more side dishes than will fit on a plate in three trips to the buffet.

We haven't been to a Friday night feeding frenzy, but the weekday dinners we have ingested at the Oakhurst were awe-inspiring. Not all the food was four-star level, mind you; we wish the baked chicken hadn't been sitting out on the steam table quite so long, and some of the pie fillings were a bit gummy for our taste. But the fillin' (extra-lush mashed potatoes) was superb; and we hit the roast beef just as it was getting carved from the haunch; and the cracker pudding for dessert proved to be a genuine regional treat.

The business card of the Oakhurst Tea Room says that all the food is "prepared with skill and patience to tempt the most jaded and pampered appetites." We don't know too many jaded and pampered people, but we can tell you this: few restaurants anywhere mount such a devastating assault on an eager appetite.

OLIVIERI'S PRINCE OF STEAKS
READING TERMINAL MARKET, 12TH & ARCH STREETS, PHILADELPHIA, PA (215) 625-9369

F or those so culinarily deprived that they don't know what a cheese steak is, let us explain: take a loaf of crisp-crusted Italian bread and slice it horizontally. Slap in a heap of hot, luscious, thinly sliced beef that has been sizzled on a grill along with a good measure of greasy onions, then blanket the mess with cheese. It is an odoriferous jumble, impossible to eat without dripping massive amounts of assorted kinds of ooze down your chin and shirt and onto the sidewalk (most cheese steak connoisseurs like to eat theirs out in the open, standing up, bent forward at the waist so the tips of their shoes are out of range of falling meat shreds and dripping cheese).

Although all cheese steaks share the Platonic configuration, variations are infinite. The basic differences concern quality of the bread, tenderness of the meat (you don't want it gristly, but it can be *too* tender to provide proper tooth resistance), inherent flavor of the meat and its necessary accompanying grease, placement of the cheese (on the bread underneath the meat, or atop the meat). Two of the most controversial issues are the proper type of cheese (mozzarella, provolone, and Cheez Whiz all have their partisans) and whether the grill operator ought to hack up the meat and onions together on the grill, thus hefting them into the sandwich as a single entity, or cook and insert them in the bread as two separate ingredients.

Cheese steaks are a Philadelphia passion; and most traditionalists prefer to eat them surrounded by the sass and commotion of the Italian market (outdoors) or the Reading Terminal Market (indoors), where the insolent cuisine is complemented by the insolence of the counter help and the press of street people with fists full of cheese steaks and cheese fries (French fries drizzled with melted cheese) eager to push you out of their way as they head for the hot sauce, peppers, or other condiments. If you are brave and hungry and want to eat a cheese steak with all such proper ambience, we recommend Olivieri's in the Reading Terminal Market.

Olivieri's is the funkiest of eateries, where the staff, while not what you'd call rude, go about their business of constructing great steak sandwiches with all the hauteur of a gourmet chef who considers customers a rather vulgar annoyance. Steam from the grill rises up all around them as they slam the top of the Cheez Whiz dispenser for a big squirt directly onto the bread, then throw in the beef (in large flaps and some gristly, fatty pieces) with plenty of its own natural grease, then heap on the big oily onions and present you with a masterpiece, all the more appetizing because of the harsh overhead fluorescent lights of the market, the bustle, and the noise.

Olivieri's is probably the most impudent cheese steakery in town, and therefore—because impudence, as much as bread or meat or cheese, is a crucial ingredient in cheese steak greatness—it is our choice for number one, well-deserving of its self-proclaimed title, "Prince of Steaks."

PAT'S
1237 E. PASSYUNK, PHILADELPHIA, PA (215) 468-1546

Y ou want dining ambience? Observe the splattered hot sauce underfoot, the dropped and crushed French fries on the sidewalk plaque that honors the place where Sylvester Stallone once stood. Listen to the rumble of trucks going past on their way to or from the Italian market. Smell the mingling of cheap after-shave lotion and fancy fragrances on customers in line—both aromas overwhelmed, as the line approaches the take-out window, by the reek of steak and onions sizzling on the grill.

Pat's claims to have invented the cheese steak in 1930. Whether or not this is true, this restaurant's shaved-beef-and-cheese sandwiches on serious Italian bread have stood for over half a century as the benchmark against which all other cheese steaks are measured. The sandwich is greasy, slippery, downright ignominious, and a barrel of fun to eat. Thin flaps of less-than-prime beef are sizzled on a grill alongside onions and hefted into a roll, then a trowel of melted Cheese Whiz is dripped on top. That's the classic steak sandwich; and if you wish to dude it up, there are big glass jars with hot sauce and peppers: help yourself.

It is a perfect combination of low-grade ingredients that transcend their mediocrity and become something wonderful. Side your sandwich with a cupful of cheese fries (French fries blanketed with more of that melted Whiz), and eat standing up on the sidewalk under harsh lights in this most glorious open-air ode to kill-or-cure gastronomy.

PEOPLE'S RESTAURANT
140 W. MAIN ST., NEW HOLLAND, PA (717) 354-2276

P eople's is a regular kind of place where you can order a normal-size dinner if you are not in the mood to pig out. Nor is the menu relentlessly local; the kitchen makes handsome ordinary American meals of roast turkey and sausage filling, or roast tenderloin of pork. Of course, there *are* some exemplary Lancaster County delicacies here, including crackling tubes of luscious sausage made in the nearby community of Ephrata, crustless chicken "pie" (actually a creamy stew) served on broad egg noodles, and wilted lettuce or dandelion (in season) salads topped with sweet-and-sour hot bacon dressing.

The best of the local eats will be found on People's dessert list: an only-in-Pennsylvania repertoire of pies that includes funeral pie (the local nickname for raisin pie, so-called because it is customarily served at wakes), custard, pecan, apple crisp, apple crumb, sour cream apple, pumpkin, shoofly (wet-bottom and dry bottom), graham cracker custard, coconut, and even a completely non-Amish but nonetheless tasty grasshopper pie the color of an after-dinner mint. Our absolute favorite from the list is the wet-bottom shoofly—an amiably cloddish, molasses-sweet hunk of pastry served warm with ice cream melting fast on top.

PLYLER'S
ROUTE 28 & 322 (EXIT 13 OFF I-80), BROOKVILLE, PA (814) 849-7357

P lyler's was a happy accidental discovery. We had pulled in for the night at Exit 13 off I-80 in Pennsylvania. There was nothing listed in our computer's *Roadfood* database in or near the town of Brookville, so we looked in the phone book and found an ad for Plyler's. It appeared to be the best of an uninteresting bunch.

A small brick building surrounded by a parking lot, Plyler's was neat and clean; but to be frank, it did not inspire visions of great eating. Inside, the mostly local clientele seemed to be enjoying themselves at the Formica-table booths.

Then we caught a glimpse of the salad bar. Now, this was interesting. Alongside the usual greens and vegetables was an array of Pennsylvania salads with that "seven sweets and seven sours" character derived from the Amish table. It wasn't quite so copious, but there were pickled peas, three kinds of slaw, creamy macaroni salad, German potato salad, pickled red beet eggs, and two kinds of homemade bread.

The first time we ate at Plyler's, we made the mistake of loading up on salad. It was very good, but then we saw people all around us eating pizza, and we were sorry we had no appetite remaining. The salad's swell, and there is a full menu of steaks and chops and fried-fish dinners, but it is pizza that now makes us happy to spend the night in a nearby motel at Exit 13.

Two kinds of crust are available: thick and chewy or thin and crispy. We like the latter, which is svelte enough to have nothing but crunch in its center, but still offers a nice puffy ring of dough around the edge. The dough is made here, and the variety of toppings is vast, including taco-topped (spicy meat and cheese, lettuce, and tomatoes) and German-style (with sausage, sauerkraut, onions, and green peppers). Plyler's also makes the local variation of calzone, known hereabouts as stromboli—a crust-lover's pocket of dough stuffed with pizza ingredients and baked until golden brown.

These good things to eat do not really taste Italian. They are more evocative of the melting pot: Pennsylvania relishes; Italian pizza with Mexican and German toppings; and the nation's big east-west interstate rumbling past not far away. That's a real taste of America—genuine *Roadfood*.

READING TERMINAL MARKET
12TH & ARCH STS., PHILADELPHIA, PA (215) 922-2317

The old marketplaces of the cities in the mid-Atlantic states are eater's paradises, forerunners of the food courts in modern malls, but without Muzak and with a lot more urban grit. The Reading Terminal Market, although somewhat renovated in recent years, remains a bastion of all the food and local color that make these places such a delight for roving gastronomes. You can browse and admire beautiful produce, cheeses, butchered parts of animals, loaves of head cheese and scrapple, jams and jellies from the countryside, and huge, whole fish. And you can eat like a rapacious conqueror, everything from raw oysters on the half shell to awful pizza. Among the not-to-be-missed highlights are soft pretzels with mustard, a cheese steak from Olivieri's (see p. 380), shoofly pie by the slice, chocolate chip cookies from the 4th Street Deli, and Bassett's ice cream. It is numbingly convenient to have so much variety in so little space, a daunting experience if you hope to have a taste of everything.

RITTER'S DINER
5221 BAUM BOULEVARD, OAKLAND (PITTSBURGH), PA (412) 682-4852

Ritter's is a 'round-the-clock breakfast hot spot where night owls congregate in the wee hours and local truckers and tradesmen come for pre-dawn infusions of good, strong coffee; but the reason we recommend it is lunch.

Ritter's is a stronghold of upstanding blue-plate specials such as beef stew, stuffed cabbage, loin of pork, meat loaf, pot roast, and turkey with all the proper fixin's. Eat here on Wednesday, and the meal you want is one called turkey Devonshire, a Keystone State version of the legendary Louisville hot brown sandwich: turkey and bacon on toast, baked under a mantle of cheese sauce. It just might be the best lunch in town. Don't ease on down the road without dipping a spoon into Ritter's yeomanly rice pudding.

TICK TOCK COFFEE SHOP
KAUFMANN'S DEPARTMENT STORE, 5TH & SMITHFIELD, PITTSBURGH, PA
(412) 232-2682; EXTENSION 2307

There are two unique eating experiences that no visitor to Pittsburgh ought to miss. The first is chipped-chopped (pronounced "chip-chopped") ham. This is a strictly western Pennsylvania foodstuff that is served just like the lowliest junk food from the dime store deli or convenience store counter: processed ham shaved tissue-thin and piled inside a burger bun or between two slices of spongy white bread. Phil Langdon, roadside archeologist nonpareil and author of *Orange Roofs and Golden Arches,* was the first to clue us in to the delicacy, which he said connoisseurs prefer served warmed in a frying pan with melted cheese inside the sandwich. After a meal of chipped-chopped ham, Phil suggested a drive along a country road in search of an even more obscure western Pennsylvania specialty, goat's milk fudge.

Back downtown, you will find us at the Tick Tock Coffee Shop in the basement of Kaufmann's Department Store, enjoying another only-in-Pittsburgh meal. For this gem of a restaurant, we have *Roadfood*er Patty Rowe of Riverside, California, to thank. A few years ago, Patty read a newspaper column in which we wrote about our search for America's best hamburger—in Los Angeles, Connecticut, Colorado, and Texas. "I have tried, sampled, and enjoyed hamburgers all over the country," Patty informed us. "Most are pretty much the same. But the best I ever tasted is at the Tick Tock in Kaufmann's, in America's number-one City, Pittsburgh."

Yes, indeed, this Tick Tock burger is a dandy—char-broiled to a glistening crusty crunch on the outside, yet thick enough to still be moist and rose pink in its center, served inside a big homemade bun.

Excellent hamburgers are not the only thing the Tick Tock has to offer. In fact, the oozingly drippy, two-fisted burgers are a bit of an oddity on the otherwise ladylike menu of soups and salads, dainty cream-sauced dishes of chicken and turkey, and fluffy cakes and chiffon pies.

Mid-morning, you can come for homemade muffins, butterscotch rolls, German apple bread, blueberry pancakes, or steamy pecan waffles. By lunch, a blackboard is set up outside the dining room listing all the day's specialties—most of them fancy desserts such as pecan stick torte, silk 'n' satin pie, chocolate port wine cake, and a variety of homemade ice creams.

RHODE ISLAND

ARCHIE'S TAVERN
47 MENDON AVE., PAWTUCKET, RI (401) 727-1700
(LUNCH AND DINNER, TUESDAY–SUNDAY)

Archie's is a huge place that serves huge portions of huge food. Located in a factory neighborhood, with an exterior that resembles a warehouse more than a restaurant, it is one of Rhode Island's several good titanic eating halls. In this case it is actually a few halls—a sprawling conglomeration of mismatched dining rooms added through the years, all of them packed with big parties of loud, hungry eaters on weekend nights.

All dinners come with cinnamon rolls—yeasty swirls of hot dough veined with cinnamon and sugar. It's easy to fill up on them (they keep coming) before you even see the rest of the meal. Many regular Rhode Island customers patronize Archie's to eat their rolls along with roasted, herbed chicken dinners—a traditional Ocean State combination of sweet and savory flavors, the bird and bread augmented by servings of antipasto, noodles in tomato sauce, a few vegetables *du jour,* and Jell-O.

Travelers in search of regional oddities can order snail salad, which Archie's makes as well as anyone in the state, and in greater abundance. You get piles of cool, faintly sweet, thinly sliced snails in a tangy marinade. They are chewy, delicious, and truly appetite-piquing, although they seem somewhat redundant alongside the complimentary tray of marinated mushrooms that every dinner party gets, along with a mass of California dip and crackers.

Pork chops are served three (big ones) to an order. Paella for one is enough for three. For the really rapacious customer, the menu lists "Neanderthal Cave Man Cut" prime rib—a mesa of tender red meat that oozes juice even before you break ground with knife and fork.

Archie's Tavern is one of the best examples we know of the strange gastronomic fact that America's littlest state serves America's biggest meals.

AUNT CARRIE'S
POINT JUDITH, NARRAGANSETT, RI (401) 783-7930
OPEN FOR BUSINESS AT THE END OF MAY

E ating seafood on the shore is one of the great warm-weather pleasures in Rhode Island. The state's coast abounds with open-air clam shacks and shore dinner halls so close to the ocean you can hear waves break as you eat. One of our favorites is Aunt Carrie's, by the beach in Point Judith.

You can come to Aunt Carrie's for nothing fancier than a cardboard plate piled high with fried clams. Oh, what clams: brittle-crusted nuggets with succulent marine tang inside every bite. Take your plate and eat on the front seat of your car: a true summertime feast. Or better yet, carry it out toward the water and enjoy the sand and surf (but be careful to protect your clams from gulls swooping overhead). Aunt Carrie's has a full menu with such simple pleasures as a lobster roll or a broiled flounder; you can even get a tuna fish sandwich.

As much as we love eating outdoors at Aunt Carrie's while lolling against the hood of our car or strolling along the sand, it is also fun to sit down for one of the full-bore meals in the screened dining room around the corner from the take-out counter. The inside of this eating place is a simple, unaffected mess hall that looks like a black-and-white postcard from the 1940s. Waitresses wear nurse-like white uniforms. Tables are plain, polished wood. The screened windows overlook sand and water. The view, accompanied by the mixed aroma of the ocean and the hot steamer clams, is a satisfying taste of New England.

The way to savor this setting best and longest is to order a shore dinner. At more than ten dollars, a shore dinner is the most expensive thing on the menu. It is a feast. For starters, you get chowder, fried clam cakes, and mountains of steamer clams with a bucket of broth on the side. Then comes the plate of filet of sole or flounder with corn on the cob and French fries, accompanied by brown bread and butter. Then you get your lobster, then the Indian pudding, ice cream, or watermelon. Abbreviated versions of the shore dinner are available (without the lobster, or without the fish); or you can order à la carte and get whatever combination of chowder, clam cakes, fish, or lobster you like. Aunt Carrie's offers three kinds of chowder—tomato-based (Manhattan style), milky white (New England style), or clear and brothy (southern New England style).

If it is late spring or early summer, you will want to finish off your meal with an Aunt Carrie's specialty—rhubarb pie, made fresh for as long as rhubarb is available. After a hefty meal of oceanic-flavored fried clams, the sweetened tang of rhubarb is an inspired dessert, especially if it is served warm and à la mode with a scoop of vanilla ice cream on top, melting into the steamy sweet red vegetable that does such a good impersonation of fruit.

BOCCE CLUB
226 ST. LOUIS AVE., WOONSOCKET, RI (401) 762-0155

There are many different things on the menu of the Bocce Club, a white frame house in a family neighborhood of Woonsocket. You can order steak, chops, or seafood; but the one meal you want is chicken, family-style. It was here, in the 1920s, that the Pavoni family began serving roasted chicken dinners, potatoes, and pasta shells to friends after playing bocce. The Pavonis' stepdaughter, Mary Tavernier, opened a small public dining room in the basement of the family home and continued the tradition. Since then, Rhode Island has lost its head over chicken dinners with potatoes and pasta on the side, customarily dished out on an all-you-can-eat basis.

According to Bonnie Tandy Leblang, who investigated the phenomenon for *Yankee* magazine a few years ago, nine out of ten weddings in northern Rhode Island feature family-style chicken; and Rhode Island is the only state in the Union where Kentucky Fried Chicken shops sell macaroni with their chicken. "Chicken family-style is to Rhode Island what chili is to Texas," Ms. Leblang decided, pinpointing its origins at the Bocce Club restaurant, where about three-fourths of the customers at the civilized and comfortable linen-clad tables order the exact same immoderate meal.

It begins with antipasto: ham, salamis, cheeses, tomatoes, olives, and peppers arrayed on a cool glass plate. Italian bread comes alongside. Then pasta with a rich red meat sauce, then platters of roasted chicken—steamy moist white meat and oozingly succulent dark pieces (you can pay extra and get all-white; but let us tell you, the dark meat here is a sybarite's delight). With the chicken come swell potatoes—a combination of French fries and rosemary-scented oven-roasted spud chunks. There are pies and Cool Whip–topped desserts, but it isn't likely you'll have much appetite left by the time the empty chicken platters are cleared away.

COMMONS RESTAURANT
TOWN CENTER, LITTLE COMPTON, RI (401) 635-4388

B reakfast at the Commons is particularly inviting. You can choose from among three kinds of pancakes. There are ordinary ones, which are thin, homey, and taste just great; there are johnnycakes, the traditional Rhode Island cornmeal flapjack; and there are "natural pancakes." We love the johnnycakes. These are the wide, sheer versions (some places make them silver-dollar size and thick), so delicate you can almost see through them, made using cornmeal that has been ground nearly to powder. Their taste is the sweet, sunny taste of corn, somehow purified and refined to its most delicious essence. They are served with butter melting on top and syrup (not grade-A maple) on the side. A Commons cook described natural pancakes to us as "johnnycakes plus" because they are made with different cornmeals as well as some other healthful grains. They, too, were rather elegant, although to our tongues not as exquisite as the johnnycakes, nor as distinctive.

Lunch is good, too. Sandwiches of all sorts are available, including grinders (southern New England's puzzling term for a hero or sub), lobster salad rolls, and zesty sausage-and-onions combos. And there is seafood. Wonderful brothy chowder thick with bits of clam, gilded with a golden slick of butter, is accompanied by a trio of crusty fritters. A stuffie is a quahog clam chopped up with peppers, crumbs, and spice and piled back into both sides of its shell, which are put back together before arriving at your table. On occasion, the Commons offers quahog or salmon pie.

The Commons is a casual lunchroom with a clientele that seems all local. If you come in the morning, most of them are reading newspapers that are strewn about on the waist-high partition between two sections of the small dining room; or they are chatting over coffee with each other and the waitresses. It is such a nice, cozy place to eat, at the north end of the green in a very small town—population 300.

PORT SIDE RESTAURANT
ACROSS FROM BLOCK ISLAND FERRY IN GALILEE, RI (401) 783-3821

There are a few worthy seafood restaurants in Port of Galilee, which—according to the menu of the Port Side—is the "Tuna Capital of the World." None are really fancy because Galillee is a working person's place more than a tourist's. Our favorite down near the docks is the Port Side, a real townie's eatery where the waitresses call you "hon" and where the food is as frank as franks and beans.

For starters, one can order that off-putting but actually quite delicious local favorite, snail salad—brisk, marinated slivers of mollusk that have none of the indulgent *luxe* of the hot, garlicky French variety. There are good stuffies—quahog clams chopped up with breading and spice and piled back into their giant shells; and there is some brawny, broth-based clam chowder that is peppery and smells like essence of ocean. Clam cakes have a nice crust and oily insides, but seem a wee bit stingy with pieces of clam.

The menu lists all manner of shore dinner from multi-course, lobster-based extravaganzas to abbreviated clamcakes-and-chowder suppers; they serve a tasty hot lobster roll as well as fried seafood by the plate, pint, or quart, and meat and potatoes, too. But the dish we keep coming back for is spaghetti with red or white clam sauce. This is well-made and lavishly apportioned sauce in either color, but the white is especially good—loaded with clams and clam flavor as well as bits of green onion and celery.

The beverage list is fascinating. A written notice promises: "Our bartenders are ready, willing, and able, with generous hand, to fix your favorite." If hard stuff is not your pleasure, the Port Side has a soda fountain that can make everything from basic chocolate milk and coffee milk (like chocolate, but even sweeter) to all those strange, and strangely labeled, sweet treats that are unique to Rhode Island, such as cabinets and frappes (local names for milk shakes and sodas).

The dessert of choice to end the Yankee homeboy meal you will eat at Port Side is pudding, preferably Grape-Nuts flavored. It is alabaster custard speckled with nuggets of softened cereal and a few raisins, streaked with nutmeg.

ROCKY POINT PARK SHORE DINNER HALL
ROCKY POINT PARK, WARWICK, RI (401) 737-8000

Rocky Point Park is a picnic—a Brobdingnagian picnic, served in a vast chowder dome that holds four thousand customers at one time at tables-for-thirty-six. The room tone can be as deafening as a high school cafeteria at high noon; waiters dash from the manufactory kitchens carrying loads of steamers in their bunched-up aprons, serving as much as a ton of clam cakes (clam-studded fritters shot into hot oil by specially designed clam cannons) every hour and ladling out gallons of Rhode Island–style chowder (tomato-pink but without Manhattan chowder's cornucopic vegetable array).

When you arrive at the Rocky Point Park Shore Dinner Hall, you must make a big decision: whether to sit in the section of the pavilion that serves a scaled-down menu of clam cakes and chowder, or in the section reserved for whole-hog "shore dinner" eaters. The segregation is necessary because you pay in advance, and once you are seated at a table, waiters keep bringing food until you tell them to stop. Clam cakes and chowder are a fully satisfying meal, but if your aim is to partake of real Ocean State cuisine, you want the top-of-the-line shore dinner. It is a staggering rendition of the traditional multiple-course banquet that vacationers along Yankee shores have enjoyed for well over a hundred years, and has been served at Rocky Point Park since 1847. This is what you get: olives, cucumbers, and Bermuda onion slices, clam cakes, clam chowder, white and brown breads, steamers with broth and melted butter, a length of sausage, a slab of baked fish, a lobster, French fried potatoes, corn on the cob, a wedge of watermelon, and a bowl of Indian pudding garnished with ginger-flavored hard sauce. Customers are given all they want of everything (except lobster), for as long as they care to sit at their paper-clothed communal table. (There is a slightly cheaper version of the shore dinner available with chicken instead of lobster.)

While you dine, the smell of the ocean wafts through the room, and the booming clatter of the kitchen and thunderous voices of thousands of happy eaters are interspersed with screams of people on amusement park rides all around the dinner hall. It adds up to a unique taste of nineteenth-century shoreline fun, and an unforgettable summertime feast.

THE SEA GULL
SUCCOTASH RD. (SNUG HARBOR EXIT), S. KINGSTON, RI (401) 789-2000

A summer kind of place, surrounded by the smell of salt air and birds skimming over waves on the water. There is a dining room at the Sea Gull, complete with tables and chairs and a hostess at the door to ensure that everyone who comes here is properly dressed (no shirt, no shoes, no service); and there is a complete dinner menu with such Ocean State dishes as cool marinated snail salad and a full-blown lobster feast. But the reason we recommend it is none of those things, not even the scenic location.

Clamcakes and chowder put The Sea Gull on the *Roadfood* map. Each is superb; together they are a Rhode Island tradition nearly as inseparable as a hot dog and its bun. The clam cakes are golden fritters with a knobby surface. Tear one open, hot from the kitchen, and fragrant steam vents into the air; its puffy insides are butter-rich and judiciously dotted with pink, oceanic tidbits of clam. As far as we are concerned, a clam fritter such as this, all sweet and doughy, is one of nature's perfect foods, much more appealing than some simply cooked piece of fish that has nothing to recommend it but awful grill marks on its pitiful naked flesh.

As for chowder, The Sea Gull serves all three kinds popular in this area: red (tomato-flavored), white (cream-flavored), and clear (ocean-flavored). The last is our choice to accompany clamcakes. It is vigorously seasoned, salty, loaded with chunks of clam and some potato, yet with none of the sweetness of the doughballs, and thus their perfect foil.

TWIN OAKS
100 SABRA ST., CRANSTON, RI (401) 781-9693

The food isn't necessarily all good at Twin Oaks, but we can practically guarantee that it is all great—as in *great big*. Squads of Ocean State families, high school football teams, and other such semi-professional eaters adore this immense mess hall, where customers are summoned to tables via loudspeakers, and where waiters (who never write an order, lest the writing slow them down) virtually run among the fields of boisterous tables as they carry pounds of food to and fro.

The menu, like the portions, is vast: from New England boiled dinner or meat loaf and mashed potatoes to spaghetti with three-inch meatballs, flounder stuffed with shrimp, and filet of beef stuffed with cheese and ham, as well as a full repertoire of shore dinners based on lobster, clams, and such. None of what is served resembles home-style food; it is inelegant and institutional. But it is generally agreeable institutional—made-from-scratch, respectable fare with real taste and character. Steaks are thick-cut, as are lamb chops and pork chops; even mixed drinks at the bar are huge, presented to customers with an overflow tankard containing seconds.

A full dinner at Twin Oaks is not cheap; it's about twenty dollars for the soup-to-nuts treatment, which does include soup, as well as shrimp cocktail, salad, bread, meat, vegetables, and dessert (no actual nuts, however). Never in recorded history has anyone left this restaurant unsatisfied.

The only thing we don't especially like is waiting. On a weekend night in particular, two hours in the bar is not unusual. It's a nice bar, with a scenic view; but considering the size drinks they serve, you risk serious inebriation if you use them to pass the time.

SOUTH CAROLINA

BEACON DRIVE-IN
255 REIDVILLE RD., SPARTANBURG, SC (803) 585-9387

Brace yourself. Get calm. Take a deep breath. Now walk through the entrance to the Beacon Drive-In. You have stepped into a tornado. New customers push in behind you. The line ahead moves fast. From behind the counter, white-aproned waiters scream at you to hurry up and place your order. "Barbecue," you stammer. "Pork-a-Plenty, sliced, with slaw and onions."

And before the last syllable is out of your mouth, J. C. Strobel, master of the serving line, is yelling your order back to an immense open kitchen, where dozens of cooks chop and fry and assemble meals in what seems like total chaos and confusion. You breeze down the counter, beneath signs advising, "J.C. Says It's Fine to Pass in Line" and "Place Your Money in Hand and Have Your Order in Mind So We Can Get You to the Ball Game on Time."

Now you have arrived at the drink station. This choice is easy. Although Pepsi, milk shakes, and lemonade are on the menu, nearly every Beacon customer orders tea. It is iced tea, southern-style, meaning liberally pre-sweetened, served in a gargantuan tumbler loaded with crushed ice. Forget about straws; the way to lap this tea up is with one's snout deep inside the cavernous cup.

Less than a minute has passed since the kitchen devoured your called-out order, and whammo! Here comes the food, exactly what you wanted, brought to you by whichever server yelled it out.

Now dig into some of the finest barbecue in a state where barbecue is king. Hickory-flavored ham is available as tender "inside slices," lean, with a subtle smoky tingle; or as "outside meat," with a chewy, sharply seasoned crust. Both come bathed in a sauce that smacks of cloves and vinegar. On the side, if you get a Pork-a-Plenty plate, you want French fries, plus sweet relish slaw and out-of-this-world fried onion rings.

The Beacon sells a ton of barbecue each and every day, but if pork with its accoutrements is not your dish, you may choose from a hundred-item menu that includes fried chicken, catfish sandwiches, "pig's dinner fudge sundaes," and double chili cheeseburgers with bacon, lettuce, and tomato.

If you plan on coming Friday or Saturday, be forewarned that the parking lot will be jammed. One way to avoid the crowds is to helicopter in. Airborne customers are invited to land at the Beacon's helicopter pad just across the street, which has in fact been frequented by airborne soldiers stationed at Fort Bragg. It is a real drive-in, so there is car service, which is pretty speedy; but we prefer going inside. Here you dine in one of several rooms equipped with televisions and iced tea dispensers (for seconds) and enjoy the incomparable thrill of a run through the Beacon serving line.

D & H BAR-B-QUE
412 SOUTH MILL, MANNING, SC (803) 435-2189

We have a soft spot for D & H because it was here, twenty years ago, that we detoured from writing a book about truck drivers and ate some of our first genuine southern barbecue. Since then we have spent our life looking for good food, barbecue formost among our targets; and the hunger inspired by that first real Carolina pig-out has kept us on the road for a million miles. The plain wood-slat benches and picnic tables of the D & H we remember have since been replaced by more comfortable accommodations, but the food they serve is still inspirational: whole hogs cooked over oak coals in a brick pit behind the kitchen. It is served buffet style (the traditional way) as well as by the plate, in sandwiches, and by the pound.

The menu lists chicken and an all-vegetable dinner, but it is the pork you want to eat, especially if you come in the evening and can help yourself, buffet style. D & H hacks it into shreds and pieces that are faintly smoky, sweet, and luscious, with a hint of vinegar tang from the peppery red sauce employed by the pitmaster and served at the tables. With the pork on a whole hog plate you get crunchy hushpuppies, cole slaw, and a heap of white rice smothered with hash, which is a sort of supercharged gravy made from various parts of the pig that are not eaten as barbecue or made into fried pork skin. When we learned about what went into hash two decades ago, it scared us but we soon fell in love with its greasy wanton succulence. Now we yearn for it whenever we are far from D & H and the real smoke pits of the Carolinas.

DUKE'S BARBECUE
789 CHESTNUT ST., ORANGEBURG, SC (803) 534-9418
(DUKE'S HAS A SECOND LOCATION IN ST. GEORGE)

There is no music in the dining room of Carl Duke's restaurant; but the sound you do hear while eating will be music to your ears if you love barbecue. It is the thump-whack-thud created by the lady behind the counter hacking pork with a cleaver.

Everything about Duke's is designed to focus your attention on the one thing that makes this place famous for miles around: hickory-smoked barbecued pork. It is served in big chunks and shreds without any sauce whatsoever. Just savor the meat: mild, gentle, sweet, with enough chew so that eating it makes its tender fibers explode with flavor. Duke's motto, listed in its small advertisement in the Yellow Pages, is the unprepossessing maxim "Cooked to Perfection."

There is sauce to add if you like. The red is blazingly hot; sprinkle it on sparingly. And there is yellow: yes, yellow barbecue sauce, the tangy, mustard-flavored stuff unique to central South Carolina. It is sweet and sour, creamy smooth, and is so distinctive you would want to eat it if the only thing you had to baste was a slice of white bread. On pit-cooked pork, it sings grand piggy opera.

What makes Duke's a barbecue jubilee other than the meat and sauce themselves is the way they are served. In the ancient manner of the traditional Carolina pig pickin', Duke's is open for business only on the weekends (Thursday, Friday, and Saturday). And they serve it the old-fashioned way, from a help-yourself cafeteria line where the pickings are minimal: pig meat, rice, hash (a stewlike mixture made from weird parts of the pig) for on top of the rice, the sauces, and some pickles. You dish out as much as you want for a *prix fixe* of under five dollars, put it into your partitioned Styrofoam plate, and grab the only available utensil—a white plastic fork from the barrel.

For beverage, there is iced tea (pre-sweetened, of course) and a Pepsi machine with cans of soda. That's all there is to eat, except for white bread (Sunbeam King Thin brand), which is set out in its supermarket wrapper on every table.

The seating itself suggests a serious Big Feed. Eight long picnic tables each provide enough seating space for maybe twenty people altogether (and they are jammed at mealtimes on Friday and Saturday night). Each table is spread with a red-and-white checked cloth and supplied with the bread, paper napkins, and a pitcher containing pre-sweetened tea.

The tables are laid out in a cavernous room that could only be called an eating hall, with a high ceiling that holds big overhead fans and fluorescent tube lighting. There is no decor to speak of, and like we said, no music other than the thud of the cleaver hacking pork and the moans of pleasure, slurping, and licking that are a symphonic expression of people enjoying one of the great meals of the Southland.

MAURICE'S PIGGIE PARK
1601 CHARLESTON HIGHWAY, WEST COLUMBIA, SC (803) 796-0220

Since the 1930s, when Joe Bessinger opened a cafe in Holly Hill, South Carolina, the Bessinger family name has meant great barbecue. Joe's sons Maurice and Melvin kept the tradition by opening a series of Piggie Park barbecue restaurants in the early 1950s. Maurice's Piggie Park in West Columbia has become one of the biggest curb-service drive-ins in the country.

Dining at Maurice Bessinger's is a stirring experience. It is the kind of uniquely American meal to which we would eagerly take visitors from another country if we wanted to show them the spunk, character, and quality of American gastronomy. Pardon our emotionalism, but Piggie Park inspires patriotic thoughts, and not only because the food is so darn good. The largest American flag in South Carolina waves above its parking lot.

It is possible to eat at tables inside, but most customers prefer dining in their cars, parked in Piggie Park's tin-covered car slots with illuminated menus and individual intercoms. The menu guarantees three-minute service—by carhops in crisp red-white-and-blue uniforms.

Roll the windows down, because the tantalizing smells of burning wood and sizzling hams make the lot an aromatic picnic. Piggie Park chefs cook their pork the old-fashioned way. Round the clock, every day, hogs are roasted over hickory coals (note the woodpile by the sooty chimney). Although the menu is vast, including foot-long hot dogs, chicken baskets, and beefalo burgers, pork is the star.

Our recommendation is a "Q Rib" or "Q Pork" plate. The ribs are big messy bats, their lode of meat permeated with smoke. On the pork plate, butt and shoulder meat is cut into big chunks—"inside" pieces that are pale white and tender; and "outside" strips, encrusted with roasted-on sauce. Be sure to get some skin on the side. It is dark mottled brown, fried to a crisp.

Some like the pork in a sandwich: Big Joe Q Pork or Little Joe Q Pork ("with skin $.20 extra"). The smoky-flavored meat is finely chopped and accented with a dash of sauce. The sauce is a shock if you have never had the pleasure of pig-pickin' (eating barbecue) in or around Columbia. Unlike the tomato-red stuff common everywhere else in the Q-belt, the glaze fancied by central South Carolinians is mustard-based and gold-hued. Bessinger's version is sweet as apple cider, zesty but not burning hot. The label on the bottle (which is available for purchase at Piggie Park or by mail) describes it as a "million-dollar heirloom recipe."

Mail order sauce sales: *Maurice's Piggie Park; Box 6847, West Columbia, SC 29171; or call (803) 791-5887.*

MOREE'S BAR-B-Q
HIGHWAY 527 OFF ROUTE 41, NORTH OF ANDREWS, SC (803) 221-5643

M oree's is open only two nights of the week, Friday and Saturday, and only until about nine. These hours are generally the mark of an authentic barbecue in the Carolinas, going back to the days when a pig pickin' was a social event to which people came from miles around. The pitmaster put his hogs up over the coals on Wednesday, and for the next couple of days, if the wind was blowing right, appetites throughout the county would build until the pork was ready to be served.

Two hundred years ago it was dished out almost exactly as it is served today at Moree's—from a help-yourself buffet line that offers not just love-ly, lean meat from the butt and shoulder (the crème de la hog), but also big, succulent ribs and two kinds of skin (deep-fried and sauce-basted), hog-drippin' gravy, and luscious pork hash made from sections of the hog you don't want to know about. In addition to pig parts, Moree's line offers sweet potatoes, barbecued chicken, and slices of Moree-made cake for dessert.

Fill a tray and find a place to eat in one of two dining rooms with long, communal tables. Moree's is an out-of-the-way place and its hours are not convenient for most passers-by, so nearly all who eat here seem to be regular customers who have made the feast part of their weekly culinary agenda. Most know each other; but even if you are a total stranger, you will likely feel at home. It is impossible not to enjoy the company when you are sitting elbow-to-elbow with other eager eaters savoring one of America's sloppiest and most distinctive meals.

SWEATMAN'S BAR-B-QUE
RT. 453 NORTH OF HOLLY HILL, SC (NO PHONE)

B ub Sweatman's place is a shingled farmhouse, shaded by pecan trees, surrounded by furrowed fields. No phone number. No sign outside. Open only two nights a week, Friday and Saturday. Only barbecue cognoscenti know about it; and now you do, too. Here, friends, is some of the finest eating in America, a place to partake of the most celebrated and delicious gastronomic ritual of the Carolinas—the sleeves-up party known as a pig pickin'.

Three generations of Sweatmans have been roasting pigs over deep pits full of oak and hickory coals since 1900, every weekend—first just for friends and neighbors, now for anyone with about five dollars (all you can eat) who is lucky enough to find the farm. Sweatman's country feeds are not nearly as crude as the tear-it-yourself open-air pig roasts, around hog-slaughtering time, that are the origins of southern barbecue. There are utensils to eat with, and you sit at an oilcloth-covered table. The five high-ceilinged dining rooms (formerly bedrooms, living room, and parlor) are paneled with slim wood boards glistening like varnished mahogany. In fact, Sweatman's is a gorgeous place.

The truly dazzling sight is the buffet line, faithful to the methodology of a true pig pickin', which demands the serving of the whole hog—*beard to tail,* or in French, *barbe à queue.* Each weekend, the Sweatman cooks turn about two dozen hogs into roasted pork that is carved into chunks of butt and shoulder meat, crusty ribs for gnawing, rib meat only (minus the bone), pigskin stripped and fried into mottled brindle strips with a wicked crunch, and from the jowls, liver, and other ignominious portions of the hog, pungent pork hash to be served over rice.

The chunks of barbecued pork are succulence incarnate, presented plain and glistening with their own copious juices. This meat needs nothing in the way of condiments, but if you do want to gild it there are two sauces available, one made with hot peppers and the other a typical South Carolinian sauce built around mustard.

Barbecue's charm is that it is primitive; and many barbecue parlors' appeal is that they are rough-and-tumble places. Not Bub Sweatman's. Simple and direct as it is, Bub's makes eating barbecue a well-nigh Ciceronian experience. Why, there is even some dessert for after eating pig: raisin bread pudding with vanilla sauce.

SOUTH DAKOTA

MINERVA'S
301 S. PHILLIPS AVE., SIOUX FALLS, SD (605) 334-0386

M inerva, the Roman goddess of wisdom, overlooks this vintage (since 1917) restaurant from the top of its carved wooden bar; and although antiquity holds sway over the look of Sioux Falls' reigning eatery (note the antique phone booths in the lobby, the patina of age on the wooden booths, the old-fashioned white linen that covers the tables), the menu is modern. Pasta primavera, anyone? How about sweet-sauced roasted duck with wild rice stuffing? Midnight mousse cake or cream puffs for dessert? Come and get 'em at Minerva's.

Yes, this is a swank place to dine; but that doesn't mean it is uncomfortably formal or especially expensive. You can eat a nice dinner for under ten dollars, and you are welcome in blue jeans. And although the menu lists plenty of hifalutin' continental food, there are also some regional-flavored specialties that make it a noteworthy stop for anyone in search of edible Americana.

Handsome as the pasta and roast duck may be, the items that drew our attention are the sirloins and filet mignons and the lovely pan-fried walleyed pike. The steaks are thick, juicy beauties, aged in the kitchen and charcoal-cooked; the native (not French) firm-fleshed pike, which is rarely served anywhere outside the upper Midwest, has a unique freshwater flavor that is sweet, rich, and clean as a mountain stream. To accompany whatever main course you order, Minerva's features a salad bar with fixings to mix your own as well as plenty of already-made accompaniments: rice medleys, composed salads, miniature muffins, soups, and French bread.

Minerva's desserts are spectacular. Our waitress practically insisted we get crepes: mocha hot fudge–sauced crepes heaped with whipped cream or banana-nut crepes with rum sauce. We chose the latter, which were delicate and sugary. There were layer cakes, tortes, and traditional pies, but our second choice for dessert had to be the special that night, a modern oddity that seemed to epitomize the Plains States' adoration of grandiose desserts: a nutty, achingly sweet confection known as Snickers pie.

TEA STEAK HOUSE
MAIN ST., TEA, SD (605) 368-9077

In the town of Tea, less than a half hour southwest of Sioux Falls, adjacent to O'Toole's bar underneath the big green sign on Main Street, is a dining room where they serve what may be the best steak dinner in South Dakota. Its pleasure is augmented by the ambience in this town meet-and-eatery, where the customers at the lined-up tables are a blend of laid-back farmers in worn denim and eager businessmen in permanently creased synthetics.

The pound-plus T-bone has a handsome, pillowy look before you slice it. At the first incision through its dark crust, juices flow. It's a good thing you have hash-brown potatoes on the side to soak up the beef's spillage; they are great potatoes in their own right (much better than the foil-wrapped baked potato or blah French fries). They are crusty and luscious, and although you'd never call them greaseless, they are rather clean-tasting. If you need a dose of delicious oily food, you want Steak House onion rings. With the good spuds and meat, they complete a classic steak-house meal.

Steaks aren't all the Tea Steak House serves. You can eat chicken or ham, halibut, perch, or lobster tails. Don't ask us how they taste. When we're in Tea, we'll eat beef. Don't ask about dessert, either. This place doesn't bother making any dessert. According to our waitress, they spend too much time concentrating on more important things, like meat and potatoes.

TENNESSEE

BELLE MEADE BUFFET
BELLE MEADE PLAZA, NASHVILLE, TN (615) 298-5571

"May I he'p you?" asks the server at the beginning of the cafeteria line at the Belle Meade. That is when it happens: Our minds go blank. Our jaws drop open. Our hands grow too numb to even point at what we want.

Can you recognize the symptoms? Yes, we confess: we suffer from the eater's disorder known as cafeteria anxiety. It never fails to happen when we visit the Belle Meade—as we always do whenever we are within a hundred miles of Nashville.

The problem is that no matter how firm our cravings are when we walk into the lobby, we are always flummoxed and flabbergasted as soon as the line curves around and we are faced with the sight of the actual buffet itself. It is not a huge array of foods, as cafeterias go: perhaps eight or ten entrées and a dozen or so vegetables, plus salads, desserts, rolls, relishes, and drinks. Still, it is a vista of vittles to make food lovers weep for joy: beautiful things to eat, all expertly prepared. How can we possibly choose x, y, and z (catfish, hushpuppies, and chess pie), and by choosing them, *not* choose a, b, and c (fried chicken, seasoned greens, and lemon meringue pie in a graham cracker crust)? The problem was exacerbated the last time we ate at the Belle Meade by the fact that there were *two* dessert stations in the line, at the beginning and the end; so we started our selection with chocolate pie, then concluded it with coconut cream.

The choices are especially challenging for us New Englanders, since so much of the Belle Meade spread is food that we *never* get back home. Food that we dream about, food that we crave, including jalapeño cornbread and superb squash casserole, rainbows of salads, and a dark fudge-pudding chocolate pie that, if available, cannot be ignored. There are far, far too many things we yearn to eat to fit them all on a single tray, or even two.

So we muddle through the line in a kind of anxious daze, usually winding up with ridiculously unbalanced meals. Jane will likely have two pies, a cake, a pudding, a chicken-fried steak, fried chicken, and roast beef. On Michael's tray, you might find a mountain of biscuits and breadstuffs, mashed potatoes, baked potato, fiesta rice, rice pudding, and three congealed salads (Jell-O).

Vegetables are especially noteworthy. They are cooked southern-style, which means they're customized, superseasoned, and vigorously spiced. Cabbage gets stir-fried with bacon until it sops up the porky goodness. Whipped yams are flavored with vanilla, dotted with raisins, and streaked with marshmallow.

Once the bill is toted up at the end of the line (it is impossible for two people to spend more than fifteen dollars for dinner), a Belle Meade waiter carries the trays to a table in the dining room, sometimes showing off with great flourishes and folderol as he whisks it above the heads of diners that he passes. (A tip for such service is customary.) The room is brightly lit; and just as the serving line moves fast, people eat fast, too. Since the whole meal is set out before you, there's no waiting between courses. And when you're done, you don't have to flag down the waiter for a check. Few people spend more than an hour at the Belle Meade, start to finish.

Cafeteria dining such as this is one of the glories of southern gastronomy. Even the big cafeteria chains, such as Morrison's, Furr's, and the Piccadilly, usually set out a fine spread. But believe us when we tell you, the Belle Meade is something special; it's a cut above.

BOBBY Q'S BARBEQUE & CATFISH
1070 N. WASHINGTON AVE., COOKEVILLE, TN
(615) 526-1024 OR 528-5000

B obby Q's menu describes the pork as "famous" and the beef as "not-quite-famous-yet." We are not betting on the beef—it doesn't have the succulence of Bobby Q's pulled pork shoulder; it is sliced thin and it is a little too lean to glisten the way flaps of four-star barbecued beef usually do, although an application of peppery hot sauce fixes it up mighty nice. The pork benefits from sauce, too; but not because it *needs* it. It is opulent meat, hacked into big tender shreds and lots of crusty outside pieces that fairly glow with flavor. With a bit of sauce, it's just about perfect.

Sweet barbecued beans and cole slaw accompany meat if you order a barbecued plate, but it is worth paying extra and replacing the standard "new slaw" with "pool room slaw," a mighty hot concoction with its own kind of sauce that is made from a recipe Bobby Q got from an old pit man in Nashville.

Catfish can be ordered boneless and filleted, which is easy to eat and very unfishy, or as a couple of whole (but headless) fiddlers on the bone. Catfish meat is easy to pick off the skeleton, and the meat from the whole ones (two to an order) is heavy with juice and high-flavored. It is sheathed in a thin, crisp, sandy crust and accompanied by a couple of spherical hushpuppies.

Bobby Q's is a dramatic exception to the rule that barbecue restaurants serve drab dessert. Every day there is something different—a multi-tiered cake, an ice box pie, or, if you are very, very lucky, banana pudding. Striations of whipped cream and threads of buttery brown sugar are veined through silken yellow custard and heaped together with crumbled vanilla wafers and bananas. The gentleness of this balmy dish is an inspired conclusion to a meal of torrid barbecue. In our book, it is one of the great desserts in all the South.

BOZO'S
HIGHWAY 70, MASON, TN (901) 294-3400

H eading into Mason, you can see hickory smoke cloud the air half a mile away from Bozo's. Step out of the car and the smell of smoldering coals and cooked pork shoulders is a dizzying invitation to enter one of western Tennessee's most enduring barbecue restaurants, open every day but Sundays since 1923.

The interior decor bespeaks superb *Roadfood*: Tired wood paneling, Formica-topped tables, and wooden chairs; a well-scuffed linoleum floor; pale green stools lined up at a gray counter; and a Chevrolet-time clock on the wall.

There is a large menu listing shrimp, chicken, salads, and steak, but the singular reason to come to Bozo's is pork. In particular, you want a "white and brown pulled pig plate." That means succulent white meat, from the inside of the shoulder, and crustier brown meat, from the outside, pulled into shreds and hunks and heaped on a plate along with saucy barbecue beans and sweet cole slaw. (There are chopped plates, too, as well as sandwiches.) The pulled meat is like pot roast infused with southern soul—some of it tender enough to fall apart when prodded with a fork, other pieces burned and crusty. Sauce is served on the side in mild and hot versions; and although the hot stuff is a rather pretty translucent red-orange, note the pepper flecks in it—and beware. Anyway, Bozo's classic pit-cooked meat is too good to want any sauce at all.

BUNTYN
3070 SOUTHERN AVENUE, MEMPHIS, TN (901) 458-8776

A two-room cafe by the tracks, next to a seed and feed store, Buntyn is a lesson in southern lunch. For Yankees unaccustomed to the forcefulness of cafe cooking in the mid-South, it is shocking to taste turnip greens this porky, or banana pudding so sweet, or a bread basket so handsomely stocked with such enormous rectangular yeast rolls and moist pie-shaped cornbread wedges. And how about this startlingly juicy fried chicken, its brittle crust impregnated with pepper and spice?

Simply stated, Buntyn serves exquisite food. It is southern cafe food, mostly configured into what some people hereabouts know as "meat and threes," meaning one main course accompanied by a trio of vegetables, always with a basket of breads.

About those breads: yeast rolls are enormous rectangular bolsters with tender tan crusts, usually still warm when they arrive at the table. Alongside them are pie-shaped wedges of grainy, butter-yellow cornbread. Delish.

For a main course, that fried chicken cannot be beat, but you might also consider meat loaf, catfish steaks, chicken and dumplings, liver and onions, country-fried steak, barbecued ribs, or turkey and dressing. The menu is different every day, but in all the times we have eaten at Buntyn, we have never had anything less than wonderful. In fact, the main courses are almost hard to focus on because the vegetables that come with them are so extraordinary. Pick three from among a choice that frequently includes creamed potatoes, fried or buttered okra, spinach casserole, buttered hominy, buttered squash, turnip greens, and assorted peas and beans cooked with hambones that infuse them with porcine luxury.

By the time we hit dessert at Buntyn, anxiety is mounting. The quandary: banana pudding or toasted coconut pie? Each is a paragon, the former an ethereal veil of moist meringue, tepid custard, broken vanilla wafers, and banana slices. We don't know if Elvis ever ate at Buntyn, but this pudding is a dish the King of Rock and Roll, and of Nursery Food, would have adored.

We could go on about this cafe, spreading adjectives like nasturtium petals at a bride's tea; but let us simply say that if we had to have lunch in one restaurant anywhere in the world, *right now* (or almost any time), it would be at Buntyn.

CHARLIE VERGOS RENDEZVOUS
52 S. SECOND ST. (GENERAL WASHBURN ALLEY), MEMPHIS, TN
(901) 523-2746

Nearly everyone who writes about the ribs of Memphis notes that they are served either wet (heavily sauced) or dry (imbued with rubbed-on spice). There are dozens, perhaps hundreds, of barbecue parlors in the city that make wet ribs of varying degrees of excellence. As far as we have been able to ascertain, there is one and only one restaurant that serves them dry. That is Charlie Vergos Rendezvous, whose ribs are weird and beguiling and technically not even barbecue. They are charcoal-broiled. Being traditionalists, we favor wet, sloppy, hickory-cooked pork; but these dry bones demand serious attention.

There is no sauce at all on them. They are blanketed with massive amounts of a paprika-colored spice mixture that bakes onto the meat and forms a kind of spice envelope around it, holding the juices in and flavoring it at the same time. They are beautiful crusty brown, as lean as any rib we have ever eaten, and the meat inside the spice crust is stunningly tender. Even through the heavy veil of spice you taste charcoal smoke and the sweet goodness of the pork itself.

It is a kick to eat at the Rendezvous (once you get a table—there is often a considerable wait). The dining room is a cellar-level eating hall festooned with customers' business cards and dusty old signs. It is noisy, impolite, and smells as much of beer as barbecue.

DOTSON'S
99 E. MAIN ST., FRANKLIN, TN (615) 794-2805

Breakfast at Dotson's is a engrossing taste of morning cafe life in the South. Any day when you come in early for coffee and oven-hot biscuits and perhaps a toothsome slab of pan-fried country ham, you will see townsfolk of every stripe stopping by for a bite to eat and a little conversation. Many of them come and sit a spell at the big communal table in the back of the dining room, creating an ongoing discussion that continues throughout the morning. The men drift in, chat 'n' chew, then drift out until Dotson's is quiet for a short while before the noontime rush begins.

Lunch at Dotson's is anything but leisurely. Service is fast, conversation is loud, and many people are in and out in less than half an hour. But even the quick eaters don't come for a drab sandwich. This venerable cafe is famous for hot lunch. That can be as simple as pan-fried steak and gravy or a slice of knobby-textured meat loaf with mashed potatoes and turnip greens. Or it can be truly elegant cafe food, such as Dotson's pan-fried chicken, which is sheathed in a dark, hard batter and bursts with juice at first bite; or fine, brittle-crusted catfish with hushpuppies and slaw. There are always plenty of highly seasoned, well-cooked vegetables to go with the hot lunches: casseroles of squash and sweet potatoes, pungent greens, beans rich with the flavor of a ham bone.

For dessert, the menu lists ordinary, sturdy-crusted pies as well as extra-ordinary Tennessee fried pies—pockets of tender dough folded over around stewed apricots, peaches, or apples.

The food at Dotson's is very good, has been since it opened as a snack shack over on First Avenue in 1947; but it's not just food that has made this place a favorite haunt for generations of Tennesseeans. It's that big table in the back; it's tradition.

ELLISTON PLACE SODA SHOP
2111 ELLISTON PLACE, NASHVILLE, TN (615) 327-1090

It has been about half a century since the Elliston Place Soda Shop opened for business. Walk in under the hanging neon sign above the sidewalk on Elliston Place and you are transported back in time.

It isn't only the sight of the gleaming stainless steel and Naugahyde interior that is nostalgic—the burgundy and yellow upholstered booths, the working soda fountain, the tiny hexagonal floor tiles; it is the *aroma*. Every day at noon, the smells of plate-lunch cooking evoke an era when nearly everybody expected to enjoy a square meal of meat and three vegetables for their lunch, or if not that, then a nice, slowly sizzled (not fast-food) hamburger from the grill with piping hot French fries on a genuine crockery plate (not Styrofoam).

"Meat-and-threes" is what they call the full treatment down here: choose baked, sugar-cured ham, salt-cured country ham, southern-fried chicken (white or dark meat), a pork chop or liver 'n' onions, then select three vegetables from a daily roster of at least a dozen. Or if you want to skip the meat altogether (Elliston Place vegetables are so good, you might just consider such a strategy), there is a four-vegetable plate, accompanied by hot bread, for about three dollars. Among the daily-changing vegetable repertoire printed on mimeographed menus you will likely find whipped potatoes, turnip greens, baked squash, fried bite-size rounds of okra, black-eyed peas, baked squash, and congealed salad (the local name for Jell-O). All these things are made the old-fashioned way, with plenty of dramatic seasonings and the expert touch of cooks who have been working in the kitchen for decades.

Consider breakfast at the Elliston Place Soda Shop, too. Although morning is not a good time to avail yourself of the great vegetables or of the soda fountain specialties they make so well (especially a classic triple-dip banana split), it is the ideal time to relish country-style ham, accompanied by red-eye gravy suitable for dipping.

Selecting dessert can be a real problem. Those sundaes, splits, and malts are top-notch; and the atmosphere of this spanking clean soda shop makes the thought of them even more alluring. However, there are also some commendable old-fashioned southern-style sweet things you won't want to miss. They make a silk-smooth and sugar-sweet chess pie that is just wonderful to eat in the tiniest increments along with a long, slow cup of coffee. And when the temperature is up, it is hard to resist a cool, frosty wedge of the simple and nearly breathtaking Dixie classic, lemon ice box pie. After a hearty meal, or for a mid-afternoon cooler with a glass of iced tea, this pie is one of the South's greatest contributions to the science of personal refrigeration on a hot day.

FOUR WAY GRILL
998 MISSISSIPPI AVE., MEMPHIS, TN (901) 775-2351

"Every meal is supervised by top professionals," the Four Way Grill menu reassures customers; and once you look at the big, crusty pieces of fried chicken coming forth from the kitchen, you have no reason to be skeptical. The Four Way Grill is Memphis's premier soul-food restaurant, a plain storefront where spectacular cooking has been a tradition seven days a week, from seven in the morning to late at night, since the Cleaves family opened for business back in 1947.

There are two dining rooms—a casual front room with booths and a television set to watch, and a quieter back room with white-clothed tables. We like the front, which isn't quite as polite, but is definitely more sociable. Here each place setting is carefully composed by a white-uniformed waitress who brings a pitcher of ice water and puts down a paper napkin, then silverware, then another napkin, creating a lovely, however humble, tableau on the oilcloth table cover.

Other than the best fried chicken in town, the thing to eat at the Four Way is pig meat: chewy slabs of salt-shocked country ham for breakfast, served with cracklin' red-eye gravy and hot biscuits; crusty pork chops with dressing and collard greens for lunch or dinner; even such adventurous soul-food exotica as pig's feet (with brown sugar gravy), boiled sow's ears, ham hocks, and chitlin's. The breads to go with all these foods are terrific, from the fluffy morning muffins to coarse-crumbed cornbread. Side dishes are great, too, and include dirty rice and stewed apples, sticky-sweet yams, potent greens, and various beans and peas cooked with pieces of pig long enough to transcend their starchy plainness.

Cobblers are the great dessert, especially peach in the summertime: a great chunky mélange of flaky crust, fruit, and sugary syrup. There are pies and rice pudding, too, and a nursery-nice banana pudding.

If people-watching is what you like, the time to come to the Four Way Grill is after church, when whole families, outfitted in their Sunday best, crowd into the bustling cafe to enjoy lavish feasts of baked ham or turkey with all the fixin's. It's as corny and down-home as a Norman Rockwell painting, but with a twist of Memphis soul.

GRIDLEY'S
6065 MACON RD., MEMPHIS, TN (901) 388-7003

The ribs Gridley's serves are known to Memphians as wet ribs to distinguish them from the dry ribs sold at Charlie Vergos. Wet means they are glazed with a sticky, fruit-sweet paste that bakes on and into the meat and makes the tender shreds that pull off the bone literally drip with flavor. There are crusty parts, too, all along the edges, pieces of meat nearly blackened by their long, slow smoke over burning hickory wood. These darkened areas striate the lean patches of glazed red meat and make these the most picturesque barbecued ribs you will ever eat; but it is their impossible lusciousness that puts them into the barbecue hall of fame. In our not-so-humble opinions, they are the best ribs in town. That's saying a lot considering that Memphis boasts of itself (with good reason) as America's pork capital.

Gridley's is renowned for ribs, but many regular customers come for big, messy, oversauced, and intoxicating chopped pork sandwiches; and frequently even we ravenous tourists who come to town with nothing but ribs on our mind switch gears and order Gridley's shrimp. They come in their shells; they are full and firm and rich-tasting; and they, too, have a zesty pepper sauce (on the side, for dipping) that makes eating them a merry mess. For about twenty dollars, two people can order a "best of both worlds" dinner: impressive portions of ribs and shrimp.

The accessories for rib and/or shrimp dinners are more than proper: a hot loaf of chewy bread, excellent for mopping and dunking ("Sop your bread in the sauce," suggests the menu); zesty beans with plenty of pork, spiked with cumin; cool cole slaw; and onion rings. Your waiter, outfitted in mustard-colored jacket and bow tie, will also supply you with a box of toothpicks and moist towelettes—both *de rigueur* when eating wet ribs.

To top off these magnificent Memphis meals, there is a choice of pies: creamy lemon meringue in a brittle crust or nutmeaty pecan that is sweet as syrup. Both seem wickedly extravagant after a full plate of ribs; and both are divine.

THE HUT
ROUTE 64, SOMMERVILLE, TN (901) 465-3458

H ave you ever eaten a pig salad? Here is a good place to acquaint yourself with this strange aspect of barbecue cookery, popular for about a hundred miles east and west of America's pork capital, Memphis, Tennessee. A pig salad, also known as a barbecue salad, is conceptually similar to a chef's salad in the sense that it combines green, leafy things with meat and cheese. In this case, however, the meat is pork barbecue, usually cut into logs or neatly shredded and strewn on top of the more ordinary salad ingredients. But that's not all. The salad is then dressed; and most restaurants that serve it—including The Hut of Sommerville—offer customers a choice of topping: salad dressing or barbecue sauce.

At The Hut, the barbecued pork is wonderful. On a sandwich bun or on a plate with beans, onion rings, French fries, and cole slaw, it is classic western Tennessee pig meat—saucy wet, very spicy, finger-licking good, served with squeeze bottles of hot, sweet-and-sour sauce to add. For a pig salad, the pork is heaped, still warm, onto a pile of lettuce, tomato, and American cheese, then quickly sauced and served. In lieu of Thousand Island or bleu cheese dressing, we usually choose barbecue sauce for our salad; The Hut's zesty brew is just as good on lettuce as it is on meat. Believe us, this salad, however bizarre, is a likable combination of temperatures, textures, and flavors. To accompany the culinary crazy quilt The Hut will serve you tall glasses of iced tea (oddly, not pre-sweetened) that are refilled by the waitress throughout the meal.

Pig isn't all they serve. There are catfish, steaks, and shrimp, and a big selection of outstanding homemade pies, the best of which are caramel and lemon ice box.

LEONARD'S
5465 FOX PLAZA DRIVE (BETWEEN MT. MORIAH AND MENDENHALL), MEMPHIS, TN (901) 360-1963

E lvis was not a big barbecue man, but when he did get the craving for a pork sandwich, Leonard's was where he went. Since 1922, long before the Presley family came north from Tupelo, Leonard Heuberger's pit has set the pork standard in Memphis. In fact, barbecue historians credit Mr. Heuberger with *inventing* the barbecued pork sandwich: shreds of smoked shoulder meat topped with tomato-sweet, vinegar-tangy sauce, weighted with a heap of creamy, cool cole slaw. Dozens of parlors throughout the city and the mid-South continue to serve it that way, but Leonard's version, prepared by cooks who have been with the business for decades, is the paragon—a mesmerizing confluence of sugar and spice, meat and bread and sauce.

There are three Leonard's in Memphis; and although the one on the way to Graceland has closed, the branch on Fox Plaza Drive has inherited its sign (as well as its eighty-four-year-old cashier and its veteran pitmaster), a sign that is one of the great images in all of porklore: a neon pig, all decked out in top hat and tails, wielding a cane, captioned "Mr. Brown Goes To Town." For years, we were perplexed by what Mr. Brown was supposed to signify. Then last year, when we visited the Mount Mariah store, which was sprucing up to resemble Leonard's of the 1950s, our waitress, Loretta, explained: "Mr. Brown was the term used for brown-meat barbecue. It is the outside of the shoulder that gets succulent and chewy from the sauce and the smoke in the pit. The inside part of the roast, which is moist but has very little barbecue flavor is known as Miss White. People in Memphis used to ask for plates and sandwiches of 'Mr. Brown and Miss White.'" We were mesmerized by Loretta's explanation, but the smell of pit smoke and hot pork wafting off our sandwiches drew our attention to the meal at hand, and we forgot to ask Loretta why Mr. Brown, that delicious pig, is going to town. Might that mean that the sandwich is "dressed up" with slaw? No apology is needed to return to Leonard's, but in addition to the main reason for visiting—sensational pork sandwiches—the answer to that question is a fine excuse to lure us back posthaste.

LITTLE TEA SHOP
69 MONROE, MEMPHIS, TN (901) 525-6000

Around the corner from legendary Cotton Row on the banks of the Mississippi River, the Little Tea Shop opened in 1918 and continues today as a favorite eatery of commodities traders and financial types who work in the capital city of the mid-South. Despite the high-powered nature of its customers, the Little Tea Shop is indeed a little tea shop, serving only lunch on weekdays between 11:00 A.M. and 2:15 P.M. (with a take-out bakery open earlier for breakfast). There isn't a meal on the menu that costs over ten dollars.

Low prices do not mean grubby clientele. Cotton is still king in Memphis, and you can see the regular lunch crowd—dressed in luxurious and oh-so-conservative natural-fiber threads—every day at noon gathered around the "Cotton Table" set aside for them. There is a "Mayor's Table," too, christened because former Memphis Mayor Frank Tobey used to come to the Little Tea Shop every day and order a slice of lemon pie.

Traditions reign in this modest town lunchroom, where the menu is headed with a "Lacey Special," named for cotton broker C. A. Lacey. It is a chicken breast set between two crunchy, sweet-meal corn sticks, ladled with gravy and sided by rice and spicy apple jelly.

Many everyday people come for club sandwiches or BLTs or chicken salad; but if you are visiting just once, we recommend a traditional Dixie meal. Each day of the week has its own lunch special, from Creole chicken giblets and rice on Monday to catfish steak on Friday. These flowers of the southern kitchen are accompanied by soulful vegetables such as black-eyed peas, candied yams, or scalloped tomatoes. If you really want to get into the spirit of the southern kitchen, you can make a meal of four vegetables without any entrée at all. Or you can base lunch around a mound of turnip greens.

Turnip greens are always on the Little Tea Shop menu, with salt pork, with baked ham, or with onions. They are *serious* greens, whole-leaf heaps of heavy vegetable goodness, soft and dark green, with a commanding tonic flavor enriched by the pork with which they have been cooked. To make them tender, greens are boiled for an eternity. They soften, they absorb the porcine succulence of the cracked ham bone or fatback with which they share space in the water, and they come out of the pot a most amazing food: strong, heady, satisfying like no other vegetable.

After the greens are cooked to a fare-thee-well and removed, what is left in the pot is considered a delicacy. It is known as pot likker, and it really is like some kind of invigorating liquor, only good for you. It is the essence of green leaves, the kind of liquid nutrition Popeye might drink to make his muscles bulge. Because it is so intense, so porky and focused, the Little Tea Shop serves it only by the cupful, with a couple of corn sticks, as a breathtaking appetizer before lunch.

THE LOVELESS CAFE
HIGHWAY 100, NASHVILLE, TN (615) 646-9700

The Loveless Cafe, attached to the Loveless Motel on the highway heading west out of Nashville, is the quintessential country-western eatery: wood-paneled walls, red-checked tablecloths, waitresses with sorghum-sweet mountain accents, and out-of-this-world down home vittles. For a long time it has been a favorite haunt among Grand Ol' Opry performers, whose pictures line the vestibule, and whose tour buses frequently can be seen parked toward the back of the lot. The Loveless has gotten a lot of good press in the last few years, praised by everyone from CBS-TV to Martha Stewart; but we are happy to say that national renown hasn't spoiled it one bit. Yes, there are some Loveless souvenirs to buy near the cash register, including a fancy print of the cafe and motel (suitable for framing); but they still serve some of the best fried chicken for miles around, and they make the blackberry and peach preserves every week in a big old pot on a kitchen stove.

Those preserves (which, by the way, are available by mail) are reason enough to celebrate the Loveless. The peach is the color of a summer sunset, sweet and deeply fruity, just perfect in conjunction with a faintly sour biscuit. The blackberry is more tart: wonderful on biscuits or toast or waffles, or on ice cream, or (we confess) spooned straight from the jar.

Even more than its homemade preserves, ham is the pride of the Loveless kitchen: it is country ham, slow cured and salty, fried on a griddle until its rim of fat turns translucent amber and the coral pink meat gets speckled sandy brown. It comes with a bowl of red-eye gravy for dipping, cream gravy, sorghum molasses, honey, and bowls full of each of the preserves. What delirious fun it is to permutate all these good things: dip the biscuits, spread the sorghum, make little sandwiches with ham. And the best thing is, the biscuits keep coming, fresh and hot throughout the meal.

MARY BOBO'S BOARDING HOUSE
LYNCHBURG, TN (615) 759-7394
(MIDDAY MEAL ONLY, BY RESERVATION)

When we met Miss Mary Bobo, she was about to celebrate her one-hundredth birthday. She was standing at the door of her boarding-house, wishing Godspeed to each of twenty guests who had just enjoyed a midday family-style dinner of southern fried chicken, mashed potatoes, hot biscuits, peach cobbler, and lemonade. We walked onto Miss Mary's front porch and scanned the heat-baked streets of Lynchburg, Tennessee. It was easy to imagine what the town was like seventy-five years earlier, when Miss Mary began taking in boarders. In fact, if you took away the cars, you wouldn't see much evidence of progress at all.

That was more than ten years ago; and although she no longer took in lodgers, dinner at Miss Mary's place was a nostalgic event, harkening back many decades to a time before motels and franchised food. Mary Bobo died in 1983, and the boardinghouse closed. A year later, Lynne Tolley, who grew up in Lynchburg, reopened it. She hired back Miss Mary's cooks; she weeded the vegetable gardens that provide ingredients for summer casseroles; and she polished the brass bell that rings at one o'clock every afternoon to announce dinner's beginning.

There are four dining rooms at Mary Bobo's, each presided over by a hostess who shows guests through the ropes. First, all the people at the table introduce themselves. Then everybody's on their own: take what you want, pass the platter to the left—unless you are sitting at the round table downstairs. That one has a lazy Susan in its center, making it easier to concentrate on eating (as long as you are quick enough to grab what you want when it spins past).

Fried chicken cooked in iron skillets is almost always on the table, augmented by a second main course such as pork chops, gently cured Tennessee ham, or turkey and dressing. At our most recent dinner, we missed the fried chicken . . . until we spooned into a platter of chicken and pastry that made us swoon. There are biscuits and cornbread muffins, and usually about a half-dozen vegetables. Extraordinary vegetables, *southern-style* vegetables, make no mistake about it: cooked with fatback or ham bone, sweetened and enriched. Carrots or cabbage luxuriate in casseroles oozing butter or cheese and topped with cracker crumbs; sweet corn straight off the cob is pan-cooked with thick-sliced bacon; okra, deep-fried to a brittle crisp, wins our nomination as one of the very best plates of okra ever; apples are sautéed with butter and sugar until they turn limp and caramelize. The voluptuous meal concludes with a fairly demure dessert, such as pecan ice box pie, meringue-topped raspberry pie, a chewy little square of whipped cream–topped chess cake, or sweet potato pudding—a textured ambrosia that is southern to its soul.

PAYNE'S
1762 LAMAR AVE., MEMPHIS, TN (901) 272-1523

Let's be honest: to the connoisseur of *Roadfood*, ambience is an important aspect of the dining experience. We all like to say that it's only good eats that matter, wherever they may be; but who among us doesn't shiver with delight and anticipation when we hear about a restaurant in a converted filling station? Ambience like that almost always guarantees a four-star meal.

Case in point: Payne's. Former gas station. Minimal menu. The smell of smoldering wood and roasting pork. This is heaven! When you order a sandwich, a chunk of shoulder meat is forked off the rack and hacked into pieces, sauced and heaped onto a bun and topped with spicy slaw. Because it has only just been cut, the meat is unbelievably moist, dripping juices that combine with the sauce and slaw to create something awfully close to perfection. There are ribs, too. And that is all you need to know.

THE PIT
ROUTE 12, ASHLAND CITY, TN (615) 792-7708

The big question you will face when you dine at The Pit is whether or not to eat barbecue. As the name of this restaurant implies, barbecue is a specialty; and as Sheriff Andy Taylor of Mayberry might have said, it is goo-ood. Crusty pork ribs are hung with big, lush strips of skin you want to pull off with your teeth; tender chunked pork is served hacked up and undressed. Add your own sauce from the bottle provided on the tables. It is sauce at once sharp and deep, and resonates for hours on your taste buds. We begged to buy a bunch to take home; but the master of the kitchen refused, offering us a bag of barbecued pig skin instead.

For pit-cooked food alone, The Pit would be a *Roadfood* classic. Add to that now all the vegetables and side dishes there are to select to go along with such robust meals as meat loaf, pork chops, fried chicken, and catfish, and you have a serious dilemma. No one person can eat a big plate of barbecued ribs and also eat fried chicken with all the fixin's. And these are some fixin's. There are creamed potatoes, white beans, glorious macaroni and cheese, greens and peas of various shapes and textures, and an impressive variation of the mid-South's preferred breadstuff, cornbread. They told us it is hot water cornbread—vaguely similar to hoe cakes, but better and creamier-textured.

Now, the *coup de grace:* dessert. On two occasions, we have eaten two different desserts at The Pit, both of them memorable. There is chess pie, a shivery, glistening, translucent wedge poised this side of tart; other times there is blackberry cobbler, which proves the adage that dessert in the South can never be too rich or too sweet.

POPE'S CAFE
ON THE SQUARE, SHELBYVILLE, TN (615) 684-7933

R *oadfood* heaven, here it is. Even from the outside, Pope's Cafe looks just right: an ancient place (since 1945) on the square in Shelbyville, with a sign lettered on the storefront window boasting of Tennessee ham. The inside is well-weathered, its yellow walls lined with red coathooks front to back. There are six tables on the right, each of them topped with glass under which are hundreds of business cards from patrons, and a long counter with stools to the left. Jukeboxes are arrayed every few seats along the counter and at each table, and the last time we stopped in, the waitress kept feeding quarters into the machine and playing the loveliest country tunes.

The one problem we have with Pope's is that we never can decide whether to plan our travels so we come for breakfast or lunch. Breakfast is classic: salty, chewy, resonantly flavorful ham with (or sandwiched inside) buttery tender biscuits. If such ham is too powerful, try Pope's good sausage; or even gentler (and more succulent) are tenderloin patties that are made to slip inside one of these good biscuits.

If you come for late breakfast, look back into the kitchen and you'll see them making lunch. Ladies at big, steamy pots and skillets are seasoning and stirring such regionally flavored vegetables as fried apples, buttered corn kernels, spinach and eggs, spiced peaches, even—for heaven's sake—baked spaghetti. These, among a list of at least a dozen every day, accompany main courses of roast pork, roast beef, country-style steak (that's like chicken-fried), ham, or pork barbecue. No meal, not even the precious country ham, costs over five dollars.

Then there's pie. Fabulous, homemade, only-in-the-Southland pie, including baby-food-gentle chess pie, fudge pie, meringues of all kind, pecan pie, and a Pope's specialty named after singer Charlie Pride. Charlie Pride pie is a kind of mud pie—all dark and fudgy, but with cream cheese and Cool Whip heaped inside and a mountain of chocolate pudding on the top. Like we said, it's *Roadfood* heaven.

RIDGEWOOD RESTAURANT
ROUTE 19E, SOUTH OF BLUFF CITY, TN (615) 538-7543

S ince we declared the Ridgewood Restaurant to be the best barbecue in America ten years ago, we have eaten a lot of pork. Challengers have come close to the profundity of Mrs. Proffitt's pit-cooked hams, hand-sliced into gorgeous, moist, smoky flaps with crunchy edges, and glowing with the smack of sauce. Yes, indeed, we have eaten at plenty of very excellent barbecue restaurants in Texas and the Deep South, even some misplaced good ones in California and Connecticut; we have eaten barbecued beef, mutton, and goat; but nothing we have eaten—not one plate or platter—measures up to the standard of the pig at the Ridgewood in the hills of eastern Tennessee.

What makes it superior is its balance. First there is the textural variety of the meat itself, which includes some shreds so tender they verge on self-disintegration, as well as firm, chewy strips from the outside of the ham, crusted with cooked-on sauce. Then there is the way the complex flavors of the hickory-piqued pork are amplified by that sauce—a thick, powerful, but polished brew that is added to the meat by the kitchen staff before plates and sandwiches are served. (Customers, Mrs. Proffitt's theory goes, might add too much or too little, thereby upsetting the balance.)

Did we mention the beans that come on the side? For these alone we would sing hosannahs: served in a small crock, in a saucy broth thick with hunks of meat and dotted with bits of sweet onion, each bean is a little silk pillow of legume lusciousness. And sparkling cole slaw, and lovely French fries, and even really good rolls . . .

But wait, we are babbling, and we don't want to give the impression that the Ridgewood rates so high because of all these wonderful side dishes and extras. They truly are grand, but when it comes to barbecue, the meat's the thing. And this meat is peerless, the quiddity of Q.

It is served by a staff of queenly ladies in a lovely restaurant with a wood-slat ceiling and comfortable booths that provide a view of the waitresses at work. We have read reports that these good ol' gals can be brusque or downright rude to customers, but we have never been insulted. Usually, they are perfectly polite; and if they seem haughty or strict on occasion, it is only because they take their work as seriously as it deserves. After all, they aren't just slinging hash here. They are carrying perfection.

Two problems about the Ridgewood: it isn't necessarily easy to find; and when you do find it—especially on the weekend—you may have to wait awhile in line. The best strategy: call ahead to check the hours, and arrive at an odd time.

SATSUMA TEA ROOM
417 UNION ST., NASHVILLE, TN (615) 256-5211

S pecializing in civilized, inexpensive meals since 1918, the Satsuma is smack in the heart of Nashville, and is a favorite place for politicians, shoppers, and visitors who crave real southern-style cooking. The pleasure of a Satsuma meal begins as you wait for a table in the vestibule, lined with an appetizing display of baked goods for sale: chess pies and lemon cakes, dinner rolls and cinnamon buns.

Once you are seated, you look over the menu (printed every day), and write your own order on a small pad set upon the table. The waitress, in white uniform and red apron, looks over the list and doesn't even blink at four desserts for two hungry people.

Fluffy cupcake-shaped rolls and corn sticks accompany such fare as turnip greens and hog jowl or country sausage, as well as more ladylike entrées including turkey à la king or shrimp salad stuffed into a tomato. The dessert repertoire is major: moist lemon cake, prune cake that is thickly woven with shredded bits of prunes, sky-high chocolate pie, with its hovering meringue cloud and crunchy nut crust. There are fresh berry shortcakes and cheesecakes, too, but the single great dessert at Satsuma is ice cream: coffee-sherry or eggnog-sherry, pale and served nearly soup-soft, a sweet, comforting taste that summarizes everything good about tea room dining.

SYLVAN PARK
4502 MURPHY RD., NASHVILLE, TN (615) 292-9275
(LOCATIONS ALSO AT 221 6TH AVE. N., NASHVILLE,
255-1562; 5207 NOLENSVILLE PIKE, NASHVILLE, 781-3077)

S ylvan Park is a square lunchroom that serves square meals, cheap and good. There are about a dozen tables, pretty red-checked curtains on the windows, and minimal decor except for a few eight-by-ten pictures signed by celebrity clientele and a marvelous oil painting of a black woman holding out a big slice of meringue pie.

"Meat and Threes" is the name Nashvillians give to the type of cuisine served by this plain-looking but distinguished eatery, meaning the kitchen sends forth dinners that consist of one meat and three vegetables with a pair of powdery biscuits or buttery sections of cornbread on the side.

There are half a dozen meats to choose from every day, including the likes of baked chicken and gravy over rice, roast beef, wieners with kraut, and fish cakes. Sylvan Park ham is especially gentle—sugar-cured and meltingly tender, almost bland-seeming at first bite (compared to most salty country ham), but sweet and ever more ingratiating as you eat it. Fabulous vegetables: whole-leaf, pungent turnip greens; really sweet sweet corn; butter-tender stewed apples; black-eyed peas; mashed potatoes; cool cucumbers and onions in a sweet-and-sour marinade; we even like the little blocks of jiggly congealed salad with fruit cocktail.

Service is nearly instantaneous, on unbreakable partitioned plates; and when you are through you will want pie. There are two kinds made each day, including some wonderful meringues and a stunning dark fudge; but the one to choose, if they have it, is chess. Golden yellow, nearly candy-sweet, rich and addictive, it has even garnered praise from a local magistrate, Bill Higgins, whose autographed photo on the wall includes a proclamation, written in his handwriting, officially judging it to be the best chess pie in the world.

WOODLEY'S BAR-B-QUE
ROUTE 64 (PULASKI HIGHWAY), FAYETTEVILLE, TN
(615) 433-2405 OR 433-4231

Woodley's has been serving barbecue for decades. A little green-painted wood-frame house way west of Fayetteville, it has a menu limited during the week to one item only—a barbecue sandwich—and expanded on Friday nights to include chicken and rib plates. For taking home, you can also buy whole cooked pork shoulders and pulled pork (already cut and shredded) by the pound.

When you order a sandwich, Gladys Bryson will ask if you want it hot or medium. Don't worry about this decision: even hot isn't all that fiery; in fact, we think it adds just the right amount of zest to the shreds of pork that get piled on a bun. This meat is atypical of Tennessee barbecue, actually more like the kind you'd expect in eastern North Carolina, which is to say that it is pale, cream-tender, and essentially sauceless. What you taste and appreciate here is not sauce, or smoke, or spice, but the pork itself. Sauce, a peppery and nearly clear vinegar-based brew, is applied only to accentuate its goodness.

For about a dollar more than the cost of a sandwich, you can get a bag of chips and a soda (help yourself to the latter from the soda machine). A lot of Woodley's business is take-out, but there is a scattering of tables with mismatched kitchenette chairs around the makeshift dining room (which also includes a television tuned to afternoon soaps) as well as a few shelves of knickknacks just like home.

TEXAS

ALLEN'S FAMILY-STYLE MEALS
1301 E. BROADWAY, SWEETWATER, TX (915) 235-2060

The only choice you will be given when you enter Allen's Family-Style Meals is whether or not you want iced tea. (Don't ask us what happens if you say no.) You will be seated somewhere in the plain dining area at a big table along with strangers; then the food starts coming. Here's what was brought to the table last time we ate at Allen's: buttered corn kernels, black-eyed peas, turnip greens in pot likker, pickled beets, honeyed summer squash, green beans, red beans, potato salad, mashed potatoes, sweet potatoes, macaroni and cheese, hot cornbread, dinner rolls, tossed salad, hot apple cobbler (that's dessert), and also plates of beef brisket, ham steaks, and fried chicken.

The vegetables seemed to be tasty (who can keep track?), the cobbler was shockingly but not unpleasantly sweet, the brisket was a bore, and the ham steaks were perfectly okay; but what we like best—and what has made Allen's a Sweetwater landmark for nearly half a century—is the fried chicken. It is sheathed in a lovely, crackling-crisp crust, juicy and loaded with flavor inside, a perfect blend of spice, crunch, juice, and balmy bird savor. It's the kind of chicken you gleefully eat down to the bone, then worry the bones for every bit of flavor—even though new, meaty pieces keep coming to the table.

The Allen family have been cooking this superb fried chicken in Sweetwater since the forties, when Mrs. Allen opened a little restaurant and catering company at the freight depot down on Broadway and Oak. They still cater parties and make picnic baskets, and serve lunch every day but Monday in their eatery here on Business Route 80. If you hanker for a groaning board feast while traveling west of Abilene, this is the place to go.

ANGELO'S
2533 WHITE SETTLEMENT RD., FORT WORTH, TX (817) 332-0357

Beef brisket, slow-cooked over hickory until it is nearly ready to disintegrate, is cut into limp slices and piled high on a roll. It is supremely mild-flavored beef, soft and savory, true cowboy comfort food. If you want something spicier, get Angelo's highly spiced, crackle-skinned sausages, also cooked in the pit and scented with wood smoke. There is pit-cooked ham, too. Along with a cold beer, these are the makings for one of Fort Worth's legendary barbecue lunches. In the evening after five, the sandwich menu is supplemented by pork ribs: big bats with enough flavor in their supremely gnawable meat to send you into a hickory-perfumed reverie for hours as you eat.

Angelo's has style befitting its cuisine. It is a dimly lit eating barn with a stuffed Alaskan brown bear and a moose head in the foyer and countermen who can draw a beer and push a beef sandwich down the counter simultaneously. Everything in it smells like barbecue smoke; and you will, too, when you leave.

AVALON DRUG COMPANY
2516 KIRBY, HOUSTON, TX (713) 529-9136

Confession: we love all food served in drugstores, even more than food served in Woolworth's. Any such short-order lunch is swell by us—a reminder of older, fading urban eating habits; and as far as we are concerned, nothing mingles better with the aromatic tang of wafer-thin American cheese sandwiches sizzling on an ancient grill than the medicinal scent of Ben-Gay.

Drugstore eateries are rarer all the time; and ones that serve basic and totally satisfying lunch-counter fare are real treasures. Behold, then, the Avalon Drug Company, famous for its thin, gray, delectably greasy hamburgers on lightly toasted buns, its crisp French fries and chocolate malts, and freshly squeezed lemonade. Residents of River Oaks come on weekends, too, to read the weekend papers and eat waffles or omelettes. None of what is dished out (other than the distinguished pecan waffle) is four-star food; but when the craving for a skinny burger and a milk shake strikes, four-star food could never satisfy. The cuisine of the Avalon, ordinary though it may seem, admits no competition.

BISHOP GRILL
321 N. BISHOP AVE., DALLAS, TX (214) 946-1752

Gennie's Bishop Grill has moved to bigger and more comfortable quarters across the street in a vintage 1925 building, but it's still hard to find a place to park. Once inside, you are on easy street. Stroll through an abbreviated but nonetheless magnificent cafeteria line that is everything good about southern-style Texas cookery. Vegetables are bought daily at the farmers' market, seasoned with brio, served with homemade yeast rolls to accompany serious blue-plate vittles like meat loaf, beef stew, chili, catfish fillets, and stuffed peppers. The best meal in the house, and one that is always available, is chicken-fried steak with cream gravy, accompanied by a big heap of mashed potatoes and pungent turnip greens.

Rosemarie Hudson, whose mother Gennie started the grill in 1971, told us that she and her husband Gus "serve only the freshest and best food available at a price the working people can afford." But you don't have to wear a blue collar to appreciate the Hudsons' plebeian perfection; the banana pudding and peanut butter pie are country aristocrats.

BLUE MESA GRILL
5100 BELTLINE RD., DALLAS, TX (IN ADDISON) (214) 934-0165

We have eaten funky fajitas in roadhouses and Tex-Mex border cafes, we have eaten mass-produced chain restaurant fajitas all across America, we have even eaten ridiculously fancy fajitas in New York City. But no fajitas are quite as tasty as those we ate at the Blue Mesa Grill, a nice, upscale dining establishment in Dallas where the kitchen specializes in very trendy (and very, very good) southwestern cooking.

It's the beef we like best: big, dark hunks of it veined with enough fat so it is profoundly juicy, and so tender that it is easy to bite. The beef is redolent of mesquite smoke, as mild as the best pot roast you ever ate, and there are heaps of it. It arrives sizzling on the hot skillet among ribbons of cooked tomatoes and peppers and sweet, caramelized onions. And, too, there are piles of dignified black beans, complex tomato relish, guacamole that is chunky with avocados yet silky smooth, and of course hot stacks of freshly made, faintly adhesive tortillas eager to wrap themselves around fistfuls of these sublime constituents. You can get chicken fajitas, and they too are excellent. Like the beef, the chicken is fall-apart tender, glowing with the flavor of pepper and smoke.

Fajitas are just one item on a menu that includes made-to-order (at your table) guacamole, enchiladas and tacos of all kinds, adobe pie (chicken, cheese, and roasted peppers), and even the ultra-exotic likes of duck taquitos with ranchero sauce, "painted desert salmon," and garlic shrimp with angel-hair pasta and a goat cheese sauce.

Blue Mesa is a comfortable place to eat: a pink adobe building with blue window frames and brick floors, lots of skylights, and table service reminiscent of Tex-Mex Fiesta Ware, in shades of blue, yellow, and pink. At the entrance to the restaurant, the foyer is guarded by a pair of adobe-colored statues of six-foot tall, howling dogs—like immense Chia-pets without their grass-seed fur.

CAPTAIN BENNY'S HALF SHELL
8506 S. MAIN, HOUSTON, TX (713) 666-5469

For fresh Gulf seafood in party-time surroundings, you will find no place more raucously satisfying than Captain Benny's, a berthed fishing boat across from Luther's Barbecue. Actually, it has grown since it used to be nothing but a little trawler just down the street, impossibly crowded with just enough stand-up space for hungry customers to sardine themselves inside. Now, there's some elbow room, although Captain Benny's still attracts a close-quarters, party-time crowd who come to relish raw oysters from Matagorda Bay, shrimp that are simply boiled or expertly fried in a cornmeal coating, plus crisp-crusted catfish and bowls of gumbo.

The beverage list is limited to beer and soda; there are no side dishes other than potatoes; napkins are paper; shuckers are brusque; and the ambience is unapologetically rude: a perfect recipe for satisfaction on the half shell.

CITY CAFE
520 WALNUT, COLUMBUS, TX (409) 432-8009

We ate at the City Cafe on our first cross-country trip back in the early 1970s. The lunch they served was so good—in an understated, home-cooking kind of way—that it inspired us to think that maybe we should try to write a little guidebook to restaurants like this one where travelers could eat well and cheaply and get a taste of real America. You are now reading the newest incarnation of that book; and the City Cafe, which helped inspire it, is still simply wonderful.

Breakfast or lunch: you can't go wrong. In the morning, it is especially nice to get cinnamon rolls hot from the oven, or a piece of the light, braided Czech pastry known as a kolache (also frequently available stuffed with savory things such as ham or ground beef). The rest of the day, whatever else you order, you want something from the cafe bakery: dinner rolls or fresh-baked bread, fruit pies, cakes, or cookies. Many local people come only for pies, cakes, or rolls to take home; and it is rare to see someone leaving the City Cafe without at least a little bag of bakery goodies.

Hot lunches are archetypal Texas cafe cooking: huge, hand-breaded chicken-fried steaks with pepper gravy; good hamburgers and French fries; Mexican lunch every Wednesday; German sausage and fiesta rice dotted with peppers and diced tomatoes. Friends, this is good eating . . . especially when topped off with a big slice of flake-crusted cherry or Dutch apple pie. If every town in America had a City Cafe, we could drive forever.

CITY MARKET
633 DAVIS, LULING, TX (512) 875-9019

We were directed to the City Market by royalty. The Watermelon Queen of Luling, touring the Southwest on behalf of her city's annual Watermelon Thump, advised us that if it was great barbecue we were after there was only one place to go, and it was in her hometown. We lost touch with the queen many years ago, but always half expect to see her sitting in a booth whenever we visit the City Market, which has stayed high on our list of great Texas eateries ever since we took her advice.

It is a dining room in a grocery store. The pit is at the back: go there first and order your meat. The choices include brisket by the pound, hot links by the piece, and pork ribs by the slab. The pitmaster puts your order on a piece of heavy red paper and bunches the paper up around the meat so it is easy to carry. Now tote your meat and pay a visit to the counter in front where you select whatever accoutrements you need—beans, potato salad, sauce, soda pop, utility towel napkins. Meal in hand, find an available knotty-pine booth along either wall of the big room and dig in.

It is truly thrilling to slice into one of the City Market's links. It bursts open and juices flow and suddenly you catch a whiff of pit smoke that the link has been containing. They are luscious tubes of meat, rich and spicy. The slices of brisket are lovely, lean except for the thin ribbon of fat that bisects them, each slice rimmed with blackened crust and permeated with the flavor of burning oak wood. The sauce available to flavor these meats has a sweet mustard flavor that would be fine if one were eating ordinary hamburgers or meat loaf. But the links and beef at the City Market need no sauce at all; they are perfect as they come from the pit.

CLARK'S
HIGHWAY 377, TIOGA, TX (817) 437-2414

We tip our caps to Jim Hayes of Denton for directing us to Clark's, which he figured was just the right place to send a couple of out-of-staters hankering for a real taste of Texas. We were in Dallas on a book tour, eating a steady diet of room-service club sandwiches and vending-machine snacks, so we took Jim's advice and took off in search of the minuscule municipality of Tioga, which is practically in Oklahoma. Here we found one of the finest *Roadfood* meals ever, served in an unlikely dining room decorated with customers' business cards and pictures of horses and the Old West. Under a stamped-tin ceiling, a slow-spinning fan, and the gaze of a deer's head mounted on the wall, customers from miles around sat at Clark's sauce-spattered red-checked tablecloths eating beef and pork ribs in the respectful semi-silence that only the most superb pit-cooked food engenders.

The beef is brisket, striated with just enough veins of fat so that it feels almost nectarous, cooked long enough (three days) to develop a sheath of sharp, pungently smoky, blackened crust, yet at a low-enough temperature so the inside stays bright, blushing pink. No prime rib or high-priced steak was ever so luscious. The ribs are lean and their meat has a real porcine sweetness that goes so well with the taste of smoke. To accompany these highlights, Clark's serves all the usual side dishes as well as fried corn-on-the-cob and bull's balls.

HERMAN SONS STEAK HOUSE
HIGHWAY 90 E., HONDO, TX (512) 426-2220

The business card we saved from Herman Sons Steak House boasts, "We feed you not fool you." We're not ones to quibble, but we have been fed *and* we have been fooled at this big barn of a restaurant on the highway heading east out of Hondo. We submit as evidence Herman Sons' cheeseburger pepper steak. Two patties of coarsely ground beef are sandwiched around a heap of chopped-up jalapeño peppers, onions, and cheese. This Dagwood is available in three degrees of hotness; and the folks who work here told us not to worry—that even the hot wasn't too bad. So that's the way we ordered it. Sure enough, it was easygoing for the first few bites—a fine combination of meat's richness and chili's bite. Then the peppers began to detonate on our tongue. Yow! Actually, it was delicious—not merely hot, but hot and really flavorful. Now we get it hot every time, but we suggest you not be lulled into complacency, as we were that first time: when the menu says hot, it means it.

In fact, there is something direct and very honest about Herman Sons. It's a wide-open, wood-paneled eatery decorated with beer signs and some hanging plants. And it seems to be a place where locals like to hang around and shoot the breeze over beers and burgers. We have never failed to find ourselves in some sort of conversation with dining room denizens—about different kinds of chili peppers, local scenery, and the best place to eat barbecue in these parts (The Salt Lick, in Driftwood).

Other than the cheeseburger pepper steak, which is served with nice big steak fries, Herman Sons is known for its rib-eye steak, as well as sirloins, T-bones, and quail-and-steak platters (fowl 'n' growl?). We liked the steaks when we tried them several years ago, and we also liked the guacamole they served; but now whenever we are headed for Hondo, we only have eyes for that distinctive cheeseburger pepper steak—hot, if you please.

HIGHLAND PARK CAFETERIA
4611 COLE ST., DALLAS, TX (214) 526-3801

Of all the most reputable cafeterias across America, the Highland Park of Dallas is the *crème de la crème*. Since 1926, when it began as a small cafe with eight tables and thirteen stools, it has grown to become a gastronomic institution, and along the way it has garnered a reputation not

only for exquisite made-from-scratch southern-style food, but for politeness and civility. A low-priced eatery patronized by everyone from blue-
collar working people who arrive in pickup trucks (and try to wash their
eternally grimy hands before getting in line) to society's upper crust whose
limos wait outside (the swells wash their hands, too), the HPC provides an
eating experience that is a taste of genteel democracy.

Your meal begins with a course in American history. Before arriving at
the trays and silverware, the line of customers (there is *always* a line—but
it moves fast) files past a wall with portraits of every President from George
Washington through George Bush. It is difficult to concentrate on this hall
of honor, however, because the great men are on the right, and compelling
though their comparative physiognomies may be (the early ones grimace,
the recent ones smile), the food is on the left—and it is too gorgeous to
ignore.

Above the food are a series of black-and-white television screens
broadcasting hungry customers' favorite show: lists of everything the Highland Park Cafeteria cooks have made that day. And what lists they are!
Dozens of different salads, dozens of vegetables ranging from the simplest
steamed or boiled healthy ones to great, oozy casseroles enriched with
cheese, eggs, bread crumbs, and butter. There are biscuits, cornbreads,
clover-leaf rolls, sticky buns, and muffins. There are pies, puddings, cakes,
cobblers, and cookies. As for entrées, some of the more memorable ones
include fork-tender chicken-fried steak and gravy, buttery slices of beef
brisket, prime rib portions severed from the mother lode of beef when
ordered and presented in a sea of natural gravy, rosy-pink baked ham,
turkey and dressing, pork tenderloin, and shatteringly crisp fried chicken
(white meat or dark). The number of choices available at any one meal is
staggering; and we promise you this: not one plate of food we have ever
eaten at the Highland Park Cafeteria (and we have been eating here as
often as possible for the last fifteen years) is less than excellent.

Many of the recipes still used today by the HPC kitchen are those
developed by Sallie Temple Goodman when she opened the restaurant
sixty-seven years ago; and there are certain dishes, like cranberry sauce,
jalapeño cornbread, southern hash, utterly simple (and impeccable) macaroni and cheese, buttermilk pie, and millionaire ice box pie, that are practically legendary among Dallas eaters as well as among traveling
chowhounds for whom the HPC is a culinary beacon. Ourselves, we are
mesmerized by the variety and color of the gelatin salads available on any
single day. Their numbers include classic perfection salad, ambrosia (with

shredded coconut), cherry salad spiced with red hot candies, guacamole mold, blocks of gelatine with prunes and cream cheese, and pastel-tinted vegetable soufflés. In this part of the country, these jiggling dainties are known as congealed salads; like everything else dished out at the HPC, they are visions of loveliness.

JOE'S BAKERY & COFFEE SHOP
2305 E. 7TH ST., AUSTIN, TX (512) 472-0017

Tourist, beware of the salsa on the tables at Joe's. It looks innocent enough, sitting in a small jar of the type that might hold pickle relish or some such wan condiment in an ordinary cafe. It is pale green, chunky, loose enough to seep and slither into the wrinkles of your enchiladas as soon as a spoonful is ladled on. Wow, is it ever hot! Hot enough to clear your ears, nose, and throat, open your eyes wide, and send a shiver down your spine. Hot enough to set your tongue buzzing for hours after you have finished eating.

Shocking as it is, the salsa is part of what makes Joe's Bakery and Coffee Shop feel so *real*. Located on East 7th Street, a mostly Spanish-speaking neighborhood in Austin, Joe's is one of the capital city's acclaimed Tex-Mex restaurants, patronized equally by local Chicanos and Anglos, blue-collar folk and students from the University of Texas.

The first thing you see when you enter the hunkering cinderblock building are shelves of cookies, cakes, and doughnuts—fanciful pastries the likes of which one finds only in Mexican bakeries. Here are wide-bodied gingerbread pigs, sheet cakes with bright pink icing, cinnamon-sheathed fried dough, and sweet rolls in a dozen different configurations. Many customers come to Joe's for bags of pastries to go.

Beyond the bakery cases is a wide dining room with seating at booths and tables where menus are semi-permanently encased underneath plastic tablecloths. Fans spin overhead. Decor is south-of-the-border eclectic, including a velvet painting of a bullfighter, scenic vistas of Mexico, high-tone art prints, and a souvenir banner from Niagara Falls.

We were strangers when we entered, and a bit timid, but the man at the cash register made us feel welcome. He guided us to a table and explained that Joe's is famous for having the best menudo (tripe stew) in town. Menudo and chili, he advised, were available by the pint or quart, to go, if we needed to get any dinner to take home.

The chili is terrific—hot and truly Texican, and the menudo was fine (if you like tripe stew); but it is breakfast at Joe's we enjoy most. Wonderful *huevos rancheros,* the over-easy eggs embellished with chunky red salsa, served alongside fried potato disks, bacon, and refried beans. Instead of toast, you get a covered plastic bowl holding warm flour tortillas. The other great breakfast is *migas,* a mess of scrambled eggs, broken-up corn tortillas, and chorizo sausage. It looks like a haywire omelette, made with an exuberant hand that heaps everything together with no worry about how it looks. Our waitress explained that many customers like to customize their *migas.* They order cheese, sautéed onions, extra sausage, or potatoes to be mixed in with the eggs. And of course, those who are serious about getting the true Tex-Mex experience dollop their *migas* with four-alarm hot sauce.

JOE T GARCIA'S MEXICAN DISHES
2201 N. COMMERCE, FORT WORTH, TX (817) 626-4356

Joe T's is legendary, the place in Fort Worth to feast on giant portions of good Tex-Mex chow from an era before Tex-Mex was fashionable. Located in a neighborhood on the north side of Fort Worth, not far from where the stockyards used to be, it is a white house, trimmed in green, that looks like it is about to cave in. Since it opened in 1935 it has been expanded many times, and now the various dining areas, indoors and out, are an incomprehensible maze.

Wherever you sit, you will eat and drink well. The Tex-Mex meals are dished out family-style with mess-hall efficiency. There is a menu from which you can order such à la carte items as fajitas, flautas, and chili rellenos, but our recommendation is to ignore the menu and tell the waiter you want the full and complete, traditional *dinner,* then let it come. You will get tortilla chips, red salsa, quesadillas hot enough to snap your taste buds to attention, then bubbling enchiladas, trailing yellow strings of molten cheese, and refried beans, and seasoned rice, and tacos, and *real* guacamole, and steamy soft corn tortillas, spread with butter. It all comes fast and furious, to the music of clattering pots and pans in the roaring kitchen: not a mellow meal, but a thrilling one. To satisfy a sweet tooth at the end of this banquet, there are good cookies and praline candies.

KINCAID'S
4901 CAMP BOWIE, FORT WORTH, TX (817) 732-2881

Here is one of America's great hamburger-eating experiences. It is half a pound of beef, charred and well-seasoned, lean yet drippingly juicy, sandwiched between thick halves of a big warm bun that oozes a surfeit of condiments, onions, tomato slices, and shreds of lettuce. What an unholy mess it is, compounded by the fact that Kincaid's accommodations are—how shall we say it—less than deluxe.

In fact, it is the ambience of Kincaid's that gives these hamburgers their extra pizzazz. You see, it is not really a restaurant at all. It is a grocery store, without tables and chairs, but with wooden doors laid out, chest high, on the tops of the shelves, so customers can find a convenient place to scarf down lunch. We saw one old couple arrive with their own folding chairs, wait in line at the counter, get their burgers, find an unoccupied door, tuck napkins into their collars, and dig in with gusto. They told us they eat lunch at Kincaid's at least three days every week.

We don't want to suggest that Kincaid's is Spartan or unobliging. The makeshift tables are strewn with magazines for reading while you chew. And dangling from above is what must be called interior decoration: a menagerie of plastic yellow happy faces, inflatable anthropomorphic hot dogs, and similar amusing gewgaws.

KREUZ MARKET
208 S. COMMERCE, LOCKHART, TX (512) 398-2361

In this part of the country, barbecue implies one kind of meat, and that is beef. It also suggests a specific kind of eatery, attached to a grocery store. In fact, the original Texas barbecue parlors were begun so butchers could do something with unsold hunks of brisket that would otherwise spoil. What they did was to lay them on a grate over a very slow fire for about eighteen hours, by which time the stringy cuts of meat would turn butter-soft.

That is exactly the way they have made their barbecue at Kreuz Market since opening day in 1900. To get to the food, you walk through the market and arrive at a pit in back where you order beef by the pound. The pitmaster forks a brisket out of the pit, whomps off a few slices, lays them on a piece of butcher paper, and hands 'em over. There is a counter where you can buy a whole onion, whole jalapeño peppers, and whole tomatoes as condiments, and stock up on saltine crackers to accompany the meat.

Heft your butcher paper loaded with its assembled meal and try to find a place to eat. In the old dining room, tables are made of wood and the management generously supplies one knife to all customers (it's chained to a post); the new dining room provides such amenities as Formica-topped tables and plastic utensils for everyone as well as good air-conditioning. It really doesn't matter where you eat, although purists probably wouldn't want their barbecue in an air-conditioned room; perspiring while eating is part of the time-honored ritual of Texas barbecue. But such considerations fade away fast at the first bite of this superlative beef. Inside its chewy, charred crust it is nectarously juicy with a meaty wallop haloed by the taste of wood smoke. *Roadfood* Nirvana.

LA BAHIA
HIGHWAY 77 AT REFUGIO RD., GOLIAD, TX (512) 645-3651

The best enchiladas we ever ate in Texas were at La Bahia. They were hot green chili enchiladas, made with truly memorable tortillas that had real corn character and a texture actually enriched rather than diminished by the sauce atop them; and they were blanketed with a wondrous, intricately seasoned condiment made of the Mexican green tomatoes known as tomatillos. We also ate what the management calls beef fajitas tacos, made with strips of skirt steak rather than ground beef, and they, too, were many cuts above the kind of soulless food that passes for Tex-Mex chow up north, not only because the beef had a real savory smack and the salsa on them actually tasted like tomatoes but because the warm white corn tortillas that enclosed them tasted as though they had been lifted hot from the kettle just before the plate of food was assembled. You can also get them wrapped around ground beef, chicken, or guacamole tacos; but even if you order picadillo or a seafood platter, don't be so enraptured by the complex comino zest of the entrée that you forget to spend some quality time admiring and savoring these excellent rounds of faintly gritty, earthy-flavored corn.

Despite its low prices, casual atmosphere, and neighborly personnel, La Bahia is more than a mere taquería. It is a comfortable, friendly restaurant with a menu that includes low-priced and handsome steaks (we haven't eaten any yet), shrimp, and fajitas with rice, beans, guacamole, and flour tortillas. Its name, by the way, derives from the nearby Presidio La Bahia, which fell to Mexican troops three weeks after the Alamo. Later at the battle of San Jacinto, Texas independence fighters fired their passion by shouting, "Remember the Alamo, remember Goliad!" To which we add: Remember La Bahia!

(Our thanks to Jan Sharpless of Brookline, Massachusetts, for this tip.)

LOUIE MUELLER
206 W. 2ND ST., TAYLOR, TX (512) 352-6206

The building in which Louie Mueller's pitmaster cooks and serves food was built as a gymnasium in 1906. It was later a grocery store and a repair shop, and in 1963 it became a barbecue parlor. For nearly thirty years now, smoke from the pit has gradually turned the green plaster walls a gorgeous mahogany color as dark as the creaky wooden floor. Even the glass skylights in the ceiling are semi-opaque from years of oak smoke drifting heavenward as some of the Southwest's master barbecuists have worked their magic. The aura in this ancient, two-story room today is less that of a restaurant than of a cathedral. Even when all of the square wooden tables strewn across the floor are occupied, there is a cavernous hush that suggests reverence. When you come to Louie Mueller's, you are at the Mecca of Texas barbecue.

Beef brisket is slow-smoked over oak wood then wrapped in butcher paper to steep until it becomes more tender than pot roast. Tell the pitmaster how much you want and he forks a big chunk from the pit and lops off enough to fill your order. Each individual slice is gorgeous, halved by the ribbon of fat that runs through a brisket, separating the leaner, denser meat below from the lusher stuff on top. All around the edge there is a smoky-tasting crust; and if you want to add a bit of punch to this gentle-flavored meat, you are provided with a little cup of brothy sauce speckled with red pepper flakes. Side dishes are inconsequential and exist only to provide a breather from the intense pleasure of the meat: white bread, potato salad, cole slaw.

The other great thing that comes out of the Louie Mueller pit is sausage: pit-cooked links that literally burst with juice when you slice into them. Coarse-textured, muscular, and spicy, the sausages alone would put this restaurant on America's good-eats map. Barbecue places Louie Mueller in the Pantheon.

MAGNOLIA BAR & GRILL
6000 RICHMOND AVE., HOUSTON, TX (713) 781-6207

A big, clamorous roadhouse with slow-spinning fans hanging from its high ceiling and a monumental carved back bar flanked by televisions that blare mercilessly when an important football game is being broadcast, the Magnolia Bar & Grill is a bastion of nice, clean Gulf Coast seafood.

By "nice" and "clean" we mean fairly mild. There isn't too much garlic on the loaf of garlic bread that comes with dinner; the classic étouffées are gently spiced; even the fried oysters and cornmeal-crusted catfish taste demure. Despite the sometimes maddening din of the dining room, this is a polite place to eat, tended by a courteous staff in white shirts and long aprons, with a menu of the once-arcane but now-familiar seafood specialties that have become popularized in recent years as Cajun cooking. In fact, the Magnolia Bar & Grill is the creation of a group of Louisianians who are passionate about their native cuisine.

Most of what you will eat here is the real thing, which means the menu lists no blackened food. ("If my mama—who was Cajun—blackened anything," one of the proprietors told us, "she threw it out.") Among the swamp country classics that always are available are smoky, sausage-loaded gumbo, red snapper stuffed with sweet lump crabmeat, and a long list of ways with crawdads (including boiled, fried, étouffée, au gratin, court bouillon, jambalaya, and crawfish pie). We have eaten memorable pasta and seafood dishes (including pasta diablo and a swell appetizer-size plate of crab and crawfish tortellini) as well as such fish-frowner delights as baked duck ("Opelousas-style," which means perfectly luscious) and sweet-meat, charcoal-grilled pork chops.

You don't have to pig out on full-bore Cajun feasts at the Magnolia. The menu also lists fairly wieldy po' boy sandwiches, a number of safe-and-sane "heart healthy" dishes (cold crab salad, poached red snapper, baked chicken), and even a meal-size version of that strange only-in-Louisiana salad that comes heaped with pickly marinated vegetables and a hefty dose of chopped green olives. In Cajun country, this dish is listed unabashedly on menus as "Wop Salad." At the Magnolia Grill, you will find it by its more tasteful and inoffensive name, "Italian salad." Still, it's darn good.

MASSEY'S
1805 8TH AVE., FORT WORTH, TX (817) 924-8242

"Home of Chicken Fried Steaks," says the sign outside Massey's, which is the best place we know to ease the edge of a fork through a cutlet of cowboy comfort food. Massey's has specialized in chicken-fried steak since the 1930s; we met one customer who swears he has been eating it four times a week here for the last half century, another one who was slicing her steak into tiny pieces to feed to her goo-gooing infant.

The steaks are breaded and fried to order, arriving under clouds of steam, crusty gold, sided by plates of warm buttermilk biscuits suitable for mopping gravy. There is, of course, plenty of gravy (chicken-fried steak would be incomplete without it); and you have your choice of how that gravy arrives. On a lunch special, there is one cutlet on the plate, smothered with gravy; order à la carte and you get two chicken-fried steaks *on top* of their gravy. For serious chicken-fried steak aficionados, this is a big issue. Waves of rib-sticking gravy blanketing the meat are a lovely sight, but it can be argued that the crispness of the crust suffers.

Massey's is an unprepossessing cafe with a full menu of hot lunch and sandwiches, but nearly everyone comes for this single famous dish. "If there was ever one day when I didn't have chicken-fried steak on my menu," Charles Massey told us, "I think there'd be a revolution in Fort Worth."

THE OASIS CANTINA DEL LAGO
6550 COMANCHE TRAIL, AUSTIN, TX (512) 266-2441

Deep in the heart of the Lone Star State in a picturesque land of lakes, prairies, and wildflowers known as "the Hill Country" there is a restaurant that calls itself the Sunset Capital of Texas. The Oasis Cantina del Lago, on Lake Travis, attracts hordes of revelers every night who come to enjoy good food and incomparable scenery. Hundreds of feet above the lake, on big open-air patios facing west, customers sit at umbrella-topped tables sipping margaritas and munching nachos as the sun sinks slowly into the placid waters of the lake.

There is no way to adequately describe the beauty of the vista, a great natural wonder all the more delightful because it is accompanied by platters of Tex-Mex food. It is not pristine nature; evidence of people is everywhere. Pleasure boats crisscross paths on the waters of Lake Travis, which are so far below that the boats seem nearly silent. And the hubbub of fellow diners and the rush of waiters carrying chips, dips, and drinks is raucous indeed. Still, there are few places we know where you feel in such direct communion with the sunset. And as the slow luminous descent is accelerated by the evening haze into a climactic crimson burn, the restaurant falls into an eerie quiet. The light softens and is gone, and everyone breaks out with a hail of awestruck applause. Then it's back to good times and good eats in the temperate Austin evening.

We have often declared that it is food, not scenery, that wins our hearts every time; and we must tell you that the fajitas served by The Oasis are not nearly as astonishing as the sunset, but like the nightly spectacle, the food here will not fail to satisfy. The drinks are big and frosty; the nachos are goopy and plentiful; and there is a full array of Tex-Mex plates that include big portions of enchiladas, tacos, chili rellenos, rice, and beans, as well as meals of Monterey shrimp and chicken-fried steak. The fajitas, which are casual and hopelessly messy, are especially appropriate in this outdoorsy place. To be honest, it hardly matters what you order to eat. Everything at The Oasis is tasty, and the view is incomparable. If you are in Austin and hanker for some natural drama with your dinner, you'll enjoy it.

OTTO'S
5502 MEMORIAL DR., HOUSTON, TX (713) 864-8526; FOR BARBECUE CALL (713) 864-2573

There are two reasons to come to Otto's: the hamburger and the brisket. Each is served in its own half of this bifurcated barbecue and burger joint. Up front at Otto's burger bar, the patties are blue-plate delights: grilled thin and well, served on spongy, lightly toasted store-bought buns, with potato chips the only possible accompaniment. They are not gourmet burgers, that's for certain; but in their less-is-more way, they are perfect. If there is a lunch counter in heaven, these are the nice, greasy little patties they serve there, with a glass of milk on the side.

In back at Otto's, in a pine-paneled dining room decorated with gag photographs of monkeys, barbecued brisket is served by the sandwich or the pound. Crude as the surroundings may be, this is truly elegant meat, each slice of it an idealized portrait of smokehouse beauty, its edge rimmed with blackened crust, its pale, roseate center heavy with beef juices. To bring it to the peak of perfection there is a tangy, rust-colored sauce: apply it yourself. The menu also lists hot links, which are wonderfully spicy, ribs, and ham; but if you are coming to Otto's only once, it is the brisket you want to eat.

PARIS COFFEE SHOP
704 W. MAGNOLIA, FORT WORTH, TX (817) 335-2041

The exact right time to eat lunch at the Paris Coffee Shop is 11:00 A.M., Monday through Friday. That will be well after the breakfast crowd has gone, and a bit before the noontime bunch arrives, so you'll have a choice of tables. But the real reason to come mid-morning on a weekday is pies: coconut, chocolate, banana meringue; cherry, apple, and pecan; lemon on Friday; egg custard every day. By 11:00 A.M. the day's selection is ready to serve.

If you are lucky, as we have been each time we've eaten lunch in this businesslike downtown cafe, the pies will be cooled to proper eating temperature at the precise time you are mopping the last of the chicken-fried steak gravy from your plate.

Slices will arrive at the table still slightly warm, the custard set but jiggling precariously, a bit of steam still escaping from underneath the top crust of the apple pie.

Eating pie in the Paris Coffee Shop—even if you dine here at 2:00 P.M. and the morning's selection has reached room temperature—is one of America's distinctive culinary experiences. Pie and coffee in a home-cooking cafe, after all, is as American as . . . well, as apple pie.

We must tell you, though, that it isn't only custard pies that have endeared the Paris Coffee Shop to the people of Fort Worth since Vic Paris opened it in 1926. Meals that precede the pies are classics, too. Here is cafe cooking unadulterated by food trends and fancy notions of gourmet cuisine. Every Monday you can come to the Paris for turkey and cornbread dressing with giblet gravy. On Tuesday, they make meat loaf; Wednesday, beef brisket; Thursday, chicken and dumplings; Friday, fried chicken. Any day, you can come to the Paris for a serious chicken-fried steak smothered in gravy, accompanied by a mountain of mashed potatoes. Another meal we like is "the Arkansas traveler": a slab of cornbread topped with hot roast beef, accompanied by mashed potatoes, pinto beans, and biscuits for mopping up the gravy. Breakfast features yeast-rise biscuits and bacon cream gravy, bone-in country ham, and hot sweet rolls.

We don't recommend the Paris Coffee Shop to everyone—only to people who really like to eat.

SARTIN'S OF NEDERLAND
NEDERLAND AVE., NEDERLAND, TX (409) 724-.6663

Noisy, crowded, and messy, Sartin's is a glutton's dream. People drive here all the way from Houston for what is known as "platter service," which costs a hefty $15.95 but means massive amounts of terrific seafood, accompanied by hushpuppies, French fries, and cole slaw, presented on platters for as long as you want to continue eating it. The exact meal you get varies depending on the day's catch (Sartin's serves only fresh), but a typical evening's platter service will consist of cold boiled crabs, stuffed crabs, spiced fried barbecued crabs, crab claws, fried shrimp, maybe crawfish, and maybe snapper. For a few dollars extra, you can augment the fried-and-boiled bonanza with plates of raw oysters. It is also possible to order a normal, portioned-out meal; but what's the fun of that?

Sartin's is designed for serious eating: paper towels are provided to customers who sit at picnic-style tables sided by big garbage cans for all the debris that serious seafood-eating creates.

SMITTY'S
6219 AIRPORT RD., EL PASO, TX (915) 772-5876

Smitty's decor has changed. All the old familiar neon beer signs are still there, some a little lopsided on the pale yellow walls and above the bar; but on one wall, where the booths are lined up, there is now something new: a huge American flag, so big it seems to occupy nearly half the wall. The flag is accompanied by a "Welcome Home, Desert Storm Troops" sign. This is no knee-jerk patriotic gesture. Fully half the customers at Smitty's are men and women from nearby Fort Bliss; and during our last visit, while browsing through the local paper, we read one interview in which a returning soldier said that the first thing he did when he got back to El Paso was to go to Smitty's for a pound of beef and a pint of beans.

We know the feeling. Although we didn't serve in the Persian Gulf, we feel seriously deprived whenever we spend too much time away from El Paso, and from the likes of Smitty's. This is West Texas barbecue par excellence, served with a small crock of some of the best, hot pickled jalapeño peppers for miles around. Beef is what's best: smoke-perfumed flaps of brisket, bordered by a ribbon of fat unless you order extra-lean, which we don't recommend. The fat adds just the right amount of juice to the fairly dry, but tasty beef. We also like Smitty's hot links: bright red sausages seasoned in such a way that they taste almost sweet, but have a noticable pepper kick. The beef, the links, and also pork, ham, and ribs are available on platters with good beans, slaw, slices of raw onion, pickle chips, and a pair of stupendous "German fried potatoes," which are about a quarter of an Idaho spud, skinned and deep fried. Smitty's also sells sandwiches. And the table is set with a squeeze bottle of excellent vinegar-based red barbecue sauce that we like to squirt on just about everything.

Located in a strip mall just five minutes from the airport, Smitty's is a place all hungry airplace travelers want to know about. If you are just arriving in the West, it's a handy launch pad for a tour north into chili country or east toward Tex-Mex and barbecue. And if you are leaving these parts, a Smitty's meal is a good war to say a fond farewell to a muscular cuisine and a blunt ambience that simply does not exist anywhere else.

SONNY BRYAN'S
2202 INWOOD ROAD, DALLAS, TX (214) 357-7120

Here is noble Texas barbecue, served in a smoke shack in the middle of a dusty parking lot. Good ribs, good ham, but what you want to order is a beef sandwich: brisket, thick-sliced and so succulent it falls apart if you look at it hard. The sauce is sensational—tangy and powerful, an inspired complement to the mild-flavored meat. On the side, there are French fries, onion rings, cole slaw, and pork-dotted beans.

There are less than a dozen seats fashioned out of child-size school desks inside this disheveled cook house, so customers frequently have to wait for a place. A lot of business is take-out, and there are always plenty of happy people sitting outside in cars, eating barbecue off the dashboard. It is a lunch-only establishment: when the day's ration of meat is sold, usually by 3:00 or 4:00 P.M., Sonny Bryan's closes its doors.

SOUTHSIDE MARKET
109 CENTRAL, ELGIN, TX (512) 285-3407

In Texas, Elgin is sausage central. The muscular ground pork tubes made here (known among connoisseurs as Elgin hot guts) are sold in grocery stores all across the state; but to eat them in their natural habitat, in the back room of the Southside Market, is a unique *Roadfood* experience.

There is a new, wood-paneled dining room at the Southside Market that is air-conditioned; but for maximum enjoyment, we recommend you try to find a place at a table or at the long bench facing the tiled wall in the old (not air-conditioned) room. Here, the air is thick with smoke from the pit; old whiskey bottles filled with tangy hot sauce are lined up along the counter; and regular sausage-eaters engage in conversations of grunts and single syllables as they lick, slurp, chew, and savor the wonderful food.

The sausage is red with flecks of hot pepper, and old-timers tell us that its heat has been tuned down over the years; but it still packs a nice punch. It is served on butcher's wrapping paper; and although the only "side dish" available for sausage is a stack of saltine crackers, there are other good meats turned out by this pit. Mutton, cut into juicy chunks, its vivid flavor tempered by smoke, is frequently on the menu, as are beef and pork ribs until supplies run out (which can happen before supper). You can always order brisket, which is some of the best in the West: butter-tender with a profound beefy flavor. It, too, is served on paper, sold by the pound.

We recommend eating in the old dining room not only because it is more colorful and true to smoke-pit traditions. After you spend a busy lunch hour in this close-quarter smokehouse, you yourself become imbued with the perfume of smoke and walk out onto the streets smelling as good as an Elgin hot gut.

THREADGILL'S
6416 N. LAMAR, AUSTIN, TX (512) 451-5440

Threadgill's is a juke joint that grew out of a gas station after Prohibition and is known as much for its musical heritage as its prodigious food. Janis Joplin recorded "St. James Infirmary" here in 1962, and her picture, with Mr. Threadgill, hangs on the wall; and in earlier times, the dining room has been rocked by the sounds of innumerable yodelers, pickers, and blues singers. Now, even if nobody is singing live, the jukebox is superb; and the food would be worth a visit if all they played was Muzak.

Don't be disoriented by the size of Threadgill's portions. It is easy to be so flabbergasted by the size of the chicken-fried steak, for example, that you almost don't notice just how good it is. Brittle-crusted, thrillingly seasoned, tender but with enough chew to provide a meal's worth of pleasure to your mouth, this is chicken-fried steak we would be tempted to call elegant if it weren't so damn big. Now, those mashed potatoes on the side. One portion would be most other restaurants' serving for two or three; and the spuds, too, are stupendously good, as is the gravy on top. Indeed, this is a paradigmatic Texas feast, one of the best you will eat anywhere.

So many tempting dishes, so little appetite. Frankly, we feel inadequate to the challenge of Threadgill's kitchen. We come here every chance we get, but cannot honestly say we have eaten our way through the menu. "American food, southern-style" is how Threadgill's describes its own cuisine; and most of it does indeed have that extra-luscious quality that characterizes so much down-home Dixie cooking. Some of the highlights in our memory book include a dazzling meat loaf with Creole sauce (also enormous), roasted pork with sweet-and-sour sauce, a divine plate of liver (calf's) and onions, and glazed ham with yams. Then, too, there was a grand "Austex Breakfast": eggs scrambled with jalapeño peppers, tomatoes, and cheese, accompanied by beans, potatoes, and high-rise biscuits.

Threadgill's is vegetable paradise, a place where you can have a hearty meatless feast if you want. In fact, the menu always features multi-veggie meals ranging from three or four on a plate to the top-of-the-line "Nine Veggie Orgy," selected from the day's list. Among the kitchen's regular offerings are mashed or French fried potatoes, black-eyed peas, lima beans with ham hock, yellow squash, buttered carrots, creamed corn, stewed cabbage, pinto beans, stewed okra, San Antonio squash (a squash casserole with cheese, jalapeño pepper bits, and onions), and turnip greens, as well as several kinds of slaw and salad. You also get good bread for mopping up: homemade white or cornbread.

Like everything else here, desserts are big and handsome. Buttermilk pie is particularly wonderful—a huge, supersweet slab that reminds us of hard sauce with a gilt top. There are good apple and pecan pies, and a dandy, actually quite demure, banana pudding served in a medium-size bowl with two vanilla wafers sticking up out of the sunny custard like Mickey Mouse's ears.

Much of the fun of eating at Threadgill's is the roadhouse ambience—casual in the extreme, with several dining rooms, all apparently added on without architectural logic at various times in Threadgill's history. The place is packed full at mealtimes, and as you wait in the bar for a table, surrounded by a hundred neon beer signs on the wall, waiters push through the crowds across the creaky wooden floor, their arms loaded with trays piled high with delicious-looking food.

UTAH

CAPITOL REEF INN & CAFE
360 W. MAIN, TORREY, UT (801) 425-3271

A few years ago a traveling gourmet named Sherry Browning of St. Louis wrote to introduce us to a place she described as "an incredible find in a physically beautiful but palate-starved place." It was the Capitol Reef Inn and Cafe near the Capitol Reef National Park and the Dixie and Fishlake National Forests in southern Utah. Ms. Browning hit a sensitive spot: we've always felt bad about being unable to find much *Roadfood* in the Beehive State, although we relish motoring through whenever we travel west because it is such a gorgeous place. Now we know we can eat well in addition to enjoying the scenery.

On Main Street (Route 24) on the west end of the buildings that the town of Torrey comprises, the Inn is not by any means a grand or elaborate hostelry. That's fine; you would not expect or want anything too fancy in this territory. There is no way a mere hotel, however swell, could compete with the splendor of the red sandstone cliffs whose gray-domed tops reminded pioneers of the U.S. Capitol in Washington. There are seven inexpensive rooms for rent, with TV but without telephones; and there is the humble but immensely satisfying Capitol Reef Cafe.

Could it be? Are the broccoli and carrots fresh? Yes, indeed. And the

444

corn-on-the-cob, served in season only, tastes only recently picked. The inn boasts that it gets its vegetables from local farmers whenever possible, and delivered from Salt Lake City when the locals have nothing good to offer. They do not served canned or frozen things here. One house specialty of which they are especially proud is the ten-vegetable salad, which is served as part of an all-vegetable dinner along with a wild rice and brown rice medley and a whole-wheat roll. Healthy eating like that is rare anywhere, extraordinary in this rugged part of the world.

The Capitol Reef Inn bakes its own bread, including onion buns, rye bread, scones, and whole-wheat rolls, and white bread for sandwiches. Even the junk food you can eat here doesn't taste junky: the brittle-crisp onion rings are exemplary; we recommend them alongside a roast turkey sandwich with cranberry sauce and real, not-from-a-can turkey gravy.

The *pièce de résistance* and the dish for which Utah is best-known, at least among outdoors people who catch and prepare their own, is rainbow trout. It is local, from spring water streams, served smoked as an appetizer or as a side dish, filleted in a sandwich with salad, soup, and onion rings, or whole, broiled with butter and lemon—a memorable dinner.

One thing you will easily find in restaurants throughout Utah is exuberantly sugary, rich dessert, and this place is no exception. Choose a mountainous wedge of chocolate mousse pie or banana sour cream pie, or have a breakfast breadstuff after dinner, such as the Inn's giant yeast-leavened cinnamon roll or orange-almond scone with butter and jam. To accompany these sweets, you can get real espresso, cappuccino, cafe au lait, or café mocha (chocolate-flavored cappuccino).

VERMONT

COLD HOLLOW CIDER MILL
ROUTE 100, WATERBURY CENTER, VT (802) 244-8771

You can buy Yankee maple-themed food products at Cold Hollow, as well as cold or hot apple cider, cran-cider, local crafts, kitchen implements, and all kinds of tacky (and not-so-tacky) souvenirs; but the one thing you can get here that you cannot get anywhere else is a freshly made Cold Hollow apple cider doughnut.

It looks like a plain raised doughnut: no frosting, no filling. Just a neat brown ring of dough. At first bite, it feels pretty much like a plain doughnut, too, pleasantly crisp on the outside, soft and crumbly once you break inside that faintly brittle shell. Then, suddenly, you begin to taste it. You taste apple cider and cloves in the tawny dough. It is sweet, but more spicy than sugary—a unique and memorable circle of delectable pastry. The best thing is that it is *fresh*. Any time you come to Cold Hollow Cider Mill, you can see the doughnuts being made, watch the hoops of batter dropped into hot oil, watch them fry, then eat them while they are still warm.

To accompany the superior sinkers, Cold Hollow will sell you a cup of their hot spiced cider (made by blending several kinds of apples), which is great for dunking, or a cup of coffee that *Yankee* magazine writer Rollin Riggs once testified was "the best cup of coffee I have ever had. Ever."

KEEP ON TRUCKIN' CAFE

P & H TRUCK STOP, EXIT 17 OFF I-91 AT ROUTE 302, WELLS RIVER, VT (802) 429-2141

Outside, you smell diesel fumes, but the first thing you notice when you enter the Keep on Truckin' Cafe is yeast-scented, freshly baked bread—shelves of homemade loaves ready to be sold whole or sliced and toasted to accompany breakfast (served all day) of bacon and eggs. Even if you aren't a hungry trucker, the view inside is mighty appetizing. Beyond the bread, dozens of homemade pies are displayed on their own shelves in the big, wide-open dining room.

The menu, encased in plastic and emblazoned with a crude drawing of a truck bursting through a wall, is a roster of honest if inelegant truck-stop grub—such rib-stickers as pot roast, meat loaf, pork chops, hot turkey sandwiches, ham steaks, and great big sandwiches made on rough-hewn slabs of sturdy toast. It is familiar fare to anyone who has eaten a few meals in truck stops, except here every item is listed in French as well as English to accommodate drivers from Quebec.

The cuisine has a regional accent as well. At breakfast pancakes and French toast are served with pure Vermont maple syrup (*sirop d'érable pur* on the bilingual menu). Among desserts are down-east puddings made with Grape-Nuts and gloriously robust pies loaded with blueberries or piled high with sweet maple custard. And there is almost always a chowder of the day on the blackboard menu. Our favorite is corn chowder: with a few slabs of good toast, it is stalwart enough to be a meal unto itself.

The Keep on Truckin' Cafe is a gearjammer's delight, from the wallpaper pattern of Macks, Peterbilts, and K-Whoppers to the bunkhouse rooms upstairs, complete with shower and lounge privileges, including color television. Next to the cash register, a bulletin board is thumbtacked with messages from deadheaders who need loads heading west, and shippers looking for a reefer (refrigerated truck) going down to Florida.

MISS LYNDONVILLE

ROUTE 5, LYNDONVILLE, VT (802) 626-9890

Having begun life as a monitor-roof diner with a short counter and stools, Miss Lyndonville has come up in the world, but is in no ways uppity. It is still a diner with a counter and stools, but now there are tables and chairs, too, and a snazzy western-style rustic exterior façade. The menu is diner deluxe, with a lot of admirable vittles to be found among the ordinary-seeming list of breakfast specials, soups, and sandwiches.

The bread made into toast with breakfast eggs is homemade, and sturdy-good. Many Miss Lyndonville customers like to order it made into French toast, which is in fact French-fried toast: puffy, lush, and irredeemably naughty. There are hefty pancakes, too, served with real Vermont maple syrup, as well as a complete repertoire of eggs and omelettes. In New England it might seem strange to find less-than-great muffins; but here they are—too cakey, too sweet, with none of the gentility of truly great ones. We have begun to believe that there is a northern boundary to Yankee muffin country, above which loaf bread, which seems more likely to be homemade the farther north you go, is always more interesting than muffins (just as there is certainly a southern border of Muffinland, below which doughnuts—then, even further south, bagels [then biscuits, then beignets]—are the breakfast bread of choice).

Last time through Vermont we ate lunch at Miss L, and it was just fine. The special of the day, pork tenderloin, was fried and made into a sandwich (on that good bread) and served along with a cup of hearty vegetable soup. From the large choice of hamburgers, we selected our perennial favorite, the North Country special, which is a nice-size patty on toast with cheddar cheese, tomato and onions, and sauce (a Big Mac sauce clone), along with French fries and cole slaw. For dessert, we ate strawberry pie, a specialty of this kitchen. It was sweet, chocked with berries, bright, and satisfying. And the coffee that came with it was good and strong.

SKYLINE RESTAURANT
ROUTE 9, HOGBACK MOUNTAIN, MARLBORO, VT (802) 464-5535

There is a bygone flair about the Skyline Restaurant that suggests the joy of traveling before interstate highways cut across the land and food got franchised. It is an eatery on a scenic two-lane; it is aimed at tourists; it is proud of its hospitality and regional flavor. The menu advises customers that they are eating in "a Vermont restaurant operated by a native Vermonter." The dining room is paneled in pine like a scenic lodge ought to be; and it has a cozy fireplace near the entrance and a few chairs for warming up if you enter during ski season. In warm weather, there is lawn furniture outside where you can sit and admire the view that includes the Sugarloaf ski area, Marlboro College, the White Mountains of New Hampshire, and the Berkshires of Massachusetts. Or you can watch the birds that fly among the dozens of bird houses and bird baths set up all around the restaurant. The Skyline aims to show travelers the beauty of Vermont while serving up traditional local foods.

This is a fine place to breakfast on waffles made of stone-ground flour, served hot off the griddle topped with plenty of butter; or griddle cakes made from scratch (not a mix), served with genuine and ever-more-rare Yankee maple syrup. On the side, the Skyline serves its own peppery country-style sausage or Vermont sugar-cured ham. Doughnuts are made fresh each morning, as are turnovers, pies, brownies, and the moist date-nut bread that accompanies most hot dinners.

Turkey (Sunday only) and roast beef dinners are as homey as you will find in any restaurant, served with all the fixin's for the evening meal; then at lunch the next day, if there is any left over, you can count on hefty triple-decker turkey or roast beef sandwiches (available, of course with big slabs of Vermont cheddar cheese).

Desserts are uncommonly ravishing. We swooned when we dipped into the Skyline's Indian pudding, a stalwart but tender-spirited cornmeal and molasses cereal faintly seasoned with ginger, served warm with a scoop of vanilla ice cream melting into its fissures and crevices. There was classic down-east strawberry shortcake (in strawberry season), served on an unsweetened biscuit, and tart apple pie accompanied by the sharp cheddar Vermonters like so well (the pie makes an excellent breakfast as well as dessert). The most wondrous dessert of all was maple pecan pie, served with a cloud of real whipped cream on top.

"Why is the Skyline so unusual?" asks a brochure available near the cash register. The answers include a "breathtaking 100-mile view from the dining room," "many kinds of birds feeding and nesting nearby," "easy access from your car," and "beautiful flowers." All these things are true, as are the brochure's promises of "fine, home-cooked New England style dinners," "famous waffles and griddle cakes," and "clean rest rooms."

WAYSIDE RESTAURANT
ROUTE 302, BERLIN, VT (802) 223-6611

The Wayside Restaurant is as true a taste of Vermont as we have ever found on one menu.

When you drive past the Wayside on Route 302 just south of Montpelier, it does not appear to be anything special: a plain brick rectangle, mustard-yellow, surrounded by a parking lot, with an American flag flying high on a pole out front.

Inside it's modern and comfortable—a wide wood-paneled cafe with easy listenin' on the radio and a couple of counters and rows of booths bustling with locals.

There is nothing precious about the menu; the kitchen isn't trying to prove its regional character to anyone. In fact, it is entirely possible to come for a hamburger or a BLT or a plate of scrambled eggs. Of course, those are not the meals that have endeared the Wayside Restaurant to us.

Instead, we recommend dishes such as milk oyster stew or fish chowder, baked haddock (Friday) or fresh native perch, hot blueberry muffins or pancakes with real maple syrup. Or how about American chop suey? There aren't a lot of restaurants that offer this dowdy old dish, but somehow it seems so right here at the Wayside. It is a favorite Yankee way of getting the most out of one's larder by creating a one-dish meal of ground beef with macaroni and tomato sauce. The menu lists it as the "Vermont Special."

The most old-fashioned dish you can eat here is a plate of salt pork and milk gravy. Like American chop suey, it is a meal reminiscent of frugal farmhouse cookery. You see, way back when, most farm cellars held a pork barrel in which slabs of salt pork were kept in brine. The pork (or occasionally the brine itself) was used to season stews, vegetables, chowders, and main courses of beef or venison. But on those occasions when there was no meat, no vegetables, nothing from which to construct a chowder, inventive Yankee cooks figured out ways to turn the salt pork itself into a satisfying meal. We've *never* seen salt pork and milk gravy served in any other restaurant. But in this part of Vermont, there are enough old-timers around to know just how delicious it can be; and so it is on the menu of the Wayside Restaurant once a week.

Most days, the kitchen offers hash. On occasion it is red-flannel hash, made from a traditional New England boiled dinner of corned beef, potatoes, carrots, and beets (whose juices dye it the color of a farmer's long-johns). It is served mounded high in a boat-shaped dish—a damp heap of stick-to-the-ribs north country comfort food. On the side you get a basketful of freshly baked dinner rolls.

This is maple country, and so the dessert repertoire includes ice cream sundaes dripping with amber syrup and—our favorite way to end a Wayside meal—a slice of maple cream pie in which a toffee-thick layer of maple filling is topped with a lightweight ribbon of whipped cream.

VIRGINIA

BARBARA'S COUNTRY COOKING
2034 LAKE SIDE DR., LYNCHBURG, VA (804) 385-5051

We like Barbara's early, early in the day, even before the sun comes up. One bleary summer morning we plunked ourselves down in this cozy eatery and without even asking what we wanted, the waitress brought us coffee, along with biscuits so recently pulled from the oven that steam fluttered up as we pulled them into halves. The combined aroma of those oven-hot biscuits and coffee was about the nicest wake-up call we've ever had. All that was needed to complete the happy tableau was a slab of Barbara's sizzled country ham, whose savory piquancy is a *real* eye-opener, and a sublime complement for the gentle biscuits. These were the makings of a Ciceronian breakfast, all the more satisfying because it was criminally cheap and served with utter nonchalance by uniformed gum-snappers in a blue-plate restaurant patronized by working people.

Lunch is like that, too: meat and potatoes, but oh, what *good* meat and potatoes. Take, for instance, this fried chicken. Listen to its crust when you cleave into it. Inhale the scent of butter-rich chicken juices as they flood forth and drip down your wrist and onto the plate. Quick, mop them with a hot dinner roll, or sop a forkful of mashed potatoes through the juice. Then plow into vegetables cooked with panache and, in most cases, with plenty of fat to make them rich as a vegetable can be—greens, beans, squash, yams. Served on plain plates and at low prices, this is a feast. Other good lunches: smothered steak, barbecue, or chicken and dumplings. For dessert, of course there are pies, including lovely meringues and some made with fruit; but the one we like best is strawberry shortcake, which is southern style—sweet and gloppy, pretty and fun.

BROOKS RESTAURANT
ROUTE 11, VERONA, VA (703) 248-1722

"Are you sure you like country ham?" our waitress asked cautiously when we sat down at Brooks Restaurant and ordered a couple of ham buns without even looking at a menu.

Yes, we love country ham, especially the way they serve it at this pleasant plate-lunch restaurant with a sign outside boasting of its ham bun's fame. A ham bun, as presented here, is similar to the traditional southern ham biscuit, which is a downsized sandwich made by inserting a small slab of salty, well-aged, dark pink country ham into a sliced, oven-hot buttermilk biscuit. Ham biscuits are delicious, especially for breakfast, and most especially if the ham is well-aged and the biscuits are freshly made. Brooks' variation of the formula starts with excellent, deeply fla-vored ham, but a bigger piece, and sandwiches it inside a huge, round-topped bun. It is an inspired idea, because the sweetness of the yeasty dome of bread becomes a foil for the ham. This combination, brought to consummation by liberal amounts of butter, is divine—a simple but ele-gant meal.

There are many other things to eat at Brooks Restaurant, including highly recommended (by our waitress) halibut, "really fresh" crab cakes, flounder, and catfish, as well as some lovely fruit cobblers that we person-ally can recommend as the perfect way to put a point on a ham bun meal. As for the other entrées, however, we have never tried them. Maybe some-day we will, but only if we are hungry after eating our fill of Brooks' singu-lar buns.

THE OWL
ROUTE 13, NORTH OF ACCOMAC, VA (804) 665-5191

Serious eaters know the narrow patch of Virginia above the Chesapeake Bay Bridge as oyster country, famous for its beds of Chincoteagues, as well as for crabs and clams. You can enjoy these Tidewater treats, as well as big slabs of classic country-style (salty) ham or fried chicken, if you stop for dinner at The Owl, a small, family-run cafe attached to an inconspicuous motel.

For forty years now, the comfortably fading dining room, decorated by a clock on the wall that says "Chevrolet Time" and a pair of faded 1950s-vintage pictures of the family boys (now men) in their best Roy Rogers suits has been a beacon for hungry wayfarers who come for fried oysters in the summer, oyster stew in the winter, and silken blocks of southern-style spoonbread all year around. The Roach family who run the place are traditionalists; and although their menu holds few surprises, the plates of food that emerge from this kitchen are sometimes truly breathtaking.

Fried chicken, skillet-cooked if you are willing to wait (you are!), arrives with a golden skin that fairly crackles when you sink your teeth into it, then into the lush, steamy, profoundly flavored meat inside. The spoonbread available as a side dish with dinner is a true southern glory—creamy-soft and luxuriously rich, a perfect complement to the rugged-crusted bird. And if you don't want spoonbread (you do, you do!), or as a somewhat redundant but irresistible addition to it, the kitchen also makes some swell squash fritters. One other good starch worth knowing about: The Owl claims to be the place where French-fried sweet potatoes were invented, a claim we have seen no other restaurant even attempt to stake.

The person who first told us about The Owl many years ago, a native Virginian named Edith Rosenthal, mentioned none of these fine foods in her postcard. Her call to glory was the kitchen's chocolate rum pie, an uncharacteristically swank pastry consisting of a microthin sugar crust, a stratum of meringue, and profoundly rich chocolate filling. It reminded us of a high-class Mallomar cookie. When we eat at The Owl, we always order at least two pieces of pie. One is chocolate rum if they have it; the other is another regional treasure, sweet potato, which we believe is appropriate any time of day with any meal, and not necessarily for dessert. With a plate of country ham or fried chicken, or by itself with a cup of coffee, this pie—like the restaurant that serves it—always seems just right.

PIERCE'S PITT BAR-B-QUE
137 ROCHAMBEAU DR., LIGHTFOOT, VA (804) 565-2955 (THERE IS ANOTHER
LOCATION AT WATERSIDE, DOWNTOWN NORFOLK)

Shortly after it opened for business in 1971, we stopped at Pierce's Pitt
and ate ourselves silly, declaring its splendid hand-shredded Boston
butt and accompanying hot sauce to be among the world's best.

Over the years, Pierce's had its ups and downs, was leased by the
Pierces to someone else then taken back, and has expanded from a small,
Day-Glo orange and yellow cinderblock smoke shack with picnic tables in
the middle of a vacant lot into a real restaurant with tables and chairs
indoors (but still painted in eye-aching colors). The barbecue is now as
good as it was twenty years ago: truly succulent stuff, an amazing array of
big, pillowy hunks of sweet pork combined with crisp bits of roasted skin,
long chewy shreds, resilient chunks, and savory little fibers imbued with
spice. All this meat has sucked in a fine hickory perfume and reaches
absolute perfection when combined with Pierce's sauce—a tingling brew of
sugar, vinegar, spice, and tomato.

The meat comes on a sandwich or on a plate with hushpuppies and
slaw. A lot of Pierce's business is take-out. Ourselves, we have always
treated this restaurant as a last-chance indulgence when returning from a
trip through the Southeast. North of here, there isn't much good barbecue
to speak of. We buy quarts of Pierce's, make a run for home, and try to
make it last as long as possible.

The odd spelling of *Pitt*, by the way, was originally a sign-painter's
error. The Pierce family liked it because they thought it was distinctive.
They trademarked the name and Pierce's is now the only legal pitt in
America.

ROANOKER
2522 COLONIAL AVE., ROANOKE, VA (703) 344-7746

The "Home of Good Food Since 1941" has moved a few times and
spruced up over the years. It now has wallpaper and luxurious booths
and laminated tables, and today seems like a sanitary, pleasant, but fairly
bland restaurant . . . until you take a deep whiff early in the morning. You
smell coffee, which is good, and hot grits, which give the air a distinct
granular aroma unique to southern cafes, and peppery sausage gravy blan-

keting biscuits, and country ham—the rank perfume of which is a signal that anything-but-bland breakfast is on its way.

What a gorgeous sight this ham is on its plate: fanned out across the giant platter are wafer-thin slices edged with an amber piping of semi-translucent fat. They are nearly as deep red as mahogany, and they are partially submerged in a pool of the wondrous viscous gravy known as red-eye. There is nothing to this piggy stuff, really; it's merely drippings of the ham cooked down with a little water until the liquid darkens and attains maximum flavor to complement its meat. With a few of this kitchen's knobby, squared-off cat-head biscuits for mopping up, the ham makes a powerful morning meal that will keep you happy (and thirsty!) for hours.

There is ham steak for dinner, too, served with red-eye gravy; and there are all kinds of other good, truly southern things for lunch, inclding crisp corn sticks and vast arrays of yams, potatoes, congealed salads (Jell-O), slaws, au gratins, beans, and greens, as well as good sugar-crusted apple and pecan pies.

THE ROWE FAMILY RESTAURANT
ROUTE 250, STAUNTON, VA (703) 886-1833

Nearly a decade ago, the manager of the Rowe Family Restaurant—a favorite *Roadfood* stop of ours for many years—wrote to say, "So many travelers are in despair. Fast food has been putting all the good places out of business. But we feel the trend has been reversed and good food is due for a large-scale revival."

He was right. There is plenty of fast food wherever you go, but that doesn't mean that cooking with character is gone. Institutional burgers are fine in their predictable sort of way, but they could never take the place of the authentic barbecues, oyster bars, and catfish parlors that can make eating one's way across America a delectable adventure. Any time you need reassurance about that fact, we suggest you travel Interstate 81 through Virginia and get off at Exit 57 for pork chops, candied yams, and baked apples at The Rowe Family Restaurant.

Mrs. Rowe, her daughter Brenda, and her son-in-law Terry LeMasurier maintain uncompromised culinary standards that have made their roadside eatery a good-eats beacon for nearly half a century. *They care.* The menu advises: "The waitress will cheerfully accept the return of any food or beverage that is not perfect as to quality, neatness, temperature, seasoning, etc." In nearly a decade of visits to this humble dinner house in Staunton, we have yet to consider sending anything back.

Savor, for example, these mashed potatoes. *Real* mashed potatoes, mounded high on the plate, starchy white swirls laced with butter, whipped smooth except for an occasional telltale nugget of unmashed spud. Sometimes a person can forget just how good ordinary mashed potatoes can be. These are a reminder.

Buttermilk biscuits are plain, too; but there is no breadstuff better than Rowe's fluffy rounds, hot out of the oven . . . unless you prefer the yeasty chaw of the butter-topped rolls that come with dinner.

Ah, dinner. We are in love with Rowe Family chicken, pan-fried until golden-brittle crisp. How good is it? Years ago we heard a true story about a very pregnant woman who sat down at a table in Rowe's, placed her order for a half bird, then promply went into labor. "I'm not leaving until I have fried chicken and mince pie," the woman declared. Her husband got her to the hospital only when Mrs. Rowe promised to bring her a plate of chicken after the baby was born.

Although the fried chicken and the pork chops and the minced barbecue and the homemade rolls are all swell, it is dessert that makes The Rowe Family Restaurant irresistible: Old Dominion specialties such as meringue-leavened banana pudding, flakey-crusted pecan or apple pie and—when the weather turns cool—hot mince pie, made with Mrs. Rowe's genuine mincemeat, topped with custard rum sauce. Our personal favorite dessert is Rowe's banana pudding—gentle as a sigh, the yummy yellow custard leavened with swirls of frothy white meringue. Sheer heaven!

SALLY BELL'S KITCHEN
708 W. GRACE ST., RICHMOND, VA (804) 644-2838

You cannot eat at Sally Bell's. The red brick house across from Richmond Metropolitan Hospital is a take-out bakery. There are some very nice lawns nearby (at the Virginia Museum of Fine Arts in particular) that look right for picnics; or if you are a passer-through, as we were, you might have to eat in your car.

Front seats are an excellent place to eat Sally Bell's food, because the specialty of the house is box lunch—tidy meals perfectly suited for dining with minimal amenities in make-do circumstances.

Lunch is sold in a white cardboard box inscribed with Sally Bell's nostalgic logo—a cameo silhouette of a Colonial dame. The contents of the box include a sandwich, a cup of salad, half a deviled egg, a cheese wafer, and dessert.

Sandwiches are made of chicken salad or Smithfield ham, or tea-time spreads such as olive and mayonnaise or cream cheese and nut or pimiento cheese. The bread is homemade, thin-sliced, and delicate. Naturally, its crusts have been removed.

The deviled egg is lush. Potato salad is bright with crisp bits of cucumber and onion. The cheese wafer is a heartwarmingly old-fashioned little cracker tile with half a pecan on top. For dessert, choose among upside-down devil's food cupcakes (on which only the top is unfrosted), yellow cake with caramel or chocolate icing, or a variety of powdered-sugar-dusted fruit tarts.

There is one extra bakery item we did nab to take with us on our journey: a bag of beaten biscuits. They are one of Sally Bell's specialties, and have been since the bakery opened in 1926. In fact, beaten biscuits go way back to Colonial gastronomy. Unlike soft, fluffy American-style biscuits, these are biscuits in the English sense of the word: hard and crisp—what most of us would call a cracker. They go great with soup, or as a munchy to accompany cold cuts (country-cured ham in particular), or—in our case—as emergency rations for the motel room late at night.

Sally Bell's is a body- and soul-satisfying experience. But it is frustrating for those of us who are merely driving through town and cannot avail ourselves of the fabulous array of cakes, breads, buns, and muffins lined up on the bakery shelves—most of which call for a table, a fork, and a leisurely pot of coffee for full enjoyment.

SOUTHERN KITCHEN
ROUTE 11, NEW MARKET, VA (703) 740-3514

The Southern Kitchen is the first place we ever tasted peanut soup, nearly twenty years ago, and it is still one of the roadside eateries we like best—a casual place catering to locals as well as to families of tourists on their way through the Shenandoah Valley to the Luray Caverns. Sometimes when you walk into the friendly little cafe on Route 11, there will be no place to hang your coat: all the hooks on the coat rack will be occupied—by hanging country hams for sale. The walls are decorated with deer heads and old, faded pictures of tourists visiting the Caverns. Placemats are paper; and service, by uniformed waitresses, is speedy and pleasant.

The Southern Kitchen is a good place for breakfast: eggs and a slab of pan-sizzled country ham are a combination hard to resist. (Too bad the Southern Kitchen no longer offers biscuits, the only breadstuff right with the high-flavored ham they serve.) Any other time of day—or even at breakfast, we recommend you start your meal with peanut soup. The Southern Kitchen's version is a luxurious bisque enriched with butter, but not thickened with cream, onion-sweet and velvet-smooth. It is a satisfying soup, but it leaves you enough appetite to move on to one of the other gratifying cafe meals available here, such as ham with raisin sauce, fried chicken, or pan-fried trout from the James River. To finish any one of these exemplary western Virginia spreads, have a wedge of apple pie.

STONE'S CAFETERIA
ROANOKE RD., E. OF CHRISTIANSBURG, VA (703) 382-8970

According to a postcard available at Stone's Cafeteria, this friendly eatery on the outside of Christiansburg is "One of America's Top 100 Independent Regional Restaurants." The card does not mention who declared this fact, nor does it list the criteria; but if you eat here, and if you enjoy real southern-style cooking, you won't likely disagree.

Pick up a tray and choose your pleasure cafeteria-style. The ladies behind the counter dish it out from pans that regularly include catfish (fried), cod, tenderloin tips, and the dish we most highly recommend, fried chicken. This is fried chicken of the thin-crusted kind: really elegant pieces of bird with an acute crunch to their skin, but no lumpy batter between that crunch and the moist, flavorful white meat or even moister and more succulent dark meat below.

To go with that chicken, you will want a big pile of mashed potatoes and gravy, and a selection or two from the wide array of vegetables for which Stone's is known. There is a memorable casserole of squash and bacon textured with bread crumbs and swimming in luscious juices; there are yams and greens and beans and salads, too; but don't fill up your tray without leaving room for dessert.

Pies are a specialty. They make a grandiose strawberry pie piled high with layer upon layer of berry; and our personal favorite, coconut cream pie—rich and summery in a fragile lard crust. The crust, we realized as we plowed into this grand classic of southern cafes and cafeterias, is a crucial element of coconut cream pie greatness. You need that brittle, luxurious texture to go along with the luxury of the coconut cream on top.

As southern cafeterias go, Stone's is among the small and cozy ones—

much smaller than the Morrison's and Piccadilly chains that occupy shopping centers throughout the Southland. It is a very personal kind of business in a building that once, no doubt, was modern with its orange Naugahyde booths and low-slung architecture. Now, compared to the franchises that line the strips outside of most small cities and towns, it seems quaint and old-fashioned. There is a family feeling to it, encouraged by the teams of chatty southern ladies who dish out the food behind the line.

THE SURREY HOUSE
VA. 10 & 31, SURRY, VA (804) 294-3389

Surry, Virginia, a small town north of Wakefield from which the ferry goes to Williamsburg, is smack in the heart of peanut country. Here you find Helen and Owen Gwaltney's Surrey House (yes, spelled differently than the town), and some of Virginia's finest peanut soup. It is a light version of the Tidewater favorite, with a consistency more like broth than like peanut butter, although it does have that nice toasty taste that makes peanut soup so distinctive. It comes garnished with chopped peanuts.

In addition to peanut soup, The Surrey House offers some vegetables (from the Gwaltney garden) sprinkled with peanuts, salads with peanuts, chocolate-peanut sundaes, and the ultimate peanut butter sandwich—a do-it-yourself sandwich board that includes breads, jelly, raisins, apples, cheese, a banana, bacon, honey, and a jar of peanut butter. "Peanuts are to Surry County what honey is to bees—our greatest crop!" notes the Surrey House menu. But nuts are not the only reason we recommend this comfortable, knotty-pine-paneled cafe.

It is a fine place to eat ham, too: lovely pale pink pig meat, aged only long enough to develop piquancy, but not so long that it turns to the scarlet leather hard core ham junkies prefer. There are fried apples and ham-layered eggs Benedict in the morning, freshly made crabcakes and apple fritters at noon, and a delicate, cream-textured lemon chess pie in case you have OD'd on peanuts and cannot face the formidable (and delicious) house special, peanut-raisin pie.

TIFFANY'S SEAFOOD
456 IVY RD., CHARLOTTESVILLE, VA (804) 293-5000

We can always count on Charlie and Adair Burlingham of Massachusetts for worthy *Roadfood* tips as they travel; and just last spring, as we were packing for a trip into the mid-South, they sent us word of Tiffany's. We were on our way to what turned out to be an immensely satisfying meal. "If it's from Tiffany's, it's fresh" is the house motto of this clean and modern combination restaurant, raw bar, take-out shop, and fish market in the University Shopping Center. Aside from a couple of steaks and hamburgers and chicken teriyaki plates for fish frowners, the menu is all seafood—from shrimp gumbo and raw bivalves on the half shell (buy 'em by the piece) to hefty slabs of flounder stuffed with crabmeat.

Tiffany's serves platters with French fries or baked potatoes, cole slaw or salad, bread, and tartar and cocktail sauces, built around such entrées as crab cakes, shrimp, scallops, crab casserole, stir-fried things, and garlicked scampi. We were impressed by the breaded oysters, which were delicately done and still fragrant with ocean freshness, and by a boundless combination platter that juxtaposed crab cakes, steamed shrimp, and fried clams. In addition to the platters, Tiffany's sells steamed shrimp and Maryland-style steamed blue crabs by the pound, accompanied by a panoply of hot sauces, drawn butter, and crackers for serious seafood feasting. Lucky us, soft-shell crabs were in season; and we also sampled a truly luscious soft-shell crab sandwich on a buttered roll—good onion rings and hushpuppies on the side.

There are some nice-looking desserts at Tiffany's; but frankly, we were too stuffed with seafood to try them. Next time, we'll leave room for cherry cobbler à la mode, "baked apple walnut delight," and a swell-looking double fudge brownie sundae.

VIRGINIA DINER
HIGHWAY 460, WAKEFIELD, VA (804) 899-3106

Wakefield, Virginia, is peanut country. They grow on vines in fields for miles around. Roadside stands sell them by the bag and bushel. Hams from nearby Smithfield got famous because the pigs around here eat these outstanding peanuts, which allegedly make pork sweet.

Until you try them, it's hard to believe that one kind of nut can be so superior to others; so we suggest you taste for yourself at the Virginia

Diner. Here you can buy shelled and salted, boiled and roasted Virginia jumbos: peanut perfection. What crunch! They crack into pieces at first bite. Then as you chew each brittle seed, it quickly turns to satin-smooth peanutty pulp, dark and profound and rich as dairy butter, with an enchanted creamy resonance no ordinary peanut butter could ever rival.

The Diner sells nuts any way you like them: salted or un-, butter-toasted (even more sybaritic), in or out of their shells, and in blocks of aristocratic peanut brittle. The menu also lists a special dish made with nuts: peanut pie. It is packed with peanuts, less cloying than most pecan pies, more a glorification of nuttiness than of corn syrup sweetness.

We recommend the Virginia Diner for good eating beyond peanuts. This happy-go-lucky tourist-oriented cafe with its red-checked tablecloths and inexpensive down-home menu is a nice place to sample a variety of Tidewater delicacies, including thin-sliced pepper-coated ham, which is brick-red and *salty* the way true country hams ought to be. It comes with a pair of buttermilk biscuits, a blimp of a yam, and a heap of greens sopped with keen pot likker. Or you can get fragile-jacketed southern fried chicken. Or try them both on a combination plate. And every March, peanut soup is on the menu.

The Virginia Diner is easy to find. Just follow the billboards along Route 460, leading motorists to "The Peanut Capital of the World." These old-fashioned road signs are a bit of nostalgic fanfare reminiscent of tourism before there were interstate highways.

VIRGINIA HOUSE
ROUTE 11 ON THE SOUTH SIDE OF TOWN, LEXINGTON, VA
(703) 463-3643

Salty country ham on steamy hot biscuits, copious arrays of vegetables embellished by cheese and butter, and homemade pies in elegant, fragile crusts: it's a classic recipe for good eating, southern-style. To savor it, we recommend a meal at the Virginia House of Lexington.

The Virginia House is an unassuming place separated from the road by a broad parking lot, looking like an idealized, depopulated post-linen postcard from the 1960s. Inside, tables are covered with white cloths; waitresses wear crisp uniforms. Above the cash register is a velveteen painting of a barefoot Spanish maid leaning to get a drink from a fountain, and there are a few postcards for sale; that's all there is as far as dining room decor goes. Off to the side, you can see a small-function hall with a Kiwanis flag that seems to be permanently hung up behind the podium. At the back of the dining room is a kitchen that features lovely vintage-1930s cabinetry and lockers for the groceries.

The food is time-honored southern cafe cooking. At least half a dozen well-cooked vegetables are available each day, including such standards as sweet-crusted yam, macaroni and cheese, stewed apples, black-eyed peas, cheese-sauced broccoli, and a sublime corn pudding dusted on top with cinnamon sugar that caramelizes as the pudding bakes, giving the tender custard and kernels a crusty sweet edge. The Virginia House menu features an inexpensive three-vegetable plate: your choice from the daily repertoire, accompanied by two delicious biscuits. They are small, golden-topped biscuits with a scrumptious buttermilky tang to their fluffy insides.

The biscuits are also featured in the Virginia House's superb version of ham biscuits, for which they are simply bisected and adorned with a small slice of country ham. Lexington is serious ham country, and this is serious country ham: salty, chewy, luxuriously flavorful, with an enigmatic character that makes country ham one of those magic foods that can inspire ecstasy in connoisseurs of edible regional Americana.

You never want to visit the Virginia House without leaving room for a piece of pie. These people know how to make the kinds of pies for which the South is famous. There is a simple, light-crusted, and well-nigh perfect apple pie; there are chess, chocolate chess, and lemon chess, each of which is excruciatingly fragile-flavored; and there is a powerhouse chocolate pecan, with fudgy veins of bittersweet chocolate among the amber, nutty sweetness.

It has been over a dozen years since we first ate at the Virginia House researching the original *Roadfood,* and we are amazed and delighted every time we stop there to see that nothing ever changes. If you are heading down through the Shenandoah Valley, do yourself a favor and stop in this pleasant cafe on the south side of Lexington for ham biscuits or fried chicken, or a plate of southern-style vegetables, or a couple of slices of some of the best pies around.

WASHINGTON

521 CAFE
521 THIRD AVE., SEATTLE, WA (206) 623-2233;
BREAKFAST AND LUNCH, MONDAY–FRIDAY

With the courthouse just across the street, the 521 Cafe is a favorite haunt of lawyers and politicians; but we like it anyway. In fact, the hobnobbing and consorting of the regular clientele, who pack the booths and counter of the little soda shop cafe at noon, adds a fitting Runyonesque quality to the cuisine of 521, which we would describe as metropolitan hash house deluxe.

Maybe not deluxe. Let's say hash house at its essence. Have a seat at the counter and inhale. Yes, those grilling hamburgers smell good, and so do those beefy ribs they serve. Listen above the din of the noon crowd to the milk shakes being mixed and the chatter of the counter help. What a comfy feeling it is to be among those smells and noises—a step back to a nearly forgotten style of culinary innocence and to cheap, good city meals that are harder to find as cities renovate themselves and go modern.

Modernity is unheard of at 521. The menu, in addition to about a dozen different kinds of hamburgers (recommended) lists such daily fare as chili, vegetable-beef soup, and meat loaf. All are homemade, inelegant, and satisfying. Mashed potatoes are the real thing, creamy rich and wonderfully spuddy. Double chocolate malts (made from scratch with cold milk, syrup, and chocolate ice cream) are thick, abundant, and profoundly nostalgic. At breakfast there are eggs, pancakes, homemade granola, and good, strong coffee.

At under five dollars for a full meal, the 521 Cafe is unassailable urban *Roadfood*.

BAKEMAN'S
122 CHERRY ST., SEATTLE, WA (206) 622-3375

U nless someone clued you in, you wouldn't likely stop at Bakeman's, down a half-flight of stairs on Cherry Street. Once inside, nothing you see immediately reveals the culinary pleasures that await. There is a bar on one side of the restaurant, separated by a bamboo curtain from a short cafeteria line. The tables in the restaurant are worn wood. Many customers sit in the red Naugahyde booths between mealtimes drinking—but not liquor. The drinks of choice at Bakeman's are the Seattle favorites: espresso, caffee latte, cappuccino.

The choices in the cafeteria line are minimal. There are different soups each day: turkey noodle, beef vegetable, or, on one memorable occasion, Chinese eggflower soup, a kind of egg drop variant made with cucumbers and mushrooms. There are Waldorf or potato salads and such, but they aren't very interesting. Nor is dessert a thrill: chocolate or lemon poppyseed cake, sliced like bread, or fruit pies, or the day's yogurt flavor. It's the sandwiches that make Bakeman's great.

Turkey or meat loaf on white or whole-wheat: here is sandwich perfection. The bread is homemade, stacked up at one end of the cafeteria line. It isn't spectacular bread on its own, not like some elegant French baguette. It is bread for sandwiches: tender and simple slices that come to life when spread with mayo and/or mustard and/or cranberry and/or shredded lettuce, then heaped with turkey or slabs of meat loaf.

If meat loaf is your dish, we recommend it on whole-wheat with catsup and shredded lettuce. The meat is tightly packed but tender, gently spiced, and with a dizzyingly delicious aroma. As for turkey, get it any way you like, because this is superb, *real*, carved-from-the-bird turkey with subtle homey flavor. The dark meat is lush; the white meat is moist and aromatic; either variety has an occasional piece of skin still attached, a nice reminder of just how real it is. The way we like it is, in the words of the countermen who hustle things along at breakneck pace, "white on white; M

& M," which means white meat turkey on white bread with mustard and mayonnaise. You can also get it dressed with shredded lettuce and an order of cranberry relish. Turkey sandwiches get no better than this!

THE CRUMPET SHOP
PIKE PLACE MARKET, 1503 FIRST AVE., SEATTLE, WA (206) 682-1598

One of the silliest souvenirs we ever bought came from this snug little tea room at the top of the Pike Place Market in Seattle. It was a clock in the shape of a full-size toaster; as the second hand went around, two pieces of artificial toast rhythmically rose up from and receded into the slots on top. It was an odd way to remember some of the tastiest morning meals you can eat in Seattle, none of which feature toast from a toaster.

What the memorable meals do feature are crumpets: thick, warm, toasted little muffins laced with holes dripping honey. Crumpets are like English muffins, but chewier and richer-flavored. Made from batter and cooked on a griddle, they have a lush consistency and a craggy-textured surface that begs to be heaped with butter and fruit-clotted marmalade.

The Crumpet Shop serves crumpets for breakfast, brunch, and lunch. You can get them simply buttered, or with a choice from among nearly two dozen different kinds of preserves and honeys, or as the foundation for open-faced sandwiches of cheddar cheese, ham, cream cheese and cucumber, or smoked salmon. On the side, have a cup of cappuccino or, better yet, imported tea. It's a great way to start a day of exploring the Pike Place Market, or to take a civilized mid-morning breather.

And do bring home a souvenir. Last we visited, there was only one tacky toaster-clock in the house, and it was not for sale; but The Crumpet Shop does sell dozens of kinds of truly exotic teas from around the world, as well as a fabulous assortment of honeys and preserves, oatmeals, grains, and cereals from the Northwest and the British Isles. Their crumpets are available, too: sold by the six-pack, ready to take home, heat, and eat.

EMMETT WATSON'S OYSTER BAR
1916 PIKE PLACE, SEATTLE, WA (206) 622-7721

Oyster lovers, take note of this pint-size cafe just across the street from the Pike Place Market in a back-street nook inside the Soames-Dunn Building. It's a little treasure known to bivalve-and-beer cognoscenti, where the ambience is as much fun as the oysters. There is a sunny, flower-adorned courtyard behind the building for warm-weather dining at rickety little tables, and an indoor area with booths protected from the weather.

Few people come to Emmett Watson's to eat a serious meal; the point is to linger over many beers, and many dozens of freshly opened Quilcines, Shoalwater Bays, Minterbrooks, or Canterburies on the half shell. For bigger appetites there are platters of fish and chips, smoked salmon with sweet and sour mustard, smoked trout with homemade dill mayonnaise, even Hangtown fry omelettes in the morning, most of these accompanied by good French bread and butter. When there is a chill in the air, the dish we like best is one of the house soups: clam and salmon, or shrimp soup Orleans, a spicy gumbo made with tomatoes, garlic, and loads of small shrimp. Utensils are plastic, plates are paper, but the flavors of the food, and the smell and sound of the market just outside and upwind, are impeccably authentic.

JULIA'S 14 CARROT CAFE
2305 EASTLAKE E., SEATTLE, WA (206) 324-1442;
BREAKFAST DAILY; DINNER TUESDAY–SATURDAY

A laid-back eatery, casual and comfortably disheveled, where customers include shaggy university types, newspaper addicts, coffee hounds, and a few pin-striped business people. When you walk in the door, you smell the powerhouse Stewart Brothers coffee that is served in thick mugs and hottened up as often as required. And you see vistas of glorious good food, piled high on plates, overcrowding the small unclothed tables.

What to eat? It's a tough decision. Even putting aside lunch and dinner, breakfast presents a befuddling set of choices. For omelettes, there are nineteen different fillings, including five kinds of cheese; on the side come hash browns and your choice of toast, English muffin, or streusel-yogurt coffee cake. The coffee cake is a big moist crumble-topped block, served with a crowning sphere of butter as big as a Ping-Pong ball. For fifty cents extra, you can get Julia's cinnamon roll instead of the regular breadstuffs. "Large and gooey" is how the waiter describes the roll—a vast spiral pastry with clods of raisins and veins of dark sugar gunk packed into its warm furrows. It, too, comes blobbed with a ball of melting butter.

If eggs aren't your dish, how about hotcakes, sourdough or regular, with sliced bananas, apple slivers, or blueberries, with bacon on the side or cooked into the 'cakes? You can order hot oats with dates and cashews, homemade granola, sourdough French toast, or a grander French toast known as Tahitian toast, gilded with a thin layer of sesame butter.

At lunch and dinner, there are salads and soups, deluxe desserts, and vegetarian burgers.

OLYMPIA OYSTER HOUSE
320 W. FOURTH AVE., OLYMPIA, WA (206) 943-8020

In 1925 oyster fishermen in Olympia opened a seafood bar in the culling house of the Olympia Oyster Company. They served little more than oyster cocktails and pan-fried oysters, and the place became known by the name that many today still call it, the Oyster Bar. Officially, it is the Olympia Oyster House, as the name "bar" was deemed illegal for any restaurant that did not serve liquor (now, this one does have a bar); but whatever you call it, the Olympia Oyster House is an excellent place in which to sample the marine specialties of the Pacific Northwest, including Hangtown fry, the northwestern omelette that enfolds a couple of handfuls of oysters that have been quickly fried to crusty succulence. Oyster Bar Hangtown fry is served for lunch only, made with large, chopped Pacific oysters.

Other than Hangtown fry, the main thing you want to eat here, if you can, are Olympia oysters—tiny little nuggets of marine sweetness, served breaded and fried in the fall and winter when they become available, but only intermittently. The menu advises that the Olympia Oyster House is "known 'World Wide' for the famous Olympia Oyster which is now a bit extinct." Don't worry, though, if "Olys" are extinct the day you visit. There are lots of other good things to eat beyond them: salmon, prawns, halibut, pan roasts, crab Louis, and, for shellfish-frowners, prime rib, and the western version of a roast beef-on-a-roll known as French dip.

The Oyster Bar is in the same building where it started in 1925—significantly expanded now into a comfortable restaurant with a patio that is a fine place to linger over a long, cool Olympia beer, and look at the water.

THE SPAR
114 EAST FOURTH AVE., OLYMPIA, WA (206) 357-6444

This cavernous old lunch counter is the place to come for low-priced, high-quality, big-portion meals in the company of Olympians of every stripe, from politicians (Olympia is the capital of Washington), lawyers, and reporters to civilian connoisseurs of real milk shakes.

For breakfast, you want a cinnamon roll with your eggs, or if you are really hungry you might want the logger's favorite—biscuits blanketed with sausage-laden cream gravy. There are omelettes, French toast, and waffles, too. Lunch at the Spar can be as simple as a good hamburger with French fries or a terrific turkey sandwich (from a cooked bird, not a compressed "turkey roll"). There is always local seafood on the lunch and dinner menus, including pan-fried oysters, crab or shrimp Louis, halibut, and salmon. Whatever else you eat, the one dessert you must have is bread pudding, made using leftover cinnamon rolls, baked and creamed and sugared until they metamorphose, turning into a wondrous bready custard.

Ambience at The Spar is vintage lunchroom, going back to the 1930s when it was a favorite among loggers and dock workers who came to eat, drink, and play pool. By the way, a spar is the trunk of a felled tree once it has been stripped of all its branches.

SUNLIGHT CAFE
6403 ROOSEVELT WAY NE, SEATTLE, WA (206) 522-9060

Once you are seated in one of the Sunlight Cafe's rather ordinary coffee-shop booths (the tables of which hold little signs advising that the kitchen stocks a full list of additive-free beers) you observe many of the customers wearing the beards, serapes, sandals, and peasant blouses that are marks of Woodstock generation leftovers. A few of them signify their counter-culture attitudes by eating salad with Third World chopsticks instead of middle-class forks. This restaurant is run by, and for, serious health nuts. But don't let that dissuade you, even if you love to eat meat, fat, and sugar. The food here is pretty swell.

The healthy folks who hang out at the Sunlight are mellow dudes; neither customers or staff will lay a heavy trip on you if you are wearing a sports jacket or if your hair is too neatly combed. In fact the clientele is a mixed group: not only woolly-haired types, but local business people, too. If, like us, you are card-carrying middle class people who appreciate homemade food, this is one nifty place to know about, where you can feel right at home.

Have a waffle for breakfast. It's eggless, but it's crisp and steamy-good, spangled with sesame seeds. Pancakes are made without eggs, too. In fact, there are no eggs used in the kitchen for anything, so breakfast is basically bread. But it is terrific bread: gooey cinnamon rolls, banana-apple muffins, blueberry-almond coffee cake, seven-grain English muffins.

Beyond eggs, other proscribed foods include chicken, red meat, and even certain dairy products for which rennet (derived from cow innards) is used.

At lunch one day, the blackboard above the counter listed spinach-lentil-barley soup, Mexican chilaquiles, country garden dressing for the salads, and the burger of the day. Yes, the burger of the day, this day made from ground nuts, rice, and vegetables. Desserts included various cheese-cakes and an apple crisp. The regular menu, which—untrue to the natural-is-better spirit of the cafe—is *laminated,* lists such vegetarian favorites as humus (mashed chick peas, tahini, and garlic), all kinds of salads (fruit and vegetable) with herbal dressings, and a hearty tostada heaped with refried beans, cheese, sprouts, olives, salsa, sour cream, and avocado.

There are also some mighty substantial sandwiches on the Sunlight's superb homemade dark wheat bread. It is sliced by hand, big enough so that half a sandwich makes a nice meal. The one we liked best is an open-face version of Elvis Presley's favorite sandwich: peanut butter and bananas. At the Sunlight, they use freshly ground peanut butter and top it with raisins. And whereas Elvis liked his on white bread fried in plenty of butter or bacon grease, here the bread is merely toasted. Although not quite as calorific as Elvis's, it's delicious.

WISCONSIN

BENJAMIN'S DELICATESSEN
4156 N. OAKLAND AVE. (IN SHOREWOOD), MILWAUKEE, WI (414) 332-7777

Benjamin's is an old-fashioned deli in a modern shopping area. It is an authentic taste of Milwaukee, by which we mean it offers a reassuring menu of old-country ethnic dishes (chicken-in-the-pot, cabbage rolls, fried matzoh) along with plenty of midwestern Americana, such as a Friday night fish fry, a deluxe hamburger plate with French fries, and that mysteriously named midwestern meal-in-a-skillet, hoppelpoppel, for which no ethnic group we know has ever taken credit. Benjamin's hoppelpoppel is listed as a "Benjy's Special" and you have your choice of ordinary hoppelpoppel (browned potatoes, salami, and scrambled eggs all cooked together) or *super* hoppelpoppel, which adds peppers, mushrooms, and melted cheese to the formula. Either way, it's delicious.

The other specialties of the house are deli food: piled-high corned beef sandwiches on rugged-crusted sour rye bread, lox-and-bagel platters, sweet-and-sour cabbage borscht, and crisp potato pancakes, served with apple sauce. For dessert, we recommend noodle kugel (a cheesecake-rich block of cooked egg noodles and sweetened cheese), served hot with sour cream. And for a beverage to drink with your meal, Benjamin's offers true melting pot variety: domestic or imported beer, kosher wine, soda in cans, chocolate phosphate (seltzer water and chocolate syrup), or 2¢ plain.

BODER'S ON THE RIVER
11919 N. RIVER RD., MEQUON, WI (414) 242-0335

When we get homesick for the Midwest, we sometimes thumb through our pamphlet of *Favorite Recipes from Boder's on the River* that we picked up last time we were there. It is no mere list of recipes; it includes the whole history of the Boder family and their restaurant, including snapshots of their Model A Ford (named "Fritter"), of Fred Krautkramer dressed as Frederika (Santa's assistant) for the annual Christmas party, of Jack Boder digging up the septic system, of various Boders getting married, and of Chico the runaway horse. You won't likely see any of these things if you head out to the country to find Boder's, but we can guarantee you a memorable taste of Great Lakes cooking that is delightfully, deliciously behind the times.

Boder's on the River has been a family-run restaurant for four generations, going back to 1929, when John and Frieda Boder bought an old homestead in the country outside of Milwaukee and turned it into a rural lunchroom. Their specialty then was afternoon tea, served to city folks who came to enjoy not only the good food, but a visit to Boder's bathing beach on the river or a stroll through the cornfields just outside the dining room. The Boders' casual country place was known also for the animals the family kept around, including Tommy the Turkey, who was famous for peering into the dining room as customers ate, and Peter the Parrot, who was once accused of calling out "Hi, Fat!" to a neighbor. (Actually, he was saying "Hi, Jack" to the Boders' son.) Customers' children rode on a horse named Brownie or played with Charlie the St. Bernard. It was not unusual, after a cold spring rain, for dinner to be delayed because all the Boder's employees were outside rescuing baby ducklings from the cold. The little birds were brought inside and placed in the kitchens' slightly warm ovens until they were dry enough to be taken to the barn.

Today, Boder's isn't quite so eccentric or casual, but it remains a treasure trove of country cooking from the heyday of country-style tea rooms in the 1930s, and a favorite destination for Milwaukeeans in search of family-style dinners of grandmotherly goodness. All meals are anchored by soul-satisfying bakery goodies such as pecan rolls, cherry muffins, and baking powder biscuits, as well as Boder's legendary oversized corn fritters, served with maple syrup. Begin by forking into a tray of bygone luxuries that once symbolized polite, family-style restaurants: demure carrot or zucchini relish along with macaroni salad with sweet pineapple chunks; then move on to Jell-O (with Boder's-made mayonnaise); then to such solid-citizen main courses as steaks or chops, Lake Superior whitefish, or Wisconsin's own crisped roast duck with wild rice.

If you know tea-room cuisine, you know that no matter how demure the rest of the meal, dessert is almost always a grand finale. That goes double for Wisconsin, America's Dairyland, where cream is king. Boder's roster of desserts includes poppyseed chiffon torte, banana split ice cream pie, peanut swirl ice cream pie, butter brickle pie (Graham cracker crumbs and chopped walnuts with locally made butter brickle ice cream), and the stunning specialty known as a schaum torte—featherweight, meltingly sweet meringue shells filled with ice cream and strawberries or raspberries.

For those who want a short-form feast, Boder's menu has a section entitled "Not Hungry?" Here you can order a full meal minus the main course: muffins, relishes, soup, a fritter, and dessert. As much as we like the whitefish and the duck, it's all these extras that make a Boder's meal outstanding.

HEINEMANN'S
665 W. WISCONSIN AVE., MILWAUKEE, WI (414) 291-5240

A big bakery with a coffee shop up front, Heinemann's serves all kinds of sandwiches (on made-here whole-wheat, rye, oatmeal loaf, Welsh wheat, or white) including burgers topped with everything from cheese and bacon to Thousand Island dressing; and there are salads and soups every day; and grilled and fried seafood; and fabulous hot fudge and hot caramel sundaes and a toffee supreme hot fudge and caramel sundae to make you swoon. But the reason we return to this bustling urban eatery is breakfast.

We order grilled cinnamon coffee cake, which the menu immodestly advises "was featured in *National Geographic* magazine!" It is a chunk of cake veined with gobs of cinnamon and sugar, lodes of raisins, and heavily buttered, cooked on a grill only until it is warmed through and faintly crisp: the stuff of which breakfast legends are made. They also grill their bran bread with cinnamon sugar and honey. The other morning foods we love here are waffles and pancakes. Although on many occasions the batter of the day is made with oatmeal, the 'cakes even then are featherweights, easy to eat.

Sometimes we don't order coffee cake or pancakes or waffles. We get plain old eggs, because at Heinemann's the plainest eggs soar. They are accompanied by toast made from the likes of zucchini bread or English muffin bread, or—our less-is-more favorite—a puffy, freshly baked hard roll, sliced and spread with good Wisconsin butter.

JACK PANDL'S WHITEFISH BAY INN
1319 HENRY CLAY, WHITEFISH BAY, WI (414) 964-3800

Great Lakes whitefish, broiled so that a paprika-flecked crust encases the sweet, moist meat; Friday fish fries and prime rib on Saturday night; schaum tortes (crisp meringues with crusty amber tops) dolloped with freshly made custard: here is a mighty fine taste of Milwaukee, accompanied by steins of Augsburger beer or glasses of sweet May wine.

Jack Pandl's (since 1915) serves its German-flavored Dairyland cuisine in a friendly, wood-paneled dining room with a wall of windows overlooking elegant Lake Drive. Waitresses wear dirndl skirts and there is lots of Old World memorabilia for decor (including one of the planet's biggest collections of beer steins), but the menu is at least as midwestern as it is middle-European. At lunch, when the steel-banded tables are set with functional paper placemats, you can eat a julienne salad or a Reuben sandwich made with Wisconsin cheese, or pork chops, or a Denver omelette. You can even have a diet burger. In addition to the superlative broiled whitefish ("always purchased fresh," the menu guarantees), there is that lean but luscious midwestern specialty, walleyed pike, fileted and broiled to perfection. Wisconsin duckling is available every weekend.

Start your meal with farina dumpling soup, and be sure to tear into a piece of sour Milwaukee rye somewhere along the way; and no matter what else you order at Jack Pandl's, be sure to get at least one German pancake for the table. This gorgeous edible event, a Jack Pandl's specialty, is a big puffy cloud of batter similar in texture to Yorkshire pudding, but sweeter, available with bacon or sausage if desired. It arrives at the table piping hot and shaped like a big bowl, its circumference crisp and brown, risen high in the oven, its center moist and eggy. Dust it with a bit of powdered sugar and give it a spritz of lemon, creating a sophisticated syrup, then dig in immediately. It is a big plate of food—a meal unto itself, or a wonderful thing to share.

JESSICA'S DRIVE-IN CUSTARD STAND
524 E. LAYTON AVE., MILWAUKEE, WI (414) 744-1119

Although our business is searching out unique regional specialties wherever we travel, our hobby is hamburgers. No matter how remarkable and exotic the local culinary passion might be—from Santa Fe's *carne adovada* to southern Indiana's turtle soup, you can be sure that if you are in America, there are interesting culinary twists on the hamburger somewhere nearby; and it is our pleasure, between sampling the regional trademarks, to find those burgers and to eat them.

In and around Milwaukee, for example, the great local flavors include wursts and sausages of every kind, sour-crusted rye bread, schaum tortes (meringues loaded with freshly made custard), and wondrous German, Czech, Polish, and Serbian dishes found in few other cities in America. Milwaukee and vicinity also happen to be hamburger heaven.

Who could resist one that is served wrapped in blue paper inscribed, "Hamburger, pickle on top: makes your heart go flippity flop"? That's the way you get them at Kewpee Lunch, a 1920s-vintage hash house down in Racine (home of that wonderful pastry known as kringle), where the counterman starts with a sphere of beef about the size of a walnut and mashes it down on the grill, cooks it until it is crusty-brown, then heaps it into a toasted bun with the works. And how about Moss Bros.' on West Capitol Drive in Milwaukee, where the specialty is a "maniac burger"? And the Nite Owl on Layton Ave., where the menu assures customers that the Jumbo burger is the "largest post-war burger in the area"? We also like Solly's Sliders on Port Washington Road—diminutive disks of burger meat secreted inside a tangled heap of stewed onions and served on French bread. And, too, there is the Centurian burger at Century Hall on N. Farwell Ave., where the beef comes topped with cheese, bacon, tomatoes, onions, mayo, lettuce, steak sauce, and green olives. Whew!

One of the most memorable burger-eating experiences in the area is at Jessica's Drive-In Custard Stand—known for years as Al's (until Al sold it to Jessica). Dine in your car at Jessica's—its out-of-the-way location across from Mitchell Airport has made it a favorite spot not only for chowhounds but for daters who want to be alone with each other and their burgers. Jessica's patties are dished out as at many places in the area—awash in tides of butter. (Wisconsin *is* the Dairy State.) They are modest-sized, sizzled to luscious perfection on the grill, then heaped into a toasted sesame-seed bun along with lettuce, tomato, mayonnaise, and grilled onions. What makes these glistening buttered burgers especially excellent, aside from their low price, is the fact that you can get them with a tall, foamy chocolate malt made with superb custard.

It was the custard as well as those great, buttery little hamburgers that put Jessica's into our little black book of favorite eating spots. A local passion, custard is like ice cream but better: plusher and creamier (generally made from higher-butterfat cream), served just soft enough so you can swirl into it with a spoon. Other than in a malt, the way to taste it at Jessica's is in a sundae or a banana split topped with strawberries and chocolate or hot fudge, or in a four-star turtle sundae with hot fudge and caramel, or in a pig's dinner known as the Jessica's Special, billed on the sign behind the serving counter as "lots of creamy custard, your favorite topping, roasted pecans, cream cherry." To be honest, we never tasted a Jessica's Special. We were too full up on those swell buttered burgers.

MIRO'S
2499 BARTLETT, MILWAUKEE, WI (414) 964-9220

Miro's is an inconspicuous corner tavern in a residential Milwaukee neighborhood of tree-shaded streets and modest family homes. Out back, it has a sunny outdoor patio where, on any weekend night, you will smell lamb and suckling pigs roasting on an outdoor grill. Serbian music plays quietly on the sound system. The walls inside are decorated with native crafts and souvenirs. There is nothing high-pressure about the ethnic pitch. This place is the real thing: a local tavern patronized by local clientele. At the small bar in the front room, locals sit reading the foreign-language newspaper and chatting in Serbo-Croatian.

The Serbian kitchen is known for grilled meats, spicy sausages, zesty kajmak cheese (like Greek feta), and the big layered pastry known as a burek. Find a place at a red-and-white-clothed table, order a bottle of "Big Nik" (Niksicko) beer, and get ready to enjoy the kind of ethnic meal that makes eating in Milwaukee an everlasting pleasure.

For those of us who are strangers, Miro's has proven to be a friendly little eatery, where the waitress patiently explains that the tangy kajmak cheese and ajvar (eggplant and pepper mix) are meant to be spread on pieces of bread as an appetizer. She suggests raznici for dinner: it's a grand meal of skewered marinated pork, charcoal broiled and served atop a bed of brilliantly seasoned rice with chunks of tomato and green pepper and little blocks of cheese. Cevapcici are also wonderful: skinless beef sausages cooked until crusty brown over an open fire. Of all the dishes Miro's serves, it is the burek that is the most distinctively ethnic. This is a Mediterranean pastry not unlike a pizza in concept, but made instead with a kind of phyllo dough wrapped around cheese, beef, or spinach.

What's great about these meals is how homey they are. The food is food you would expect to get in a little cafe in Serbia, or at the table of someone's immigrant grandmother. The unaffected sustenance, the affable corner-tavern setting, the music, the accents of the staff: they add up to a taste of melting-pot America at its best.

NORSKE NOOK
7TH & HARMONY STS., OSSEO, WI (715) 597-3069

Look at the northwest corner of Wisconsin on a map. See the profile? It is known as Indianhead country; and if your map happens to be a road atlas, all you need do is follow I-94 southeast from the Indian's lips. It leads across the tongue, down the throat, and beyond; the place to get off is at the bottom of the double chin.

Here you find a village named Osseo. It is a sleepy hamlet without obvious points of interest to lure travelers from the Interstate. There is hardly more to it than a short Main Street with a hardware store and a small-town cafe named the Norske Nook.

You might imagine from its name that the Norske Nook specializes in Norwegian food. Not much, except during the fall, when lutefiske and lefse and rollepolse are made according to Scandinavian tradition. The everyday menu is middle-American cafe cuisine: hamburgers, hot roast beef, tuna salad on white.

And yet, look at the cars parked outside: license plates from Illinois, Minnesota, Iowa, and beyond, from coast to coast. On a summer weekend, you might have to wait in line, on the sidewalk, for a place inside. Why is the Norske Nook one of the great gastronomical magnets of the upper Midwest?

Answer: the pies, which you'd have to be blind and scentless not to notice the minute you step inside. In a brightly lit display case in the center of the dining room, with an occasional overflow lined up along the counter, the pie inventory of this inconspicuous cafe is a sight to make any dessert lover fall to his knees and thank fortune for providing a slice of heaven on earth. Or maybe two or three slices, à la mode.

The pie prodigy of the Norske Nook is a lady named Helen Myhre, a mother of six who learned to cook from her own mother. When Helen and her husband, Ernest, used to operate a nearby dairy farm, she developed quite a reputation among friends for the desserts she used to serve. They kept telling her she really ought to open a restaurant. In the early 1970s, Helen and Ernest took the plunge, purchasing the Star Cafe at 7th and Harmony streets. They named it the Norske Nook in honor of the mostly Norwegian clientele, and they worked up a straight-shooting hot-lunch menu, offering a choice of four or five kinds of pie for dessert.

The specialties were sour cream raisin and rhubarb, both of which stunned our callow palates when we first visited in 1976. We ate a couple of slices and knew with the certainty of religious converts that we had tasted ultimate excellence. From that moment on, we have been insufferable Norske Nook proselytizers, arrogantly comparing every inferior pastry to the Great Ones of Osseo.

Back then, Helen used to set the pies out to cool on newspapers spread across the counter. The sour cream raisin pie—a specialty seldom found outside Midwest dairy country—is what made us eternal partisans of the Norske Nook; it is the flavor you must try if you are passing this way only once. Cut into titanic slices, its quivering, cream-sweet ivory custard is clotted with swollen raisins, heaped high with ethereal meringue, and piled into a wafer-crisp crust. Rhubarb, served in huge slices that seemed to be a quarter pie each, was tart, sweet, butter-dripping rich—still warm, and staggeringly flavorful. We took pictures of the pies, the way tourists take pictures of the Seven Wonders of the World, so we could show our friends at home and amaze them with the sights we have seen, and eaten.

In the last twenty years, Helen's restaurant has become a *Roadfood* landmark; Charles Kuralt has praised it on the radio; and Helen Myhre's output has grown to more than fifty pies per day: blueberry, raspberry, mincemeat with hot rum sauce, banana cream, butterscotch . . . you get the idea. The pies are stellar, but it's hard to resist sampling some of Mrs. Myhre's other pastries, too: lush carrot cake, caramel rolls, date bars, cookies, apple turnovers. With a cup of good Norske Nook coffee, any one of these is a prescription for culinary satisfaction that will last a thousand miles.

SCHULZ'S RESTAURANT
1644 CALUMET DR., SHEBOYGAN, WI (414) 452-1880

A Sheboygan brat (say "braat") is generally cooked outdoors. It is picnic food; and when food writer Marialisa Calta investigated the subject a few years ago, she discovered that over the July Fourth weekend, the people of Sheboygan (which stands unchallenged in its claim to be "The Bratwurst Capital of the World") eat approximately eleven tons of this favorite locally made pork sausage. In fact, what distinguishes a Sheboygan brat from other pork sausages is not necessarily any of the spices that go into it; what makes it special is the way it is cooked—over hot coals.

You can study this phenomenon at Schulz's restaurant. Visible from every seat at the double horseshoe counter, Schulz's grill man wields his long-handled tools over an aromatic charcoal fire, turning and flipping brats, along with hamburgers and boneless butterflied pork chops, occasionally pulling out a small shower head and spraying the fire to keep the flames low and the coals smoldering. You will note that Schulz's brats are not sausage links (heresy to some aficionados); they are patties—flat cakes of sausage meat that because they are so thin can absorb maximum fire flavor. What's missing is the nice pop when you bite into a cased sausage; on the other hand, that extra char flavor gives these brats an extra kick. They are served, as per tradition, in a sandwich with the works, including mustard and onions, single or double; and because this is Wisconsin, the roll on which they come is generously buttered.

Don't leave Schulz's without also trying one of those butterflied pork chops. This is a fairly unsung specialty in this part of Wisconsin, and it is surprisingly good. The chop is a well-seasoned, flattened slab of pork, laced with a few streaks of fat (so you know it's not a reconstituted pork-product-patty), cooked until nicely charred on the outside, but still plenty moist. Like the brat, it is served on a rugged-crusted, buttered roll, with creamy potato salad on the side.

SMOKY'S CLUB
3005 UNIVERSITY, MADISON, WI (608) 233-2120

The great carnivorous moment of dining at Smoky's Club, other than actually putting a juice-heavy pink triangle severed from the T-bone into your mouth and beginning to chew, is listening to the steak hit the plate on its way to your table. The T-bones, strips, and filet mignons are slapped onto a superheated metal plate, setting off an explosive sizzle and sending the succulent aroma of searing beef into the air.

When you plunge your wood-handled knife below the blackened crust of one of these magnificent meat mountains, it glides almost effortlessly down into the delicate-fibered beef and juice begins to flow onto the platter. Eat the piece you sever, savor it, relish its protein-packed delight; but quick, without delay, fork into your hash browns and push a little heap of them through the hot juices on the platter. These spuds are grand, every bit as memorable as the meat itself: skillet-fried until crusty on the outside, but with lots of tender white potato pulp within.

What a meal! There are crudités, good rolls, soups, and pickled beets to start; but you will pay little attention to them, nor will you likely be very impressed by the Loony Tunes decor, which hangs on the wall and dangles from the ceiling and includes a stuffed baby alligator, a vintage carpet sweeper, ships' wheels, and bowling trophies. At Smoky's Club, no one seems to have any problem focusing on what really matters: meat and potatoes.

TIFFANY STORE AND CAFE
TIFFANY, WI (TAKE THE SHOPIERE EXIT OFF I-90, JUST NORTH OF BELOIT)
(608) 365-7252

The Tiffany is one of two businesses in Tiffany, Wisconsin. The other is Laders' Tiffany Feed and Supply across the road. In the morning and at lunch, this farm country town can get almost crowded, what with all the people from surrounding villages and travelers from nearby I-90 who come to the Tiffany to eat. They come for buttermilk pancakes or for perfectly cooked eggs that the cafe's proprietors get from a nearby farm, accompanied by bacon and sausage from a butcher just down the road. They eat freshly baked caramel rolls, and sit at counter stools (made from old milk cans) and drink good coffee long into the morning.

Lunch is nice, too. There are always soups: vegetable beef and chicken noodle are the two we have tried, and both were chockablock with good ingredients. There are sandwiches and a hot-lunch special every day. We relished stalwart Salisbury steaks smothered in mushroom gravy.

But one would never want to eat so much at the Tiffany that there wasn't plenty of appetite remaining for dessert. The pie and cake selection is a midwestern bonanza: always about half a dozen kinds of pie, including a grand one made with Michigan cherries late in the summer, as well as peach, blueberry, and creams. Our favorite desserts are the old-fashioned cakes, cut into titanic slices. There are chocolate, banana, carrot, and a stupendously good pineapple-upside-down cake. It's good to know that such riches are only minutes from the highway; however, Tiffany is not on the map. When you get off I-90, ask directions from a local. If you get lost—we do every time—you will be lost in lovely farmland.

WATTS TEA SHOP
761 N. JEFFERSON ST., MILWAUKEE, WI (414) 276-6352

B eing a lady is not a significant goal for most women these days, but ladies' lunch is an event that all of us, whether gal or guy, ought not to undervalue. This fine old gastronomic ritual, for which the fairer sex has customarily forgathered to chat and chew, is an opportunity to savor American cookery's finer aspect.

Bread, for example. Observe the breads served at the Watts Tea Shop, on the third floor of George Watts & Son in Milwaukee, where ladies (and gentlemen) come for nourishment in the middle of their busy shopping day (as well as for breakfast Monday through Friday and for tea in the afternoons). Sandwiches of egg salad, chicken salad, and tuna salad are served on homemade bread—nice, tender whole-wheat bread, nothing snazzy or outrageously crusty; and there are big, steamy English muffins, made in the kitchen each morning. That gentle tan bread can be made into cinnamon toast or ginger toast if you like. Some customers stop in the Tea Shop for nothing more than an order of buttered toast, accompanied by a pot of hot chocolate or hot Russian chocolate (coffee and chocolate together, with whipped cream on top). They sip and they nibble and they listen to quiet music piped in to aid digestion as waitresses in tidy black-and-white uniforms glide through the blue room making people happy.

With bread, a lady likes soup. What lovely soup Watts Tea Shop serves: unadorned hot chicken broth, chicken rice, and always one voluptuous bisque—spinach, vegetable, or tomato. The daily special is a bowl of soup and half a sandwich.

There are hot meals, too, at least one per day—pleasant curries or seafood-and-cream dishes reminiscent of shrimp wiggle; and there are salads, some of them stuffed into tomatoes, others garnished with big, plump strawberries.

Desserts are sensational, displayed on a cart near the entrance to the dining room; and although ladylike and dainty to look at, they are as satisfying as a manly wedge of pie. The house specialty is filled sunshine cake, a moist, triple-layer sponge extravaganza with buttercream filling and artistically swirled seven-minute frosting on top. There are other tortes and cakes, ice cream and sherbet, but sunshine cake is the *pièce de résistance*.

WHITE GULL INN
FISH CREEK, WI (414) 868-3517

At this clapboard hotel in the downeasterly village of Fish Creek in Door County, they suspend two immense kettles over an oak wood fire each Wednesday, Friday, Saturday, and Sunday night throughout the summer (and Wednesday and Saturday in the winter). Locally caught whitefish is cooked using an unvarying and unimprovable technique: fish steaks and new potatoes, along with pounds of salt, are boiled furiously together until the fish is perfectly cooked.

This ritual is known as a fish boil, or more specifically, an Icelandic fish boil, supposedly because the tradition was begun by Icelandic lumbermen who settled the rugged peninsula between Green Bay and Lake Michigan's western shore. They had minimal kitchenware at the lumber camps, so they built fires, hung up pots of water, and tossed in some of the fish that were so plentiful in the bay. A second explanation for the primitive cooking technique is that it was devised by returning fishermen who entertained their families on the beach by building massive bonfires fires and boiling up their catch.

The fish boil is a gastronomic event virtually unknown outside this one finger of the Wisconsin shore north of Sturgeon Bay. But among locals and vacationers, it is a summer picnic with a sense of place and history, a meal that symbolizes Wisconsin's culinary heritage. Hand-scrawled signs advertising impromptu fish boils line the road through small towns like Egg Harbor, White Fish Bay, and Ephraim; some of the nightly cookouts are so popular that you have to make reservations weeks in advance.

A fish boil is always cooked outdoors on the beach or in a backyard, usually eaten by the light of the moon and paper lanterns and the crackling wood fires over which the fish is boiled. The fun part of the ceremony comes when the Master Boiler deems everything done to a turn. He tosses kerosene onto the flames below the pot. The flames lick up in pyrotechnic splendor and the water boils over, naturally skimming the oil off the surface and yielding up firm steaks ready to be plucked from the bubbling caldron.

The hot-from-the-pot meal is drizzled with melted butter and strewn with lemon. On the side, the White Gull dining room provides cole slaw and a trio of breads including orange-date-nut and pumpkin. Dessert at a fish boil is always cherry pie.

Note: reservations for a fish boil at the White Gull Inn are required, and sometimes must be made as much as two weeks in advance.

INDEX

483